THE WAR IN CROAT

AND

BOSNIA-HERZEGOVINA

1991–1995

THE WAR IN CROATIA

AND

BOSNIA-HERZEGOVINA

1991–1995

Editors
Branka Magaš and Ivo Žanić
The Bosnian Institute (London)

Foreword by Noel Malcolm

FRANK CASS
LONDON • PORTLAND, OR

First published in 2001 in Great Britain by
FRANK CASS PUBLISHERS
Crown House, 47 Chase Side, Southgate,
London N14 5BP

and in the United States of America by
FRANK CASS PUBLISHERS
c/o ISBS, 5804 N.E. Hassalo Street
Portland, Oregon, 97213-3644

Original edition *Rat u Hrvatskoj i Bosni i Hercegovini 1992–1995*,
Naklada Jesenski i Turk (Zagreb) and DANI (Sarajevo 1999); explanatory notes
and translations from English by Ivo Žanić.

Translations into English for this edition by Saba Risaluddin.

Website: www.frankcass.com

British Library Cataloguing in Publication Data

The war in Croatia and Bosnia-Herzegovina, 1991–1995
1. Croatia – History – 1990 – 2. Bosnia and Herzegovina –
History – 1980 – 3. Bosnia and Hercegovina – Politics and
government – 1990 –
I. Magaš, Branka II. Žanić, Ivo
949.7'03

ISBN 0-7146-5204-0 (cloth)
ISBN 0-7146-8201-2 (paper)

Library of Congress Cataloging-in-Publication Data

Rat u Hrvatskoj i Bosni i Hercegovini 1991–1995. English.
The war in Croatia and Bosnia-Herzegovina, 1991–1995 / edited by
Branka Magaš and Ivo Žanić.
p. cm.
Includes bibliographical references and index.
ISBN 0-7146-5204-0 (cloth : alk. paper) – ISBN 0-7146-8201-2 (pbk.
: alk. paper)
1. Yugoslav War, 1991–1995–Campaigns–Croatia. 2. Yugoslav War,
1991–1995–Campaigns–Bosnia and Hercegovina. I. Magaš, Branka. II.
Žanić, Ivo, 1954–. III. Title.
DR1313.4 .R3813 2001
949.703–dc21
2001002918

Typeset in 10.25/12pt Sabon by Cambridge Photosetting Services
Printed in Great Britain by
Creative Print and Design, Wales, Ebbw Vale

Contents

List of Tables

List of Maps

Notes on Contributors

Dušan Bilandžić: political scientist and historian; graduated in law at the University of Belgrade, doctorate in economics at Zagreb University; full professor at Faculty of Political Sciences, University of Zagreb (retired) and full member of Croatian Academy of Sciences and Arts; during the 1960s and 1970s principal of the Centre for Social Research of the Presidency of the LCY Central Committee in Belgrade, then of the Institute for History of the Labour Movement in Zagreb; member of the Assembly of the Socialist Republic of Croatia. After the first democratic elections (and until the adoption of the Constitution in December 1990, when the body was abolished), member of the presidency of the Republic of Croatia; from 1996 to 1998 expert adviser in the Office of the Republic of Croatia in Belgrade. Author of *Ideje i praksa društvenog razvoja Jugoslavije 1945–1973* [The idea and practice of social development in Yugoslavia 1945–1973] (1973), *Jugoslavija poslije Tita 1980–1985* [Yugoslavia after Tito 1980–1985] (1986), *Historija SFRJ* [History of the Socialist Federative Republic of Yugoslavia] (1985), *Hrvatska moderna povijest* [Modern History of Croatia] (1999).

Vladimir Bilandžić: political scientist; former deputy principal of the Institute for South-Eastern Europe, and lecturer at the Central European University in Budapest; master's degree in political science from McMaster University, Hamilton, Canada, doctorate in international relations from the University of Belgrade. Did research at the Institute for International Policy and Economy, Belgrade; visiting associate at the Institute for East–West Security Studies, New York; delegate to Conflict Prevention Centre of OSCE, Vienna. Has published numerous papers in international academic publications; co-author of *SDI and European Security* (1987) and *Razoružanje u Evropi* [Disarmament in Europe] (1987).

Norman Cigar: senior associate of Public International Law and Policy Group, Washington, DC; previously professor of National Security Studies at US Marine Corps School of Advanced Warfighting, Quantico, Virginia.

Worked as senior military–political analyst at US Land Forces HQ at the Pentagon. Master's degrees from University of Columbia and Joint Military Intelligence College, doctorate from Oxford University. Has published: *Genocide in Bosnia: The Policy of 'Ethnic Cleansing'* (1995), *The Right to Defence: Thoughts on the Bosnian Arms Embargo* (1995) and (as co-author with Paul Williams) *War Crimes and Individual Responsibility: a Prima Facie Case for the Indictment of Slobodan Milošević* (1996); consultant to The Bosnian Institute.

Daniele Conversi: sociologist, lecturer at Central European University in Budapest, author of *The Basques, the Catalans and Spain: Alternative Routes to Nationalist Mobilization* (1997).

Jovan Divjak: brigadier-general of the Army of Bosnia-Herzegovina (retired). Military education at the Military Academy in Belgrade and the École d'état major in Paris. Commanding officer of the Territorial Defence (TO) of the Socialist Republic of Bosnia-Herzegovina in Mostar 1984–89, Sarajevo 1989–91; dismissed and court-martialled by the JNA for issuing an unauthorized order for firearms and ammunition to be handed over to the TO of Bosnia-Herzegovina. In April 1992 appointed deputy chief of staff of the General Staff of the TO of B-H; from 1993 to the end of the war, deputy chief of staff of the General Staff of the Army of B-H, responsible for cooperation with civilian institutions and organizations. From 1994, president of the Citizens' Foundation (since 1998 Association) *Obrazovanje gradi BiH* [Education Builds B-H], which supports the education of war orphans; member of the Association of Independent Intellectuals *Circle 99*. Awarded Légion d'Honneur 2001.

Indijana Harper: freelance translator and interpreter (of Bosnian origin), long resident in Great Britain; during the war in B-H worked first for the Bosnian Information Centre, then 1994–95 for the Bosnian Embassy in London. After Dayton, worked in B-H as translator and assistant to Christian Schwarz-Schilling, international mediator for Federation of Bosnia-Herzegovina.

Adrian Hastings: historian, emeritus professor of theology and religious studies at Leeds University, editor of *The Oxford Companion to Christian Thought* (2000). Author of numerous books, including *Church and State: The English Experience* (1991), *A History of English Christianity 1920–1990* (1991), *The Church in Africa 1450–1950* (1996) and *The Construction of Nationhood: Ethnicity, Religion and Nationalism* (1998). During the war published privately three editions of his *SOS Bosnia*; in 1994 attended the founding assembly of the Serb Civic Council in Sarajevo. A founder-member in 1993 of the Alliance to Defend Bosnia-Herzegovina; trustee of The Bosnian Institute. Died 2001.

Marko Attila Hoare: historian, master's degrees from Cambridge (England) and Yale (USA), doctoral dissertation *The Establishment of the People's Republic of Bosnia-Herzegovina 1941–1946*, Ph.D. Department of History, Yale (2000). Has published several academic articles on the war in former Yugoslavia and the pamphlet *The Politics of the Armed Forces of B-H, 1992–1995* (forthcoming). Currently a British Academy postdoctoral fellow at Cambridge.

Tarik Kulenović: sociologist, academic assistant at the Faculty of Political Sciences, University of Zagreb; executive editor of *Polemos – Časopis za interdisciplinarna istraživanja rata i mira* [Journal for Interdisciplinary Research into War and Peace].

Branka Magaš: historian, journalist and commentator on former Yugoslavia, author of *The Destruction of Yugoslavia: Tracking the Break-up 1980–1992* (1993), and editor of *A Question of Survival: A Common Education System for Bosnia-Herzegovina* (1998). One of the founders of the Croatian Peace Forum in 1991, and of the Alliance to Defend Bosnia-Herzegovina in 1993. Former editor of *Bosnia Report*, and a consultant to The Bosnian Institute. Currently completing a book on the history of Croatia.

Rusmir Mahmutćehajić: professor of applied physics at the University of Sarajevo, where he also lectures on the phenomenology of the sacred. In 1991 appointed deputy premier of the Republic of Bosnia-Herzegovina, then served as minister of power and industry; in late 1993 resigned from all governmental posts because of his opposition to the country's ethnic partition. Founder and president of International Forum Bosnia (Sarajevo), an NGO which advocates the strengthening of civil society in B-H. Co-editor of the periodical *Forum Bosnae*, author of numerous historical-philosophical, sociological and political articles, and of *The Genocide against the Bosnian Muslims* (1991), *Living Bosnia: Political Essays and Interviews* (1996), *O nauku znaka* [On the Doctrine of Symbols] (1996), *Bosnia the Good* (2000), *The Denial of Bosnia* (2000).

Stjepan Mesić: at the time of the Croatian Spring, member of the Assembly of the Socialist Republic of Croatia; in 1972 subjected to a political trial. Founding member and secretary-general of the Croatian Democratic Community (HDZ), from 30 April 1990 prime minister of the Republic of Croatia, and from 24 August 1990 Croatian representative on the SFRY presidency. Prevented on 15 May 1991 from assuming the rotating post of SFRY president as required by the Constitution, he formally took up his post on 1 July in the presence of EC representatives. As former Yugoslavia's last legal president, he resigned on 5 December 1991, retroactive to 8 October when the Croatian Sabor broke off all state-legal relations with the rump Yugoslav Federation and its members. Thereafter president of the Sabor, until he resigned in early 1994 and left the HDZ, because of its policies towards Bosnia-Herzegovina. Vice-president of the Croatian People's Party until February 2000, when following the death of Franjo Tuđman he was elected president of the Republic of Croatia.

Nermin Mulalić: lawyer from Sarajevo, wounded defending the city; 1994–96 worked in the B-H Embassy in London. An associate of The Bosnian Institute and an independent researcher on legal and economic conditions in B-H, he co-authored *From Daytonland to Bosnia Rediviva* (2000).

Warren Switzer: retired senior officer of the US Army, in which he served for 25 years, including in Vietnam and on the General Staff at the Pentagon. Has been adviser to ministries of defence in a number of countries; for nine months during 1997 served as military adviser to the Federation of B-H through MPRI. Now senior program analyst at AB Technologies, Inc., where he works on the use of computer models and simulations as a means of resolving complex internal and transnational situations, in particular low-intensity conflicts. Doctorate in political science, the Catholic University of America, Washington, DC. Author of numerous papers on socioeconomic strategy.

Martin Špegelj: general of the Croatian Army (retired). Military education at academies in Yugoslavia; 1982–85, commanding officer of the Territorial Defence (TO) of the Socialist Republic of Croatia; from 1985 until his premature retirement in May 1989, commanding officer of the 5th Army (North-Western Theatre) of the JNA, with its headquarters in Zagreb. On 1 September 1990 joined the government of the Republic of Croatia as minister of defence; 15 June 1991 appointed commanding officer of the country's ZNG (National Defence Council), but resigned because of disagreements with the political leadership related to the country's defence. From 25 September 1991 until his retirement on 1 January 1993, chief superintendent of the Croatian Army. Adviser on military affairs to President Mesić. Recently published his memoirs, edited by Ivo Žanić.

Anton Tus: general of the Croatian Army (retired). Military education in academies in Yugoslavia, the Soviet Union and the United States; from 1985 to 8 May 1991, commanding officer of the Yugoslav Air Force and Anti-Aircraft Defence; dismissed by decree of the president of the SFRY Presidency for opposing the involvement of the military in political issues. With the formation of the general staff of the Croatian Army on 21 September 1991 he became chief of staff, but was relieved of these duties on 22 November 1992. Until his retirement at his own request in early

1996, chief military adviser to the president of the Republic of Croatia, with special responsibility for international military cooperation. Vice-president of the Croatian Movement for Democracy and Social Justice.

Paul Williams: professor of law and international relations at the American University in Washington, and principal of the Public International Law and Policy Group. Ph.D. University of Cambridge 1998, J.D. Stanford Law School 1990; 1991–93 served in the Office of the legal advisor for Europe and Canada in the US State Department, with special responsibility for issues relating to the dissolution of SFRY and the Soviet Union; subsequently, senior associate with the Carnegie Endowment for International Peace. Legal adviser to the government of the Republic of Bosnia-Herzegovina at the Dayton negotiations. Author of *The Treatment of Detainees* (1990), and co-author with Norman Cigar of the politico-legal study *War Crimes and Individual Responsibility: A Prima Facie Case for the Indictment of Slobodan Milošević* (1996). Consultant to The Bosnian Institute.

Ivo Žanić: freelance writer and researcher; doctorate from the Faculty of Philosophy, University of Zagreb (with a dissertation on the relations between political communications and traditional culture). 1994–98 editor of *Erasmus – a Journal for the Culture of Democracy;* has published numerous papers on political myths, symbols and rituals, in Croatian and other academic journals, including a survey of Croatian and Bosniak political myths for *Der Jugoslawien-Krieg: Handbuch zu Vorgeschichte, Verlauf und Konsequenzen* (1999). Author of *Mitologija inflacije: govor kriznoga doba* [The mythology of inflation: Report From a Time of Crisis] (1987), *Smrt crvenog fiće: ogledi i članci 1989–1993* [Death of the red Fiat: Essays and Articles 1989–1993] (1993), and *Prevarena povijest: guslarska estrada, kult hajduka i rat u Hrvatskoj i Bosni i Hercegovini 1990–1995* [History deceived: the gusle-player's stage, the cult of the bandit and the war in Croatia and Bosnia-Herzegovina 1990–1995] (1998).

Ozren Žunec: sociologist and professor at the Department of Sociology, Faculty of Philosophy, Zagreb, where he founded the Chair of Sociology of Military Issues and War. Founder and chief editor of *Polemos – Časopis za interdisciplinarna istraživanja rata i mira* [Journal for Interdisciplinary research into war and peace]. Author of *Planet mina: taktičko-tehnički, humanitarni, socijalni, ekološki i međunarodno-pravni aspekti uporabe kopnenih mina u suvremenom ratu* [Planet of mines: the tactical, technical, humanitarian, social, ecological and international-legal aspects of the use of land mines in contemporary warfare] (1997), and *Rat i društvo: Ogledi iz sociologije vojske i rata* [War and society: essays from the sociology of the military and war) (1998). Co-director of the private, independent, non-party institution Strata Research, editor of *Hrvatska vojska 2000: Nacionalna sigurnost, oružane snage i demokracija – materijal za raspravu* [Croatian Army 2000: national security, the armed forces and democracy – discussion papers] (1999), and with Anton Tus coordinator of *Projekt 108*, under whose auspices the study was carried out. In February 2000 placed in overall charge of Croatia's intelligence services, but resigned a month later.

Abbreviations

ARBiH	Armija Republike Bosne i Herzegovine – Army of the Republic of B-H
B-H	Bosnia-Herzegovina
CC	Central Committee
CPY	Communist Party of Yugoslavia (pre-1952)
FRY	Federal Republic of Yugoslavia (Serbia, Montenegro, Kosovo and Vojvodina)
HDZ	Hrvatska Demokratska Zajednica – Croat Democratic Community
HDZBiH	Hrvatska Demokratska Zajednica Bosne i Hercegovine – Croat Democratic Community of B-H
HOS	Hrvatske Obrambene Snage – Croat Defence Forces
HV	Hrvatska Vojska – Croatian Army
HVO	Hrvatsko Vijeće Odbrane – Croat Defence Council
HZ(H-B)	Hrvatska Zajednica (Herceg-Bosne) – Croat Community (of Herzeg-Bosna)
INA	Industrija Nafte – Petroleum Industry (of Croatia)
JNA	Jugoslovenska Narodna Armija – Yugoslav People's Army
LCY	League of Communists of Yugoslavia (post-1952)
MPRI	Military Professional Resources, Inc.
MUP	Ministarstvo Unutarnjih Poslova – Ministry of Internal Affairs
NDH	Nezavisna Država Hrvatska – Independent State of Croatia
OS	Oružane Snage – Armed Forces
OSRBiH	Oružane Snage Republike Bosne i Hercegovine – Armed Forces of Republic of B-H
PEN	International Association of Poets, Playwrights, Editors, Essayists and Novelists
PL	Patriotska Liga – Patriotic League

SANU	Srpska Akademija Nauka i Umetnosti – Serb Academy of Sciences and Arts
SAO	Srpska Autonomna Oblast – Serb Autonomous Region
SDA	Stranka Demokratske Akcije – Party of Democratic Action (B-H)
SDS	Srpska Demokratska Stranka – Serb Democratic Party (B-H/Croatia)
SFRY	Socialist Federative Republic of Yugoslavia
SNO	Srpska Narodna Obnova – Serb National Renewal (Serbia)
SPO	Srpski Pokret Obnove – Serb Renewal Movement (Serbia)
SPS	Socijalistička Partija Srbije – Socialist Party of Serbia
SVK	Srpska Vojska Krajine – Serb Army of the Krajina
TO	Teritorijalna Odbrana – Territorial Defence
TORBiH	Teritorijalna Odbrana Republike Bosne i Hercegovine – Territorial Defence of the Republic of B-H
UDBA	Ured državne bezb(j)ednosti – Office of State Security
UNPA	United Nations Protected Area (in Croatia)
UNPROFOR	United Nations Protection Force (in Bosnia-Herzegovina)
VJ	Vojska Jugoslavije – Army of Yugoslavia
VRS	Vojska Republike Srpske – Army of Republika Srpska
ZNG	Zbor Narodne Garde – (Croatian) National Guard Association

Foreword

Noel Malcolm

Few events in recent history have been so intensively written about as the 1991–95 war in Croatia and Bosnia. The scale of scholarly (and not-so-scholarly) production on this topic has been quite breath-taking. Two years ago, when Quintin Hoare (the Director of the Bosnian Institute) and I compiled a critical listing of books about the Bosnian war, we found to our surprise that it was necessary to read 347 of them – and these were only works in English and other West European languages, excluding the huge number of items published in the former Yugoslavia itself. So what possible justification can there be for the appearance of yet another book on this subject?

The answer, in this case, is simple; it is also rather extraordinary. The main focus of this book is on a particular topic: the internal military–political history of the war in Croatia and Bosnia-Herzegovina. In other words, it examines the actual policies of the military and political leaderships in those two countries, and the ways in which those policies were formed or deformed by political purposes, strategic aims and military-logistical constraints. It is a topic central to any proper understanding of how and why the war developed as it did. And yet the extraordinary fact is that not one of those 347 previously published books gives any adequate treatment of this subject at all.

Instead, the existing literature offers almost all other conceivable perspectives on the conflict – some of them valid and important, others tangential or tendentious. Thus we have a huge body of literature about nationalism, ethnicity, identity-politics and so on, much of it consisting of political scientists juggling with their conceptual categories. We also have many accounts of how Western policy towards the conflict was made and

---

In addition to being a leading authority on Thomas Hobbes, Noel Malcolm is the author of *Bosnia: a short history* (1994) and *Kosovo: a short history* (1998). In 2001 he was elected a Fellow of the British Academy.

implemented, and of the law, politics and ethics of humanitarian and military intervention. Serious studies of the intra-Yugoslav political origins of the war are much rarer, though valuable ones do exist (notably Silber and Little's *The Death of Yugoslavia*, based as it is on in-depth interviews with the participants and the use of an unparalleled archive of contemporary video footage). Yet even these tend, once the war has commenced, to shift their focus away from the local leaderships in Zagreb and Sarajevo, towards the decision-makers (and indecision-makers) in New York, Washington, London and UNPROFOR headquarters.

Why has such a central topic been so inadequately treated by previous writers? One obvious reason is that much of the relevant information has emerged only gradually after the war, in sometimes obscure local publications. Some of the key players have written memoirs, and others are in the process of doing so; new nuggets of information are constantly being disclosed. (Many important details, indeed, are revealed for the first time in this book.) Yet this is hardly a full explanation. A surprising amount of relevant information was available from local sources even during the war, to those diligent enough to seek it out – as Norman Cigar's finely documented study of the internal weaknesses of the Bosnian Serb military machine clearly demonstrates.

Looking at the whole range of Western writings about the 1991–95 war, it is hard to avoid the conclusion that there is an almost systematic inadequacy to it. One might say, cramming the issue into one awkward but useful word, that the general problem with most previous coverage is its non-Clausewitzianness. The central insight of Clausewitz's work is that war must be understood in the context of the policy-aims of the participants. This does not mean, of course, that war can be simply reduced to politics, or that military conflicts, once embarked upon, can always be ended by waving political magic wands. But it does mean that the conduct of every war must be looked at in terms of the long-term intentions of the leaderships who are waging it. Such insight, in many previously published studies (but not all – there are honourable exceptions) has been strangely lacking.

This, in turn, reflects and reinforces a more important weakness: the fundamental inadequacy of analysis and policy-making by Western governments towards the Croatian and Bosnian war. Lurking at the back of many minds in London, Washington and elsewhere was the idea that the whole conflict was little more than an eruption of primitive, ever-recurrent and therefore unstoppable 'ancient ethnic hatreds'; one distinguished British military historian even announced, half-way through the war, that he had found the key to the conflict while reading a book about Stone Age Indians in the Amazonian jungle. Even those who did not explicitly advance such views were often in implicit accord with them: politicians and diplomats spoke routinely about trying to end a single, undifferentiated thing called 'the violence' or 'the fighting', without paying much attention to who was fighting whom, and why. The arms embargo, similarly, was defended on the grounds that lifting it would merely 'add petrol to the flames' – as if the war were single and simple thing, like a fire, that would grow or diminish in merely quantitative terms.

Most surprisingly, the failure to engage in serious military–political analysis was most intense in the one place where one might have expected such issues to be considered with due care: the headquarters of the UNPROFOR commander in Sarajevo. No moderately well-informed observer of the Bosnian scene who turns to General Sir Michael Rose's account of his time in Sarajevo can fail to be struck by its extraordinary errors and omissions: its breezy account of the origins of the war which mentions Milošević only in passing; its mis-dating of the crucial Bosnian elections of 1990 by two years; its strange claim that the Vance–Owen peace plan was destroyed by the Bosnian government; or its bizarre re-assignment of the Serb exodus from the Krajina to after the Dayton Agreement. Here was a general who thought that the Yugoslav Army officers on the Serb side had received training from 'their Soviet masters', and who apparently believed that even though the military balance had begun to shift against the Bosnian Serb Army by the summer of 1994, arming the Bosnian government side would have no effect except to cause its forces to be 'overrun by the Serbs'. And if the inadequacies of Rose's analysis are an extreme case, they can almost be paralleled by the beliefs of several senior figures in the American military, who convinced themselves that the Bosnian Serb Army – a largely static and ill-motivated army dependent on its superiority in heavy weaponry and its control of towns, main roads and bridges – was a 'guerilla' force as resourceful and formidable as the Viet Cong.

Readers of this book will learn that the truth was very different. They will find much that may make them reassess the nature of Western policy during the war; they may also learn important new facts (many of them far from creditable) about the local leaderships in Zagreb and Sarajevo. One of the things that emerges most strongly is the degree of President Tuđman's co-responsibility for the war in Bosnia – which, while it may not reach full equivalence with the responsibility of Milošević, must now be seen as approaching it more closely than previous evidence had suggested. The inadequacies of the Bosnian leadership, and the narrowing of its internal political agenda, are also clearly exposed here. When this book was first published in Serbo-Croat (Croatian, Bosnian), it caused a sensation both in Sarajevo and in Zagreb, where it stayed on the bestseller list for many weeks. In both places there is a hunger to understand what really happened in 1991–95; indeed, it may be doubted whether the future of either Croatia or Bosnia can be secure until such hunger has been adequately satisfied. The appetite for such understanding in the West may be less strong. But unless such understanding is supplied – as it can be, to a significant extent, by this vitally important book – Western policy-makers will only continue to repeat, in future, the errors of the still recent past.

Introduction

Norman Cigar, Branka Magaš and Ivo Žanić

It is not often that the world is able to watch a war day by day on the television screen, as was the case with the recent wars in Croatia and Bosnia-Herzegovina. But despite the unprecedented media coverage, and despite the fact that these two interdependent wars were the greatest armed conflict in Europe in the second half of the twentieth century, they have not been systematically studied with a view to understanding their background and conduct; nor have practical lessons been drawn in anything more than a general manner. This is all the more surprising since their impact on the region's political landscape is still visible today and is likely to continue for the foreseeable future.

A realistic understanding of these wars is an important element in building a sound basis for the future of the successor states of former Yugoslavia, and for better relations between them. An analysis of their successes and failures is needed to serve the establishment of more stable and cooperative regional security.

This book is the outcome of a conference on the War in Croatia and Bosnia-Herzegovina 1991–1995, held in Budapest from 25 to 27 September 1998 under the auspices of the Bosnian Institute in London and the Institute for Southeastern Europe, part of the Central European University in Budapest, with the former assuming primary responsibility for editing the proceedings. The organizers are particularly grateful to Professor Ivo Banac, then director of the Institute for Southeastern Europe, for his generous support for the project, although he himself, unfortunately, was unable to take part in the conference due to his commitments at Yale University. In addition to the participants represented in this book, invitations were extended also to Generals Ramiz Dreković, Atif Dudaković and Sefer Halilović of the Army of Bosnia-Herzegovina, and to Generals Karl Gorinšek and Antun Tus of the Croatian Army; they were unfortunately unable to attend. General Tus submitted his contribution subsequently, for which we are most grateful to him. We also owe thanks to two prominent journalists: Ines Sabalić, of the editorial staff of *Globus* (Zagreb), and Vildana Selimbegović, of the editorial staff of *Dani* (Sarajevo), who helped in the preparation of the book.

General Martin Špegelj, the creator of the strategic basis for the successful defence of Croatia, who from the very start advocated the creation of a broad front of the states of former Yugoslavia at risk from the aggressive policies of Belgrade, was the first, in his discussion with the journalist Darko Hudelist in the Zagreb magazine *Erasmus* and weekly *Globus*, to raise the issue of the dysfunctionality of civilian–military relations in Croatia during the war. He thus made visible the gulf between overt and covert policy that characterized these wars, and opened the possibility of public debate, one of the results of which is this book. The organizers wish to thank him for his early support for the idea of the conference, and for his vital contribution to the success of the whole project.

Although there are a great many journalists' reports and scholarly studies covering the period 1991–95, as well as interviews with and memoirs by some of the participants, up to now there has been no attempt at a comprehensive analysis of these two interdependent wars, which would integrate their military and political aspects. It is this continuing gap in knowledge, not only abroad but also in the region itself, that the conference organizers sought to fill, by facilitating an exchange of ideas and discussion so as to provide the dimension hitherto lacking. The intention was to provide an open forum in which key participants in the two wars would be brought together for the first time to share their experiences. It was hoped that this would provide a unique opportunity for former military commanders and government officials from Bosnia-Herzegovina and Croatia to exchange personal knowledge, to explore new ideas and to engage in debate with other regional and foreign scholars.

While it is possible to argue that a definitive history of these events must await the release of official documents from the archives of relevant states, this opportunity may be a very long time in coming. In the meantime, the chance to establish direct communication with some of the key actors in the events, now sufficiently distanced from the heat of battle for a detached perspective, offers a unique advantage that with time, as memories fade, will no longer be available. Bringing together senior military officers, politicians and experts did indeed prove very stimulating and rewarding, and generated a lively discussion, as this record testifies.

The organizers believed it was important to look at the wars in Croatia and Bosnia-Herzegovina not only as a contribution to forming a reliable historical record, but also as providing lessons for an understanding of the conduct of political–military affairs.

Some of the contributions clarified the decision-making process and the nature of the political options and objectives which were considered and finally adopted, including those which relate to the role of the international community. It is to be hoped that a clearer appreciation of what occurred and how will provide insights into the current situation and suggest alternatives for the future in similar situations. One particular goal was to assist in setting the historiography of this key period on a sound footing before the weight of time and political correctness reshapes the memory of the past. Indeed, both in the countries of former Yugoslavia and abroad, official versions of events have rapidly emerged as a substitute for a balanced analysis, with a tendency to become the basis for new myths and conventional wisdom. A proper understanding of these wars will help to stabilize regional security and political cooperation.

The main aim of the conference was to highlight the symbiotic interplay of military and political affairs, as stated long ago by Carl von Clausewitz: 'war is a true political instrument, a continuation of political intercourse carried on with other means'.[1] Hence, every effort was made to relate military events to the domestic and international political environment, and to examine the impact of political options and decision-making on the conduct and outcome of the wars. Key areas of discussion suggested to the participants were:

The road to war. What was the sequence of events which led to war? Did the participants prepare effectively for war, both politically and militarily? What options were considered and what decisions taken?

The conduct of the war. What were the characteristics of these wars? Did the political leadership set realistic goals and did these change with time? What were the military objectives and strategies? Were they appropriate to and supportive of political objectives? What were the key phases of the military campaign and the decisive turning points? How did they reflect upon the political situation? Were the force development strategies adopted appropriate to the given goals and available resources?

Serb war effort. What were the Serbian political and military objectives? How effective was the Serb war effort? What were its strengths and vulnerabilities? Why did the Serb leaders stop the war when they did?

Civil–military nexus. Were civil–military relations effective or dysfunctional? Did the political leadership play an appropriate role? What influence did the political leadership have on military commanders and on the conduct of military campaigns?

The international dimension. What was the impact of the international factor during the lead-up to the war, on the conduct of the war and on its termination? How did the local political and military leaders react to that factor or make use of it for their own ends? What effect did the arms embargo have on the war? What was the influence of the United Nations and, later, NATO forces?

---

[1] Carl von Clausewitz, *On War*, ed. and trans. Michael Howard and Peter Paret, Princeton, NJ: Princeton University Press, 1976, p. 87.

War termination. Why did the wars end when they did? Did the political leaderships end the wars at the appropriate time? If not, why not? What was the political and military impact of the decision to end the wars?

All wars, including those examined here, are similar as far as their nature or unchanging physiognomy is concerned. Thus one will readily recognize Clausewitz's 'paradoxical triad' of war, which he defines as composed of 'primordial violence, hatred and enmity, which are regarded as a blind natural force; of the play of chance and probability within which the creative spirit is free to roam; and of its element of subordination, as an instrument of policy, which makes it subject to reason alone'.[2]

At the same time, however, Clausewitz stressed that the character of individual wars can indeed differ, given the complexity of this phenomenon, and that no two wars are exactly alike: 'War is more than a true chameleon that slightly adapts its characteristic to the given case.'[3] As the papers of this collection illustrate, to understand the wars in Croatia and Bosnia-Herzegovina it is necessary to be sensitive to all these facets and, above all, to be cautious in applying preconceived templates often developed mechanically from other times and situations which, despite their seductive simplicity, may obscure rather than illuminate. Most significantly, the results of this conference suggest a number of conclusions that challenge what has already become established as conventional wisdom about these wars.

These conflicts did not arise from 'centuries-old enmities', but from political rivalries with a significantly more recent dynamic and engineered by specific political elites. Rational, albeit in some cases ruthless or venal, elites defined concrete political objectives, crafted plans to attain them and adopted policies designed to achieve them. Most of the population, while in favour of self-determination and ready to defend itself, had little predisposition to participate in aggression against their neighbours. The poor response to mobilization and limited commitment to the war effort of the average Serb, in particular, supports such an interpretation, especially considering the intensive propaganda campaign organized by the government, together with urgings by the Orthodox Church, intellectuals and many opposition political leaders.

This is not to deny the existence of Serb fear of another genocide, played upon during the period leading up to the war by Serbian government propaganda. This fear is an important and thus far insufficiently researched phenomenon. Even though it had no real basis at the time of the transfer of government in Croatia, nor later in Bosnia-Herzegovina, it was a psychological and social fact independent of external manipulation, which to an extent must have influenced the political stance of the Serb population, especially in rural and relatively isolated communities.

[2] Ibid., p. 89.
[3] Ibid.

The participants also agreed that these wars were not triggered off by the international community's alleged 'premature recognition' of Slovenia, Croatia and Bosnia-Herzegovina, but were the result of a well-planned and long-prepared policy responding to domestic political needs in Belgrade, and to a lesser extent subsequently in Zagreb in the case of the war in Bosnia-Herzegovina. The aggression would probably have occurred in any case without international recognition. In the case of Slovenia and Croatia, such recognition followed only after they had already ensured their independence through their own efforts on the battlefield. If anything, international recognition of the independent republics erected at least some obstacles, however tenuous, to a Serbian victory in the long run, by depriving Belgrade's (and in the case of Bosnia-Herzegovina also Zagreb's) actions of legitimacy; while the international community's feeble response and its imposition of a blanket arms embargo, to the benefit of those with existing arsenals (especially Serbia and its Serb partners in Bosnia-Herzegovina), constituted an effective 'green light' for the stronger parties – Serbia and subsequently also Croatia in Bosnia-Herzegovina – to seek a decision through the use of force. Only credible deterrent action by the international community could have averted these wars at the time Yugoslavia broke apart.

When considering why there was no such action, it is worth taking into account the attitudes, stereotypical perceptions and cultural habits which, quite apart from the specific challenges posed by the war, existed in Western academic circles, political elites and sections of the public. Those reporting at the end of the 1980s and in the early 1990s on events in former Yugoslavia, those with public influence and academic authority who supplied explanations in the media, were often prone to cultural and ideological prejudice, not to speak of intellectual laziness. Quite a few succumbed to the propaganda of one or other of the 'warring factions', chiefly – both chronologically and quantitatively speaking – that of the Serbian side.

For some, Tito's Yugoslavia represented both the only successful model of a 'third way' and a unique multicultural idyll which, all of a sudden, primitive ethno-nationalists were beginning to destroy, aiming to create claustrophobic fiefdoms for their own criminal interests and thus running counter to the world-wide process of integration and globalization. Others promoted the cautious view that Yugoslavia was a highly explosive mixture which only the communist dictatorship had succeeded in holding together, so that, as soon as that era ended, it was natural and unavoidable that hatreds transmitted from generation to generation would rise to the surface; it was not possible either to restrain them or to explain them according to the categories of modern, Western political thought or scientific discourse.

In both cases the result was the same: a significant part of the public and the political elite did not understand the war in its real terms, its real time and space, but treated it as a kind of dehistoricized drama. For the first group, dehistoricization occurred in line with their perception of an objectively complex state as a kind of child's picture book, in which East and West, North and South, the Latin and Cyrillic scripts, mosques and churches, customs and cuisines, passed in succession without ever being linked to any real sociocultural and political categories. A passive surrender to the aesthetic of the superficial repressed the need for an active thematization and eventual problematization of the content. For the others, dehistoricization arose from the stereotype that the contestants were steeped in dark passions and sinister memories of long-past events, intertwined into bizarre relations in an area devoid of any content with which the public could positively identify. The term 'Balkan', which in the West had long since acquired a pejorative overtone as connoting a region organically foreign to Western civilization, was now being used as justification for such a passive stance.

Labouring under the influence of Serbian propaganda and the attitudes of their own governments, the Western public became susceptible to messages which further distorted its perception of reality. The propaganda was based on the evocation of trauma from the recent or distant past, especially from the Second World War but also from the period of Ottoman rule in the Balkans, and on generalization or extrapolation of individual experience to the collective level.

The platitudes of Nazi revival and of 'history repeating itself', in which Croatia appeared as a satellite of a renewed and expansionist German Reich, struck a nerve among the Western public, whose democratic value system incorporated a powerful resistance to right-wing totalitarianism, and fed into the unease and dilemmas occasioned by the reunification of Germany. The platitude of the 'danger of an Islamic state at the heart of Europe' also reached many credulous ears – both at the start when it was put about by Belgrade, and in the later phases of the war when the same rhetoric about Bosnia and Bosniaks was taken up officially in Zagreb – set as it was in the context of the Israeli–Arab conflict, terrorism in Algeria, international military action against Iraq and tense relations with Iran, and helped by the unease and tensions arising in Western societies from an ever-increasing inflow of immigrants from Islamic countries.

When considering whether these were civil or interstate wars (a largely legal distinction), one may conclude that in real life the clear-cut distinctions typical of social science models do not always exist. In the case of former Yugoslavia, while one can certainly discern elements of a 'civil war' once the wars were fully under way, armed parties being engaged against their neighbours at the local level, the wars' origins and predominant traits, and the factors which ensured their continuation, show the external dimension as decisive.

While there was political rivalry between the various national communities within Croatia, Bosnia-Herzegovina and other republics at the time of Yugoslavia's dissolution, there is no evidence that its dynamic made armed conflict inevitable. On the contrary, all the indications are that without direct intervention from Belgrade (and later also from Zagreb in the case of Bosnia-Herzegovina), without organization from without of elements bent on obstructing a peaceful resolution in favour of armed confrontation, and without the removal of local leaders willing to seek a peaceful settlement, there would have been no armed conflict at all. Even when these wars were well under way, without the direct and continual involvement of Belgrade (and in Bosnia-Herzegovina also of Zagreb), they would have ended more rapidly, with much less destruction and far fewer casualties.

As for the question whether these conflicts were conventional or unconventional – i.e. waged by uncontrollable elements armed haphazardly and with no motives other than hate and plunder, with all that this implies for command and control, strategy and responsibility – one can find elements of both. But once again these papers, concentrating on the key factors, argue that it was conventional forces, leadership and policies that predominated and determined how these wars were waged and what was their ultimate outcome.

Furthermore, as many of the papers show, the wars were conducted at two levels of reality: the actual and the imaginary, the physical and the symbolic, since the aggressors deliberately introduced into them a psychological energy and a system of normative values which elided the boundary between the two.

The destruction of sacred objects and cultural monuments, the razing of graveyards and the changing of place names are especially painful for all communities: they represent an attack on the symbols of their identity, on the referential framework that enables them to orient themselves in space and time. The papers in this book show that this was an important way of appropriating territory and creating conditions in which, even in the event of military and political defeat, it would be almost impossible to return to the pre-war situation. All such barbarous acts directly served the war objectives, and were not a mere side-effect or an unavoidable phenomenon associated with military activity. The systematic and consistent destruction in areas where there was no armed conflict at all speaks for itself; but even where there was bitter and long-lasting armed conflict, including street fighting, scarcely an example is to be found where it can be convincingly demonstrated that the destruction of a cultural, historic or religious monument was the unavoidable consequence of war or a mere accident.

Attacking symbols deeply rooted in time and place, symbols of psychological and social cohesion, especially in smaller communities, had a two-fold purpose. On the one hand, like the systematic mass rapes and other forms of humiliation, this subjected the 'wrong' population to additional terror and pressure to flee, since the creation of ethnically and religiously homogeneous areas was a fundamental component and objective of the war. On the other hand, since the destruction continued even after the population had been deported or killed, one can conclude that those very monuments of their material presence were treated in principle as a weapon with which competing communities hold a given territory and which must, therefore, be destroyed with other weapons – typologically different, but essentially the same – so as to 'liberate' the territory in question, i.e. appropriate it in all its dimensions. This is confirmed by the fact that in many such instances – in which the Yugoslav People's Army (JNA), followed by the Serb armies that emerged from it, set the example from the start, an example later to be copied also by Croat forces, especially in Herzegovina – one can recognize ritual and theatrical elements. The statements of the perpetrators or members of the military and political elite themselves testify not only to their unconcealed satisfaction but also to their efforts to imbue the destruction with the meaning of 'rectifying historical injustices', of 'legitimate restoration of the original historical situation', and such like; paradoxically, then, as the 'construction' of a world from the past.

What also emerges from these papers is the conclusion that virtually in every case the war efforts were hampered by dysfunctional civil–military relations, as political objectives set by the governments often had less to do with military effectiveness and political feasibility than with the consolidation of the elites in their positions of authority within the emerging domestic political system. Typically, the failure to specify the intended borders of the projected Greater Serbia in any but vague terms provided Slobodan Milošević with political flexibility in the event of defeat; but it also complicated the setting of appropriate military objectives and made it more difficult to achieve the necessary support for the war effort among the Serb military.

These papers lead also to the conclusion that the international community's principle of 'even-handedness' and dogmatic insistence that only a 'political solution' to the wars was possible, serving as they did as substitutes for a more robust response, were more damaging than beneficial. At the very least, this attitude encouraged the strong to initiate and persist in their armed aggression, sure that they could do so without fear of effective military or political sanctions. Almost all wars end 'politically', with a negotiated settlement; but how and when a war ends is certainly affected and often determined by the situation on the battlefield. On the basis of the contributions discussing relations between the military and the political actors, it can be asserted that the wars moved towards termination only when it became evident that the Serbian government's objectives would be impossible to achieve, prompting the international community to ensure a certain balance of power on the ground.

The conference also saw the attribution of a quasi-mythical power and prowess to the JNA and its Serb offsprings as due for revision. Despite an overwhelming initial advantage in equipment and organization, the Serb war effort was beset by a low level of commitment, poor morale, personnel shortages, poor leadership and dysfunctional civil–military relations. Instead of being able to conduct a short, decisive war as expected, Belgrade found itself enmeshed in costly and protracted conflicts, though the international arms embargo undercut the ability of its opponents to defend themselves.

The achievement of a mere balance of power with Belgrade's field forces, well short of parity and reached with far fewer forces than the international community had considered necessary to bring about change on the ground, was sufficient to force Belgrade to renounce its ambition to achieve its objectives by armed conflict. Unable to reach a decisive victory, and faced with a collapse of morale and the ever more manifest possibility of defeat, Serb forces had no choice but to end the wars by coming to terms. Nevertheless, thanks to Zagreb's specific foreign policy interests, which frequently lent support to Belgrade's interests in Bosnia-Herzegovina, and to international pressure, Belgrade was in the end able to achieve more than its military success warranted.

The greatest benefit to be gained from a study of these wars is the lessons which can be drawn from them and applied to future conflicts. Nonetheless, the international community only in part applied these lessons to the war in Kosovo, which followed a few years later. This is all the more surprising since the conflict in Kosovo was a continuation of the wars fought in Croatia and Bosnia-Herzegovina and part of the same process of disintegration of Yugoslavia. It can even be said that Milošević was more easily able to embark on the war in Kosovo, with its accompanying atrocities by Belgrade's military and police, because his experience in Croatia and Bosnia-Herzegovina had reinforced his belief that the international community would act tentatively and slowly, allowing him to end it with a deal which would favour Belgrade. It seems that the international community, in the shape of NATO, did however draw some positive lessons, including the need to act early and resolutely by, if necessary, military means, although it perhaps did not do so to the extent that many considered optimal.

The deeply rooted perception of Serb military prowess and tenacity, although refuted by the recent wars, resurfaced to affect NATO's plans to use military force. The consequence was the unfounded assessment that it would be difficult to carry out any kind of ground campaign which, if it had happened, would have led to a clearer end-game and might thus have sealed Milošević's own political fate. As it was, Milošević had to take further unprecedented steps before at least some in the international community became convinced that he could not be a valid partner in negotiations, as he had been regarded at the time of the wars in Croatia and Bosnia-Herzegovina.

The papers also confirm the impression, already present at the outbreak of the wars in former Yugoslavia, that the international community was not just a passive observer or even a neutral intermediary in the search for a peaceful solution, but an active participant, introducing its own individual and collective objectives and interests which were often decisive for the conduct of the wars and the achievement of peace. Since they were constantly being adapted to the behaviour of the international community, the wars were shaped by its attitudes and conduct, and it is really difficult to understand them fully if one ignores the contribution of the international community to all three elements of Clausewitz's 'paradoxical triad'.

As the guardian of access to the United Nations, the international community, for example, was in a position to chart the range of 'contingency and likelihood' in the context of which the Yugoslav republics and regions could 'legitimately' be attacked, regardless of the fact that at the start of the war only Serbia had an organized armed force. While the media in the West expressed their abhorrence of 'tribal' or 'ethnic' wars, Western politicians readily accepted the creation of ethnically pure territories in Croatia and, especially, in Bosnia-Herzegovina, the partition of which was built in to the very start of negotiations on its future and continued in ever more grotesque forms to be imposed upon the country even after its international recognition.

It is possible that in the early autumn of 1991 Western politicians were indeed convinced that the military machine launched by Belgrade had already won the war in Croatia; but this had already become untenable by late autumn, when the Croatian Army halted the invasion from Serbia and liberated much of western Slavonia. It remains an open question why the international community not only insisted on the Vance Plan for the occupied regions of Croatia, but built into it a withdrawal, in fact redeployment, of the aggressor's military forces and hardware to neighbouring Bosnia-Herzegovina, where various illegal structures were already being armed for a violent occupation and/or division of this member state of the former Yugoslavia.

What the international community had excluded from its consideration of these wars, by all appearances, was the popular commitment to self-determination as a right to freedom, and the strength of the resistance which resulted. The embargo on the import of arms for the defence of Bosnia-Herzegovina was not only a form of direct intervention in that war, but also a sign of the international community's surprising readiness to accept the country's partition. It was not impossible to foresee, even as early as the end of 1992, that the inability of Belgrade and Zagreb as well as of Sarajevo to bring the war to a quick end would feed the forces of anarchy at the base of society, and would reinforce the power, both within and outside the country, of ruthless and corrupt circles to whom the prolongation of the war served only as a means of strengthening their personal power.

As many of the papers show, the fig leaf of humanitarian aid with which Western politicians attempted to disarm critics of their policy of appeasement towards Belgrade, the chief source of armed aggression in former Yugoslavia, merely fed the horrific war in Bosnia-Herzegovina. The unworkable Bosnia-Herzegovina devised at Dayton, resulting not from the *victory* of anti-Bosnian forces but negotiated after their military *defeat* near Banja Luka, is a visible sign of the presence of the international community as a key participant in the wars in former Yugoslavia. We still await an answer to the question whether its diplomatic and military efforts are leading to lasting stability in the region.

The Budapest meeting posed many questions concerning the involvement of the international community in the wars in former Yugoslavia, and provided some answers. To the extent that an integral Europe, its peace and development, are important for international relations in the future, this book should be of use also to those who were not directly involved in military and diplomatic battles connected with the disintegration of the former Yugoslavia. And while it is true that the attitudes and behaviour of the international community were at all times built into the wartime plans of the ruling elites in Bosnia-Herzegovina, Croatia and Serbia, it was their own ambitions and their ability to realize them that in the end proved decisive.

We believe that the meeting, and the book that resulted from it, will throw some light on the objective effects of their actions, and it is to be hoped that it will stimulate further research in that direction.

MAP 1
Territorial constitution of the JNA before 1987/88 – army system

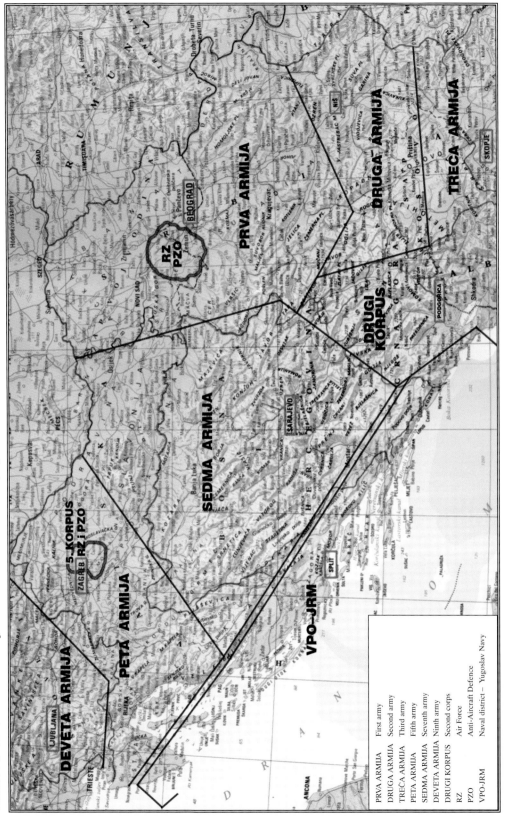

PRVA ARMIJA	First army
DRUGA ARMIJA	Second army
TREĆA ARMIJA	Third army
PETA ARMIJA	Fifth army
SEDMA ARMIJA	Seventh army
DEVETA ARMIJA	Ninth army
DRUGI KORPUS	Second corps
RZ	Air Force
PZO	Anti-Aircraft Defence
VPO–JRM	Naval district – Yugoslav Navy

MAP 2
Territorial constitution of the JNA after 1988 – theatre system

Structure and numerical strength of the armed forces of the Socialist Federal Republic of Yugoslavia (Armed Forces = JNA + Territorial Defence – TO) in peacetime and war:

JNA: peacetime personnel: 180,000 (15 per cent); wartime personnel: + 1,200,000 (85 per cent)

TO: peacetime personnel: approx. 1,000 (2 per cent); wartime personnel: + approx. 1,200,000 (98 per cent)[1]

Armed Forces total in wartime (with full mobilization of 8 per cent): 2,400,000, of whom approx. 550,000 in production and logistics, with the remainder combat troops.

Land Army: structure: 17 corps, plus 1st guards division (Belgrade) and 63rd parachute brigade (Niš) as independent troops of the general staff; heavy weapons: 2,100 tanks, 1,000 armoured transporters, 8,000 artillery pieces and 1,300 anti-armoured missile pieces.

Navy: structure and resources: 1 brigade torpedo boats (14 vessels), 1 brigade guided-missile frigates and destroyers (16 vessels), 1 brigade patrol boats (4 vessels), 1 division minesweepers (9 vessels), 1 submarine brigade (11 vessels), 1 maritime sabotage detachment and 3 marine brigades.

Air Force and Anti-Aircraft Defence: structure: 5 corps (Zagreb); 1 corps (Belgrade); 3 corps (Skopje); resources: 512 fighter aircraft, 104 transport aircraft, 152 helicopters and 118 other aircraft, with 5,100 anti-aircraft guns and 2,800 anti-aircraft rocket weapons.

[1] The TO of Kosovo (130,000) existed only on paper, since after the first demonstrations by Albanians in spring 1981 it was disarmed and its arms transferred to Serbia. Kosovo Serbs and Montenegrins were left armed or later armed via parallel, extra-institutional channels.

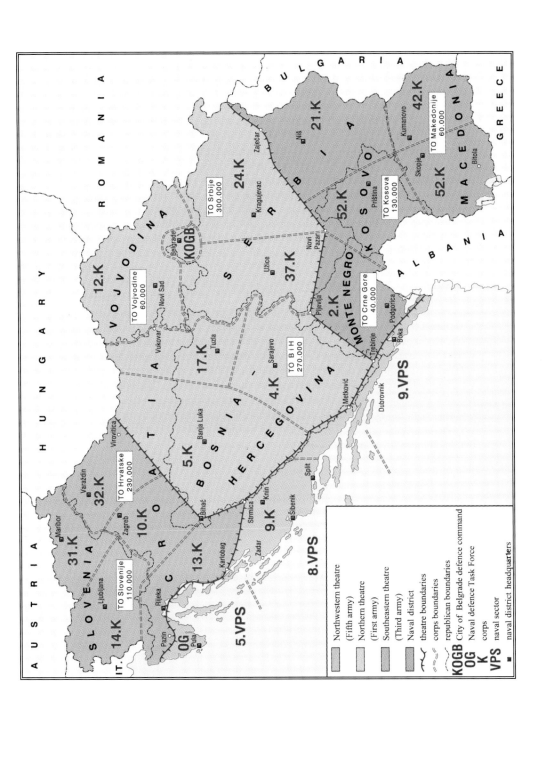

AUSTRIA

HUNGARY

ROMANIA

BULGARIA

GREECE

ALBANIA

IT.

SLOVENIA
14.K
31.K
32.K

Maribor
Varaždin
Ljubljana
Zagreb

TO Slovenije 110.000
TO Hrvatske 230.000

VOJVODINA
12.K
Novi Sad

TO Vojvodine 60.000

KOGB
Beograd

SERBIA
24.K
21.K
37.K

Zaječar
Niš
Kragujevac
Užice
Novi Pazar

TO Srbije 300.000

KOSOVO
52.K
42.K

Priština
Skopje
Kumanovo
Bitola

TO Kosova 130.000

MACEDONIA
52.K

TO Makedonije 60.000

CROATIA
10.K
5.K
13.K
9.K

Virovitica
Vukovar
Banja Luka
Bihać
Karlobag
Strmica
Knin
Zadar
Šibenik
Split
Pazin
Pula
Rijeka

BOSNIA - HERCEGOVINA
17.K
4.K

Tuzla
Sarajevo

TO BiH 270.000

MONTE NEGRO
2.K

Pljevlja
Trebinje
Podgorica
Boka
Metković
Dubrovnik

TO Crne Gore 40.000

OG
5.VPS
8.VPS
9.VPS

Northwestern theatre (Fifth army)

Northern theatre (First army)

Southeastern theatre (Third army)

Naval district

theatre boundaries

corps boundaries

republican boundaries

KOGB   City of Belgrade defence command

OG   Naval defence Task Force

K   corps

VPS   naval sector

■   naval district headquarters

MAP 3
The battle for Vukovar, August–November 1991

Apart from suffering damage in the general destruction of the town, the hospital was many times specifically targeted. On 26 August it was hit by two air-to-ground missiles fired from an aircraft, on 2 October by 37 artillery shells, the following day by a 500 kg bomb, which smashed through all the floors and landed in a space crammed with wounded but did not explode, and on 12 October by between 120 and 130 missiles from multibarrelled launchers positioned in Bačka; in November 100 or so shells were falling on it daily. After the first direct attack on the town at the end of July, an operating theatre was set up in the basement, and the second floor was vacated. From the end of September, when the whole building above ground was destroyed, all surgical interventions were carried out in improvised conditions in the basement, in the former clinics and the premises where plaster-casts were made and in other auxiliary rooms. During the 88 days of the siege 2,500 wounded were treated in the hospital, including several members of the belligerent forces; 80 of the wounded died. During the same period 14 children were born. When the town fell, the hospital was sheltering 350 wounded and about 1,000 civilians who had taken refuge there. On the basis of an agreement reached on 17 November between the International Red Cross, the Croatian civilian authorities, the hospital manager Dr Vesna Bosanac and the JNA, all the wounded, medical personnel and civilians in the city (some 15,000) were to be evacuated to free Croatian territory. But the JNA and Serb militias entered the hospital on 18 November at about 13.00, paying no attention to the International Red Cross representatives or the EU observers. During the following two days, both in the town and in the surrounding area, especially on the Ovčara farm, many individual and mass executions were carried out. About 100 people went 'missing', i.e. killed, from the hospital itself: 18 employees, 25 members of the technical support staff, 60 civilians and about 200 wounded.

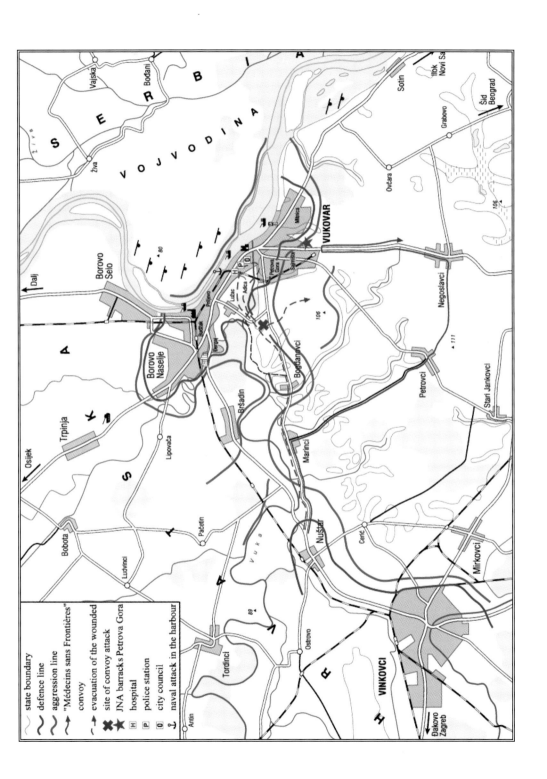

Legend:

- state boundary
- defence line
- aggression line
- "Médecins sans Frontières"
- convoy
- evacuation of the wounded
- site of convoy attack
- JNA barracks Petrova Gora
- H hospital
- P police station
- 0 city council
- naval attack in the harbour

SERBIA

VOJVODINA

Živa

Vajska

Bodani

Dalj

Borovo Selo

Borovo Naselje

Trpinja

Osijek

Bobota

Ludvinci

Pačetin

Lipovača

Bršadin

Antin

Tordinci

Ostrovo

Marinci

Nuštar

Cerić

VINKOVCI

Đakovo Zagreb

Mirkovci

Stari Jankovci

Petrovci

Negoslavci

Bogdanovci

VUKOVAR

Lužac

Adica

Petrova Gora

Sajmište

Mitnica

Priljevo

Bačak

Borovo

Sotin

Ovčara

Grabovo

Itok
Novi Sa

Šid
Beograd

Vuka

106

111

89

106

80

MAP 4
The siege of Sarajevo, April 1992–October 1995

The tunnel that runs beneath the airport runway is 900 m long, 85 cm wide and 160 cm high, on average. Conceived by the General Staff of the Army of the Republic of Bosnia-Herzegovina, it was excavated by members of the Civil Defence who were not fit for active service. The digging began in April 1993, in the basement of the relatively well-sheltered house of the Kolar family, in the sub-urb of Butmir, and was completed on 30 July of the same year. On the Butmir side it was held up by wooden props and on the Dobrinje side by metal ones, since there was no wood in the city. It often flooded, and heavy rains would bring down sections of it, so a special 10-member team was charged with maintaining it. It is estimated that there were at least 3,000,000 crossings through the tunnel; some people went through it more than 100 times. Among the people who used it were the wounded, civilians, soldiers and many foreign delegates, ambassadors (US, Austria) and members of the government. Electricity and water, and fuel pipes, ran through the tunnel, which was also used to bring in humanitarian aid – food, medicines – as well as ammunition and military equipment. Until the sign-ing of the Dayton Accord, except for a very short period when the Blue Road over Igman existed, the tunnel was the only link between the besieged city and the out-side world.

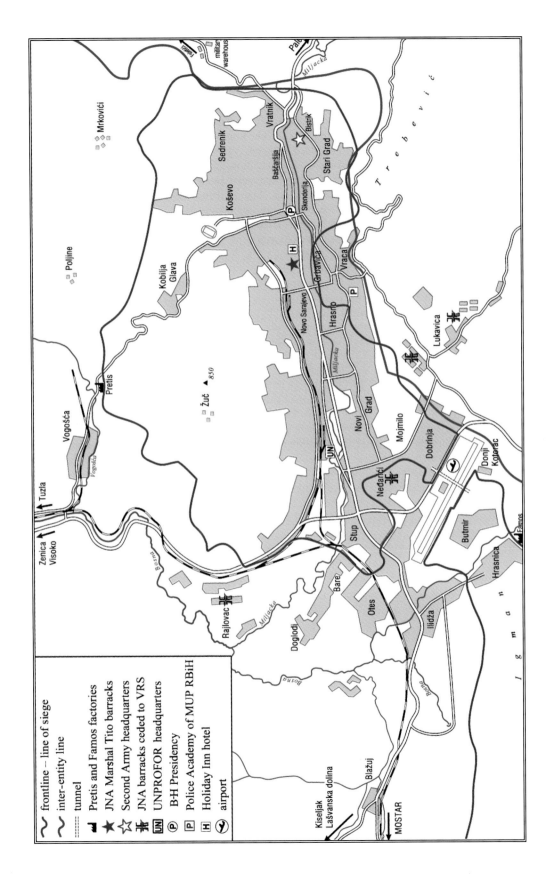

Legend:

- frontline – line of siege
- inter-entity line
- tunnel
- Pretis and Famos factories
- ★ JNA Marshal Tito barracks
- ☆ Second Army headquarters
- 卍 JNA barracks ceded to VRS
- UN UNPROFOR headquarters
- Ⓟ B-H Presidency
- Ⓟ Police Academy of MUP RBiH
- Ⓗ Holiday Inn hotel
- ✈ airport

Map labels:

Mrkovići, Poljine, Vogošća, Pretis, Žuč ▲ 850, Kobilja Glava, Sedrenik, Vratnik, Bistrik, Baščaršija, Stari Grad, Skenderija, Koševo, Trebević, Grbavica, Vraca, Novo Sarajevo, Hrasno, Miljacka, Lukavica, Novi Grad, Mojmilo, Dobrinja, Nedžarići, Donji Kotorac, Butmir, Hrasnica, Igman, Stup, Bare, Otes, Ilidža, Doglodi, Rajlovac, Miljacka, Bosna, Vogošća, Zenica, Visoko, Tuzla, military warehouse, Pale, Kiseljak, Lašvanska dolina, Blažuj, MOSTAR, Famos, Bosut

MAP 5
Extent of Serb occupation

In July 1995 Srebrenica, a UN 'safe area', after being completely surrounded for more than three years, fell into the hands of the Army of Republika Srpska (VRS) and paramilitary units that had joined it. The largest massacre in Europe since the Second World War then took place – about 7,400 people, of a total of 30,000 who had been trapped in the city. The testimonies of survivors, and the investigations of *Christian Science Monitor* journalist David Rohde and of the independent Bosnian–Herzegovinian media (*Dani*), from the start pointed to the shared responsibility borne by official representatives of the international community. Although the United Nations tried for a long time to hush the case up, and expressly to deny the massacre (Akashi), they were forced by public pressure to launch an investigation at the end of 1996. It was led by David Harland, and its report, published in November 1999, confirmed that UN Secretary General Boutros Ghali, UNPROFOR Commander Bertrand Janvier and UN Special Envoy for Civilian Affairs Yasushi Akashi, as well as the Dutch UNPROFOR battalion in Srebrenica, shared the blame. On 10–11 July 1995, the battalion's commanding officer had more than once called for air strikes against the Serb troops to put an end to the attack against the town: Akashi and Janvier first ignored him, then explicitly rejected the final request, since it was not submitted in the prescribed form. About 4,300 Bosniaks, boys and adult male civilians, who had taken shelter in the UNPROFOR base in the village of Potočari, were handed over to the VRS by the Dutch troops; they were killed in a series of mass executions ending on 17 July, while more than 3,000 other civilians were killed in the forests and mountains as they fled towards Tuzla. Many of them were killed when they came into the open after seeing soldiers with blue berets, not knowing that these were in fact VRS soldiers who had 'borrowed' that part of their uniform from the Dutch UNPROFOR troops. Harland's full report is available on http://www.un.org/News/ossg/srebrenica.htm

SLOVENIA
CROATIA
HUNGARY
VOJVODINA

ZAGREB
BILO GORA
Virovitica
Grubišno
Polje
HV   Beli
       Manastir

Sava
C   R   O   A   T   I   A
Osijek

Delnice
Karlovac
HV
Sisak
Kutina
Pakrac
HV
HV   Vukovar

Kupa
Ogulin
Petrinja
Sunja
Vinkovci

Gvozd
Hrvatska Kostajnica
Okučani
Nova Gradiška
Slavonski Brod
Ilok

HV
Una
Sava
HV
Srijemska
Mitrovica

Slunj
Velika
Kladuša
Dvor
Prijedor
Derventa
Odžak
Orašje
HV

ABiH
Cazin
Gradačac
Brčko
Sava

Otočac
Korenica
Bihać
Sanski Most
Banja Luka
Doboj
ABiH
ABiH
Bijeljina
Šabac

HV

Gospić
Udbina
Ključ
Maglaj
Tuzla
ABiH

HV
Donji
Lapac
Drvar
Jajce
HVO
Žepče
ABiH
Zvornik

Gračac
Travnik
Vareš
ABiH

Obrovac
Bosansko
Grahovo
Zenica
HVO
Srebrenica

Zadar
Benkovac
Knin
Glamoč
Vitez
ABiH
Žepa

Biograd
Vrlika
Kupres
Kiseljak
HVO
ABiH

HV
Drniš
Livno
HVO
Prozor
Konjic
SARAJEVO
Goražde
ABiH

Šibenik
HV
Sinj
Tomislavgrad
HVO
ABiH

Split
Imotski
Mostar
HVO
Foča

Nevesinje

Ploče
Stolac
HVO

Ravno
Nikšić

Trebinje

Dubrovnik
MONTE NEGRO
Podgorica
Cetinje

SERBIA
BOSNIA

under Serb control in
Croatia (around 28%)
and B-H (around 70%)
~~~ international border
ABiH forces of B-H Army
HVO Croatian Defence Council
HV Croatian Army

MAP 6
Operation Storm, 4–10 August 1995

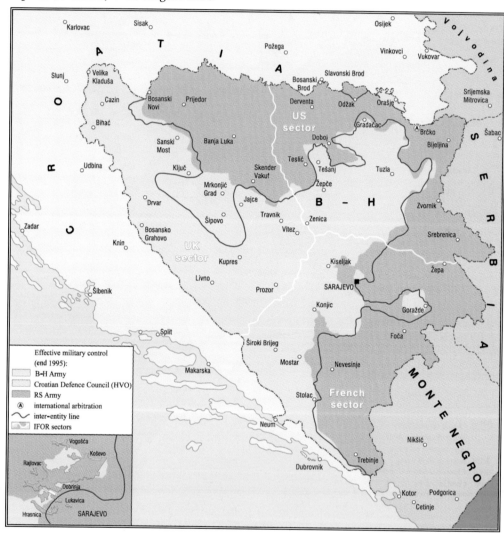

Effective military control
(end 1995):

B-H Army
Croatian Defence Council (HVO)
RS Army
Ⓐ international arbitration
inter-entity line
IFOR sectors

MAP 7
Bosnia and Herzegovina as determined by Dayton Accord, December 1995

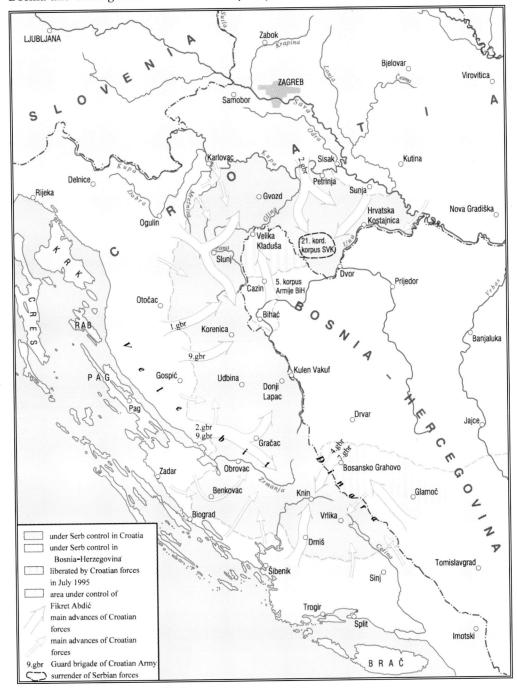

MAP 8
Ethnic distribution in Bosnia and Herzegovina according to 1991 population census

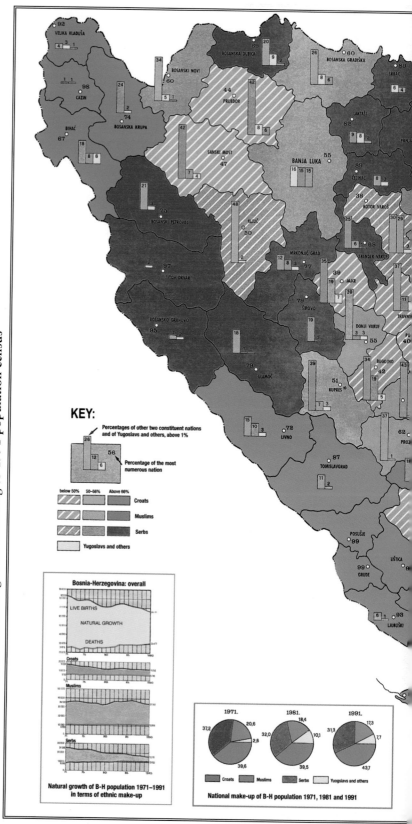

KEY:

Percentages of other two constituent nations
and of Yugoslavs and others, above 1%

Percentage of the most
numerous nation

below 50%   50–66%   Above 66%

Croats

Muslims

Serbs

Yugoslavs and others

Bosnia-Herzegovina: overall

LIVE BIRTHS
NATURAL GROWTH
DEATHS

Croats

Muslims

Serbs

Natural growth of B-H population 1971–1991
in terms of ethnic make-up

1971.   1981.   1991.

National make-up of B-H population 1971, 1981 and 1991

Croats   Muslims   Serbs   Yuogslavs and others

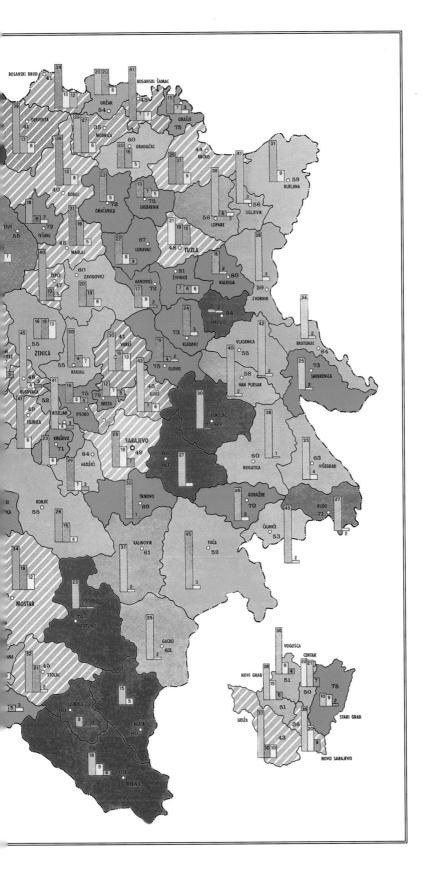

MAP 8
Ethnic distribution of Bosnia and Herzegovina, 1991

Bosnia and Herzegovina (total population): 4,354,911

Sarajevo (total) 525,980
    Centar 79,005
    Ilidža 67,438
    Novi Grad 136,293
    Novo Sarajevo 95,255
    Stari Grad 50,626
    Vogošća 24,707
    Hadžići 24,195
    Ilijaš 25,155
    Pale 16,310
    Trnovo 6,996
Banovići 26,507
Banja Luka 195,139
Bihać 70,896
Bijeljina 96,796
Bileća 13,269
Bos. Dubica 31,577
Bos. Gradiška 60,062
Bos. Krupa 58,212
Bos. Brod 33,962
Bos. Novi 41,541
Bos. Petrovac 15,552
Bos. Šamac 32,835
Bos. Grahovo 8,303
Bratunac 33,575
Brčko 87,332
Breza 17,266
Bugojno 46,843
Busovača 18,883
Cazin 63,406
Čajniče 8,919
Čapljina 27,852
Čelinac 18,666
Čitluk 14,70
Derventa 56,328
Doboj 102,546
Donji Vakuf 24,232
Drvar 17,079
Foča 40,513
Fojnica 16,227
Gacko 10,844
Glamoč 12,421
Goražde 37,505
Gornji Vakuf 25,130

Gračanica 59,050
Gradačac 56,378
Grude 15,976
Han Pijesak 6,346
Jablanica 12,664
Jajce 44,903
Kakanj 55,857
Kalesija 41,795
Kalinovik 4,657
Kiseljak 24,091
Kladanj 16,028
Ključ 37,233
Konjic 43,636
Kotor Varoš 36,670
Kreševo 6,699
Kupres 10,098
Laktaši 29,910
Livno 39,526
Lopare 32,400
Lukavac 56,830
Ljubinje 4,162
Ljubuški 27,182
Maglaj 43,294
Modriča 35,43
Mostar 126,067
Mrkonjić-Grad 27,379
Neum 4,268
Nevesinje 14,421
Novi Travnik 30,624
Odžak 30,651
Olovo 16,901
Orašje 28,201
Posušje 16,659
Prijedor 112,470
Prnjavor 46,894
Prozor 19,601
Rogatica 21,812
Rudo 11,572
Sanski Most 60,119
Skender Vakuf 19,416
Sokolac 14,833
Srbac 21,660
Srebrenica 37,211
Srebrenik 40,796

Stolac 18,845
Šekovići 9,639
Šipovo 15,553
Široki Brijeg 26,437
Teslić 59,632
Tešanj 48,390
Tomislavgrad 29,261
Travnik 70,402
Trebinje 30,879
Tuzla 131,861
Ugljevik 25,641

Vareš 22,114
Velika Kladuša 52,921
Visoko 46,130
Višegrad 21,202
Vitez 27,728
Vlasenica 33,817
Zavidovići 57,153
Zenica 145,577
Zvornik 81,111
Žepče 22,840
Živinice 54,653

NOTE: Data for Kupres relate to 1981, since the census officials were unable to carry out their duties in 1991. Rounding-up of numbers in some municipalities results in a total percentage of 101.

AUTHORS: Ante Markotić, Ejub Sijerčić and Asim Abdurahmanović

SOURCE: *Population Census 1991. Statistics Bulletin No. 219*, Republic Statistics Institute, Sarajevo, May 1991; *Population Census 1981. Statistics Bulletin No. 86*, Republic Statistics Institute, Sarajevo, November 1982.

PUBLISHERS: Altermedia d.o.o. – NUB BiH, Sarajevo 1991.

Part I

The War in Croatia

1

The Road to War

Stjepan Mesić

It is difficult to consider the war in Croatia in isolation, because both in its preparation and during its actual course it remained closely linked to events in Bosnia-Herzegovina, as it had also been with the short war in Slovenia, the three areas functioning like joined vessels. Even now the war has ended, we see that every problem emerging in Bosnia-Herzegovina has its reflection in Croatia and vice versa. So before the armed conflict ever broke out it should have been realized that war in the Balkans could only result in a full-scale tragedy. But unfortunately the international community did not send out sufficiently firm signals: it allowed the war to happen, and there were even those who not only allowed it, but actually wanted it.

In my capacity first as vice-president, then as president of the Presidency of the Socialist Federative Republic of Yugoslavia (SFRY), I did my best to persuade the international community to become involved, because Yugoslavia could no longer be sustained – all its internal integrative factors had ceased to exist. I called, in particular, for international forces to be stationed on the borders between Croatia and Serbia and between Bosnia-Herzegovina and Serbia, to prevent direct contact between the forces of war in Serbia and their followers in Croatia and Bosnia-Herzegovina. But Milošević's stubborn pursuit of the war option, and later Franjo Tuđman's obstinacy in continuing the war in parts of Bosnia-Herzegovina, indicate collusion between the forces wanting to destroy that country. According to the 1974 Constitution of SFRY the republics were states; their acquisition of independence could actually have led to a peaceful resolution of the crisis. But those outside the country who wanted war, thinking that Bosnia-Herzegovina would then be split apart along a Serb–Croat seam, acted as mentors of those in the country itself who also sought war.

HISTORY OF THE GREATER SERBIA IDEA

The preparations for war began long before it effectively broke out in 1990. It was basically a war for a Greater Serbia. The project of creating a Greater Serbia has failed twice: first in the 1941–45 war, with the formation of a Federal Yugoslavia; and again in the 1990–95 war, with Yugoslavia's disappearance, i.e. with the independence of Slovenia, Croatia, Macedonia and Bosnia-Herzegovina. This project has a long, well-known and stubborn history; here I shall refer only to some of its basic aspects from the past six decades.

One of its key proponents was Slobodan Jovanović (1869–1958), professor of state law at the Faculty of Law in Belgrade. He became actively involved in politics only on the eve of the Second World War, following the 1939 Agreement – between the leader of the Croatian Peasants' Party (HSS) Vlatko Maček and Yugoslav Prime Minister Dragiša Cvetković – which created Banovina Croatia as an autonomous administrative unit within Yugoslavia.[1] Allergic to every expression of Croatian political individuality and above all to any sign of its being recognized by Serbs, proponents of a Greater Serbia organized a campaign against the agreement in which a prominent role was played by the Serbian Cultural Club. It was then that Jovanović joined the club and became its ideologue. Their demand was for the whole of Yugoslavia apart from Slovenia to be united administratively under the common name of the Serb Lands, with the capital in Skopje.

After the collapse of Yugoslavia in April 1941, Jovanović accompanied the king to London and became prime minister of the government in exile. From that position he presented the Chetniks and their leader Draža Mihailović as the principal resistance movement in occupied Yugoslavia. He strengthened Mihailović's position by getting him promoted general, and by appointing him minister of armed forces in the homeland, with himself as his representative in the government. The rapid capitulation of the Kingdom of Yugoslavia in April 1941 was seen by advocates of the Greater Serbia idea as advantageous for their cause. A whole series of studies and projects were developed, all based on the idea of a 'Greater' and 'homogeneous' Serbia and on the alleged right of the Serbs to be the leading nation in the Balkans, for which they must first be brought together in a single, ethnically homogeneous state.

The first major programmatic document, 'Homogeneous Serbia' or 'Homogeneous Serbian State', dates from as early as 30 June 1941. It was

---

[1] Banovina Croatia included large areas of Bosnia-Herzegovina (especially in western Herzegovina and Posavina). While Croats were in a relative or absolute majority in many of these, the Bosniak population was simply ignored when drawing the new banovina borders; only the ratio of Croats to Serbs was taken into account. The borders represented a total disregard for the political, legal and historical identity of Bosnia-Herzegovina.

written by Stevan Moljević, a Banja luka attorney, who submitted it to Mihailović and in May 1942 went to the latter's headquarters and became his political adviser. 'The Serbs must have hegemony in the Balkans', he wrote, 'and to have hegemony in the Balkans, they must first have hegemony in Yugoslavia', which they would 'instil with their spirit and give it their stamp.' Homogeneity, i.e. the complete separation of the Serbs from neighbouring peoples, was to be achieved by 're-settlement and population exchange', while Serbia thus conceived was to encompass by far the greater part of Yugoslavia – everything except Slovenia and the north-western region of Croatia, including part of its coast at Kvarner – and would border directly on Slovenia in the Karlovac area. It would also include some territories to be taken from Hungary, Romania, Bulgaria and Albania.[2] The military force behind this project would be Mihailović's Chetniks, to which the government-in-exile gave the legitimacy and status of successor to the pre-war regular Yugoslav army.

This megalomaniac, explicitly expansionist and ultranationalist programme was not achieved at that time. In 1943 majority-Croat Partisan troops inflicted a defeat on the Chetniks at the river Neretva from which they never recovered. Tito's Partisans came out of the war as victors, and as part of the global anti-fascist coalition. It is true that the Partisans were led by communists, who after the war established a dictatorship by manipulation and the use of terror; but the Partisan movement itself, especially in Croatia and Slovenia, was essentially pluralistic and brought together a broad coalition of anti-fascist democrats and patriots.

The project of establishing a Greater Serbia up to the Virovitica–Karlovac–Karlobag line has remained to this day – more or less covertly, and with modifications according to circumstances – as a goal in the minds of militant Serb nationalists; it became the model for contemporary Serb nationalists and for Slobodan Milošević in the 1980s, when they revived the idea of Greater Serbia, the principal cause of the war in former Yugoslavia.

When General Kadijević writes that there were 'two main pillars of the defence of Yugoslavia – the Serbian people and the JNA',[3] it becomes clear how Moljević's ideas on the historic mission of Serbs and their special role in Yugoslavia were stubbornly retained even in the minds of those who publicly expressed their revulsion against the Chetniks, glorified their own Partisan past and represented themselves as 'true Yugoslavs' and fighters

---

[2] All these documents and studies have been published in *Zbornik dokumenata i podataka o narodnooslobodilačkom ratu naroda Jugoslavije* [Collected documents and data on the Yugoslav peoples' national liberation war], vol. XIV, book 1, Belgrade 1981. Moljević's study has been republished in Božo Ćović (ed.) *Izvori velikosrpske agresije – rasprave, dokumenti, kartografski prikazi* [Origins of the Greater Serbian aggression: discussions, documents, cartographic surveys], Zagreb 1991, pp. 141–7.

[3] Veljko Kadijević, *Moje viđenje raspada: vojska bez države* [My view of the break-up: an army without a state], Belgrade 1993, p. 89.

for equality, brotherhood and unity. The great manipulator Milošević succeeded in convincing many people throughout the world that he and his movement were struggling to preserve Yugoslavia. Before the war broke out he insisted that the existence of the Autonomous Provinces of Kosovo and Vojvodina was preventing Serbia from establishing its statehood to the same degree as the other republics. But after abolishing the autonomy of Kosovo and Vojvodina, he took up the position of defending Yugoslavia from the separatism of the 'anti-Yugoslav' republics – first Slovenia, then Croatia, and so on down the line. Now that he has led Serbia into war and genocide, it must be clear to everyone that he never wanted any kind of Yugoslavia at all – neither federal, nor confederal. His persistent advocacy in the mid 1980s of a 'modern' federation to replace the existing one was simply part of the campaign for a Greater Serbia.

As is well known, in 1990 Croatia and Slovenia had worked out the concept of a confederal agreement. They called for a confederation to be established for a certain period, from three to five years, after which, if it proved unworkable, each would go its own way. Serbia never accepted this option (and the government-controlled Belgrade press mocked the proposal), supporting only a 'modern' federation that simply meant the other republics would suffer the same fate as Kosovo, Vojvodina and Montenegro, whose governments were brought down by Milošević through populist campaigns involving a series of coordinated rallies on the pretext of solidarity with 'threatened' Serbs in Kosovo. Coordinated coups took place in Vojvodina and Montenegro in autumn 1988, and in Montenegro again in January 1989 after the first attempt had failed. Milošević had the support of the leaders of the Serb Orthodox Church, the Serbian Academy of Sciences and Arts (SANU), the Writers' Association of Serbia, the Serbian PEN, and other such institutions.

In 1986 a group of SANU members drew up a 'Memorandum on Current Social Issues in Our Country', in which they analysed the crisis in the Yugoslav economy and society, and the position of Serbia and the Serb nation in Yugoslavia. They claimed that Serbia was exploited, and that the Serb nation suffered discrimination. They cited Slovenia and Croatia as leaders of an anti-Serb coalition, and sought a solution in the physical separation of Serbs from other nations.[4] At the same time they launched the ridiculous but insidious assertion that Serbia and the Serbs have always been victors in war and losers in peace.[5] Militant Serb nationalists took this call

---

[4] The text of the Memorandum, first published by the Belgrade daily *Večernje novosti* on 24–25 September 1986, can be found in Ćović, *Izvori velikosrpske agresije*, pp. 256–300. On the genesis, conception and programme of the Memorandum, see Olivera Milosavljević, 'The abuse of the authority of science', in Nebojša Popov (ed.), *The Road to War in Serbia: trauma and catharsis*, Budapest 2000, pp. 274–302.

[5] See note 2, p. 5.

to close ranks as a call to military conquest and genocide. It is true that other republics too claimed they were disadvantaged in Yugoslavia. Croatia claimed that the central government was extorting from it the foreign currency it earned from tourism and shipbuilding, Bosnia-Herzegovina that it was obliged to sell its coal and other raw materials in the domestic market more cheaply than it could in European and global markets, and so on. Every republic had something to complain about, and it was evident that the model that had obtained until then was no longer satisfactory.

BLAME FOR THE WAR

Attempts to relativize the blame for the outbreak of war are doomed to failure. The principal culprits are Milošević and his regime, in conjunction with the military leadership, i.e. the staff of the supreme command (the Yugoslav Federal Presidency), headed by federal secretary for people's defence, General Veljko Kadijević. Aggressors often seek to justify their action as protection of their fellow countrymen living in the states they are going to attack, but war is usually fought for territory. And thus did Milošević too plan and launch a war for territory, including genocide against non-Serbs. The mask of defending Yugoslavia fell from the moment the call 'All Serbs in a single state!' was heard, and when the decision was made to withdraw the JNA from Slovenia. The withdrawal of the Federal army from Slovenia meant the release – or expulsion – of Slovenia from the Federation: the Greater Serbia ideologues were not interested in that republic (indeed, it was even a nuisance to them), because there was no indigenous Serb population there that could have formed the basis of an insurrection and later a quisling government. It must have been clear then to the most politically naïve that the JNA had ceased to be multinational: it had become a Serb army under Milošević's direct command. In a very short period the JNA had evolved from an army that, in earlier days, had fought for self-managing socialism and Yugoslavia into an army fighting for Orthodoxy and Greater Serbian nationalism.

After the Dayton Accord was signed and peace imposed in Bosnia-Herzegovina, it became clear to everyone that Milošević could not have contemplated the war option without the treacherous role of the military leadership, bringing the JNA over to his side.[6] The army should have

---

[6] As president of the SFRY Presidency, I formally personified the supreme command and it would have been normal for the generals and military leaders to maintain contact with me, but no general ever came to me, nor did I ever receive any information from the JNA commanders. During all this time the JNA was under Milošević's command, hatching the plans whose results we know all too well, while presenting themselves in public as the only ones in the country who were obeying the supreme command and respecting the constitution.

remained outside the negotiations which the republics were conducting with the SFRY Presidency, or followed the line of the decisions issued by that Presidency, instead of which it embroiled itself in political life in order to seize as much territory as possible from the ruins of Yugoslavia, since it was seeking a sponsor able to sustain the bloated body the JNA had now become.

Those who bear the responsibility for this war and its aftermath must be brought before the Hague Tribunal. And FRY, i.e. Serbia and Montenegro, must pay war damages to the victims of aggression: to Slovenia, Croatia and Bosnia-Herzegovina. Under the leadership of Slobodan Milošević and former president of Montenegro Momir Bulatović, Serbia and Montenegro invested their entire military, economic and human potential in the war; only compensation to the victims of their aggression can lead to the democratization of FRY. The fact that Croatia has not asked for damages has allowed Milošević to claim success for his war aims. But if Serbia were compelled to pay reparations, forces would emerge in that country demanding to know who was responsible for the fact that the whole of Serbia has to pay for the pursuit of unrealizable war aims. Insistence on war reparations, regardless of whether they would be paid or not, would make it possible for pro-European forces to emerge in Serbia too. The fact is that Serbian aggression has experienced total defeat, and Milošević has not achieved a single one of his war aims; but the Greater Serbian hypnosis can come to an end only if Serbia and Montenegro face up to the fact, as they will have to do if they undertake to pay war damages, or if they are persistently required to do so. By taking this stance, Croatia, Slovenia and Bosnia-Herzegovina would set in motion a wave of democratic change in Serbia and free the region of former Yugoslavia from this destabilizing factor in Europe.[7]

---

[7] On 2 July 1999 Croatia did file a claim against FRY (Serbia and Montenegro) with the International Court of Justice in the Hague, basing it on the 1948 Convention on the Prevention and Punishment of the Crime of Genocide, and seeking war damages. The claim states, among other things, that FRY has 'committed aggression against Croatia in that it supported, armed, incited and directed the actions of various groups within Croatia to rebel against the democratically elected authorities', and that it was responsible not only for the 'ethnic cleansing' of the non-Serb population in Croatia (20,000 killed, 55,000 injured, 3,000 missing and 600,000 displaced: the numbers in November 1991), but also for the 'exodus of the Serbs after Operation Storm – ordering, encouraging and inciting Croatian citizens of Serb nationality to evacuate'. Officially, the claim was filed only then because all the data had finally been gathered and 'the political circumstances have matured for a final analysis of the truth about what happened from 1991 to 1995' and 'political conditions have been created for the situation in the whole region to stabilize' (see *Jutarnji list*, *Večernji list* and *Vjesnik*, Zagreb, all of 3 July 1999). One is left, however, with the impression that the claim, although justified, was motivated primarily by diplomatic and political speculations after the NATO intervention in FRY. See also the exposition by Jovan Divjak in this volume, pp. 152–77.

Yugoslavia had three basic integrative factors: Tito and his charisma; the League of Communists (LCY) as a multinational party; and the JNA as a multinational army. Seven and a half years after Tito's death, following the notorious 8th session of the Central Committee of the League of Communists of Serbia in September 1988, at which Milošević got rid of his most important internal opponents in the party and state structures of Serbia, he began to take over – i.e. eliminate – the other two cohesive Yugoslav factors. At the 14th session of the LCY, in January 1990, the Federal party organization was broken up and the Serbianization of the JNA began. The betrayal of the military leadership, headed by General Veljko Kadijević and General Blagoje Adžić, cleared the way for Milošević's military adventure. The so-called 'anti-bureaucratic revolution' removed the autonomy of Kosovo and Vojvodina, as well as the state leadership of Montenegro. The president of the Federal Executive Council, Ante Marković, with his economic reforms and US support, and the republics of the so-called anti-Serbian coalition, Slovenia and Croatia, were still blocking the way to the homogenization of Serbia and the outbreak of war. Marković and his government offered reforms that, had they been achieved, would have made possible a peaceful examination of political options for the country. That was precisely what Milošević, and later Tuđman, did not want, so they both insisted that Marković be brought down. The United States supported Marković and his reforms, since it considered that if he succeeded Yugoslavia could be maintained as an external, international legal framework, regardless of its internal organization. Neither the United States nor Marković, however, took into consideration the power of those who at that time wanted to move from politics to war as soon as possible. Milošević was merely seeking a pretext for war.

On the day the JNA attacked Slovenia, 27 June 1991, the Slovenian member of the Federal Presidency, Janez Drnovšek, called me in great distress from Ljubljana to say: 'Look, man, this is banditry: they want war at any price!' My adviser, a Serb, called me from Belgrade and said: 'The military will not be able to break Slovenia, the people will prove stronger!' I was completely unable to make contact with either Kadijević or his deputy Stane Brovet, while Ante Marković assured me by telephone that he had not been informed about troop movements in Slovenia either. 'It's not possible to explain what's happening, let alone justify it by decisions of the Federal Executive Council! Someone is trying to discredit the Federal government's reform efforts in the international arena.'[8]

---

[8] Stjepan Mesić, *Kako smo srušili Jugoslaviju: politički memoari posljednjeg predsjednika Predsjedništva SFRJ* [How we destroyed Yugoslavia: political memoirs of the last president of the Presidency of SFRY], Zagreb 1992, p. 49; 2nd edn: *Kako je srušena Jugoslavija: Politički memoari* [How Yugoslavia was destroyed: political memoirs], Zagreb 1994.

On 17 October of that year, just before missiles launched by the JNA Air Force hit Banski Dvori (The Ban's Court, office of the Croatian president) and almost killed Tuđman, Marković and myself, Marković stated that he had believed the generals' promises that in no circumstances would they attack Zagreb, and that he hoped we could form a new Federal government to carry out the peaceful reform of Yugoslavia. But Jović, Milošević and Kadijević considered him from the very start 'unacceptable and undependable', 'a direct agent of the USA charged with the destruction of the system', and even a covert 'Croat separatist'. Some ten days before the Serb insurrection began in Knin, they agreed that he 'must be brought to his senses' and the Yugoslav crisis be brought to a conclusion while Jović headed the Presidency, since 'after that we would be completely helpless'.[9]

That from 1989 a significant part of the JNA command was involved in planning for a war to achieve the idea of Greater Serbia is confirmed by the reorganization of the JNA in the second half of the 1980s, the subsequent placing of the Territorial Defence (TO) forces under the Federal military command, the disbanding and reorganization of the TO of Kosovo, and the decision to disarm the TO in areas outside the army's control. The real meaning and purpose of this disarmament, carried out in May 1990, can be deduced from the fact that it was strictly carried out only in Slovenia and Croatia – of course, without the knowledge of the political leadership of those republics.[10] The armed forces of SFRY were composed of the JNA, the regular army and the TO, which had two lines of command: one was to the local republican leadership, the other to the supreme command, i.e. the Federal Presidency. The changes meant that the TO forces lost all effective connection with their own republics.

The 'anti-bureaucratic revolution' in Serbia, with continual threats against Slovenia and Croatia, provoked resistance in those republics to possible Serbian aggression. The result was a homogenization of Croats and Slovenes, but also a strengthening of national sentiment. In other words, it was the 'anti-bureaucratic revolution' itself which produced an increasingly nationalist opposition; Milošević's militantly imperialistic policies played into the hands of nationalist parties in the western republics.

The armed destruction of SFRY in accordance with the Greater Serbia concept began in Croatia on 17 August 1990 with the planned and directed Serb insurrection in the Knin *krajina* and Lika. Milošević needed an insurrection of Serbs in Croatia to ignite war in Bosnia-Herzegovina,

[9] Borisav Jović: *Poslednji dani SFRJ: izvodi iz dnevnika* [The last days of Yugoslavia: excerpts from a diary], Belgrade 1995, p. 196.
[10] On the disarmament of the TO, see pp. 21, 158–9 and note 88 on p. 99 in this volume.

and Belgrade used Jovan Rašković to bring it about. When he was used up, the political and military operations were entrusted to Milan Babić, Goran Hadžić, Milan Martić, Mile Mrkšić and others, but the aim remained the same – the formation of a Belgrade–Knin–Pale axis.

OBSESSION WITH THE DIVISION OF BOSNIA-HERZEGOVINA

Milošević's raising of tension and incitements to war encouraged Tuđman's naïvety and passionate desire to extend Croatia's borders. He was convinced that Bosnia-Herzegovina would in the very near future be partitioned along a Serb–Croat seam, and that the world would allow it to happen. The two of them agreed on this in Karađorđevo and Tikveš, where Milošević succeeded in convincing Tuđman that Serbia would surrender Bosnia-Herzegovina to him up to the borders of the 1939 Banovina, and even give him the additional territory of so-called Turkish Croatia: Cazin, Velika Kladuša and Bihać.[11]

When Serb villages in Croatia began to be supplied with arms, we were informed about it. The arms came from the JNA arsenal in the local garrisons: these were not just defensive weapons, but high-quality arms for use in serious fighting. I was in Belgrade at the time and said to Borisav Jović, my Serbian colleague on the Federal Presidency, that we had full information about this and that it would lead to a catastrophe in which Serbs in Croatia would be the greatest losers, since they, being only 10–12 per cent of the population, could not oppose the whole of the rest of Croatia. I asked him why Serbia was following such suicidal policies to the disadvantage of their fellow nationals, since, I said, it was obvious that Serbian policies in Belgrade were behind this.

He replied that Serbs in Croatia were of no interest to Serbia: 'They are your citizens, do with them what you will, you can impale them if you want, it's no business of ours.' 'Are you interested in Croatian territory?' I asked him. He replied that they were not interested in Croatian territory either, and he meant it: during and after Operations Flash and Storm Milošević did not lift a finger to help these Serbs, but left them to their

[11] Turkish Croatia is a name for the territory between the rivers Una and Vrbas which, until the Turkish conquest in the second half of the sixteenth century and its inclusion in the Bosnian *pashalik*, belonged to the medieval Croatian kingdom (but in large part also to medieval Bosnia under King Tvrtko I Kotromanić). Although it was occasionally used earlier, this name was first used consistently by Austrian military topographers who, after the Peace of Karlovci of 1699, worked in the Austro-Ottoman border commission. In the mid nineteenth century it began to be replaced in cartography by the term Bosanska Krajina, which became the invariable term after the Austro-Hungarian occupation of Bosnia-Herzegovina. On coming to power, Tuđman began to revive the anachronistic term 'Turkish Croatia' as a means of devaluing Bosnian statehood.

fate. I then said to Jović: 'If that is so, let's sit round the table and avoid war. What are you really interested in?' 'We are interested in 66 per cent of the territory of Bosnia-Herzegovina, and this we shall take. It was Serb, it is Serb and it will remain Serb.' 'Then let's sit round the table, and let the Bosnian problem be internationalized. We don't need war for either problem, we can resolve everything by political agreement. Are you for sitting round the table, Tuđman and me on the one hand, and Milošević and you on the other?' Jović agreed. We waited for Milošević's response, and when he agreed too, I went to Zagreb, where Tuđman also agreed. After some time, Tuđman informed us that the Croatian political leadership was going to Karađorđevo; when they came back, he said that Milošević had offered Croatia the Banovina borders plus Cazin, Kladuša and Bihać. They had also agreed to wait before bringing down Ante Marković. Tuđman said that he had guarantees that the JNA would not attack Croatia. I do not know what happened at their second meeting in Tikveš, but we all know what ensued.

Before the outbreak of war, Tuđman, relying on the Karađorđevo agreement, predicted that the JNA would not try to resolve the political crisis by military means. He insisted that he had Milošević's and Kadijević's guarantees for that. He was convinced that the rebellious Serbs would in time return the Croatian territory they were holding, in one way or another, and that he would extend Croatia through the partition of Bosnia-Herzegovina.

Verbal support for the survival of Bosnia-Herzegovina was not hard to see through: Milošević created Republika Srpska in Bosnia-Herzegovina, and Tuđman the Croat Community or Croat Republic of Herzeg-Bosna: the absorption of the first into Serbia and the second into Croatia was to be only a matter of days. However, with the formation of the Army of Bosnia-Herzegovina – according to my information, 250,000 soldiers by the end of the war – all partitioning plans were dead in the water. Despite this, the Croatian and Serbian controlled media continued to demonize the Bosniaks. In debates in the Croatian parliament it was said that there could be no coexistence of peoples in Bosnia-Herzegovina, and that it would be best to redraw the borders. Hundreds of thousands of people were expelled from their homes by ethnic cleansing, later called 'humane population resettlement'. Instead of encouraging and assisting the return of refugees and displaced persons, the advocates of partition have done everything they could to maintain the status quo. The principled stance of the international community, and especially of the United States, that borders must not be altered, and the ever stronger awareness of the citizens of both Bosnia-Herzegovina and Croatia that an integral Bosnia-Herzegovina is both possible and essential, encourages the advocates of peace to persevere with the Europeanization of former Yugoslavia.

CONCLUSION

Milošević and his regime are responsible for the war in Slovenia, Croatia, Bosnia-Herzegovina and now also in Kosovo. The JNA is also indisputably guilty. When it found itself an army without a state, it had two options: either to surrender its weapons and allow its personnel to return to civilian life, or to rent itself out to someone. The JNA opted for the second solution: to be the mercenary army of Milošević's Serbia.

Part of the responsibility for the conflict between Bosniaks and Croats in Bosnia-Herzegovina is certainly also to be borne by Tuđman's coveting of territory. By further analysis it is not difficult to establish that the Vance–Owen plan for the cantonization of Bosnia-Herzegovina provided an additional incentive for the partition of that country, so that the international community too bears a responsibility. So its messages to those who are to blame for the aggression against Croatia and Bosnia-Herzegovina need to be much more resolute. They must be such as to encourage democratic forces in the whole of former Yugoslavia, so that those responsible for the outbreak of war, and for the destruction and suffering it has brought about, leave the political arena as soon as possible. This would be far more helpful than bombarding us with ambiguous or even illogical statements such as, for example, those made by Ambassador Warren Zimmermann – a decent man and pleasant interlocutor – who at the height of the crisis in 1991 kept rejecting the appeals of Slovenia and Croatia for help, repeating meaninglessly: 'We do not believe that Yugoslavia can remain intact except as a democratic country, nor do we believe that Yugoslavia can become a democratic country unless it remains intact.'

It is my belief that the fundamental causes of the war have not yet been removed and that the international community still has a great deal to do in our region. We can attain a durable peace only if it remains clear and persistent in its stance that aggressors should not profit from wars.

2

The First Phase, 1990–1992: the JNA prepares for aggression and Croatia for defence

Martin Špegelj

This chapter represents the first attempt at a systematic examination of the causes, conduct and consequences of the war in former Yugoslavia, so we can be forgiven if there are omissions or mistakes. I shall begin by observing that the multinational JNA as such is not guilty for having been drawn into the war, whereas both its leadership and many of the new, younger Serb officers who attained important positions in the armed forces between 1975 and 1990 do bear great responsibility for the outbreak and subsequent course of the war.

The catch-phrase publicly launched in the late 1980s that the army was the 'seventh republic' originated with its top people, with specific ideological and political aims in mind. In reality, of course, this JNA 'republic' was greater than any of the republics, since it controlled the whole of Yugoslavia. After Tito's death the military leadership began to consider itself responsible in a special way for Yugoslavia's political and state order. During 1989 and in the spring of 1990 its intention was to get rid of both Milošević and the leading people in the western republics – not only the leaders of the newly created parties, but also Milan Kučan and Ivica Račan – since in its eyes they were all 'nationalists'; and to return Yugoslavia to the centralist model of the late 1940s and early 1950s, which meant revoking the 1974 Constitution and many of the reforms associated with it. The idea of recentralizing Yugoslavia did not originate with the radical Serb leadership, but with the military structures which 'saw in the Constitution of 1974 itself the basis for the break-up of Yugoslavia'.[1] Its hostility towards the existing Constitution was maintained right up to the start of the disintegration of the JNA itself.

My theme is the genesis of the war on the territory of the Socialist Federal Republic of Yugoslavia (SFRY) and its first phase, 1990–92, the

---

[1] Veljko Kadijević, *Moje viđenje raspada: vojska bez države* [My view of the break-up: an army without a state], Belgrade 1993, p. 108.

war in Croatia. In order to address the military issues of the genesis of the war, it is necessary first to set out some essential factors among its causes.

JNA REORGANIZATION AND RELATIONS WITH THE TO IN THE EIGHTIES

The framework for the prolonged war in SFRY was created over a period of decades. The fundamental shortcomings of the political structures in both Yugoslavias, the Kingdom and Tito's, their undemocratic and repressive natures in particular, provided a favourable environment for perpetual clashes arising out of the historical, national and religious differences within the state and especially from the uneven economic potential of its regions. From 1918 to 1990 both integrative and disintegrative forces were constantly in play, but the disintegrative forces, taken as a whole, were always stronger. This was still the case even after the Second World War, when, thanks to the victorious anti-fascist struggle, integrative forces came to the fore: the ideology of brotherhood and unity, the welfare state, Yugoslavia's high international standing and Tito's charisma, together with the appearance of liberal tendencies in the running of its state and economy that marked Yugoslavia's last twenty years or so.

Kardelj's famous lectures at the end of the 1960s recognized this fact: divergent interests were acting destructively, shaking the entire Yugoslav state structure. His view was that Yugoslavia would not survive in its existing organizational form, but only if a fundamental and qualitative decentralization of state and society was rapidly achieved, entrusting each socialist republic with maximum possible responsibility for its own development, including its own defence within 'the Yugoslav community'. It is well known what an uproar there was from unitarist circles at this fully justified statement by Kardelj (then effectively the second most important man in Yugoslavia and Tito's right hand), in which SFRY appeared for the first time as a 'community' coordinating the relations between its parts, rather than as the site of governmental or ruling power. There followed the adoption of the new Constitution of 1974, in which the Federation became an institution for reconciling the diverse interests of the Yugoslav republics and provinces.

The Constitution defined the Yugoslav Armed Forces as composed of two equal components: JNA and Territorial Defence (TO). According to the Law on National Defence, these components were equal as to training and acted as a single operative force in the event of external aggression. There was no question of their unity in other circumstances, however. TO forces were trained and run by the leaderships of the republics and autonomous provinces, while the JNA's training and operational-strategic use fell within the jurisdiction of the Federal Presidency, which after Tito's death replaced him in his role of commander-in-chief.[2]

The new concept of defence was motivated both by the need to create an effective defence against superior forces in the event of an attack by NATO or the Warsaw Pact, especially the latter, and by the need to safeguard the rights and powers of the republics and provinces enshrined in the new constitution. This is important to bear in mind when considering the subsequent development of both branches of the armed forces. Nothing was said openly about this at the time, but it was known at the highest levels that the arrangement was intended to act as guardian of the essentially confederal elements of the 1974 Constitution. Right from the beginning, and from various motives, hard-line integralists and unitarists attacked the Constitution and the new defence law in particular. They clashed fiercely with supporters of further decentralization and continued to do so with increasing bitterness throughout the 1980s, with minor oscillations in the conflict but no essential retreats.

From the end of the 1970s, the military leadership, which had acquired considerable independence, was developing what was known as the military–industrial complex: in 1985 it exported US$2 billion worth of products, which was very high for Yugoslavia. Apart from acquiring this unique economic independence, the military command also sought after Tito's death to win greater political and institutional independence, which was when the notion of the JNA as a 'seventh republic' emerged. It was put about by the military command itself, as a signal that it saw itself as an essential participant in the resolution of all fundamental issues of state and society.

It was already clear what the military's preferences were. It stood for unitarism, as did the Serbian leadership, which claimed that the majority Serb nation was disadvantaged by the 1974 Constitution, which should, therefore, be amended to minimize its confederal elements. The term 'majority' was deliberately misleading, since the Serbs formed only 37 per cent of the population of Yugoslavia: they were the most *numerous* nation, but not a *majority*. Moreover, there were in principle no majorities and minorities in the Federation, all constituent communities being equal.[3]

---

[2] See Table 1 for the command structure of the SFRY armed forces, and Map 1 for the territorial disposition of the JNA, at this stage. Table 2 and Map 2 show the same after the 1988 reorganization.

[3] According to the 1981 population census, SFRY had 22,424,711 inhabitants of whom 8,140,452 were Serbs, 4,428,005 Croats, 1,999,957 Muslims (Bosniaks), 1,753,554 Slovenes, 1,703,364 Albanians, 1,339,729 Macedonians, 579,023 Montenegrins, 426,866 Hungarians, plus some smaller groups; 1,219,045 declared themselves 'Yugoslavs' in the national sense. See *Statistički godišnjak Jugoslavije 1990* (Statistical Annual of Yugoslavia 1990), Federal Statistics Institute, Belgrade 1990, p. 129. Data from the 1991 census were treated only at the republic or autonomous province level, since by that time the Federal administration was

Table 1
Command structure of SFRY armed forces before the 1988 reorganization

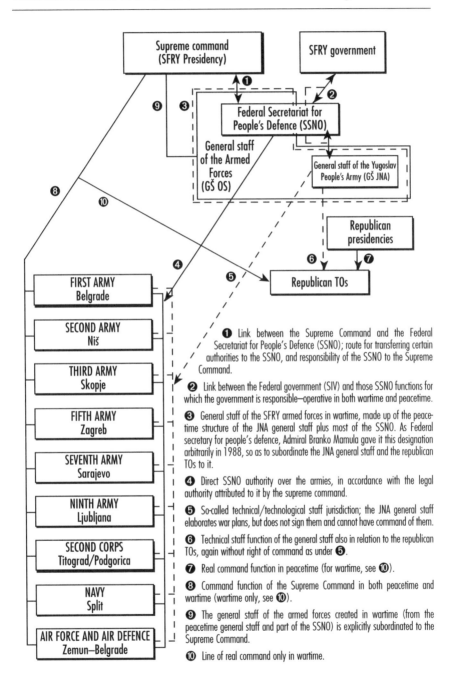

❶ Link between the Supreme Command and the Federal Secretariat for People's Defence (SSNO); route for transferring certain authorities to the SSNO, and responsibility of the SSNO to the Supreme Command.

❷ Link between the Federal government (SIV) and those SSNO functions for which the government is responsible—operative in both wartime and peacetime.

❸ General staff of the SFRY armed forces in wartime, made up of the peacetime structure of the JNA general staff plus most of the SSNO. As Federal secretary for people's defence, Admiral Branko Mamula gave it this designation arbitrarily in 1988, so as to subordinate the JNA general staff and the republican TOs to it.

❹ Direct SSNO authority over the armies, in accordance with the legal authority attributed to it by the supreme command.

❺ So-called technical/technological staff jurisdiction; the JNA general staff elaborates war plans, but does not sign them and cannot have command of them.

❻ Technical staff function of the general staff also in relation to the republican TOs, again without right of command as under **❺**.

❼ Real command function in peacetime (for wartime, see **❿**).

❽ Command function of the Supreme Command in both peacetime and wartime (wartime only, see **❿**).

❾ The general staff of the armed forces created in wartime (from the peacetime general staff and part of the SSNO) is explicitly subordinated to the Supreme Command.

❿ Line of real command only in wartime.

It was the military leadership which in 1988 initiated a debate on, and the adoption of, amendments to the Constitution which ultimately led to a redistribution of military power to the centre, under the pretext of overcoming the disunity of the Yugoslav armed forces, the uncoordinated management of the republican economies, the duplication and triplication of economic capacity, etc. The military leadership favoured a state-run 'socialist' economy. The desired amendments were not immediately accepted, but their proponents did not give up. Various moves were made that year – announced both in veiled formulations and in open lobbying among delegates to the Federal Assembly – to push through amendments to the Law on National Defence as 'modernization' of the armed forces. As soon as they were adopted, it became clear that 'modernization' boiled down to abolition of the existing military organization based on armies. The Yugoslav armed forces had been organized as six armies (plus an independent corps stationed in Montenegro and a naval division based at Split), with commands located in the republican capitals and territories approximately coinciding with the republican borders. This was now replaced by regional theatres: three of ground troops – central, south-eastern and north-western, with their headquarters in Belgrade, Niš and Zagreb respectively – and one naval theatre with its command headquarters in Split as before.

The thinking behind this move is illustrated by a privately-voiced admission by Lt-Gen. Milan Daljević, who had worked hard in 1986 to change the Armed Forces Law: 'The republic-based armies must be abolished', he said, 'to prevent them from becoming too close to the republican leaderships.' General Kadijević in his book on Yugoslavia's disintegration confirms that this was the real aim, when he writes that the 1987–8 reorganization of the command and of the strategic and operative-strategic groupings of the JNA and TO forces meant that the military leadership had 'essentially' won the battle, since the territorial delimitation of the three new theatres *completely ignored the administrative borders of the Republics and Provinces*.[4]

completely dysfunctional, and armed conflict had already broken out. Presumably the ratios were more or less the same, apart from a significantly reduced number of declared 'Yugoslavs'. Probably those who had formerly declared themselves as such were fairly equally distributed among Serbs, Croats and Bosniaks, so that the ratio would not greatly alter.

[4] Kadijević, *Moje viđenje raspada,* p. 77 (italics in original). It is worth noting the use of 'administrative' for the republican and provincial borders.

Sefer Halilović, former chief of staff of the armed forces of Bosnia-Herzegovina and until September 1991 an officer in the JNA, has also recognized this reorganization as important evidence of an alliance between the JNA and advocates of a Greater Serbia, and of preparations for the creation of a Greater Serbia by force. The three new military theatres 'completely ignored the existing republican borders' and 'were meant to correspond with the future borders set by the [SANU]

Table 2
Command structure of SFRY armed forces after the 1988 reorganization

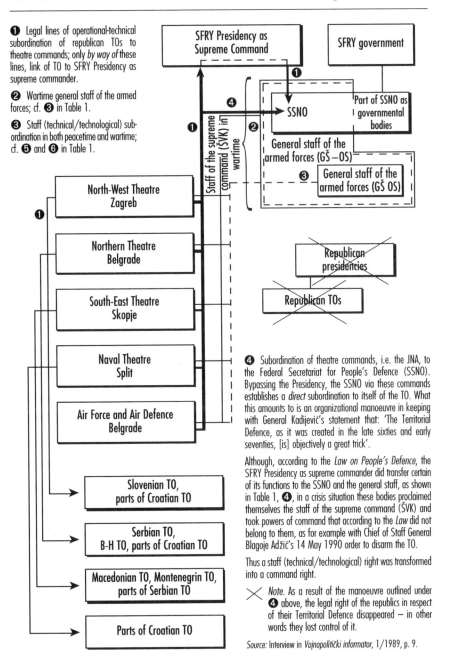

❶ Legal lines of operational-technical subordination of republican TOs to theatre commands; only *by way of* these lines, link of TO to SFRY Presidency as supreme commander.

❷ Wartime general staff of the armed forces; cf. **❸** in Table 1.

❸ Staff (technical/technological) subordination in both peacetime and wartime; cf. **❺** and **❻** in Table 1.

SFRY Presidency as Supreme Command

SFRY government

SSNO

Part of SSNO as governmental bodies

General staff of the armed forces (GŠ–OS)

General staff of the armed forces (GŠ OS)

Staff of the supreme command (ŠVK) in wartime

North-West Theatre Zagreb

Northern Theatre Belgrade

South-East Theatre Skopje

Naval Theatre Split

Air Force and Air Defence Belgrade

Republican presidencies

Republican TOs

Slovenian TO, parts of Croatian TO

Serbian TO, B-H TO, parts of Croatian TO

Macedonian TO, Montenegrin TO, parts of Serbian TO

Parts of Croatian TO

❹ Subordination of theatre commands, i.e. the JNA, to the Federal Secretariat for People's Defence (SSNO). Bypassing the Presidency, the SSNO via these commands establishes a *direct* subordination to itself of the TO. What this amounts to is an organizational manoeuvre in keeping with General Kadijević's statement that: 'The Territorial Defence, as it was created in the late sixties and early seventies, [is] objectively a great trick'.

Although, according to the *Law on People's Defence*, the SFRY Presidency as supreme commander did transfer certain of its functions to the SSNO and the general staff, as shown in Table 1, **❹**, in a crisis situation these bodies proclaimed themselves the staff of the supreme command (ŠVK) and took powers of command that according to the *Law* did not belong to them, as for example with Chief of Staff General Blagoje Adžić's 14 May 1990 order to disarm the TO.

Thus a staff (technical/technological) right was transformed into a command right.

✕ *Note.* As a result of the manoeuvre outlined under **❹** above, the legal right of the republics in respect of their Territorial Defence disappeared — in other words they lost control of it.

Source: Interview in *Vojnopolitički informator*, 1/1989, p. 9.

The essential point about this reorganization of the armies into regional theatre commands was that these were subject, in the chain of sub-ordination, to the commander-in-chief, which was the Federal Presidency – not the Federal secretary for national defence or his chief of staff, but the Presidency as commander-in-chief. And since the Presidency was responsible in time of war for the TO forces as well, it was logical that the republican TO commands should also be subject to the theatre commands, since – this is the essential point – only thus would the Presidency be able to issue orders to them. But since the Presidency could not command without the Staff of the Supreme Command – i.e. the army command and Veljko Kadijević – it is clear that the TO forces were now *de facto* subjected to the JNA. This is the essence of the whole charade about changing the Law on National Defence. Kadijević best explains what it was all about when he refers to 'decisions initiated by the JNA [between 1984 and 1988] regarding the organization of the armed forces, command and operation, the purpose of which was to alleviate the negative consequences of the constitutional provisions in this area'.[5]

By such devious means, by the back door, the republics were deprived of their constitutional rights of involvement in, and jurisdiction over, their TO forces, a clear indication of what preoccupied the army command at this time and how it would proceed. The new Law on National Defence also abolished the TO forces of Kosovo, since that region was considered to be a zone of continual unrest, a danger zone.[6] It is not generally known, since it was a secret kept within the army leadership, that for the entire period beginning with the second half of the 1960s Albanian conscripts from Kosovo were treated differently from any others. A plan was drawn up by which, in the case of external threat from the Warsaw Pact or NATO – the perpetual theme of the plans drafted by the Yugoslav armed forces – Albanian conscripts would be marched or otherwise dispatched to distant zones, internment camps in effect, where they would be kept quiet until the danger had passed. All the details were worked out: how many

Memorandum'. From his perspective, 'the most marked and, for B-H, the most striking example is the Belgrade theatre [i.e. the First or Central theatre], which comprised Serbia as far south as Niš, the whole of B-H and eastern and western Slavonia. Under the pretext of operational-strategic needs, a Knin division [in reality a corps] was formed in Knin, which almost completely covered the Serb krajina in Croatia.' The western boundaries of that theatre and the Knin division were 'almost identical with the borders of Milošević's homogeneous Serbia: Karlobag – Ogulin – Karlovac – Virovitica'. Sefer Halilović, *Lukava strategija* [A devious strategy], Sarajevo 1997, pp. 69–70.

[5] Kadijević, *Moje viđenje raspada*, p. 100.

[6] 'A decision was taken and implemented to disband the Territorial Defence of Kosovo because it was chiefly composed of separatist forces. After its disbanding, there began the formation, from Yugoslav-oriented people, of many smaller Territorial Defences of Kosovo.' Kadijević, *Moje viđenje raspada*, p. 78.

lorries and railway wagons would be required, which routes the transport would take, the specific locations where the men would be interned, etc. I mention this here since it has considerable bearing today, twenty years later, on the situation in Kosovo.

As early as 1984 the JNA leadership had worked out a secret mechanism to make it impossible for the republics to conduct autonomous defence policies; it was set in motion immediately after the first multiparty elections in January 1990 in Slovenia. On this Kadijević writes: 'One of the most important means of paralysing the dangerous [1974] constitutional concept of the armed forces was the *Decision on Withdrawal of TO Arms and their Placing under JNA Control*. Many protested against this decision, especially the Slovenes'[7] – but their veto was ignored.

The first multiparty elections in Croatia were held on 22–23 April (first round) and 6–7 May (second round), and the transfer of authority was announced for 30 May; 15 May, a week after the second round, was also the date for the regular rotation of presidents in the Federal Presidency, when Milošević's man and Serbia's representative Borisav Jović was to be replaced by Slovenia's representative Janez Drnovšek. On the eve of that rotation, the last day of Jović's mandate, the JNA General Staff took a secret decision to take control of TO arms, with two aims in mind: to put pressure on the democratic forces within the western republics, and to make it impossible for those republics to offer armed response to possible attack from the Federal centre, i.e. prevent their effective and legitimate defence.

By the start of the war in Slovenia and Croatia, fundamental changes had been made in the JNA personnel in those republics. I shall give data only for Croatia, but I could also for Slovenia, since I was commander of the north-western theatre and know all the personnel details. At the time when I commanded the 5th army, over 50 per cent of its command positions were filled by Croat generals and senior officers. But on the eve of the war General Života Avramović, an officer who had earlier occupied a minor position and was unknown to me personally (all I knew was that he was a Serb from southern Serbia) became commander of the north-western theatre. General Dobrašin Praščević from Montenegro became chief of staff, Andrija Rašeta deputy commander, while Vladimir Trifunović, Dušan Uzelac, Mićo Delić, Milan Popović and Marijan Čad became corps commanders. In Knin, where the corps commander was Špiro Niković, the notorious Ratko Mladić became chief of staff in the early summer of 1991, soon taking over the leadership of the corps *de jure* as well as *de facto*. The command structure of the north-western theatre now contained no

---

[7] Ibid., p. 78 (italics in original). As he says a little further on, the TO was disarmed 'before the armed conflicts began in Yugoslavia', but with one exception which was to have an important function in future actions: 'Of course, we used the Territorial Defence of the Serb regions of Croatia and Bosnia-Herzegovina in joint actions with the JNA' (p. 94).

Croats and just one Slovene (Čad), and, except for Rašeta who comes from Lika, not one person who was even born in Croatia or Slovenia.

MILITARY LEADERSHIP IN SEARCH OF A STATE

This change could not go unnoticed. The inevitable conclusion was that the army leadership was getting ready to resolve the growing political crisis by force of arms. Serb radicals – Milošević and his group – were following all of this carefully. They concluded that the army leadership was working in their interest and, since a unitary Yugoslavia would mean domination by the numerically largest national group, they should not impede but covertly support it on its course towards a radical resolution of Yugoslavia's future. The army leadership was openly making its aims known as early as spring 1990, by insisting that 'only a strong unitary state can overcome the present crisis, and this is the only way the JNA can regain the state it has lost'. General Kadijević told the generals assembled at a meeting convened in Topčider (Belgrade) in autumn 1988, at which I was present, that he was ready to fight with arms for socialist and communist ideas. Admiral Branko Mamula (retd) was also there, and made no comment. There followed some discussion in which this stance was barely challenged.

So Kadijević had concluded that the JNA did not have its own state, and that it must demand one and fight for it. He saw this state as Yugoslavia, but without its republics, because ever since the republics had taken over chief responsibility for the economic and political structure of government, and also for the TO, his kind of Yugoslavia had ceased to exist. So Kadijević asserted that the JNA had no state, and asked what sort of an army it was that allowed itself to be placed in such a situation.

His book is permeated with lament for the strong centralized state that existed until the mid 1960s and the start of the economic, legal and constitutional reforms finally formalized in the 1974 Constitution. Consequently, as he emphasizes right from the introductory pages, the JNA 'first constitutionally and legally ... and then also in reality became an army without a state'.[8] So at the end of the 1980s and the beginning of the 1990s, that army, in alliance with Milošević, began to seek a state that it could experience as *its own*, began to create *its own* state and determine its borders, for it was 'absolutely certain that without a clearly defined new Yugoslav state' it could not maintain itself as it had been and

[8] Ibid., p. 5. This thesis, which he also uses as the subtitle of his book, he repeats in a number of places, as for example on p. 76, or on p. 89, where he says that 'we in the army, probably more than anyone else, felt what it meant to be without a real state'.

would like to be.[9] Milošević offered it that state, and the army command put itself at his service.

However much they both continued to call that state Yugoslavia, however much Kadijević subsequently strove to explain that 'the chief motive for this stance of ours lay not only in the need for the JNA to have its state, but above all in the belief that there were people, nations in Yugoslavia who really wanted to live in a common state, so such a state had to be created',[10] it is clear that this state really was – or was to be – Greater Serbia. He himself, somewhat later, admitted that what was being created was 'a new Yugoslav state of the Yugoslav peoples who wish for it, at this stage the Serb and Montenegrin peoples'.[11]

WEAKNESS OF THE JNA AND OVERTURES
TO THE SERBIAN LEADERSHIP

The radical Serb leadership concealed its objectives, but these emerged into the public domain via intellectual circles in Belgrade, where it was argued that as the Serbs were numerically the largest nation, a unitary Yugoslavia suited them best; but if that was impossible to achieve, the other option was a Greater Serbia with its western borders on the Virovitica–Karlovac–Karlobag line, so that all Serbs would be brought together into a single state. After its defeat in Slovenia the army leadership too focused on that very line, but these planned western borders also had to be abandoned. They could not have been held, because things happened very differently from the way the army and the radical Serb leadership had imagined.

Powerful nationalistic currents emerged also in Croatia and Slovenia, partly as a reaction against aggressive Greater Serbianism, partly because national sentiments in the communist era had been repressed or belittled, but naturally revived as the former regime weakened. The aim of the new governments was to amend the 1974 Constitution to create a confederative community of sovereign states; alternatively, if that were impossible, if it proved unacceptable, to form wholly independent states. After a while Macedonia and Bosnia-Herzegovina adopted the same concept. The aims of the army and the Serbian leadership, on the one hand, and the leaderships of the western republics, on the other, were absolute in the sense that both sides were determined to achieve them at any price.

Some think it was possible to act politically to reconcile these opposing positions and thus avoid military conflict. I was not then, nor am I now, an adherent of this view, although I deeply respect all attempts at a peaceful resolution. I know that it would have been much better, but I was a

[9] Ibid., p. 78.
[10] Ibid., p. 90.
[11] Ibid., p. 93.

realist and did not want to waste time reaching for the moon. Events anyway came to the boil before the anti-war forces could have any say. [12]

Such contradictory options led towards a hot war for yet another reason. The unitarists and Serb radicals had reckoned that they had absolute superiority, which was a delusion. They thought they had the JNA under their thumb, and the TO forces of all the republics too via the general staff of the supreme command, while the police forces of the republics were technically inferior and smaller in number. We know what we inherited in terms of police, not only in Croatia but also in Slovenia, Bosnia-Herzegovina and Macedonia: everything was outdated and in every respect inferior. So, relying on power and arms as usual, they thought: 'If we have the JNA, and now the TO forces as well, and their police are not up to much, that is additional reason to seek a military resolution, perhaps with a limited military coup, so that war won't actually flare up, since – because of the imbalance of power and under threat of the JNA's superiority of arms – the republics will have to give in and accept the internal solution we want.'

But this was an illusion which could persist only so long as the JNA was not used in actual armed conflict. Once used it ceased to exist, for numerous reasons, key amongst which was its multiethnic nature: it became a mere heap of weapons without soldiers, a ship without a crew. Every demographer knows that the Serbs, because of their low birth rate, have very few young people to send to war. In peacetime the JNA ran at about 20 per cent of capacity, and in the event of war it needed to draft about 80 per cent non-Serb soldiers. In the north-western theatre in 1990, for example, some 30 per cent of the eighteen-year-old recruits were Albanians, 20 per cent Croats, 8 per cent Slovenes, 10 per cent Bosniaks, a considerable number Hungarians, and only 15–20 per cent Serbs and Montenegrins, most of whom, like the majority of the officer class, were not ready to risk their lives in a war against Slovenia and Croatia.

Some politicians in Slovenia, Croatia and Bosnia-Herzegovina did not understand this. Stipe Mesić knows that, when I spoke in Croatian inner circles about how the JNA would fall apart the moment it was used, Tuđman interrupted me very authoritatively: 'No, that is not correct. The JNA is the fourth – or the third, I don't remember exactly – military force in Europe.' It was not understood that this structure could be used

---

[12] See the book written by my friend and colleague General Ilija Radaković, a Serb from Lika, who spent his entire working life in the JNA before retiring in 1985, when he had reached the position of deputy federal secretary for national defence. He gives a good deal of consideration to the possibility that war could have been avoided by negotiations conducted in good faith: Ilija T. Radaković, *Besmislena YU ratovanja* [The senseless YU wars], Belgrade 1997, published by Društvo za istinu o antifašističkoj narodnooslobodilačkoj borbi u Jugoslaviji (1941–45) [Society for the truth about the anti-fascist national liberation struggle in Yugoslavia (1941–45)].

effectively only in the event of external danger, in defence against external attack, especially from the East, from the Warsaw Pact. Not so effectively in the case of attack from the West, because for the population of Yugoslavia, especially the youth, the West had always been the storehouse of wealth and the symbol of many other good things: democratic order, freedom of expression and assembly, cultural diversity, etc. There was plenty of discussion about this when we, the top commanders, analysed our war plans; it was openly spoken about in the army command itself; but General Kadijević and his circle of armchair generals simply could not or would not face up to reality.

However, regardless of this weakness of the JNA, there was no question of waiting with arms folded to be threatened by it and its material force, so in 1990 I began to arm Croatia. When threatened by a force capable of raising 2.5 million people, you could not sit and do nothing, considering the terrifying and destructive effects it could have on the functioning of the new governments in the western republics. So we began to procure arms and to train people: by the end of February 1991 we had succeeded in mobilizing and training 65,000 lightly armed soldiers. And here we are today, meeting in the country from which we first obtained weapons!

The army command and the Serb leadership planned to achieve their aims not only by use of the regular forces, but also by an armed insurrection of Serbs in Croatia. Individual JNA officers – e.g. General Rašeta, at one time my chief of staff, and the newly appointed Colonel Mladić, at that time unknown to me – openly armed the rebels and used military movements to prevent the Croatian police from reaching the rebel zones. Was Borisav Jović sincere when he said that he did not care about the Serbs in Croatia, or did he say it only to mollify us, to sap our will to suppress the insurrection with a combination of negotiations and limited force? Was not this, as Kadijević confirmed later in his book, all to do with establishing the western border of Greater Serbia on the Virovitica–Karlovac–Karlobag line?

Soon after, at the end of February 1991, I learned of the existence of a plan, already at an advanced stage, to intervene in Slovenia and Croatia. Several Croatian generals had known about it from before: it was part of the *Sutjeska 2* or S-2 plan by which, in the event of a NATO attack, military forces would move from eastern Yugoslavia into Croatia and western Bosnia so as to occupy a particular line of defence. With some modifications and alterations it was also suitable for intervention against Slovenia and Croatia. The intervention was conceived at first as a military coup to bring 'healthy forces' to power. Veljko Kadijević went overnight to Moscow, to persuade USSR Minister of Defence Dimitri Yazov to support the coup, for he believed it would not be possible to carry it out without some major external support. But he did not succeed. Indeed, Yazov told him: 'Not only will we not support you, but we shall have to condemn you like the West.' Kadijević came back empty-handed. Which was why, at the dramatic 12 March meeting of the Federal Presidency, Borisav Jović could hardly wait for Bogić Bogićević, Bosnia-Herzegovina's representative, to say that he would not sign the decree proclaiming a state of emergency, before bringing the meeting to a close.

This failure led Kadijević to begin to consider a military campaign against Slovenia, for which it was necessary to ensure that Croatia would not intervene. He obtained this assurance from the Croatian leadership, meaning Franjo Tuđman, who told him: 'We shan't meddle in your dispute with Slovenia.' I was horrified by this, and it was then that I began to consider resigning, because it was stupid to remain passive when it was obvious what would follow after the intervention in Slovenia. The action against Slovenia was to discover how the JNA, that multinational though already somewhat Serbianized army, would behave: whether it would be capable of reaching the western borders and ensure a takeover of power, what kind of resistance it would come up against, and so on. It was a test and, if the action went well, General Petar Gračanin, then Federal minister of the interior, would follow Kadijević into Slovenia with 2,000 specials and a group of Slovenes to take over the government. Few people know that in advance of the operation General Gračanin had gone by air to a JNA base near Ljubljana, where he awaited the outcome of Kadijević's action; but since Kadijević experienced a catastrophic defeat within ten days, the great General Gračanin climbed back into his aircraft and fled to Belgrade. And that is how the plan failed.

The year 1991 saw a coalescence of the groups that were heading for war and later waged the war. In the army command there were Generals Kadijević and Adžić, and that very dubious Slovene Admiral Stane Brovet, while in the background stood Admiral Branko Mamula (retd) and a few others. They formed a closed group. General Čubra, who was at the very highest level of command (he was responsible for the JNA's economic and financial affairs) has testified that even he was kept out of their most secret discussions. The Serbian leadership involved Milošević, Jović and Gračanin. Dr Jovan Rašković, a psychiatrist from Šibenik and close friend of Dobrica Ćosić, worked in association with them; and one must certainly also include here, as emissaries and instigators of the armed insurrections in Croatia, a number of other generals, such as Dušan Pekić and Boris Rašeta, Colonel Mladić and a hundred or so others. So in the spring of 1990 we experienced a regular invasion of decrepit generals in Serb villages in Banija and Kordun, in Lika, Knin and eastern Slavonia. Relying on old acquaintances and relatives, and on the reputations they had gained in the Second World War, they proceeded very systematically and deliberately to revive old traumas and to convince the bewildered people that a revival of the Ustasha state, with consequent expulsion of Serbs, was being planned by the new Croatian government.

On the opposing side were the leaders of the republics of Slovenia and Croatia, who had agreed on military cooperation at the beginning of 1991. The agreement was signed on 20 January for the Slovenes by Minister of Defence Janez Janša and the Minister of Interior Igor Bavčar, and for the Croatian side by myself, as minister of defence, and Minister of Interior Josip Boljkovac. One might get the impression from that brief document, consisting of a mere two or three clauses, that the agreement amounted to very little, but the truth is that we had created a very detailed plan for a united defence of Slovenia and Croatia.[13] It was obvious that if Slovenia and Croatia were to achieve their objectives, they had to have armed forces. This was a view which I stubbornly upheld until July 1991, when I submitted my resignation to President Franjo Tuđman.

The debacle in Slovenia fully confirmed my earlier judgement of the problem the JNA was bound to face in this campaign: that it would fall apart. This does not mean that the Slovenes did not offer armed resistance; on the contrary it was a very serious armed conflict and not just for show, as some subsequently claimed. But the fact remains that my predictions of 1990, that in an internal war the JNA would inevitably dissolve into its components, proved true. For example, one tank regiment, which set off for the border to take control of the frontier posts, simply stopped at one point and the officers and men abandoned the tanks and made off into the woods or joined the local population. They simply refused to drive the tanks any further. Such was the effect of the multinational character of the JNA.

It was by the good will of the Slovenian leadership that the JNA was able to withdraw some of its heavy weapons from Slovenia to Bosnia-Herzegovina, Serbia and parts of Croatia, though there were some other reasons. One was a message to the Croatians: 'Since you did not want to join us in defence, we shall pass the rest of the JNA weapons to the east.' I once debated on TV Ljubljana with Slovenia's President Milan Kučan and a few other politicians, and I told them: 'You had a good breakfast (meaning you successfully faced up to armed intervention); you had a still better lunch (you defeated it), but you had no dinner (you did not hold on to the armour and put it at our disposal, so that we too could defend ourselves).' Kučan's reply was brilliant: 'You know, General, after a good breakfast and a good lunch, it is best to omit dinner, because then one sleeps more easily.'

[13] The text of this Croatian–Slovene defence agreement is in Slaven Letica and Mario Nobilo, *JNA: rat protiv Hrvatske* [JNA: the war against Croatia], Zagreb 1991, p. 73.

JNA PLAN FOR THE ATTACK ON CROATIA

From the military point of view the plan for the attack on Croatia was excellent. Even I, who criticize the JNA high command as armchair generals, have to acknowledge that any military expert would find it difficult to make a better plan.

1. Strong JNA forces were placed in all the garrisons in Croatia, to form a deep incursion into the enemy rear, as Kadijević literally said. Next, part of the forces from these garrisons, under the pretext of separating the Serb insurgents and the Croatian forces, would intervene, ostensibly to prevent clashes, but in reality to support the rebels and enlarge the zone of rebellion. This zone extended south from the river Sava, from Croatian Kostajnica as far as Zadar, embracing Banija, Lika, Kordun and the so-called Dalmatian Plate: Bukovica, Ravni Kotari and the Šibenik hinterland. In the other direction the zone encompassed western Slavonia from Gradiška to Virovitica and Orahovica, and in eastern Slavonia and western Srijem the area between Osijek and Ilok, as well as Baranja which the JNA occupied early on. These were the positions from which the attack on Croatia began. As Kadijević wrote, the campaign, aimed at intersecting Croatia in five directions, began with the main forces – one army, a very strong one, composed of the 12th Vojvodina (Novi Sad) corps and the 1st Guards division, which was not really a division but a very strong corps[14] – acting from Bačka and the Serb part of Srijem together with four corps coming from Bosnia-Herzegovina.

Achieving 'the general political objective – the creation of a new Yugoslavia of the people who wanted it' was planned as follows: the

---

[14] The guards division of the JNA had three motorized brigades, two tank regiments (about 300 tanks), two artillery support regiments, a regiment of anti-tank artillery, a mixed regiment of anti-aircraft defence and a mixed (pioneer and pontonier) engineers' regiment, i.e. 18,000–20,000 men. When this impressive convoy set off for Vukovar on 19 October, a crowd of citizens on the western roads out of Belgrade and along the road towards Srijemska Mitrovica gave them a great send-off with flowers, applause and cheers. But as soon as they entered Croatia, they clashed near Tovarnik with a small ZNG formation, which destroyed several tanks and armoured vehicles. That was a shock for them. A conflict broke out between professional soldiers and conscripts, a significant number of whom simply went home. The JNA had trouble getting the division moving again. We did not know at the time that many tanks in perfect working order and fully equipped for war, but without crews, were standing for several days along the Šid to Ruma road.

The mobilization base of the guards division was northern Serbia, a strip about 70 km wide south of the Sava and Danube. This lowland territory had a village population of traditional outlook, with very low birth rates; probably this mentality, and fear for every 'male head', had considerable influence on their reluctance to go to war.

JNA's task was to ensure that 'all areas with a Serb majority be thoroughly freed from the presence of the Croatian army and Croatian authorities', and 'to continue the transformation of the JNA throughout the whole of Yugoslavia into the army of the future Yugoslavia, both in regard to internal national and organizational structure and territorial location'. In the first phase this was to be done 'with the intensive organization and preparation of Serb insurgents in Croatia', and in the next 'by a united operational-strategic offensive operation' so as to defeat the Croatian forces.

The concept of the manoeuvre was composed of the following basic elements:

- a full air and sea blockade of Croatia;
- to link as directly as possible the lines of attack of the main JNA forces with the liberation of Serb regions in Croatia and of JNA garrisons deep in Croatian territory. For this purpose to intersect Croatia on the lines Gradiška–Virovitica; Bihać–Karlovac–Zagreb; Knin–Zadar; and Mostar–Split. With the strongest units of armoured mechanized forces to liberate eastern Slavonia, and then rapidly to continue the action in the west, joining with the forces in western Slavonia and extending up towards Zagreb and Varaždin, i.e. towards the Slovene border. At the same time, with strong forces from the Herceg Novi-Trebinje region, to blockade Dubrovnik from the land and strike into the Neretva valley, coordinating their action with the forces advancing along the Mostar–Split axis;
- after attaining these objectives, to secure and hold the borders of Serb Krajina in Croatia, then withdraw remaining JNA units from Slovenia and unoccupied parts of Croatia.[15]

This is how the JNA high command saw Croatia: as reduced to territory west of the Virovitica–Karlovac–Karlobag line.

The Croatian Ministry of Defence learned of this plan, in its main lines at least, as early as March 1991 and informed the Slovenian leadership about it, as well as many of the responsible political people in Bosnia-Herzegovina – not as officials in institutional positions but as individuals, responsible citizens and patriots. If we had formally notified the institutions in Sarajevo – the Presidency, the parliament, the government, etc. – Milošević's, Kadijević's and Karadžić's people would inevitably have come to know about it, since as members of the Serb Democratic Party (SDS) they were part of the structures of government. This illustrates how the legal bodies of governance were forced to act illegally.

[15] Kadijević, *Moje viđenje raspada*, pp. 134–5.

The last two plans for the defence of Croatia, those of June and July, were drafted as a response to this kind of threat. It was clear to me that no coup was possible with the forces the JNA had in Croatia, because for the most part they consisted of military hardware lying in depots more accessible to our own mobilized units than to anyone in the JNA, so that we could far more easily get hold of it than they could. For that reason I was not really afraid of a military coup, not even at the end of January 1991 when Tuđman, Mesić and Josip Manolić were in Belgrade and that notorious spy film about me was shown on Belgrade television.[16] I was not afraid that they would launch a military coup, because they would have paid a high price for it. It was possible that the entire JNA could have been defeated there and then, so there would have been no war, or at least not such a terrible war as it was.

2. It was necessary to continue negotiations with the leadership of the Republic of Croatia at all levels and to encourage the belief that everything could be resolved by negotiation. The army command did this, with General Kadijević stating convincingly on several occasions that

---

[16] This film, whose purpose was to prepare the ground for the legitimation of military intervention, was made by the military film company *Zastava-film*, and broadcast by TV-Belgrade and TV-Sarajevo in coordination on 25 January 1991. The following day it was repeated on TV-Belgrade, and in the evening it was shown on Croatian television with expert commentary. The moment was carefully chosen: the entire Croatian leadership was in Belgrade in discussions with the Federal leadership – the president of the republic, the presidents of the government and the Sabor, and the Croatian member of the SFRY Presidency. On 24 January a statement from the political administration of the Federal Defence Ministry was read in every JNA garrison, announcing the extension of JNA authority in order to stamp out 'counter-revolution', which raised war psychosis to its peak. The essence of the film was this: an authentic, secret recording of discussions with General Špegelj, in which the main subject of debate was the difference between inter-state and civil war, was edited and cut so that a generalized description of the characteristics of the latter (street battles, the extensive use of side arms, extreme viciousness towards civilians, forced entry into apartments and so on) could be presented as Špegelj's actual plan for the massacre of Serbs in Croatia.

An overview of the reaction in Croatia, relevant documents, and a selection of orchestrated reports in the Belgrade and Sarajevo press which heightened the impact of the film on an uninformed and frightened public, can be found in Letica and Nobilo, *Rat protiv Hrvatske*. The author of the film himself – a publicist and political scientist with a master's degree in mass communications systems, who was also a graduate of the Military Academy and who until the beginning of 1995 served as head of the Information Service of the JNA/Yugoslav Army – later described the making of the film and the atmosphere at that time in the Yugoslav army command. At the beginning of December 1990 he was given about ten secretly filmed video cassettes and all the necessary equipment, with the task of completing a finished version by 10 January 1991, which he did. See Ljubodrag Stojadinović, *Film koji je zapalio Jugoslaviju* [The film which set Yugoslavia alight], Belgrade 1995.

under no circumstances would they attack Croatia or launch any kind of military coup. According to some sources, more than one hundred negotiating meetings were held at all levels of governance in Croatia and the JNA.

3. A special war was to be organized against the western republics: ostentatious movements of tanks and heavy artillery and low-altitude overflights, but also the use of agents to collect and make public data about individuals and institutions. The spy film was certainly part of this. I was careless for a moment, and their agent gained access to certain data. The film was shown on television on 25 January 1991. Propaganda from the army and Serbian leadership also harped on about an Ustasha revival in Croatia and said that the events of 1941 were repeating themselves, which unfortunately was partly true. The Ustasha ideology was imported from abroad with the return of extremist *émigrés* – not those who had really been NDH officials, but those who thought they could use this ideology for their own benefit now that a new order was being established in Croatia. And they did indeed benefit and acquire power; because of them, because of their presence in politics, the structures of power have remained shaky and there are major problems to this day. That fact, together with the blowing up of Serb houses in the spring of 1991, caused greater damage to Croatia's defence than the entire JNA aggression, and the aftermath can be felt even today in neo-fascist manifestations of various kinds.

THE PLAN FOR CROATIA'S DEFENCE

Croatia's defence plans, produced in June 1991 and again at the end of July 1991, were based on the following:

1. To carry out the preparations for mobilization in two levies. The first, smaller levy, as a first step in the military protection of the republic, was organized in the late autumn of 1990. We were in a position to mobilize 60,000–65,000 soldiers, to be armed with imported weapons or with those that remained in Croatia despite the disarmament of the TO. These were light arms, but highly suitable for the kind of actions I envisaged in the event of a military coup. The second levy was prepared in spring 1991, and provided for the mobilization of about 100,000 officers and men in all three military branches and every combat arm and service, the weapons for which would be taken from JNA depots and garrisons. It was fortunate that military conscripts and officers in Croatia had previously, in the mobilization schedules of the JNA, been responsible for these same weapons and trained to handle them. The JNA had no other teams for these weapons: they would have

to be drafted in from Serbia, and might well not be capable of handling such equipment, nor be willing to come to Croatia anyway.

2. To extend and fundamentally reconstruct the police levies, some 30,000 strong, and to use them to control territory and the movements of JNA military formations.

3. To use the first mobilized levy and part of the police force to keep the garrisons and depots of the JNA under observation, and in the event of attempted military action to surround and occupy them. They were to undertake this latter action only if the JNA launched a military coup or armed attack against Croatia. Kadijević writes that the JNA had decided to enter into armed conflict only if they were attacked,[17] while I took the position that we would only respond to an actual armed attack by the JNA. So we were both holding off, waiting to see who would go first. Of course, once armed attack began, the question of who was first would no longer be asked (except by the international community), but only whether it was being carried out effectively. Police units were also meant to block the armed insurrection and prevent it from spreading, especially in western Slavonia, towards Zadar, and in eastern Slavonia. By mid May 1991 the first defence levy, of little more than 60,000 men, was fully operational.

4. To hold military and political negotiations in order to gain time, and to engage in propaganda focusing on the multi-ethnic composition of the JNA, thus making it a problem and embarrassment for the JNA command. That we did very well. Almost no one from the JNA in Croatia took part in the attack on the republic; by the time the attack came they had all dispersed in various directions. Between mid-June and the end of July 1991 we took care of 12,000 youngsters from the JNA in the vicinity of Zagreb, most of them from Serbia, who had deserted from JNA barracks in Slovenia and Croatia, including the naval sector. They expected their parents to come and take them home, but the parents often just sent them abroad. In short, the army as a body simply broke up, and not even the officer class, for the most part, including some of the Serbs and Montenegrins, was inclined to take action against the Republic of Croatia. More than 3,000 officers and generals, most

[17] Explaining 'the fundamental thinking about the use of armed force' in the situation after multiparty elections in Slovenia and Croatia, Kadijević cites the following 'essential decision: Consciously to allow the enemy to make the first attack so that the whole world would clearly see who was the aggressor and what they wanted. This was a crucial decision for which we were often criticized, even called traitors and suchlike.' Kadijević, *Moje viđenje raspada*, pp. 93–4; see also pp. 86–7: 'defenders of Yugoslavia's unity' must not be the first to apply force, for the 'secessionist' media would use this to accuse them before the world of 'destroying the democratically elected regime by force'; or p. 133: judging that the phrase 'prevention of national conflicts' had been used up in Croatia, the JNA 'must first wait for open attack, visible to everyone', and 'only then strike back'.

of them non-Serbs, had joined the Croatian Army by the time the JNA began open hostilities. My 1990 judgement that the JNA was absolutely incapable of taking part in an internal war was fully confirmed.[18]

5. To try to form an alliance of the republics and provinces threatened by the attempt to create a unitary Yugoslavia. In this we failed: they all acted discordantly, each for itself, with the partial exception of Slovenia and Croatia, which did reach an agreement initialled by President Kučan and President Tuđman. Although even this Slovenian–Croatian cooperation fell apart at the start of the war in Slovenia, such an alliance was a possibility and posed a threat to the war planners in Belgrade, worrying them a good deal.

We held discussions in Zagreb with people from Bosnia-Herzegovina, Kosovo and Macedonia. I shall speak about just one such case. We held discussions over a period of a few days with a group of Kosovar Albanians, 15 of them headed by Ibrahim Rugova, and at one point I took Rugova and his two colleagues to meet President Tuđman. They were offered coffee and then Tuđman said in effect: 'You Kosovo Albanians need to solve your problems in Belgrade, not in Zagreb', whereupon Rugova simply wound his famous scarf round his neck, got up and went out, leaving his coffee untouched. I was sorry, because we had very thoroughly prepared and conducted the negotiations with them, as well as with people from Sandžak and Bosnia-Herzegovina.

DEVELOPMENT OF THE WAR ON THE TERRITORY OF CROATIA

With JNA assistance the rebel zones gradually extended, and long lines of refugees left the occupied areas. At every stage, wherever one turned, there was the smell of war, ethnic cleansing and crimes of all kinds. Gradually our first call-up levy and police took up positions facing the rebel zones. The first significant skirmishes began with the intervention of the Croatian police in Plitvice; there followed on 1 March 1991 fighting in Pakrac, and at the beginning of May the events in Borovo Selo. In Plitvice the JNA was securing the future borders of the Serb Autonomous Region of Krajina: it was ostensibly separating our police and the insurgents, but in reality protecting the insurgency in Korenica

---

[18] The Slovenes made an identical and clearly accurate assessment. The report 'Possible situation for the partial or complete use of National Defence tactical units in the Republic of Slovenia', drafted at the beginning of September 1990, states that JNA 'morale is low' and because of its 'mixed national structure such an army cannot effectively intervene in an internal conflict'. Janez Janša, *Pomaci: nastajanje i obrana slovenske države 1988–1992* [Moves: formation and defence of the Slovenian state 1988–1992], Zagreb 1993, p. 52.

and Plitvice. From the military perspective, controlling and limiting the insurrection were the most difficult and uncertain tasks in the defence of Croatia; but I never succumbed to the temptation to order the insurrection to be crushed, which would have been very difficult to do.

The first plan, drafted in 1990, to eliminate the Knin insurrection was more or less feasible, but later it all became more and more difficult. The local Serb population had for almost five decades been the strongest force for a unitarist Yugoslavia and the most solid and conservative Communist Party bastion in Croatia; it was not possible to defeat such a force just like that. The insurrection could be brought to an end only by the removal or neutralization of the JNA.

We began to strengthen what I hoped was imperceptible surveillance and blockade of the JNA barracks and depots, which was carried out in three ways: by cooperation with many officers and generals in those very buildings; by openly supervising their activities; and finally by barriers of various kinds, including armed force. The resulting experience convinced me that we could gain access to the arms in the depots without incurring casualties, and that the second mobilized levy could be trained in a relatively short period of time. Once it was trained, we would be able to carry out a strategic deployment, and then sit down at the negotiating table. Once a balance of power had been reached, it would be possible to achieve a peaceful solution, for no one would dare to shoot. All we had to do was choose the best moment, and the best moment to obtain the JNA armaments was provided by its campaign against Slovenia between 25 June and 10 July 1991, when it finally engaged in open internal war. It was then at its most vulnerable. However, as a result of the Croatian leadership's well-known political calculations this was not done; an opportunity to avoid a long and bloody war was lost.

The second mobilized levy of the Croatian Army was armed later, from the end of September, in very much more difficult conditions than those that prevailed in June. By occupying JNA depots and garrisons in Croatia we acquired 250 tanks, 400–500 heavy artillery pieces, about 180,000 firearms and some 2 million tonnes of ammunition and other military hardware, which brought about a fundamental alteration in the balance of military power. If we had not done so, the aggressor would have reached the Virovitica–Karlovac–Karlobag line. The Croatian Ministry of Defence then sent a troop of the ZNG to eastern Slavonia and Srijem (the Ilok–Tovarnik–Vukovar region), and then gradually, as the mobilization was carried out, brought in forces towards the rebel zones, in the direction of possible attacks from Bačka, Baranja and Srijem and from Banja Luka, Knin and Mostar. We took up position at the points from which we anticipated hostilities. At the end of October, which was the wrong time (tank movements in autumn, in that deep Slavonian mud!), General

Kadijević decided to attack eastern Slavonia with a powerful army and begin the battle for Vukovar.

This was a fortuitous battle; no one in the Croatian Army, myself included, had planned to defend the town. But the ZNG forces withdrawing from Ilok took cover in Vukovar and regrouped there, so that it became a bastion of our defence and hence vital for the JNA's further advance. This resulted in a senseless destruction of the town, while the monstrously incompetent policy of the Croatian leadership made it impossible for the siege to be lifted in time and for everything possible to be withdrawn from it. Vukovar carried out its military task extremely well, and in doing so clearly demonstrated that even a Serbianized JNA was incapable of resolving the crisis militarily.

The town fell on 19 November 1991, but the JNA's advance, intended to link up with garrisons in the interior and the rebel zones, was deeply compromised. The major breakthrough was to Ernestinovo, near Osijek, after which the JNA was completely blocked and brought to a halt. The Croatian Army began a counter-offensive at the end of November with newly mobilized forces from the Virovitica–Orahovica line and simultaneously through the Sava valley: from Zagreb and from Slavonski Brod to the rebel zone in western Slavonia. In only twenty-five days the Croatian Army retook most of western Slavonia, right up to the Pakrac–Požega line. The conditions for further advance were excellent, but on 26 December an order transmitted by a secret HDZ line of command halted all offensive actions in the area.

Why? Even today I do not understand it. No one within the military structures of the Croatian Army was told why. Only HDZ officials knew the reason. I presume that they must have decided that it was no longer necessary to wage war in Croatia, where security was basically achieved since the JNA did not have the forces to achieve its objectives, and that operations should move into Bosnia, while a permanent truce should be established in Croatia with a view to reaching a peaceful settlement in eastern Slavonia and the Knin Krajina. It is curious that I, as inspector-in-chief of the Croatian Army (HV), and General Anton Tus, its chief of staff, were not informed that the brigades had been ordered to end the operation. It was done behind our backs, and I shall show shortly that such actions by the Croatian leadership (meaning Franjo Tuđman personally) were not the exception but the rule. In any case, the situation was frozen at the very moment when the HV was at its greatest strength, and on 2 January 1992 a permanent ceasefire was signed in Sarajevo. This situation lasted for four years, until operations Flash and Storm in 1995. On the other Croatian fronts the JNA had practically no further successes, but was left with what had been seized in the insurrection. Southern Croatia was not cut off; all the front lines were stabilized. Although the HV had grown to 250,000 and opportunities for new offensives presented themselves, everything was frozen and many units remained in barracks, unused. The war in Croatia was put on the back burner.

From the beginning of 1992 the war gradually moved into Bosnia-Herzegovina; by the end of the year and during 1993 the intention behind Tuđman's secret negotiations with Milošević, and behind that 'permanent ceasefire', was revealed as the partition of Bosnia-Herzegovina between Serbia and Croatia. The war became increasingly vicious, and promised to be long-lasting. By May 1992 the JNA had formally disappeared. It became three armies: the army of the Serb Krajina (SVK), the army of Republika Srpska (VRS) – initially called the army of Serbs in Bosnia-Herzegovina – and the army of Yugoslavia (VJ).[19] Kadijević put this on record to remind the Serbian leadership of his contribution in having provided weapons for three Serb armies. He complains that he was not able to achieve his military objectives in Croatia because neither in Serbia and Montenegro nor in Bosnia-Herzegovina had he had any chance to mobilize. Mobilization was indeed disastrously low, but that could easily have been foreseen even before the war.[20] The Croatian Ministry of Defence had always borne it in mind and, indeed, counted on it.

The war in Croatia had formally ended, though some tactical actions were carried out during 1992: the mutually agreed liberation of southern Croatia, including Dubrovnik; the inglorious Maslenica operation, which brought little except heavy casualties; the operation in the Medak pocket, ending in crimes against the Serb population; the operation on the Miljevci plateau – all with minimal results, many unnecessary casualties and, as I have said, crimes.

KEY PHASES OF THE WAR

The period between 27 June and 7 July 1991, the duration of the JNA military campaign against Slovenia, is particularly important. The army leadership's belief that it could prevent the break-up of an unsustainable political system proved totally unfounded: when used against parts of its own country and people, the JNA inevitably disintegrated. General Kadijević wrote later that the war could have been successfully concluded with the use of fresh forces; in reality, continuing the war would only have led to a complete break-up of the JNA in all areas of former Yugoslavia except Serbia and Montenegro. The war could not have been prolonged with fresh, larger forces except by mobilizing Croats and Bosniaks in Croatia and Bosnia-Herzegovina! Meanwhile, the mobilization of troops

---

[19] Kadijević, *Moje viđenje raspada*, p. 163.
[20] 'Mobilization became the crucial limiting factor in achieving all plans for using the JNA, greater than all the other problems put together.' Ibid., p. 97 – and in several other places.

from Serbia was out of the question because of the possibility of insurrection in Kosovo, Sandžak and Vojvodina. If the Croatian political leadership had used the God-given opportunity created by Slovenia's successful defence, the war could have been definitively ended within a few months.

September to October 1991 is also exceptionally important, for it was then that 250 modern tanks, 400–500 heavy artillery pieces, some 180,000 modern firearms, anti-aircraft weapons and anti-tank guns were removed from the depots and barracks of the JNA which, together with the arsenal already assembled, was sufficient for Croatia's successful pursuit of the war. Yet this was an action which our 'supreme leader' tried to prevent: the mobilizing and arming of the HV with captured weapons was carried out at lower levels and by organizational means set up earlier. This seizure of weapons and the training of the second mobilized levy was a key element of the war, yet it was carried out without the approval of the state leadership, on the personal initiative of previously organized HV levies. For example, the municipal secretary for people's defence and the commander of the municipal TO in Đakovo occupied the garrison and seized the equipment of a large anti-armoured brigade; two officers in Bjelovar, Lt-Col Stjepan Škarec and Colonel Ivo Grbovac, with their men captured 110 new tanks: all four were imprisoned by President Tuđman for not obeying him when he ordered them not to undertake these actions. There is still much discussion in our army and police about this strange behaviour.

General Kadijević writes that the JNA 'withdrew all its principal fighting units from Croatia and positioned them where they could respond appropriately to future demands. Most of the JNA garrisons in Croatia were relieved by force, and only a small number on the basis of the Vance Plan. Only a few garrisons and depots were seized by the enemy. Most of the technical capacity lost in this way was either disabled or destroyed by subsequent air action or in other ways.'[21] This is not true. What is true is that the greater part of the JNA's heavy military hardware in Croatia was withdrawn to occupied regions of Croatia and to Bosnia-Herzegovina, Montenegro and Serbia in accordance with the agreement signed by Zagreb and Belgrade with the assistance of foreign intermediaries. Moreover, all this war matériel was loaded onto ships, railway transport and lorries by Croatian military personnel, an outrage which should never have happened. If instead we had seized those arms, the war would have been over much sooner.[22]

The crucial turning point was the defeat of the JNA in eastern Slavonia, largely the result of the unsuccessful mobilization in Serbia. Once

[21] Ibid., pp. 142–3.
[22] On the withdrawal of the JNA from Croatia, see in particular Norman Cigar, 'Croatia's War of Independence: the parameters of war termination', *Journal of Slavic Military Studies*, vol. 10, June 1997, pp. 34–70.

the HV general staff, headed by General Anton Tus, had established a better command system and completed the formation of the HV, our forces moved onto the offensive at the end of November. The HV offensive in western Slavonia was crucial, since it forced the JNA to accept the ceasefire. Sixty per cent of western Slavonia was liberated in this operation by 25 December 1991, and it was realistically estimated that all of it could have been liberated by 5 January; but the operation was halted by Tuđman's intervention, about which no one in the military command was notified in advance. Brief counter-attacks in the hinterland of Zadar and Šibenik repulsed the Krajina paramilitaries, and a strong front was established between the coastal and continental parts of central and northern Dalmatia. In the south, an impregnable defence was established on the Mostar–Ston line, following which the Montenegrin Army fell into disarray, with increasing desertions on the battlefield. The area around Gospić was also liberated through offensive action. By the end of 1991 the Croatian Army had grown to 250,000 men and had in reserve or in other echelons 15 well-trained brigades. All this pointed to an extension of offensive action in western Slavonia and the liberation of the Dalmatian Plate (the Miljevac plateau–Benkovac–Obrovac line).

But this did not happen. On 2 January 1992, minister of defence Gojko Šušak signed the ceasefire in Sarajevo, after which the war moved into Bosnia-Herzegovina. The JNA wanted the ceasefire, because it was on its knees. Ceasefires were regularly signed when the HV was in a strong position of advantage, because of the incompetence of the Croatian political leadership and its obsession with the expansion of Croatia by agreement with Serbia, an aim to which everything else had to be subordinated.

The freezing of military activity from the Sarajevo ceasefire until autumn of the same year, 1992, allowed the JNA to undergo its crucial transformation into a Serb army, ready for war in Bosnia-Herzegovina.

The actions of the Croatian Army during 1992, from Dubrovnik via Zadar and Gospić to the senseless withdrawal from Bosanska Posavina, were tactical moves often carried out with essentially limited and politically motivated objectives. The HV withdrawal from Bosanska Posavina was again ordered through secret channels and without the prior knowledge of either General Tus or myself. Our general staff had planned an offensive towards Doboj, but found the brigades pulling back across the Sava to Slavonski Brod. 'What's this?' I asked. They said it was what they were ordered to do. 'Who ordered it?' 'Generals Josip Lucić, Slobodan Praljak and Pavao Miljavac came, and announced it directly to the brigade commanders.' General Tus and I were left speechless.

The final phase of the war came in 1995 with operations Flash and Storm (see Ozren Žunec's contribution below). It is interesting that the final operations in Bosnia-Herzegovina were once again halted in full swing, allegedly because they required the use of major force, not really a convincing explanation. When Croatian Deputy Minister of Foreign Affairs Ivan Šimonović was asked at a symposium in 1996 why those 1995 operations had been halted, he replied: 'If we had continued, there would have been a large number of refugees entering Serbia, and Serbia would have been destabilized.' Rather as if the Allies, in 1945, had halted their operations on the German border for fear that Germany would be defeated. My personal view is that operations were halted in the spirit of the Tuđman–Milošević agreement to partition Bosnia-Herzegovina.

RELATIONS BETWEEN MILITARY AND CIVIL AUTHORITIES AND THEIR INFLUENCE ON THE CONDUCT OF THE WAR

History shows that military and civil authorities often disagree, but what happened in this war between the leadership of the HV and the leadership of the HDZ is a special case. Here are a few examples.

1. Between December 1990 and the end of July 1991, President Tuđman rejected three plans for the defence of Croatia. He closed the discussion on the first of these with the words: 'Not only do I not want this plan, I don't want any kind of defence plan!'
2. From mid February 1991 to the end of June 1991 the president suspended the arming of the Croatian Army.
3. At the end of July 1991, only two months before the start of the aggression, President Tuđman rejected my third defence plan and exiled me abroad, despite my position as commanding officer of the ZNG. A month and a half after my departure, the HV General Staff instructed middle and lower ranks of the HV to implement my plan to seize the armaments from the depots and garrisons of the JNA, thus saving the country from disaster.
4. The president used the ZNG chief of staff, Colonel Imra Agotić, for negotiations about the withdrawal of the JNA, although the country was conducting a defensive war. The Croatian Army General Staff, which came belatedly to be headed by General Anton Tus, was established in effect at the height of the aggression.
5. The highly successful HV offensive in western Slavonia was stopped without the knowledge of the Croatian General Staff, or General Tus (chief of staff), or General Špegelj (inspector-in-chief).
6. At least ten brigades of the HV and the HVO were withdrawn from Bosanska Posavina in autumn 1992, without the knowledge of Generals Tus and Špegelj.
7. The final operation in Bosnia-Herzegovina in 1995 was halted with absolutely no military rationale.

Despite this state of affairs, Croatia successfully fought and defended itself, albeit with far too many unnecessary casualties. It emerged victorious – despite the war with the Bosniaks, catastrophic for the Croats in Bosnia-Herzegovina and for Croatia itself – because the aggressor was always the weaker party. What was finally decisive in ending the war was the emergence, to general astonishment, of a strong army of Bosnia-Herzegovina. It foiled the plans to divide that republic, which was a great surprise to both the Serbian and Croatian leaderships.

The disintegration of SFRY was, objectively speaking, inevitable. While external events affected it – the fall of the Berlin Wall, the disintegration of the USSR and other events in Eastern Europe – it was brought about by internal forces. The disintegrative factors that had been acting during its whole existence finally triumphed. The Serbs in Serbia did not wish to go to war outside Serbia and die for a Greater Serbia, while every other nation, every other republic and Kosovo, was agreed about seeking independence, albeit at the cost of heavy casualties. A large majority of the population came to think the same, and that was decisive. The JNA high command and the Serbian leadership embarked on the war on the basis of completely false judgments. They were consequently bound to lose it.

3

The War in Slovenia and Croatia up to the Sarajevo Ceasefire

Anton Tus

The direction that Greater Serbian nationalism was taking could be seen as early as 1986, with the appearance of the Memorandum of the Serbian Academy and numerous public statements following it. The illegal abolition of the autonomy of the two Autonomous Provinces and the overthrow of the governments in Kosovo, Vojvodina and Montenegro was clearly an integral part of Milošević's attempt to put things in order 'at home' before turning westwards, to the battle for Greater Serbia. After Tito's death in 1980, Yugoslavia was left with only two remaining props: the League of Communists of Yugoslavia (LCY) and the Yugoslav National Army (JNA). The disintegration of the LCY in January 1990 was the final confirmation that the destruction of Yugoslavia's multinational community would rapidly follow.[1] Thus only the JNA was left, with a pro-Serb peacetime leadership and a wartime structure that matched republican or national ratios, while the Serb component in its mobilized formations was, for demographic reasons, smaller than the Serb component in the population as a whole.

THE SERB INSURRECTION AND THE MILITARY COMMAND

When the orchestrated Serb insurrection in the Knin Krajina began on 17 August 1990, I was on holiday. I immediately returned to Belgrade and met the Federal minister of transport and communications, the Slovene Janez Slokar. I proposed that he go at once to Knin to break the traffic

[1] At the Conference of the JNA branch of the LCY in December 1989, and at the 14th Congress of the LCY in January 1990, I myself made a proposal for the decentralization and depoliticization of the army. I said that the JNA must not impede the political processes, which were clearly heading towards multiparty democracy, and that it must adapt itself, structurally, organizationally and functionally to constitutional and legislative changes, which were clearly leading towards a transformation of the Federal state into a federation of sovereign states.

blockade, and the president of the Federal government, Ante Marković, concurred. To enable him to get to Knin as quickly as possible, I provided Slokar with an aircraft to take him to Split, where a helicopter was waiting to take him to Knin. There he met the organizers of the blockade in the railway administrative offices; they already had a para-state structure headed by Milan Babić, president of the Knin municipal council. In the formal, legal sense, this was the proper approach, since Slokar as minister of transport could act simply with the purpose of resolving an organizational and technical problem within his jurisdiction, avoiding any matters that needed political negotiation. He immediately understood what was going on, and on his return informed me that we were dealing with a real insurrection with a political background, and that the leaders in Knin could not make independent decisions but were acting on instructions from Belgrade.

When, the following day, I proposed to the collegiate body of the Federal Secretariat for National Defence that the JNA should lift the road and rail barricades erected by the armed rebels, General Kadijević exclaimed: 'Do you really want the Serbs to say that the JNA is against them?' That was our first public clash. With the barricades, the crisis had moved into the phase of terrorism and special war which normally precedes aggression and military intervention.

In December of that year a wartime general staff of the supreme command was formed, to which my deputy rather than myself was appointed, though I was commander of the air force and anti-aircraft defence. This confirmed my suspicions that detailed war options were being prepared, about which I, as a Croat and advocate of decentralization and depoliticization of the JNA, was to know nothing. In the New Year of 1991 I met General Martin Špegelj in my flat in Zagreb; he was then minister of defence in the Croatian government. We were in agreement about what was going to happen and what needed to be done.

On 13 March 1991 my pilots informed me that General Kadijević had come to Batajnica, the military airport near Belgrade, where he was awaiting permission to fly to Moscow. Surprised, I went to the airport, but since Kadijević was already sitting in the aircraft with the intention of leaving covertly, I did not approach him. After waiting for four hours, he obtained permission to overfly Hungary and flew to Moscow for a meeting with Soviet Minister of Defence Dimitri Yazov. When he learned from him that the Russian Army was not after all going to carry out a coup, as it had intended, he returned disappointed to Belgrade. A coup in the USSR would have triggered one in Yugoslavia, but Gorbachev's approach to the troops eliminated or at least postponed the threat. When Yazov did try to carry out a coup in August of that year, he was no longer able to do so.

At the beginning of April 1991, in a meeting of the inner circle of senior staff officers of all branches of the military forces and from all military sectors, I opposed the new operational dispositions of the JNA. I maintained that an operational deployment of the army in the west and a programme to take control of the area was being carried out, for which there was no justification, since there was no external threat. I also asked why an armoured bridge from Pančevo was moving into Bosnia-Herzegovina, to Banja Luka; why members of the Niš parachute brigade were going to Zagreb; and why part of the JNA from Bosnia-Herzegovina was being transferred to Slovenia. I ended by reiterating that the JNA must not be used against any of the peoples of Yugoslavia, and that the air force and anti-aircraft defence, with myself as their leader, would not make war against any of our peoples. Kadijević rose and said: 'We can do without anyone who is not with us! Anyone else want to say anything?' Then General Konrad Kolšek, the Slovene commander of the 5th army district (theatre) which covered most of Croatia and Slovenia, stood up and said that he would not be able to carry out any such mission, because he would not be able to mobilize Slovenes and Croats, who constituted the war reinforcements in that sector. Admiral Mile Kandić, the Serb commander of the navy, also spoke up, and in effect repeated what Kolšek had said. Kadijević gave us ten days to think it over and repeated that the JNA could do without any of us. I replied that his message was perfectly clear and that I stood by my decision.

I had already made preparations for returning to Zagreb, and during my last days in Belgrade I always carried two pistols, one in my bag, the other in my belt. When fighting broke out in Plitvice at Easter 1991 between the JNA and Serb paramilitaries on one side and members of the Croatian gendarmerie (MUP forces) on the other, I supplied helicopters to take the wounded from both sides to hospital at the personal request of the Croatian Minister of Interior Josip Boljkovac. I was immediately criticized for 'providing helicopters to the Ustasha'.[2] On 2 May, the day of the attack on Croatian policemen at Borovo Selo, I was in Novi Vinodolski with Minister Boljkovac and we talked about the possible future shape of events. He was then informed that 12 policemen had been killed. Returning to Belgrade, I received on 8 May the decree of the president of the presidency of SFRY, Borisav Jović, relieving me of my duties as commander of the air force and anti-aircraft defence, with a note that I would be retired at the end of the year. I relinquished my post, came home to my family in Zagreb and made myself available to the Croatian authorities.

---

[2] Simo Dubajić, a Serb from Kistanje and one of the organizers of the Serb insurrection, a partisan from the early days of the Second World War and retired JNA colonel, gave an interview to the Belgrade newspaper *Politika* in autumn 1991 in which, speaking of these events, he said: 'Tus should have been immediately arrested.'

THE WAR IN SLOVENIA

It was probable that Yugoslavia would collapse, and we had to reckon that it might happen in the worst possible manner – armed dissolution; but the international community did nothing to prevent it, merely expressing its desire to halt a process that was already under way. After 1988 the crisis, already deep, produced ever more bitter clashes between Serbia, the Federal institutions and the JNA high command, on the one hand, and the remaining republics, institutions and citizens inclined towards democratic change on the other. The JNA leadership and Serbia clashed fiercely with Slovenia and its government over military organization, military service in one's home republic, the language of command in the JNA and the financing of the JNA. When the Slovenian leadership opposed the intention of the 'threatened' Serbs of Kosovo to hold a 'truth rally' in Ljubljana on 1 December 1989, the first economic blockade in history within a federal state took place: Serbia broke off trade relations with Slovene firms and prohibited the sale of Slovene goods in Serbia.

In May 1990 came the placing of TO weapons under the control of the JNA, but as a result of the way their ordnance was organized territorially, the Slovenes did manage to retain a third of them. The commander of the TO of Slovenia, General Hočevar, issued an order to hand over the weapons, following which President Kučan dismissed him, and in September 1990 Slovenia took over control of the TO and appointed its new commander, which enabled the Slovenian TO to be organized militarily and deployed successfully at the right time.

The JNA leadership was behaving more and more as a political force; the introduction of a state of emergency and preparations for a military coup became its constant preoccupation. That is why the decree on enforcement of Federal government rules, aimed at safeguarding the SFRY frontiers at border crossings into Slovenia, provided the excuse for the military leadership to go into action. At that time the aims of the JNA and Serbia did not coincide: the JNA wanted to retain the whole of Yugoslavia, while Serbia wanted a Greater Serbia within the framework of Yugoslavia, without Slovenia. This was the first discrepancy in the formulation of their military and political objectives, and the cause of the improvised and rash use of military force, with which Serbia and the JNA would be dogged throughout the wars to come.

On 25 June the assemblies of Slovenia and Croatia each adopted separate but coordinated declarations of sovereignty and independence, which implied that on the territories of those two republics the only valid laws would be those adopted by those two legislatures. The following day the Federal government pronounced both declarations null and void, and passed a decree that the JNA and Federal police should take over control of border crossings. A day later the military leadership of the JNA launched military action in Slovenia, thus preventing a peaceful dissolution of the Yugoslav Federation. The formal mission of the JNA was to occupy the border crossings into Austria, Italy and Hungary, which had been taken over by the TO of Slovenia, and enable the Federal police and customs service to be deployed there. The real objective was to take control of the borders and principal facilities in Slovenia, including Brnik, Ljubljana's airport, and thus to frustrate first Slovenia's and then Croatia's move to independence.

The JNA forces in Slovenia – the Ljubljana and Maribor corps, the airborne brigade from Cerklje airforce base and the anti-aircraft missile regiment in Vrhnica – were engaged in this action, as were forces from Croatia: parts of the Rijeka corps on the Rijeka–Ilirska Bistrica–Sežana line, the Zagreb corps on the Zagreb–Novo Mesto and Karlovac–Metlika routes, the Varaždin corps on the Varaždin–Maribor route, and the entire Zagreb airborne brigade (parachute brigade and reserve forces). The operation was planned in Belgrade by the general staff, but the corps commanders were not given the plans, just brief orders. Not even the command of the 5th army district had the plans in their entirety. Because of this secrecy, everything was improvised and irresponsible: the planners had completely failed to anticipate organized resistance supposing that the arrival of heavy weapons and tanks would terrify the Slovenes.

The JNA forces in Slovenia reached most of the border crossings, but a significant proportion of them remained surrounded in their barracks. The units from Croatia, except for the Rijeka corps under the command of the zealous General Čad, were halted by road blocks. Slovenia's TO and police together had more than 20,000 actively engaged men, with about another 30,000 in reserve. Their great advantage was their high morale, determination and skill at blockading buildings, installations and roads.

The main battles took place on 27 and 28 June; after the ceasefire had been agreed, the military leadership of the JNA and Serbia prepared reprisals in the form of massive air strikes to punish Slovenia, to free besieged JNA garrisons and to cover withdrawal of their forces from Slovenian territory, as witness the following exchange between Milošević, Kadijević and Jović on 5 July:

> We require Veljko [Kadijević]:
> 1. To respond vigorously to the Slovenes with all means including airforce [and] then to withdraw from Slovenia. A decision will be issued on this at the proper time. This will raise the morale of the troops, intimidate Croatia, and calm the Serb people.
> 2. To concentrate his main body on the Karlovac–Plitvice line in the west; Baranja, Osijek, Vinkovci – the Sava to the east, and the Neretva in the south, so as to cover all territories where Serbs live until the final resolution.

3. To eliminate all Croats and Slovenes from the army.
   If we do not launch this action in Slovenia, we shall lose in Serbia, and then the army will disintegrate. We were categorical. Veljko accepted without discussion. He thought he would need 6–10 days. We did not agree. We wanted it done in 2–3 days. He accepted. And we needn't spare them in the conflict.[3]

As part of this plan, the commander of the Zagreb airborne brigade, General Marijan Rožić, was given the task of bombarding civilian installations in Slovenia; the list included transmitters, installations in Ljubljana, etc. He was worried, and came to my house in Zagreb for advice. We agreed that this would be a war crime, and that he need not and should not carry out the mission. In the event, the military leadership abandoned the idea of massive air strikes, but General Rožić and General Kolšek, commander of the 5th army district, both Slovenes, were dismissed.

The decisiveness of the Slovenian leadership, the success of the Slovene defence forces in blockading the JNA, and a skilfully conducted media war won the victory. In that ten-day skirmish, 65 people lost their lives: the JNA 37, the Slovene TO and police 12, while of 16 civilians killed 10 were foreigners, lorry-drivers on blocked roads. The injured numbered 330.

On 7 July, with the mediation of the European Union 'troika' ministers, the republican representatives, the SFRY Presidency, the Federal government and the JNA adopted the Brioni Declaration covering a ceasefire, the arrival of international observers, the withdrawal of the JNA from Slovenia and a three-month moratorium on the implementation of the Slovene and Croatian declarations of independence. Slovenia became *de facto* independent, and the JNA and Serbia turned their backs on an unsuccessful theatre of operations. Croatia should then have recognized that it was next in line.

GENESIS AND DEVELOPMENT OF THE CROATIAN ARMY

The phase of disorganized defence

The creation of the Croatian Army (HV) began with the change of government on 30 May 1990. As part of the reorganization of the Ministry of Interior (MUP) and the formation of its anti-terrorist units, special troops were formed under its auspices, which became the National

---

[3] Borisav Jović, *Poslednji dani SFRJ* [The last days of SFRY], Belgrade 1995, p. 349. Kadijević had asked Milošević and Jović to say something to encourage the reluctant and demoralized conscripts; they told him that 'as far as the call-up is concerned, the answer lies in military action in Slovenia, not in some political gesture from us, which could have a negative effect'. Ibid., p. 350.

Guard (ZNG), basis of the future Croatian Army. By 28 May 1991, four such active units, A-brigades, of the ZNG had been created: the 1st and 2nd in Zagreb, the 3rd in Slavonia (Osijek) and the 4th in Dalmatia (Split). They were composed of MUP special troops and volunteers directed by the government and the HDZ, but their numbers and armaments were very modest – a few thousand people armed with minimal infantry weapons. The MUP retained its existing structure, and thus was able more rapidly to deploy its troops, while the TO was kept out of operation for political reasons and because of lack of confidence in it: in March and April 1991 the municipal and city TO Staffs were abolished and partly reorganized, while the TO Staff of the Republic was abolished on 12 July.[4]

In June, July and August 1991 small MUP, ZNG and Croat Defence Forces (HOS) units were formed throughout Croatia, but they were later, mostly without any problems, incorporated into the regular army. Armed and unarmed volunteer detachments and units of the National Guard were also formed. In July the government issued several decrees relating to defence: organization and formation of reserve brigades of the ZNG, appointment of territorial commanders and setting up of crisis staffs. On 30 July the ZNG Command was formed. General Martin Špegelj, who had only just been replaced as minister of defence, was appointed commander, and Colonel Imra Agotić was made chief of staff. Improvised war production began, and the flow of resources for defence from Croats increased. At that time there were four JNA army corps stationed in Croatia, as well as half the air force and the entire navy. There were two army corps in Slovenia and three in Bosnia-Herzegovina, which meant that the greater part of the JNA was in the western half of the country.

The disorganized phase of the defence, based on limited numbers of MUP, ZNG and volunteer forces together with self-organized citizens' groups, lasted until September. It was a time when the enemy was not precisely defined, when Croatian leaders did not yet consider the military option as the principal one, but maintained that everything could be resolved by political negotiation, although we were well enough informed of the intentions of the JNA leadership and Milošević's political group. However, on 3 August 1991 the government decided to form the Croatian Army general staff.

---

[4] I believe this was an error that made the organization of the army and the defence effort more difficult, and that it would have been enough to replace those in the TO who were unwilling to cooperate with the legal authorities or who were acting in concert with the JNA. It was especially necessary to preserve the mobilization structure of the TO and to rely upon it. As it was, when we had recourse to it in the deployment of the Croatian Army, we found that it was partly non-functional, since its structure had already been replaced with spontaneous, unorganized or party-backed troops.

On 17 September, Milošević, Kadijević and Tuđman signed a ceasefire agreement in Igalo in Montenegro under the auspices of Lord Carrington, but it was obvious that it would hold no better than the previous ones, so on 20 September, at 15.00 hours, President Tuđman sent a new 'Proposal to End the Conflict in Croatia' to Belgrade. He proposed that on Saturday 21 September at 19.00 hours he and Kadijević would issue simultaneous and public orders to the forces under their command: the Croatian forces would cease all offensive actions against JNA units, and local authorities would restore water, food and electricity supplies to JNA barracks, while JNA forces would cease all military operations, movements and transfer of forces into Croatia, and lift their blockade of all Croatia's harbours and air traffic. The deadline for executing the orders would be Sunday 22 September at 12.00 hours, after which talks would be held 'on regularizing all mutual relations'. This proposal was brusquely rejected by the Federal Secretariat for National Defence via its Information Service.

Saturday 21 September was a day of drama. Tovarnik was attacked with cluster bombs; there was a battle on the access routes to Grubisino Polje; the sea, land and air attack on Šibenik reached its climax, its citizens having already spent five days in shelters; while some JNA garrisons surrendered to our forces (Ðakovo, Gospić, Zadar). At about 18.00 hours General Kadijević himself issued a public statement through Tanjug and Belgrade TV which included the following:

> Yugoslavia is no longer what it was. The Presidency has been shattered. It is headed by one of the chief proponents of the establishment of a fascist government in Croatia, a proven enemy of Yugoslavia [i.e. Mesić]. The [Yugoslav] Assembly has fallen apart while the government's leader [i.e. Marković] is blatantly trying to blame others for his failings, which have fundamentally contributed to, indeed made possible, the chaos and disintegration of the country.[5]

I concluded from this that Kadijević was determined not to recognize the government of the Republic of Croatia, and that SFR Yugoslavia and its federal bodies no longer existed: that the supreme command's general staff had taken power and begun military action to 'prevent civil war', as Kadijević put it. In short, this was a declaration of war against Croatia. That same evening, after the main news on Croatian television, President Tuđman announced the decree setting up the general staff of the Croatian Army, and appointed the chief of staff and his deputy. The next phase of defence then began, marked by accelerated deployment of the HV and an organized military response; by that time the JNA had already occupied a quarter of the territory of Croatia, but thereafter it would go on to occupy only Vukovar and the Dubrovnik area.

---

[5] Quoted from a video transcript in the possession of the author.

The phase of organized defence

I became chief of staff of the Croatian Army general staff. My deputies were General Petar Stipetić and Colonel Ante Roso. The ZNG command, headed by Colonel Imra Agotić, also joined the general staff. The Croatian naval command was already established in Split, headed by Admiral Sveto Letica, and an air force and anti-aircraft defence were formed under Colonel Tomo Madić. We had first-class people – military professionals and commanders fully equal to the war situation we faced. We all wanted to do our utmost, and concentrated on what we knew best. Ante Roso and Milenko Filipović created a centre for training special troops in Kumrovec and the Zrinski-Frankopan regiment, while General Stipetić and Colonel Franjo Feldi were considered to be the best operations officers of the former 5th army district (it was said of the first that he was the best operations officer in the entire JNA). We knew the real state of affairs in the JNA – its potential, the abilities of individuals, the morale of the troops and the state of its armaments – so we were able to predict the moves it would make.

More than 80 per cent of Croat officers left the JNA for the Croatian Army to defend their people and their homeland, some in the first days of clashes with the Serb rebels, the majority in September and October, when the JNA declared war on Croatia. Without the officers who came from the JNA and their professionalism, we would have had many more casualties, losses and defeats. There were not only Croats, but Albanians, Bosniaks, and even Serbs who considered Croatia their country.[6] By the end of 1991 there were nearly 2,500 officers and NCOs who had been JNA professional soldiers, and over 400 who fought in the ranks (for example, there were two pilots in Sisak whom we had had no opportunity to deploy in accordance with their expertise).[7] To this must be added more than 18,000

---

[6] Serbs fought in the Croatian Army, many of them as volunteers. According to two official statements issued by the Croatian government at the start of 1997, some 9,000 Serbs fought as part of the Croatian Army, where they formed the 'largest ethnic group'. See Vesna Škare-Ožbolt and Ivica Vrkić (ed.), *Olujni mir: kronologija hrvatske misije mira na Dunavu* [Stormy peace: the chronology of the Croatian peace mission on the Danube], *Narodne novine* [National Gazette], Zagreb 1998, pp. 159 and 203.

[7] They had come over to the Croatian Army without their aircraft. The first pilot who, not wanting to take part in the aggression, left the JNA with his aircraft landed on 21 October 1991 in Celovec/Klagenfurt, in Austria, where his MiG-21 was held, in accordance with international law. The first fighter interceptor aircraft MiG-21bis flew into free Croatian territory from the 117th JNA fighter squadron in Bihać on 4 January 1992 and became part of the Croatian Air Force as no. 101; it was lost in a reconnaissance action in the Prijedor region on 26 June 1992. Another two such aircraft flew over from Užice (Serbia) on 15 May 1992 – one landed in Zagreb, the other in Split.

reserve officers and NCOs, which means that we had more than 20,000 well-trained soldiers with the professionalism we needed. Another element of the officer corps of the Croatian Army was formed of Croat members of the French Foreign Legion and the armed forces of other countries who had returned home. A third group – the most numerous from 1992 onwards – consisted of the new generation of officers who had risen through the ranks in combat and were accepted by their peers as leaders. It was worth giving them a military education to provide them with the skills needed to fill more senior positions and carry out more complex missions.

There were very few misunderstandings between former members of the JNA and other volunteers: we were all patriots with the same mission. Problems were created by radical nationalists in the ruling party and the Ministry of Defence, who considered that former members of the JNA should be made use of and then dismissed. These people created an atmosphere of intolerance towards former JNA members, who were just as much volunteers as all the others.

I was fully aware that we could not prevent the occupation of parts of our territory until we had deployed our army and formed an unbroken line of defence from Vukovar to Dubrovnik. The major problem was that the main JNA forces and rebel Serbs were on our territory, so we had to be prepared to defend ourselves against not only external attack, but also internal clashes. Our greatest error was that after the successful non-violent blockade of the garrisons in summer 1991 we did not go on in September and October to occupy all the JNA garrisons and depots in Croatia. It is not true that in that case Zagreb, Rijeka and Split would have been destroyed. They could have attacked us with heavy weapons from the Marshal Tito barracks in Novi Zagreb, for example, for only about 20 minutes or at the most half an hour, since they were surrounded and helpless. The JNA learned its lesson from Croatia, and later in Bosnia-Herzegovina withdrew all its troops from barracks in the towns to deploy them in dominant positions.

But the Croatian leadership acceded to the demand of the European Community and the United States at the end of June – formalized by the Brioni declaration of 7 July – to suspend the Croatian and Slovenian declarations of independence for three months, provided the JNA returned to barracks. However, the JNA did not withdraw to barracks in Croatia but continued to occupy territory, and we lost valuable time between June and September 1991 when we could have been deploying the army and setting up our defence.

We in general staff were not slaves to classroom models, and had from the very beginning abandoned the classic army units of division and corps, since we would not have been able to deploy and use them operationally.

Instead, along with operational zones, sectors and brigades,[8] we formed a large number of battle, tactical and operational units, and battlefield commands. The creation of operational commands and the division of the territory into six operational zones (Osijek, Bjelovar, Zagreb, Karlovac, Rijeka and Split) and two operational sectors (Zadar and Dubrovnik) were of particular importance, since this enabled us to unite our defence forces in the regions under attack. At the same time we removed the right of command from the regional (civilian) crisis staffs, which had fulfilled their mission and become a brake on the more efficient use of our new troops, and redirected their activities towards mobilization and logistics. We moved from local defence to the defence of broader zones and lines, so that a given place could be defended from a distance of 10 kilometres or more, not immediately beside the first houses in the town.

We wanted above all to defend the larger towns, and the main road and rail routes so that the JNA could not cut them. We concentrated especially on maintaining the Drava and Adriatic highways and the Zagreb–Rijeka road and rail links, and on defending the Pag bridge, the only remaining firm link between the interior and Dalmatia. We banned all departures of those fit for military service from Dubrovnik, Zadar, Vinkovci and Osijek, because we would not have been able to defend abandoned towns.

Up to that time too many of our troops had remained to the rear, unused, while we had insufficient forces on the front lines. The formation of operational zones fundamentally changed the situation: smaller units were successfully linked, and the command hierarchy began to be respected, although we were still short of weapons, and had to rely for a while longer on a defensive strategy, with intermittent joint offensive actions. Mobile units of operational and tactical groups with greater fire-power were organized, and at the same time we began to develop new brigades and complete those already formed. At the beginning of October 1991 we had 24 acceptably equipped and armed brigades, and another 10 in formation, plus the Croatian navy, air force and anti-aircraft defence troops. With these forces, and another 20 newly formed units at the brigade level, we halted the JNA advance in October and November and formed a united battlefront 1,200 kilometres long, from Donji Miholjac to Dubrovnik. The 2 January 1992 truce found us with an army of 230,000 armed soldiers in 65 brigades, and many independent units in all three branches of the armed forces, as well as around 40,000 police from the Ministry of the Interior, of whom one third were deployed in war positions.

---

[8] We reinforced the 1,200-strong TO brigades with one battalion and support forces, so that a standard HV brigade had 1,800 people.

September and October – the turning point of the war

One of our most important tasks after forming the Croatian Army general staff was to transform the passive blockade of the JNA garrisons into an active one, and to occupy the depots. To be able to engage more effectively with the forces that were coming from outside – Baranja was already occupied, and the battles for Vukovar, Vinkovci, Osijek, Pakrac, Nova Gradiška, Novska, Sisak, Gospić, Šibenik and Zadar had begun, while that for Dubrovnik was about to start – we had to neutralize the forces already on Croatian territory: the 5th army district, the naval district and the 5th air force corps and anti-aircraft defence of the JNA. When we finally began the operation to occupy the depots and barracks throughout Croatia, we disarmed the entire 32nd (Varaždin) and half the 10th (Zagreb) corps and those parts of the 13th (Rijeka) corps which were located in Gorski Kotar (Delnice) and Lika, as well as parts of the air force and navy. Only the Knin corps, most of which had already been deployed in the operational area, remained beyond our reach, 'defending the threatened Serb population', i.e. occupying northern Dalmatia and Lika. We managed to halt them just outside Šibenik and Zadar.

October 1991 was the most difficult month of the entire Patriotic War, for on the 5th of the month the JNA launched a general offensive, with operations in all the regions, aimed at crushing Croatia within 20 days. They were even intending to attack Zagreb, from the Karlovac and Sisak direction. We expected the fiercest offensive on the Kupa, so that is where we concentrated most of our forces. The defence of the Kupa valley from Sisak to Karlovac foiled the JNA's attempt to break through and free the troops surrounded in their barracks in Zagreb, Jastrebarsko and Dugo Selo, with the intention of simultaneously taking Sisak and Karlovac and breaking the blockade of the Rijeka and Varaždin corps. We stopped them, and at the same time disarmed parts of the besieged corps.

We knew then that we would win – we might still lose the odd battle, but there was no longer any doubt that we would hold Croatia.[9] In all we captured almost 200 tanks, 150 armoured personnel carriers and infantry combat vehicles, as well as about 400 artillery pieces, 180,000 rifles and automatics, 18 ships of various types, and significant quantities of ammunition, bombs and mines. We also recovered part of the armaments of the former Croatian TO, which the JNA had been holding in those same depots. The Croatian Army was formed and organized almost unimaginably

---

[9] I had a visit at that time from a high-ranking Western NATO general, whom I had met earlier. We met in Zagreb on 7 October, and he told me that in NATO's judgement we would not hold out for more than two weeks. I promised him I would call him two weeks later so that he could see for himself. After a few months we met again in Paris. He acknowledged that they could not believe we would really hold out. The JNA itself had planned to complete the operation in about 20 days.

rapidly, in just a few months. In September and October alone we formed dozens of solidly armed brigades and support troops. Those two months marked a turning point in the war.

In October and November a special operation was carried out to defend the main communications: the main roads along the Adriatic and the Drava and the roads from Zagreb to Rijeka, which we could not allow to be cut. The defence of Dubrovnik and of the river Neretva from Metković to Ploče lasted through October, November and December 1991, when Serbia's access to the Neretva and Dalmatia was cut. The battle for Dubrovnik and our halting the enemy before Ston were the key events in the defence of southern Dalmatia.

The arms embargo was unjust, since it assumed an equivalence between the unarmed victims of aggression and the aggressors who had sufficient arms and equipment for several years of warfare. Though we were conducting a defensive war we could not carry out a full mobilization, but only a gradual one as arms and ammunition became available to us.

The equipping of the Croatian Army can be classified into different periods. During the first year of war, in 1991, the army was primarily equipped by captured weapons and local production, which was improvised, certainly, but had a good base in our extensive industrial potential and expertise, and the high level of professionalism of our people. We manufactured light infantry weapons: machine guns, various types of rifle, explosives, mines, hand grenades, grenade launchers, and light artillery weapons such as recoilless cannon. We also produced improvised armoured personnel carriers, and adapted light aircraft from local flying clubs for war use, and speed boats for battles at sea. Croatia's mechanical engineering capacity and parts of the electronics and chemical industries were already able to produce numerous items necessary for the conduct of war. Some equipment was also obtained from abroad, though in limited quantities. After 1991, there were fewer captured weapons, while foreign purchases and domestic production increased.

THE BATTLE FOR VUKOVAR

Encirclement of the town and setting up the defence

In the broader sense, the battle for Vukovar began in the second half of July 1991. The situation in the region was marked by an increase in armed attacks by Serb rebels, the laying of mines on roads and rail and in buildings, the barbarism of local and incoming Chetniks, and the removal of animal stock and crops to Serbia. During that and the following month, the JNA began operational deployments in the region of Baranja and eastern Srijem, right up to Osijek and Vinkovci, occupying the area and inciting the Serb population to rebel, while itself arming them. The first tanks with reservists from the 12th (Novi Sad) corps from Vojvodina came over the bridge at Batina, then at Erdut, while forces from the 17th (Tuzla) corps, reinforced by units from the 14th (Ljubljana) corps after its withdrawal from Slovenia, were brought in over the Sava bridge at Županja, which we later destroyed. The main forces, from the Belgrade army district and the Serbian TO came in via Šid, Tovarnik, Ilača, Oriolik, Negoslavci. The JNA grouped in Negoslavci, Bršadin, Trpinja, Pačetin, Bobota, Borovo Selo and on the Danube.

Deployed in this way, encircling the area, these troops were soon able to take control of it and attack Vukovar from three sides: Negoslavci–Sajmište, Borovo Selo–Borovo Naselje, and Bršadin–Borovo Naselje, so that the town was surrounded from these three principal directions before 1 October. By occupying Erdut, Dalj and Almaš at the beginning of August, the aggressor formed a bridgehead from the Drava–Danube confluence up to Vukovar.

The battle for Vukovar itself had two phases: the phase when it was partially surrounded, before 1 October, and from then on, when it was completely surrounded, the JNA 252nd armoured brigade having occupied Marinci, until the aggressor's entry into the town on 18 November 1991. Since the beginning of hostilities Vukovar had suffered from missile and artillery bombardment from the area of Bačka, across the Danube, and from warships on the Danube itself. The 4th regiment of the 3rd brigade and troops of the ZNG's 1st brigade were in Vukovar: only about 400 guards in all, with 300 Ministry of Interior troops from Vukovar, Slavonski Brod and Varaždin, and some ZNG forces who had arrived after the gradual loss of western Srijem. They were joined by another 1,100 Homeguard volunteers raised from local communities. They were only partly armed, with very little heavy weaponry. These forces defended their positions and carried out surprise assaults, ambushes and attacks on rebel units; offensives against the JNA were at first forbidden. We began to send them significant quantities of arms only after the occupation of the JNA barracks in September – Vukovar and Dubrovnik were our priorities, followed by exposed cities such as Karlovac, Gospić, Osijek, Vinkovci and Zadar.

The all-out offensive against Vukovar began on 24 August with air and artillery strikes. As well as needing arms, ammunition and troops, the city needed assistance in organizing its defence, so on 31 August Mile Dedaković as commander, and Branko Borković as his deputy, came and organized a ring defence – a defence of the town by sector. There were six sectors, with one unit responsible for each, but they acted as a single entity within the 204th brigade formation; they had some grenade launchers and anti-tank guns, and a large quantity of mines. But the defence was unable to resolve the problem of the encirclement of the town, nor were our forces in the town able to deal with the Petrova Gora barracks: it was a great mistake not to have occupied it before Vukovar was completely surrounded. It formed the base for the aggressor's attacks; occupying it would have greatly strengthened the defence.

It was rather different with the Danube bridges. Their destruction would have greatly hampered the JNA manoeuvres, but not made them impossible, since they were not the only way into Croatia. The aggressors could have grouped in Srijem and come in from that direction. Their river fleet was bombarding Vukovar from the Danube and had no need of the bridges; it also attempted a landing, which the defenders repulsed.

First attempt at a breakthrough

On 29 September, with the noose tightening around Vukovar, I issued the order to concentrate our forces with the aim of breaking through to the town. Volunteers from Zagreb, Varaždin and other Croatian towns began to move to Vinkovci, along with troops from the Croatian Army general staff and Ministry of Interior special troops, all at combat strength. The breakthrough operation was planned for 10 October. It was to be led by the commanding officer of the Osijek Operations zone, General Karl Gorinšek, with Lt-Col Ivan Basarac, commanding officer of the 3rd brigade of the ZNG, which was to be the first strike levy of the breakthrough, as operational commander. Meanwhile, the commanding officer of the Vukovar defence, Mile Dedaković, made the decision, on his own account, to leave the town, breaking out with a small escort under attack through the cornfields and canals along the river Vuka, in order to get support sent in more rapidly. Since he knew both our and the enemy forces and positions well, I appointed him commanding officer of the breakthrough operation, and later commanding officer of the operational group that was to enter the town, while I appointed Borković, who had remained in Vukovar, commanding officer of the Vukovar defence.

The 3rd brigade, the tank company of the 109th Vinkovci brigade, units of the 106th and 122nd brigades, special defence troops from general staff and part of the Ministry of the Interior special brigade were all concentrated in Nuštar. It was a high quality formation, with very solid support from one of the reinforced artillery divisions. Its task was to make for Marinci and occupy it. Marinci was defended by a reinforced JNA battalion and units of Serb volunteers. Since our forces did not manage to concentrate in time, given that we had to withdraw them from other areas, our offensive began two and a half days later, on the morning of 13 October. During the night of 12 to 13 October we preceded it with diversionary actions which were to destroy specific enemy hotspots and disguise the direction of the main breakthrough. After artillery preparation our forces set off along two parallel routes towards Marinci, and, albeit with significant losses, by noon already held half Marinci. Perhaps one could say that at that moment the battle for Vukovar could have been won, since the Vukovar road was now open.

However, at 9 a.m. on 13 October President Tuđman called me and asked me to suspend the action. He said that the European Community and Minister Hans van den Broek were demanding it of him, since they wanted to send a convoy of the international humanitarian organization Médecins Sans Frontières into Vukovar to evacuate the wounded. I told him that we could not interrupt a successful breakthrough, and that was how things remained for the moment.

At 12 noon, when we were already in Marinci, he again called me and ordered me to suspend the operation, since otherwise the European Community would accuse Croatia of violating the ceasefire and withdraw their observers. But when we began the breakthrough there had been no ceasefire in this theatre of operations. I told the president quite explicitly that the operation was going successfully, that our troops were already in Marinci and that there was absolutely no reason to stop; and that Médecins Sans Frontières, if they were to enter Vukovar that day, would not be able to leave but would have to spend the night in the JNA barracks, so that the aid they brought with them would be taken by the Serbs. I ended by saying: 'There is no reason for them to go in today. Let them go in tomorrow, and by then we shall have completed our breakthrough.' 'I am ordering you to stop the operation at once!', he replied. 'Mr President, we are in the middle of the operation, and if we stop now, we shall have more casualties. We must not turn back now!' The conversation ended, and I remained convinced that the breakthrough would be continued according to plan, but then General Gorinšek called me from the field and said that the president had called him and ordered him to suspend action.

We then allowed the humanitarian convoy to pass, but the JNA carried out manoeuvres along with it (ostensibly for security reasons), holding it up near Marinci and turning it back to Vinkovci, whence it set off again on 14 October; but the JNA diverted it to its Petrova Gora barracks in Vukovar. They manoeuvred the convoy around the area for two days, making it impossible for us to continue the breakthrough. In those two days the enemy mined the area around Marinci and brought in new forces; the 252nd armoured brigade of the JNA occupied the area and cut the road to Vukovar.

The convoy did carry out its mission to evacuate some of our wounded, but the JNA used it to reconsolidate positions they had already lost. From then on two of their motorized brigades carried on uninterrupted combat against our forces in the town itself and against those we had positioned between Osijek and Vinkovci, thinking that they would proceed according to military logic, bypass Osijek, blockade Vukovar and Vinkovci, and effect a breakthrough towards Đakovo, whence they could have reached the Drava highway to link up with units of the 5th (Banja Luka) corps, which had penetrated towards Virovitica from Okučani.

Instead, the Serb leadership concentrated on Vukovar, and took the strategic decision to occupy it at all costs. It was for this purpose that the JNA guards division from Belgrade and the command of the 1st army district came to the assistance of the 12th (Novi Sad) corps, with major fire-power support.

On the other hand, this gave us time to strengthen the defence in depth: during October we prepared four lines of defence as far as Našice, which the JNA was unable to breach after the Vukovar battle was over. Kadijević wrote that he was left without strike forces, that 'the lack of forces and the time it took to assemble them was the only reason that the operation could not maintain the pace and momentum planned at the outset',[10] and that as a result 'the main formation of JNA ground troops, principally armoured-motorized elements from eastern Slavonia', after the 'so-called Battle for Vukovar', was not able to accomplish its other mission, 'to be the chief manoeuvring force of the Supreme Command for the breakthrough towards Zagreb and Varaždin'.[11]

The JNA's increasing difficulties with manpower, especially in the Banja Luka and Tuzla corps, were compounded by a new circumstance. As early as 20 September the military and political leadership in Belgrade noted with dissatisfaction that 'resistance has arisen among the Muslims' in Bosnia-Herzegovina 'against the army which has set off from Serbia towards Krajina and Okučani, and from Montenegro towards Mostar'.[12] Two weeks later, the president of the Presidency of Bosnia-Herzegovina, Alija Izetbegović, publicly called upon the citizens of Bosnia-Herzegovina not to respond to the call-up. Bosnian-Herzegovinian Croats had not responded from the start (nor had the JNA counted on them), while Serb military potential had by now been exhausted. The message had a powerful impact on Bosniak military conscripts, at whom – though this was not stated explicitly – it was principally aimed. But there were still plenty of

---

[10] Veljko Kadijević, *Moje viđenje raspada: vojska bez države* [My view of the break-up: an army without a state], Belgrade 1993, p. 108, p. 143.

[11] Ibid., p. 137.

[12] Jović, *Poslednji dani SFRJ*, p. 386. It was planned that JNA formations which had entered western Slavonia from Bosnia-Herzegovina would get five brigades, but 'because of unsuccessful mobilization' they got 'only the equivalent of one and a half brigades, and those that did reach the front deserted during combat'. Kadijević, *Moje viđenje raspada*, p. 138. Milošević, Jović and Montenegrin Presidency member Branko Kostić did not agree, at the meeting on 24 September 1991, with Kadijević's judgement that the 'call-up was such a failure', since 'it had raised 50,000 people'. Jović, *Poslednji dani SFRJ*, p. 387. Kadijević spoke at the same meeting 'of the great mistrust of Serbs even towards loyal non-Serb officers'. The Tuzla corps also had major problems, getting underway slowly and with great difficulty, since its mobilization base was Bosanska Posavina, with a majority population of Croats and Bosniaks.

frightened and disoriented young people among them, whom the JNA was counting on as cannon fodder for the final strike against Croatia.[13] Kadijević called for another call-up in Serbia for a further offensive, but instead Milošević decided to pacify the occupied territories in Croatia and launch the war in Bosnia-Herzegovina. Hence Vukovar had to be occupied at all costs.

Vukovar was now completely isolated, but we continued to supply it from the air. We formed an air force platoon from aircraft of the agricultural air service and sports clubs, which dropped arms, ammunition and medical equipment on the town. They flew by night at an altitude of 3,000 metres, out of range of artillery and small missiles, dropping their cargoes right into the centre of town, by the hospital. They were able to do so because the squadron commander, Captain Marko Živković, had built JPS devices into the aircraft which ensured precision targeting within 10 metres.[14]

---

[13] This was the *Message to the Citizens of Bosnia-Herzegovina* that Izetbegović read out on television. Saying that the citizens of Bosnia-Herzegovina could not prevent this 'blood-letting', he said: 'What we can do is to refuse to participate in this madness. ... It is your right and duty as citizens of Bosnia-Herzegovina not to respond to the call-up . ... I call upon you to find the courage to refuse to take part in these evil deeds. Remember, this is not our war. Let those who want it, wage it. We do not want this war.' See *Muslimanski glas* [The Muslim voice] (Sarajevo), 11 October 1991; *Behar* (Zagreb), 3, XI–XII.1993–I.1994, *Behar Journal* supplement, p. 3. The HDZ in Croatia and Bosnia-Herzegovina is still manipulating the statement by taking 'this is not our war' out of context and citing it as proof that Izetbegović and the Bosniak leadership as a whole were not concerned about Croatia. It is true that Izetbegović defined the *Message* as a proclamation of the 'neutrality of Bosnia-Herzegovina in this war', that he called it a 'civil war', and that he did not name names; but from the entire context it is obvious that it was a call to boycott the JNA, that the expression 'this is not our war' does not relate to the Croatian defence effort, but to the JNA and Serb paramilitaries' aggression against Croatia, and that 'these evil deeds', 'this madness', and 'this senseless act' related in particular to the destruction of Vukovar. It was not the Croatian Army that was carrying out mobilization in Bosnia-Herzegovina.

[14] For data on the types of aircraft (from flying clubs, businesses and agricultural organizations) and their combat use, and the types of manufactured and adapted weapons (with photographs), see Vojislav Jeber and Danijel Frka, *Hrvatski zrakoplovi* [Croatian aircraft], Zagreb 1994. For example, adapted rocket-propelled grenade launchers, of types Osa 90mm and Zolja 64mm, were fixed under the wings of the sports aircraft UTVA-75, and 'boiler-bombs' were manufactured from boilers and pressurized containers for acetylene, etc. The agricultural biplane An-2 was used in the eastern Slavonia battlefield as a bomber, since it had a large cabin in which bombs could be carried and launched through the side doors. These aircraft also supplied both medicines and arms, by parachute and by landing, since they could both land on and take off from unprepared terrain in limited space. In a night combat action on 2 December 1991, ground to air missiles brought down an An-2 not far from Vinkovci, in which commanding officer Živković, his deputy Captain Mirko Vukušić and two crew members – Rade Griva (Serb) and Ante Plazibat (Croat) – were killed. This was the Croatian air force's only combat loss in 1991: two An-2s were lost in non-combat flights.

Second attempt at breakthrough and fall of the town

Despite the way things had developed, I had not given up the idea of break-ing the encirclement but decided on a new breakthrough action, with much stronger forces, to be organized by 10 November. The major JNA offen-sive had been crushed on all Croatian fronts in October, leaving us still in control of Osijek, Vinkovci, Pakrac, Nova Gradiška, Novska, Sisak, Karlovac, Gospić, Zadar, Šibenik and Dubrovnik, and enabling us to begin to liberate the area around Daruvar, Novska, Nova Gradiška and Otočac. So the general staff was able to set aside the 105th Bjelovar brigade to enter Vukovar as second levy; the first levy was again to be formed by Colonel Gorinšek from his troops and the ZNG 3rd brigade. On the eastern Slavonian front we also readied the 101st Zagreb brigade, to cover the areas near Vinkovci made vacant by the Vukovar operation.

The second breakthrough action used the same two routes as the first. The main one ran from Nuštar towards Marinci, with the difference that this time Marinci would be bypassed, since we needed rapidly to occupy territory towards Vukovar. The reserve route went from Osijek via Trpinja to Borovo Naselje, but it had many weak points and required extensive manoeuvres for which we had no time. The first route was the shortest and most advantageous, given that Nuštar was our most forward position and that we had our strongest artillery support near Vinkovci. The best artillery we then had was positioned on the route to Vukovar – more than 100 field guns of various calibres. Over 10,000 shells were fired from the Osijek–Vinkovci line at the Serb positions. Since the shelling continued for days without let-up, we used a large number of grenades, and just before the breakthrough action of 5 November itself we had to occupy the JNA barracks in Delnice in order to resupply.

The action was a joint effort of our forces in Vukovar and the reinforce-ments near Vinkovci: the first defending an area extending 2–4 kilometres from the town, the second shelling the Vukovar access routes. One shell which hit a tank killed the commanding officer of the Novi Sad corps, General Bratić.

Our breakthrough was intended to reinforce the defenders and to enable evacuation of the wounded and civilians. On the evening of 12 November, we began to shell enemy positions and the approaches to the town. The fighting lasted all next day. The operation had been thoroughly planned, but the breakthrough was slow because the JNA had concentrated strong armoured forces with a large quantity of artillery and rocket weaponry, and routed our first wave of attack with exceptionally fierce fire. Our first levy, led by the commanding officer of the ZNG 3rd brigade, sustained heavy casualties and destruction of tanks. One of its units, which was to have opened up the area near Bogdanovci so that the 105th Bjelovar corps, as the second levy, could enter the town and continue fighting there, with-drew with heavy losses, and the strength of the enemy fire did not allow us to fill the gap. The order was then given to remain on the front lines, to keep the enemy engaged and to receive the defence forces and civilians when they broke through from the town.

There was no possibility of continuing the offensive, and on 14 November the break-out action from Vukovar began, as did the final JNA assault on the town. The last air drop by the hospital was made during the night of 17 November. The Vukovar defence command then joined the break-out, though they had wanted to stay with the wounded. If they had stayed, I believe they would immediately have been killed. The groups from Borova Naselje did not break out, since they were completely surrounded, and most of them were killed.

We lost about 1,100 defenders in Vukovar, to whom must be added most of the 2,600 listed as missing (defenders and civilians), while about 1,000 defenders were killed on the approaches to Vinkovci and Osijek, bringing our losses in eastern Slavonia to about 4,000: half our total losses in 1991. According to foreign estimates, the enemy (JNA, Serbian TO, various paramilitary forces, some local, some from Serbia) lost 6,000–8,000 in eastern Slavonia; our estimate would make it certainly more than 5,000 (Serb sources published losses only for the Novi Sad corps, which amounted to more than 1,300 dead). About 600 armoured vehicles and heavy weapons and more than 20 aircraft were destroyed. The guards division was practically annihilated, and the Novi Sad corps was exhausted, while the Tuzla corps suffered heavy losses from which it never recovered. After the occupation of Vukovar the JNA no longer had the forces to penetrate westwards between Vinkovci and Osijek via Đakovačka Greda, which had been the principal mission of these units.

There are two reasons for the success of the anti-tank fighting in the town. First, the defence was very well positioned in each sector, and it was possible to manoeuvre between sectors as long as the enemy had not gone in so deep as to be able to cut them off. Second, the battle was carried on both above and below ground: defenders were able to get through to their objectives unobserved, via cellars, channels and ditches, with help also coming from our forces outside. The 12-member diversionary group from Vinkovci, under the leadership of Andrija Andabaka, destroyed 32 enemy tanks and other armoured vehicles on the access routes from Šid towards Negoslavci and Vukovar.[15]

---

[15] Andrija Andabaka is one of the heroes of Croatia's war. During his regular military service in the JNA he had been trained to operate *maljutka* targeted anti-tank projectiles and at the beginning of the aggression against Croatia, as a freelance leader without formal rank, he organized his own fighting group. I wanted him to survive and write a book about it all, so after the fall of Vukovar I did not send him into action again. But in summer 1992 he went as a volunteer to Bosanska Posavina and was killed near Derventa by an artillery shell. He was awarded the posthumous rank of battalion commander.

A three-month resistance under day and night assault by shells, missiles and grenades, living in damp cellars, channels and ditches, without water, light or medical supplies, and often without food, is an astonishing achievement. But complete destruction of a city with many thousands of victims, civilian and military, with tens of thousands forced to flee the town, is a crime on the part of the aggressor which cannot be forgotten. Nor can the international community have an easy conscience about it.

OPERATIONS IN WESTERN SLAVONIA – SWATH-10 AND HURRICANE '91

The defeat of the JNA in the Vukovar–Vinkovci–Osijek area made it possible to liberate parts of western Slavonia. The Croatian Army began this operation in December; we needed only another five to seven days to reach the Sava, and without the ceasefire we would have done so. Every action until then had been at tactical level; this was the Croatian Army's first offensive at operational level, codenamed Hurricane '91. It was carried out in autumn and winter 1991 by troops of the Posavina Operational Group formed by the 1st brigade of the ZNG Tigers and the 121st Croatian Army brigade.

The operational group composed of the 127th Virovitica and 136th Slatina brigades pushed through from the north, from Virovitica and Slatina, in Operation Swath-10. The first phase began on 31 October and ended on 4 November, with the liberation of occupied regions of Bilogora, from which the enemy had been attacking the area of Virovitica, Grubišno Polje, Podravska Slatina, Daruvar and Bjelovar with artillery and mortar fire. In the second phase, which began on 4 December, the Papuk region was liberated. Up to the time when the 127th brigade was unexpectedly halted on 25 December it had advanced successfully, completely shattering one brigade of the Serb 28th Partisan division, composed of the local population and JNA officers (three infantry units of local Serbs, one JNA infantry unit, a battery of cannon and 120mm mortars, and a mixed armoured-motorized platoon – in all about 1,750 men), while on 5 December the Grubišno Polje independent ZNG battalion had destroyed the White Eagles, paramilitaries from Serbia, at Papuk.[16]

---

[16] On this operation, see Ivica Debić and Ante Delić: *Otkos* [Swath], Bjelovar 1999. As the authors say, by the middle of August there were already 600 to 800 members of local Serb paramilitary units in Bilogora, armed and organized by the JNA (p. 59). The order to prepare operation Otkos was issued at the beginning of October by the commanding officer of the Bjelovar Second operational zone, Colonel Miroslav Jezerčić; it was planned by its commanding officer, Colonel Franjo Kovačević.

Operation Hurricane '91 halted the Banja Luka corps of the JNA, whose objectives were to occupy Novska, Pakrac, Kutina and Nova Gradiška, to relieve the besieged barracks in the Zagreb area, and to reach the north-western borders of the projected Greater Serbia. The Croatian Army then went on the offensive for the first time in the Patriotic War and liberated more than 170 square kilometres of territory, destroying 21 enemy bastions and liberating 21 inhabited areas.

The operation was planned and prepared in mid-October in the command centre of the Posavina Operational Group as part of the general staff's plan to liberate western Slavonia; the plan was put to me, as chief of staff, on 25 October, and approved. Troops of the Posavina Operational Group advanced to within 2 kilometres both west and east of the road between Pakrac and Okučani, the backbone of the so-called Serb Autonomous Region of western Slavonia, but were unable to cut it. The road was cut in Operation Flash, three and a half years later, by troops of the Ministry of the Interior special police and the 81st guards unit, advancing along the same routes. The importance of Hurricane was as a model for Operation Flash, which in early May 1995 liberated the remaining occupied territories of western Slavonia; the maps of the two operations are almost identical, except as regards the fire power of the supporting forces. The planners of Flash followed the Hurricane planners in almost every detail, even on the direction of the offensive from Nova Gradiška in the east and Novska in the west towards Okučani. The Hurricane plan, achieved by Flash, was to break through from the Kričko and Novsko hills to the Novska–Okučani road and attack Jasenovac, both of which objectives were entrusted to the 125th Novljanski Brigade.

If the 127th brigade, commanded by Đuro Dečak, now a general, had not been held up for four or five days, we would already have been at the Sava, with the whole of western Slavonia liberated and the motorway reopened; then everything in the Banija, in Bosanska Krajina, in Bosanska Posavina and in our Danubian region would have turned out very differently. The reasons why the formation advancing from the north did not follow the plan of the general staff, so that its advance was halted on the Bučje–Kusonje–Pakrac road on 25 December, remain to be investigated by military historians. It is true that the 127th brigade had suffered significant losses, which may have been a reason. In the event the entire offensive was halted by order of the president, with the explanation that the Vance Plan and the general ceasefire had been accepted.

Offensive operations in western Slavonia were finally halted on 3 January 1992, when the Sarajevo ceasefire came into force. Our forces only needed perhaps one more day at that point to reach the motorway, which would have left the enemy surrounded, as was later achieved in Operation Flash.[17]

In 1992 a reorganized Croatian Army, now better trained and equipped, successfully carried out its second major offensive operation, the liberation of southern Dalmatia. The regular forces of the JNA, defeated, abandoned the territory of the Republic.

POLITICAL CLASHES AND DEPARTURE

From September 1991 to the end of 1992, when I left my post as chief of staff of the Croatian Army, there were several occasions when I walked out of meetings with President Tuđman, for both political and military reasons. Of course, politics determines national goals, while it is for the military to carry them out; but politicians do have to take account of military knowledge and professionalism, and to know when objectives can be realized by diplomacy and when by military force. While waiting for such political decisions, or when confronted with some that ignored the need for harmony between political and military aims in operational activities, I had to react.

The first time was when the JNA was removing arms from Croatia, from besieged garrisons and depots, in order to use them against us later. I recommended that they be allowed to leave only with personal arms, not with heavy weapons. In front of the president, I warned the European mediator, Lord Carrington, that the JNA would use the weapons they were removing against Croatia and to launch war in Bosnia-Herzegovina, Kosovo or Macedonia, which Europe must not allow for the sake of its own conscience. I said to him explicitly: 'Your conscience will not be clear, since the JNA will again attack Croatia with these weapons and start a war in Bosnia-Herzegovina or some other region.'

There was tension again when the Ministry of Defence proposed that the Croatian Army adopt certain NDH terms; I resolutely opposed this, and left the president's office in protest. The president rejected the proposal, but some of the controversial names were used later in the titles of HVO units in Bosnia-Herzegovina.

Nor did I agree with the fifteenth ceasefire, on 2 January 1992, marking the end of the war, and I refused to attend its signing in Sarajevo. The Vance Plan was in fact intended to secure for the Serbs the territory they

---

[17] For an exhaustive overview of the operation, see Rudi Stipčić, *Napokon smo krenuli* ... [We're on the way at last], Zagreb 1996. The author, a JNA colonel, joined up in September 1991 and on 9 October was appointed commander of the Posavina Operational Group. He took for his title the exclamation of a soldier of the 1st guards brigade returning from action on 25 October, when for the first time in the Patriotic War two complete units were committed to the enemy rear.

had seized in Croatia, so that they could move into a new phase of the war for Greater Serbia. That was the essence of the ceasefire and the peace plan linked to it. I was opposed to halting while more than a quarter of our territory remained occupied.

It was actually the illegal and incomplete Presidency of SFRY itself that wanted peacekeeping forces to come in 'at the moment when almost all the territory on which there was a majority Serb population had been liberated',[18] and when they needed to reduce the international pressure to which they had been exposed and free the army for the war in Bosnia-Herzegovina. Borisav Jović's diary for 15 November 1991 triumphantly reads: 'The operation has succeeded', i.e. the Security Council had opened a debate on sending in Blue Berets, with Great Britain and France formally requesting it since the rump Presidency of SFRY had no legal standing, 'so that the uninitiated won't grasp what's up', as he commented, not without good cause.[19]

Only Milan Babić, president of the Serb para-state in Croatia, did not understand that they were thereby *de facto* becoming a state, so they had great difficulty with him at the 'Presidency' session of 2 February 1992, at which it was precisely 'the army, and especially the commanding officers from the front lines, who insisted that the session could not be adjourned or completed without a positive decision', i.e. the decision to accept the plan.[20] They knew very well how our forces had grown, while the JNA was on the verge of complete collapse, since all its non-Serb members had left. They were unable to carry out any further mobilization

[18] Jović, *Poslednji dani SFRJ*, p. 432. Belgrade's manipulation of 'majority Serb areas' often fooled international representatives. According to the 31 March 1991 population census, Croats formed a majority in two occupied Danubian municipalities (Beli Manastir: 22,740 Croats and 13,851 Serbs; Vukovar: 36,910 Croats and 31,445 Serbs); moreover, there were 8,956 Hungarians in Beli Manastir, and 2,284 Ruthenians, 1,383 Slovaks and 1,375 Hungarians in Vukovar, towards whom the aggressor had the same attitude as towards Croats. Serbs were also in a minority in occupied parts of Osijek and Vinkovci municipalities. In the south, in Dubrovnik, of a population of 71,419, 4,765 were Serbs. In western Slavonian municipalities they were also in a minority except in Pakrac, where they were the largest group (12,813 Serbs out of a population of 27,589). Nor was the Serb population in a majority in all the municipalities in central Croatia which were wholly or largely occupied (Slunj: 12,091 Croats and 5,540 Serbs; Drniš: 18,732 Croats and 4,974 Serbs; in Petrinja the ratio was almost exactly equal: 15,790 Croats and 15,969 Serbs). The whole of the occupied territory contained only a third of the total Croatian Serb population of 581,663 (12.2 per cent of the population of Croatia). These numbers reveal the real nature of Belgrade's and the JNA's claim that they were 'protecting the Serbs'. See *Census of Population, Households, Residences and Agricultural Economy, 31 March 1991: population by nationality in each area of settlement*, Republic of Croatia, Republic Statistics Institute, Zagreb 1992.

[19] Jović, *Poslednji dani SFRJ*, p. 411.

[20] Ibid., p. 434.

in Serbia, so they opted for UN peacekeeping forces. According to Jović, the essence of Vance's concept was to 'consolidate the territory under the protection of the United Nations. That territory is chiefly inhabited by Serbs, and the peacekeeping forces are there to protect them. That is, to protect Serbs from Croatian aggression.' Further, 'the current political authorities, that is, the government of the Serb nation' remain in power in the region, while the Constitution of Croatia does not apply 'nor does the Croatian government have any authority whatsoever in this region'.[21]

Every relevant international mediator assured him and others among the Serbian leadership that this interpretation of the plan was correct, while Tuđman believed that UNPROFOR would be helping him to return the refugees and Croatian constitutional order to the occupied territories.

The documents relating to the UN peacekeeping operation stated that simultaneously with the arrival of UNPROFOR both the JNA and the Croatian Army must withdraw from the territories under their control, i.e. that the JNA must withdraw from Croatia entirely: 'In parallel with the UN forces taking up their duties in UNPA [United Nations' Protected Area], all JNA units deployed elsewhere in Croatia will be transferred outside that republic.'[22] The expression 'elsewhere in Croatia' referred to Lastovo, Vis and the Dubrovnik area. The JNA immediately began, in February and March 1992, to supply Serb territorials in, for example, Banija with heavy weapons, and transferred some of its officers from both active and reserve units to the Serb TO units, later known as the Serb Army of the Krajina (SVK). This was very dangerous for Croatia, since it was clear that they intended to remain on key territories with the most powerful weapons and best prepared officers possible. The peace plan had laid down that TO arms, which *de jure* belonged to Croatia, should be retained in those areas; but as the original TO was not equipped with heavy weapons, the Serb troops now formally claimed them as their own and retained possession of them.

Since joining the Croatian Army I had not allowed duality of command, but had required the Ministry of Defence to carry out its own numerous tasks and not involve itself in army activities. This was, on the whole, respected throughout 1991. Explicit interference of HDZ politics in the army began in 1992; clashes were evident in particular in appointment policy and in Croat–Bosniak relations in Bosnia-Herzegovina. Naturally, I could not accept the later events in Bosnia-Herzegovina either, since I believed that we must not have two enemies, but in alliance with the Bosniaks, or rather the Army of Bosnia-Herzegovina, should end the war

[21] Ibid., p. 432–3.
[22] See 'Plan mirovne operacije UN u Jugoslaviji (studeni-prosinac 1991)' [Plan for the UN peacekeeping operation in Yugoslavia (November–December 1991)], in Anđelko Milardović (ed.), *Dokumenti o državnosti Republike Hrvatske* [Documents on the statehood of the Republic of Croatia], Zagreb 1992, p. 162.

by destroying the Serb forces and the idea of Greater Serbia. At the time this could have been achieved: the JNA had disintegrated in Croatia and could not go any further, it had also been brought to a halt everywhere in Bosnia-Herzegovina, while the climate in international relations was also favourable to us. But the president's position was that Bosnia-Herzegovina did not exist as a historical state, that – like Yugoslavia – it could not be preserved, and that Croats in that region had to be 'protected'.

I told the president that we could not wage war against two enemies, especially a war in two different theatres of operation. To go to war in Bosnia-Herzegovina with a new opponent while the Serb aggressor held more than a quarter of our state territory would be madness. The president responded that these were political, not military, issues, and that the world did not want a Muslim state in the heart of Europe! In the war between the HVO and the Army of Bosnia-Herzegovina the Croats came to the verge of defeat. When it began, the HVO controlled more than 20 per cent of the territory of Bosnia-Herzegovina; just before signing the Washington Agreement, it was less than 10 per cent. For both sides it was a disastrous war for territory, a war with the wrong enemy, the effects of which we are still suffering today. I have always been convinced that the survival of an independent Bosnia-Herzegovina, with its state borders on the river Drina and at the point where the frontiers of Croatia, Bosnia-Herzegovina and Montenegro meet, is in the vital interests of Croatia. Otherwise the Serb entity in Bosnia-Herzegovina would occupy almost half that country, which would increase our border with Serb territories by more than 400 kilometres: 280 kilometres on the Sava, 120 kilometres on the Una and almost 15 kilometres above Konavle.

Because of all these disagreements, I left the post of chief of staff of the Croatian Army at the end of 1992.

4

Operations Flash and Storm
Ozren Žunec

The other day I was complaining to a Croatian general that I had butterflies in my stomach at the thought of making a speech to professionals who had graduated from military academy and been ministers of defence and commanders of strategic operational units, while I, without formal military education, would have difficulty in talking relevantly about military operations. He smiled and said: 'Military matters are not the real problem in our case'. This wasn't much comfort to me, but there was quite a lot of truth in his words, especially as regards the part of the war about which I am going to speak. It is a part that embodies all the political lines of force that converged during the war as a whole; even the last two operations of the Croatian Army on Croatian soil (not in the entire war, since the Croatian Army later operated in Bosnia-Herzegovina) are not exclusively military in nature, but have a political dimension and function.

If we take Clausewitz as the accepted wisdom for understanding the phenomenon of war as an aspect of human relations, we know that it is a compound of military and political causes and factors. This is incontestable: we cannot understand any war if we do not, at least at the outset, analyse it in terms of these two elements. Yet it seems to me that the war in former Yugoslavia shows such a preponderance of political, social, ideological and even symbolic factors (just think of the flag, the coat of arms and the other symbolic elements which provoked important moves during the course of it) that we can say that though, like all wars, it had political objectives, it would seem that, at least in part, it was waged for its own sake.

I do not mean that it was war for war's sake, but that the war was itself a political objective: herein lies its difference from many other wars and uses of armed force. In December 1972, Nixon's decision to begin massive strategic bombing of North Vietnam, including the most important urban centres of Hanoi and Haiphong, with 200 B52 aircraft, was designed to relaunch the peace process, since the Paris negotiations were stuck. Individual military operations always have some political reasons, but it seems to me that the war in former Yugoslavia is a special case in that it was not conducted in order to achieve some specific political project *at the cost* of the destruction of people and resources, with loss of time and perhaps territory too. No, the actual launching and conduct of the war, and especially what was done in its aftermath, were themselves the principal political aim. The political objective of a war aimed not only at ethnic cleansing, but at the total destruction of the civilian and social values of the societies concerned, could only be to ensure that the effects and dimensions of the war should continue even after it was ended. This can be seen from the last two elections in Bosnia-Herzegovina (perhaps a little less in the most recent one than in 1996), since most of the votes on all sides went to the parties that had waged the war and administered its aftermath.[1] So the project was a success.

What, then, is achieved by a war of the kind we have seen and experienced? First, it makes possible a greater mobilization of human resources, political, economic and military, and also extraction of material resources especially from the population, than could be expected in other circumstances and for other objectives. Second, the destruction of infrastructure, which also destroys communities by creating a more primitive lifestyle, enables the authorities to become the permanent arbiters of the basic, everyday needs of the population, not only during the war but afterwards. The population has become the hostage and client of the authorities; the state is no longer a civil body serving the public good, but the allocator of all possible resources even for the most elementary, everyday needs. This makes it possible to monopolize the distribution of property, and thereby ensure permanent loyalty of the population to the parties, politicians and others who administered the war and its aftermath.

I say this because I want to emphasize that even the final battles, Operations Flash and Storm, cannot be understood outside this political complex. They were military operations, of course, but conducted within the ambit of a war whose main political objective was to create lasting after-effects – or the permanent presence of war. On the other hand, the predominance of politics seriously interfered with the military logic. In many discussions with Croatian military experts and generals, the theme always comes up that during the war, politics, at least in Croatia, always halted operations just when the Croatian Army was in the most favourable situation. Generals Špegelj and Tus have mentioned the dual command lines from their own experience. For the later development of civilian–

---

[1] On this see Ozren Žunec, 'Socijetalne ratne štete u Bosni i Hercegovini: zašto je narod ponovo izabrao patnju?' [Societal war damage in Bosnia-Herzegovina: why did the people again choose suffering?], *Erasmus*, vol. 20, 1997, pp. 19–36. Also Ozren Žunec, *Rat i društvo: ogledi iz sociologije vojske i rata* [War and society: enquiries from the sociology of the military and war], Zagreb 1998, pp. 177–212.

Table 3
Major actions and offensives of Croatian Army (May 1992–August 1995)

Code name	Objective of the action/operation	Start	End	Op. area	Duration
Tiger	Liberation of the Dubrovnik region and lifting of the blockade of Dubrovnik	18.5.1992.	01.30h 23.10.1992. issue of command to cease offensive	1,500 km^2 (25×60)	159 days
	Liberation of the 'pink zone' in the Miljevac region	21.6.1992.	22.6.1992.	150 km^2	24 hours
	Liberation of the territory round the Maslenica bridge, the Zadar hinterland and Rovanjska	07.00h 22.1.1993.	Transition to defence 20.00h 25.1.1993.	1,050 km^2 (35×30)	85 hours
	Liberation of the 'Medak pocket' (Gospić)	05.00h 9.9.1993.	18.00h 9.9.1993.	225 km^2 (15×15)	13 hours
Flash-1	Liberation of western Slavonia	05.00h 1.5.1995.	16.00h 3.5.1995.	500 km^2	59 hours
Summer 95	Occupation of Bosansko Grahovo and Glamoč	25.7.1995.	28.7.1995.	1,200 km^2 (30×40)	4 days
Storm	Liberation of northern Dalmatia, part of Lika, Kordun and Banija	05.00h 4.8.1995.	c. 13.00h 10.8. 1995. Croatian Army as a whole gained control of state borders	10,500 km^2	152 hours

Source: Croatian Army general staff

G   *raph*
Croatian Army Offensive Operations, 1992–1995 (by regional action of operation)

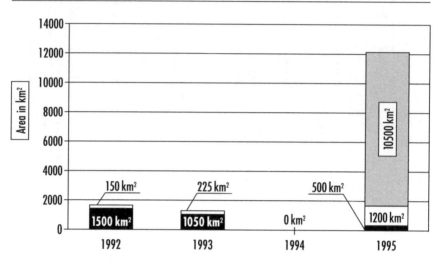

military relations in Croatia, we should note that in Posavina during summer and autumn 1992 there was a command line via the general staff, or its command centre in Đakovo where General Petar Stipetić was stationed, *and* a party logistical line for supplying Posavina that ran via the Ministry of Defence and relied on General Ivan Čermak, now owner of the tanker firm Crodux. Such a situation is unthinkable in any normal defence set-up and it made any kind of operation almost impossible.

General Špegelj has already covered what went on in the individual operations on Croatian soil between 1992 and the end of 1994. I would only add that the much-talked-of Maslenica operation at the beginning of 1993, seen with hindsight, and regardless of the extent to which, at the time, it raised the morale of both the population and the army, was from the military point of view a disaster. The Croatian Army attacked with all its forces along the entire confrontation line, entered territory which the Serbs had been holding until then, met with counter-attacks and was driven back, so that a brigade from Osijek had to be brought in as support, there being no reservists in the zone of action; it could have ended with Zadar falling into Serb hands. Casualties were catastrophic: there were more than 150 dead in one brigade alone. When one knows that there were to have been elections in Croatia some 15 or 20 days later, it suggests that the whole operation was mounted as part of the election campaign. I don't like to say so, but it is a rather striking coincidence. I shall now pass to the situation on the eve of the final operations of 1995.

NEITHER WAR NOR PEACE

Table 3 sets out the principal offensive actions from 1992 to 1995. Except for the first, codenamed Tiger, which was for the relief of Dubrovnik, they were all brief operations. More important than the table itself is the graph that follows (see opposite), which shows the offensive operations according to the territory covered by combat action in square kilometres.

These are the operations conducted on Croatian territory during the four years from 1992 to 1995. The graph shows that the offensive actions of the Croatian Army declined from 1992 to 1994, when there was not a single major action, let alone operation, in Croatia, and that then in 1995 there was first a very small operation, Flash, covering between 500 and 600 square kilometres, followed by a large one, Storm, covering more than 1,200 square kilometres. At the end of 1991, at the time when the cease-fire was agreed, the Croatian Army had raised some tens of reserve brigades, already had well-organized professional troops with significant combat experience, had managed to acquire arms and equipment for more than 200,000 men, had launched a strategic initiative in western Slavonia, and in eastern Slavonia, in Vukovar (a 'fortuitous battle', as General Špegelj calls it) had broken the back of the whole JNA offensive – so why did it then become completely passive?

The answer is very simple – because of the war in Bosnia-Herzegovina. The action moved into that country, and Croatia's own theatre of operations was left quiet. The situation is, of course, completely absurd: the area where these enemies had formerly been fighting was left in peace so that the same opponents could move across to another theatre of operations. When the JNA, later the army of Republika Srpska, began intensive operations in Bosnia-Herzegovina, and was committing appalling crimes and wreaking destruction there, there should then have been *more* action in the Croatian combat zone, so as to get results there immediately, in 1992 or at the latest 1993; or possibly to wait for the Army of Bosnia-Herzegovina to form, so that joint actions could be organized and the Serbs be finally defeated in the entire region west of the Drina. But instead operations eased up. Such behaviour is completely indefensible, and there must be political reasons behind it. The freezing of the fronts in Croatia was purely a matter of political logic, in the service of the notorious plan to partition Bosnia-Herzegovina. This is the only logical answer to the question why nothing was happening in the Croatian war zone at that time.

Let us go a step further. To understand the defeat of the Serbs in Croatia in 1995, in Operations Flash and Storm, we have to see what was the strategic and political basis of Serb thinking: what their conception of defence was, and how they had expected to remain on that territory and defend themselves by force of arms. The defence strategy of Republika

Srpska Krajina and its armed forces, the Krajina Serb Army (SVK), was based on the awareness of the rebel Serb leadership in Croatia that the Republic of Croatia was about ten times more powerful than they were. The pan-Serb 'think-tank' thought about it too and came to the conclusion that the Serb position in Croatia was the 'weakest link in the chain of the Serb national programme', and that no long-term defence of it was feasible.[2] They had already concluded this in the autumn of 1993.

Considering the position in which they found themselves, it was perfectly clear how the rebel Serbs would organize their defence. They had to rely on the political and military support of Republika Srpska and FRY. Republika Srpska Krajina and Republika Srpska did sign an agreement on mutual military cooperation, in Prijedor in October 1992, but they never activated it; there was never any real cooperation in defence. They did cooperate in offensives, for example against the 5th corps of the ARBiH in Bihać, but never in defence of Serb positions.

Since its militarily more powerful enemy had abandoned the military resolution of the situation in Croatia thanks to its involvement in Bosnia-Herzegovina, and was gradually being drawn into a war of attrition with the Serb para-state on its territory, the para-state in question considered ways of responding to a possible Croat attack, and concluded that it could be done by massive reprisals with artillery and rockets. It had the weaponry, it had the ammunition, it also had positions very close to the vital centres of Croat infrastructure. Karlovac, Sisak and Zagreb were a mere 25 kilometres away from the firing positions of the SVK, to say nothing of other cities in the area of the front. The second prop of the Serb defence was, then, the threat of massive artillery and rocket reprisals.

But it was a feasible strategy only so long as it was not tested in practice, since it was based on false assumptions and assessments. First, neither Republika Srpska nor FR Yugoslavia ever intended to come to its aid, nor were they able to do so. Second, massive reprisals would not have been technically possible, since wherever Serb positions were close to Croatian urban, commercial and industrial centres, they were equally close to the Croatian Army, so that every attempt at reprisals would have boomeranged upon them. In 1992 Knin did from time to time come under artillery attack. So there really was no opportunity for using a strategy of massive reprisals. But this raises another, fundamental question relating to that period of neither war nor peace which, on the model of 1939–40, we could call *une drôle de guerre*, a phoney war. Why did Croatia not attempt, during all those years, to liberate the greater part of the occupied territory? Why did it wait until 1995?

---

[2] Radovan Radinović, 'Odmazdom do pobede' [By reprisals to victory], *Duga*, 513, Belgrade, 23 October–5 November 1993, p. 78.

One possible response is that the Croatian Army was not ready. But it was no more ready in 1995 than in 1992. There had been no essentially new procurement of arms and military equipment, nor had any new military personnel been trained. In 1995 the Croatian Army was organized very much as at the end of 1992: there were no strategic-operational groups or tactical units, no armoured brigade which could have made a dash into Slavonia and do what such brigades do; there was still the existing guards brigade as the first echelon, there were motorized brigades (infantry brigades with one armoured battalion) and reserve infantry, light brigades. Even these had difficulties in many areas and had to use mainly commandeered vehicles: without even a vehicle pool for troop movements, they travelled by bus as earlier in the war. There had been no essential growth of the Croatian Army in the meantime, such as would have made possible more extensive operations; rather, it was in the same state as in 1992, 1993 and 1994, apart from demobilization. This had been considerable during 1992–24; more than 100,000 men left the Croatian Army in that period, which is really inexcusable in conditions of open conflict.

Was it that the Croatian Army had not been able to carry out these operations in those three years because conditions simply did not permit, whereas in the middle of 1995 conditions suddenly changed and made it possible? To that one must reply that good conditions existed in October 1994, when the 5th corps of the ARBiH made a sortie from Bihać. The situation in August 1995 was no more promising than it had been in October and November 1994, when the 2nd (Krajina) corps of the Republika Srpska Army was already engaging the Bosnian 5th corps. Conditions existed then which could have led to a liberation operation. Looking once more at the graph of Croatian Army Offensives in 1992–93, I can only conclude that the only reason for the let-up in military operations in Croatia was political, and must be sought in the war in Bosnia-Herzegovina. This concludes my contextual introduction.

PARAMETERS, PREPARATION AND EXECUTION

As I said at the start, the political assumptions of the entire war, its political meaning or essence, are most obviously in evidence in Flash and Storm, which seem at first sight to be clear-cut military operations: blitzkrieg operations of short duration, from 30 to 100 hours, looking as though they were carried out according to military principles and military logic. But when we read their official appraisals from the Croatian side, we see that they are overestimated from the military point of view. Admiral Domazet insists in several texts that the two 1995 operations – Flash in May and Storm in August – were a turning-point from which the

Croatian Army became a regional power.[3] This is an interesting slip of the tongue, since surely only a state, not an army, can become a regional power. It reveals, in my view, a highly dubious judgement.

Second, Storm is taken as an operation of the kind 'which in its scope and complexity has been seen only during Desert Storm in the Gulf'.[4] The comparison, already suggested by the choice of code-name, was later made explicit with the conclusion that this was the only realistic comparison for the liberation of Croatian territory. The Ministry of Defence made this official.

Third, Flash and Storm are described as operations in which 'the fundamental principles of air and land battles can be recognized in the operations of the Croatian Army', which, it is added, were conducted 'in an integrated battlefield'.[5] In other words, these two operations were conducted according to the doctrinal decisions of an army which has at its disposal the most sophisticated armed forces in the world. Since there is a special doctrine of air–land battle for Europe called 'follow on forces attack', meaning attack on forces as they arrive, some even maintain that no one except the Americans can carry out air–land battles, and certainly not the Croatian Army in the given context.

I shall try to round out the information about Flash. From the military perspective, it was the only Croatian Army operation in the recent war which was conducted according to logical military criteria. The offensive was carried out in two principal and two support directions, which were well chosen, and the Serb forces in the western Slavonia enclave were cut off. New forces were then brought in to the very hilly territory around Lipik and Pakrac, to 'cleanse the terrain' and engage in combat with one of the remaining light brigades of the SVK. The collapse of the Serbs, that is of the entire 18th corps of the SVK in western Slavonia, was catastrophic, and both the army and the population fled. It is especially shameful that as early as the first day of the operation, 1 May, the commandant of the 18th corps himself crossed the Sava into Bosnia. The Serb army experienced not only defeat but disgrace in a very real sense.

Flash set the parameters for further developments. It became clear that the Serbs had not the means to defend themselves against the Croatian Army, which really was superior in numbers, even if in no other way. The strategic position of the entire Republika Srpska Krajina, and especially the western Slavonia enclave, was disastrous; it was incapable of being

---

[3] See Davor Domazet Lošo, 'Završne operacije Hrvatske vojske: uvjerljivost vojne moći i(ili) promjena strategijskog odnosa [Final operations of the Croatian Army: credible military power and/or changes in strategic relations], *Hrvatski vojnik*, vol. 7, no. 22, 1997 (Zagreb), pp. 12–21.

[4] Marijan Pavičić, '*Oluja*: ime hrvatske pobjede [*Storm*: the name of Croatian victory], *Hrvatski vojnik*, vol. 8, no. 38, August 1998, p. 9.

[5] Lošo, 'Završne operacije Hrvatske vojske', pp. 20–1.

defended under any circumstances, and it was perfectly clear that it would fall. The logical consequence of the disorganization of the SVK in that region, of local social disintegration and population drainage, and ultimately of the whole ideological project of Greater Serbia, which excluded all possibility of living with Croats, was the departure of the Serbs as soon as Croatia took over the region. In Flash we saw for the first time what would later be the rule in Bosnia-Herzegovina too: it was possible and feasible to defeat the Serbs militarily, but this would unfailingly lead to the departure of the inhabitants affected by such operations. It became clear that when the next operation began, all the Serbs would leave the region where it was being carried out. I foresaw this, wrote about it and published it before Storm, in June of that year, and that was indeed what happened.[6]

I single out Operation Flash, then, as solidly conceived, planned and conducted, militarily speaking, with well-chosen directions; it was well carried out, and demonstrated that the Serbs could not count on help from anyone. The Republika Srpska Army could have shelled the motorway from Bosnia, attacking the Croatian forces which were passing below Okučani and entering it, but this did not happen; or if it did, it was entirely sporadic. It was obvious that the local Serbs had been left to their own resources, at least in this phase of the war. When Martić tried to use massive reprisals and fired a number of rockets at Zagreb, Milošević appeared on television and condemned both the Croatian attack on the western Slavonian enclave, and the Serb rocket attacks on Zagreb. It was a clear sign to the Serbs that the story was over.

Croatia began to prepare Storm in autumn 1994, continuing during the whole of the winter and up to summer 1995 with a slow advance via Kupres, which Croat forces entered in November 1994, followed by occupation of the Dinaric heights, and completed by entering Glamoč and Grahovo immediately before Operation Storm. This was the key to entering Knin from the rear, from the 'wrong' side, which was crucial for the success of the entire operation; all the Croatian forces entered Knin from that area. As for the operation itself, the principal objectives were occupied by 10 August, so that Storm lasted six or seven days. Seen as a whole, it was carried out in some 30 directions with highly concentrated forces, especially in Banija, where an unbelievable number of brigades were lined up; on one route they were shoving up against each other as if in a crowded tram. Croatia deployed a very large quantity of troops and succeeded in overcoming four enemy corps in a very short time. On the first day, targets deep in enemy-held territory were hit by artillery and air attacks, on the second day an advance began in depth, and after that came the

---

[6] See Ozren Žunec, 'Okučanski zaključci [Conclusions from Okučani], *Erasmus*, vol. 12, 1995, pp. 7–20; also Žunec, *Rat i društvo.*, pp. 99–128.

withdrawal of Serb troops, especially in the southern part. In fact they abandoned the battlefield, and there was no really major fighting, especially in the Lika and northern Dalmatia theatre of operations. However, this was a shallow field of operations, whereas in Banija and Kordun it was significantly deeper, and there were problems there. The Croatian Army had no significant difficulties or great losses in the south, but on the Jasenovac–Kostajnica route where the operation had begun with an attack across the Sava, as soon as the depth increased somewhat there were 90 deaths on the first day, even before Kostajnica was reached.

For the most part, the Serb army simply fell apart. Its 4th corps and special forces corps were being used mainly against the ARBiH 5th corps, and on the front lines the latter was trying to hold round the Bihać enclave; then for some reason all those forces were turned in the other direction. When the Croatian offensive began, the command and communications disintegrated, slowly at first, later more rapidly. The brigades were all fighting for themselves; there was no coordination even at corps level, let alone in the army as a whole, and the Serb forces began to depart along whatever routes they could find. In Banija and especially in Kordun the 21st corps was surrounded and later surrendered, while the Banija corps of the SVK crossed over via Dvor into Bosnia in a stampede such as one seldom sees, along with civilians in a terrible state. The Knin and Lika corps also crossed into Bosnia by the only remaining route, via Gornji Lapac. The population fled with the army; estimates of population vary from 90,000 to 200,000; in any case, there were so few inhabitants left that it is fair to say that all the Krajina Serbs left Croatia before the operation was completed – something which, as I have said, could have been foreseen after Flash.

Croatia has always hushed up the fact that before daybreak on 4 August, just before Storm was launched, four US Navy aircraft attacked radar installations at Udbina and Knin, which may have led the Serbs to think they were facing a coordinated attack by NATO and the Croatian Army.

CAUSES OF THE DEFEAT OF THE KRAJINA SERB ARMY

The key to the success of the operation in the southern theatre of operations was the Croatian Army's reaching the Knin hinterland via Kupres and the Dinara range. The attack on Knin from the rear by the whole 4th brigade, followed by its occupation as an abandoned town on 5 August, the second day of the operation, proved the key to success in that area. But it is interesting that the preparations for it took place across territory which was in the zone of responsibility of the VRS. Kupres and Glamoč were not held by local forces of Serbs from Croatia, but by Bosnian Serbs who did not lift a finger to prevent the Croatian Army's advance towards Glamoč, nor, during the final operations, the occupation of Glamoč, Bosanski Petrovac and other places. The VRS did not offer anything beyond purely symbolic resistance to the Croatian Army and the HVO, which had been attacking since November 1994. It is said that Glamoč was defended by seven people, and the troops deployed in the region were neither supplied nor equipped to offer any kind of resistance.

Why did the VRS not defend this territory? In August 1994 Milošević for the first time publicly distanced himself from Karadžić and Mladić because they had rejected the plan to divide Bosnia-Herzegovina 50:50, insisting on retaining the 70 per cent they held. Milošević realized that it was impossible, both because of the growth of the ARBiH and because of international factors: he had to put pressure on his proxies in Bosnia-Herzegovina to abandon their project. It seems that Karadžić, however unwillingly, understood that he must give up a part of Bosnia; forced to choose, he chose well, since the area of Kupres, Drvar, Grahovo, Glamoč and Petrovac had the sparsest population and the poorest resources in the whole of Bosnia-Herzegovina. Giving it up to keep the Banja Luka basin, for instance, was a wise decision; if any of us had been faced with the choice of giving up something, we too would probably have renounced the southern part of the Bosnian Krajina. And Karadžić's decision meant that the Serbs in Croatia must fall with southwestern Bosnia.

Of course, the fall of the Serb para-state in Croatia is linked to the weakness of the whole Greater Serbia project. The Serbs in Croatia formed a kind of rural guerrilla community; they had not succeeded in creating any of the elements of a state, in achieving international recognition or economic independence, but had remained in complete, unsustainable isolation. These were the internal factors which caused their rapid collapse.

CROATIA AS A REGIONAL POWER AND
STORM AS AN AIR–LAND BATTLE

Comparing Storm with Desert Storm is an exaggeration. Calling it an 'air–land battle' and relating it to American military theory and the operations of the US Army in 1991 can serve only as political propaganda, dangerous for the development of the situation in the whole region and especially dangerous for civilian–military relations in Croatia. The theory of air-land battle was developed for confrontation between the US Army in Europe and the forces of the Warsaw Pact, in conditions in which the opponent's forces were numerically superior; it was reliable and useful in the situation for which it was designed. It arose from the expectation that the Americans in Europe, in a very shallow theatre of war such as Germany up to the Channel, would find themselves faced with numerically

Table 4
Comparison of forces of the Croatian Army and Krajina Serb Army at time of Operation Storm

Category	Croatian Army[a]	Krajina Serb Army	Ratio[b]
Men	130,000	40,000	3,3 : 1
Brigades/regiments	51	20	2,5 : 1
Tanks	320	385–430	1 : 1,3
Armoured transporters	240	195–210	1,1 : 1
Cannon	812	515–570	1,4 : 1
Aircraft	36	20–25	1,4 : 1
Helicopters	12	10–13	1 : 1,1

Note: a – including all personnel and troops which participated directly in combat actions, and all equipment
b – higher values taken for purposes of calculation

Sources: Paul Beaver (ed.) Jane's Sentinel: the Balkans. Jane's Information Group, Coulsdon 1995.

Mladenka Šarić: 'SAD nisu dale zeleno svjetlo za Oluju, ali su stavile do znanja da akciju neće spriječiti. Dosad nepoznati podaci o akciji Oluja koje je VL ustupio general zbora Zvonimir Červenko, tadašnji načelnik GSHV' [The United States did not give the green light for Storm, but let it be known that they would not prevent it. Hitherto unknown facts about Operation Storm made available to VL by General Zvonimir Červenko, then chief of staff of the Croatian Army general staff], Večernji List, Zagreb, 6 February 1998, pp. 4–5.

superior forces being continually reinforced, since for the USSR, or the Warsaw Pact, the narrowness of the front was an advantage, enabling their huge forces and manpower to be continually brought into battle. 'Air–land battle' was the response to that threat, providing a theoretical solution to the problem of how the US Army could defeat a numerically superior enemy in the conditions presented by the European theatre of war. This is why the army was reorganized and new, sophisticated equipment introduced. The air–land battle did take place in the end, in a sense, during Operation Desert Storm, since the Iraqi forces roughly corresponded to the parameters of the forces of the Warsaw Pact in a war in Europe; it was a similarly organized army with similar hardware and other elements.

It is obvious, then, that comparisons between Operations Storm and Desert Storm are inappropriate, since the situation in Croatia was quite different from that which led to the theory of air–land battle, as Tables 4–7 show.

Table 4 shows the Croatian Army as generally superior in manpower, and manpower was the only resource in which there was any significant inequality. The Croatian Army in fact played the role of the Warsaw Pact. This is the first point showing that the whole theory is irrelevant.

Table 5
Relation between manpower and equipment in selected armed forces

Armed force	Soldiers per tank	Soldiers per helicopter	Soldiers per aircraft	Soldiers per APC/ armoured combat vehicle
United States, Great Britain, France, 1994	70	123	247	
7th corps US Army, 1991 (Desert Storm)	89	636 (excl. transport helicopters)		95
India, 1994	408	4,924	1,161	
China, 1994	275	6,567	442	
Croatia, 1995 (Storm)	407	10,833	3,611	541
Standard for Europe	146–149	1,395–1,458	419–434	94–98

Sources: AntonŽabkar: 'Preoblikovanje strategijskog odnosa sila i oružanih sukoba na kraju tisućljeća – novi istraživački izazovi' [Transformation of strategic power relations and armed conflicts at the end of the millennium – new research challenges], *Polemos*, vol. 1, January 1998, pp. 125–47.

Frank N. Schubert and Theresa L. Kraus (eds), *The Whirlwind War: The United States Army Operations Desert Shield and Desert Storm*, Center of Military History, United States Army, Washington, DC, 1995.

Croatian data from Table 4.

Table 5 shows how the Croatian Army's equipment was structured. It shows that it was very poorly equipped at the time of Storm, even in comparison with India, which is considered a regional power. Take a look at what that regional power represents from the technological aspect compared with Croatia at the time of Storm.

Third, an air–land battle is conducted at very high speed, which the Croatian Army was far from achieving. The tempo of individual brigades in Storm occasionally reached 20 kilometres a day in the concluding phases of the operation when the enemy had already been scattered, while in Operation Desert Storm the US Army achieved an *average* tempo of more than 100 kilometres a day. So the comparison does not work here either. Furthermore, 'air–land battle' is primarily a doctrine of combat in depth, attacking forces entering the contact zone from deep in the rear, whereas the Croatian Army suffered badly wherever the depth of territory was

Table 6
Iraqi matériel destroyed in Operation Desert Storm (1991) and resources of Krajina Serb Army (SVK) seized by Croatian Army in Operation Storm (August 1995)

Resources	Desert Storm (1991)			Total in SVK	Storm (1995)	
	Total in Iraqi Army	Destroyed	Per cent destroyed		Seized by Croatian Army	Per cent seized
Tanks	4,550	3,847	84.5	385–450	60	14–15.5
Armoured vehicles	2,880	1,450	50.3	195–210	Not known	Not known
Aircraft				20–25	11	44–55
Helicopters				10–13	1	7.7–10
Motor vehicles				Not known	600	Not known
Cannon	3,357	2,917	86.9	515–570	300	52.6–58.2
Anti-aircraft guns				295–340	Not known	Not known
Ammunition				Not known	More than 10 wagon-loads	Not known

Sources: James Blackwell, *Thunder in the Desert: the strategy and tactics of the Persian Gulf War*, Bantam Books, New York 1991.

Data for the calculated according to Šarić.

Table 7
Comparison of the Croatian Army's daily consumption of material (logistic) resources during Operation Storm (1995) with standard average daily consumption of a Russian infantry division and a US army infantry division (ID) (average for attack, defence, pursuit and reserves) and with the actual consumption of the US Army 7th corps in attack in Operation Desert Storm (1991)

Logistical resource	Average standard consumption Russian ID (12,736 men)		Average standard consumption ID USA Army (16,290 men)		Consumption 7th corps US Army (142,000 men)		Consumption Croatian Army in Operation Storm – troops in combat actions (130,000 men)				
	total (tonnes)	per soldier (kg)	total (tonnes)	per soldier (kg)	total (tonnes)	per soldier (kg)	total (tonnes)	per soldier (kg)	per cent standard cons. Russian ID	per cent standard cons. ID US Army	per cent standard cons. 7th C US Army
ammunition	773	60.7	1309	80.4	6075	42.8	1200	9.2	15.2	11.4	21.5
fuel	910	71.5	461	28.3	21,000	147.9	400	3.0	4.2	10.6	2.0
food and water	63 (food only)	4.9 (food only)	79 (food only)	4.9 (food only)	12,500 (water only)	88.0 (water only)	300 (food & water)	2.3 (food & water)	46.9	46.9	2.6

Calculated from the following sources: James F. Dunnigan, How to Make War. comprehensive guide to modern warfare for the post-cold war era, William Morrow & Co, New York 1993.

Schubert and Kraus, *The Whirlwind War* (See Table 5).

Šarić, see Table 6.

greater. In Kordun and Banija three brigades of the SVK counter-attacked towards Karlovac and Sisak before being repulsed. Near Petrinja the Croatian 2nd guards brigade was actually repulsed, and had to begin its attack again elsewhere. Those were precisely the places with greater depth, and one wonders how Operation Storm would have developed if the depth had been greater still.

Table 6 gives comparative data on destroyed and captured equipment in Desert Storm and Storm, for further assessment of the Croatian victory over the SVK.

The categories are not really comparable, but the differences can be approximately seen in the quantities of military resources destroyed in Desert Storm and captured in Storm. Croatia has no data on enemy resources destroyed in Storm. This is understandable: there must have been very little destroyed, given that the Serb army neither accepted any serious combat nor defended itself, so it can be presumed that it either fled or, as in the case of the Kordun corps, was captured as a whole. Table 7 compares the consumption of certain logistical resources with the average, theoretical standard consumption of a Russian infantry division and an infantry division of the US Army. In the case of the 7th corps of the US Army, actual consumption during Desert Storm is given, while the five right-hand columns give the consumption of the Croatian Army in Storm, calculated only for units in combat action, that is, not including the troops deployed in eastern Slavonia and the southern battlefield to prevent possible Serb counter-attacks from Serbia-Montenegro or Bosnia-Herzegovina. In making the calculations for this table, I almost thought that my computer and calculator must be faulty: it seemed unbelievable that the Croatian Army in operation had consumed less than 50 per cent of the food consumed by Russian or US armies, and that it was supplied with 2.6 per cent of the water consumed by the American 7th corps in Desert Storm, while the Croatian consumption of fuel and ammunition stands at 2 per cent–21.5 per cent of the quantities consumed in that operation. Clearly this is a very primitive military force, with small technical resources, and manpower subject to very harsh treatment. It is all very far from what could be called zero-death warfare, war without casualties, as assumed in the theory of air–land battle.

CONCLUSIONS

I propose the following conclusions from all this. First, the timing, performance and consequences of this final operation in Croatia can be seen as the logical result of the political assumptions of which we have spoken, which are summarized in the formula: 'war as a political objective rather than the means of attaining political objectives'. The operation to destroy the SVK was carried out when the time was ripe politically: the time of the conflict between Karadžić and Milošević and the surrender by Republika Srpska of southwestern Bosnia. It was launched only partly because favourable military conditions had arisen, by which I mean the actions of the Croatian Army and HVO in the Glamoč and Kupres region. Since these actions were also politically determined, the dominance of political factors becomes still clearer.

Second, Operation Storm, like Flash, achieved one of the classic objectives of the entire conflict, the ethnic cleansing of the area and, in parallel, as is too easily forgotten, the complementary ethnic repopulation of the area.

Third, the defeat of the Serbs was political rather than military. The Serbs never had a clear objective, nor a clear review of resources for achieving their objective. Hence they had no clear strategy, nor the required consensus. They created no state or any of the other preconditions for completing their project. All this applies to what they did in Croatia, indicating that the political focus was elsewhere.

Finally, the official appraisal of Storm as an air–land battle by which Croatia transformed itself into a regional power has absolutely no basis in reality. It is a mere political slogan designed to serve two basic purposes. One is to reinforce Croatia's policy of involvement in Bosnia-Herzegovina, an involvement which includes reluctant agreement to the preservation of Bosnia in some form, but is always waiting for opportunities to take part in its dismemberment. This is why Croatia has to be a 'regional power'. The second purpose is to present the Croatian Army as a mythical force, well demonstrated by Admiral Domazet's slip confusing or conflating the categories of army and state. A state institution is trying to mythologize itself in readiness for involvement in political life; and this, of course, is the most disastrous possible result of those final operations.

5

Termination and Aftermath of the War in Croatia

Dušan Bilandžić

It can never be said often enough (so I shall say it at once) that events in the Balkans, including the war we are discussing, must always be viewed in the context of the broad historical processes occurring in Europe. The powerful effect of the terrible events which have happened in the Balkans leads many to think that the Balkans are special: things happen there which could not happen elsewhere in Europe. I do not think that is the case; I believe we are dealing with a global historical development which has characterized Europe over the past two centuries.

With this in mind, I shall begin with a true story from Zagreb, from the electoral campaign preceding the first multiparty elections in Croatia. About 1,000 people were gathered in a big hall, where I spoke in the name of the League of Communists of Croatia – Party for Democratic Change, now the Social Democrats. I said: 'Beware of the possibility that a people may go mad, lose their heads and head for destruction, not seeing where they are heading!' I did not say that Croats, or Serbs, or Bosnians or Slovenes would go mad, but that a people, a nation, might go mad; but the audience protested strongly. To extricate myself, I offered the following argument: do you recognize that Germany is a great nation? I would. If you were to eliminate the German contribution to our common civilization – to the arts, to the natural sciences, to philosophy – Europe would pretty well return to the Middle Ages. And yet in 1939 that great nation launched a war that was lost before it began, aiming to conquer the whole of Europe, including Russia, to break up the British Empire, to occupy huge areas of Africa and Asia, etc. We know it was an unattainable objective, since it has shown itself as such; but German youth continued to make war even after Hitler's suicide in April 1945, thinking that there was still a hope of victory.

(GREATER) STATE IDEOLOGIES AND THEIR REVIVAL IN THE SECOND YUGOSLAVIA

The war in former Yugoslavia was caused by a clash of national-state ideologies. Since the population in this region is ethnically mixed, each of these national ideologies faced the problem of unassimilated 'foreign' populations on the territory which it already controlled; or aspired to territory outside its ethnic region, alleging an historical right to inherit some particular area. In 1908, just before the annexation of Bosnia-Herzegovina, the Serbian anthropologist and geographer Jovan Cvijić wrote a study entitled 'The Annexation of Bosnia-Herzegovina and the Serb Issue', with the thesis that Bosnia-Herzegovina was the 'central region and core' of the Serb nation.[1]

If you look at a map, you can see that Bosnia is to the west of Serbia, and cannot, in all sanity, be the central Serbian land; but if you look at it from the point of view of Serbian national ideology, Bosnia-Herzegovina is not west of real Serbia but in the middle of imaginary Serbia. Imaginary Serbia comprises, or should comprise, all Serbs: not only those who live to the west of the Serbian motherland, but also those who live to the west of Bosnia-Herzegovina, in Croatia or still further west, which really does make Bosnia-Herzegovina look like the central region. According to Jovan Cvijić, writing at a time when Serbia had 2.9 million inhabitants, there were 10 million people in the region between the Karavanke, Salonika and Istanbul who had not yet become an ethnic unity, but who were coalescing around Serbia and would become the Serbian nation.

In the same month, the leader of the Croatian Peasants' Party, Stjepan Radić, published a book with the title 'The Live Croatian Right to Bosnia-Herzegovina' with a similar thesis from the Croatian angle, albeit slightly differently defined and argued. According to Radić, Bosnia-Herzegovina had made significant progress of every kind while it was an Austro-Hungarian protectorate, so that Sarajevo was catching up with Zagreb and Belgrade in intellectual and other capacities. This showed that Austria-Hungary had proved itself the most capable agent for ensuring peace, legal order and progress in Bosnia-Herzegovina. It was absolutely natural for Croatia to take over the task, within the framework of Austria-Hungary, not only because it surrounds Bosnia-Herzegovina on three sides but also because it is ethnically closest to it. Moreover, Bosnia was 'the core of the old Croatian state'.[2] Frano Supilo, a leading Croatian politician at the beginning of the century, said something rather different,

---

[1] Jovan Cvijić: *Aneksija Bosne i Hercegovine i srpsko pitanje* [The annexation of Bosnia-Herzegovina and the Serb question], in *Govori i članci* [Speeches and articles], Belgrade 1921 (1908), vol. I, p. 213.

[2] Stjepan Radić: *Živo hrvatsko pravo na Bosnu i Hercegovinu* [The live Croatian right to Bosnia-Herzegovina], Zagreb 1908, pp. 27–37.

roughly: 'if, God willing, the Kingdom of Serbia gets Bosnia, we shall be pleased and will congratulate them; but if Croatia were to get Bosnia-Herzegovina within the projected Trialist solution,[3] then the Serbs should congratulate us on having worked it out that way rather than having Bosnia-Herzegovina remain a protectorate.' Clearly the roots of these different viewpoints go very deep.

During Tito's time we communists (I was a communist from 1939 until the fall of communism and was for a while on the Croatian party's Central Committee; I also have a Partisan certificate of service from 1941) were convinced that the defeat of the Greater Serbia and Greater Croatia ideologies had been final and irreversible; that after the defeat of Draža Mihailović and Ante Pavelić, nationalism had been so thoroughly crushed that there was no danger of its reappearance within Yugoslavia. We were deluding ourselves; after the defeat of Pavelić and Mihailović in the Second World War, nationalism and chauvinism slowly began to revive everywhere. Some documents which I have been reading recently show how mistaken we were. I shall give just two examples.

In March 1962, in the utmost secrecy, Tito held a three-day Communist Party session attended by 70 political leaders from the whole of Yugoslavia, at which he said that he realized Yugoslavia might break up and that something must be done to save it. Serbia's leader Petar Stambolić added: 'I have been reading an UDBA report on what our Party cadres are talking about among themselves. I compared it with an UDBA report from 1945 on what was being said in bourgeois circles in Belgrade, and I realized that the two reports are identical. If you just change the names, the ideas are exactly the same.' The ideology which we communists had thought was dead had, in some 20 years, resuscitated itself.

The revival of Greater Serbia ideology was a long process, spreading slowly by osmosis through the intelligentsia in Serbia. They began to say, as if awakening from a dream: 'Well, we Serbs have lost Macedonia in Tito's Yugoslavia; we have lost Bosnia-Herzegovina too; we are about to lose Vojvodina and Kosovo. We must do something because, if we surrender without a fight, it means giving up our gains from the First and Second Balkan Wars and the First World War. If we are not to sink, as a nation, into being nobodies and nothing, we must achieve the great historical deed of preserving the heritage of a hundred and fifty years of Serbian expansion. We *must* – if need be, by war. We mustn't hold back, we have no choice but to face that painful challenge; we have to resist and regain our former greatness.'

Certain individuals among the Yugoslav leadership were pretty well aware of this. Edvard Kardelj said at another, also secret, meeting of 80

---

[3] The proposal to transform Austria-Hungary constitutionally so as to introduce a third, Yugoslav unit with its seat in Zagreb.

leading people from all the republics and the Federation, held on 12 and 13 November 1965:

> Our theory that the nations would fade away is wrong. The nations are not fading away but becoming ever stronger. If we want to save Yugoslavia, we shall have to move to a confederation or an alliance of sovereign states with so much state autonomy that there would be no threat to anyone's national identity.

The meeting lasted two days and no one, not a single member of the Central Committee, referred to Kardelj's proposal. Instead, they talked about economic reform, the state of the economy, finances, foreign currency reserves, balance of payments deficits, productivity and so on.

In Croatia, too, during the events of 1971,[4] nationalist romanticism began to spread osmotically, and Greater Croatia ideas occasionally appeared on the political scene, but they were really marginal, and within those complex events mere harmless political folklore. They were preserved chiefly by the 1945 Ustasha emigrants in their diaspora enclaves, and by smaller groups from later political emigrations who, as if nothing had occurred in the meantime, inclined to the nineteenth-century concept of Croatian State Right, or even to nostalgia for the NDH. But in Serbia during 1969 and 1970, the intellectual scene began to hum with the idea that Serbia should not defend Yugoslavia but should establish new borders for Serbia and abandon the rest, because, they said, that 'fierce Slovenian and Croatian nationalism cannot be tamed'. With the view that Serbs should forget Yugoslavia and turn instead to the creation of a new enlarged Serbia, the Serb intellectual elite was slowly returning to the positions of Ilija Garašanin, Vuk Karadžić, Jovan Cvijić and Stevan Moljević; this meant that war was unavoidable.

MILOŠEVIĆ'S FIVE TRUMP CARDS

In the second half of the 1970s, after Tito had replaced the younger and more modern political generations in the republics, and then set in motion the adoption of the 1974 Constitution of SFRY, Serbia was constantly expressing its dissatisfaction with the way in which the status of the provinces was defined in the new constitution, while the other republics, and the communists in Croatia especially, hung on to its provisions for all they were worth. After Tito's death and the Albanian demonstrations in Kosovo which soon followed, Ivan Stambolić, president of Serbia, held negotiations for six years with the republics and provinces, saying that

---

[4] For the events of 1970/71 in Croatia, see note 14, pp. 119–20. below.

something must be done to strengthen the position of Serbia as a state. But the constitutional procedures Kardelj had devised made it impossible to launch any initiative in that direction without the absolute consensus of all eight members of the Federation. Kosovo and Vojvodina had the right of veto as well as the republics. Since the republics resisted any kind of change, Milošević said to himself: 'I shall not negotiate any more, or rather, I shall negotiate but also initiate parallel, extra-institutional moves, and follow both tracks.' Thus in 1987–89 macro and micro policy coincided. The national ideology of Serbia was revived among the intelligentsia, while Milošević and the Serbian ruling elite believed that it was enough to issue a threat for everyone to capitulate at once. Milošević had five menacing trump cards over the other republics:

1. He had absolute international support from both East and West. This was not, of course, for him personally, but for Yugoslavia; but as he posed as the defender and preserver of Yugoslavia, the whole world, in supporting Yugoslavia, effectively supported Milošević.
2. He had the JNA, to which socialism and Yugoslavia were sacrosanct.
3. He had, or thought he had, the LCY.
4. His fourth trump card was his financial capital, i.e his *de facto* control of the National Bank of Yugoslavia.[5]
5. He controlled the diplomatic service.

All these factors gave Milošević a terrifying power over his opponents, and he concluded that it was the moment to make his move. But then came something which rarely happens in history: a carefully prepared project began to be implemented, but, overnight, circumstances changed so much that everything that had seemed to favour it disappeared. The Berlin Wall fell, and out of the ruins of the Cold War with its bipolar geostrategic dispositions a new European constellation began to arise. Yugoslavia was no

---

[5] On 8 January 1991 the Assembly of Serbia unconstitutionally passed a law on 'Borrowing by the Republic of Serbia from the National Bank of Yugoslavia', to the tune of over 18.2 billion dinars, i.e. about US$1.5 billion. This involved plundering the bank to Serbia's advantage and making the whole of Yugoslavia pay the bill through rising inflation. It is interesting to note the sarcasm with which this was described by the then president of the Presidency of SFRY, Borisav Jović, in his diary. For formal cover the decision was published in the Official Gazette, 'in a confidential edition', of which 'someone' then informed the Federal government. Božo Marendić, a Croatian member of the Federal Executive Council, called for 'those responsible in Serbia to be arrested', and was supported by Ante Marković and also by Aleksandar Mitrović, a Serbian member of the Council. But the government was divided, and reached the indeterminate conclusion that 'the matter should be investigated and the funds returned, if they have been used'. Borisav Jović, *Poslednji dani SFRJ* [The last days of SFRY], Belgrade 1995, p. 239. Soon after, Mitrović changed sides and joined Milošević.

longer the favourite of either West or East; there no longer was a West or an East in the old sense. Goaded, the non-Serb nations awoke to the threat of Greater Serbian hegemonism; the League of Communists of Yugoslavia collapsed; and the JNA, as General Špegelj has shown, began to split along national lines. This was the moment for Milošević to say to himself: 'Stop! Things have changed. I won't make war, I'd be bound to lose!' But then what I have called national madness began to take over.

What does Milošević do? He, or rather the leaders of the JNA, had meant to defend the Yugoslav border on the Karavanke, but when they couldn't reach the Karavanke, they said to themselves, 'Very well, the Sutla, and if we can't manage that line either, let's go to the Una, and if that doesn't work, we'll take up position on the Drina' – and that's what happened.[6] So we have a protracted withdrawal, a reduction of objectives and programmes, but no giving up, which again reminds me of Germany. The Wehrmacht advance was broken in the winter of 1941–42 outside Moscow; Leningrad did not fall, and Zhukov launched a counter-offensive. It was perfectly clear that a change of strategy was needed, but Hitler did not change it. Nor did he see the consequences of the surrender of von Paulus' 6th army at Stalingrad at the beginning of 1943. In summer 1943 came the battle of Kursk, the greatest tank battle of the Second World War; the Soviets were victorious, but again Hitler did not draw the obvious conclusion. In June 1944 the Americans landed in Normandy, and yet again he failed to see the consequences. He withdrew, but did not change his objectives. What Milošević did was no mere Balkan phenomenon.

There is something else of which one must take account in the Balkan situation, and thus within former Yugoslavia: intense and increasing internal conflict. Yugoslav contradictions reflected those in the rest of the world. Take just one economic index: the ratio between national per capita income in the most developed Federal unit, Slovenia, and the least developed, Kosovo, was 6:1. In 1932, at the height of King Alexander's dictatorship, the leader of the Croatian Peasant Party, Vladko Maček, said to a Czech journalist that he was just managing to avert a Croatian insurrection, since he knew that nothing would come of it and that it would simply give rise to still greater evils, because Yugoslavia was supported by the Versailles system. What supported Tito's Yugoslavia was the Cold War. It was supported 75 per cent by the United States and the Soviet Union and

---

[6] The Karavanke is the mountain range on the border between Slovenia/Yugoslavia and Austria; the Sutla, a river in the northwestern sector of the Croatian/Slovenian border, is often taken symbolically as the whole border between the two republics; the river Una symbolizes the western border of Bosnia-Herzegovina with Croatia, though the border actually coincides with it for only a short distance; the Drina is symbolically, and in large part in fact, the border between Bosnia-Herzegovina and Serbia.

25 per cent by its own internal forces. When the Berlin Wall fell, the war broke out.

CROATIA'S PYRRHIC VICTORY

Were Croatia's war aims achieved? Hard to say. The only certainty is that the war west of the Drina is over, and we shall see what happens to Kosovo and to Serbia in general. The American politician Lawrence Eagleburger once advised waiting for us all to bleed to death, when the war would end of itself.[7] Something similar happened in Europe in 1945, when it lay bloodied and ruined. The Germans lost 6 million soldiers alone, while 13 million refugees arrived in Germany; Russian deaths are said to have numbered 29 million, and the country was incapable of making war any longer, although Stalin threatened to strike against the West with the help of communists in western European countries. Today we have no more cannon fodder either; we have no more soldiers.

The main question now is what will become of us after the war, in the coming few decades. The Croatian regime insists that the country is in good standing economically, politically, psychologically and in every other way, but I have to say that in these past nine years it has sharply declined in civilizational terms. Here are some indicators. First, what may be called de-industrialization: ten years ago Croatia had 1,690,000 people in employment, now there are about 1 million: 700,000 jobs have been lost, mostly in industry. Second, there is an ongoing degradation of the nation's intellectual and spiritual life. As always happens in bloody revolutions, many illiterate or semi-literate people, with no knowledge of how to govern society, have risen to important positions. Under their rule the former engines of economic development, such as the Končar, Nikola Tesla or Prvomajska factories, have to a large extent been transformed into warehouses, and workers in the once powerful Đuro Đaković enterprise in Slavonski Brod have dropped from 18,000 to 3,500. Scholarship is also in decline, in the sense that it has absolutely no influence on social life. Croatia has a state-run Economics Institute, founded before the Second World War and afterwards revived by the Croatian communist government,

[7] Lawrence Eagleburger, US ambassador to Yugoslavia until 1989, then assistant secretary of state in the Bush administration, gave a lecture in autumn 1992 at the Centre for Security Policy in Washington, in the course of which he said: 'I have said this 38,000 times and I have to say this to the people of this country as well. This tragedy is not something that can be settled from outside and it's about damn well time that everybody understood that. Until the Bosnians, Serbs and Croats decide to stop killing each other, there is nothing the outside world can do about it.' See Branimir Anžulović, *Heavenly Serbia: from myth to genocide,* New York and London 1999, p. 170.

but these days no one turns to its expertise to resolve the economic problems of the country. Deurbanization has also begun. Although Zagreb prides itself on being a Little Vienna, and is indeed beautiful, it is really a huge Potemkin village, while everything outside is having a hard time. We are also undergoing depopulation, since young, qualified people are leaving for foreign countries. Taken as a whole, all this leads to the conclusion that the civilization of the country is collapsing.

I shall conclude with the following story. I once appealed to the international community not to leave us alone in the Balkans, for alone we could solve nothing, whereupon the state-controlled daily newspaper *Vjesnik* produced the headline 'Bilandžić calls for occupation of Croatia.' Fortunately for us, there is no Stalin in Moscow and no Hitler in Berlin, while in Washington nothing has changed. Our chances are better today than before, but the international community must help us. The stain left on the Croatian nation by the crimes committed in the war cannot be removed, and, especially as regards Bosnia-Herzegovina, will remain a national stigma for a very long time. It can be alleviated by humanism, tolerance, liberal democracy, but it can never be wiped clean.

Discussion: The War in Croatia

(Chaired by Norman Cigar)

Rusmir Mahmutćehajić

The presentations we have heard make it clear that what we have been calling 'the war in Croatia and Bosnia-Herzegovina' was really a war *against* Bosnia-Herzegovina, even though none of the speakers explicitly defined it as such. I think we have to confront this failure to define the issue. Despite their negative view of Tuđman's politics, moreover, none of the speakers said clearly that Tuđman's war in Bosnia-Herzegovina was not against the Serbs but against Bosnia-Herzegovina, with an aim made explicit a year before the start of the war, when he said: 'Territorial concessions must be made to the Serbs so as to eliminate the reasons for Serbian imperialistic policies'[1] – 'concessions' which implied the destruction of Bosnia-Herzegovina.

[1] At the end of 1991, Tuđman organized a reception for the chief editors of most Croatian newspapers and Croatian radio and television, in the course of which he responded to their questions. Two topical issues dominated the meeting: the announcement of the European Union that, following the decision of the Badinter Commission, it would recognize Slovenia and Croatia on 15 January 1992; and the JNA-supported Greater Serbia insurrection in Bosnia-Herzegovina. Commenting on a recent statement by Milošević on the 'coexistence of Serbs and Muslims in B-H', in which the absence of reference to Croats could be understood as an indirect offer to Croatia of parts of that country, he said: 'Willingness to change borders could mean that war is not inevitable in B-H ... It may be possible to reach an agreement as in 1939, but on even more favourable terms.'

A journalist from *Slobodna Dalmacija*, Olga Ramljak, asked: 'How will the creation of a Serb region in B-H affect Croatia?', to which he replied: 'There are now two million Serbs living west of the Drina. It is more dangerous to maintain relations of hatred and intolerance ... than to eliminate the reasons for incessant rivalry and dispute. It can be done in such a way as to achieve Serbia's national aims so that she has no further reasons for expansion; at the same time the regions of Croatia would be joined up, since the present Croatian *croissant* is unnatural ... It is in Croatia's interest to solve the problem in a natural way, as when the Banovina was formed. Part of the [ancient] "Little Bosnia", where the Muslims

We all know about the SANU Memorandum, but there was also a Croatian response or ideological rebuttal of it entitled the 'Antimemorandum', in which the author asks at one point what the purpose is of the falsehood that Croatia (and Slovenia) are exploiting Serbia, and replies that it must be:

> the destruction of brotherhood, accord and the possibility for Croats and Serbs to live together, the replacing of harmonious coexistence and mutual respect by legalized Greater Serbia imperialism and creation of a Greater Serbia state on the entire Serbo-Croatian territory by direct, unconcealed conquest, as intended by plans and programmes which have been circulating for a long time ... throughout Yugoslavia, and which dominate the *émigré* Greater Serbia press.[2]

Reducing the problem to relations between Serbs and Croats, and the whole geopolitical region to 'Serbo-Croatian territory', implies denying the existence of Bosnia-Herzegovina. So 80 years after Jovan Cvijić wrote that Bosnia-Herzegovina is 'the central region and heart' of the Serbian nation, the same stance has appeared in Croatia. For both authors the solution to the Serb–Croat dispute presumes the complete negation of Bosnia-Herzegovina and the establishment across it of new borders between Croatia and Serbia.

Bosnia-Herzegovina remains fundamentally both a Serbian and a Croatian question, but only because of views like this; it will cease to be a 'question' as soon as it is clearly recognized that it is neither Serbian nor Croatian.

Indijana Harper

I wonder if Mr Bilandžić could expand on his claim that the part played by foreign powers in maintaining Yugoslavia as a state amounted to 75 per cent, while the peoples themselves, the citizens of that state, and their political structures, only had a 25 per cent stake?

---

would be in a majority, could remain, making a buffer state of Bosnia between Croatia and Serbia. The B-H which was a colonial creation would cease to exist.' He also claimed that the proposals for partition came from Bosnia-Herzegovina itself, 'from Serbs, Muslims and Croats', and that Izetbegović had 'allowed' such discussions. See *Slobodna Dalmacija*, 31 December 1991–1 January 1992, p. 3. On the Croatian Banovina of 1939, see note 4, p.00 above.

[2] Miroslav Brandt, 'Antimemorandum: bilješke uz "Memorandum" SANU' [Antimemorandum: notes on the 'Memorandum' of SANU], in Božo Ćović (ed.), *Izvori velikosrpske agresije: rasprave, dokumenti, kartografski prikazi* [Origins of the Greater Serbian agression: discussions, documents, cartographic surveys], Zagreb, 1991, p. 239.

Dušan Bilandžić

I have been astounded by some discoveries I have made in the research with which I am currently occupied. For example, I counted up all the armed forces on the ground in former Yugoslavia during 1941–45, and came to a startling conclusion. I counted up the Partisans, the Ustasha, the Domobrans [Home Guards] in the NDH, Rupnik's Home Guard in Slovenia, the Slovenian White and Blue Guards, all the Chetniks – Serbian, Montenegrin, Bosnian, Herzegovinian and Lika-Dalmatian – and the Albanian 'Balists' in Kosovo, Albanians in the Skenderbeg SS division, the Muslim militias in Bosnia-Herzegovina, the Muslims or Bosniaks in the Handžar SS division, the anti-communist militia under the auspices of the Italians (MVAC), and so on, then divided them into pro-Yugoslavs and anti-Yugoslavs. Conclusion: right up to the end of the war the anti-Yugoslav forces were numerically stronger than the pro-Yugoslav ones.

I was troubled at first about what to do with Draža Mihailović's Chetniks, but in the end I classified them among the anti-Yugoslav forces, since the Yugoslavia for which he insisted he was fighting was really Greater Serbia. Mihailović had a maximum of 100,000 soldiers (I will not now go into their quality), but in summer 1944 his forces, plus 39,000 members of Nedić's Serbian State Guard, plus 10,000 members of Ljotić's Serb volunteer corps, amounted to about 150,000 people under arms. Tito was able, if he concentrated all his forces, to send at most 28,000 people into Serbia. That included seven divisions in Bosnia (of which two were from Vojvodina) and two Croatian divisions, i.e. nine divisions with at most 2,000 people in each, which adds up to 18,000 people. Koča Popović (appointed chief of staff of the People's Liberation Army and Partisan detachments of Serbia) had five divisions of 2,000 people each, i.e. 10,000 fighters. It was thus impossible for the Partisans to occupy Serbia. But then Stalin gave Tito nine infantry divisions plus General Zhdanov's motorized corps, plus four air divisions, plus the 2nd Bulgarian army: these are the forces which crushed Serbia. Milovan Đilas said, at a session of the Politburo in 1945, after the liberation of Belgrade: 'We must treat Serbia as occupied territory, because she is all royalist.'

West of the Drina the situation was different. The armed forces of the NDH from 1941 to 1945 were equal in numbers with the armed forces of Partisan Croatia (incidentally, from summer 1942 to summer 1944, exactly 50 per cent of all Yugoslav Partisans, of whom Serbs were 28 per cent to 30 per cent, were under the command of the Croatian general staff). But no decisive battle between the armed forces of the NDH and the Croatian Partisans took place, nor were the NDH armed forces militarily defeated; the Wehrmacht withdrew them to Austria. Even in Slovenia, where the situation was most straightforward, at the end of the war there were 40,000 Partisans and 20,000 'anti-Partisans'.

Looking back for a moment to the First World War, four of the future Yugoslav Federal units (Slovenia, Croatia, Bosnia-Herzegovina and Vojvodina), as components of Austria-Hungary, fought for four years against the Kingdoms of Serbia and Montenegro and their allies in the Entente. Even after the surrender of Austria-Hungary, Croatian divisions and corps, together with Bosnian Muslims, resisted the Italians: it lasted only a day or two, but even so – they continued the struggle.

But things were not as simple as Serb nationalists wish to make out when they insist that the Serbs, as a nation, were on the 'right' side and the Croats on the 'wrong' side, so that the latter should be grateful to the Serbs for having heroically freed them and unselfishly allowed them to go unpunished. This simplistic, historically inaccurate and chauvinist account of events has been repeated so persistently that it has been accepted, with whatever ulterior motives, by numerous foreign diplomats. The last US ambassador in Belgrade, for example, spoke often of 'Serbia's heroic role on the winning side in World War I', while he said of Croatia that in 1918 it 'joined the new state [of Yugoslavia] in order to be among the winners of the war'.[3]

There was certainly strong sympathy for Serbia among Serbs in the Austro-Hungarian Empire; they joined the Serbian army individually and in groups as volunteers, but so did many Croats, seeing in Serbia a Yugoslav Piedmont which would liberate them from Vienna and Pest. But most Serbs from Croatia, Vojvodina and Bosnia-Herzegovinia, like all other military conscripts in the monarchy, fought wherever they were deployed, even in operations against Serbia: sometimes with great enthusiasm, since in the region of the former Military Border, for example, there was for various reasons a strong emotional link with the Habsburgs.

General Gojko Nikoliš, former head of the Partisan medical corps, and one of the first in Serbia to come out openly against Milošević's policies, told a significant, and in its way tragic, story heard in his childhood from Serb villagers in Kordun, where he comes from. When the Austrian Army crossed the Drina into Serbia in 1915, one of its formations, composed of Serbs from Croatia, was surrounded by Serbian soldiers who began to shout at them: 'Surrender, Kraut!' They yelled back: 'We aren't Krauts, we're Serbs from Lika. A Serb never surrenders alive. You haven't a chance, as long as any of us are here.'[4]

And suddenly, people with different historical experiences and traditions, different legal systems, political cultures and cultural preferences, different

---

[3] Warren Zimmermann, *Origins of a Catastrophe*, Random House, New York 1996, pp. 5–6.

[4] Gojko Nikoliš, *Memoari: korijen, stablo, pavetina* [Memoirs: root, tree, creeper], Zagreb 1980, p. 9. He cites several examples of those 'old warriors' who were proud of having fought for the Kaiser and who were often 'greater Krauts than any Franz from Linz'.

levels of economic development, different social structures and degrees of ethnic and religious homogeneity, with fresh memories of bloody war during which they had served in armies on opposite sides, found themselves all inside one state.

Yugoslavia was created in 1918 by the internal situation: the people in the former Austro-Hungarian territories were economically exhausted by the war; the woods and hills were full of armed deserters, revolutionary ideas were coming from Russia, the impoverished peasantry was radicalized, famine was looming, the imperial army had disintegrated, and civilian administrative structures were falling apart. There was a legal vacuum, since the state of Slovenes, Croats and Serbs, proclaimed in Zagreb and comprising the southern Slav territory formerly under Habsburg rule, was not given international recognition. At the same time the Italian army, a member of the victorious Entente, crossed the Soča [Isonzo], entered Istria and made for Ljubljana, while in the south it occupied northern Dalmatia, achieving thereby its old imperialist aim of encircling the Adriatic. For Croats and Slovenes there was really no alternative to forming a joint state with Serbia, to get international recognition and protect their national territory and their very survival within this stronger framework. Thank God a federation was not created in 1918! I provoked a scandal one day when I said on a public platform: 'Thank God Trumbić abandoned a federal solution when he signed the Corfu Declaration.' The audience were amazed and told me I had gone mad, but, as I explained, 'If Trumbić had said to Pašić that he did not want Yugoslavia until the borders of the federal units had been established, where do you think the western border of Serbia would be now?'[5]

So the Corfu Declaration, signed by the two of them on 20 July 1917, defined the future state in general terms as a constitutional, democratic and parliamentary monarchy, with the proviso that after the war a

---

[5] Ante Trumbić (1864–1938), Croat politician and opponent of Austria-Hungary, emigrated at the start of the First World War, and in 1915 became president of the Yugoslav Council working to liberate the South Slav peoples in Slovenia, Croatia, Bosnia-Herzegovina and Vojvodina from Habsburg rule, and to unite them with those of Serbia and Montenegro. After the creation of the Kingdom of Serbs, Croats and Slovenes in 1918, he became minister of foreign affairs in the first government; but after three years, disappointed and disillusioned, he resigned. To the end of his life, as a committed federalist, he collaborated in various ways with Croatian political movements under the leadership of Stjepan Radić and Vlatko Maček.

Nikola Pašić (1845–1926), Serbian politician, for many years prime minister of Serbia and of the Kingdom of Serbs, Croats and Slovenes; centralist and monarchist; accepted the creation of the South Slav state – instead of simply an extended Serbia – against his own convictions, under the pressure of international circumstances and internal Serbian opposition; remained to his death firmly convinced that the new state could be founded only on the supposed proven statehood of Serbs.

constitution would be adopted that would take account of 'self-governing entities, distinctive characteristics, social and economic circumstances'. What actually happened was another story, since both the unification in 1918 and the Constitution adopted in 1921 contradicted the principles of the Corfu Declaration, while the administrative division of the country in 1921 (into regions) and in 1931 (into banovinas) broke up historical, political, economic and cultural units if they had a non-Serb or a majority non-Serb population.

Yugoslavia was a conflict-prone state, even more than the Soviet Union, since the Russian nation had the capacity to hold the USSR together as long as it could survive in global relations, but the Serb nation formed only 36 or 37 per cent of the population of Yugoslavia. (When I saw Lord Carrington after the fall of Vukovar, I told him that I still favoured Yugoslavia, but on one condition: the establishment of English-style parliamentary democracy. Then even if all Serbs voted for the same Serbian party, they would be only a little over one third in the parliament, and would not be able to rule with that percentage.) Serbia was not on the same level as Croatia and Slovenia in terms of culture and civilization, which meant that it did not have the capacity to govern; yet a state was created in which it was dominant. This is what I had in mind when saying that Yugoslavia was maintained more by external powers, within the context first of the Peace of Versailles and then of the Yalta and Potsdam accords, than it could have been by its own internal power.

The international community was largely unaware of what was happening here. I think that they actually ignited the war, though not deliberately. When President Bush or Secretary of State Baker said that they were 'both for the unity of Yugoslavia and for the right of each people to self-determination', Milošević read only the first part of the sentence and put a full stop after it; while the western republics blanked out the first part and took cognisance only of the second. It was as though a message was sent to both saying: 'you all have rights: *you* have the right to self-determination and *you* have the right to maintain Yugoslavia'.[6] Which is how Yugoslavia was lost.

---

[6] The best-known, and most controversial, example was Baker's visit to Belgrade on 21 June 1991, five days before the proclamation of sovereignty of Slovenia and Croatia was issued. He met separately with the presidents of the republics (Kučan, Tuđman, Izetbegović, Milošević, Bulatović, Gligorov) and the president of the Federal government, Marković, but did not wish to meet with members of the SFRY Presidency, since he maintained that with Serbia blocking the election of Mesić as president it had ceased to be legitimate. Baker made no official statements after these meetings, but only responded in passing, briefly and in general terms, to the questions of some journalists, who then made public what he had said.

According to an account in the *New York Times* of 22 June 1991 by Thomas Friedman, who was both well-informed and close to Baker, he did say that the United States wanted to see Yugoslavia preserved, and that when speaking with

Jovan Divjak

Mr Mesić says that while he was in Belgrade as a member (or as president) of the SFRY Presidency, no general came to tell him what was happening. Not even one of Croat nationality, since there were some of them there too?

I should also like to know why Croatia has not filed a case against FRY? Bosnia-Herzegovina did so as early as March 1993, basing its case on the 1948 UN Convention on the Prevention and Punishment of the Crime of Genocide, and some other conventions, such as the 1907 Hague Convention IV Respecting the Laws and Customs of War on Land, and the 1948 UN Universal Declaration of Human Rights. If the International Court of Justice finds FRY guilty of genocide, it will have to pay damages to Bosnia-Herzegovina and its citizens. Our country will persist in this case, despite various attempts to get us to abandon it. I do not think the people of Bosnia-Herzegovina would ever allow the case at the International Court in the Hague to be withdrawn. I don't know how to interpret the fact that Croatia has not done the same. You have said that FRY would have to pay war damages for democracy to emerge in Serbia. With or without payment of war damages, it will take a very long time for a democracy movement to arise.

It was also said that in 1990 the TO armaments were transferred to JNA depots and that this was strictly carried out in Slovenia and Croatia. Unfortunately, it was strictly carried out only in Bosnia-Herzegovina. Slovenia went about things much more smartly and resolutely.[7] I think that Croatia also managed to save something.

Kučan and Tuđman he had opposed 'unilateral decisions which could provoke clashes'; but the emphasis in all the meetings was on the need for parliamentary democracy, the rights of minorities and respect for the will of the people, as well as, in particular in the meeting with Milošević, on the inevitability of greater independence for the republics and strong condemnation of any possible moves towards military intervention.

For an account of Baker's memoirs, *Politics of Diplomacy: revolution, war and peace 1989–1992*, New York 1995 (co-authored with Thomas M. Defrank), see Damir Grubiša, Diplomacija na 'kraju povijesti' [Diplomacy at the 'end of history'], *Erasmus* vol. 18, 1996, pp. 90–6. The article analyses various interpretations of Baker's visit to Belgrade.

[7] During the session of the Assembly of Slovenia on 17 May 1990, when the new government was elected, the first calls were received from the leaders of certain municipalities that the JNA was removing TO arms from the municipality depots and taking them to an unknown destination. After initial confusion, the Presidency of Slovenia despatched to all local authorities a confidential telegram telling them to stop handing over the arms. 'The majority of the arms of 12 municipal TO headquarters and part of the arms and ammunition of 30 defence brigades were saved, something less than one third, while more than 70 per cent of the weapons and equipment of the Slovene TO remained under JNA control. Janez Janša, *Pomaci: nastajanje i obrana slovenske države 1988–1992* [Moves: formation and defence of the Slovenian state, 1988–1992], Zagreb 1993, p. 40.

Martin Špegelj

I cannot tell you exactly what weapons were taken from the Croatian TO, since without access to the military archives in Belgrade it is not possible to give precise data. But a fairly reliable estimate can be made. Since the Croatian TO could deploy 240,000 men, it must have had 200,000 firearms of various types, about 1,400 mortars of various calibres, some 10,000 grenade launchers, about 10,000 artillery pieces, about 8,000 anti-aircraft guns, about 500 armour-piercing rocket systems, and some quantity of mines and explosives. It can safely be estimated that more than 200,000 short- and long-range weapons and many combat sets were removed.[8] I should add that later, when we occupied the JNA barracks and depots, we found a significant proportion of these weapons and got them back.

I can be more precise about what we saved. We held on to 9,000 weapons of various calibres, from pistols and rifles, including semi-automatic pump-action rifles, to some high-quality 40mm Bofors guns. The items located in depots under the direct control of the republic's executive authorities were saved, for example in Sveta Nedjelja near Samobor, where the guards were simply unwilling to hand over arms intended for defence of the republic. The depots in the harbours and in some factories were also saved, in Đuro Đaković in Slavonski Brod, OLT in Osijek, part of what INA had warehoused in its oil fields in Podravina. In the joint refinery and railway depot in Sisak we held on to two batteries of very high-quality, modern 20mm artillery pieces, twin-barrelled and three-barrelled, with extremely well-trained and practised crews.

Jovan Divjak

So at least you saved those 3 or 4 per cent of rifles, but they took literally everything from us, since we believed that there would be no war. I was in the TO at that time and am one of those who sent its weapons to the JNA depots.

It was stated that the aggressors did not benefit in this war. But Croatia did benefit: it was multinational, and now it is mononational; it no longer has that problem, and behaves accordingly. If Croatia was 12 per cent Serb before and is now about 4 per cent, the authorities in Croatia have benefited. Moreover, Tuđman has widened the *croissant* formed by the country's south-western borders and will not easily allow Serbs to return to Glamoč, Drvar or anywhere else where they lived before. In three municipalities of the Bosnian krajina – Glamoč, Drvar and Grahovo, with an area of about 2,800 square kilometres – there were some 37,000 inhabitants, chiefly Serbs (with 2,000–3,000 Bosniaks and a few isolated Croats). In the

[8] Regarding this estimate, see Slaven Letica and Mario Nobilo, *JNA: rat protiv Hrvatske*, Zagreb 1991, pp. 63, 72.

Bosanska Posavina, only half as large with wonderfully rich and fertile ground, perhaps the most valuable in Bosnia-Herzegovina, there were 180,000 people; the municipalities of Bosanski Brod, Bosanski Šamac, Odžak, Orašje and Derventa do not even amount to 1,400 square kilometres in all. Of that population, Croats formed more than 50 per cent, and their numbers were larger still if one adds some populated areas on the margins of Doboj and Modrića municipalities, which also fall within the Posavina. I have included Orašje, though it largely defended itself, not only from the JNA and the Chetniks but from Tuđman's intention to give it up to Karadžić. Yet a population exchange took place, and the Posavina is now part of Republika Srpska, since Tuđman gave it up for a piece of the *croissant*'s hinterland. I am sure that was how it was seen, since there is no logic in it: that a hilly, stony wasteland with no Croat population is considered more valuable than fertile plains where more than 100,000 wealthy Croats live.

Everything said about the behaviour of the JNA holds good, but for the sake of truth we must say that there was resistance in the JNA too. I was glad to hear General Špegelj say that some 3,000 officers of the former JNA immediately joined the Croatian forces, but even those who did not were not particularly keen to go to war; on two occasions the army command pensioned off some 150 generals. You recall General Trifunović in Varaždin: though you had occupied the barracks, he behaved most honourably, believing that he should not make war against his own people.[9]

We all heard Milošević in 1989 saying in Gazimestan that there would be war;[10] we listened too when Vuk Drašković spoke, in the programme

[9] Vladimir Trifunović was commander of the Varaždin corps of the JNA; in September 1991, ZNG forces surrounded him in the barracks. Though there was firing on the town from the barracks, including the use of heavy weapons, during the seven-day blockade and negotiations, Trifunović did not use his authority to order reprisals against the town nor to breach the blockade regardless of casualties, but reached agreement with the Croatian authorities: he handed over the barracks and arms (74 tanks, 61 armoured vehicles, etc.) and in return was allowed to leave for Serbia together with his staff (about 220 men on military service, with about 60 officers and military officials with their families). In Belgrade, besides being subjected to media persecution, he was sentenced to 11 years' imprisonment for treason, but was pardoned after little more than a year, though not rehabilitated. In 1993 the criminal court in Varaždin sentenced him *in absentia* to 15 years' imprisonment 'for war crimes and crimes against humanity and the international law of war'. Convinced that he had behaved correctly in the circumstances – saving the lives of his men and ensuring that the destruction of Varaždin was kept to a minimum – Trifunović is still fighting for his complete rehabilitation in Serbia, and has appealed for a new trial in Croatia.

[10] On 28 June 1989, Milošević as president of the Presidency of the Socialist Republic of Serbia made a speech in the Gazimestan quarter of Prishtina as part of the great state-sponsored celebrations of the 600th anniversary of the Battle of Kosovo. He said: 'For six centuries the Kosovo heroes have inspired our creativity, nourished

of his party, the Serb Renewal Movement, about Serbia's western border being on the Virovitica–Karlovac–Karlobag line, a border that had long figured in Greater Serbia projects. But why was there no common stance of democratic forces in Yugoslavia to prevent such a bloody outcome? I agree that nationalism in Serbia aroused nationalism in Croatia; if things had not been as they were in Serbia, I do not think the Greater Croatia idea would have taken hold in Croatia.

Again, I do not think Yazov was so definite in his refusal to help Kadijević's planned coup. He left him in doubt: neither told him that he would nor that he would not help him. But a military coup is what it was: no vote in the Presidency would have changed anything, because all the essential moves had already been made. As you yourself have said, Mr Mesić, the process had been going on for ten years.

General Špegelj said that he held discussions with Bosnians. With whom? About what? Is it not strange that the Bosniaks, who were the military and political leaders of Bosnia-Herzegovina, have not made public your proposals, or your assessments about what was happening in their country, and have not said why they did not accept them? When you talked about the plans to attack Croatia, you gave no indication that you as a neighbour thought that a military attack would be launched also against Bosnia-Herzegovina.

Bosnia-Herzegovina was the army's testing range for the attack on Croatia. The war in the former did not begin at the start of 1992, nor with the attack on Sarajevo in April of that year, but as early as the beginning of October 1991 with the attack on Ravno, which is B-H territory. Indeed it began in early September, when the Užice and Podgorica corps of the JNA, together with volunteers, entered eastern Herzegovina and Mostar, where they terrorized the inhabitants. When we come to talk about the war in Bosnia-Herzegovina, we shall discuss the actions of the Croatian military in its various phases, including the concluding phase. For now I merely mention, since Kupres has already been referred to, that the battle for Kupres was fought not only by the HV but also by the ARBiH. They

our pride; let us not forget that we were once militarily great, brave and proud … Six centuries later, today, we are again battling, and facing battles. They are not armed, although even that possibility is not yet excluded.' See *Politika*, Belgrade, 29 June 1989.

The state-controlled Serbian media said there were more than 1 million people present, but in fact there were an estimated 300,000–400,000 Serbs. Apart from the leadership of the republic of Serbia, there were also present at the celebrations the entire leadership of the Serbian Orthodox Church, with Patriarch German at their head, and the president of the Federal government, Ante Marković, together with the members of the Presidency of the Central Committee of the LCY and the Presidency of SFRY – other than the member from Croatia, Stipe Šuvar. The meeting was boycotted by the US ambassador and all members of the European Community and NATO except Turkey.

did at least liberate territory jointly in some areas. The HVO too took part in the liberation of Bosnia-Herzegovina, since Bosnia-Herzegovina was occupied first by the JNA and then by others. But we shall come to that tomorrow.

I like Mr Žunec's conclusion on the operations. Theoretically, we know what operations are: each has its objective, forces, resources, territory and timing, and no operation, regardless of who plans and conducts it, can last precisely 56 or 158 hours. It has its own duration and its forces on both sides. Though what kind of forces were these, if the Serb army simply fled and took the population with it? But can you explain why the Americans allowed you to do it? Is it true that there were teams of American retired military professionals with you (the ones who are today training the Federation Army), and did their presence somehow imply what the United States later officially accepted: Dayton, and the two- or three-way division of Bosnia-Herzegovina. The United States took part in that, and continues to support it. So I cannot understand why they are now insisting on the implementation of Annex 7 in B-H, connecting this with Croatia, and saying that Serbs must return to Knin and the Knin Krajina: that there can be no return of Bosniaks to the regions of Bosnia-Herzegovina from which they were expelled, to Foča or Banja Luka, until Serbs have returned to the parts of Croatia they left through 'humane resettlement'. I do not understand why in August 1995 the Americans allowed Operation Storm and its results, and then in December of the same year insisted that everybody must return to wherever they were expelled from.

Certainly Storm should not be called an operation. We in Bosnia-Herzegovina have a tendency to declare two or three battles an operation, and I see that it is no different in Croatia. Our colleague Žunec's tables show that 130,000 soldiers of the Croatian Army took part in Storm, but according to normal military standards, in such situations more than 60 per cent of the soldiers are involved in logistics. So there could not have been more than 70,000 active troops in Storm, too small a number for it to be called an operation. Another of his charts shows that from 1992 to 1995 Croatia was not engaged in war on its own territory, but was engaged in Bosnia-Herzegovina and very fiercely at that. Sadly, more Croatian soldiers were killed in battles against the ARBiH than fighting in Croatia itself, against either the JNA or the Serb krajina forces. In those two years the Serbs were resting in preparation for their next attempt. What they did not achieve in Croatia they achieved in Bosnia-Herzegovina, with long-lasting effects.

Dayton, alas, accepted the military outcome on the ground. We may say that there are no winners in war, but the greatest losers in human and territorial terms are the Bosniaks, who had no intention of making war on anyone, unlike some of their neighbours.

Stjepan Mesić

When I came to take up my duties in Belgrade, I stated publicly that I would most probably be the last president of Yugoslavia. The reaction was hostile, but I was only being realistic. No federal institution was functioning, everything was blocked, and there was no logical reason to believe that my commitment, whether physical or intellectual, could change anything. I could do nothing except state that in Yugoslavia as it was then, no president would be elected after me. And I was right. Milošević did not want any kind of Yugoslavia; he did not want even to talk about the confederal concept; he was interested only in Greater Serbia.

As for the JNA, I still say that it contained many sensible and patriotic officers, reluctant to participate in a war against any of the nations in SFRY, who tried to forestall the madness. They understood that times were changing, and wanted to adapt to democratic standards, but they were overruled and subjected to severe pressure. Some succumbed, but many joined the defence of the republics under attack. On 20 September 1991 alone, 38 JNA officers came over to us in Zadar, not all of whom were Croats. But General Kadijević's army command had other intentions, and certainly bears major blame for the war.

This was the force in which Milošević put his trust and it finally ended up under his command. I repeat, no general from the General Staff or the Ministry of Defence ever came to me. I visited Kadijević a few times, thinking that he was more sensible and might take heed of what I said, and finally because I wanted to hear what he thought, since both he and Tuđman kept insisting that there was no one in Serbia to talk to except Milošević, because everyone else was even more of a Chetnik than he. The only general who met and talked with me was Nikola Čubra, who had been best man at my wedding. I think he acted very properly. On the other hand, General Zorko Čanadi, my neighbour in my native town of Slavonska Orahovica, never even contacted me, though my father and uncles were with him in the Partisan army and had remained on good terms with him.

As for who gained what from this war, I still say that Croatia did not benefit. If, as Professor Bilandžić has said, Croatia has become deindustrialized, if its principal resource – people – has been destroyed, if whole areas of Croatia have become depopulated, then that is a loss for the whole of Croatia, regardless of the fact that the abandoned areas were inhabited by Serbs rather than Croats. This cannot be made good in the short term: anyone who eventually settles there will need decades to recover the area economically. Then there are the huge changes in mentality: Croatia has reverted to being a peasant society. A country whose standards were close to those of Europe is now down to the level of the most backward. Legal institutions are not functioning, the economy is ruined, the education and health care systems are destroyed. I really do not know what benefit Tuđman has obtained. Even his borders have not moved by a millimetre.

It's the same with Milošević's insistence that Serbs outside Serbia had to be protected. His line was that Yugoslavia was formed of sovereign *peoples* not republics, hence that all Serbs, wherever they lived, had the right to self-determination. But by the 1974 Constitution it was the republics and provinces, as constituent elements of the federation, which had the right to self-determination. It is only on that basis, of recognized republican borders, that any referendum could be organized to establish the will of the citizens; not by Serbs or Croats or Slovenes voting through-out the whole of Yugoslavia. We could have reached a peaceful solution to the crisis on the basis of the 1974 Constitution, if the military had not intervened by force in political affairs. I agree with General Špegelj that war could no longer be avoided once the JNA entered the game, but we ought to realize how much was negotiated within the framework of the Presidency of SFRY, later expanded to include the presidents of the republics. But then the Presidency was sidelined, and the presidents of the republics began to negotiate directly among themselves.

Perhaps we have failed to say decisively enough that Croatia and the Croatian Army fought a war for parts of Bosnia-Herzegovina, but I can only say that the Croatian parliament, of which I was head, never took any such decision, and according to our Constitution only the Sabor can order deployment of the army outside Croatia. Anyone who led the Croatian Army across the borders was acting against the Constitution. Sooner or later, investigations will reveal who was responsible for this, seeing that this use of the military led to crimes which will be remembered for decades. There is nothing here for Croatia or the Croatian people to be proud of.

There were other forces besides the Milošević and Tuđman regimes which wanted to divide Bosnia-Herzegovina. How else can one interpret the fact that Sarajevo endured three years of siege without anyone doing anything about it? Croatia actually blocked the aid intended for Bosnia-Herzegovina: little of it reached its goal, most being appropriated in various ways by Croats, HVO or others, either at the borders or *en route*. I think Russia had let it be known via Milošević that Bosnia could be divided along a Serb–Croat line, with the Bosniaks, if they survived, remaining as a minority on one side or the other. It was reckoned that some of them would leave the country, some would be assimilated, and some would remain with minority status. Tuđman received similar messages from Great Britain and France, though I cannot determine whether these originated with their respective intelligence services or as official policy: this was one reason for his stubborn insistence that Bosnia-Herzegovina must be divided. We disagreed violently about this, but his only argument was: 'Don't you see that the world wants Bosnia divided?' If Sarajevo had fallen, Bosnia-

Herzegovina would indeed have been divided, but the formation of the ARBiH upset all reckonings. It was ready to fight for the next 30 years, which would have been disastrous for Europe and for the world; then, and only then, the decision was made to stop the war.

I have my own first-hand information about this. At one of the secret sessions of the Croatian state leadership, Tuđman produced what he claimed was a copy of a memorandum from British Prime Minister John Major to his Foreign Secretary Douglas Hurd. It said something like: 'Dear Foreign Secretary, the Bosnian problem is a very serious one for Europe and for the world. All your public statements must support the survival of Bosnia-Herzegovina as a state, but our real policy is that the country should be partitioned between Croatia and Serbia, and the Muslims cease to be a factor in the region.' I immediately told Tuđman it was impossible, it could only be a forgery. Even if Major had wanted to say such a thing to his foreign secretary, he would have said it covertly, not left written evidence of a policy which condemned a nation of 2.5 million to disappear. Tuđman thought it was authentic. We consulted the British ambassador who, of course, said it was a forgery.

However, on my recent visit to London, organized by The Bosnian Institute, I visited the Foreign Office; not at the highest level, but high enough to obtain reliable information. The Major government had fallen, and Blair had come to power, so I asked them if they knew about such a letter from Major to Hurd, given that it had created a terrible stir in Croatia. An official told me: 'Yes, I know something about it, it is certainly a forgery, and I know that it was bandied around in Zagreb. I don't know who planted it on Tuđman. *But that was the policy.*' The letter was a forgery, but it did reflect the policy of the then British government. I tell this story to show that it was the destroyers of Bosnia who received messages encouraging them to carry on, not we who defended the inviolability of borders and territorial integrity of the republics.

When I say 'republics', by the way, I do not mean that the former provinces do not have similar rights. The Badinter Commission said that constituent units of the Yugoslav Federation had the right to self-determination, not just republics; so Kosovo, which was a constituent unit, has that right and perhaps a solution could be found for it along those lines.[11] Kosovo is

---

[11] The Arbitration Commission of the Conference on Yugoslavia was founded in autumn 1991 by the European Community, with the task of issuing legal judgements in the Yugoslav crisis. The president of the French Constitutional Court, Robert Badinter, was appointed chairman. The Commission published an Opinion No. 1 on 7 December 1991, stating that 'the Socialist Federative Republic of Yugoslavia is in the process of dissolution', and relating the right of self-determination in 'a federal-type state' to 'communities that possess a degree of autonomy and, moreover, participate in the exercise of political power within the framework of institutions common to the Federation'. See Marc Weller (ed.), *The Crisis in Kosovo 1989–1999*, Documents and Analysis Publishing Ltd, Cambridge 1999, p. 81.

where everything began and General Divjak has reminded us that Milošević's message from Gazimestan was that 'armed conflict lies ahead'. The people then in positions of political responsibility thought this was just rhetoric, a political trick, his way of getting more support from Serbs who had moved out of Kosovo. But Milošević knew very well what he was saying and where his 'anti-bureaucratic revolution' was leading.

Dušan Bilandžić

I agree with Mesić. But I would like to add something on the question of whether Croatia was a victor. I have always said that the departure of the Serbs was a defeat for Croatia, both morally and economically. There is not a living soul now between Karlovac and Zadar. The area won't be repopulated for 50 or even 100 years; Croatia will feel the loss for a very, very long time. As far as Yazov is concerned, I am a little closer to General Divjak; I too think Yazov did not come out clearly against a coup, but left Kadijević in a dilemma, at least as far as one can judge from Jović's diary.

Martin Špegelj

Mr Mahmutćehajić has rightly observed that the period 1992–93 is not covered here. Ms Magaš knows how hard we have tried to find a speaker on those events, someone who was at the centre of them, but we were not successful. So I should like to say something about it briefly myself.

I agree that the war in Bosnia-Herzegovina began at the same time as in Croatia, in 1991, with the attack by the JNA and local Chetniks on the village of Ravno near Trebinje. I see the geostrategic area of Bosnia-Herzegovina and Croatia as an indivisible whole, so that everything that happened militarily in Croatia had implications for Bosnia-Herzegovina, irrespective of whether it took the form of a military operation. All the events in Bosnia-Herzegovina and Croatia are interdependent and must be viewed together, especially from April 1991, when a Croatian Army unit engaged the 2nd (Montenegrin) corps of the JNA in the Neretva valley. After Slano was liberated on 25 May 1992 and in the following two days the JNA driven back from the immediate neighbourhood of Dubrovnik, a political agreement was reached between Belgrade and Zagreb, which turned the operation into a combination of advance and retreat: a disorderly advance of General Janko Bobetko's forces and a disorderly retreat of the Montenegrins. Bobetko was at the time concerned more with the north than with Dubrovnik, where the outcome was clear.

Later, in spring 1993 during the war against the ARBiH, the HVO found itself in great difficulties even though the equivalent of three or four Croatian Army brigades had gone to the region. You will recall that

106

General Bobetko describes in his book how they stripped off their HV insignia and replaced them with those of the HVO. The officers were told to represent themselves as members of the HVO and say they were from Bosnia-Herzegovina.[12] It was a very poor improvisation which anyone could see through.

Stjepan Mesić

The coffins were coming back to Croatia.

Martin Špegelj

Yes, the coffins were coming back to Croatia, so it was evident where those officers and men came from. In spring 1993 the HVO, even with these reinforcements, was severely pressed in almost every area where they were in confrontation with the ARBiH. The danger was that it would end in a disorderly withdrawal to the Neretva valley and western Herzegovina, and that the enclaves in central Bosnia would be lost. There was panic in Zagreb and recourse to negotiations. Anyway, after the Croatian Army moved into Bosnia-Herzegovina from the south along the Neretva valley, it spent several months waging bitter battles with the ARBiH, and unsuccessfully at that. I know about this crisis, since, though my position in regard to Bosnia-Herzegovina was well known, I was actually asked to rescue the situation. Not only did I refuse, I made a statement to the press that it was an unjust war, and in fact a war against Croatia. Tuđman said I was anti-Croat.

The period from 1992 until 1993 and the end of hostilities between the HVO and the ARBiH must, because of the continuity, be analysed from 1990 up to Storm and the final operations in Bosnia-Herzegovina. The things that Mr Žunec and I have spoken of are not sufficiently well known, especially that middle period, which people in Croatia want to play down. A few days ago, in an incoherent speech, Tuđman said that the Croatian Army fought the ARBiH because at that time, spring 1993, the latter was aiming to reach the sea and occupy Ploče, which would mean the whole of Croatia south of Neum. Every corporal knows that the ARBiH was in a terrible military situation at that time, and would not have dreamt of undertaking anything of the kind.

The objectives of Bobetko's group are well known: to occupy as much territory as possible with a view to dividing Bosnia-Herzegovina with Serbia. He has himself admitted that there were 9,000 dead in this fighting, not with Chetniks but with the Army of Bosnia-Herzegovina. Generals involved in it say that more than 13,000 Croat soldiers were killed. In

[12] See Janko Bobetko, *Sve moje bitke* [All my battles], self-published, Zagreb 1996.

Slavonski Brod, Đakovo, Zagreb and elsewhere there are graves of soldiers and officers killed in Bosnia-Herzegovina – and many were never brought home at all.

After April 1992 when the Serbian aggression against Bosnia-Herzegovina began, and after the beginning of 1993 when war began between the HVO and the ARBiH, a controlled war was being waged in Croatia. Peace did not reign, but Milošević and Tuđman issued prescribed doses, as far as they were able. Croatian Army operations were halted for political reasons without military justification, which is also true for the Serbian side. The war was brought under control so as to allow freedom, potential and resources to both parties for their engagement in Bosnia-Herzegovina. Almost half the tank arsenal left Croatia for B-H; about 70 Croatian Army tanks were in action there, as well as about 200 heavy artillery and missile weapons, half of our then arsenal, and almost all this war matériel was fired into east Mostar. It is all known, but not addressed: a void that must be filled.

Rusmir Mahmutćehajić

The war which the Croatian state, under Tuđman's command and leadership, waged in Bosnia-Herzegovina was a war for Greater Serbia, since the actions which led the Croatian Army and the HVO to the brink of defeat in spring-summer 1993 also prevented the defeat of the Serbian army in Bosnia-Herzegovina. For just afterwards, when Bosnia-Herzegovina, already closed by Serb forces to the east, north and west, was also closed to the south, and when there were bloody clashes along all the Croat lines of contact with Bosnian forces, the resistance in eastern Bosnia, in Podrinje and Posavina, was broken. This success was not due to the strength of the Serb army, since in those areas it was in chaos and close to defeat. It could not have reached strategic deployment anywhere in that region at the time, had Tuđman not enabled it to do so.

I think that Croatia was unable to commit greater resources to the Bosnian theatre of war for fear of exposing itself to the risk of a total defeat by the Serbs, which after all was their original plan. But Croatia's involvement in the war in Bosnia-Herzegovina made possible the creation of Republika Srpska. If it had not been attacked from behind, the ARBiH would never have allowed a stable military situation to develop, even in Podrinje.

That is why I interrupted you, since to understand the issues one must realize that Tuđman's war in Bosnia-Herzegovina was *de facto* a war for Milošević. Without that, the present situation in Podrinje would have been impossible. Tuđman directly assisted in the disintegration of Bosnia-Herzegovina even in areas which were of no interest to him – Podrinje, Semberija and eastern Herzegovina. This fact is simply forgotten, or ignored, as though that part of the war in B-H did not concern Croatia. But this issue is crucial, as you yourself have confirmed. Bosnia-Herzegovina and Croatia are a single geostrategic region, but in most of the presentations here the whole thing is reduced to the Croatian component.

Martin Špegelj

I agree. In the space of four years I was expelled from the army three times: in 1989, when the JNA dismissed me two years before my retirement date; in 1991, when I was expelled not only from the Croatian Army but from Croatia, and had to live for two months in Germany; and in 1992, because of the decision to move the war into Bosnia-Herzegovina, as Mr Mesić knows. At that time General Tus and I judged that the Serbian forces in both Bosnia-Herzegovina and Croatia were losing the war and were in complete disarray, and that the Croatian Army, in alliance with the ARBiH and using everything hitherto uncommitted in Croatia, could reach the Danube and the Drina by autumn 1992, finish the war, and totally defeat Serbia. I insist that this would have been beneficial also for Serbia itself, since it needs to go through a process of catharsis to enable it to take the first steps towards democracy.

Norman Cigar

As far as the war's victors are concerned, I believe Croatia will pay very dearly in the long run for its relative success in Bosnia-Herzegovina: instead of having a friendly state as far as the Drina, it now has an enemy state along the Sava; and that state may not remain merely Republika Srpska, an entity within the overall structure of Bosnia-Herzegovina, but might one day become Serbia proper: which is a strategic defeat. Second, I think the protracted war destroyed institutions in Croatia, or hindered their development, since war makes everyone close ranks, so that neither the parliament, nor the press, nor opposition parties can be effective, and that will cost Croatia dear. The departure not only of Serbs but also of Croats, young people who have left and will never return, is also a tragedy. That is the third defeat. Tuđman may have emerged a victor, but Croatia has not.

As to what General Špegelj said about the involvement of the Croatian Army in B-H, I have a personal experience. I was in Zagreb in September 1993, when operations were being conducted both in the war against the ARBiH and against the Krajina Serb Army in the Gospić area. Some things surprised me very much. One was the link between military affairs and domestic politics in Croatia – though I do see foreign policy as always and in every country linked with domestic politics, with Croatia being no exception. Second, I was astonished that in Zagreb, although the front was so close that at night one could see the reflection of artillery fire in Pokuplje, people were sitting in cafés and living perfectly normally – but this too is common enough in situations of neither peace nor war. The third thing that astonished me was the connection with events in Bosnia-Herzegovina. Relations were very bad, Croatia was engaged on two fronts, one of which was certainly unnecessary, and its resources – money, arms and manpower – were being sent to the second front, in Bosnia-Herzegovina. Even a superficial glance at the newspapers of that time reveal uncertainty about what the priority was: it was very hard to tell. I think all this was crucial for the later war effort in 1995, and that a reversal was necessary; people then understood at last that the war in Bosnia-Herzegovina was a major error which would hinder the reintegration of Croatia itself.

Ozren Žunec

Before I respond to Mr Mahmutćehajić and General Divjak, I want to draw your attention to something else, which I consider very important. It did not surprise me when General Špegelj mentioned President Tuđman's assertion that the JNA was the third or fourth military power in Europe. He is still saying it today on various public and official occasions.[13] So far as I know, no comparative data in any relevant categories have ever been supplied, nor has it ever been said upon what sources or perceptions the assertion is based. So for eight years a dogma has been spread among the public which is already gaining the dimensions of a myth. It is easy to see its function as political propaganda. First, it boosts Tuđman's charisma,

---

[13] Speaking at Grobnik above Rijeka on the occasion of the '750th anniversary of the battle with the Tatars at Grobničko Polje', Tuđman said that 'Croatia has overcome the third military force in Europe' (*Slobodna Dalmacija*, 23 June 1992). He repeated this four months later, at the celebrations in Gruž after the liberation of Cavtat and Konavle, stressing that Croatia 'has fought against the third most powerful military force in Europe' (*Slobodna Dalmacija*, 30 Oct. 1992). During a speech at the Third Convention of the Croat World Congress in Brioni he mentioned that the internal Serb insurrection was followed by the attack of 'the fourth military power in Europe' (*Vjesnik*, 7 July 1996). The commander of the B-H Army, General Rasim Delić, indicating the ratio of forces in 1992, stated during an interview: 'The fourth or fifth military power in Europe, at least in terms of conventional arms, attacked us.' See Zehrudin Isaković and Nedžad Latić (eds), *Armija Bosne i Hercegovine* [The Army of Bosnia-Herzegovina], Sarajevo 1997, p. 89 (reprint of interview originally published in the weekly *Ljiljan*, 14 December 1994). The assertion was taken up uncritically by foreign authors: the JNA was 'Europe's fourth-largest army', claim Laura Silber and Allan Little in *The Death of Yugoslavia*, Penguin/BBC, London 1995, p. 195; while it was called the 'third-largest armed force in Europe' by an American physician of Croat origin who participated in the identification of war victims: Jerry Blaskovich, *An Anatomy of Deceit: an American physician's first-hand encounter with the realities of the war in Croatia*, Dunhill, New York 1997, p. 112.

Table 8
Armoured forces of selected European countries, 1990

Country	Military budget (billions US$)	Men	Tanks	Armoured/ Combat vehicles	Artillery weapons	Combat aircraft
SFRY	1.21	180,000	1,863	3,760	1,034	455
Warsaw Pact countries						
USSR	117.5	3,998,000	61,500	50,000+	66,880	8,800+
Bulgaria	2.2	129,000	2,888	2,851	2,788	215
Czechoslovakia	3.2	198,000	3,995	7,078	3,685	312
DR Germany	11.9	137,000	2,920	4,500	2,203	191
Hungary	0.72	94,000	1,516	2,858	1,084	86
Poland	0.7	312,000	2,960	4,150	2,359	516
Romania	0.79	163,000	2,817	3,349	3,803	370
NATO countries						
Belgium	2.9	92,000	467	2,021	379	n/p
France	35.1	461,250	1,493	6,018	1,337	n/p
FR Germany	31	469,000	5,045	6,462	2,492	n/p
Greece	3.79	162,500	2,143	2,097	1,850	n/p
Italy	18.98	389,600	1,533	4,790	1,955	n/p
Netherlands	7.5	102,600	913	3,210	849	n/p
Spain	7.98	274,500	838	2,217	1,310	n/p
Turkey	3.28	647,000	3,828	3,210	4,191	n/p
Great Britain	33.4	306,000	1,584	5,302	717	n/p
Other countries						
Austria	1.61	42,500	170	460	n/p	48
Finland	1.8	31,000	115	290	n/p	73
Sweden	5.5	64,500	985	600	n/p	415
Switzerland	3.78	3,500	870	1,350	n/p	271

Source: Military Balance 1990–91.

so that he can present himself as a strategic visionary, the 'wise leader' who has defeated such a powerful force. Second, it neutralizes criticism in advance, for when confronted with such a force, the implicit message is that one simply cannot do wrong. Just as when faced with an earthquake, there is no space for rational alternatives and combinations, you will either be crushed or you will survive; and if you do survive, you will owe it to an equally supernatural force: the god-given leader.

There are plenty of people who take these statements for granted; if they doubt them, they still repeat them, because they are afraid that a realistic estimate of the JNA in the European context would devalue the Croatian, and later the Bosnian-Herzegovinian, defence effort. The truth is that the war was distinctly unequal, but also that the JNA does not deserve these compliments. Whether they put it third, fourth or fifth in Europe, such assertions simply do not hold up by any criteria, as Table 8 demonstrates.

Thus, according to these objective, quantitative criteria, the table makes the JNA approximately the tenth military force in Europe.

But the combat power of armed forces is not revealed only by quantitative data, since significant factors in assessing combat power are the way the forces are organized, the way the command structure functions, the quality of equipment and manpower, and the level of morale. The JNA had significant weaknesses here. Its forces were broken up into small units; there were no strategic operational groups capable of serious and heavy combat action and of being rapidly deployed. Its peacetime composition included many small units and commands which were intended to be the core of war units, so that the complement of existing units was at a low level. A large number of soldiers were in non-combat units: on the day the war began in Slovenia, 27 June 1991, the JNA was maintaining 1,400 guard posts, which means that about 20,000 servicemen, out of a total of around 110,000 doing military service, were permanently on guard and could not be used for combat action. The JNA owned 14,000 facilities of various kinds, with the larger troop units such as corps in possession of tens and even hundreds of buildings, barracks, depots, etc.; there were communications difficulties, supply difficulties, and failure to agree on larger structures. Almost all the forces were widely scattered and not up to full complement: for example, in summer 1991 the 32nd (Varaždin) corps had 8 garrisons and 55 buildings, but only 1,800 men.

A large proportion of the weapons and equipment was outmoded and non-standard, which was as true for tanks and armoured/combat vehicles as it was for the air force; most equipment was based on 1950s concepts, such as the T-55 tank or the MiG-21bis aircraft. Communications systems were obsolete, and there was a lack of modern quartermaster supplies. For example, camouflage uniforms, already standard for decades in European armies, were only just being introduced. Weapons included equipment which had long since been overtaken by developments in military technology, such as the 76mm B-1 small mountain piece, with its short range and poor penetration.

At the end of the 1980s the JNA had begun yet another major reorganization of its command structure (the division of the country into three sectors), which had not been completed when war broke out, nor ever tested in practice. There was a lack of motor vehicles, fuel and spare parts. Because of the budgetary restrictions imposed by the country's economic difficulties, such as the hyperinflation of the late eighties, exercises – and even target practice with basic weapons – had been abandoned. The command structure also suffered from the presence within the armed forces of autonomous political and security organs with their own parallel lines of command.

One may conclude that the JNA, on quantitative data approximately the tenth military power in Europe, was in fact much weaker in combat potential, which was significantly reduced by poor equipment, poor leadership, deficient training, and complete unpreparedness for the type of war it launched. But these facts in no way diminish the achievement of the practically unarmed, but highly motivated and resourceful, defence forces of Croatia and Bosnia-Herzegovina.

Let me now return to what I really wanted to say. I believe that General Špegelj has given an excellent response to Mr Mahmutćehajić's question: why any mention of the involvement of the Croatian Army in Bosnia-Herzegovina is avoided when talking about the war in Croatia. I would just add that we in Croatia have a perceptible predisposition – which I sense in myself and many of my colleagues – to avoid speaking of the involvement of Croatian forces in B-H except in actions which appear uncontroversial. I did personally include in something I wrote on the war in Croatia some operations which took place in Bosnia-Herzegovina, since they decisively affected the outcome of events in Croatia. I mean the southern battlefield and Bosanska Posavina, two key operations which were – one in its entirety, the other in part – conducted on the territory of Bosnia-Herzegovina.

It still remains that we do have some kind of inhibition when faced with these issues. But I think enough has now been said to show what Croatia's role and objectives were: the aim was radical destruction of the existing social order in Bosnia-Herzegovina, together with its basic values; what was done involved destroying an entire society. So much for that. I believe we shall overcome this problem; in any case, I recognize it in myself.

As to winning, it is really hard to say that Croatia won the war. It won in the sense that it regained its 1990 borders, the so-called AVNOJ borders, except in the small disputed area of Prevlaka. But as Dr Cigar has said, the price was enormous, disastrous, and will be paid for a long time to come. Moreover, the victory is the victory of the national oligarchy, and the price that Croatia has paid and is paying is the retention of power by that oligarchy. The victor is not Croatia but the regime, in so far as they can be distinguished. So much for this very important issue.

And now two specific questions from General Divjak: why did the United States allow Storm and what were professional teams of retired generals and senior officers from the US Army doing in Croatia? By his own account, the US ambassador to Croatia, Peter Galbraith, informed the State Department on 21 July that Storm was being prepared, and suggested that nothing be done. Those are his words. He also explained, roughly, why he did so. It seemingly had to do with the fact that after the fall of Srebrenica on 11 or 12 July, and as a result of the threat to Bihać and the incapacity of UNPROFOR to do anything at all, an absurd situation had arisen: about 30,000 soldiers, fully trained and with a command line, very well armed with infantry weapons and equipped with lightly armoured combat vehicles, had ended up in an 'acute hostage situation', of the kind in which individual members or small units of UNPROFOR in Bosnia-Herzegovina had already several times found themselves. It is not at all clear to me how an army can finish up like helpless passengers in a civilian aircraft, but there we are, it happened. Once again, political reasons led to a militarily unimaginable situation – soldiers handcuffed to lamp posts.

So I presume that Galbraith's idea was that the United States should do nothing to hinder Croatia from saving what UNPROFOR had been unable to save, since it was expected that Bihać would fall. According to the data I have, ammunition and food had run out there and the humanitarian situation was very bad: I don't know how many months, if not years, had elapsed since the last convoy had reached the town. I believe this was the Americans' motive.

However, there still remains the question why they allowed, if indeed they did allow – why they turned a blind eye to what really happened in Storm: all the Serbs fleeing, leaving behind 900 corpses, of which 450 were civilians; Serb villages burned wholesale (apparently the French alone counted 20,000 burned-out houses). Did the plan presented to Galbraith really include offensives in all directions? Or, as was proposed in one text published in Croatia, only the occupation of individual installations, success to be followed by political exploitation through UNPROFOR and the international community, so that the Krajina Serb Army would be defeated, but without the catastrophe of cleansing the territory. This proposal was in the public domain. But the Croatian Army moved in 30 directions, frontally, everywhere that it could, so that the Serbs withdrew completely. It remains an open question whether the Americans knew what was really being prepared and what would in fact happen. I have no answer, but I doubt if they did. The question is, what was shown to Galbraith.

As for the US teams, the Croatian Army has always denied that they took part in drawing up the plans for Storm. Certainly Military Professional Resources, Inc. (MPRI) had been present in Croatia for years. This is a private US company which brings together retired generals and senior officers with the purpose of training those military forces in the world in which the State Department or the administration has expressed interest and given the go-ahead. They came to Croatia with a mandate to introduce the values of democratic society into the administration of the defence sector. The Croat side nominally accepted this, but also requested the company to participate in the tactical training of its forces, and to introduce combat principles. This was done, so the combat principles of the US Army are now those of the HV. I do not know why MPRI was asked to do this when the combat principles in question are publicly available. Even more amazingly, it involves transferring a leadership principle from the US value system to the European, to which it is inapplicable. Hierarchies in Europe and authority in the United States are two quite different stories.

In one way or another, MPRI finally became involved in many functions of the Croatian Army, but I have no confirmation and cannot claim that it took part in planning the operation. I do know something else; the employment of MPRI meant the exclusion of a whole series of Croatian professionals from working on HV projects. Thanks to the engagement of one mercenary team, hundreds of local people were driven out of projects which were already under way. In 1992 the Centre for Strategic Studies of the Croatian Army had 250 civilian experts engaged in a variety of development projects, from anthropometric research for standardization of uniforms onwards. All these projects were stopped, probably with the intention of excluding from the defence sector people who might be able to use their expertise to exercise civilian control over the military.

A mercenary company can supply its expertise and collect its fees, but is free of responsibility for any further development of the situation. Local professionals can act responsibly, use their expertise to raise important questions, and oblige those with whom they are working to act. Foreign mercenaries are under no such obligation. So the MPRI issue concerns not just the involvement of foreigners in individual operations, but also civilian–military relations. I think the firm's involvement was extremely damaging, since it squeezed out the local potential which might have been able to change the defence sector in Croatia, in a disastrous state today, to a system appropriate to a democratic country.

Branka Magaš

I should like to come back to Professor Bilandžić's thesis that war was inevitable and basically reflects the unresolved national issue in the Balkans. In other words, the war has really been going on for 150 years, and everything that has not been war has been a kind of interregnum. You spoke of the deep roots of the war and linked it to the Greater Serbia and Greater Croatia ideas. You said that the communists had thought that these ideas had been defeated, but then within a decade they re-emerged; even Yugoslavia itself proved to be unimportant – perhaps the instrument of this or that national idea, but in essence irrelevant. I think we are looking at something quite different. Though the national question did exist, there was also an evolution.

This evolution, which included the creation of Yugoslavia, was caused by a combination of the international with the internal balance of power, so that at the end of the First World War Yugoslavia was formed both at the wish of the Entente and by the decision of local politicians. Its creation gave rise to a new balance of power, in which there was a clear and on the whole positive evolution. The start was a centralized state, but later a federation was created, and then this loosened and became a *de facto* confederation. The process sometimes went on easily, sometimes with difficulty, but it was a positive evolutionary process. So after the Second World War a state system was created on Yugoslav soil which articulated political relations in the region. These became not so much a question of unresolved national issues as of the old-fashioned principle of the balance of power. That balance of power within Yugoslavia was, of course, always closely linked to the balance of power outside Yugoslavia, which with the fall of the Berlin Wall was suddenly disrupted. The moment came when Yugoslavia had to make a move in one direction or another. One prevailed. If war was inevitable, it was because Belgrade wanted it, because Milošević and the circle around him wanted it. That option prevailed, and opened up once again the question of the balance of power in Yugoslavia, or in the region as a whole. With Milošević, Serbia became absolutely independent of all the federal institutions and, as Mr Mesić has said, these no longer had any function in reaching a solution to the problem. When Kadijević and his generals say that the JNA had no state, they are right, since they sensed that they were slowly losing it. Their reaction to the creation of the territorial defence system came before the emergence of Milošević. When Ante Marković wanted to introduce economic reforms through the existing institutional system, it was already disintegrating. There were obviously some evolutionary reasons for this, but there was also the break that occurred with Milošević's entry onto the stage. The history of the balance of power in this region is an integral part of European history. But it gradually became articulated as a question of relations between states, no longer of relations between national groups.

Adrian Hastings

There are two points I would like to make. The first, a general one, follows on from what Branka has said. It seems to me that in history, as situations develop, there is often more than one real possibility. When there is a balance of possibilities, one particular personality can be decisive; in this case, if Milošević had not been there, everything might have gone in a different direction. The world holds various possibilities, but in some situations a particular character – Milošević, or Hitler or Napoleon – forces things to go one way, once that person has got into a situation of power.

My second point takes up what Professor Bilandžić has said, that Croatia could not be said to have won, since, among other things, it has lost a huge number of jobs in industry – 700,000, I think he said. This may not actually be a result of the war, but something that derives from the economic situation in Europe, like the loss of jobs in Eastern Germany, northern France, the former industrial areas of Britain, etc. Of course, the war meant that Croatia was less well placed to respond to the general change in the European economy, particularly perhaps because of an outdated system of industrial organization; but the rising unemployment cannot be ascribed solely to the war, but also to the general economic situation in Europe.

Dušan Bilandžić

To take up the issue of what is historically possible, perhaps if we had accepted a Western system in 1945 things might have been better; but nations do not choose what they want but what they must. Generally they have no choice. The civil war came to an end in Yugoslavia that year, not because the reckoning within Yugoslavia had been completed in accordance with some logic of its own, but because the Second World War was over, so peace had to break out in Yugoslavia as well. When the war ended Yugoslavia had to be recreated, regardless of what Serbs, Croats, Bosniaks, Macedonians and others thought about it, since the anti-Hitler coalition of great powers decided in principle to recreate every state that Hitler had destroyed. That was written into the Atlantic Charter and repeated in Teheran and at Yalta.

So the country was recreated after the civil war, and what happened then? In 1945 Churchill said to Yugoslav ministers in exile in London something like: 'I am taking the destiny of Yugoslavia into my hands and will no longer allow you to handle politics. Why? Because you support Draža Mihailović, who is making war against us and will make it possible for the Communists to come to power.' Churchill then replaced the government, and King Peter II Karađorđević wrote in vain to Roosevelt: 'Mr President, Churchill demands of me that I disown Draža Mihailović. But Mihailović is a legend, he is the salvation of Serbia.' Then Churchill looked for someone among the refugee Yugoslav politicians who would agree to negotiate with Tito and found only Ivan Šubašić. The idea was that Šubašić and Tito should form a joint government – half the ministers communists, half of them royalists – and so ensure a future for the old system.

Then the war was over. Was Serbia defeated in April 1941? Yes. Was Mihailović's army of 100,000 Chetniks defeated? Yes. But back to Belgrade came president of the Democratic Party Milan Grol, back came president of the Radical Party Miša Trifunović (successor to Nikola Pašić); back came the leftist and well-respected Dragoljub Jovanović, president of the Farmers' Party. They came for the elections, since Tito had agreed to a multiparty system. But he did not in fact allow any such thing, so he proved a trickster; but he could not have done anything else. Why? Because the recreated Serbian parties demanded the abolition of Macedonia, Bosnia-Herzegovina and Montenegro as federal units, regarding them simply as Serb lands.

Dragoljub Jovanović, then vice-president of the People's Front of Yugoslavia, personally told me: 'I went to the Marshal [Tito] and said to him: Comrade Marshal, the Serbs and Montenegrins are one people, which was divided by two dynasties. Now, when we no longer have either Karađorđevićes or Petrovićes, let that people come together in a single state.' In other words, there should be no more Montenegro. 'And what did the Marshal say?' 'He said: I have nothing against it. Look, there are going to be elections; if the people so decide, let Montenegro unite with Serbia.' But since he, and not Jovanović, held power, he broke up all parties except his own. What do you think would have happened if he had allowed freedom of action to political parties in Serbia? Another civil war in Yugoslavia, that's what! And then pro-Ustasha forces would have come to power again in Zagreb and the civil war would have been extended and prolonged. What is one to do in such a situation? What Tito did was introduce a dictatorship.

At one point Đilas came out in public calling for a multiparty system. I was condemned along with him, since as a political commentator I had interpreted his eighteen articles in Borba as the party's new line. But Tito said: 'We must stop Đilas, because if we allow a multiparty system, we embark on civil war.' So they imprisoned Đilas to avoid civil war. When the student protest broke out in Belgrade in 1968, Tito said that the NKVD was behind it, because the Russians wanted to use the students to destroy the government. He did not want to use the army against the students, but appeared on television and said: 'Students, I am with you, you are right', and they cheered: 'Tito – Party! Tito – Party!' and went back to their studies. As simple as that.

What am I saying? Only that Yugoslavia was a conflict-torn community. I cannot agree that we should have done something at that time to bring down the system. The East Germans tried to do so in 1953, and got Soviet tanks on the streets; the Hungarians in 1956: tanks again; the Czechs in 1968: more tanks; and the Poles, several times . Any attempt to change the system was just adventurism. A child cannot be born until the nine months of pregnancy are over; things must mature, and even today you cannot do just what you want. Theoretically, I could go to Ban Jelačić Square in Zagreb and urge people to rise up against the authorities, but only if I were mad or an adventurist. It can't be done like that in political life; time is needed, new forces, new situations, which bring about change through their own logic.

Some great human illusions also have to be dissipated. In 1949 the decree was issued to begin collectivization. In January, Kardelj said: 'Comrades, we must collectivize our entire agriculture so that all Yugoslavs will be in a kolkhoz by the end of 1951.' A five-year plan was drawn up and a propaganda campaign began; as a political commissar I had to tell my own father that he had to join a peasant cooperative. He replied: 'My son, that's where good-for-nothings go; an honest peasant does not need a cooperative.' I said: 'Dad, have you ever stayed in bed after sunrise? No, you've always been out in the fields by then; but now there'll be tractors, and at ten o'clock the mobile kitchen will come and bring you breakfast, and then there'll be lunch, and then you'll go back home by tractor, and everything will be just fine.' My father saw that his son was deluded by ideology, and complained to his wife: 'What will become of Dušan? He's forcing me into a collective, but I won't go.' His wife was more sensible, and said: 'Tell him you will, and when he leaves, don't go.' So what happened? They found that he had not fulfilled some obligation or other, not given enough grain, and they came and arrested him and gave him two months in gaol. That was what we had to live through and survive.

You want a system of values. I know my answer has not satisfied you, but I am not trying to convince you that we were right, but simply to remind you how complicated it all was. When the Mass Movement began in Croatia,[14] Kardelj said to Miko Tripalo: 'Miko, don't stir up trouble for

[14] The complex, turbulent events in Croatia in 1967–71 often known as the Croatian Spring were in communist circles especially in Serbia usually termed (with pejorative undertones) the *maspok,* from *masovni pokret* [mass movement]. Heterogeneous and often contradictory elements took part – from younger, reforming elements in the ruling communist elite via cultural and academic institutions to students and public employees. Their principal demands were the introduction of a mixed economy, political pluralism, linguistic equality (especially in the JNA), greater autonomy for the federal units, etc. Students from Zagreb University – with the support of students in Split and Zadar – began a strike on 23 November 1971 in support of political and economic reforms, calling in particular for changes to the foreign trade and foreign currency system, so that foreign currency would no longer be centralized in Belgrade but remain in the hands of those who had earned it, which at the time meant chiefly the dynamic Croatian economy (tourism, ship-building, maritime trade). Their slogan, and that of the events as a whole, was *For Straight Accounts!,* which directly referred to the economy but extended to the entire system.

The movement was crushed at the beginning of December 1971 by centralist forces, with the threat of the entry of JNA tanks into Zagreb, and was followed by a series of show trials. But Tito's balancing act between centralists and autonomists

me. The Petöfi clubs provoked the Russian intervention in Budapest in 1956; the 2000 Words charter had the same result in Prague; the Russians will come here too.' When Miko told me, I said that perhaps Kardelj was right, to which he replied: 'What do you mean, right? He's scared, he's a coward, there's no way the Russians will come.' But who knows? Maybe they would have come, maybe not. When the Warsaw Pact invaded Czechoslovakia, Tito held a meeting with the country's political leadership on Brioni. I was there myself, and it was seriously discussed whether the Russians would also subjugate both Romania (which was internally ultra-Stalinist but opposed the USSR in foreign policy and had refused to take part in the invasion) and Yugoslavia. I just want to say: it wasn't easy.

Stjepan Mesić

I should like to add something about our state of mind after the collapse of the Croatian Spring. Professor Bilandžić was a member of the Central Committee, while we who took part in the Spring were facing gaol sentences (I did finish up in gaol). We were friends, and would meet (which was very risky for him) in the basement of a house belonging to one of his cousins. I said: 'Look, Duško, we weren't looking for anything more than a bit more civil liberties, a bit more democracy. And straight accounts.' But Duško said: 'All very fine, but the way you went about it wasn't feasible. A student movement can't turn itself into an indefinite strike demanding amendment of Yugoslavia's foreign currency law. Were the Federal Assembly, the League of Communists, the JNA and all those mechanisms really going to be so afraid of Ivan Zvonimir Čičak, Dražen Budiša and their students that they would amend the federal foreign currency law?

led to confederal elements being built into the 1974 Constitution of SFRY, very much along the lines demanded during the Croatian Spring.

Miko Tripalo (1926–1995), a Second World War partisan who represented Croatia in the Executive Bureau of the LCY Presidency and on the Presidency of SFRY, was the leading political personality of the Croatian Spring, together with Savka Dabčević-Kučar (1923–), premier in the Croatian government and president of the CC of the League of Communists of Croatia. Ivan Zvonimir Čičak (1947–), until recently president of the Croatian Helsinki Committee, and Dražen Budiša (1948–), since 1990 president of the Croatian Social Liberal Party and unsuccessful candidate for the country's presidency after Tuđman's death, were the chief student leaders at the time of the Croatian Spring. After the movement was defeated, Tripalo was pensioned off, while Čičak and Budiša were gaoled for four years. Stjepan Mesić (1934–) was a representative in the Sabor during the Croatian Spring and president of a municipality in Slavonia, where he was the first person to make use of the law allowing the formation of a private company (with 18 employees), on account of which Tito accused him of 'restoring capitalism'. After the defeat of the Croatian Spring he was sentenced to two years and two months in prison.

It was absurd to imagine it. It might have got us a yet more powerful dictatorship, and I don't want to say anything more about it.' He said, in fact, that what we were calling for was fine and could be achieved, but in another way. And that other way produced the 1974 Constitution of SFRY, without which we would not have our state today.

Tarik Kulenović

Professor Bilandžić's eloquence is hard to follow, but I would like to say something about the issue of war aims and whether the warring parties achieved them. Unlike most of the participants here, I think that all the national groups involved in the war – Slovenes, Bosniaks, Croats and Serbs – actually have achieved their war aims; in different ways, of course, since their aims differed.

Public discussion in Slovenia in the second half of the 1980s (most obviously expressed in the articles of *Mladina* and in the popular motto *Slovenija, moja dežela* [Slovenia, my country])[15] centred on the problem of Slovenia's links with the rest of Yugoslavia, and asked whether Slovenia really had anything to do with Yugoslavia, whether it was gaining or losing from being in Yugoslavia. Their tendency and principal objective was separation from the Yugoslav cultural sphere – and to some extent from the Balkans. For the Croats, the fundamental issue was the state, for throughout its history since the end of the medieval kingdom Croatia has been part of various complex state structures, but never enjoyed full statehood, with full sovereignty and autonomy. The Bosniaks were preoccupied primarily with the question of identity and national emancipation, not

---

[15] Until the mid 1980s the weekly *Mladina*, organ of the Socialist Youth Alliance of Slovenia, did not differ essentially from similar mediocre, boring publications under official auspices, but it then became the first to address some taboo subjects, especially relating to the constitutional status of the JNA, the corruption within its leadership, and civilian alternatives to military service (notably in articles by editor Franci Zavrl and the journalist Janez Janša, later to be independent Slovenia's first minister of defence). It dealt with attitudes towards minorities and marginal groups in society, the role of the secret police, the treatment of political prisoners, communist reprisals against members of non-partisan armies and civilians at the end of the Second World War, etc. After a few years it had a circulation of over 100,000, was widely read in Croatia, and became a model of courageous investigative journalism and a symbol of democratic yearnings, not only in Slovenia.

The motto *Slovenija, moja dežela* arose in the spring of 1987 as an advertisement for tourism, without any ideological or political connotations; but since the pro-Milošević press in Serbia rapidly began to stigmatize it as an expression of Slovenian separatism, the Slovenes themselves began to adopt it as such, sticking it on cars or printing it on T-shirts as a sign of awakening national awareness in the face of aggressive centralism. In 1989 the stickers appeared in Croatia and even in Sarajevo, as an expression of political solidarity with Slovenia, which was being seen as a symbol of resistance to Milošević and centralism.

only within Yugoslavia since 1918 but as early as 1878, with the loss of their status as a constituent people in the Ottoman Empire. Who are we, in reality? was the question constantly asked among Bosniaks. For Serbs, the issue was territory: how far does Serbia extend, what and where is the real Serbia?

All these issues were being discussed before the war, and each of these national groups achieved its respective aims, to a degree, through the war which followed. Slovenia detached itself from the Balkans and became an associate member of the European Union, so that the border of the symbolic Balkans shifted from the Karavanka to the Sutla. Croatia became an independent state, clearly expressed at the symbolic level in official and even unofficial iconography, and recognizable in reality as well: as the Croat state leadership imagines the state, so it creates it in practice. I think that the Bosniaks have, after this war, attained self-emancipation as a nation: they have become aware of themselves as a nation, and have grounded themselves nationally, and this cannot now be altered or called into question. And Serbia has gained territory in the shape of Republika Srpska, both formally, since that part of Bosnia-Herzegovina is now officially known as Republika Srpska, and substantively, since it really is in every way Serb land alone. Every trace of the presence of others has been completely destroyed.

Thus, all the parties involved in the war have achieved their basic objectives. I do not know whether they can be called war aims or whether these pre-war issues have really been resolved by the war; I should like to hear answers in further discussion. And now a remark to Professor Bilandžić, who referred to national madness. The theory of national madness in former Yugoslavia was first proposed by Dr Jovan Rašković, a psychiatrist and founder of the SDS in Croatia. He had the Serbs in mind, though where political processes are concerned the allegation of madness is apt to be a way of escaping responsibility.[16]

When one examines the conduct of the 'anti-bureaucratic revolution', and how the groups behaved that gathered around Miroslav Šolević who launched it, one sees that it was conducted in a very rational and

---

[16] Jovan Rašković, president of the Serbian Democratic Party (SDS) founded in Knin on 17 February 1990, on several occasions in the late 1980s promulgated his quasi-scientific ethno-psychological thesis about the 'national characteristics' of Serbs, Croats and Bosniaks. The phrase 'national madness' attained a certain notoriety when a recording of his discussion with the newly elected President Tuđman was published. To Tuđman's remark that the Serbs in Croatia were rebelling and arming themselves for no good reason, since the new government guaranteed them all their rights, Rašković responded: 'They're a crazy people – I'm a psychiatrist – they're a crazy people, I tell you, crazy' (*Danas*, 441, 31 Sept. 1990, pp. 12–15). The title of his collected political speeches and interviews is *Luda zemlja,* [Crazy country], Belgrade 1990.

practical way, and that Šolević himself was an extremely rational individual and an impressive organizer,[17] with no sign of any mental illness, disturbance or irrationality.

Adrian Hastings

It is quite impossible for everyone to have gained. Either Kosovo will be a complete loser or Serbia will completely lose Kosovo. If Serbia loses Kosovo, it will lose something essential to its self-definition. If it is true that Republika Srpska is really part of Serbia and will remain so, Bosnia has lost decisively, and historic Bosnia has been destroyed. Either Bosnia has lost or Republika Srpska has lost. Bosnia-Herzegovina will either regain West Mostar or it will not: if it does, Tuđman and Croatia will have lost; if West Mostar remains essentially part of Croatia, then Bosnia will have lost. It is a grave mistake to think you can say: 'Well, at the end of it all everyone has gained what they wanted.' That is quite impossible. We are not at the end, not nearly at the end, and only in the coming years shall we see who has gained and who has lost.

Jovan Divjak

I do not think the three new states had equivalent war aims. Slovenia had no war aims, nor did it go to war: it had political objectives which were not necessarily linked to armed conflict. The Bosniaks did not have war aims either, nor did they begin the war; war was imposed on them, and then their objective became survival as a nation: preservation not only of their territory, but of their national being. The only person who had war aims from the beginning was Milošević; later Tuđman came to have similar aims in relation to Bosnia-Herzegovina.

Professor Hastings says that we still do not know what will become of Kosovo: will Milošević hold on to it or not. But Serbia has already lost Kosovo, as it was after abolition of the autonomy conferred on it by the

---

[17] Miroslav Šolević (b.1948), by profession an electrician, lived in Kosovo Polje, a suburb of Prishtina founded in 1921 by Serbo-Montenegrin colonists. From the beginning of the 1980s, as a compelling populist speaker, he was a prominent member of the non-institutional leadership of the Kosovo Serbs. In 1987–90, in collaboration with the Yugoslav secret services and under the pretext of 'protecting Serbs' and 'defending Yugoslavia', he organized a series of mass demonstrations calling for the expulsion of Albanians, the abolition of the Autonomous Provinces and the centralization of Yugoslavia. On the organization of these meetings and Šolević's activities and world view, see Darko Hudelist, *Kosovo: bitka bez iluzija* [Kosovo – a battle without illusions], Zagreb 1989. For Dobrica Ćosić's statement on how he helped Šolević and gave him advice, see Laura Silber and Allan Little, *The Death of Yugoslavia,* Penguin/BBC, London 1995, p. 33.

1974 Constitution. Both the problems and the war in former Yugoslavia began in Kosovo, and will end in Kosovo; and however it ends in Kosovo, so will it be in the other regions of Yugoslavia.

Warren H. Switzer

I do not believe that anyone has emerged a victor in the series of recent wars. If any activity is judged in the light of its effect on living people, then it seems to me that political, economic, social, security and many other reasons indicate that no one has gained. Everything is at least slightly more uncertain than before. I should like to speak for those not present among us, the dead on all sides: I believe that, if asked, they would agree.

Paul Williams

Before asking my one question, I want to say something following on from Switzer's comment. I think almost all the parties involved are losers, and some of them big losers. Bosnia, of course, is the biggest: subjected first to genocide, then to partition, the Dayton Accord has essentially sealed its fate. I often think that the European Union should be counted as a big loser: it will be a long time before it has a common foreign and security policy and is able to take the lead in security issues in Europe, let alone in any other part of the world. I think that lack of EU leadership in resolving the Kosovo crisis is an effect of the war. More generally the international community, and the United Nations in particular, are big losers, since they have proved highly reluctant to become involved in Kosovo, in the renewed conflict in Rwanda, in the conflict in the Congo, etc. NATO, with its failure to apprehend the war criminals, looks like becoming a casualty as well.

My question is this. What are Slobodan Milošević's objectives in Kosovo? Is he seeking to cleanse a large part of it of Albanians? Is he seeking to partition it, as proof that he has achieved a kind of victory by retaining part of it? Or is he just seeking to secure it within Serbia, with no intention of driving Albanians out of it? I am being continually asked by State Department and Pentagon officials, and by the US media, what his objectives are. If they are ethnic cleansing or partition, we need a military solution with NATO involvement. If he has some other objective, which could lead to a peaceful resolution, then the US government could act in accordance with the Interim Kosovo Accord. My personal opinion is that the Interim Accord will prove a failure and there will be a need in the end for some type of involvement. I would be grateful for your views on Milošević's long-term intentions in Kosovo, given your experience with him in Croatia and Bosnia-Herzegovina.

Rusmir Mahmutćehajić

Ivo Banac recently wrote in the Croatian press that interpretation of the former regime provides a commentary on the war and the post-war situation in former Yugoslavia. The Yugoslav communist system was the most malevolent of all the totalitarian regimes in Eastern Europe. This is demonstrated by the way in which it came to an end, by what happened after its political breakdown, and by the fact that most people in former Yugoslavia could identify what was happening precisely because they had grown up with the regime and were so close to it that they had no objective standards by which to assess it, but only imaginary referents. Hence, a vital question for our discussions is: can we find some model that will make sense of the previous system, about which we know very little, and which the West – Western sociologists, political scientists, strategists and analysts of all kinds – demonstrably failed to understand?

The pretence that Yugoslav communism was better than the Soviet or Romanian kind misled the West and made Yugoslavia its client, which makes the West responsible – if one can speak of responsibility at all in the circumstances – for the tragic denouement of both the system and the country.

The events of 1990 cannot be explained apart from what already existed in former Yugoslavia and unless its rationale is first established. Its after-effects have been more severe here than in Russia or anywhere else. Apologies for a regime which ended in war, a terrible war and one that is not yet over, lead nowhere except to new delusions. Bosnia is like a patient surviving on a life-support machine; the question of its recovery, of its future, is one of the fundamental questions facing humanity, not only people in Bosnia but everyone everywhere. No apologetics on behalf of the previous regime will contribute to her recovery.

What we need to do now is to create the premises on which to forecast future events. Professor Hastings is right: to say that anyone has gained in this war is completely unacceptable. No one in this region, regardless of whether he was among those who opened hostilities or those who were forced into taking up arms in self-defence, can say that he has gained. Everyone has substantively lost, everyone is completely spent, regardless of whether his energy went on attack or defence. We are now in qualitatively new circumstances, and the fundamental question is how things will develop in the future.

General Divjak, ready like all of us to avert his gaze from evil, says optimistically that there will be no more war. I think this is false. In that case, our scholarly reconsideration of the future has absolutely no purpose. The probability of war in the Balkans as a whole, or even in the whole of Europe and the world, does exist, and is what should concern scholars more than anything else. Our task, the task of those who research such things, is precisely to assess that probability, however small it may be.

In June 1991, I put forward my hypothesis that war was inevitable, that uncontrolled militaristic belligerence would finally be directed against Bosnia-Herzegovina, and that the Bosniaks or Muslims would be subjected to expulsions and killing, before one of Yugoslavia's most eminent generals. He replied: 'That is an absolutely unfounded, ridiculous prognosis. I created that army, I know what that army is; it could not sink to that.' His opinion was based on ideological blindness. It was that ideology which was the problem in former Yugoslavia, and the cause of its tragic end; but it cannot be understood in isolation from the outside world, since it was not engendered in Šumadija, or Moscow or Dresden. It is a human condition which must be understood if we are to influence changes in the way events are moving, and overcome our inability to make predictions.

We can pray to God that there be no more wars in the world, but I do not think that anyone can confidently state that there will not be. Everyone in Yugoslavia said that; they said so in Bosnia on the very eve of war; but it is our responsibility to say that there is liable to be war, and to mobilize forces that can prevent it. It seems to me that even now we are disempowering ourselves for meeting our obligations to the future, by saying that tomorrow will be good, there will be no wars in tomorrow's world, because the Croats achieved something and the Serbs achieved something. The Serbs are the most tragic people in the whole region. A Serbia that is not free, Serbs who are not free, means a Croatia and Croats that are not free, however repugnant this may seem to some people. There are people without rights in Bosnia, but those who think they have achieved something have even fewer rights.

Stjepan Mesić

There is no sense in making apologies for the former regime, but everything that has happened in history has happened, and it is pointless to argue about what has not happened. I agree with Professor Bilandžić's account of the events that followed the Second World War. If every last Croat and every last Bosniak had joined the Ustashe, if they had all fought on the side of the Axis powers, if not a single one had joined the Partisans, the Second World War would have ended just as it did. The Kingdom of Yugoslavia would have had embassies in Moscow, London, Paris and Washington, the king would have returned and Croats and Bosniaks would mostly have disappeared. Some would have fled, some would have been killed by Mihailović's Yugoslav Army in the Homeland, and the rest would have assimilated. It is precisely thanks to our fighting on the side of the Allies that we were able to survive as a national body.

Could Tito have gone for democracy at the time of his clash with Stalin? Yes, probably, but then he would have lost power. Could he have gone at that time for a confederal model? Certainly he could, but again he would have lost power. Theoretically speaking, if Yugoslavia had not had any integrative factors and the Yugoslav segments could have joined Europe, then the communists would not have remained in power and there would have been no dictatorship. That is what could have happened; but it didn't. No one wanted to give up power. Tito was a hedonist, but also a dictator; more accommodating than some, to be sure, but only when pressed. So let us not give in to speculation. The model which later emerged was not the result of internal democratic development, but once again was imposed by Tito, which he was able to do precisely because he was a dictator. He could impose whatever he wanted – a confederation, a multiparty system, joining Europe – but then things would have gone on to develop without him and despite him, as they did elsewhere in Europe.

Many people are trying to work out what Milošević really wants. I know one of his devices. He lost the war in Croatia, but he must not and will not admit to his people that he was defeated by those Croats, cowards and lackeys of the Germans, so he blames the international community for everything: for meddling in the war and even allowing the Croats to expel the Serbs.

Norman Cigar

Officially, Serbia was not at war.

Stjepan Mesić

Yes, Milošević claims that he was not at war, but he has to explain to his people why things happened as they did. His explanation is that the international community interfered. In Bosnia-Herzegovina, though Republika Srpska may have 49 per cent of the territory, it is economically and functionally unsustainable, which is why I agree that the process is not over. It is clear to Milošević, too, that Serbia cannot have anything to do with it any more. The process has to take an entirely different turn. This means that here too the international community has sent him packing. And then comes the problem of Kosovo.

What is Milošević looking for now in Kosovo? Some say that he wants to herd all the Albanians together in one small area: persecute them to make them move and thus ethnically cleanse part of Kosovo, leaving them one area, a little Kosovo, which would formally remain part of Serbia but where the Albanians would be allowed a modicum of local autonomy, while he would retain for himself the larger, ethnically cleansed part of the region. Others say that as long as Kosovo remains part of Serbia it is

Serbia's greatest problem, which is why Milošević is really begging for international intervention, so that he will be able to say: 'Those European pariahs the Shiptars didn't force us out of Kosovo, it was the international community that did it; but I succeeded in obtaining guarantees for our historical monuments and monasteries. Having got all that I can leave Kosovo, since the international community is after all stronger than Serbia.' I find it difficult to judge where Milošević is heading; I only know that both options are open.

Jovan Divjak

Will someone tomorrow make a serious attempt to explain how and to what extent it was nationalist parties that led us to war, instead of laying the blame exclusively on the League of Communists of Bosnia-Herzegovina?

Norman Cigar

Well, Milošević is still a communist.

Stjepan Mesić

I think he's more of a fascist.

Dušan Bilandžić

As far as my so-called apologies for the old regime are concerned, I think that our colleague misunderstands me. There is a tendency to assume there is nothing to be said about the old regime: it was so meaningless and un-natural that it is best simply to say it was a kind of dark ages and leave it at that. But that is simply intellectual laziness, an excuse for historians and other researchers not to study the period. How are we to illuminate the darkness? Even during Tito's lifetime I wrote and explained that Yugoslavia was the most conflictual state in Europe and would have difficulty in sur-viving if it did not democratize, decentralize and join the European processes. It did not do so. So I was no apologist. In 1981 and 1982 I was thrown out of the CC and the Sabor; I've never told anyone that, not even Mesić or Špegelj know it.

Stjepan Mesić

I do happen to know.

Dušan Bilandžić

After the population census of 1981, I wrote that the 400–500 per cent rise in ten years of those identifying themselves as Yugoslavs in a national sense was a sign of the sickness of Yugoslavia, and that a Yugoslav nation could not exist.[18] That is why the top man in the LCY personally denounced me from the platform during the 12th Congress, and the Belgrade newspaper *Politika* wrote that I had a pathological hatred of Yugoslavia and socialism. The CC took no action, but I was struck off the list when the elections for the Sabor came along a few months later. Six months later came elections for the Croatian Central Committee and I was struck off that list too, after 15 years on the CC. It is not a question of apologetics. Simply, as a historian I have to research those times and say it was like this and not like that.

---

[18] For the 1961 population census the Yugoslav authorities introduced a category of 'Yugoslav in the sense of national affiliation', which 317,124 citizens opted for; the number fell to 273,077 in the 1971 census, but rose ten years later to 1,219,045. See *Statistički godišnjak Jugoslavije 1990* [Statistics annual of Yugoslavia 1990], Federal Statistics Institute, Belgrade 1990, p. 129.

Part II

The War in Bosnia-Herzegovina

6

The Road to War

Rusmir Mahmutćehajić

The war against Bosnia-Herzegovina is part of events that took place in the wider region, and cannot be understood outside that context, whether as to its causes or its long-term consequences, not only in Bosnia-Herzegovina but also in the neighbouring countries and significantly further afield. As far as I know, no consistent, credible model for interpreting that process has been offered so far, either in Bosnia-Herzegovina or elsewhere. So I shall begin by emphasizing the wording of my original title 'The war *against* Bosnia-Herzegovina', since this is very important for understanding the propositions that follow. The war against Bosnia-Herzegovina also explains what occurred in Croatia, both politically and militarily, and what happened in Serbia, all within the context of the repercussions and influences of European and global processes. The break-up of SFRY involved the question of Bosnia-Herzegovina, which remains the central issue after that break-up, as it also was of what we have called the war in Croatia. Events in Croatia and Serbia were crucially important for the war against Bosnia-Herzegovina; they are neither independent nor parallel phenomena, but hierarchically subordinate to that war.

In all partial approaches to the issue thus far, two interpretations of Bosnia-Herzegovina have been offered as basic premises. To construct a consistent and credible model for understanding the issues we are discussing here, it is necessary first to consider these two premises and adopt one of them. One sees Bosnia-Herzegovina as an indivisible organic unity, the other as an artificial creation of separable parts. The first viewpoint is held by those who have been steadfast in the defence of Bosnia-Herzegovina as a whole, whether they were conscious of it or not; while the second is characteristic of those who repudiate it and seek its destruction. The would-be destroyers of Bosnia-Herzegovina in the immediate neighbourhood have always claimed that it is unnatural and divisible. Standing against them have been various actors, in B-H itself and in a wider environment, who assert that it is an organic whole which can be decomposed only by the application of massive external force along with protracted internal destructive action.

The matrix, model or paradigm of the destruction of Bosnia-Herzegovina is formed of three essential elements, three ethno-national blueprints: the Greater Serbian, the Greater Croatian, and the Muslim or Bosniak.[1] They are not equal either in magnitude or in power, nor as regards their time of origin, nor in their sequence in that matrix, nor as to degree of guilt; but they are equal in principle. They are also rational, albeit deeply permeated with irrational rhetoric, religious content and an emotional reading of history.

THE SERBIAN ETHNO-NATIONAL BLUEPRINT

The first, original or active, stimulative or impellent blueprint is the Greater Serbian. Understanding it requires insight into the convergence of four factors that can make an ethno-national blueprint operative to the point where it produces destruction along with the energy it generates. The four essential dimensions of the Greater Serbia blueprint are:

1. its ethno-national elite, publicly personified by Milošević as manager of the activity directed towards the ethno-national goal; he is not the most important intellectual expression of the blueprint, but merely the administrator of what the writer and ideologue Dobrica Ćosić propounded and disseminated;
2. its ethno-national ideology of Greater Serbdom, similar to other ethno-national ideologies which characterized Europe in the eighteenth and nineteenth centuries, but which has not undergone the metamorphosis that has affected phenomena of the same kind all over Europe;
3. its organization: essentially the state of Serbia, with such trans-Serbian instruments as can be mobilized or subordinated to this Greater Serbia blueprint; in other words, the state potential and capacity of Serbia, which in a region like ours are rather powerful; and
4. its executors, i.e. that wide circle of people who, within the hierarchy of the ethno-national elite/ethno-national ideology/ethno-national organization, are prepared to submit themselves, absolutely or almost absolutely, to that system and to carry out orders from above regardless

[1] There is no time here to elaborate on these concepts, but I refer those who are interested and who would like to have a deeper understanding of what is being discussed here to my book *Kriva politika: Čitanje historije i povjerenje u Bosni* [Warped politics: a reading of history and confidence in Bosnia], Tuzla, Sarajevo, Zagreb 1998, translated as *The Denial of Bosnia*, University of Pennsylvania Press, PA: 2000.

of their scale and nature, including genocide as organized destruction of a people and all that belongs to it.

This blueprint is known to the majority of observers, even to those with limited knowledge of the Balkans. Its goal is the establishment of an ethno-national state over a wide region which, with inconsistent logic, is postulated as Serb, sometimes on the basis of the ethnicity of the population, sometimes on the basis of a common language, sometimes on the basis of geostrategic interests, sometimes on the basis of historic right, etc. In the whole collection of diverse arguments it is possible to recognize in the final instance an extreme arrogance which justifies right by might: whatever can be achieved by the force at our disposal or the capacity of our organizations is permissible. In this concept, Yugoslavia was seen as an instrument for achieving the ethno-national goal. To that extent Yugoslavia was indeed 'a basic Serb interest', as frequently asserted by the historian Milorad Ekmečić, one of the key proponents of the shift within the Greater Serbia project from the idea of Greater Serbia to the idea of Yugoslavia, i.e. of identifying Yugoslavia with Greater Serbia. Anything opposed to the interest thus defined is seen as anti-Serb.

However, since we are dealing with a rationally established ethno-national blueprint, in real life, like any other such blueprint, it soon came up against significant resistance, as also happens in physics, where things are much more precise and founded on pure premises.

For Yugoslavia to be a state within which all Serbs could live and achieve political dominance on the basis of numerical advantage, it had to have a centralized administrative system. The de-Serbianization of the Yugoslav state, the emancipation of non-Serb nations and the relative decentralization of the mid 1970s, prompted the Greater Serbian strategists and theoreticians to view communist Yugoslavia as incompatible with their fundamental objective: a state that would realize Greater Serbian interests. Viewing the presence of non-Serb ethnic and historical identities in the Yugoslavia created in 1918 as a historical excess or incomplete historical process, they were convinced that demographic development would lead to the definitive inclusion of a significant number of Croats, Bosniaks, Montenegrins and others within the Serb demographic corpus. But, in post-war conditions of stability, the normal demographic development of the entire region demonstrated that Serb ethno-national homogeneity (an essential premise of the ethno-national blueprint) rather than becoming stronger was actually growing weaker.

Systematic analysis of the understanding of these circumstances by the intellectual leadership of Greater Serbia (operating, of course, under the mantle of the communist idea) would reveal a kind of mental disturbance, often manifested in public as panic in the face of a situation in which Serbs, it was said, were losing what they had gained in war. Claiming that Serbs are 'losers in peace' shows an essential lack of readiness to face up to the real facts of the situation, except through an ideological image postulated as a new religion.[2]

[2] This reading of Serb history was originally formulated by Dobrica Ćosić in a lecture delivered on the occasion of his election to the Serbian Academy of Sciences and Arts on 29 March 1978, entitled 'Literature and history today'. He wished to use the opportunity, he said, to give 'a more intimate expression of my understanding of the history of the Serb nation in the 20th century'. During that period Serbia had taken part in four wars, endured huge human and material losses, and, according to Ćosić, 'had always been on the right side' and come out as a victor, fighting unselfishly at the same time for the freedom of other South Slav nations. The essential question, however, was this: 'What kind of nation, what kind of people are we that die in such numbers fighting for liberty yet in victory remain without it? How is it that those among us, those living in the same house, can deprive us of what far stronger enemies could not deprive us on the battlefield? How is it that a people who are so dignified, proud and courageous in war, accept lasting humiliation and subjugation in peacetime? … It is tragic to be the heirs of those forced to be stronger in war than in peace; who, after the greatest and most difficult victory in Serb history, remained powerless to validate it in peacetime.' Dobrica Ćosić, *Stvarno i moguće: Članci i ogledi* [The real and the possible: articles and essays], Rijeka 1982, pp. 171–2.

By that 'greatest victory' which remained invalidated in peacetime, Ćosić meant the creation after the First World War of Yugoslavia instead of a national Serbian state, a Greater Serbia, within borders which became a goal once again at the end of the 1980s. The Serbs were deprived of their supposedly legitimate war gains by 'those living in the same house', the Croats and other non-Serb nations, or rather all those who advocated decentralization of Yugoslavia, any kind of recognition within it of cultural, historical and ethnic differences, and the participation of non-Serbs in its administration. His ideas were soon reduced to the maxim that 'Serbs (always) win in war and lose in peace', which became the axiom of a tragic understanding of national history and gave a new impetus to the myth of Serb heroism, creating a readiness to wage another war. For Ćosić's own interpretation of this 'paradoxical thought', which condenses 'the tragic existence of the Serb nation' and forms the basis of his novel cycle *Vreme smrti* [Time of death], see Slavoljub Đukić, *Čovek u svom vremenu. Razgovori sa Dobricom Ćosićem* [A man of his time: Conversations with Dobrica Ćosić], Belgrade 1989, pp. 236, 336.

Ćosić and others (Matija Bećković, Vuk Drašković) promoted the slogan both before and during the war. It appears in the SANU Memorandum, and its axiomatic nature was further strengthened in a series of interviews in *Politika* in the summer of 1991, when the SANU academicians were asked: 'Could the Serb nation once again win the war and lose the peace?' For some of the answers see Olivera Milosavljević: 'Zloupotreba autoriteta nauke' [Misuse of academic authority], *Republika*, Belgrade, no. 119–20, 1–31, July 1995, pp. xxvii–xxix (the section is omitted in the reprint of the text in Nebojša Popov (ed.), *Srpska strana rata*, English translation details in footnote 4 on p. 6 above).

One sees the same construct in Danko Popović's novel *Knjiga o Milutinu* [The book about Milutin], Književne novine, Belgrade 1986. His 'collective hero', the Serb peasant Milutin, embodying centuries of folk wisdom, laments the 'fatal error' the Serbs had made in liberating their 'brothers' in two world wars so as to form a common state with them, and then being exploited and undervalued by those same 'brothers'. It is therefore time for Serbs to get smart and take care of themselves,

A deeper interpretation of the SANU Memorandum shows that it does not repudiate Yugoslavia, though many see this as its main theme. It postulates Yugoslavia as essential to Serbia, but calls for its reform, asserting that its existing structure is anti-Serb, so that not only is the Serb national issue not resolved, but its solution is becoming more and more difficult and the Serbs more and more endangered. Defining Yugoslavia's problem as fundamentally a Serb problem opened the door to transforming all Federal institutions and organizational components into Serb components. The idea of Yugoslavia, in which communism was supposed to be the homogenizing or cohesive factor, would simply be transformed (as many of yesterday's contributions showed in relation to the JNA) into something which, for a large number of people raised within that ideology, would be identical with Serb interests, since Serb interests were regularly identified with Yugoslav interests and vice versa.

Raising the question of the need to reorganize Yugoslavia changed the Yugoslav question into the Serb question, a process that lasted until its culmination in the war. But it was not fully concluded with the end of the war; it would continue to develop for a long time in the same direction, albeit in different forms.

THE CROATIAN ETHNO-NATIONAL BLUEPRINT

The reorganization of Yugoslavia according to the Serbian ethno-national blueprint involves confrontation with factors opposed to it. Crucial among these is the Croat question, or the existence of the Republic of Croatia, or the existence of legitimate Croat interests. These legitimate Croat interests will offer resistance to the Greater Serbia blueprint, provided they do not take a purely reactive form. Thus from the very start of the moves to reorganize (or destroy) Yugoslavia, the Croatian ethno-national response displays the same ingredients as the Serbian, defining Yugoslavia as also a Croat problem and seeing the resolution of that problem only in the two blueprints which, with natural and logical justification, we can call the Greater Serbian and the Greater Croatian. This blueprint is identical in nature and principle to the Greater Serbian. True, in the hierarchy of causes and consequences, it comes second to the Greater Serbian, but it adopts the latter's essential elements, and has all its four dimensions. It too has

i.e. wage a war whose gains they will successfully preserve. The novel had a huge sale and was an essential factor in shaping the mass psychosis in Serbia on the eve of the war. Some of Milutin's phrases were carried on placards during pro-Milošević demonstrations; cases are known of ritual group recitation by memory of excerpts from the book at public gatherings, and its phraseology entered the vocabulary of the new populism. See Mirko Đorđević, 'Populist wave literature', in Nebojša Popov (ed.), *Srpska strana rata*, pp. 351–72.

an ethno-national elite personified by Franjo Tuđman, except that the Ćosić–Milošević duo is not paralleled in the Croatian case, since Tuđman is at one and the same time the spokesman, the intellectual shaper of the blueprint, and its executive leadership. It too has an ethno-national ideology, which can be explained in all its elements by reference to the elements of the Greater Serbian ideology. Since the goal of the Greater Serbian blueprint is the familiar mantra 'All Serbs in a single state', which disregards the demographic, ethno-national, cultural, religious and every other profile of the region, the response comes in a word-for-word identical formula: 'If Serbia's demand for all Serbs to live in a single state is met, then no one can deny the same right to Croats.' Which is precisely the stance that Tuđman adopted.[3]

Thus for both blueprints the fundamental question becomes that of new borders between what is defined as the attainment of Serbian and Croatian national interests as a whole, a paraphrase of the formula in the public statement made after the Tuđman–Milošević meeting at Karađorđevo: representatives of Croatia and Serbia had agreed to respect 'the interests of the Serbian and Croatian nations as a whole'.[4] The phrase 'as a whole' meant, in essence, that the existing borders within Yugoslavia were to be abolished and new borders established which would realize the fundamentally identical goal of both parties – the creation of two new states on the ruins of Yugoslavia with a simple, sustainable border between them.

[3] Tim Judah: 'Creation of Islamic buffer state discussed in secret', *The Times*, 12 September 1991. As Judah testifies, 'a senior adviser' of Franjo Tuđman, i.e. Mario Nobilo, confirmed to him that secret negotiations were taking place between Tuđman and Milošević 'to resolve the Yugoslav conflict by reshaping the Republic of Bosnia-Herzegovina and establishing an Islamic buffer state between them'. Nobilo said that discussions about such an agreement, which was 'perhaps the best chance of a lasting solution', were held 'at at least two meetings'.

[4] According to the official statement distributed by the state agency HINA, the two presidents met on 25 March 1991 'in the border region of the two republics' during the preparations for the meeting of the six presidents of the Yugoslav republics on 28 March in Split; their 'discussions were held in an effort to remove the options threatening the interests of the Croat or Serb nations as a whole and to seek a durable solution respecting the historical interests of those nations'. *Vjesnik*, 26 March 1991.

It quickly became known that the meeting had been held in Karađorđevo, a state property on the Vojvodina bank of the Danube. In the first Yugoslavia it was owned by the Serb royal house of Karađorđević, while after 1945 it was confiscated and transformed into an exclusive hunting lodge for the new military–political elite. In December 1971 a session of the state leadership was held there, at which the reform leadership of Croatia was removed from office (see note 14, p. 119 above). From then on it became for the Croatian public a symbol of repression and Serb hegemony, so that 20 years later many were convinced that the choice of such a place for the meeting was yet another clear, and very cynical, Greater Serbian message. However, Tuđman remained unperturbed.

But the existence of Bosnia-Herzegovina was a key obstacle to the attainment of this goal. The new border, if it was to conform to their 'interests as a whole', would have to cross Bosnia-Herzegovina, as would be explicitly repeated on many occasions in public: clearly by Tuđman, with considerable restraint by Milošević; but when Milošević is silent one should listen to what Ćosić says, or said.

Both sides, of course, agreed that Bosnia-Herzegovina was an artificial creation, an unnatural construction, which had emerged as a result of unfortunate historical circumstances, for which the presence of Muslims in it was the crucial argument. Since the execution of the plan implied a gradual process, as soon as Tuđman began to demand, understandably and legitimately, the independent statehood of Croatia, he would come up against the fact that the same publicly stated criteria on which he based his demand would also require recognition of the statehood of Bosnia-Herzegovina. The grounds on which Croatia established its right to international recognition after the collapse of Yugoslavia established this right for Bosnia-Herzegovina too. This is a paradox which has remained unexplained: Tuđman publicly recognizes Bosnia-Herzegovina, while tenaciously working to destroy its statehood.

Thus Bosnia-Herzegovina, whose statehood is based on the same legal grounds as Serbia and Croatia, represented a fundamental obstacle to both the Greater Serbian and the Greater Croatian ethno-national blueprints. From the very start of the Yugoslav crisis Bosnia-Herzegovina became directly or indirectly a fundamental question for both Tuđman and Milošević, so that they had to agree at the outset that without its destruction it would be impossible to achieve the objectives in their ethno-political blueprints. Hence, the most important topic at their meetings in Karađorđevo on 25 March and Tikveš on 15 April 1991 was the Muslim issue, with most of the discussion being devoted to the question of how to reduce Bosnia-Herzegovina from an organic whole to three separate parts.

THE REDUCTION OF BOSNIA-HERZEGOVINA
AND THE BOSNIAK CONSENT

It was crucial that the substance of Bosnia-Herzegovina be reduced to what was Bosniak or Muslim, and the more Muslim the better. In this sense the question of B-H ceased to be about the whole country, but was reduced to a Muslim question. Taking into account European prejudices against Islam, it was intended to ensure that the world would understand the problem of Bosnia-Herzegovina as a problem of Islam and a Muslim threat. In his public statements Tuđman frequently expressed overt Islamophobia, trying to find interlocutors in the West or to represent himself as some kind of authorized 'guardian of Christianity' in South Eastern Europe.

This is how we should understand the encouragement for a third element in the projected destruction of B-H: namely, a Muslim state.

From mid 1993, and with significant international assistance, the idea of a Muslim state was becoming a reality on 33.5 per cent of B-H's territory, as postulated in the notorious peace package crafted on the British aircraft carrier *Invincible*, when definitive agreement was actually reached to resolve the crisis by the creation of three states in Bosnia-Herzegovina. The Bosniaks, or more exactly their political representatives headed by Izetbegović, were promised their own state on 33.3 per cent of the territory, and its borders were determined. Drawing borders between the so-called Serb and so-called Croat areas of B-H was not regarded as a problem. Both sides, Boban and Karadžić, or Tuđman and Milošević, said they could easily resolve that problem; the essential thing was for the Muslims, i.e. Izetbegović, to consent to the plan.[5]

Thus the idea of a separate ethno-national state of Bosniaks was legitimized, and the struggle for Bosnia-Herzegovina boiled down to the Bosniaks' renunciation of the country as an organic unity. The Bosniak ethno-national oligarchy agreed that Bosnia-Herzegovina was an assemblage that could not be held together in the circumstances of the war, so that the best solution was to dismantle it. Izetbegović agreed merely to his own ethno-national blueprint, once again constituted as an ethno-national elite and an ethno-national ideology. Political realism demanded the acceptance of a Muslim state, which in the eyes of B-H patriots meant consenting to the suicide of both the Bosniak people and Bosnia-Herzegovina as a state. So the Bosniak political leadership is not blameless for the successive weakening of the Bosnian patriotic alliance and Bosnian state consciousness. This was when the Bosniak organism itself became polarized between forces of resistance and forces of acceptance.

The whole Yugoslav problem, moreover, the entire war against Bosnia-Herzegovina, was thus reduced to the Muslim problem, which Tuđman asserted would be resolved by giving the Muslims a bit of territory around Sarajevo (though obviously, when his calculations are taken into account, no more than about 20 per cent). On 14 January 1992 he spent more than an hour assuring Warren Zimmermann that Bosnia must be partitioned between Serbia and Croatia, but that Croatia was not insisting on a fifty-fifty division.

> Let Milošević take the larger part; he controls it anyway. We can do with less than 50 per cent. We're willing to leave the Muslims a small

---

[5] On the negotiations in Geneva and Brussels in December 1993, when the principle of partition agreed on *Invincible* was worked out in terms of territory, see Hrvoje Šarinić: *Svi moji tajni pregovori sa Slobodanom Miloševićem 1993–95 (98)*. [All my secret negotiations with Slobodan Milošević 1993–95 (98)], Zagreb 1999, pp. 69–84.

area around Sarajevo. They may not like it, but a stable Balkans is possible only if there's a change in Bosnia's borders, no matter what the Muslims think. There's nothing sacred about those borders. Bosnia isn't an old state, like Croatia.[6]

SECESSION FROM THE CENTRE

And now we return to the situation in 1990 and 1991. It was already possible to recognize, in the public arena, all the essential elements of the crisis and its development to the present day; it is vital for contemporary history to demonstrate how certain of these essential elements were seen from the perspective of Bosnia-Herzegovina itself. In the 18 November 1990 B-H elections, three political parties were established whose electoral constituencies lay in the three main ethno-national groups. This happened when what had been Yugoslav had already fundamentally shifted towards being Greater Serbia, when the dissolution of Yugoslavia had already occurred in substance as a result of activities directed from Belgrade. The purpose of those activities was to gain legitimacy through a struggle for Yugoslavia, while bringing about the kind of changes in the whole area that would eventually reduce it to the desired Greater Serbia. Of course, this was not said publicly; it was all about 'protecting Yugoslavia'. But the whole process was leading to a significant homogenization of power in Belgrade, and to its centralization via the JNA and via the usurpation of currency flows, diplomatic resources and so on.

The agents of this project generated reactions centred on Ljubljana, Zagreb, Sarajevo and elsewhere, but then those who had usurped power in Belgrade used these peripheral secessionist trends to bring about the dissolution of Yugoslavia from the centre; not, however, along natural lines of division, but on the basis of newly established borders. If by secession we understand the separation of peripheral elements from the centre, we fail to perceive that it was the 'centre' itself that was secessionist. From the perspective of the Greater Serbian blueprint, the separation of Slovenia really assisted the transformation of the rest of Yugoslavia into Serbia, which is why the 'centre' incited and supported those phenomena that would make the collapse of Yugoslavia inevitable and at the same time push integrative forces into the arms of the Greater Serbian elite. Once the process had begun and the inevitability of secession had become the dominant line of thought, it became possible to call into question the integrity of Yugoslavia's component parts as well as Yugoslavia as a whole. The dissolution of Yugoslavia into the republics of which it had been

[6] Warren Zimmermann, *Origins of a Catastrophe*, Random House, New York 1996, p. 182.

composed was rejected in favour of a wholesale alteration of internal borders in pursuit of the postulated ethno-national unification. If the secession of Slovenia had been accepted as part of a process of wider dissolution, this would have implied returning sovereignty to the republics, which was the interpretation accepted by the Badinter Commission. The republics, moreover, had the constitutional right to resist being broken up. Belgrade was aware that coordinated resistance in the republics to the destruction of the constitutional order would bring the secessionist forces to a halt; for that reason it sought a partner to support it in its efforts to destroy the constitutional order of Bosnia-Herzegovina, in order to prevent the simple dissolution of Yugoslavia into its component parts, the republics.

Mr Mesić has already spoken about this, but yesterday's discussions did not bring out the fact that the real reason why Milošević's plan failed was the resistance in Bosnia-Herzegovina. The plan was absolutely impossible and unrealizable if Belgrade and Sarajevo were to cooperate: if Bosnia-Herzegovina decided to remain in Yugoslavia and reject strategic cooperation with Croatia, so as to stop the dissolution process, then Croatia would not be able to attain its own goal of independence even within its current, internationally recognized borders. The plan was also impossible in the case of an alliance between Zagreb and Sarajevo, for then Serbia would be denied a partner in Croatia with whom to partition Bosnia-Herzegovina and extend its own borders. So the executors of the Serbian ethno-national blueprint offered to the executors of the Croatian ethno-national blueprint the abolition of Bosnia-Herzegovina, though it meant they had to freeze all other conflicts between their two blueprints, including those on Croatian territory, with the idea that in the closing moves, after the conflict with the Bosniaks and the imbroglio in B-H, the Croatian ethno-national blueprint would fail of its own accord. Milorad Ekmečić, who along with Dobrica Ćosić was the key shaper of the Greater Serbian blueprint, clearly said in my presence at a meeting in the first half of 1991 that the blueprint for the partition of Bosnia-Herzegovina would be very useful in achieving Serb aims, since the Croat project would rapidly fail of its own accord at the very moment when it thought it had succeeded.

I am talking of the actual perspective from which the Serbian side offered the Croatian side an agreement about Bosnia-Herzegovina. What lay behind the offer was not any conviction that partition could really be achieved, but rather an intention to involve Croatia in B-H in such a way that, in the context of a general reconstruction of the whole post-Yugoslav region, the Greater Serbian plan would attain its fullest scope, to the detriment of both Bosnia-Herzegovina and Croatia.

At the time we well understood the meaning of Milošević's message to Karadžić that Slovenia might leave Yugoslavia if it so desired, but

Croatia could do so only after redrawing its borders with Serbia.[7] Croatia's demands for state independence imposed on the B-H leadership the need to define their own positions in the coming process. At that time, at the end of 1990, they formulated, and later consistently applied, their strategic position in regard to the Yugoslav crisis: that Bosnia-Herzegovina, as a state, must have the same legal position as Serbia and Croatia in the new situation in the region, and that its relationship with Serbia could be no different from that of Croatia. Seen with hindsight, there were perhaps some deficiencies in the way this position was maintained; but strategically it was entirely correct and ensured the impossibility of destroying Bosnia-Herzegovina.

THE CONCEPT OF ETHNO-NATIONAL TERRITORIALIZATION

The formation, when the old state organizations and institutions were still functioning, of three parties in Bosnia-Herzegovina – the Serbian Democratic Party (SDS), the Croatian Democratic Community (HDZ) and the Party for Democratic Action (SDA) – gave those seeking to implement the Greater Serbian (and later the Greater Croatian) ethno-national blueprints a basis for their attempt, in line with the principle of homogenization from the centre, to link the B-H Serbs with Belgrade and the Croats with Zagreb, so as to block the institutions of Bosnia-Herzegovina itself. From the beginning of 1991 we were confronted with the fact that representatives of the HDZ and SDS on governmental bodies were attempting to block those bodies and subordinate them to Belgrade and Zagreb, so that the situation in Bosnia-Herzegovina should develop in accordance with the original agreement that the country should be destroyed. The military situation was designed for the same purpose. During 1990 and 1991 the JNA disarmed the TO, so as to prevent any legitimate armed resistance by the state of Bosnia-Herzegovina to its destruction, while at the same time members of the SDS were armed. The Bosnian leadership submitted evidence of this to the Federal premier Ante Marković, and Defence Minister Veljko Kadijević, but they either did not want or were not able to do anything about it.

A significant proportion of the JNA's military capacity was relocated to Bosnia-Herzegovina, and people from Serbia were put in command

---

[7] As Slovenian President Milan Kučan later told the American ambassador, immediately after the multiparty elections in Slovenia in November 1990, 'Milošević said to me several times that Slovenia was free to leave Yugoslavia, but he always added that Croatia, with its Serbian minority, must never leave', Zimmermann: *Origins of a Catastrophe*, p. 145. Such public statements by Milošević from the first half of 1991 are also cited by Laura Silber and Allan Little: *The Death of Yugoslavia*, Penguin/BBC, London 1995, p. 142.

positions in all sectors of the army throughout the territory. As a result, the state authorities in B-H were faced with disintegrative trends in the police force, which was internally split and linked to Belgrade, with the JNA as a *de facto* Serb army in every city, and with evidence that the agreement to destroy and partition Bosnia-Herzegovina was already functioning. This was made clear as early as spring 1991, with the emergence of well-defined Serb autonomous regions, followed by the definition of Croat autonomous regions under the joint name of the Croatian Community of Herzeg-Bosna. These structures covered almost the whole of Bosnia-Herzegovina: the first comprised 32,222 square kilometres (62.94 per cent of the territory) and the second 10,689 square kilometres (20.88 per cent of the territory), with another 6,468 square kilometres (12.63 per cent of the territory) overlapping and claimed by both of them, while the remaining area was a mere 1,818 square kilometres, or 3.52 per cent of the territory.[8] Mate Boban once cynically remarked that something had to be left for the Muslims so that they would have graveyards to bury their dead.

So the fact that ethno-national territorialization was the most important tactic adopted in the attempt to destroy Bosnia-Herzegovina testifies to an awareness, on the part of the protagonists of both greater-state blueprints, that the country's very nature was a crucial obstacle on the road to their goals. The 1991 census indicated that B-H Serbs were distributed throughout 94.5 per cent of the territory, Bosniaks through 94 per cent and Croats through 70 per cent; and that they were everywhere so densely intermingled that territorialization, on whatever criteria it was carried out, could only demonstrate the falsity of the assertion that Bosnia-Herzegovina was an artificial construct of three elements. It had never had separate ethno-national or ethno-religious territories. The more the distribution of the population was analysed in detail and in a deeper historical perspective, the more clearly it could be seen to stand in opposition to any idea of destroying the country's real nature. Its organic unity arose from its deepest inner nature, as waters meeting at the mouth of a river, or two ocean currents coming together, merge in layers and depth. It was, in short, a very complex demographic archipelago in a continual state of intermingling. This is not the result of any kind of superficial, rational plan, but of the organic unity of Bosnia-Herzegovina, whose inmost existential instinct calls for intermingling, whereas the rational model yearns for homogeneity, as is clear from the ethno-national blueprints of Milošević and Tuđman.

For these blueprints to be carried out, it was necessary to apply external force, or war, for no kind of political agreement on the creation of ethno-national territories could have produced the desired decomposition of Bosnia-Herzegovina. This required, first of all, dividing the

---

[8] A map and calculations are given in Mahmutćehajić, *Kriva politika*, p. 161.

country politically – division at the level of the ethno-political blueprint – which the HDZ achieved by subordinating the Croat population's political will to Zagreb. The SDS did the same with the B-H Serbs, so that the Bosniaks, as the third component, were pushed into the kind of apparent behaviour that is seen by the world as most negative, the kind of behaviour that will be regarded as proof of the Huntington theory that this is a clash of civilizations – which, in the case of Bosnia-Herzegovina is a fundamentally inaccurate and unprovable construction, but completely in accord with Milošević's and Tuđman's project. It is not surprising therefore that some writers in Zagreb say that for Tuđman, Huntington's theory has become more important than the Bible.[9]

Those of us who were active in the state leadership of Bosnia-Herzegovina were confronted with the fact that the two ethno-national blueprints, both founded on premises incompatible with the survival of

---

[9] US political scientist Samuel Huntington formulated the theory that, after the fall of communism, the basic sources of conflict would no longer be primarily ideological or primarily economic. Instead, the great divisions within humanity, and the dominant causes of conflict, would be cultural in character. Political and ideological borders are replaced by the divisions between civilizations, of which there are eight: the Western, Islamic, Confucian, Japanese, Hindu, Orthodox, Latin American and African. The next great conflict is to be anticipated along the Christian–Islamic fault line. He first advanced the hypothesis in the debate 'The Clash of Civilizations', *Foreign Affairs*, vol. 72, no. 3, Summer 1993, then developed it in *The Clash of Civilizations and the Remaking of World Order*, Simon & Schuster, New York 1996.

A serious critical reaction already appeared in the following issue of *Foreign Affairs*, and again following publication of the book. Numerous critics argued that Huntington's concept of 'civilization' was flawed, and his theory mechanistic and incoherent, burdened with stereotypes and tendentious in its selection of examples, especially in the case of Islam but for the West as well. However, his theory was immediately taken up and enthusiastically promoted in Croatia by the state-controlled media, including television (the assertion of one author that Huntington's 'understanding of global relations coincided with the views of Dr Tuđman' was typical: *Vjesnik*, 13 September 1997). Tuđman himself also referred to the theory directly. In official policy it was welcomed because it enabled the war in Bosnia-Herzegovina to be (re)defined as a clash between Islam and Christianity, and the old concept of the need to divide Bosnia-Herzegovina to be strengthened on a pseudo-scientific basis, as well as reviving the anachronistic metaphor of Croatia as 'ante muralis cristianitatis' and 'the defender of (western) Europe' for new ideological purposes, stereotypes which from the beginning of the break-up of Yugoslavia existed in high international politics, whether unconsciously or as a mask for other interests.

For a selection of international and Croatian critical reactions to Huntington's theory, along with a translation of his first paper, see *Europski glasnik*, Zagreb, vol. 3, no. 3, 1998, pp. 297–415. For a review of reactions, critiques and apologetics in the Croatian press during 1997, see Anđelko Milardović, *Poraz Europe* [The defeat of Europe], *Politološki ogledi 1991–1998*, Panliber, Osijek, Zagreb, Split 1998, pp. 246–67.

Bosnia-Herzegovina, proposed to resolve the crisis by reducing it to a Muslim problem. Thus, as they cynically stated, it would not be insensitive to the legitimate interests of Muslims, i.e Bosniaks, to form their own state in central Bosnia as a revival of the 'little country' of Bosnia mentioned by Constantine Porphyrogenitus in the tenth century, as Tuđman said at the end of 1991.[10]

Internal activities in the institutions of government themselves were going the same way: elements subordinated to Belgrade and Zagreb were seeking to bring about the dissolution of all governmental bodies. Nor is it irrelevant that the forces which understood this and tried to oppose it were weak. They could not offer opposition by appealing to the previous [communist] system. That system did claim to protect Bosnia-Herzegovina, but in the eyes of the people it was dead and completely discredited, since in their view the state should have been the instrument for establishing human rights, the rule of law and democracy for their benefit, all of which communist Bosnia-Herzegovina had failed to do. Bosnia-Herzegovina, like Yugoslavia itself, was for the majority of its population not an instrument for achieving their rights but a way of subordinating those rights to a narrow ideological oligarchy.

Hence there came about an astonishing, impossible congruence between people who were committed to the defence of Bosnia-Herzegovina, but were not formally part of the existing ideological-party system, and the most powerful element of the population in educational terms: people trained in the JNA and formally part of the system, but also committed to the preservation of Bosnia-Herzegovina. The majority of the latter viewed what was happening in Yugoslavia with contempt. They despised Milošević and Tuđman, but they also despised Bosniak politics, which they saw as merely reactionary. But they themselves offered no way out, indeed they impeded the establishment of an effective patriotic alliance. They even deepened the rift between themselves and the small group of former dissidents (ideological, religious and political) who – since the former regime was not conducive to their education and training, since they had been persecuted and retained numerous complexes from their time in prison and their position as outsiders – were incapable of forming and leading a patriotic front such as would overcome the existing ideological disintegration and external pressures.

Such were, approximately, the circumstances in which those who were for defending Bosnia-Herzegovina found themselves. Belgrade and Zagreb had assumed that there could be absolutely no opposition within B-H to the military power already present there in the shape of a *de facto* occupation; that the authorities were in complete disarray and disaccord, hence incapable of offering the people a consistent patriotic basis for defending

[10] On this statement, see note 1, p. 92 above.

the country. To the advocates of destruction and partition it seemed that there was a historic opportunity which must not be lost, and that the task could be very rapidly accomplished, as one individual who had had many discussions with key participants in that destruction told me personally. It was assumed that the war in Bosnia-Herzegovina would last at most three months, and also that some degree of opposition to its destruction was even desirable, as explained by the commander of the JNA Sarajevo corps, General Milutin Kukanjac: 'Small-arms fire by small groups of people, which can be labelled as terrorism, can only provide justification for this huge and invincible force [the JNA] to finish the job.' Of course, in agreement and open collaboration with our western neighbour.

INTEGRISTS AND EXCLUSIVISTS

In April 1991 a number of meetings of B-H intellectuals were held to discuss the political and military situation and analyse possible developments. I have not wished to speak of this before, but now that I have a clearer insight into what was being planned and proposed, I shall outline how the strategy to defend Bosnia-Herzegovina was in fact defined.

First, there was a firm assumption that the country must be defended in its entirety, in all its complexity and diversity, both from Serbia and from Croatia, as a country which could ensure its own survival and the rights of its people; as the country of all those living in it, Serbs, Croats and Bosniaks. All forms of integration with neighbouring countries were desirable, on condition that their point of departure was Bosnia-Herzegovina's complete equality with Serbia and Croatia on the same basis of statehood.

Second, it was judged that the formation of para-state and para-military structures was directly in the interest of those out to destroy Bosnia-Herzegovina and would contribute to the further destruction and collapse of the country, so that it was unacceptable for any kind of preparation or action to develop separately from the state institutions. Since more and more individuals, worried by what was happening, were leaving the JNA and showing themselves ready to join the process of preparing and organizing for defence, they were offered what we called the Patriotic League: not an organization, but a rallying point in regard to current and anticipated developments.

So the country was going to protect itself through its institutions and by affirming its difference from its surroundings; on the basis of a patriotic alliance of all its people, not of one group alone; and in a long time-scale, since in any conflict it was impossible to resolve Bosnia-Herzegovina's crisis, or to block the long-term plan for the destruction of B-H that was being implemented in various forms (with, as I have said, three centres:

147

the Greater Serbian, the Greater Croatian and the Bosniak), if the conflict was brought down to any other than a B-H policy.

This approach, of course, came up against resistance, especially in the intelligence services and other non-public elements of the old system. Those who sought to destroy Bosnia-Herzegovina, meanwhile, soon recognized that their key enemies were not the advocates of exclusivism, whether Serb, Croat or Bosniak (who were, on the contrary, desirable), but the B-H integralists: those who asserted that coexistence in Bosnia-Herzegovina was not merely possible, but an essential condition for the survival both of the Bosniaks and of all B-H's people, and that the blueprint for the country's destruction was not only anti-Bosniak but also anti-Serb and anti-Croat. When one looks at what was being written in Croatia, and indeed in Sarajevo and elsewhere in Bosnia-Herzegovina itself, about those who were creating B-H's defence system, one sees a systematic attempt to vilify the integralists in the eyes of international public opinion, and to promote and support precisely those forms of religious, political and military behaviour which contradicted the integralist idea.

Our attitude was that everything tending towards a general patriotic forum was desirable, if it involved seeking ways to oppose the destruction of the state. This was our stance when the TO was constituted as an organ of Bosnia-Herzegovina's armed resistance, and the Patriotic League was fully integrated into that legal structure, significantly strengthening it, not as a separate organization but as a broad patriotic forum. The start of the war thus did not find the B-H forces, including a significant part of the political and state leadership, unprepared. Contrary to all expectations, the Army of Bosnia-Herzegovina arose very rapidly out of the Patriotic League, and by mid 1993 was established as such a large force that the Milošević–Tuđman plan had to fail. Its emergence provoked changes in strategic relations, for it became clear that the war could last for a long time, and that while Bosnia-Herzegovina could be seriously damaged it could not be finally destroyed.

International factors were also exerting pressure on the Bosniak leadership to give up the idea of an integral Bosnia-Herzegovina. When, after the Vance–Owen plan was abandoned in mid 1993, the international community began to shape a solution based on the so-called union of three (ethnonational) republics, Lord Owen 'advised [Izetbegović] to start negotiations [with Boban and Karadžić] as soon as he judged opinion in his country could accept his doing so'. Izetbegović responded that he was 'worried' that the public in Bosnia-Herzegovina was against the ethnic partition of the country, while he himself 'had grasped the reality that the face of Bosnia had changed', that 'partition had taken place on the ground'.[11] Somewhat later Izetbegović agreed to negotiate, which 'showed that [he] was now

---

[11] David Owen, *Balkan Odyssey,* Indigo, London 1996, p. 208.

moving towards a separate Muslim republic and that realistic talk of keeping Bosnia-Herzegovina together was over'.[12] From Owen's perspective, the Bosniak leadership's giving up the idea of Bosnia-Herzegovina was good news, since it at last made possible what he called 'realistic negotiations' or 'realistic policies'. While exerting such pressure, the international community deliberately concealed the nature of the war and of the crimes being committed, and denied the primacy of justice, promoting instead the formula of 'sympathy for the victims', 'saving the Bosniak people from complete destruction' or 'preserving whatever can be preserved'.

Within the Bosniak leadership too, i.e. among politicians of Bosniak nationality, a marked polarization began. Because of powerful external support for the forces of destruction and disintegration, the advocates of Bosnia-Herzegovina's integrity were systematically pushed aside and excluded from the decision-making process. But they survived and are the guarantee of a future for the country, whatever the pressures from Belgrade and Zagreb, and whatever the activities of the third component, the Bosniak exclusivists, all of whom enjoy various forms of external assistance.

THREE ILLUSIONS ABOUT BOSNIA-HERZEGOVINA

I now want to outline briefly a few points which are often overlooked. First, Yugoslavia and Bosnia-Herzegovina are often compared, with the assertion that both were created unnaturally, forcibly and artificially, so that the break-up of the first implied the break-up of the second. But these two states are not comparable: Bosnia-Herzegovina has existed culturally, historically, and indeed politically, for more than 1,000 years, while Yugoslavia was a historically short-lived collection of different, separate identities, joined in a fundamentally artificial way and thus liable to disintegrate. Application of the same logic to Bosnia-Herzegovina is unfounded; when it appears, it clearly forms a part of the ideology of an anti-Bosnian blueprint.

Second, the assertion, often made, that Bosnia-Herzegovina is a multicultural country is basically inaccurate. On the contrary, Bosnia-Herzegovina is culturally, historically, politically and linguistically more homogeneous than any of its neighbours, so that it is possible to speak of the multicultural content of Serbia, even of Croatia, but not of Bosnia-Herzegovina. From its westernmost to its easternmost point, from its most northerly to its most southerly, there are no fundamental differences in language. The majority of the population are of the same ethno-genetic stock, and the finest anthropologist in the world could not find any anthropological difference among the people of Bosnia-Herzegovina, whatever they may be called.

[12] Ibid., p. 224.

Of course, Bosnia-Herzegovina is a multireligious country, and its enemies attempt on this basis to present it as an historical freak, where people cannot live together but need to be separated, as Dobrica Ćosić and Franjo Tuđman publicly agree. When coopted by ethno-national blueprints, religion certainly is a key factor in producing inner pressures and conflicts. But during the past two centuries, the period of ethno-national projects, religion has been undergoing a process of atheization; it has lost its essentially religious content, so that in Bosnia-Herzegovina today the understanding of religion has lost any sense of universality. The country's religions are totally subordinated to the ethno-national blueprints, making it possible to use religion for purposes of domination. The revitalization of Bosnia-Herzegovina requires the revitalization of attitudes towards religion, and its liberation from its current subordination to political, ethno-national, oligarchic and particularist interests. It seems to me that such changes are already visible in all three major religions, though not yet as powerful or recognizable as they need to be. This is something to be thought about by all those whose intentions towards the future of Bosnia-Herzegovina are good. As I have said, reduction of the country to different cultural components is fundamentally part of the anti-Bosnian blueprints, since these components are reduced entirely to religious differences, to present-day religious consciousness, and subordinated to exclusivist blueprints. For Bosnia-Herzegovina to be revitalized, its cultural unity must be understood and the misuse of any differences must be combated.

Third, it is often, and inaccurately, stated that Bosnia-Herzegovina was unprepared for resistance. It was in Bosnia-Herzegovina that the most sophisticated preparations were made and a resistance offered which has prevented our enemies from fulfilling their original plan for the final destruction of the country. We cannot say at this point that Bosnia's defence has won, but it certainly was not defeated, which is a huge success, given the forces in operation. This has given us a basis for attaining the final objective: a normal society in which the freedom of peoples necessarily requires the freedom of individuals. As long as there is a single Serb in Bosnia-Herzegovina who does not consider himself free to enjoy all his human rights, Bosnia-Herzegovina is not free; and the same is true for Bosniaks and Croats.

In the present situation created by the war, the goodwill of international players – who rarely act as a community – is concentrated on preventing the possibility of new conflicts (the presence of NATO makes the likelihood of such conflicts insignificant or non-existent), while foreign aid is concentrated on the economic revival of the country and its state institutions. All this is vital, but not sufficient, since the real potential in Bosnia-Herzegovina, which was not taken account of in the ethno-national blueprints, calls for greater assistance. I am thinking of reconstitution of the knowledge and feeling of B-H unity, which the war did not destroy. Unfortunately, outsiders often have no understanding of this kind of thinking, though it is Bosnia-

Herzegovina's best protection as a state of equals where the rights of all are protected regardless of their differences: a state which is an instrument for protecting those rights and the rule of law, as well as a framework for democratic development and integration into broader democratic trends. So Bosnia-Herzegovina continues to be exposed to powerful external influences, not only in the form of propaganda, but in many practical forms.

FOR A DIFFERENT POLITICAL LOGIC

Since the logic of neighbouring states is based on the ethno-national concept, which in Bosnia-Herzegovina could lead only to ethno-national separatism and then to the country's disintegration, what can ensure its survival is support against the involvement of neighbouring states and for the establishment of a different political logic. Such support is not at present sufficiently forthcoming, whereas economic renewal (an entirely rational concept) is given even more support than is needed. The many-faceted character of B-H culture is ignored, as is the complex issue of how long-lasting outside influences can create a mentality of distrust. This must be met by building confidence, but not on the basis of a simplistic understanding of tolerance as indifference towards other traditions, but of a tolerance which finds its source at the deepest level of our ethnic and religious – particularly religious – affiliation.

Bosnia-Herzegovina has not survived during these thousand years merely as a rational concept. Its history witnesses that Catholics, Orthodox Christians, Muslims and Jews could live together, not in paradise, which does not exist on earth, but in life as it could be lived. That co-existence did not derive from a balance of power or terror, but from mutual respect derived from the very essence of the sacred traditions to which these people belonged. The new era did not produce its own response by discursive political thinking, so the people of Bosnia-Herzegovina found themselves in a dilemma between their own feelings, which led them to love their neighbours regardless of their religion, and the cerebral, reductionist concepts of the ethno-national programmes, which invited them to coalesce as a unity – with an external centre – despite their own interests and despite their obligations towards their neighbours.

Because events changed rapidly and external circumstances were unfavourable, Bosnia-Herzegovina was not able to overcome the contradiction and create a consistent, rational self-interpretation. I hope that, after the failure of the war against it, this task will after all be carried out; and that Bosnia-Herzegovina will find that consistent self-interpretation in the majority of its people, and upon it build a society in which the state will be able to protect all collective and individual rights.

7

The First Phase, 1992–1993: struggle for survival and genesis of the Army of Bosnia-Herzegovina

Jovan Divjak

Despite all the effort put into the preparation, organization and realization of this seminar, it cannot provide full answers to the questions posed by the war in former Yugoslavia, since for that the people who bear responsibility for the aggression against Croatia and Bosnia-Herzegovina should also be sitting here. I would like to see such people as Andrija Rašeta or Milutin Kukanjac at seminars like this. We see Belgrade and the JNA as the main culprits, but the accused are not in a position to give their assessment of the events of 1991–95. I have been to several international seminars, and in every case one of the 'warring parties'[1] was absent, which meant also an absence of academic objectivity. Since we too made mistakes and bear part of the responsibility for the war in what was until recently our common homeland, I have to say how glad I am that on this occasion we have heard considerable criticism of what happened in our own countries. But enough of that, and to work.

In the first part of my presentation I shall give a broad overview in which I shall address the issue of the military organization of the aggressor: basically the JNA, volunteers from Serbia and Montenegro, and paramilitary units of B-H Serbs.

MILITARY AND POLITICAL PREPARATIONS FOR AGGRESSION AGAINST BOSNIA-HERZEGOVINA

From the earliest days of the formation of the government in Bosnia-Herzegovina after the first democratic elections, the Serb Democratic Party

---

[1] I put the phrase in quotation marks, since neither UN Security Council resolutions nor the Dayton documents have ever named the aggressor, but always spoken of 'warring parties'. Security Council Resolution 724 is an exception, but of that more later.

(SDS), which was a participant in every governmental body in proportion to the number of votes it had obtained, obstructed the vote in the Assembly and sought to destroy the legitimate government. Acting as a fifth column, in many regions of the republic it took on the role of a collaborationist body with links to the government of Serbia, as many documents prove. By November 1991, of a total of 109 municipalities more than 50 had been taken over by these unconstitutional procedures, though more than 20 of them did not have an absolute Serb majority. These municipalities came together into five Serb autonomous regions (SAO): on 12 September the SAO of Herzegovina was proclaimed, on 16 September the SAO of Bosnian Krajina, on 19 September the SAO of Romanija; later another two were formed, in Semberija and in the Ozren-Posavina region. During a debate in the B-H Assembly, broadcast live on television, Karadžić publicly threatened the Bosniaks with extinction, since they would not be able to defend themselves if war broke out.[2]

Serbian extremists organized an illegal and unsupervised plebiscite on 9–10 November, which offered Serbs a choice between an independent

---

[2] The four-day session of the B-H Assembly, several times interrupted, debated the motion according to which Bosnia-Herzegovina was to be 'a democratic, sovereign state of equal citizens – the peoples of Bosnia-Herzegovina – Muslims, Serbs, Croats and the members of other peoples and nationalities who live there' (*Oslobođenje*, 15 October 1991). That motion, submitted by the SDA with the support of the HDZ, was to be presented at the Peace Conference in The Hague as a *letter of intent* of the B-H authorities. Karadžić, who was not a member of the Assembly nor had any state function but nonetheless regularly participated in Assembly debates, took the floor in the evening of 14 October and said at the top of his voice that 'we have ways' of preventing Bosnia-Herzegovina from 'going the way of Slovenia and Croatia. Don't think that you will not lead Bosnia-Herzegovina into hell, and the Muslim nation perhaps to annihilation, since the Muslim nation cannot defend itself if there is war.' Izetbegović replied, 'The Muslim nation will not raise a hand against anyone, but will energetically defend itself, and will not, as Karadžić says, disappear … We really have no intention of living in a Yugoslavia built on the basis of messages such as Mr Karadžić's.' The president of the Assembly, Krajišnik (SDS), ignoring the rules of procedure, then proclaimed the session concluded and the SDS representatives ostentatiously left the hall.

The vice-president, Mariofil Ljubić (HDZ) took over as chair of the meeting. Since it had been determined that there was a quorum for passing valid resolutions, on 15 October at 3 a.m. the representatives voted for a Memorandum, basically a confirmation of Amendment LX to the B-H Constitution and the B-H Presidency's Working Paper on the position of Bosnia-Herzegovina and the future structure of the Yugoslav community. Both documents had contained the crucial stipulations that Bosnia-Herzegovina was 'a sovereign and indivisible state' equal in status to Serbia and Croatia, that it would not remain in a truncated Yugoslavia (without Slovenia and, especially, Croatia), and that it did not recognize resolutions of the rump Federal bodies. See *Oslobođenje* or *Vjesnik* of 15 and 16 October 1991. For a short description of the session see also Laura Silber and Allan Little: *The Death of Yugoslavia*. Penguin/BBC, London 1995, pp. 237–8.

Bosnia-Herzegovina and remaining within Yugoslavia, then on the basis of falsified results announced that the majority had voted for the second option. On these grounds the SDS Deputies' Club in the B-H Assembly renamed itself the Assembly of the Serb Nation in Bosnia-Herzegovina and from then on ceased to implement the decisions of the legal bodies of the republic and began to receive their orders direct from the government of what was then still the Socialist Republic of Serbia. Finally a 'sovereign' Serb Republic of Bosnia-Herzegovina was proclaimed on 9 January 1992 in Pale, composed of the five SAOs and some districts; and on 27 March the self-styled Assembly of the Serb Nation in B-H even proclaimed a Constitution of the Serb Republic of Bosnia-Herzegovina (later abbreviated to Republika Srpska). As the height of cynicism, this was done in Sarajevo, in the building of the B-H Assembly, and the session was chaired by Momčilo Krajišnik, still president of the joint Assembly of Bosnia-Herzegovina.

At the military level, preparations were being carried out which gave the JNA the task of 'protecting the Serb nation in Bosnia-Herzegovina'. Following orders from the general staff of the armed forces of SFRY, as well as of political and military figures in Serbia and Montenegro, the JNA was systematically arming members and sympathizers of the SDS. When the command of the 2nd (Sarajevo) military sector left barracks on 3 May, we seized documents which showed that this arming of Serbs had begun in the Foča region as early as 1990, and that during 1991 arms from JNA depots were distributed to individuals and units in Vogošća, Ilijaš, Hadžići, Breza, Visoko, Doboj, Brčko, Bihać and other places where there had been garrisons before or new ones had been organized in the meantime. These documents of the 2nd military sector showed that by 19 March 1991 the JNA had distributed about 51,900 firearms to Serb volunteer units, and that members of the SDS had received 23,298 firearms.

At the beginning of hostilities, during April, May and June 1992, some firearms were found in apartments in Sarajevo where members of the SDS were living. One of the three snipers arrested on 6 April by Ministry of Interior special police while they were firing from the Holiday Inn on the crowd gathered in front of the B-H Assembly building was Branko Kovačević, deputy secretary for national defence of Sarajevo and before that personal secretary to Radovan Karadžić. I know also that some of my officer colleagues allocated to the TO had commanded units carrying out attacks on Croatia.

General Veljko Kadijević speaks without a twinge of conscience of the involvement of the JNA in the hostilities against Croatia and Bosnia-Herzegovina. He says that the JNA, 'in exceptionally unfavourable international and internal circumstances, completed the missions it had been given'. In Croatia, 'together with the Serb people it liberated Serb Krajina and forced Croatia to accept the Vance Peace Plan'.[3] In Bosnia-Herzegovina it

> made it possible for first the JNA, and then the Army of Republika Srpska which the JNA set up, to liberate Serb territory, protect the Serb people and create a military situation in which the interests and rights of the Serb people in Bosnia-Herzegovina could be achieved by political means, to the extent and in the conditions which international circumstances permitted.[4]

After the ceasefire in the Croatian war was signed on 2 January 1992, some of the JNA units from Croatia were relocated to the Bosnian Krajina, Tuzla, Derventa and Brčko, while new corps were formed where previously there had been none. The deployment of JNA units to Bosnia-Herzegovina was carried out without the agreement of the B-H Presidency. Thus in April 1992 the 4th, 5th, 13th and 17th corps and the 5th air force corps (in Bihać) were all stationed in the 2nd and 4th military sectors, which covered the territory of Bosnia-Herzegovina. The Zadar artillery training centre was moved to Sarajevo, and part of the Knin corps arrived in Bihać. Its commanding officer, with the rank of colonel, was Ratko Mladić, who had been appointed commanding officer of the Serb army in B-H, the Army of Republika Srpska (VRS), on 15 May 1992. The overall strength of these corps amounted at the time to between 90,000 and 100,000 well armed men, cadets and officers, 750 to 800 tanks, about 1,000 armoured personnel carriers and other armoured vehicles, more than 4,000 mortars and artillery weapons, and up to 100 fixed-wing aircraft and 50 helicopters.

JNA units occupied and controlled the operational-strategic routes leading from the Drina to central Bosnia, which means that they were able to keep under surveillance everything going from Serbia towards Sarajevo and Tuzla. They took up positions around the major towns – Sarajevo, Tuzla, Bihać, Mostar – and joined in the genocide of Bosniaks and deportation of the non-Serb population. The occupation of positions around Sarajevo began as early as the end of 1991, with the excuse that they were carrying out exercises of artillery units in preparation for defence of the city in the event of attack by the West.

The first JNA action was carried out by units of the Užice and Podgorica corps, which included formations and volunteers from Serbia and Montenegro. It is worth recalling that at the end of November or the

---

[3] Veljko Kadijević, *Moje viđenje raspada: vojska bez države* [My view of the break-up: an army without a state], Belgrade 1993, p. 162. See also p. 128.

[4] Ibid., p. 162. He says elsewhere that 'commands and units of the JNA formed the backbone of the Army of Republika Srpska kitted out with arms and equipment', p. 148.

beginning of December 1991, the rump Presidency of Yugoslavia (representatives of Macedonia, Slovenia, Croatia and Bosnia-Herzegovina had already left) had passed a resolution that volunteers would not be treated as such, but would form part of the regular standing army. The entry of the JNA and 'volunteers' into eastern Herzegovina as far as the area above Mostar was justified with the pretext that it was protecting Mostar's military airport and the Serb population of eastern Herzegovina from the 'Turks' – an expression frequently used in the rhetoric of Ratko Mladić, Radovan Karadžić and Momčilo Krajišnik to evoke associations with the Kosovo myth, and thus make it easier to mobilize the local Serb population. In this way the JNA occupied Bosnia-Herzegovina by stealth, without resistance. General Milutin Kukanjac once said, after his departure from Sarajevo: 'I handed over territory with the borders of Republika Srpska to Mladić, and he lost it.'

The hostilities in Bosnia-Herzegovina began with a massacre of older members of the population in a wide area around the village of Ravno, after they were accused of attacking JNA units which were at the time fighting in Croatia and attacking Dubrovnik. Since its formation the VRS had operated from positions established by the JNA. Its first objective was to reach the left bank of the Neretva, with which it would gain control of the whole of eastern Herzegovina, and of the valley of the Krivaja river to the north, and the line Doboj – Maglaj – Zavidovići – Olovske luke – Romanija. This would divide Bosnia-Herzegovina into two, and completely block any kind of manoeuvres by resistance forces. They already had the Bosnian Krajina under their control. The aim was also to occupy the entire Posavina region, making the Sava the border with Croatia. At Sarajevo, the objective was to reach the left bank of the Miljacka. This added up to the 66 per cent of B-H territory which Karadžić had from the start described as belonging to the Serbs.

General Špegelj and Professor Mahmutćehajić have already spoken of the national composition of the JNA at this time, but I want to add something further: of 15 command positions at the rank of general in the corps of the 2nd military sector, which took part in the occupation by stealth of Bosnia-Herzegovina, 12 were held by Serbs, one by a Montenegrin, one by a Croat and one by a Bosniak (the Croat was in the operations centre of the 4th corps, the Bosniak in the TO).

WHAT ENABLED BOSNIA-HERZEGOVINA TO SURVIVE THE FIRST PHASE OF THE WAR?

The aggressor obviously set an unrealistic aim for the occupation of Bosnia-Herzegovina, under conditions when he was engaged in a war with two adversaries and on very extended fronts. We have data about plans to take Sarajevo within seven to ten days, and the whole of Bosnia-Herzegovina within three or four months; but that goal was shattered from the start, since the JNA had greatly underestimated the human factor. Apart from numerical advantage, the defence enjoyed high morale, had strong patriotic feelings and was able to rely on the population, especially in the larger cities.

After an initial success in attacks on towns in the Drina valley and the rapid conquest of most of eastern Bosnia, the aggressor was compelled to cut back his unrealistic plans to attainable goals as soon as he came up against the first organized resistance and began to suffer losses. The euphoria began to evaporate, and from then on the enemy attempted to proceed step by step, a little in this direction, a little in that, moving ahead faster where he succeeded and stopping where he did not. The early impetus also faded because in May 1992 the UN Security Council ordered the JNA and other paramilitary units from Serbia and Croatia to leave Bosnia-Herzegovina, which had in the meantime been recognized as an independent state by the European Union.

Due to the defeatist behaviour of the Bosnian government (on this I perhaps differ from Professor Mahmutćehajić), its incompetence and superficial knowledge and monitoring of the military and political situation, the defence amounted to no more than sporadic and spontaneous armed resistance by individuals and groups on the outskirts of residential areas surrounded by hostile forces. How else to describe the early assessments of the situation by those in responsible positions in the government? First, that there would be no war in Bosnia-Herzegovina; then that while it was possible that war would break out, it could never do so in Sarajevo; after which they said that an agreement would be reached with the JNA to transform part of that force into the TO of the Republic of Bosnia-Herzegovina! And while the government was still getting its bearings, patriotic forces organized in the Patriotic League, the *Zelene beretke* [Green Berets] (or various of its units designated as Bosna-1, Bosna-2, etc.), together with police detachments were, at first spontaneously but soon in organized fashion, putting up a more or less successful resistance against the aggressor.

On 4 April the JNA and the Chetniks began to shell the suburbs of Sarajevo and the city itself. This was actually test firing, to get the correct range for artillery fire. The following day the police station in Vraca, Sarajevo, was attacked, and on 6 April the JNA and the Chetniks attacked Foča and began their mass killings and expulsions of Bosniaks, with looting and destruction. At the 4 April session of the B-H Presidency it was resolved that 'TO units of each municipality and of the city of Sarajevo be mobilized, including communications units', that the entire police force be mobilized, and that 'the competent bodies of the JNA be required to return to TO units, and to municipal and regional TO headquarters, the arms, military equipment and other material and technical resources handed over to them for storage'. Every municipality could, according to this resolution, decide on the mobilization of its own TO.

A key moment in the defence of Bosnia-Herzegovina was the Presidency's decision on 8 April 1992 to form the Territorial Defence of the Republic of Bosnia-Herzegovina (TORBiH), following the abolition of the republican TO Staff, whose command structure, all Serbs, with its commandant General Vukosavljević, had crossed over into the 2nd military sector of the JNA and thus betrayed the state. Colonel Hasan Efendić was appointed commanding officer of the TORBiH Staff, with Colonel Stjepan Šiber as its chief of staff and Colonel Jovan Divjak as deputy chief of staff and chief operations officer. At the same session a resolution was passed declaring an immediate threat of war, and it was resolved that decisions on the use of the TO should be made by the Presidency, abolishing the dual command in TO headquarters.

ROLE OF THE TO AND FORMATION OF THE ARMY OF BOSNIA-HERZEGOVINA

I do not know if there is another case in history of a state being internationally recognized, as was Bosnia-Herzegovina on 6 April 1992, without having an organized army with which to defend its constitutional and territorial integrity. According to the 1990 Constitution of Bosnia-Herzegovina, the TO was responsible for defence of the republic against internal enemies; but it was prevented from fulfilling its function because it had been disarmed and because its command structure included people who supported the idea of Greater Serbia. It had handed over more than 300,000 assorted firearms to the JNA depots – rifles, light mortars and artillery weapons, and the small quantity of armour in its possession – and was the only republican TO fully to conform to the decision of the JNA's General Staff of May 1990 that all armaments be placed under JNA control.

The 8 April decision of the Presidency to form a TO was rapidly put into effect. That same day and the day after, 40 out of 48 former staff members indicated in writing their loyalty to the new TO staff, and by 12 April the report on the organization of regional staffs was on Colonel Efendić's desk. In 1990 there had been nine regional TO staffs in Bosnia-Herzegovina, and of those seven confirmed in writing that they accepted the decision of the state Presidency to form a new TORBiH staff, as did 73 municipal staffs out of a total of 109. These were municipalities with Bosniak and Croat majorities, while the others had a Serb majority or – as in the case of Foča, Višegrad, Zvornik and Bijeljina – the Bosniak majority had already been expelled. That same day we had a list of 75,000 people of all nationalities who had presented themselves to local TO commands volunteering to defend their country. The Presidency decision required all units of the Patriotic League, the *Zelene beretke*, etc. to join the TO by 15 April, and for the TO to unify all the armed defence forces and develop an organized resistance. The general staff of the Patriotic League joined the TORBiH staff immediately, on 12 April.

According to the Law on Defence and the Presidency Decision, the armed forces of B-H were composed of the Army of the Republic of Bosnia-Herzegovina (ARBiH), the Croatian Defence Council (HVO), the military police and the TO units of larger factories and institutions. An argument is still raging in Bosnia-Herzegovina to this day about who first came to the defence of the country and who made the greatest contribution in the first phase – the Patriotic League and other extra-institutional groups, or the TO, or the police. We have heard what Professor Mahmutćehajić thinks about that. I know that General Sefer Halilović also takes the view that it was the Patriotic League that organized country-wide resistance to the aggressor. On the other hand, we who were in the TO from the first day strongly contend that it was the TO that defended Bosnia-Herzegovina in the first phase, together of course with other patriotic forces.[5] A Directive for defence of the sovereignty and independence of the Republic of Bosnia-Herzegovina was drawn up by the TO staff on 12 April, and forwarded to the subordinate staffs. I have reliable knowledge that the essential elements of this Directive were formulated as early as the end of 1991 by people in the Patriotic League, and since one of the League's organizers and conceptual framers was Professor Mahmutćehajić himself, I should like him to tell us something about that later.

I shall quote a few excerpts from a copy of the Directive that I have personally retained, as one of its authors:

Concerning the enemy forces: Enemy forces (units of the TO SAO and Yugoslav Army) have succeeded in part, through their military and political activities to date, in destroying the system of governance and tearing Bosnia-Herzegovina apart ... The basic objective of the enemy's action is to occupy territory and to form artificial national borders, to establish a Serb Republic of B-H and, in the next phase, to merge it with the Republic of Serbia.

Concerning our own forces: TORBiH forces and the armed population are unified under the sole command of the TO Staff of the Republic of Bosnia-Herzegovina, and shall continue the further expansion,

[5] For these opposing views, see Sefer Halilović: *Lukava strategija*. [A devious strategy], Sarajevo 1997, and Hasan Efendić: *Ko je branio Bosnu*.[Who defended Bosnia), Sarajevo 1999. Halilović was one of those who organized the Patriotic League and was later chief of staff of the General Staff of ARBiH, while Efendić was the first commander of TORBiH. The Directive referred to here is reproduced in Efendić's book, on p. 127.

consolidation and successful defence of the entire territory of the Republic with the basic objective of protecting the lives and material wealth of the citizens of the Republic of Bosnia-Herzegovina.

Meriting particular attention: Clause 6.1. Emphasize the significance of supplementing combat units with members of the Serb and Croat nationalities, with the objective of restoring confidence and creating the conviction that our only possibility is coexistence and not the partition of Bosnia-Herzegovina.

Unfortunately, because of poor security or poor cryptographic protection, our Directive reached Radovan Karadžić's desk that same day, and he immediately used it as confirmation that 'the Muslims are launching a war against Serbs'.

After the initial spontaneous self-mobilizations of the people in April 1992 – on the streets, in residential areas and local communities, headed by self-appointed local commandants who posted security guards opposite the sentry-posts and positions where Bosnian Serb paramilitaries had previously been posted – by May and June people were joining organized TO units: platoons, companies and battalions. Brigades were formed in June and July, corps from September to the end of 1992.

For the sake of truth it must be said that in many places the police, who were better organized and armed in April and May, played a decisive role in the defence of areas with a majority Bosniak population, especially in Sarajevo. The defence of the cities of Sarajevo, Tuzla, Mostar, Goražde, Bihać, Maglaj, Kalesija and others, of vital strategic importance for the defence of Bosnia-Herzegovina as a whole against the more powerful aggressor forces, bought time for organizing and planning the defence. Many problems arose during this first phase of defence, which went on right up to the end of the war.

- Shortages of arms, munitions and all forms of military hardware and technical resources (signals; engineer/sapper corps; atomic, biological and chemical defence). It was really incredible that we were able to defend Sarajevo at all, given the lack of sophisticated weapons and engineer and signals resources, and since we did not even have shovels to dig simple trenches, to say nothing of mechanical diggers, especially in the cities which had been surrounded from day one.
- Lack of adequate uniforms, footwear and other quartermaster stores. About 75 per cent of the members of the armed forces spent the first year of the war in civilian clothes and shoes, in jeans and trainers, and I even found some youngsters at their posts in winkle-pickers. Some wore the blue uniform of the Civil Defence, and some even the clothing of volunteer youth workers brigades. Their insignia were very diverse

too, from TO and Patriotic League badges via the coats of arms of various towns (Tuzla, Mostar) to armbands.

- Lack of professional personnel to fill the most important posts in the command of brigades and corps. On the one hand, as in Croatia, there was widespread mistrust of JNA officers, not only those who had joined the defence at the beginning of the war but also those who had long been in retirement. Thus it happened that one highly trained JNA major, who had graduated from the technical faculty in Zagreb, joined the TO and was killed as an ordinary soldier on the front line. On the other hand, many brigades were commanded by people who had not even done military service, and in one, with more than 5,000 men, they were actually boasting that they did not have a single officer or NCO from the former JNA! It took a long time for the leadership to understand that a militarily uneducated patriot who might have made a significant contribution to the defence of parts of the town, defending his street along with his mates, simply did not have the knowledge to go about lifting the siege of the city.

- The training and exercises of command units were not at the level required to be effective in combat. In Sarajevo, furthermore, there was nowhere to carry out such activities, nor would it have been possible because of the uninterrupted military activity, unlike the situation in Croatia from 1992 to 1994, when the army had both weapons and the time and place for training. Because of this, the results of the fighting were poor: there were many casualties, while the results were not commensurate with the number of victims.

- Until mid 1993 the war took the form of classic trench warfare as in the First World War. In Sarajevo, for example, two thirds of the defence lines remained unaltered from June 1992 to December 1995, a period of three and a half years. At the beginning of the war the aggressor held Sarajevo in a 46 kilometres ring, but by the end of 1993 we had expanded that to 64 kilometres, and that was how it remained until the end of the war. The first victories, which ensured that besieged Sarajevo could breathe, were the seizure, or retaking, of positions in Dobrinja and Mojmilo. This was an area of some 600 square metres dominating the Lukavica and Pofalići barracks, a residential neighbourhood with a Serb majority population that had been wedged in at the outset of the aggression, when it had been armed and directed to link up with forces aiming to bisect Sarajevo from Vraca to the Marshal Tito barracks. The area was occupied and extended during 1992 and 1993, and the situation did not alter until the end, though every three or four months the ARBiH organized and carried out assaults in various directions where possible breaches were anticipated.

- During the whole of the war the army and the minister of interior failed to cooperate fully, though the military police were an integral part of the armed forces.

The progress of the army from its initial formation to a firm organizational structure, from classic defence to active attack, had its ups and downs, in which the civilian authorities played a negative part. They failed to ensure the material resources needed for a more effective armed struggle, and meddled excessively in the command and control of the armed forces. Rusmir Mahmutćehajić was one of the few members of government who devoted his energies to developing military production, but he was not well understood; so a lack of material resources resulted from double or even triple management. This was especially true of supplies, which were in the hands of a group of people directly connected with the SDA party leadership. At the beginning there were as many as four management channels: the TO had its own system, but the Patriotic League continued for a long time to conduct some actions according to its own plans. The influence of the SDA as the leading Bosniak party grew stronger and stronger, and the subsequent politicization of the army impacted on the defence.

All this, together with the involvement of clergy and the introduction of religion into the armed forces during 1993, led to the genesis of a mononational structure and politics that contradicted the presidential platform for the defence of multinational, multireligious, multicultural Bosnia-Herzegovina. The country thus lost the democratic image it had at the beginning, when all its peoples were defending it against aggression.

SIEGE AND DEFENCE OF SARAJEVO

Taking the 1st (Sarajevo) corps of the ARBiH and the 1st (Sarajevo-Romanija) corps of the VRS as examples, I shall show the ratio of forces in Sarajevo during the war.

Neither as the TORBiH nor as the ARBiH did we ever have manpower problems. As early as May 1992 we had 75,000 volunteers, although the authorities for reasons unknown to me claim that the number was smaller, somewhere between 15,000 and 20,000. The following year we had as many as 200,000 people on our list in the country as a whole, though not all of them were armed. In 1994 we reached a total of 250,000. The basic problem was that we did not have even one rifle per soldier. The city of Sarajevo itself, with 350,000 inhabitants, had some 30,000 to 35,000 people under arms, or rather in units, although with better organization there could have been more. But we had, for example, only six semi-automatic sniper rifles; and in all other categories, as the table shows, we were greatly inferior to the enemy. And that was in the corps which was the largest, numerically speaking, at that time, and which was protecting Sarajevo, and to some extent the whole country, though there had at one time been a plan to move the Presidency and government to Zenica, in which case Sarajevo would have ceased to be the pivot of Bosnia-Herzegovina.

Table 9 Manpower and equipment of the 1st (Sarajevo) corps of the Army of Bosnia-Herzegovina, 1992–95, and the Sarajevo–Romanija corps of the Army of Republika Srpska, 1992–95

Manpower/arms 1st corps, Army of Republika Srpska	Sarajevo–Romanija corps, Army of B-H			
	1992	1995	1992	1995
Manpower	28,900	20,670	35,400	40,500
Infantry weapons				
Semi-automatic rifles	8,267	5,155	1,694	3,114
Automatic rifles	8,717	11,341	2,340	23,521
Sniper rifles	285	196	6	75
Automatic rifle–machine guns	996	1,031	128	724
Machine guns	354	295	154	630
M-48 rifles	45	35	96	131
60mm mortars	11	132	35	155
80mm mortars	108	97	28	446
Automatics	10	10	20	30
Anti-tank weapons				
Zolja	782	310	95	1,328
Osa	523	206	24	77
Recoilless rifles	30	38	18	73
Zis	25	21	–	–
SO90	3	–	–	–
T-12 cannon	4	5	–	–
Anti-tank guided missiles	–	10	–	5
SA 76/90	–	9	–	–
POLK 9K11 launchers	42	35	2	9
Anti-aircraft defence				
Anti-aircraft machine guns	93	116	14	45
Anti-aircraft cannon 20–40mm	95	64	5	34
2M guns	3	1	–	–
Artillery				
120mm mortars	45	62	19	32
76–105mm cannon	26	22	10	22
122mm howitzers	20	31	–	–
152mm howitzers	3	2	–	–
155mm howitzers	24	6	–	–
Self-propelled weapons 122mm	8	–	–	–
130mm cannon	–	3	–	–
Armoured vehicles				
T-34 tanks	13	14	–	2
T-55 tanks	73	75	1	9
T-84 tanks	5	5	–	–
APCs	42	46	2	4

Source: Opsada – odbrana grada Sarajeva [Siege and defence of the city of Sarajevo], general staff of the Army of Bosnia-Herzegovina, 1996; and author's own calculations.

So in the year the country was being saved from destruction, our armoured-mechanized resources were only one T-55 tank, one APC and one combat vehicle. For a front that was at first 46 kilometres and later 64 kilometres long, we had at our disposal 128 machine guns, i.e. one per 500 metres. The ratio was later maintained in some places and somewhat enlarged elsewhere. We had only 63 60mm and 80mm mortars, and in August and September we had brigades that did not have any, let alone 120mm mortars, which are increasingly becoming normal infantry weapons. Later, however, the number of mortars increased significantly, and by the end was almost eight times as many: from 82, of all calibres, to a total of 633. The table does not show the stages between the initial situation and how it was at the end; if it did it would show that for almost the entire period we had only two anti-tank 9K11 launchers. At the end, immediately before the signing of the Dayton Accord, the situation markedly improved, and on the eve of the attempt to lift the siege in June and July 1995, the number of our automatic rifles had jumped from 2,340 to 23,521 – a ten-fold increase.

But we had only one tank, which was not in the city itself but in the surrounding district; later we acquired another, a T-34, also outside the city; so at no time did the 1st corps have a modern T-84 tank, whether inside or outside the ring, while the Serb Romanija corps had five throughout. Speaking of tanks, at the end of the war, just before Dayton, the ARBiH had a total of 80, while the VRS had about 250, or probably nearer 300.

In short, the VRS Romanija corps was superior in all forms of infantry, artillery and anti-aircraft weapons: we had barely 4,000 automatic and semi-automatic rifles in all, and they had at least 17,000; we had only 6 sniper rifles, while they had 285; and so on. The aggressor had field-pieces with a calibre in excess of 12.7mm to the number of 35 per kilometre of the front-line encircling Sarajevo, as was confirmed by UNPROFOR when the Romanija corps was required to place its heavy weapons under their control, after the NATO ultimatum at the beginning of 1994. By way of comparison, the greatest concentration of artillery in the Second World War was that of the Red Army against Berlin, with 25 pieces per kilometre of front.

Why, then, did the Army of Republika Srpska fail to enter the town? There are several reasons. First, as the table shows, they had somewhat less than 29,000 people on a front of 64 kilometres, which is an insufficient density for any significant infantry attack, and they could not use their hardware in any significant quantities in the city, because it was impossible to carry out any kind of manoeuvres. Second, of course, the defence stopped them. Third, if they had entered the city, they would have become responsible for gas, electricity, water and food, but as it was they controlled these supplies and allowed through only as much as they considered necessary. Fourth, however crazy it may seem, the international community too had some control over the level of conflict. They had their own positions in parts of the town from which they could determine whether they would let us try to lift the siege or the Serbs try to come in. But such 'permission' notwithstanding, I maintain that the enemy was *unable* to enter the city.

The 2nd (Tuzla) corps of the ARBiH was a little better off, since they had surrounded the barracks, which the JNA had to evacuate by the end of May 1992, and had seized part of the equipment (in Kozlovac they got 9,000 infantry weapons). It was the same at Zenica, where TO units of the Zenica regional headquarters captured 20 tanks, 19 20mm anti-aircraft guns and some infantry weapons. The Bihać regional TO headquarters also took some equipment from the JNA. When one considers the relative strength of the armies, many of the results achieved by our army were surprisingly good; but expectations that still more could be achieved, especially in the case of Sarajevo, were not realistic. There were many casualties in and around Sarajevo during attempts to lift the siege, for the situation was this: if we tried to break through from the north, the enemy would shell us from the south; if our forces moved to the west; they were hit from the east, and so on.

And now something about the organization of the ARBiH 1st corps. In spring 1992, in April, May and June, as I have said, squads, platoons, companies and battalions were formed, as well as municipal and regional TO staffs and the staff of TORBiH, while during the summer brigades were formed, and in autumn corps too, with more or less the same structure across the whole country. In spring 1993 the brigades were reorganized, since they had up to that time been variously structured: in Sarajevo there were some brigades with between 1,500 and 2,000 men and some with 5,000. To begin with they only held defensive positions and did not undertake any offensive action. In some cases the TO staffs were not keen to send their units from one quarter of town to another. With the reorganization into mobile brigades, some units even left Sarajevo for battlefields around the city and later, in the second half of 1993, for combat with HVO forces. Until the end of that year the structure remained the same, and then at the beginning of 1994 operational groups were formed, and mobile battalions within the brigades, since it had become clear during the previous year that the brigades did not have sufficient manoeuvring capacity to be effective. The battalions now took on the organizational structure of a modern army.

But, as can be seen from the arms available to the 1st corps, none of our brigades, even at the end of the war, was structured like, for example, NATO brigades, for the simple reason that we did not have enough equipment. ARBiH did obtain some combat equipment, but nothing else – no engineers and signals equipment, etc. In the winter of 1994/95, the municipal and regional TO staffs were disbanded, and replaced by neighbourhood commands. The 1st corps' zone was extended to include sections of the 2nd, 3rd and 6th corps, which had in the meantime been reorganized. The 6th corps was abolished and the 7th corps was formed. Finally, in spring 1995, the operational groups were disbanded and mobile brigades and divisions formed.

POSITIVE AND NEGATIVE ASPECTS OF THE INTERNATIONAL COMMUNITY'S INFLUENCE

The best illustration of the attitude of the international community to the hostilities against Bosnia-Herzegovina is the statement of a senior official in the US administration, George Kenney, senior diplomat on the Yugoslav desk in the State Department up to August 1992, who later revealed the games that were being played in certain Western states' diplomatic services at the beginning of the Balkan crisis:[6]

> The positions of the Bush administration on the Yugoslav crisis between February and August represent the worst kind of hypocrisy. I know this, because I wrote them for seven months in addition to other duties. While working in the State Department's Yugoslav Section, I was responsible in Washington for drafting most public statements about the crisis in Bosnia-Herzegovina. My job was do this in such a way that the US would appear active and worried about what was going on there, and at the same time not give the impression that the US were actually ready to do anything about it. From the beginning the aim was not a good public policy but good relations with the public, and if things looked that way the administration had achieved a magnificent success – it had succeeded in diminishing the seriousness of the crisis and confusing its substance.[6]

At the international conference on the documentation of genocide in Bosnia-Herzegovina, held in Bonn in 1995, the prominent American humanitarian worker Dr John Gould said: 'For the most part we sat idle while the genocide raged like wildfire through the streets, houses and fields of Bosnia. Of course, we issued statements, of course we expressed our dismay, but we did nothing.' One of the few bright spots in the US administration was the case of the five State Department officials who resigned, giving as their reason their frustration at the refusal to formulate an effective and timely US response. Among them was Marshall F. Harris,

---

[6] George Kenney, 'See no evil, make no policy', *The Washington Monthly*, November 1992.

who headed the Bosnia-Herzegovina desk, established after the break-up of SFRY and the consequent reorganization of the Yugoslav desk. Harris said at that time that he could 'no longer serve in a Department of State that accepts the forceful dismemberment of a European state and that will not act against genocide and the Serbian officials who perpetrate it'.[7]

The international community is responsible for failing to prevent the genocide and reducing its involvement to merely providing humanitarian aid and localizing the conflict so that it would not spread to the rest of the Balkans. Policy-makers concentrated chiefly on avoiding any move that might threaten those two objectives, even as 'ethnic cleansing' was going on. The statement of General Michael Rose in March 1994, discussing the role of the UNPROFOR mission, may serve as proof of this attitude: 'It is not our job to impose peace by force.'[8] A day earlier he had explained to a French journalist that the imposition of peace was incompatible with 'our first priority', which was 'to ensure the passage of humanitarian aid. As soon as we become involved in the fighting – look at what happened in Somalia – we become helpless.'[9] On other occasions, too, he showed his indifference to the situation in which he found himself. In a BBC documentary film he justified his decision not to allow the use of air strikes to prevent Serbian attacks on the civilian population by saying: 'We are not here to protect or defend anything except ourselves and our convoys.'[10]

---

[7] Quoted in Owen, *Balkan Odyssey*, p. 221.

[8] Quoted in an AFP report of 4 March 1994, published in FBIS-EEU-I4-043, 4 March 1994, p. 22.

[9] In an interview with Renaud Girard, *Le Figaro*, 28 February 1994, reproduced in FBIIS-EEU-94-039, 28 February 1994, p. 30. The 'Mogadishu syndrome' seriously affected the debate on the role of international troops in Bosnia-Herzegovina: see Owen: *Balkan Odyssey, passim*. The principle of moral equivalence which it gave rise to was articulated in particular by UNPROFOR commander General Michael Rose, using his troops in a supposedly 'neutral' but effectively pro-Serb way, because 'peace-making means taking sides in the conflict'; see Silber and Little, *The Death of Yugoslavia*, p. 362.

The concept of 'peace keeping' is based on Chapter VI of the UN Charter and founded on the consent of all parties involved, while the concept of 'peace enforcement', also derived from Chapter VI, permits the use of force even without the consent of all parties. According to Rose, in Bosnia there was no question of crossing the 'Mogadishu line' between the two concepts. The commonsense untenability (since in Bosnia-Herzegovina there was no peace to keep) and lack of legal foundation for this view in relation to UN resolutions is analysed by Noel Malcolm in his review of Rose's book *Fighting for Peace: Bosnia 1994* (Harvill, London 1998), in Quintin Hoare and Noel Malcolm (eds), *Books on Bosnia: a critical bibliography of works relating to Bosnia-Herzegovina Published Since 1990 in West European languages*, The Bosnian Institute, London 1999, pp. 140–59.

[10] Quoted in Daniel Williams, 'General Rose's Mission: Recoup Pre-Bosnia Bloom', *Washington Post*, 5 February 1995.

The international community was not in agreement about the hostilities and genocide in Bosnia-Herzegovina. Some European governments, especially the Greeks, rejected every condemnation of the Serbs, while Russia refrained at that time from any criticism, while the hierarchy of the Greek Orthodox Church and the red–brown, communist–fascist coalition in Russia fiercely defended Serb policies. Great Britain and France were also involved in concealing the seriousness of the situation, and did so over a long period, so as to avoid the need for any greater involvement on their part. In the Islamic world, Iraq and Libya stood aside because of their long-established links with Belgrade and their own interests.

The fundamental premise to which international mediators clung was entirely false. It was claimed that this was at bottom a civil war, that it reflected long-lasting, deeply-rooted hatreds, that all sides were guilty for what was happening and that all had the same basic objectives. Serb propaganda about ancient ethnic hatreds between Serbs, Croats and Bosniaks dominated Europe for a long time. Western leaders like Clinton, Mitterrand, Major and Hurd accepted these assertions and stereotypes and even disseminated them. The British military historian John Keegan constantly tried to present the war in Bosnia-Herzegovina as a tribal conflict, and the journalist Robert Kaplan wrote about the ancient and ineradicable ethnic hatreds in our region.[11] Reacting to these assertions, Noel Malcolm has written:

---

[11] John Keegan contributed regular comments to the *Daily Telegraph* along these lines, throughout the war years. For Robert Kaplan's book *Balkan Ghosts* and its influence on the US political elite, n. 5, p. 322 below. Among many such statements one may single out that of Bill Clinton, that the end of the Cold War 'lifted the lid of the cauldron in which centuries-old hatreds had been seething' (Ann Devroy: 'President cautions Congress on "simplistic ideas" in foreign policy', *Washington Post*, 26 May 1994), or that of Secretary of State Warren Christopher that Bosnia-Herzegovina is 'an unresolvable "problem from hell" for which one cannot expect a solution from anyone', and that this was in part a 'tribal feud which no outsider could hope to subdue' (Thomas L. Friedman: 'Bosnia reconsidered', *New York Times*, 8 April 1993). For one similar British instance among many, see Noel Malcolm, 'New light on Owen', *Bosnia Report*, 2, December 1993, which quotes Lord Owen's characterization of the war in former Yugoslavia as 'revenge' for what had happened in the Second World War, with 'ethnic violence' repeating itself in two great 'cycles' in the 1940s and 1990s. François Mitterrand said at a press conference in Munich on 8 September 1992 that there had been centuries of hatred in the region which had been subdued by the Yugoslav state and the communist authorities, and that 'we are facing something that was created by history and which is the reason these people have been fighting each other for centuries' (*Le Monde*, 10 July 1992). Expounding his policies towards Bosnia-Herzegovina, the French foreign minister even appealed to the literary authority of Ivo Andrić who 'wrote long before the war that Sarajevo is a city of hatreds' (Alain Juppé: 'Sarajevo: ce que je crois', *Le Monde*, 21 May 1994). On the political manipulation of a theme from Andrić's short story *Pismo iz 1920. godine* [A letter from 1920], to which Juppé refers, see Ivo Žanić: 'Pisac na osami: Upotreba

That hatreds and rivalries existed in Bosnia's past is certainly true; those writers who have reacted in the last two years by portraying Bosnia as a wonderland of permanent inter-religious harmony have over-reacted. But a closer inspection of Bosnia's history will show that the animosities which did exist were not absolute and unchanging. Nor were they inevitable consequences of the mixing together of different religious communities. The main basis of hostility was not ethnic or religious but economic ... This hostility was not some absolute or irreducible force: it varied as economic circumstances changed, and was also subject to political pressures ... These animosities were not permanently built into the psyches of the people who lived in Bosnia; they were products of history, and could change as history developed.[12]

The judgement that ours was a civil war was used in the West as justification for not acting on behalf of the endangered Bosnian Muslims, since intervention could be interpreted as taking sides. UN Security Council Resolution 713, of 25 September 1991, on the imposition of a general and complete embargo on the export of arms to former Yugoslavia, prevented the Bosnian government from procuring any significant quantities of arms and ammunition, while Karadžić's forces were not in the least affected, since they had taken over the entire JNA arsenal, and were kept continually supplied during the war by Serbia and Montenegro. Thus the legal government of Bosnia-Herzegovina and the Bosniaks, though the main victims, were put on an equal footing with the well-armed aggressor.

For a very long time many European governments based their 'neutrality' on the powerful Serb propaganda which presented the situation in Bosnia-Herzegovina through pseudo-historical assertions. Since Western analysts did not know much about the history of our country, they accepted Belgrade's assertions, which were based on myths and falsehoods. According to one such myth, Serbs owned 60–65 per cent of the land in Bosnia-Herzegovina, so that their occupation of 70 per cent of Bosnia's territory in 1992 was explained as an attempt to defend their own land, not as an act of aggression. General Charles Boyd, who was deputy commander-in-chief of US forces in Europe from 1992 to 1995, was taken in by this when he wrote: 'In short, the Serbs are not trying to occupy new territory, but only to hold on to what is already theirs.' He even said that there would be no peace in Bosnia-Herzegovina 'until the US government perceives the essential similarity in the behaviour of the Serbs, Croats and Muslims', and accused the Bosniak authorities of

Andrićeve književnosti u ratu u BiH' [A writer in isolation: use of Andrić's literature in the war in Bosnia-Herzegovina], *Erasmus*, 18, 1996, pp. 48–57, and Dževad Karahasan, 'Europe's Wild West', *Bosnia Report* 12, September–December 1995.

[12] Noel Malcolm, *Bosnia; a short history*, Macmillan, London 1994, p. xxi.

shelling the citizens of Sarajevo in order to attract world attention and collect political points.[13]

The historical facts tell a different story. The traditional landowners in Bosnia-Herzegovina during the four centuries of Ottoman rule were the Muslims, and it can be seen from the last census carried out during the Austro-Hungarian period, in 1910, that Serbs owned only 10 per cent of the land. Just before the recent war, *private* land ownership according to the land registers (cadastral records) was: Bosniaks 44.8 per cent, Serbs 42.6 per cent and Croats 12.6 per cent. But nowhere in the modern world is the ethnic or religious affiliation of a land owner a legal category.

The general impression from 1992 is that while resolutions were being passed giving clear messages to end the war, UNPROFOR was 'neutrally' monitoring what was happening on the ground and protecting only itself. UN Security Council Resolution 752 of 15 May 1992 unequivocally recognizes the presence of the JNA and the Croatian Army in Bosnia-Herzegovina's neighbours and requires them to leave. Thus the Security Council

- demands that all forms of interference from outside Bosnia-Herzegovina, including from the JNA and elements of the Army of Croatia, cease forthwith and that Bosnia-Herzogovina's neighbours take urgent steps to end such interference and to respect the territorial integrity of Bosnia-Herzegovina;
- demands that all units of the JNA and elements of the Army of Croatia withdraw immediately or submit to the authority of the government of Bosnia-Herzegovina or disband and disarm, and place their weapons under international supervision, and requests the Secretary General to consider without delay what international assistance can be found in this respect;
- further demands that all irregular troops in Bosnia-Herzegovina be disbanded and disarmed;
- calls upon all parties and others concerned to ensure that the forcible expulsion of persons from the areas where they live, and all attempts to alter the ethnic composition of the population, wherever it may be in former Yugoslavia, cease forthwith.

When speaking of the influence of the international community, we tend to forget the recent history of Europe and the world, from which the conclusion can be drawn that the international community practically always behaves as it behaved towards the genocide and aggression in Bosnia-Herzegovina. The Allied governments soon became aware of the existence of the Nazi concentration camps, but did nothing; in Kampuchea the United

---

[13] Charles G. Boyd, 'Making Peace with the Innocent', *Foreign Affairs*, September–October 1995, pp. 28–9.

States favoured the Khmer Rouge, because the Vietnamese were against them; the West protected Indonesia when it invaded East Timor; and it was the same with the conflict in Rwanda, when the time came to determine responsibility for violations of human rights and to punish the guilty.

BACKGROUND TO THE CLASH BETWEEN ARBIH AND HVO

The 'war within a war' began with the destruction of the state of Bosnia-Herzegovina and the creation of para-state structures: first the Serb SAOs, soon thereafter the Croatian Community of Herzeg-Bosna (HZ Herzeg-Bosna) as the civilian authority for organizing the HVO (Croatian Defence Council), a military structure whose purported task was to defend areas of B-H where the majority population was Croat. While Milošević's attitude towards Bosnia-Herzegovina clearly followed the formula that all Serbs must live in a single state, the Croat position had a number of variants:

a joining western Herzegovina to Croatia, as Vojislav Šešelj had offered the Croats before war of any kind broke out;
b dividing Bosnia-Herzegovina in the proportion of 25 per cent for the Croats, 20 per cent for the Bosniaks and 55 per cent for the Serbs, which was Gojko Šušak's idea;
c Tuđman's project of dividing Bosnia-Herzegovina between Serbs and Croats along the borders of the Croatian Banovina of 1939; and
d 'Croatia to the Drina', the objective of the Ustasha radicals.

The Croatian political leadership in Bosnia-Herzegovina was throughout dependent on Zagreb; overtly it was pro-Bosnian, but covertly it worked to bring about the country's partition. HZ Herzeg-Bosna was established on 18 November 1991, and the political leadership called upon Croats to vote for the independence and sovereignty of Bosnia-Herzegovina in the referendum of 29 February and 1 March 1992. Very soon after, on 8 April 1992, the HVO was formed, outside the command structure of the government in Sarajevo. To understand the overall situation and attitudes among B-H Croats, we must be aware of the sudden awakening of national consciousness; solidarity with the newly established Croatian state, which immediately after its creation found itself dangerously threatened; the existence of a nationalist political party with populist ideas; pride in the creation of the country's own armed forces; and Croatia's expressed interest in Bosnia-Herzegovina. All of this powerfully affected the national and political commitment of the HDZBiH and the B-H Croats.

For the sake of the 'historic moment' in which Croats were erecting a state on the basis of the 1939 Banovina project, Zagreb and Tuđman ignored the real interests of this numerically smallest nation in Bosnia-Herzegovina. The interests of Croats living in Bosanska Posavina, Bosanska Krajina, parts of central Bosnia and the larger cities were sacrificed to the aim of thickening the Croatian 'croissant' or, as Tuđman put it, securing the strategic hinterland of Dalmatia. He was convinced that the Serbs would quickly and easily defeat the Bosniaks, and that the partition of Bosnia-Herzegovina could thereby be reduced to a pragmatic resolution of Serb and Croat interests. At the same time as concluding a limited pact with the Bosniaks as 'natural allies', Zagreb made a lasting pact with the Serbs at the expense of their Bosniak victims. Tuđman was sure that the world would eventually decide to compensate Serbia, which, even if it could not preserve Yugoslavia or achieve the whole of Greater Serbia, should certainly get a Little Greater Serbia. And then Croatia would get a Little Greater Croatia, while the left-overs would go to the Bosniaks, who, being surrounded by more powerful neighbours, would rapidly atrophy as a nation in that 'buffer state' or 'little Bosnia' which Tuđman had offered them in his New Year address to Croatian journalists even before the beginning of the war.[14]

There was a very cynical joke being told at this time. An SDS Serb and an HDZ Croat were conversing across the Neretva and, having agreed that the Serbs should have the area to the east of the river and the Croats the area to the west, wondered: 'But what shall we do with the Muslims?', and immediately shouted in unison: 'Into the Neretva with them!'

In such military and political surroundings, and between such mentalities, the Bosniaks had only one option: Bosnia-Herzegovina was all they had, but only inasmuch as it belonged also to the other two peoples. The Bosniak departure from Yugoslavia was met with serious threats: Vojislav Šešelj warned the Muslims 'not to become once again a weapon in the hands of Croatian criminals', and Radovan Karadžić that 'one [Bosniak] nation could cease to exist'. So the Bosniaks had to fight for their bare physical survival, and had no choice but to depend on the Croats and Croatia, who were already militarily organized, as their only access to the outside world, and thereby to buy time to organize and arm themselves.

The legality and legitimacy of the newly recognized state of Bosnia-Herzegovina, after the formation of these two sets of unconstitutional civilian and military–political structures, was preserved by those institutions that survived from the past, reinforced by the leftist opposition and a significant number of Croats and Serbs who had opted for Bosnia-Herzegovina. This is most evident in the numerical composition of the TO, which rapidly grew into the ARBiH: the proportion of Croats was higher than their proportion of the overall population of Bosnia-Herzegovina, while the number of Serbs stood at about half their percentage proportion

[14] On this statement, see note 1, p. 92 above.

of the population. In the general staff of TORBiH, later ARBiH, there were about 18 per cent Croats and 12 per cent Serbs. Within our defence system in Sarajevo there was the Kralj [King] Tvrtko Croat brigade, and in the 2nd (Tuzla) corps there were two brigades each with more than 75 per cent Croats. Many police units were over 20 per cent Croat. As you know, the 1991 census showed that Croats were 17.3 per cent of the population and Serbs 31.3 per cent.

Unfortunately, it was like this only at the beginning, since, as the Serbs and Croats had done earlier, the Bosniak side, or more precisely the SDA, soon radicalized its position and began to follow flawed policies in the army and police. It started saying that the Bosniaks were the 'central nation' in Bosnia-Herzegovina and appropriated the name Bosniak, which historically refers to all inhabitants of Bosnia, thus relegating local Serbs and Croats to their 'reserve homelands'. As a result the percentages I have just quoted began falling as early as the end of 1992 and the beginning of 1993. SDA extremists also falsified the country's history, with the clear aim of making the Bosniaks the principal – if not the only – factor in the state on the basis of their numerical superiority. All this played into the hands of Serbs and Croats who were accusing Izetbegović of creating a Muslim state.

The war which the Serbs launched against Croatia and Bosnia-Herzegovina, like the later Croat–Bosniak war, arose from the conflicting interests of three national communities concerning division of territory and zones of influence. Under the auspices of the Portuguese diplomat Jose Cutileiro as the European Community's envoy, Karadžić, Boban and Izetbegović adopted a Statement of Principles on new constitutional arrangements for Bosnia-Herzegovina in Sarajevo on 18 March 1992. Bosnia-Herzegovina was to be an independent state of 'three constituent units, based on national principles and taking into account economic, geographic and other criteria', only for all these other criteria to be effectively rejected in the next sentence, which states that the basis for the proposed working groups is to be a 'map based on the absolute or relative national majority in each municipality'.[15] Some ten days later Izetbegović rejected

---

[15] For the full text of the Statement, which was 'adopted' but not 'signed', see translation in Foreign Broadcast Information Service, Daily Report: Eastern Europe, 19 March 1992. Although reached in Sarajevo, it is called the Lisbon Agreement since it was in that city on 12 February that Cutileiro's series of meetings began with the leaders of the three ethno-national parties from Bosnia-Herzegovina, as a kind of offshoot of the September 1991 European Community Peace Conference on Yugoslavia in The Hague, chaired by Lord Carrington. The general principle of 'constituent national units' was worked out in Lisbon, and later at the fifth meeting in Sarajevo the European Community offered a survey map of municipalities based on the 1991 population census as the 'starting point' for negotiations on the constitutional arrangement of the country, which were to have continued on 30 and 31 March in Brussels. According to this map, the Bosniak unit would

the plan after all; but he had legitimized the 'national' criterion for dividing territory which was followed by all subsequent plans and thus, even
before the war broke out, acted willy nilly to invite mass population dis-
placements and massacres aimed at achieving national homogeneity in the
desired areas.

Thus the Vance–Owen plan, set out in Geneva on 2 January 1993, proposed that the Bosniaks should hold power in four provinces, the Serbs in
three and the Croats in two, while ten provinces would be mixed
Bosniak–Croat.[16] The Croats began at once to implement the agreement,
even before it was adopted. In March 1993 they called upon the Army of
the Republic of Bosnia-Herzegovina to submit to the military authority of
the HVO in areas where Croats were to hold power. In the name of principle but in fact with transparent hypocrisy, they said that the HVO would
submit to ARBiH in the proposed Bosniak provinces, these being regions
which the HVO had not been counting on as parts of its future 'state' and
from which it had persuaded Croats to depart: for example, Vareš, Žepče,
Tuzla and Usora. Thus a latent conflict was transformed into open and
savage warfare.

But the Croat–Bosniak war was not the fruit only of imperialist Greater
Croatia politics, but also in part a struggle for living space. The Serbs had
seized more than 60 per cent of the territory of Bosnia-Herzegovina, from
which Bosniaks and Croats alike had been expelled. The former, especially,
had found refuge for the most part in central Bosnia, which led to fundamental changes in the demographic equilibrium. The influx of Bosniaks into
areas that had previously had a Croat majority was viewed by the political
and military leadership of the HDZ as taking territory away from the Croats,
so it committed the HVO to isolating central Bosnia. As a first step the bridge
over the Neretva at Bila, which had been the logistical route into Bosnia,
was destroyed. Then on 12 January 1993 Gornji Vakuf came under heavy
attack, with the idea of creating a united Croat ethnic territory from

be composed of 52 municipalities (44 per cent of the territory of Bosnia-
Herzegovina), the Serb unit 35 (44 per cent) and the Croat unit 20 municipalities
(12 per cent of the territory). The absurdity of the concept can be seen from the
fact that 50 per cent of Serbs would still be living outside the 'Serb region', as
many as 59 per cent of Croats outside the 'Croat region' and 18 per cent of Bosniaks outside the 'Bosniak region'.

[16] For the origins of the plan, see Owen, *Balkan Odyssey,* pp. 94–160. Not even the
author himself, however, is consistent in explaining his ideas. One variant made
Province 7 (Sarajevo) Bosniak and Province 10 (Travnik-Livno) Croat–Bosniak.
Another variant made Province 7 into a kind of 'capital city district' common to
all three nations, and Province 10 Croat only, so that each would have three
'cleansed' provinces and share the 'uncleansed' Sarajevo. Silber and Little, *The
Death of Yugoslavia,* pp. 306–7, meanwhile, offer the interpretation that Sarajevo
would have power-sharing between the three groups, while Province 10 would be
Bosniak-Croat.

Duvno and Prozor via Gornji Vakuf to central Bosnia – Fojnica, Busovača, Vitez and Novi Travnik – which would have established a line of communication completely isolating the Neretva/Bosna valley north of Mostar (not far from the imaginary border of the Croatian Banovina of 1939). The Croats experienced the war as a Bosniak attempt to take from the Croats, as a minority nation, what the Serbs had been unable to take, while for the Bosniaks it was betrayal by an ally, a knife in the back. It served the Serbs very well; for them, 1993 was effectively a year of holiday from war.

It is very important to realize that even during the fiercest clashes between the ARBiH and the HVO, the two armies were continuing to cooperate on many joint battlegrounds, from Orašje in northern Bosnia, via the Tuzla region in the zone covered by the ARBiH 2nd corps, down to Sarajevo. The bloody battles were waged in central Bosnia, which was the operational zone of the 3rd and 7th corps of the ARBiH, and in Herzegovina, where the HVO had encircled the region of which Mostar was the principal city. Throughout that 'war within a war' the HVO was trying to retain its territory and at the same time exercising pressure on Croats outside that territory, in towns such as Vareš and Kakanj, to resettle there *en masse* so as to increase the Croat population and enhance its military potential. Croats from Sarajevo, Tuzla and Zenica were supposed to move to the new 'Croat capital' of Mostar.

At the same time, those who were against the war and in favour of cooperation between the two peoples were being eliminated. Typical of this was the destruction of the Croatian opposition in Bosnia-Herzegovina, the elimination in Croatia of generals who opposed the war against the Bosniaks, and the discrediting of the Croat Peasants' Party of Bosnia-Herzegovina and the Croatian National Council in Sarajevo, which had brought together B-H Croats opposed to Franjo Tuđman's policy. At the beginning of August 1992, immediately after the JNA and Chetniks had been driven out of Mostar, the HVO military police killed the commandant of the rightist Croat Defence Forces (HOS), Blaž Kraljević, in extremely suspicious circumstances, allegedly because his vehicle had not stopped at a checkpoint at the northern exit of the town. He had been very influential, advocating Croat–Bosniak cooperation and an undivided Bosnia-Herzegovina, and the HOS itself was of mixed composition.

The Bosniaks, for their part, conducted the war so as to link their three big cities – Tuzla, Sarajevo and Zenica – and prevent the Croats from Kakanj, Vareš, Žepče, Kiseljak, Fojnica, Busovača, Vitez and elsewhere from obstructing them.

AFTERMATH OF THE CROAT–BOSNIAK WAR

The crimes committed by the HVO – massacres in Bosniak villages near Vitez (Ahmići) and Vareš (Stupni Do) and in concentration camps in Mostar and Čapljina, and expulsions of Bosniaks from Prozor, Kiseljak and Stolac – and those of the ARBiH against the Croat population in the Vareš area (Borovica, Kopijari), Vitez (Buhina Kuće), in the Neretva valley (Gornja Grabovica), in Bugojno and in Croat villages around Travnik and Zenica, remain as a bloody stain on the conscience of the political and military leaderships of the Croat and Bosniak peoples. The consequences of the war are unpredictable: human victims can never be replaced, and the razing by the Croats in particular of religious, cultural and historic monuments to their foundations is a barbaric act unprecedented in the recent history of these two peoples. Hatreds have blazed up with consequences to which no end can be seen. Bosniak nationalists often say: 'We can easily live again with Serbs, with Chetniks, but never again with Croats, with Ustashe', while Croat nationalists say: 'Never again with the *balije*!'[17]

With minor corrections, Dayton reinforced what the 'warring parties' had gained on the ground. The taking of territory by force of arms was legitimized, so that the Serbs gained most territorially speaking, in relation to their proportion of the population of Bosnia-Herzegovina, through the recognition of Republika Srpska as their entity. The Bosniaks are the greatest losers; they and the Croats find themselves in a single entity, of which the two largest compact areas with a Bosniak majority are physically separated, and they have lost the opportunity for a unitary Bosnia-Herzegovina. But the Croats, already the smallest nation, have been halved in number, especially through the war with the Bosniaks. They have lost the most fertile part of the country, Posavina, and have been halved in number in the large industrial centres; many have lost the sense of a Bosnian homeland and do not intend to return to places where they had been in a majority. Tuđman's concept of deepening the Dalmatian hinterland has prevailed, since to replace Serbs who fled or were expelled the Croatian state has settled Croats in 'liberated' areas. This is especially true of the large but sparsely populated municipalities of Grahovo, Glamoč and Drvar, which were exchanged with Milošević for Bosanski Brod, Derventa, Bosanski Šamac and other parts of Posavina, about which I have already spoken.[18]

The aftermath of the war between Croats and Bosniaks is still very much present. Relations between the two are on the brink of explosion

---

[17] *Balije* is a derogatory term now meaning, roughly, 'dirty Muslims'. The term was originally used by Muslim town-dwellers in Bosnia-Herzegovina for the more 'primitive' rural population in the hills.

[18] See p. 172 above.

from various incidents. The HDZBiH, supported by Zagreb, from time to time revives the idea of (additional) cantonization, or 'consistent cantonization', which would transform the Federation into two nationally homogeneous entities. The Bosniaks reject it, since they see it as a further partition of Bosnia-Herzegovina and a way to the future and final destruction of the state. Hence, too, their insistence on strengthening the state, which the other two sides perceive as unitarization which, given the size and birthrate of the Bosniak population, would lead to the formation of a predominantly Bosniak and Islamic state.

It is important for the future to implement Dayton Accords consistently (return of populations, punishment of war criminals, freedom of movement, etc.), to democratize society, to work methodically for reconciliation and mutual trust, and as rapidly as possible to rebuild the economy. This is a long-term process, directly linked with significant changes and development of democracy in Zagreb and Belgrade. The present political structures in former Yugoslavia, apart from Slovenia and Macedonia, are not capable of effecting democratic change, so one must rely on the international community's presence for a long time yet.

8

Civilian–Military Relations in Bosnia-Herzegovina 1992–1995

Marko Attila Hoare

The relationship of the civilian and military authorities in the Republic of Bosnia-Herzegovina went through a marked transformation in the period 1992–95. At the start of the Bosnian war, in the spring of 1992, the B-H presidency and government on the one hand, and the Republic's armed forces on the other, were the heterogeneous, disunited representatives of a multiplicity of political interests and national loyalties. By the war's end, in the autumn of 1995, the remnants of the Republic and the newly born Bosnian Army – in possession of the approximately 30 per cent of Bosnian territory not occupied by Serb or Croat separatist forces – had been effectively transformed into the private domain of President Alija Izetbegović and the Bosniak-nationalist Party of Democratic Action (SDA). Our purpose here is to trace the subordination of the Bosnian military to the political goals of the SDA, and its evolution from a multi-national state army to a purely Bosniak party army.

The history of the Army of the Republic of Bosnia-Herzegovina (ARBiH) of 1992–95 resembles in certain respects that of the communist-led Partisan force born in 1941. Formally named the People's Liberation Army of Bosnia-Herzegovina, this fought under the command of the General Staff for Bosnia-Herzegovina as a component part of the National Liberation Army of Yugoslavia (NOVJ). Both NOVJ in Bosnia-Herzegovina and ARBiH fought under the banner of Bosnian patriotism and statehood; each began life as a decentralized, makeshift resistance force and became transformed over the course of a four-year war into a disciplined regular army completely subordinate to a political party – the Communist Party of Yugoslavia (CPY) and the SDA respectively. The CPY and SDA were each headed by a dedicated and closely knit cell of political revolutionaries, the fanaticism of whose leaders had been hardened by years of persecution and imprisonment at the hands of the regimes they sought to resist.

However, while the internationalist CPY built its army as a multi-national force of Serbs, Muslims and Croats, the Bosniak-nationalist SDA

built its army on a purely Bosniak-national basis. The CPY had consequently established a territorially unified and nationally heterogeneous
Bosnian republic by 1945; the SDA established, by contrast, a territorially
truncated and nationally homogenous Bosniak para-state by 1995. The
transformation of ARBiH into the party army of the SDA ran in tandem
with the transformation of the Republic of Bosnia-Herzegovina into a
Bosniak rump-state.

OLD LOYALTIES AND DOUBLE AGENTS

The Armed Forces of the Republic of Bosnia-Herzegovina (OSRBiH),
organized under the aegis of the Bosnian government in 1992, were
founded, on the one hand, upon institutions inherited from the communist
period – Territorial Defence and Ministry of Internal Affairs forces – and,
on the other, upon the Patriotic League – the resistance organization
gradually organized by the SDA following its election victory in November–
December 1990. The Territorial Defence (TO) provided the institutional
basis, while the Patriotic League (PL) provided the organizational kernel
of the future Bosnian Army. Civilian-military relations in Bosnia-
Herzegovina following the outbreak of war in the spring of 1992 were
dominated by the triangular relationship between the PL, the TO and
the SDA regime headed by President Izetbegović.

The TO was the republican defence force created by the Yugoslav
communist regime following the Warsaw Pact invasion of Czechoslovakia
in 1968. Its organization was rooted in the Partisan system of warfare:
after the Soviet–Yugoslav split in 1948, Yugoslav defences always included
a Partisan element, according to the 'Doctrine of General People's
War'. The TO was formed by the transfer of territorially based units
from the command structure of the Yugoslav People's Army (JNA) to the
civilian authorities in each republic and autonomous province of the
Yugoslav Federation, with staffs formed at the local, municipal and
regional levels. In 1974 the TO system was further devolved, so that, in
the words of Josip Broz Tito, 'The centres of organized resistance must
be every factory, every settlement, every portion of our territory.'[1] The
consequence of such decentralization was that the Bosnian republic's
defences were dependent upon its political leadership to provide them
with structural unity. The League of Communists was naturally expected
to provide a political leadership that would unify the TO units in
each locality across the republic. However, wholly different conditions

---

[1] Milan Inđić, *Teritorijalna odbrana Socijalističke Republike Bosne i Hercegovine*
[Territorial defence of the Socialist Republic of B-H], Republički štab Teritorijalne
Odbrane Socijalističke Republike Bosne i Hercegovine, Sarajevo 1989, pp. 146–7.

were created by the fall of the communist regime and its replacement in Bosnia-Herzegovina with a coalition of nationally based parties – the SDA and its Serb and Croat counterparts: the Serb Democratic Party (SDS) and Croat Democratic Community (HDZ). The SDA could provide a political leadership to the TO in areas where Muslims formed a majority, but in Serb- or Croat-majority areas the local TO units were likely to be coopted by the SDS and HDZ for very different political agendas: while the SDA aimed to turn the TO into a Bosnian Army, portions of the TO under SDS or HDZ leadership would be incorporated into the separatist paramilitary forces whose purpose was the destruction of Bosnia-Herzegovina.[2]

The Bosnian communist authorities, prior to their fall in the autumn of 1990, had made no preparations for the defence of Bosnia-Herzegovina against the approaching Serbian juggernaut, and allowed the JNA to confiscate the armaments of the Bosnian TO without resistance.[3] The SDA–SDS–HDZ coalition that controlled the Bosnian Presidency and government from late 1990 until spring 1992 was both unable and unwilling to organize the defence of Bosnia-Herzegovina in preparation for attack by Serbia and the JNA. The Serb-nationalist SDS was violently opposed to any republican defence preparations and its central and local bodies cooperated with the JNA and Yugoslav security services in hindering such preparations as much as possible.

The Bosnian Ministry of Internal Affairs (MUP) and State Security Service (SDB) in particular had evolved over 45 years of communist rule as institutions loyal to the Yugoslav Federal centre. They were riddled with Serb and Croat nationalists as well as conservatives and double agents of all nationalities who were willing to collaborate with the efforts of Belgrade and the JNA to subvert and conquer the Bosnian state from within. Ironically, therefore, the SDA as the leading party of government was forced to organize its own clandestine resistance movement independently of the Bosnian state institutions, while these same institutions in large part collaborated with the external enemy in attempting to suppress this resistance.

---

[2] For example in Kiseljak, whose pre-war population was approximately 52 per cent Croat and 41 per cent Muslim, the HVO was formed when Croat officers seceded from the TO municipal staff soon after the start of the war and set up their own staff. See Fuad Kovač, 'U konacima Mehmeda Fatiha rođeni su hrvatski zločinci Rajić i Blaškić' [Croat criminals Rajić and Blaškić were born under Mehmed Fatih's roof], *Ljiljan*, Sarajevo, no. 185, 31 July 1996, p. 28.

[3] Fikret Muslimović, *Odbrana Republike* [Defence of the Republic], NIPP Ljiljan, Sarajevo 1995, pp. 27–8.

FORMATION AND STRATEGY OF THE PATRIOTIC LEAGUE

Preparations within the SDA for the formation of a national paramilitary force to safeguard Bosnian sovereignty and territorial integrity began soon after the party's assumption of power. In February 1991 the Executive Council of the SDA discussed the establishment of such a force outside the control of the Interior Ministry. Izetbegović gave his approval for the formation of the future Patriotic League (PL) the following month. It would provide an organizational umbrella to cells being formed for resistance by individuals at the local level. On 10 June 1991, at a gathering of 356 leading Muslim political, cultural and humanitarian figures from all over Yugoslavia, a 'Council of National Defence of the Muslim Nation' was established as the military council of the SDA and the embryonic military organization received the name 'Patriotic League'.

Divided between a civilian wing headed by Izetbegović and a military wing comprising Muslim officers who had defected from the JNA, the PL would be anchored in the structure of the SDA.[4] While the bodies that grew into the Bosnian civilian and political leaderships respectively were therefore originally two halves of the same Muslim national organization, the division of labour would ultimately engender a strategic divergence and a political conflict. At this time, however, the SDA leadership stood at the apex of a state apparatus it hardly controlled while the PL found its most dangerous persecutors to be the security services of the Bosnian Republic it was set up to defend.[5] The Yugoslav military counterintelligence service (KOS) had its agents at all levels of the Bosnian state, including the (Muslim) member of the Presidency Fikret Abdić and the (Muslim) Minister of the Interior Alija Delimustafić. The latter, as well as persecuting the PL, worked to ensure the unhindered organization and arming of Serb separatist forces on Bosnian territory.[6]

President Izetbegović and his close collaborators in the SDA leadership, having come to power in such a politically and nationally divided state, were in the position of having to reconcile these divisions. Forced into collaboration with a wide range of individuals from the Bosnian state apparatus and body politic who were outside the SDA, Izetbegović ceased to be a purely SDA figure. He set about broadening the SDA leadership into a Bosnian state leadership even as he would increasingly subsume the Bosnian state within the SDA party umbrella. Policemen, bureaucrats, JNA officers and others who had served under the communist regime moved with the times and drifted into the SDA's orbit much as former

---

[4] Hasan Čengić, interview in *Armija Bosne i Hercegovine 1992–1995* [The Army of Bosnia-Herzegovina 1992–1995], NIPP 'Ljiljan', Sarajevo 1997, pp. 124–5.
[5] Sefer Halilović, *Lukava Strategija* [Devious strategy], Sarajevo 1997, pp. 61–2.
[6] Ibid. See also Munir Alibabić-Munja, *Bosna u kandžama KOS-a* [Bosnia in the talons of KOS], Sarajevo 1996, pp. 37, 41–2, 50–1.

Chetniks, Ustashas and Muslim SS troops had drifted into the victorious Communist Party half a century before.

The character of the fledgling SDA regime changed under the impact of its broadening base; the newcomers made the regime more conservative and collaborationist in relation to their former imperial masters in Belgrade. Consequently, a split developed between the Izetbegović leadership, on the one hand, and PL commander Sefer Halilović and his followers on the other. A champion of an uncompromising struggle to defeat the Serbian enemy by military means, Halilović would increasingly clash with the pacifistic Izetbegović and the regime's newer recruits from the ranks of the JNA and KOS. While the PL worked to organize armed resistance, the SDA leadership sought to negotiate a peaceful settlement with Belgrade, the JNA and the SDS.

ATTEMPTS AT FINDING AGREEMENT WITH THE JNA

When SDS supporters set up barricades in Sarajevo after the Bosnian referendum for independence, in preparation for an attack on the capital, and Bosnian resistance members set up counter-barricades to oppose them, Izetbegović agreed on joint patrols of the JNA and Bosnian police to dismantle the barricades on both sides.[7] Following the Bosnian declaration of independence on 3 March 1992, Izetbegović continued to seek a negotiated settlement to the political crisis that was threatening to engulf his country in full-scale war. The president hoped naively that JNA units on Bosnian territory could be either transformed into a Bosnian army or withdrawn from the country without bloodshed: he would subsequently admit that after 50 years' talk of 'brotherhood and unity' he did not believe that Yugoslavia's army would engage in genocide.[8] Following the invasion of the north-east Bosnian town of Bijeljina, on 1 April 1992, by the Serbian paramilitary force under the JNA command known as 'Tigers', Izetbegović sanctioned the JNA's occupation of the town to end the Tigers' terror against the town's Muslim civilians.[9] The Bosnian Presidency would indeed not declare a state of war and full mobilization until 20 June, after nearly three months of full-scale aggression against their country.

In the absence of resolute leadership from the Presidency and government, the success of Bosnian resistance to the Serbian onslaught in a given locality depended upon the initiative of the local leadership, with all the failures of coordination that this involved. In the Tuzla municipality, government was in the hands of Social Democrats headed by Mayor Selim

[7] Laura Silber and Allan Little, *The Death of Yugoslavia*, London 1995, pp. 226–77.
[8] President Izetbegović's speech at a meeting of the Congress of Bosnian Intellectuals, 29 November 1997, as noted by the author.
[9] Ibid., pp. 247–8.

Bešlagić, and played an active role in arming and organising the TO and the militia, but this activity was not coordinated with the Tuzla PL. The municipal authorities and PL in Tuzla, indeed, organized resistance independently of each other; PL officers would later accuse the Tuzla municipal council of harassment and obstruction of their activities.[10] In eastern Bosnia, according to Halilović, PL efforts to blow up bridges on the river Drina between Serbia and Bosnia were vetoed by local SDA leaders.[11]

The Bosnian government stumbled reluctantly into a state of war as the reality of the aggression could no longer be denied. On 4 April, in response to the flight of Muslim refugees from already occupied northeastern Bosnia and under pressure from members of his Presidency, Izetbegović ordered a general mobilization of the Bosnian TO. In response, the two SDS members, Biljana Plavšić and Nikola Koljević, resigned from the Bosnian Presidency, and the following morning SDS paramilitary forces began their assault on the capital. On 8 April about 20 veterans of the Republican Staff of the Bosnian TO met at the Presidency building in Sarajevo to select a new TO commander, since the previous commander, Drago Vukosavljević, had defected to the JNA. As a result of its deliberations, the Bosnian Presidency dissolved the former TO Staff and appointed a new staff consisting of the Muslim Hasan Efendić as commander and the Croat Stjepan Šiber as chief of staff; the Serb Jovan Divjak was subsequently appointed deputy commander. The Presidency became the supreme command, while the Republican TO staff remained subordinate to the Ministry for People's Defence.

RIVALRY BETWEEN TERRITORIAL DEFENCE AND PATRIOTIC LEAGUE

The new staff proceeded to secure a pledge of loyalty in the struggle for Bosnian independence from the staff of the Sarajevo city TO and 72 other municipal- and district-level TO staffs. On 9 April, the Presidency ordered the unification of all armed forces on the territory of Bosnia-Herzegovina, with a deadline of 15 April for all existing armed units to accept this decision.[12] Halilović claims that as PL commander his approval was sought

[10] Dževad Pašić, *Zemlja između istoka i zapada: Tuzla – odbrana kontinuiteta državnosti Bosne i Hercegovine* [A land between east and west: Tuzla – defence of Bosnia-Herzegovina's state continuity], Bosnia ARS, Tuzla 1996, pp. 224–30.

[11] Šefko Hodžić, 'Kako je nastajala Armija (6): junaci i stradalnici Podrinja' [How the army was formed (6): heroes and victims of the Podrinje], *Oslobođenje*, Sarajevo, 21 April 1997, p. 15.

[12] Šefko Hodžić, 'Kako je nastajala Armija (1): traganje za komandantom' [How the army was formed (1): search for the commander], *Oslobođenje*, Sarajevo, 15 April 1997, p. 5.

for the new appointments. The division between the PL and TO at the republican centre was not resolved immediately after the start of full-scale war in early April 1992. The PL maintained its staff separate from the TO; the rivalry this inevitably produced was not ended when, a week later, the republican Staff of the TO formally assumed command of all military units in Bosnia-Herzegovina formed on the political platform of the PL.

The OSRBiH thus created were to include not only the PL and TO, but also the Croatian Defence Council (HVO), the Croat Defence Forces (HOS), the SDA militia 'Green Berets' and local resistance units set up in localities throughout Bosnia-Herzegovina. Izetbegović hoped they would also include the JNA units on Bosnian territory. The heterogeneous, disunited character of the OSRBiH was increased by the fact that the Presidency, as supreme command, included two traitors who would in time defect openly to Bosnia-Herzegovina's enemies: Fikret Abdić and Nenad Kecmanović. The Bosnian Defence Minister Jerko Doko was a Croat who gave priority in armaments to the HVO, the HDZ-controlled Croat paramilitary force. Interior Minister Delimustafić was in all probability a KOS agent.[13]

Within such a broad political spectrum represented by both the civilian and military authorities, personal relationships between individual politicians, officials and commanders would be all-important. President Izetbegović, TO commander Efendić and PL commander Halilović each pursued his own policy, often in conflict with that of the others.

Efendić, an SDA loyalist, took steps to form a joint command of the TO and JNA in Bosnia-Herzegovina, as part of Izetbegović's plan to include the JNA within the OSRBiH. However, when on 14 April Efendić faxed to his local commanders a plan for the disarming of all JNA garrisons in Bosnia-Herzegovina by the TO, it led to a breach with Izetbegović. Serbian intelligence service obtained the text of the plan, the commander of the Sarajevo corps of the JNA accused Efendić of declaring war on the JNA and Izetbegović was forced publicly to repudiate Efendić's action.[14] On 16 April Izetbegović's agreement to allow the JNA to withdraw from Bosnia-Herzegovina – with both its own weapons and those it had confiscated from the TO – was bitterly opposed by Halilović, who was planning the seizure and disarmament of the JNA garrisons.[15] Izetbegovic vetoed Halilović's plan to seize confiscated TO weapons from the JNA's warehouse at Faletići, in the northeast corner of Sarajevo, for

---

[13] Silber and Little, *Death of Yugoslavia*, p. 324. See also Marko Lopušina, *Ubij bližnjeg svog: Jugoslovenska tajna policija 1945/1995* [Kill your neighbour: the Yugoslav secret police 1945–1995], Belgrade 1996, p. 392.

[14] Šefko Hodžić, 'Kako je nastajala Armija (4): sporna direktiva' [How the Army was formed (4): the disputed order], *Oslobođenje*, Sarajevo 19 April 1997, p. 14.

[15] Halilović, *Lukava strategija*, pp. 57–8.

fear of JNA retaliation. Efendić later agreed that such an action would have been suicidal.[16]

THE INFLUX OF JNA OFFICERS

A new dimension to civilian–military relations in Bosnia-Herzegovina was added by the arrival of JNA officers, who answered Efendić's appeal of 13 April to defect to the OSRB:H. Several of the men who would come to head the ARBiH in mid-1993 defected at this time, including Rasim Delić and Fikret Muslimović. The embryonic Bosnian Army thus comprised three principal currents among its officer corps: PL, TO and JNA.[17] Izetbegović may have preferred the newcomers from the JNA, because they lacked the popular local bases of their PL counterparts and were, therefore, more dependent upon the regime's patronage. Furthermore, the vacillation of these officers between remaining in the JNA and joining the Bosnian resistance mirrored somewhat Izetbegovic's own vacillation between ordering a general war of liberation and attempting to reach a peaceful and negotiated solution with the Serbian enemy. Fikret Muslimović, who became the SDA's chief ideologue within the ARBiH and favoured candidate for the role of commander, has claimed that as chief intelligence officer of the Sarajevo corps of the JNA he attempted to facilitate talks between Izetbegović and Yugoslav Defence Minister General Veljko Kadijević so as to sideline the SDS and prevent the JNA from falling wholly under the influence of Slobodan Milošević.[18]

On 23 May Halilović replaced Efendić as chief of staff of the TO, which would be officially renamed the Army of the Republic of Bosnia-Herzegovina (ARBiH) by presidential decree on 4 July. In early June an Operational Command was established at Visoko under Rasim Delić to help organize and coordinate the formation of military units in the wider Sarajevo region. Halilović would later complain of Izetbegović giving direct orders to Delić in a manner that violated military protocol by bypassing the TO staff and without informing them.[19] The 'Visoko group' of officers would provide a pool of cadres from which Izetbegović remodelled the ARBiH in mid-1993, when he appointed Delić as ARBiH commander in place of Halilović and demoted many of the 'Sarajevo group' of officers close to the latter.

[16] Šefko Hodžić, 'Kako je nastajala Armija (8): otimanje oružja' [How the army was formed (8): the seizure of weapons], *Oslobođenje*, Sarajevo, 22 April 1997; Sefer Halilović, *Lukava strategija*, pp 58–9.

[17] Šefko Hodžić, 'Kako je nastajala Armija (7): dvojno komandovanje' [How the army was formed (7): dual command], *Oslobođenje*, Sarajevo, 22 April 1997, p. 15.

[18] Muslimović, *Odbrana Republike*, p. 20.

[19] Halilović, *Lukava strategija*, pp. 13–14.

With the Bosnian armed forces as diverse and subject to local conditions as they were, Izetbegović, Halilović and other political and military leaders depended for their influence over the military on their own personal patronage networks, giving rise to power struggles in which Izetbegović ultimately overcame all his opponents to achieve complete personal control of the army, as of the SDA.

BATTLE FOR SARAJEVO, 2–3 MAY 1992

On 2–3 May there occurred the most decisive political and military battle for control of the Bosnian capital between Izetbegović and the Bosnian resistance on the one hand and the JNA and its Muslim collaborators on the other. Those days also occasioned the most serious clash to date between Izetbegović and Halilović. On 2 May the Green Berets and Sarajevo citizenry prevented the JNA from removing the archives from the Army Office, though Ejup Ganić as Izetbegović's deputy had instructed the TO commander of the Old Town in Sarajevo not to obstruct the removal for fear of weakening Izetbegovic's negotiating position during international talks at Lisbon by presenting the Bosnian side as the aggressor.[20] In response to the obstruction, General Kukanjac, JNA commander of the Sarajevo corps, ordered a general attack on the city and capture of the Bosnian Presidency building. This was to be coordinated, it would seem, with kidnapping Izetbegović at Sarajevo airport and an attempted *coup d'état* on the part of Abdić and Delimustafić.[21]

However, in a successful counter-attack commanded by Halilović, JNA columns were surrounded or destroyed by the Sarajevo defenders while Kukanjac himself was blockaded as he advanced from his headquarters in Bistrik. On 3 May it was agreed that Izetbegović would be released in return for the Bosnian side allowing Kukanjac and his column of 400 troops to evacuate the Bistrik barracks. Halilović, however, appears to have attacked the JNA column in violation of the agreement and against Izetbegović's will as soon as the president was in Bosnian hands, much to Izetbegović's displeasure.[22]

This clash, which heralded the conflict between Bosnia's president and the commander of its army, coincided with the ending of the division of policy between the president and the Interior Ministry. The Bosnian police forces, on paper the strongest single element within the OSRBiH, had

---

[20] Šefko Hodžić, 'Kako je nastajala Armija (12): Sarajevo 2. maja '92' [How the army was formed (12): Sarajevo 2 May 1992], *Oslobođenje*, Sarajevo, 17 April 1997.

[21] Silber and Little, *Death of Yugoslavia* pp. 262–3; Alibabić-Munja, *Bosna u kandžama*, pp. 62–3.

[22] Silber and Little, *Death of Yugoslavia* pp. 263–7.

played a crucial role in the defence of the capital in April. Nevertheless, the Interior Ministry under Delimustafić had continued after the declaration of independence to act more as an instrument of Belgrade's rule over Bosnia than as an institution of Bosnian statehood, and prevented the police's full mobilization in the latter's defence.[23] Delimustafić was now replaced as interior minister on account of his suspected role in the coup attempt. Under his successor, Jusuf Pušina, the Interior Ministry would continue to clash with the army headed by Halilović, while simultaneously becoming an increasingly obedient tool of the regime as the leaders and officials of the SDA and the bureaucrats and security officers of the former communist regime melded into a new Bosniak elite.

Izetbegović's stance towards the JNA toughened following the events of 2–3 May. His refusal to allow the JNA to withdraw from the Marshal Tito Barracks in Sarajevo with its weapons led, on 16 May, to the JNA's attempt to break into the city, link up with the garrison at the barracks and cut the city in half along the line Pofalići–Vraca. The JNA's defeat in this battle, and its almost simultaneous defeat in Tuzla, ensured that the Bosnian heartland would remain in government hands. The inability of the Serb forces to conquer the Bosnian capital stemmed in large part from the nature of their political goals: their endeavour to kill or expel the non-Serb population of the territory they occupied left them with no means of holding or governing large Muslim-majority cities like Sarajevo and Tuzla, while forcing the latter's defenders to fight to the last in what for them became a life-or-death struggle.

Following the failure of the Abdić–Delimustafić coup at the start of May, Serbian forces could capture a city only by pulverising it, Vukovar style – a method that was extremely costly. But there were equally strong political reasons why Sarajevo's defenders could not break out of the besieged capital. According to some sources, successful offensives by Bosnian forces in Sarajevo against Serbian positions at Ilidža, Grbavica and Vraca in April and May were ended by negotiations carried out by treacherous members of the Bosnian leadership.[24] Criminal elements in the Bosnian armed forces may also have had a vested interest in maintaining the siege and the lucrative black market that went with it, and may have done so in collaboration with fellow criminals among the Serbian besiegers and the HVO. On the Igman front, Bosnian 1st corps commander Mustafa Hajrulahović claimed that the front lines were controlled by the mafia of all nationalities.[25] Here were located the forces of the Sarajevan gangster Jusuf Juka Prazina, which were formally part of the ARBiH but which resisted control by the General Staff; Prazina would

---

[23] Halilović, *Lukava strategija*, pp. 60–2.

[24] Alibabić-Munja, *Bosna u kandžama*, p. 64; Halilović, *Lukava strategija*, p. 10.

[25] Mustafa Hajrulahović Talijan, 'Igman je naša najružna ratna priča' [Igman is our most infamous war story], *Ljiljan*, Sarajevo, 18 March 1998, pp. 28–9.

eventually defect to the HVO. The collapse of the ARBiH's position on Igman in the summer of 1993 appears to have been the result of corruption and treason.[26]

THE POLITICAL SPLIT BETWEEN ARBIH AND HVO

A further obstacle to Sarajevo's liberation lay in the gradually escalating conflict between the ARBiH and the HVO. Following the Presidency's declaration of the unification of Bosnia-Herzegovina's armed forces on 9 April, minister of defence and HDZ member Jerko Doko stated that the HVO was 'his business' and that he would take care of its incorporation in the OS BiH. The HVO, nevertheless, rejected its inclusion in the new army and formed its own General Staff on 15 April.[27] The HVO at Kiseljak obstructed efforts by the Bosnian Army to break the siege of the capital. [28] The wholly Muslim character of the Izetbegović regime, indeed, made it impossible to challenge the anti-Bosnian HDZ's hold over the HVO.

The structure of the Bosnian regime, a coalition in which the SDA was dominant and the HDZ a junior partner, accelerated the dismantling of the Bosnian state as the HDZ pursued an increasingly separatist policy. As late as January 1993, Halilović was blaming the conflict between the ARBiH and the HVO on Croat politicians, saying that without their interference he and Milivoj Petković could have reached agreement within minutes.[29] The Izetbegović regime, however, had no defence against this interference.

The HVO was officially recognized from 20 May as a constituent part of the ARBiH. The Tuđman–Izetbegović agreement of 21 July recognized the HVO and ARBiH as distinct elements of the OSRBiH to be united under a joint staff. However, the HVO remained loyal exclusively to the HDZ leadership and, consequently, to Zagreb and, to ensure his full independence from Croatian influence, Halilović transferred the ARBiH out of the jurisdiction of the Croat-controlled Bosnian Ministry of Defence.[30]

---

[26] Ibid. Alibabić-Munja, *Bosna u kandžama*, pp. 71–7.
[27] Šefko Hodžić, 'Kako je nastajala armija (11): gdje je Hrvatsko Vijeće Odbrane?' [How the army was formed (11): where is the HVO?], *Oslobođenje*, Sarajevo, 26 April 1992, p. 21.
[28] Šefko Hodžić, 'Kako je nastajala armija (10): Kako deblokirati Sarajevo?' [How the army was formed: how to lift the siege of Sarajevo?], *Oslobođenje*, Sarajevo, 25 April 1997, p. 20.
[29] Interview with Sefer Halilović, in *Armija Bosne i Hercegovine 1992–1995*, pp. 26–7.
[30] Halilović, *Lukava strategija*, pp. 139–41.

The political split of the OSRBiH into two hostile parts – the HVO as a Zagreb-controlled Croat-separatist force and the ARBiH as the increasingly Muslim-dominated party-army of the SDA – facilitated the territorial partition of the country and the collapse of Bosnian defences in Posavina and Central Bosnia.[31] The town of Bosanski Brod fell to Serbian forces on 8 October and Jajce on the 29th. The latter defeat occurred six days after the HVO seized control of Prozor from the ARBiH and expelled its Muslim population.

The final straw leading to all-out war between the ARBiH and HVO was, however, provided by the international community, whose Vance–Owen Peace Plan of January 1993 divided Bosnia-Herzegovina into ten prospective provinces divided between the Croats, Serbs and Muslims. This was taken by the Bosnian HDZ as legitimizing its military possession of the three provinces assigned to the Croats. Bosnian defence minister and HDZ politician Božo Rajić responded by ordering all ARBiH units in the Croat provinces to submit to HVO command, and all HVO units in the Muslim provinces to ARBiH command, which resulted in fighting as the ARBiH resisted Rajić's order.[32]

REORGANIZATION OF THE SUPREME COMMAND AND ATTACK ON THE PATRIOTIC LEAGUE

Two events were decisive for the establishment of Izetbegović's full personal control of the ARBiH: the replacement of Halilović as commander, in June 1993, and Operation Trebević in October of the same year. Halilović's replacement had been considered as early as July 1992, something that has been ascribed variously to his military failures, pressure from the Croatian side and his power struggle with the Bosnian Ministry of the Interior and Ministry of Defence.[33] Halilović attributes his growing isolation within the Bosnian leadership to his policy disagreements with Izetbegović: 'He constantly spoke of an end to the war, and I of a struggle for freedom.'[34] The SDA favoured Muslimović as ARBiH commander while the Croatian lobby favoured Jasmin Jaganjac, a Muslim officer who had served both in the Croatian Army and the HVO. Halilović's position was temporarily rescued by his successful counter-offensive against Serbian forces on the Žuč hill above Sarajevo in December 1992, but

---

[31] Attila Hoare, 'The Croatian Project to Partition Bosnia-Hercegovina 1990–1994', *East European Quarterly*, Boulder, CO, vol. XXXI, No. 1, March 1997, p. 128.

[32] Ibid., pp. 132–3.

[33] Šefko Hodžić, 'Kako je nastajala armija (22): Ko umjesto Sefera?' [How the army was formed (22): who to replace Sefer?], *Oslobođenje*, Sarajevo, 8 May 1992, p. 20.

[34] Halilović, *Lukava strategija*, pp. 10, 105–8.

over the following six months ARBiH defeats in East Bosnia (Cerska, Kamenica, Srebrenica) and the intensification of the conflict with the HVO increased the pressure for his replacement.[35]

On 2 June 1993 Izetbegović announced to the collective Presidency his reorganization of the Bosnian High Command. Halilović has argued that Izetbegović lacked the requisite majority in the Presidency, and that therefore his demotion was unconstitutional.[36] The changes involved Halilović remaining chief of staff, but being relegated to the number four position in the army hierarchy. The top position would be the newly created one of commandant, to which Rasim Delić was appointed, with Divjak and Šiber as his deputies. Delić and Muslimović, both of whom had gone over to the Bosnian side as late as April 1992, were promoted to the rank of general, while two top Bosnian commanders, PL founding-members Zićro Suljević and Rifat Bilajac, were likewise promoted but simultaneously retired.

The high command received the news of the changes on 8 June with much surprise and bitterness. The reorganization was arrived at without consulting the general staff and was therefore political in motivation; one of the ARBiH's two deputy commanders (Jovan Divjak) himself opposed the changes, though the other (Stjepan Šiber) was in favour.[37] Halilović denounced the changes, in particular the promotion of Delić and Muslimović, and threatened to resign.[38] Bilajac lamented that 'The Patriotic League has been defeated. The enemy has succeeded in turning one against the other.'[39] Vahid Karavelić, another PL founding-member, described the changes as 'a direct blow to the Patriotic League'.[40] Muslimović would later accuse Halilović of having attempted to incite the staff of the high command to a *coup d'état*. The commanders may indeed have been on the verge of rejecting the changes, but Muslimović made the decisive intervention by reminding them that 'before us is the order of the High Command. Do not permit the High Command to be obstructed'.[41]

Under Halilović the ARBiH had been an autonomous body whose policies and actions were pursued independently of the Presidency and organs of government and whose functioning owed much to the chief of staff's personal control over the irregular forces in and around Sarajevo. Under Rasim Delić it would become a compliant tool of the president of

---

[35] Hodžić, 'Ko umjesto Sefera?', p. 20.
[36] Sefer Halilović, 'Samo su trezorasi gori od podrumasa!' [Only those who lived in safes are worse than those who lived in cellars!], interview in *Slobodna Bosna*, Sarajevo, no. 47, 15 June 1997, p. 11.
[37] Halilović, *Lukava strategija*, pp. 27–8.
[38] Ibid., pp. 29–38.
[39] Ibid., p. 33.
[40] Ibid., p. 35.
[41] Ibid., p. 35.

the Presidency, wholly subordinate to the Izetbegović regime's political goals and dependent in turn on the president's personal control over irregular units.

OPERATION TREBEVIĆ: ATTACK ON THE PRIVATE ARMIES

The second stage in the president's subordination of the army would occur in late October 1993, with Operation Trebević. This was a military operation conducted by the army and police against the 9th motorized and 10th mountain brigades commanded by the Sarajevan warlords Ramiz Delalić Ćelo and Mušan Topalović Caco, who controlled a large part of the besieged capital. Initially effective and obedient military leaders, Topalović and Delalić became increasingly self-willed and undisciplined during 1993 as Bosnian state power crumbled, and their units were gradually transformed into private armies in the service of their criminal fiefdoms. They paralysed the functioning of state and legal bodies in the capital and carried out a reign of terror against civilians. Topalović and Delalić appear to have enjoyed a close relationship with Halilović; Hajrulahović, as commander of Sarajevo's defences, claimed subsequently that the latter had exercised an informal system of authority over the gangsters.[42] The 9th and 10th brigades were therefore feared as units in the service of the army commander's personal policies.

On 2–3 July Topalović's and Delalić's men occupied and disarmed the police station in Sarajevo's Old Town; four days later Halilović's apartment was blown up and his wife and brother-in-law killed in what may have been a failed assassination attempt against the chief of staff organized by his enemies in the Bosnian security services.[43]

On 26 October Operation Trebević was launched under the direction of Enver Mujezinović, a former KOS officer and Muslimović's colleague, who had been transferred directly from Belgrade to a top security post in the Bosnian Ministry of Defence in May 1992. In a bloody showdown Topalović was killed and Delalić arrested while Halilović was blockaded in his headquarters. This was followed by action against other individuals and bodies considered unreliable by the regime. Halilović was immediately sacked as chief of staff and placed under investigation. The Sarajevo (King Tvrtko) brigade of the HVO was forcibly incorporated into the ARBiH on 6 November, as was the 115th HVO brigade in Tuzla at the end of the year. Dragan Vikić, commander of the Interior Ministry special forces, was dismissed in January 1994 and security chief Munir Alibabić in August.

[42] Hajrulahović, *Igman*.
[43] Medina Delalić and Jelena Stamenković, 'Kako je Izetbegović štitio kriminal (ce) i zločin(c)e' [How Izetbegović protected crime and criminals], *Slobodna Bosna*, Sarajevo, no. 95, 10 September 1998, p. 9.

Operation Trebević coincided with Izetbegović's reclaiming of the moribund Bosnian government for his regime: previously crippled by divisions between Muslim and Croat ministers, with the latter holding the premiership and Ministry of Defence, it now became a firmly Muslim and SDA body under Haris Silajdžić.

IDEOLOGICAL TRANSFORMATION:
FROM DEFENCE OF BOSNIA TO DEFENCE OF BOSNIAKS

The ideology of the Bosnian Army too underwent a transformation following Operation Trebević in that its Bosniak-national element became more pronounced. The war was increasingly presented by army commanders and spokesmen as a struggle for the survival of the Bosniak nation, its culture and the Islamic religion. According to Muslimović as chief propagandist of the reconstituted army, the successes of the liberation struggle were due to the

> high level of political organization of the Bosniak nation, to whom the SDA gave its principal meaning and stamp. Of particular service were the SDA and its cadres, and particularly the President of the Presidency of the Republic of Bosnia-Herzegovina Mr Alija Izetbegović. ... The prestige of our Army is at once the prestige of our nation, and the prestige of our nation is inseparable from the prestige of the SDA.[44]

Military operations were increasingly subordinated to the political interests of the regime. Even Delić, President Izetbegović's protégé, complained subsequently about soldiers being unwilling to fight for territories surrendered by the political leadership to the Serbs and Croats during international negotiations.[45]

The Islamic orientation of the army was increased after the conflicts and organizational changes of 1993. Rašid Muminović, chief of the Department of Religious Affairs at the army's Office of Political Affairs, stated, 'the Islamic Community does not wish to be concerned solely with "the needs of believers", but that the science of Islam and Muslim tradition be the basis for the morale of the Muslim-Bosniaks, particularly if we want "the Army to resemble its nation"!'[46] Rather than becoming an Islamic fundamentalist army committed to a religious struggle, how-

---

[44] Muslimović, *Odbrana Republike*, p. 199.

[45] Rasim Delić, interview in *Armija Bosne i Hercegovine 1992–1995*, pp. 42–3.

[46] Rašid Muminović, 'Uloga Islamske zajednice na ostvarivanju vjerskih potreba pripadnika ARBiH' [The role of the Islamic community in the realization of religious needs of ARBiH members], in *Duhovna snaga odbrane* [The spiritual force of the defence], Press Centre ARBiH, Sarajevo, February 1994, p. 86.

ever, the ARBiH was being transformed into a Bosniak-national army committed to a national-liberation struggle to which Islam was subordinated and for which it served as a badge. 'Islamic patriotism' or 'religious patriotism' were equated with the 'Bosniak liberation struggle'.[47] However, some units such as the 7th Muslim brigade and the Black Swans did adopt an ideology that tended to present the liberation struggle in essentially religious terms.[48] Units of this kind may have formed the basis for a parallel system of command exercised by Izetbegović and Čengić that, like Rasim Delić's 'Visoko group', bypassed the General Staff and thus acted as precursor to a wholly party-based army.[49]

The US-brokered Washington Agreement of March 1994 that ended the ARBiH's bloody conflict with the HVO and Croatian Army marked a further step in the dismantling of the Bosnian state and the army's subordination to Izetbegović and the SDA. The Agreement envisaged the establishment of a loose Bosnian 'Federation' that would encompass the territories under ARBiH and HVO control and supersede the existing state formations, the Republic of Bosnia-Herzegovina and the HZ H-B. The Federation was to have a 'unified military command', yet in the transitional period leading up to its establishment 'current command structures will remain in place'.[50] The ARBiH and HVO were to be united in a federation army, but retain their separate structures. On 11 March 1994 the Split Agreement was signed between General Rasim Delić and General Ante Roso as commanders of the ARBiH and HVO respectively, as preliminary to the establishment of a joint staff. This agreement was reached under the auspices of US General John Galvin, and US military representatives would thenceforth invest considerable effort into attempting to forge the two armies into a functioning unified force.[51]

While improving the ARBiH's military position, however, the Washington Agreement accelerated its transformation into a purely

---

[47] See Nedžad Latić, 'Hej, hej, nek se znade, postojale Muslimanske brigade' [Hey, let it be known that Muslim brigades did exist], *Ljiljan*, Sarajevo, no. 273, 8 April 1998, p. 10.

[48] See the interviews with Halil Brzina and Asim Koričić in *Armija Bosne i Hercegovina 1992–1995*, p. 66 and p. 70; Chuck Sudetich, 'Crni Labudovi' [Black swans], *BiH Eksklusiv*, Sarajevo, 30 June 1995, no. 140, p. 3.

[49] Vildana Selimbegović, 'Kako je nestajala Armija BiH: pojela je politika' [How the army disappeared: swallowed up by politics], *Dani*, Sarajevo, no. 54, April 1997, pp. 24–5.

[50] Framework Agreement establishing a Federation in areas of the Republic of Bosnia-Herzegovina with a majority Bosniak and Croat population, and Outline of a Preliminary Agreement for a Confederation between the Republic of Croatia and the Federation, 2 March 1994.

[51] Željko Grubešić, 'Godina jačanja ugleda Armije RBiH' [The years of growth of ARBiH prestige], *Prva Linija* [The front line], Sarajevo, no. 19, year 3, December 1994, pp. 24–5.

Muslim army. The Bosnian government and staff of the high command were immediately forced to abandon their policy of incorporating the HVO into the ARBiH.[52] Furthermore, the establishment of a Federation under joint state institutions in which the HZ H-B leaders would be guaranteed representation threatened a degree of Croatian influence over the Bosnian state and, consequently, over the army. During the course of 1994, therefore, the staff of the high command was renamed the general staff, and all remaining functions related to the army were removed from the jurisdiction of the Ministry of Defence and united under its aegis.[53] The general staff appeared intent on remaining independent of the Presidency of the Federation and was accused by Croatian sources of obstructing the formation of a joint staff, even as it demanded the full merger of the HVO and ARBiH into a unified military force.[54]

The ARBiH was becoming a party army of the SDA independent of the formal state bodies. Consequently, the personality of President Izetbegović would assume an increasingly central role in army propaganda: in April 1994 the ARBiH's Department for Morale initiated a study of 'the personal role of Mr Alija Izetbegović in the defensive organization of the nation'.[55] On 20 October 1994 at a ceremony at Zenica, Izetbegović was proclaimed 'honorary commander' of the 7th Muslim brigade.

The manifestations of Islamicization of the army that characterized the Zenica ceremony provoked a clash between Izetbegović and Vice-President Ejup Ganić, on the one hand, and the non-SDA members of the Presidency on the other. The latter, as one of the last feeble bastions of multi-ethnicity in the state, would on 30 January 1995 condemn the politicization of the ARBiH as manifested at Zenica, and its transformation into an Islamic, Bosniak and SDA army.[56] Izetbegović reacted with fury and contempt directed at his fellow Presidency members, stating that 'the 7th Muslim with its fighting has objectively done more to safeguard a Bosnia of citizens than all those self-proclaimed, vociferous democrats who sit at home and just talk about Bosnia'.[57] Although the Presidency remained officially the supreme command of the army, Izetbegović did not recognize the right of his presidential colleagues to interfere in its affairs.

---

[52] Rasim Delić, *Bosnia is Here*, Press Centre of the Army of the Republic of Bosnia and Herzegovina, Sarajevo, October 1995, p. 8.

[53] Haris Halilović, 'Efikasnijim komandovanjem do slobode' [With more efficient command to freedom], *Prva Linija* [The front line], no. 20, year 4, January 1995, p. 4.

[54] Delić, *Bosnia is here*, pp. 74–5.

[55] Esad Hećimović, 'Kako su prodali Srebrenicu i sačuvali vlast' [How they sold out Srebrenica and kept power], *Dani*, Sarajevo, special edition, September 1998, p. 27.

[56] Ibid., pp. 51–2.

[57] Ibid., p. 52.

SARAJEVO, MAGLAJ AND SREBRENICA:
POLITICAL NEEDS AND MILITARY LOGIC

The army had by 1994–95 long since ceased to play any political as opposed to military role in the struggle for a unified Bosnia-Herzegovina, but its political role in the maintenance of the SDA regime was increasingly important, at the expense of its military performance. On 15 April 1994, at the height of the Serbian onslaught on Goražde, Commander Delić spent the entire day holding conferences in celebration of the second anniversary of the army's birth, and spent the evening with his top commanders at the theatre in Sarajevo.[58] Major military operations would be undertaken less for strategic reasons than for the sake of the regime's political ambitions or to improve its political standing. General Mehmed Alagić, commander of the 7th corps and himself an SDA supporter, recalls Izetbegović demanding that he break the siege of Maglaj even though this was not militarily feasible.[59] Alagić subsequently resisted Izetbegović's surrender of strategically key territory around Kupres to the HVO as part of an agreement on 'borders' with Croatian President Tuđman.[60]

Far more costly would be the army's attempt to break the siege of Sarajevo in June and July 1995, undertaken without the requisite military conditions, which may have cost the lives of over 400 Bosnian soldiers. In the face of the exhaustion of Sarajevo's population and the unwillingness of the Western alliance to confront Serbia, Izetbegović had spoken openly of attempting to break the siege militarily on repeated occasions, beginning in April 1995. The offensive was undertaken for political reasons: to stabilize the regime and reassert its credibility.[61] At the same time, Rasim Delić would in early July call for the 'common and coordinated activity' of the party and army to ensure favourable conditions on the home front during the offensive.[62]

The counterpart to the Sarajevo offensive was the abandonment of the besieged enclaves of Srebrenica and Žepa in East Bosnia to Serbian forces in July. Izetbegović, Ganić and other SDA leaders had discussed handing over Srebrenica and Žepa to the VRS on several occasions in exchange for the Serbian abandonment of the occupied Sarajevan suburbs of Vogošća and Ilijaš that separated the capital from the rest of government-held

---

[58] Hećimović, 'Kako su prodali Srebrenicu', p. 27.
[59] Nedžad Latić and Zehrudin Isaković, Ratna sjećanja Mehmeda Alagića: rat u Srednjoj Bosni [Mehmed Alagić's war memories: war in central Bosnia]', Bemust, Zenica 1997, p. 37.
[60] Ibid., p. 49.
[61] Hećimović, 'Kako su prodali Srebrenicu', pp. 54–9; Latić and Isaković, Ratna sjećanja Mehmeda Alagića, p. 65.
[62] Hećimović, 'Kako su prodali Srebrenicu', p. 58.

territory.[63] In March 1995 Naser Orić, commander of the 28th division in Srebrenica, and 15 of his officers were withdrawn from the enclave for 'retraining' and never returned, yet in June the defenders of Srebrenica were required to launch diversionary attacks on the VRS in support of the offensive around Sarajevo, a tactic General Divjak condemned as 'insane' since it provided a pretext for the Serbian counter-offensive and occupation of the 'safe area'.[64]

The ARBiH General Staff made no military effort whatsoever to assist Srebrenica, for whose survival the regime chose to rely solely on the international community. Izetbegović himself admitted that the town could have held out for a further month had it received the support of the army.[65] On 11 July, the day the VRS occupied the town, Rasim Delić devoted only 5 minutes of his 25 minute military report to this imminent military and human catastrophe. The SDA leadership ignored the latter too, preoccupied as it was with finding a replacement for Vice-President Ganić, who had been injured in a road accident.[66] The power struggle between Naser Orić and the SDA for control of the town may also help to explain the failure of military coordination between Orić and the general staff and 2nd corps in Tuzla.[67]

CONFLICT IN ZENICA: PROFESSIONAL ARMY OR 'ARMED PEOPLE'

The failed Sarajevo offensive and the fall of Srebrenica provided the occasion for the removal of the final obstacle to the achievement of complete control of the army by Izetbegović and his followers: the attempts by Prime Minister Haris Silajdžić, an ambitious politician from outside the president's inner circle, to claim a degree of influence over military affairs. The quarrel within the Presidency over the Zenica ceremony had coincided with early rumblings of the impending storm between Izetbegović and

[63] Ibid., pp. 74–82.
[64] Ibid., pp. 45–6.
[65] Ibid., pp. 61–71.
[66] Ibid., pp. 9–13.
[67] David Rohde, *A Safe Area – Srebrenica: Europe's worst massacre since the Second World War*, London 1997, pp. 356–8. 2nd corps commander Sead Delić was an SDA supporter; he moved his elite units *away* from Srebrenica and towards Sarajevo a mere four days before the enclave fell, and resisted all calls from his officers for a military push to link up with its fleeing soldiers and civilians. See Mehmed Pargan, 'Baljkovica: najveći poraz Armije BiH' [Baljkovica: ARBiH's greatest defeat], *Slobodna Bosna*, Sarajevo, no. 88, pp. 28–30; Ismet Hasanović and Nirzad Karamujić, 'Lovačka puška bila je razlog da se bošnjacko selo opkoli sa 12 transportera UN-a' [A hunting gun provided the reason for 28 UN transporters to surround a Bosniak village], interview in *Ljiljan*, Sarajevo, no. 211, 29 January 1997, pp. 32–3.

Silajdžić which broke out at the 6th session of the General Council of the SDA on 18–19 January. To Silajdžić's increasing restlessness in the face of the government's marginalization in affairs concerning the army, Izetbegović would respond by insisting that full authority over the latter be vested in him as President of the Presidency.[68]

Silajdžić advocated the reduction of the 200,000-strong conscript army by at least 50,000 and its transformation into a professional force, which may have conflicted with the hardline-SDA vision of the army as incubator of national and religious consciousness in the Muslim 'nation in arms'.[69] He also favoured the dissolution of the military in favour of civilian administration in parts of the country and the revitalization of the Military Council of the Republic. Silajdžić had opposed the leaking of the start of the Sarajevo offensive and was aggrieved that major military operations of this kind were undertaken without prior consultation with him.[70] On 3 August 1995 he resigned his post and denounced the Sarajevo offensive for preparing the ground for the Serbian conquest of Srebrenica and Žepa.[71]

At the SDA General Council meeting of 5 August in Zenica, which censured Silajdžić following his resignation, Čengić responded by accusing Silajdžić's Ministry of Defence of having fallen under the command of the Croatian Ministry of Defence. The integration of the Ministry of Defence into a joint Croatian–Bosnian defensive system had led Izetbegović and the SDA leadership to sideline their own government so as to protect the army from Croatian influence.[72] Following the Council's censure of the premier a directive was sent to all members of the ARBiH signed by Delić, but actually written by Muslimović as chief of the Department for Morale of the general staff, claiming that Silajdžić's conduct 'wholly conforms to the consistent, well-known efforts of our enemies to sow dissension and conflict among the highest political and state leaders of our country'. The directive virulently denounced the prime minister's policies concerning the army, and reminded soldiers that 'Silajdžić's conduct was unanimously condemned at the extended session of the General Council of the SDA'. It was further said that 'in the educational and political work with members of ARBiH, [it is necessary to] emphasize our military and patriotic responsibility, which is that in every situation, including this one, our basic orientation must be the demands of our supreme commander President of the Presidency Mr Alija Izetbegović.'[73]

---

[68] Hećimović, 'Kako su prodali Srebrenicu', pp. 39–40.
[69] Ibid., p. 59.
[70] Ibid., p. 52.
[71] Ibid., pp. 61–4.
[72] Ibid., p. 69.
[73] 'Pismo Generala Delića pripadnicima Armije' [General Delić's letter to members of the army], reproduced in Slobodna Bosna, Sarajevo, no. 1, 4 September 1995, p. 17.

FUSION OF SDA AND ARBIH:
UNOCCUPIED BOSNIA-HERZEGOVINA AS A BOSNIAK PARA-STATE

The growth in the size and power of the Bosnian Army in the period 1993–95, culminating in the victorious offensives of summer and autumn 1995, did not result in any significant territorial gains other than those achieved by the 5th corps, the military unit over which, given its territorial separation from the Bosnian heartland, Izetbegović's personal influence was weakest. Indeed, the territorial settlement achieved by the Bosnian delegation at Dayton in November 1995 was scarcely more favourable than that offered by the Owen–Stoltenberg Plan of two years earlier, drawn up at the nadir of Bosnian military fortunes.[74]

The political campaign waged by the Izetbegović regime during this period culminated not in the liberation of Bosnia-Herzegovina from the Serbian and Croatian aggressors, but in the achievement of almost absolute power by the president and the SDA within the unoccupied rump of Bosnia-Herzegovina, which had assumed the character of a Bosniak-national para-state.

The Bosnian state that existed in 1992 had been a compound multi-national entity in which rival political and national forces contended for control. In the face of aggression from Bosnia-Herzegovina's neighbours – first by Serbia and subsequently also by Croatia – and the threatened extermination of the Muslim Bosniaks as a nation, in which numerous elements within the Bosnian state collaborated, the Izetbegović regime achieved security for the Bosniak nation by the most conservative means. The common institutions of Bosnian statehood were deemed unreliable and dismantled, while the Bosniak national interest was identified solely with the president, the ruling party and the army, in consequence of which these three institutions became increasingly fused. High-ranking Bosnian officials, generals and politicians who obstructed this fusion (Sefer Halilović, Munir Alibabić, Rusmir Mahmutćehajić, Haris Silajdžić and others) were dismissed or sidelined.

Furthermore, the imposition of complete control by the SDA over the army in the period 1993–95 was a means by which the regime overcame the problem of localism across the territory of the rump Bosniak state. A series of local opponents, varied in nature, were challenged, and either ousted or marginalized by the Izetbegović regime: the HVO in Croat-majority areas; Selim Bešlagić and his fellow Social Democrats in Tuzla; Jusuf Prazina at Igman; Topalović and Delalić in Sarajevo; Fikret Abdić in the Cazinska Krajina and Naser Orić in Srebrenica. By the war's end in the autumn of 1995, military power in every territory held by the ARBiH

---

[74] The principal Bosnian territorial gain at Dayton was exclusive possession of the city of Sarajevo.

was firmly in the hands of local SDA leaders loyal to Izetbegović. The Bosniak nation, as represented by the SDA, achieved in this way control of the Bosnian heartland as a militarily secure and politically stable national territory; the price to be paid was acceptance of a partition of Bosnia-Herzegovina in which the Bosniak nation would effectively cease to exist in the two-thirds of the country outside of the SDA's para-state.

The Bosniak nation has survived, but the state of Bosnia-Herzegovina is still fighting to ensure its existence.

9

Serb War Effort and Termination of the War
Norman Cigar

In looking back at the recent conflicts that have engulfed former Yugoslavia, a key area of study has to be the Serb war effort, which was a central factor in the military and political situation of the region. This study will focus on the 1991 war in Croatia and the 1992–95 war in Bosnia-Herzegovina, although the other phases of the Serbian-Croatian conflict and especially the merging of the two wars in 1995 are also germane. As part of that process, the Serbian strategy for war termination, by which is meant why and how a belligerent decides to end a war at a specific time, merits particular attention, as this phase can determine the shape of the political end-state resulting from a conflict.[1]

This chapter will argue that the Serb belligerents – whether Serbian President Slobodan Milošević, the JNA leadership or the Bosnian Serb leadership – waged war in the pursuit of concrete military and political objectives, and that it was a shift in the military situation on the battlefield that was the key factor in catalysing war termination and a political solution in each case. To be sure, as Paul R. Pillar has pointed out, the relationship between the military situation and political negotiations is a complex one: 'Combat does not influence diplomacy directly; it does so through the intervening variables of a belligerent's perceptions, interpretations, and expectations.'[2]

The relationship of the military balance with the attainment of the political objective is crucial. The latter, though not stated explicitly, in both cases had been to add territory in pursuit of the creation of a Greater

[1] Some of the material in this study is taken from Norman Cigar, 'Croatia's War of Independence: The Parameters of War Termination', *Journal of Slavic Military Studies* (Carlisle, PA), vol. 10, June 1997, pp. 34–70, and Norman Cigar, 'How Wars End: War Termination and Serbian Decision-making in the Case of Bosnia', *South East European Monitor* (Vienna), vol. 3, no. 1, 1996, pp. 3–48.

[2] Paul Pillar, *Negotiating Peace: war termination as a bargaining process*, Princeton, NJ: Princeton University Press 1983, p. 196.

Serbia. Moreover, the relationship between the military situation and domestic political situation in Serbia was key to both war fighting and war termination, with Belgrade's war effort to a significant degree a reflection of domestic interests. Ultimately, for Milošević, going to war was a mechanism to legitimate and consolidate his own political power. Specifically, Milošević saw external war as a means to direct outward and away from his regime the latent hostility from the opposition which, as elsewhere in Eastern Europe, had begun to coalesce against the holdover communist system in Serbia. Reflecting on the Serbian communists' strategy of adopting a nationalist agenda, Milošević's adviser Slobodan Jovanović concluded that if they had not done so the opposition might have turned its discontent against the government instead: 'What would have happened with the energy of half a century of suppression of Serbian nationalist feelings? Would that enormous energy have exploded, and how, and would we have had a political war among the Serbs?'[3]

THE WAR IN CROATIA

Strategic objectives

Different actors in Serbia – Milošević, the JNA, the nationalists – had different objectives *vis-à-vis* Croatia. Initially, the JNA seems to have thought that it could establish control over all of Croatia and suppress its bid for independence by defeating the nascent Croatian Army. The Serbian political leadership seems to have been more flexible than the JNA and to have thought earlier than the latter in terms of 'amputating' Croatia by seizing parts of its territory, claiming that the republican borders were only 'administrative borders' and thus liable to change.[4] This was closer to the goals advocated by Serbian nationalists and the Serbian Orthodox Church, who had called not for retaining all of Croatia, but for taking territory up to the Karlobag–Ogulin–Karlovac–Virovitica line (about two thirds of

---

[3] Interview with Slobodan Jovanović by Nenad Stefanović, 'Slobodan Jovanović: predsednikov nepogrešiv čovek' [Slobodan Jovanović: the president's infallible man], *Duga*, Belgrade, 3–16 September 1994, p. 21. In fact, in urging the JNA to attack Slovenia, the Serbian political leadership had argued that, 'If he [General Kadijević] did not move into action in Slovenia immediately, we will lose in Serbia, whereupon the Army would also collapse.' Borisav Jović, *Poslednji dani SFRJ* [The last days of SFRY], Belgrade 1995, p. 349.

[4] Borisav Jović presented the options at a meeting on 12 September 1991, attended by the Serbian political and JNA leaders, at which he asked 'for the nth time': 'Is our aim to defend the new borders of the peoples who wish to remain in Yugoslavia, or to bring down the Croatian government?' Jović himself was against this second option and called military actions deep in Croatia 'a stupidity'. Jović, *Poslednji dani SFRJ*, p. 385.

Croatia's area) which, however, would have meant the virtual dismemberment of Croatia.[5] A natural counterpart of this aim was 'ethnic cleansing' of the territory that was to be included in the Greater Serbia. Ultimately, Milošević's territorial goals extended to wherever the JNA could reach: by October 1991, instead of aiming to take two thirds of Croatia, Serbia's political leadership had decided that it was realistic to hold on only to that territory which the JNA already had under its control, 'regardless of what the Army thinks'.[6]

Operational objectives

According to the JNA's initial operational concept, as proposed by Defence Minister General Veljko Kadijević, the military goal was, 'if the situation permits, to defeat the Croatian Army completely, and without fail to the extent necessary to achieve the objectives set'.[7] The JNA thought it would achieve its military objective with an operational plan meant to slice through most of Croatia along well-defined routes. As the JNA's chief of staff, General Blagoje Adžić, concluded: 'Croatia, cut up in this manner, would be ready to capitulate.'[8] Those in the Croatian Serb leadership then allied to Belgrade, such as Milan Babić, thought that a war would be easy.[9] The JNA communicated these ambitious operational and territorial objectives to its personnel, who were confident that the new borders could be set deep in Croatia.[10] Only when the JNA was unable to succeed in the

[5] Vuk Drašković, who later established the Serbian Renewal Movement (Srpski pokret obnove or SPO), in January 1990 drafted the platform for the Serb National Renewal (Srpska narodna obnova or SNO), a party ultimately headed by Mirko Jović, which participated in the 1991 war with its White Eagles militia. According to the SNO platform, the SNO 'commits itself to the unification with Serbia of the historical and ethnic regions (*oblasti*) of our people in Bosnia, Slavonija, Herzegovina, Lika, Kordun, Banija, Knin, and the Krajina'. 'Predlog programa stranke Srpska narodna obnova' [Proposal for the SNO party programme], *Koekude Srbijo?* [Quo Vadis, Serbia?], Belgrade 1990, p. 129. Chetnik warlord Vojislav Šešelj, for his part, called for UN troops to be placed along the Karlobag–Ogulin–Karlovac–Virovitica line in November 1991; interview with Vojislav Šešelj, 'Sada verujemo armiji' [Now we trust the army], *Pogledi*, Kragujevac, 26 November 1991, p. 33.

[6] Jović, *Poslednji dani SFRJ*, p. 392.

[7] Veljko Kadijević, *Moje viđenje raspada* [My view of the collapse], Belgrade 1993, p. 134.

[8] This is what General Adžić told the Serbian leadership on 20 September 1991. Jović, *Poslednji dana SFRJ*, p. 386.

[9] According to Croatian Serb leader Jovan Opačić, in the summer of 1991 Babić had urged his more moderate colleagues not to negotiate with the Croatian government by arguing specifically that: 'It will take us only fifteen days to deal with the Croatians by force of arms.' Jovan Opačić, 'Od sveca do izdajnika' [From saint to traitor], *NIN*, Belgrade, 25 August 1995, p. 25.

[10] For example, JNA Colonel (later Bosnian Serb Army brigadier general) Slavko Lisica, then in command of a JNA mechanized unit in the Knin corps, considered

field were these objectives reduced to cutting off smaller pieces of territory, after which, according to General Kadijević, the JNA would withdraw, having first changed the borders of Croatia.[11] However, by then the JNA had also become less optimistic about what it could accomplish without significant additional forces. In fact, the JNA would have had to defeat the Croatian Army even to achieve its later, more modest goals of territorial control. As Kadijević himself admitted on 9 September, 'the JNA does not have enough forces to fully defeat the Croatian Army'.[12]

Critical vulnerabilities

The JNA, despite its overwhelming equipment advantage, had not been a very effective force under the best of circumstances, due to numerous vulnerabilities in command and control, combined arms, logistics, and training.[13] However, it was the human factor in the form of cohesion – and such elements as morale, leadership, commitment – that was probably the JNA's most serious critical vulnerability, and which not only compromised operations but also undermined national will and threatened to spawn a political backlash at home in Serbia which could have proved menacing to Milošević's position if the war had continued.

In particular, the JNA faced a serious manpower shortage, from the start, related to weak popular commitment. Relying as it did on the mobilization of reservists, the low response by the latter made it difficult for

his objective to be the Zadar–Virovitica line; interview with Slavko Lisica by Major Veljko B. Kadijević, 'Ispovest ratnika' [A warrior's confession], *Vojska*, Belgrade, 12 May 1994, p. 19. Srđan Stanišić reported that the JNA troops with whom he travelled to the front believed that: 'We are going to the Karlobag–Ogulin–Karlovac–Virovitica border': Srđan Stanišić, 'Ratni dnevnik urednika *Pogleda*' [War diary of an editor of *Pogledi*], *Pogledi*, 18 October 1991; a collection of articles from *Pogledi* was reprinted in *Za bolju Srbiju* [For a better Serbia], Kragujevac 1993, vol. 1, p. 166. Likewise, Nenad Čanak, then a drafted reservist with the JNA, reports that a 'high-ranking officer' who visited the troops on 1 December 1991 still talked of reaching the Ogulin–Metlika–Karlovac–Virovitica line: 'Dnevnik dobrovoljca' [Diary of a volunteer], *Vreme*, Belgrade, 30 December 1991, p. 28.

[11] Kadijević, *Ispovest ratnika*, p. 135.

[12] General Kadijević reported this on 9 October 1991. Jović, *Poslednji dani SFRJ*, p. 394. In his diaries Jović noted that the former 'has now replaced the overthrow of the Croatian leadership, which he has long demanded, by withdrawal of the army [from the besieged barracks]'.

[13] Critical vulnerability is defined here as a weakness 'which can be exploited to undermine, neutralize and/or defeat the enemy's center of gravity'. See Joe Strange, *Centers of Gravity & Critical Vulnerabilities*, Quantico, VA, Marine Corps Association 1996, p. 74. The concepts and terminology used here are adapted according to his work. Also see Major Phillip Kevin Giles, and Captain Thomas P. Galvin, both of United States, *Center of Gravity: determination, analysis, and application*, Carlisle Barracks, PA: US Army War College 1996.

the JNA to function effectively, as its leadership recognized. Even early in the war, mobilization had been a problem, with only a 25 per cent response rate from those called up.[14] The shifting military balance and the accompanying rise in casualties among Serbian military personnel seem to have caused morale to plummet further and discontent to rise proportionately both on the battlefield and on the home front. Desertion, draft-dodging, and political protest rose apace as the situation at the front deteriorated, and morale and discipline, which had been poor from the start, now began to unravel. The already chaotic mobilization in Bosnia-Herzegovina was gravely undermined by Alija Izetbegović with his public statement that 'this is not our war'.[15]

On the home front, in Serbia itself, morale was also becoming a serious concern for the JNA in direct proportion to casualties at the front. By November 1991 the JNA leadership was already worried that 'defeatism is spreading among the people. Columns of parents who want to bring the soldiers home are being organized in precisely those parts of the country which must support the JNA's military effort.'[16] The Serbian political leadership, in fact, had been sensitive all along to the possibility that mobilization might lead to discontent threatening the Serbian government's stability.[17]

Vukovar – the turning point

If there was a 'decisive battle' in the war which can be identified as the turning point, it may have been the siege of Vukovar. Despite the fact that the Croatians ultimately were forced to give up the city, this event was decisive in the sense that, it would appear, it forced Serbia and the JNA to revise their military assessments and expectations for victory at an acceptable cost. Opinion at the Serbian Ministry of Defence originally had been that Vukovar would be an easy target. As the minister of defence's administrative assistant remembered, 'It was believed that Vukovar would fall anytime now. It did not!'[18] Following the sobering experience of Vukovar, the JNA began to view future operations with less optimism, especially in an

[14] Jović, *Poslednji dani SFRJ*, p. 385.
[15] For more on the context of this statement, see p. 58 and note 13 p. 203 above.
[16] S. Ristić, quoting Admiral Stane Brovet, in 'Ratni sistem Hrvatske protiv armije bez podrške' [Croatia's military system against an army lacking support], *Narodna armija*, Belgrade, 9 November 1991, p. 10.
[17] At a 30 October 1991 meeting of the leadership, for example, Borisav Jović had stated that 'we cannot succeed in such a mobilization; mass protests and a political defeat could result if we keep insisting on that'. Jović, *Poslednji dani SFRJ*, p. 407.
[18] Dobrila Gajić-Glišić, *Srpska Vojska; iz kabineta ministra vojnoga* [The Serbian Army; from the office of the minister of defence], Čačak 1992, p. 70. Mrs Gajić-Glišić was administrative assistant to Lt-Col General Tomislav Simović, Serbia's minister of defence, who directed the country's TO; subsequently, she published notes compiled during her tenure in that post.

urban environment. The unexpected breathing spell was put to good use, as the Croatian Army assimilated captured equipment and developed a fighting force in a short time – in itself quite an achievement – which eventually was able to shift to the offensive in Slavonija, where the best JNA units were committed.

War termination

War came to Milošević as no surprise. Rather, this was a conscious policy decision which was necessary if he was to change the existing republic borders in order to achieve his stated goal of 'all Serbs in a single state'. However, it is not clear to what extent Milošević had thought out his entire strategy at the beginning or if he had prepared alternatives if things went badly for him. He had enjoyed a series of unbroken political successes since 1987, and was probably especially confident of his ability to get his way. As a result, neither the Serbian political leadership nor the JNA seems to have worked out a realistic war termination strategy early in the process and had to react, clumsily as it turned out, to unforeseen events.

The available evidence suggests that what motivated Milošević and the JNA to seek an end of the war in January 1992 was primarily the deteriorating military situation, the fact that they had reached their culminating point. In other words, they assessed that they had reached the point in time and space when the belligerent on the offensive, using the means devoted up to then, has attained his apogee and begins to lose momentum to the opponent.

Belgrade, with Vukovar, had reached its culminating point, and faced a decision point at which it had either to seek to end the war by negotiations or to escalate in order to regain its stalled momentum. The latter, however, was problematic. Escalation, by increasing the level of violence – such as with massive air strikes or intensified shelling against civilian targets – would have raised the cost, but it did not guarantee victory, while greater effort on the ground would have been risky in light of the JNA's serious internal difficulties.

Given the changing circumstances, apparently both the JNA and Milošević came to the conclusion that a continuation of the war would have been increasingly to the disadvantage of the Serbs. Both at Vukovar and elsewhere the Croatian Army outfought the JNA and put the JNA increasingly on the defensive by December 1991. And, as noted, the JNA was now plagued by serious morale and manpower problems, making it hard-put to continue the war.[19] In December 1991, Serbia's Ministry of Defence, which ran the republic's TO, reported despondently that: 'The

---

[19] See Norman Cigar, 'The Serbo-Croatian war, 1991: political and military dimensions', *Journal of Strategic Studies* (Washington), September 1993, pp. 320–2.

situation at the front was ever more complicated. The last of those mobilized, those who were thoroughly disciplined, had abandoned their positions. There was a danger that Serbia would have to defend itself in Zemun.'[20]

To be sure, there had been considerable mis-communication and friction between the JNA and Serbia's political leadership over the conduct of the war, as Borisav Jović records in his diary. However, given the growing difficulties, the JNA's leadership too was coming to the conclusion that the war had to stop quickly. By late 1991, according to Borisav Jović, the JNA was urging Serb political leaders to wind up the war in Croatia with a political deal soon, arguing that 'We cannot sit at the front for a hundred years and hold onto that territory!'[21] The JNA leadership probably was also worried that if the domestic opposition, much of it Chetnik-oriented, became stronger or even took power, perhaps with the support of like-minded officers within the JNA, it would seek to replace the JNA's senior officers and restructure the Army to reflect the opposition's political orientation.[22] Such a takeover would have been made easier if the JNA suffered further setbacks or fell apart, and this was, therefore, probably an additional motive for the JNA's leadership to seek an early end to the war. Thanks to the JNA's dismal showing, the timing of the war's end enabled Milošević to rein in the JNA and to discredit its leadership while at the same time avoiding the JNA's collapse. At the same time he was able to maintain a check on the domestic opposition by way of the paramilitary units which he himself had helped to form.

[20] Gajić-Glišić, *Srpska Vojska*, p. 202.

[21] Interview with Borisav Jović by Milomir Marić, 'Nikoga nismo silom terali da ostane' [We did not force anyone to remain], *Intervju*, Belgrade, 19 August 1994, p. 6. Not everyone at the lower levels in the JNA was happy with the ceasefire. For example, Lt-Col Novica Simić (later a major general in the Bosnian Serb Army) was so irritated when ordered not to fire across the Sava after his unit had withdrawn from Croatia to Bosnia in the wake of the ceasefire, that he had ordered his artillery to fire on his own position in order to blame the Croatian Army and thus justify resuming his own firing into Croatia. Simić interviewed by [Major] Veljko B. Kadijević, 'Gospodar koridora' [Lord of the corridor], *Duga*, Belgrade, 10–23 June 1995, p. 30.

[22] There were many calls in opposition circles, and even within Serbia's Ministry of Defence, to establish a Serbian Army. See Gajić-Glišić, *Srpska Vojska*, *passim*. General Kadijević believed that Milošević was his natural ally in Serbia, in part because the opposition was made up largely of Chetniks, who represented an ideological and institutional threat to the JNA. As he told Stjepan Mesić in July 1991, when asked why he was linked to Milošević: 'With whom in Serbia, if not with him? All the others on the public scene are Chetniks; I can't go with Chetniks!' Stjepan Mesić, *Kako smo srušili Jugoslaviju; politički memoari* [How we destroyed Yugoslavia, political memoirs], Zagreb 1992, p. 128. On 28 September 1991 General Kadijević complained to the Serbian political leadership that there had already been several coup attempts within the JNA by elements tied to the hard-core nationalist opposition, including in the air force and in one of the elite guard brigades. Jović, *Poslednji dani SFRJ*, p. 388.

The broader geostrategic context

In addition, the looming crisis in Bosnia-Herzegovina was probably also a significant factor for Serbia in the timing of the end of the war. Belgrade's planned annexation of most of Bosnia-Herzegovina depended heavily on the JNA's having a free hand, and therefore it needed to avoid being bogged down in Croatia.[23]

What is more, Belgrade probably concluded that it could achieve most of its key objectives despite the agreed-upon presence of UN peacekeeping forces envisioned by the ceasefire agreement. Belgrade's assessment that the international community – whether in the form of the United Nations, the European Community, NATO or other similar body – and specifically the United States, which was viewed as the key player, would be reluctant or unable to intervene effectively had very likely been a factor in its original planning for war. As Milošević had stated in a speech in the Serbian parliament in early 1991:

> I believe and assess, and those are not only my assessments, that the great powers will not intervene in Yugoslavia. The great powers will find it difficult to intervene in any European country, especially not in a country in which their [personnel] could die. We are not Panama nor Grenada.[24]

This ability to deter the international community was again a factor in the Bosnian war, with the Serb side stressing successfully the Second World War experience or Vietnam in case of intervention. The international community's failure to act more forcefully earlier, perhaps at such milestones as the initial JNA attack against Slovenia and Croatia or the sieges of Vukovar or Dubrovnik, only reinforced Milošević's view that the international presence would be a relatively minor obstacle to Serbia's ultimate political goals.

[23] Stjepan Mesić reports a conversation he had with Borisav Jović at the start of 1991, in the course of which the latter, when asked what Serbian aims were, responded: '66 per cent of Bosnia-Herzegovina is Serb and we shall take that'. Interview with Zehrudin Isaković, 'Tuđmanu i Miloševiću pripremio sam sastanak u Karađorđevu' [I prepared the Tuđman–Milošević meeting in Karađorđevo], *Ljiljan*, Sarajevo, 11 October 1995, p. 11. See also pp. 11, 12 and 138 above.

[24] Speech reported from the official minutes of the Serbian parliament proceedings. 'Bogami ćemo da se tučemo' [By God we shall fight], *NIN*, Belgrade, 12 April 1991, p. 42. On 25 March 1991, Borisav Jović had also concluded that if there were to be a 'civil war' in Yugoslavia, NATO 'will not intervene militarily; they are not anxious to die'. Jović, *Poslednji dani SFRJ*. p. 312. That the United States was an important factor in the planning calculations by Yugoslav leaders is acknowledged by Borisav Jović, who noted on 22 August 1990 that 'The overall assessments of American policy toward Yugoslavia were always very important to us, especially now that the U.S. is the sole superpower which runs roughshod over and dominates the world', p. 180.

THE WAR IN BOSNIA

The Serb war effort in the case of Bosnia was similar in many ways to that in Croatia, particularly with respect to war termination, in so far as it was also basically a shift in the military situation on the battlefield that was the key factor in catalysing an end to the fighting.

Objectives and type of war

Some foreign observers have argued that Bosnia-Herzegovina was a case of 'fourth-generation warfare', conducted essentially by non-state entities, even small kaleidoscopic groups, often acting with little apparent higher control, following their own agendas, with no strategy, in a chaotic unconventional environment.[25]

On the contrary, there is compelling evidence that despite many small-scale actions the Serbs' main strategic and operational objectives were fairly traditional and that the forces that were key were conventional forces. As Karadžić and other Bosnian Serb civilian and military leaders stressed repeatedly, their goal was to establish a state.[26] Ultimately, for the Serb leadership both in Serbia and in Bosnia, the objective, though not always stated explicitly, was to gain control of territory in pursuit of the creation of a Greater Serbia, although, as in Croatia, the amount of territory would depend on how much could be held by force of arms.[27]

---

[25] Colonel David H. Hackworth (Retd.), for example, labelled the fighting 'mindless slaughter' and 'indiscriminate violence', and its participants 'animals' and 'lawless cowboys', in 'Balkans *are* another Vietnam', *Soldier of Fortune*, July 1993, p. 50. Elsewhere, he claimed that 'the Bosnian Serbs are also essentially light-infantry guerrillas': David H. Hackworth, 'Air Power Just Won't Work', *Newsweek*, 17 May 1993, p. 32. Lord Owen, the European Community negotiator, for his part, had decided that, simply put, 'there aren't any loyalties [in Bosnia]'; interview on the 'Charlie Rose Show', PBS Network, 15 June 1994. Indeed, proponents of this type of 'fourth generation' warfare believed that Yugoslavia was a prime validation of their paradigm. See William S. Lind, Major John F. Schmitt and Colonel Gary I. Wilson , 'Fourth Generation Warfare: Another Look', *Marine Corps Gazette*, December 1994, p. 35.

[26] For example, as Karadžić told an interviewer: 'There is no democracy, there is no freedom, there is no economy without a state. We have created a state.' Interview with Radovan Karadžić , 'Srpstvo je jedini orijentir za Srbe' [Serbdom is the Serbs' only imperative], *Spona,* Frankfurt (Germany), 7 October 1993, p. 4. Again: 'The Army of the Republika Srpska has entered the most glorious pages of Serbian history. It did not lose a state, but rather created a state.' Interview with Karadžić by Radivoje Gutić, 'Branimo srpstvo' [We are defending Serbdom], *Evropske Novosti,* Belgrade/Frankfurt (Germany), 30 July 1994, p. 5.

[27] A working map, published subsequently in the semi-official *Politika*, from the proceedings of a session of Serb think tanks sponsored by the Yugoslav Army indicated additional areas in Bosnia-Herzegovina and Croatia which the participants felt should go to the Serbs eventually. These areas included outlets to the sea and

In operational terms, the JNA and its successor Army of Republika Srpska (VRS) sought to seize key terrain, such as cities, transportation and communication nodes, and access to the sea, and was prepared to engage in 'ethnic cleansing' to achieve that control. In particular, Sarajevo was considered decisive terrain, and not only for its symbolic value. Radovan Karadžić, for example, stressed that 'Here [i.e. Sarajevo], we are near the viper, and one holds a viper by the throat and not by the tail. It is here that the state must be built – Sarajevo is our city.'[28]

The military balance

As in Croatia, the evolution of the military balance over a longer period of time in Bosnia was a central factor in affecting political calculations and negotiations. Throughout the conflict the military balance was heavily tilted in favour of the VRS, thanks to the arsenal and personnel transferred to the latter when it was formed from the JNA, although in relative terms the gap in combat capabilities and arsenals narrowed over time.

The Serbs' strategic centre of gravity

The Bosnian Serbs' strategic centre of gravity, the linchpin of their decision-making which shaped their overall strategy and war effort, lay outside Bosnia, in Belgrade. Despite the image that Milošević sought to foster of his non-involvement, without the support that the latter provided the Bosnian Serbs would not have been able to fight their war for very long. It was the JNA which took control of most of the territory that was eventually held by the Bosnian Serbs. And, despite frequent denials, the VRS continued to rely on the JNA, even after it was renamed Yugoslav Army, for crucial support without which the Bosnian Serb leadership would have been hard-put to fight its type of fight, something of which Belgrade officials were not reluctant to remind Serb leaders in Croatia and Bosnia-Herzegovina.[29]

Belgrade provided to the VRS help with logistics, equipment, training, air defence coverage, intelligence, medical support, and planning, as well

---

the largely Muslim enclaves in eastern Bosnia, while the criterion was solely strategic utility, with the implication that that should be the focus of military operations. Radovan Kovačević, 'Granice crtane puškama' [Borders drawn by rifles], *Politika*, Belgrade, 8 November 1993, p. 9.

[28] Interview with Radovan Karadžić by Branka Anđelković, 'Tovarenje konja' [Horse trading], *NIN*, Belgrade, 10 February 1995, p. 13.

[29] As Ivica Dačić, the spokesman for Milošević's ruling SPS party, noted proudly: 'It would be difficult for any citizen of the Serb Republic [in B-H] or the Republic of Serb Krajina [in Croatia] to point to a single inch of Serb land which they liberated!' Interview with Ivica Dačić by Mirjana Bobić-Mojsilović, 'Partija koja seli srca u glavu' [A party which moves hearts to the head], *Duga*, Belgrade, 21 January–3 February 1995, p. 23.

as significant numbers of officers and personnel, sometimes whole formations, on loan.[30] In fact, throughout the war, the VRS officer corps continued to be part of the organizational successor of the JNA – the Yugoslav Army – receiving its pay, promotions, validation, and presumably also guidance from its parent body in neighbouring Serbia.[31] Belgrade's financial support – amounting to one-fourth of Belgrade's total budget at times – was crucial, for without it the Bosnian Serb authorities would have found it difficult in the long term to fund the basic amenities of life in order to prevent the wholesale emigration of Serbs from Bosnia.[32]

How much influence Milošević could exert over the Bosnian Serbs became clear during the war termination stage and the subsequent negotiations in Dayton. Milošević was able to induce the Bosnian Serb leadership to transfer authority to him on 29 August 1995 to negotiate on their behalf.[33] Milošević, not unexpectedly, sought to ensure that Bosnian Serb

---

[30] Independent media sources in Serbia claimed that, in mid-1993, some 10,000 Yugoslav Army personnel were operating in Bosnia; see article from *Nezavisni*, Belgrade, reprinted as 'Gde ratuje Vojska Jugoslavije' [Where is Yugoslavia's army fighting?], in *Srpska reč*, Belgrade, 7 June 1993, p. 36. Danica Drašković, a member of the Executive Council of the SPO, provided details of the Yugoslav Army's crossing into Bosnia for the Srebrenica operation in 1993, 'U Srebrenici je gorela zemlja' [In Srebrenica the ground was on fire], *Srpska reč*, Belgrade, 10 May 1993, p. 23.

[31] Stephen Engelberg and Eric Schmitt, 'Western officials say Serbia helps Bosnian comrades', *New York Times*, 11 June 1995. As Lt-Gen. Milan Gvero, chief of staff of the VRS, noted, 'not a single active duty officer got a single dinar from the Republika Srpska [Bosnian Serb authorities]. In five years of war, literally not a single dinar!' Interview with General Milan Gvero by Milija Vujišić, 'Karadžić je hteo da me ubije' [Karadžić wanted to kill me], *Intervju*, Belgrade, 13 December 1996, p. 25. Significantly, Maj.-Gen. Đorđe Đukic, the chief logistician of the VRS, who was questioned by the International Criminal Tribunal in 1996, carried a military identification card which had been revalidated only recently by the Yugoslav Army general staff in Belgrade. Ed Vulliamy, 'Serbian lies world chose to believe', *The Guardian*, London, 29 February 1996, p. 12. According to Richard Holbrooke, Milošević had a direct communication link to General Ratko Mladić, commander of the VRS; even the commander of the VRS Romanija corps responded to Milošević's orders, *To End a War*, New York 1998, pp. 6, 158.

[32] This figure is provided by Radmilo Bogdanović, a senior Serbian official, in an interview by Vladan Dinić and Slavko Ćuruvija, 'Knin je mogao da se brani barem dva meseca' [Knin could have defended itself for at least two months], *Telegraf International*, Belgrade, 23 August 1995, p. 8. According to Yugoslav government sources, between 1991 and late 1994 Belgrade had provided $4.73 billion in aid to the Bosnian Serbs and to the Serb-held territories in Croatia; D. Dimitrovska and A. Vasin, 'Drugi dinar preko Drine' [A second dinar across the Drina], *Evropske Novosti*, Belgrade, 5 August 1994, p. 5.

[33] Admittedly, this had not come easily, and was accompanied by bitter shouting matches between Milošević and General Mladić before the latter yielded and

representatives at the subsequent Dayton talks were marginalized and would not have the possibility of wielding influence on their own. As he told a US negotiator, it would be a 'waste of your time' to seek the views of the senior Bosnian Serb official at the talks, and members of the Bosnian Serb delegation complained that they were kept uninformed.[34] Milošević's influence, not unexpectedly, became easier to wield as the Bosnian Serbs' military position deteriorated. It was not surprising when, at the end of 1995, Nikola Koljević concluded:

> We must cooperate with the one who is president of Serbia, the president of our mother country, if we are not crazy or ideologically fanaticized. And I believe that this leadership is not fanatical or fanaticized. It is especially important now that we do not lead Serbia into a still more difficult situation. That cooperation is vital for the survival of the Serbian people.[35]

The Bosnian Serbs' operational centre of gravity

So far as the Bosnian Serbs' operational centre of gravity, i.e. the basis of their ability to conduct military activity, was concerned, it was clearly made up of the regular forces, and particularly the heavy units with their preponderance of equipment and their mobility. It was that portion of the Serbs' force structure which was the linchpin of their capability on the battlefield. It was the heavy regular forces – whether in the JNA or the VRS – which spearheaded the seizure and consolidation of territory and which was instrumental in dealing with the other belligerents. In particular, it was the imbalance in artillery, tanks, and armoured personnel carriers that allowed the VRS to engage in combat at a great advantage in firepower and mobility and at a relatively low cost in terms of casualties. Time and again it was the Serbs' heavy weaponry which was decisive in the

withdrew, supposedly for treatment in Belgrade for a kidney stone problem. Dejan Anastasijević, 'General na rezervnom polozaju' [General in a reserve status], *Vreme*, Belgrade, 25 September 1995, p. 11. At one point, Nikola Koljević threatened to leave the Belgrade talks, with US envoy Richard Holbrooke shouting 'Go ahead, walk out!', before Koljević agreed to cede to Milošević. Michael Dobbs, 'Pursuing Peace at High Volume', *Washington Post*, 22 September 1995.

[34] Michael Dobbs, 'After marathon negotiations, an extra mile to reach peace', *Washington Post*, 23 November 1995. Typical of the dominance Milošević sought to establish at a preliminary meeting on 19 October with the Bosnian Serb delegation, according to one of the Bosnian Serbs attending: 'He [Milošević] has the last word. He asks the questions, which he then proceeds to answer himself.' Jovan Janjić, 'Aparat u kvaru' [The machine is broken], *NIN*, Belgrade, 27 October 1995, p. 17.

[35] Interview with Nikola Koljević by Nenad Novaković, 'Ukroćena goropad' [The taming of the shrew], *NIN*, Belgrade, 20 October 1995, p. 18.

outcome of engagements and which the VRS leadership could promise in order to stiffen the wavering resolve of VRS personnel.[36]

Despite many assessments in the West to the contrary, in operational terms, the militias which were sponsored by the Belgrade government or by the authorities in Pale, while effective in 'ethnic cleansing' operations against civilians, were of limited conventional military value, and the regular VRS itself regarded them with contempt and scepticism. General Ratko Mladić, typically, commented:

> There was no need to set up militias such as we had in 1992 and in part of 1993. Most consisted of 'great patriots' who never absented themselves from TV screens, as well as 'liberators' who were able to 'do it all'. However, their groups and militias in general hovered around jewellery shops, banks and well-stocked self-service stores, and there is not a single hill which they held or liberated. All they did was to plunder well.[37]

The Serbs' critical vulnerabilities

Despite its large arsenal, the VRS was not a very effective fighting force, and was beset by numerous critical vulnerabilities – having problems with command and control, mobility, cooperation between the different military branches, i.e. the use of integrated forces, and extended logistics. However, it was internal cohesion, in particular, that could be viewed as the VRS's 'critical requirement', a necessary condition for the VRS to function effectively. Instead of being a strength, it was the human dimension (commitment, morale, leadership) which constituted perhaps the VRS's greatest 'critical vulnerability', a weakness which could be targeted and which, finally, contributed to the defeat in 1995.

What enabled the VRS to paper over its vulnerabilities for some time was the initial glaring overmatch in equipment and organization it had over its adversaries which gave it such an advantage in firepower, force

[36] The promised arrival of heavy weaponry as a morale booster was reported, for example, by General Slavko Lisica, former director of the Serbian Republic and Krajina military schools, 'Ratni memoari Generala Slavka Lisice' [The war memoirs of General Slavko Lisica], *NIN*, Belgrade, 28 April 1995, p. 56; and General Lisica quoted in Dragoš Kalajić, 'Lisica lavljeg srca [Lisica (Fox) with the heart of a lion]', saying that on the Ozren plateau front he had stopped the VRS's 'panic-stricken retreat' by promises of support with heavy weapons: 'I have ordered the tanks to come, and we will be reinforced with artillery and everything else', *Duga*, Belgrade, 14–27 May 1994, p. 32.

[37] Interview with General Mladić by (Colonel) Milovan Milutinović, 'Narodu ne treba pričati ono što želi čuti, već mu treba reći istinu' [One must tell the people not what they want to hear, but rather the truth], *Srpska Vojska*, Pale, 25 June 1995, p. 11.

protection, and mobility. The weakness of UNPROFOR's force structure and its indecision, along with the international community's largely passive reaction until 1995, also contributed to mitigating the potential impact of the VRS's internal weaknesses. In addition, the VRS was also granted a respite by the outbreak of fighting in 1993 between the Croatian Defence Council (HVO), backed by Croatia's President Franjo Tudman, and the Bosnian government forces. However, when put under stress in 1995, these problems were to lead to the VRS's operational defeats.

The limits of Bosnian Serb commitment and morale

A common assumption in the West was that the Bosnian Serbs were fanatically committed to the nationalist cause and not amenable to rational factors. However, contrary to this 'conventional wisdom', the Bosnian Serbs' willingness to risk death and maiming in combat in the pursuit of a Greater Serbia was surprisingly limited.

The Bosnian Serb leadership often had a difficult time convincing many average Bosnian Serbs to fight endlessly for what many saw as simple territorial expansion and the enrichment of a local elite, and significant numbers of Serbs from Bosnia-Herzegovina did their best to avoid serving in the army. Many left Bosnia to avoid military duty, others deserted from the VRS, while still others paid for a disability certificate or exemption from active military duty. There were an estimated 120,000–150,000 deserters and draft dodgers from Bosnia, leading the official Bosnian Serb press to lament that 'the Serbian organism is ill with desertion' and that 'never in the history of the Serbian people has there been as much desertion as during this most recent war'.[38] The number of Serbs who left Bosnia to avoid military service were so large that a new ironic term, the 'Belgrade Corps' of the VRS, was coined for them in Bosnian Serb government circles.[39]

Service avoidance created problems on two levels. First, this meant that the VRS would simply not have all the personnel it needed to maximize its significant advantage in equipment and achieve its objectives, defeat its adversaries decisively, and end the war quickly, especially since the Bosnian Serb community's population base was smaller and older than that of the Bosniaks.[40] Second, this had a negative impact on the cohesion of the VRS,

[38] See, for example, Dušan Marić, '(P)okret za zaokret' [A turnaround movement], *Javnost,* Pale, 5 August 1995, p. 25; Dragoljub Jeknić, 'Brana ratnim pretnjama' [Barrier against war threats], *Javnost,* Pale, 28 September 1996, p. 13.

[39] Željko Pržulj, 'Pozdrav "Beogradskom korpusu"' [Greetings to the 'Belgrade Corps'], *Javnost,* Pale, 19 August 1995, p. 26.

[40] One Bosnian Serb source posited in 1995 that it would take an additional 120,000–300,000 personnel for the VRS to be able to win the war. Marić, '(P)okret za zaokret', p. 25

213

as morale was hard to maintain.[41] The result was a growing war weariness already by 1994 within the VRS. The conditions were made worse by the rise in casualties: by the end of the war VRS had 18,392 dead and 36,543 wounded.[42]

The lack of personnel also dictated VRS tactics, such as long sieges of cities and the avoidance of bolder operations with casualties, especially in urban terrain, which could both deplete the VRS and undermine morale further. Even around Sarajevo, according to negotiator Lord Owen's military adviser, the VRS lacked sufficient trained artillery crews for their besieging guns, and had to shuttle personnel from position to position.[43] Moreover, the VRS found itself obliged to man a 1,500 kilometre-long front along exterior lines, with its forces often spread thin, with gaps in the defences and the need for long tours of duty, which had a negative impact on morale and combat effectiveness.[44]

The VRS had particular difficulties with ensuring a sufficient number of officers with commitment. As Karadžić complained: 'The officer corps is small in relation to such a large army. Many officers from our areas did not return.'[45] According to the deputy commander of the VRS, Lt-Col General Manojlo Milovanović, by late 1994 46 per cent of the VRS's officers had fled to Serbia.[46] This shortage was exacerbated by the penchant of many officers for service at headquarters or elsewhere in the rear

---

[41] As one indignant VRS soldier insisted: 'If we really want to fight, then everyone must contribute equally. Some have been in the trenches for two years already, while others do not even know what war is. While our bowels rot in the dampness, many [others] go strolling in dry and secure places.' Quoted in Milena Marković, 'Vreme kada se moralo protiv svega' [A time when it was necessary to oppose everything], *Evropske Novosti*, Belgrade, 5 July 1994, p. 8. An officer from an elite unit complained that: 'The handful of us who have remained here have to defend Serbdom. That hurts us. In Banja Luka people have chains of businesses. They throw someone some dinars and they are exempted from the Army. They are allowed to conduct business while we die.' Quoted in Aleksandra Bilanović, Čekaonica smrti' [Death's waiting room], *NIN*, Belgrade, 6 January 1995, p. 19.

[42] Branko Perić, Žrtve rata u Bosni – strogo poverljivi bilans' [War victims in Bosnia – a confidential audit], *Nezavisna svetlost*, Belgrade, 1–7 June 1997 (electronic edition, URL: http://www.svetlost.co.yu/arhiva/97/88/88–4.html, accessed on 10 June 1998).

[43] This was based on an estimate prepared in May 1993 for Lord Owen, in David Owen, *Balkan Odyssey*, New York 1995, p. 291.

[44] On the front lines of the Majevica theatre, although the VRS was defending its critical main supply route, a VRS colonel assessed that on the Serb side 'People no longer want to fight. They are afraid. They have had enough of war.' Nenad Stefanović, 'Na pupku srpstva; slike sa koridora' [On the Serbian world's navel: images from the Corridor], *Duga*, Belgrade, 28 May–10 June 1994, p. 25.

[45] Interview with Radovan Karadžić, 'Republiko, srećan ti rođendan' [Happy birthday, Republic], *Srpsko Oslobođenje*, Pale, 6 January 1995, p. 4.

[46] Quoted in Zoran Petrović-Piročanac, 'Kolubarska bitka na Uni' [The battle of Kolubara on the Una], *Duga*, Belgrade, 26 November–9 December 1994, p. 29.

echelons.[47] Moreover, corruption was common among the senior VRS leadership, and knowledge of this was apparently fairly widespread within the ranks in what was a small, transparent, society.

Civil–military relations

Civilian–military relations were also a problem, in part due to the differences in ideological orientation between the senior VRS officers who had advanced as part of the communist system within the JNA and the new civilian politicians in Bosnia who tended to support a revived right-wing nationalist outlook.

The turmoil caused by the public competition between the Bosnian Serb civilian and military leadership had a negative effect on the Bosnian Serbs' war effort in view of the fact that financial and material resources were directed to the police and paramilitary structures under direct civilian command, which further undermined morale. The tension in civil–military relations became worse under stress: in April 1995 at the Bosnian Serb parliament session held in Sanski Most, each side sought to blame the other in the wake of recent setbacks, for the inability to end the war and for trying to build competing political organizations and loyalties within VRS units.[48]

According to Lt-Col General Milovanović, only 52 per cent of Bosnian Serb officers had responded to the original call, which meant, according to his calculations, that with subsequent losses and departures, the VRS had only 21 per cent of the officers it needed. Interview with Lt-Col General Milovanović by Gordana Janićijević, 'Ova vlada pada zajedno sa Brčkom' [This government falls with Brčko], *Duga*, Belgrade, 14–27 March 1998, p. 29.

[47] VRS personnel lamented the tepid commitment of their own officers. According to one junior VRS officer, 'Our soldiers find it hard to accept that at our Brigade's headquarters in Dubica there are dozens of officers, and that they even have "working hours" from seven to three, as if it were a question of the quietest peace, while we are at the front. ... When it was necessary to take over a squad, it was difficult to find an officer, even though Banja Luka was full of them.' Lieutenant Zoran Petković, quoted in Marko Ručnov, 'Što ste vukli mačka za rep?' [Why did you twist the cat's tail?], *Vojska*, Belgrade, 14 October 1993, p. 19.

[48] In his two-and-a-half hour contribution, General Mladić reportedly attributed his inability to win a decisive victory to the civilian authorities' failure to provide the VRS with adequate means, the politicians' meddling in military affairs, and black market dealings with the enemy. The civilians retorted that the VRS had been unprepared for the ARBiH recent offensives and had not neutralized its 5th corps in the Bihać pocket as promised. One civilian critic added that, with the VRS's preponderance of equipment at the beginning, the latter 'should have been able to end the war in twenty-four hours, but the commanders had botched it, and provided poor assessments'. One parliamentarian even told Mladić, 'You are a hero only where there are folk guitars, but where there are no guitars no one sings about your military victories, since there are none [i.e., victories].' Proceedings reported by Jovan Janjić 'Generalske suze' [The General's tears], *NIN*, Belgrade, 21 April 1995, p. 23; and Gordana Lazarević, 'Deveta ofanziva' [The ninth offensive], *Intervju*, Belgrade, 5 May 1995, pp. 11–12.

This rift had an impact on the operations of the VRS, with a VRS spokesman accusing Karadžić of diverting money and equipment away from the VRS to the police, which Karadžić controlled.[49] As the competition remained unresolved, *Srpska Vojska*, the VRS's official journal, complained later that summer that

> The issuing of incompetent and contradictory orders [i.e., by civilians] over the radio and television with the sole intent of affirming one's personal authority ... and the ill-considered attempt to change key personnel who up to now have shown that they are capable of leading the army in combat, clearly reveals, to put it mildly, the tactlessness of such moves.[50]

The deterioration in the relationship between civilian and military leaders caused by the looming military defeat affected negatively the morale of VRS personnel. For example, as Lt-Col General Milovanović complained, the Bosnian Serb civilian leadership was prepared to yield some lands 'but did not say which ones', and 'the absence of clear objectives and missions' led to 'destructive internal activity'.[51]

War termination strategy

Neither Milošević nor the Bosnian Serb decision-makers had planned for protracted war. Originally, they had been convinced that the other communities would be so overawed by Serb power that resistance would be weak and that any war would be short and easy.[52] As Milošević was to

---

[49] [Colonel] M[ilovan] Milutinović, the VRS's deputy chief of staff for information: 'Narod je uz vojsku' [The people is with the army], *Srpska Vojska*, 25 August 1995, p. 13: 'Recently, the largest part of the Republic's budget and the benefactors' gifts meant for Defence have been diverted to the MUP [i.e. police] to set up special police forces which are being equipped and armed with the most modern means and equipment, while the Army has to wait.' In the wake of the subsequent setbacks, the friction increased accordingly, with Karadžić dismissing several top officers, and the military laying the blame for failure on the politicians and the media. See Batić Bačević, 'Olako obećana brzina' [Lightly promised speed], *NIN*, Belgrade, 20 October 1995, pp. 14–15.

[50] Borislav Đurđević, 'Podela naroda je izdaja' [Dividing the people is treason], *Srpska Vojska*, 25 August 1995, p. 44.

[51] Interview with Lt-Col General Manojlo Milovanović by B. M., 'Bez jasnih ciljeva' [Without clear objectives], *Evropske Novosti*, Belgrade, 8 November 1995, p. 7; also Marić, '(P)okret za zaokret', p. 24.

[52] For example, *Narodna armija*, the JNA journal, reported that 'In Bosnia-Herzegovina, it is not realistic to expect a repetition of the Croatian situation with the legal formation of a party army. ... It has been noted that many Bosnian Muslims would not gladly confront a stronger JNA.' V. M., 'Ekstremisti gube strpljenje' [The extremists are losing patience], *Narodna armija*, Belgrade,

admit later when discussing the war: 'I never thought it would go on so long.'[53] Hopes for a quick victory were revived in 1993, with the onset of major fighting between the Bosniaks and Croats, and General Ratko Mladić, chief of the VRS's general staff, later said disparagingly that 'Some predicted at that time [i.e., in 1993] that the war would be over in five to ten days.'[54]

Despite the rapid initial seizure of territory in 1992, the subsequent failure to achieve a rapid decision as expected presented the Bosnian Serbs and Serbia's President Slobodan Milošević with the dilemma of how to terminate the war while at the same time persuading their opponents and the international community to agree to a new *status quo* in favour of the Serbs. However, no adequate strategy was formulated beyond holding on, in the hope that the Bosnians would be bled into submission and Sarajevo abandoned; that the nominal Croatian–Bosnian alliance would fall apart; and that the international community would tire and promote a settlement favourable to Serb interests.

A major consideration was to deter the international community, and especially the United States, from military intervention. To that end, the Serbs promoted the spectre of a quagmire reminiscent of the Second World War and Vietnam and, abetted by Western policy-makers and the media, projected a false image of unshakeable military might and resolve, and presented the conflict as a centuries-old intractable struggle. Foreign initiatives designed to keep the arms embargo in place inevitably strengthened, however unintentionally, the Serb leadership's determination and negotiating position, by continuing to reassure them that they were likely to retain at least a stalemate capability on the battlefield, thus buttressing the status quo.[55]

---

5 March 1992, p. 17. Likewise, Momčilo Krajišnik, subsequently head of the Bosnian Serb parliament, spoke confidently to a small circle in London in March 1992, before the outbreak of war, claiming that 'everything is ready. In ten days, it will all be over'. Quoted in Slavko Čuruvija, 'Džon Vejn na Miljacki' [John Wayne on the Miljacka], *Borba*, Belgrade, 10–11 April 1993, p. 1.

[53] Quoted in Holbrooke, *To End a War*, p. 245. Likewise, the Serb leadership seems to have underestimated international determination, with Serbia's deputy premier, Radoman Božović, claiming that any economic sanctions would be short-lived, because they are 'against the logic of capitalism', a point which Milošević also made while speaking in the Serbian parliament: 'I believe the sanctions ... will not be able to last long.' Belgrade TV News, 28 May 1992, and 6 October 1992, respectively.

[54] Interview with General Ratko Mladić by Snježana Lalović, 'Niko nas ne može uništiti' [No one can annihilate us], *Srpsko Oslobođenje*, Pale, 6 January 1995, p. 8.

[55] Thus, when discussions to lift the embargo came to naught in late 1994, an editorial in the government-controlled *Politika* gloated that now the Bosnian government would have to enter into direct talks with the Bosnian Serbs – implicitly from a position of weakness – to 'exchange territories' and end the war. Radivoje Petrović, 'Kako do trećeg potpisa' [How to get the third signature], *Politika*, Belgrade, 5 October 1994, p. 2.

WHY DID THE WAR STOP IN 1995?

Reaching and recognizing the culminating point

Serb leaders would have liked to end the war much earlier, when their position was at its strongest and when most, though not all, of the original objectives may have been attained. During 1994 Milošević clearly came to recognize that the culminating point had been reached and that it was in the Serbs' interest to see the war end.[56] However, he probably thought this could be done on very favourable terms, and there is no indication that either Belgrade or Pale felt much urgency to make major concessions in exchange for peace. Despite the Contact Group's original 'take it or leave it' ultimatum for its plan of August 1994, Belgrade had concluded that the five member states would compromise in favour of the Bosnian Serbs, and that the international community, willy-nilly, would acquiesce to at least a reduced version of Serbia's long-term goals. Although the process might be couched in terms designed to save face for the international community, as Borisav Jović, a vice-president of Milošević's ruling party, saw it, this would still result in a Serbian victory. In his view, 'The great powers, however, are great powers. They will not admit defeat, even when they are defeated. They would rather proclaim it a victory at whatever cost. The Serbian victory, [however], is obvious.'[57] Indeed, in June 1995 Milošević felt confident enough to demand additional concessions from the US negotiators.[58]

The position of the Bosnian Serb leadership, however, had been a stumbling block to Milošević's plans to wind down the war. Although also wanting to end the war in order to consolidate their gains, the Bosnian Serb leaders, more than Milošević, believed that they could get even better

---

[56] Not only had the Croatian and Bosnian armies become more professional forces, making war more costly, but the international community had hinted on several occasions that it might lift the arms embargo which had hamstrung the Bosnian government's efforts to provide for its own security. Borisav Jović hinted as much in an interview: 'From another perspective, with the unavoidable military strengthening of the adversary, the Serbs of Bosnia-Herzegovina may reach the point where they are defeated, and where they lose that which they have conquered and that which the international community would then never again recognize [to them]. There is a great danger that Serbia and the Federal Republic of Yugoslavia will be dragged into the war, and lose this war in a catastrophic manner, with enormous suffering and consequences, for neither the FRY nor anyone else is in a position to fight against the entire international community.' Interview with Borisav Jović by Milomir Marić, 'Nikoga nismo silom terali da ostane' [We did not force anyone to remain], *Intervju*, Belgrade, 19 August 1994, p. 4.

[57] Ibid., p. 6.

[58] Dana Priest 'Hill critics query Perry on Bosnia', *Washington Post*, 8 June 1995.

terms – perhaps drawing on their successful experience with the international community's reluctance to enforce the 1993 Vance–Owen Plan in the face of their resistance, and encouraged by the weak stand taken initially by the Contact Group. As a result, they sought more land and control over strategically significant areas beyond the Contact Group's original offer in the hope that, providing the existing situation on the ground were to hold, the international community would tire and offer a better deal. In April 1995 Karadžić fell confident enough to promise that 'we will push for a final military victory'.[59]

Karadžić, in particular, felt that the United States, whose leadership the Serbs recognized as vital for the international community, was already overextended around the globe and would not be willing to get involved or to exert pressure over the long term.[60] Such perceptions were no doubt validated as recently as the apparent understanding that no air strikes would be launched in exchange for the release of UN personnel taken hostage in June 1995 and the subsequent ineffective response to the takeover of the UN-designated safe zones of Srebrenica and Žepa.[61]

Changing the military balance and political perceptions

What, then, was the catalyst that convinced the Bosnian Serbs and Belgrade to end the war when they did, given this background? Much of the credit for the political turnaround in 1995 which led to the end of the war must be attributed to the change in the military balance and the new situation in the field, which convinced both Milošević and Karadžić that the cost-benefit ratio of continuing the war would not only become unbearable but could lead to an irreparable defeat. In retrospect, it was probably the atrocities which accompanied the seizure of Srebrenica and Žepa that constituted Pale's strategic blunder, since this finally galvanized

---

[59] This was at the keynote April 1995 session of the RS assembly. Jovan Janjić, 'Generalske suze' [The general's tears], 21 April 1995, *NIN*, Belgrade, p. 23.

[60] As Karadžić told Dragoš Kalajić, in 'Srbi protiv celog sveta' [The Serbs against the whole world], *Duga*, Belgrade, 12–25 November 1994, p. 21. General Mladić, for his part, continued to believe that the West would not exert military pressure because it was loath to risk its own personnel to counter Serbian goals, noting that 'The Western countries, affected above all by the experiences which they had in the wars waged from Vietnam up to today, have drawn the lesson that they cannot draft their own children to achieve their objectives outside their homelands.' Interview with General Mladić by [Colonel] Milovan Milutinović, 'Narodu ne treba pričati ono što želi ćuti, već mu treba reći istinu' [One must tell the people not what it wants to hear, but rather the truth], *Srpska Vojska*, 25 June 1995, p. 8.

[61] John Pomfret, 'UN rejects NATO requests to bomb Serb airfield after "No-Fly" violations', *Washington Post*, 22 June 1995.

a reluctant West into reacting more robustly when a shell soon thereafter killed a number of people in a Sarajevo street.[62]

NATO *air strikes and the ground campaign*

This said, what specifically was the crucial element in operational terms that changed the situation? Many US civilian and military policy-makers believe that it was the NATO air campaign which was decisive.[63] However, one can also make a case that, although NATO air power was an important psychological factor, it was actually the combined Croatian–Bosnian ground campaign which was key in changing the military situation.

For example, the antennas destroyed at the communications sites could be replaced easily and much of the ammunition probably had already been moved out to storage. Press sources reported that the Yugoslav Army, contrary to Milošević's own commitments, was soon repairing the damage the VRS had sustained.[64] Nevertheless, Radovan Karadžić, perhaps as an excuse for the setbacks, was later to note that 'it is clear to all that the bombing by NATO caused great damage to our state and our army'.[65]

The NATO air strikes, which began on 31 August, clearly represented a departure from the earlier symbolic international military response. These air strikes, unlike previous ones, included military targets, such as command and control nodes, logistics assets, some lines of communication such as bridges, some artillery positions and even a barracks, but they were still relatively restricted. To a great extent, NATO's self-imposed restraint

---

[62] According to Secretary of Defence William J. Perry, 'This action was so outrageous that even the nations who had been resisting strong NATO action to that point realized that they had to meet this provocation with a real show of military force.' Speech at Nellis Air Force Base, 27 January 1996, published as 'Bosnia: so far, so good', *Defense Issues,* Washington DC: Department of Defence, 1996, vol. 11, no. 5; electronic version at URL:http://www.defenselink.mil/speeches/1996/di1105.html (accessed 3 September 1998).

[63] For example, speaking to the Air Force Association about the recent elections in Bosnia in the post-Dayton period, negotiator Richard Holbrooke claimed that Dayton 'wouldn't have taken place without the United States Air Force and Navy and the precision bombing', 'Holbrooke praises airpower's role in Bosnia', Air Force Association News Service, 17 September 1996, at URL http://www.afa.org/holbrel.html (accessed 5 May 1998). Not surprisingly, the Clinton administration at the time was quick to take credit for the turnaround in the situation on the ground. For example, State Department spokesman Nicholas Burns noted in the daily State Department press briefing on 21 September 1995: 'The West, led by the United States and NATO, has stopped the Bosnian Serb offensive all over Bosnia.'

[64] Stephen Engelberg and Kit R. Roane, 'Yugoslav Army Reported to Aid Bosnian Serbs Despite Promises', *New York Times,* 18 November 1995.

[65] Interview by Zoran Marković, 'Radovan Karadžić: Ne plašim se haškog suda' [I am not afraid of the Hague Tribunal], *Svet,* Novi Sad, 13 November 1995, p. 4.

was deliberately intended only to convince the Serbs to negotiate, and thereby avoided an opportunity to redress the basic military balance.[66] As US Air Defence Chief General Ronald R. Fogelman stated, 'The intent of NATO bombing was not to defeat the Serbs, but simply relieve the siege of UN safe areas and gain compliance with UN mandates and thus facilitate ongoing negotiations to end the fighting.'[67] Realistically, however, the actual physical damage to the Serb war-fighting capability was probably limited, since most of the targets that were hit had a longer-term impact and would not have affected the battle directly in the northern and western theatres where the decisive fighting was taking place.

True, manoeuvre and command and control in the VRS were made more difficult.[68] However, as the US air force chief of staff indicated, entrenched troops and front-line heavy weapons – the Bosnian Serbs' operational centre of gravity – had been explicitly placed off-limits to air strikes, and of course the leadership itself had not been targeted. Overall, perhaps the greatest impact may have been in the psychological realm, as battered VRS morale, one can suppose, suffered further. In particular, this development was unexpected, and contradicted the Bosnian Serbs' analytical paradigm, based on assumptions of international indecisiveness reinforced by past experience with foreign pinprick airstrikes.

In reality, most of the designated targets on the first target list had already been hit and, given the continued foot-dragging by Great Britain and France, expanding the air campaign to the potentially more productive targets said to have been on a follow-on list might well have been politically contentious and difficult.[69] However, what was probably important for the Bosnian Serbs' decision-making was their own assessment of

---

[66] As an unnamed Pentagon official explained the restrained scope of air strikes: 'When you are trying to get someone's attention, you don't have to knock out all their teeth so they cannot eat again'. Stephen Engelberg, 'NATO to intensify use of air power against the Serbs', *New York Times,* 7 September 1995.

[67] General Ronald R. Fogelman, letter to editor, 'What air power can do in Bosnia', *Wall Street Journal,* 11 October 1995. Troop concentrations, unless poised to attack safe zones, were also off-limits. Rick Atkinson, 'NATO weighs risks of attacking more targets', *Washington Post,* 10 September 1995.

[68] Reports indicate that, for example, the VRS lost its encrypted communications capabilities and was forced to fall back on less secure communications, compromising its operational effectiveness. Zoran Kusovac, 'Borba za Tuđmanov jelovnik' [The battle for Tuđman's menu], *Vreme,* Belgrade, 18 September 1995, p. 9. Civilian broadcast and telephone capabilities were also destroyed. Perica Vučinić 'Raspamećeni grad' [The insane city], *Vreme,* Belgrade, 25 September, p. 15. Such disruptions are also reported in Miroslav Lazanski, 'Tomahak u travi' [Tomahawk in the grass], *NIN,* Belgrade, 22 September 1995, p. 13. However, the fact that the VRS was able to transfer to the northern theatre the artillery it withdrew from Sarajevo indicates that air power did not impede the movement of the VRS forces, Holbrooke, *To End a War,* pp 164–5.

[69] Holbrooke, *To End a War,* p. 146.

future costs and the uncertainty which faced them, as they apparently believed that the air campaign would become more painful.[70] The air strikes could have continued, as seemed plausible, and escalated both horizontally to such war zones as the Banja Luka area and vertically to the systematic striking of deployed field forces trying to mass or to manoeuvre along roads, or against main supply routes. Despite confusing mixed signals from the United States, with Secretary of Defense William Perry categorically denying that there would be any escalation, other US political and military officials, including Admiral Leighton Smith, NATO's southern commander, suggested at least in public that the targets could be expanded, with the wider Option 3 list.[71] The fact that Tomahawk cruise missiles, launched on 10 September, had targeted the air defence network in the Banja Luka area seemed to set the stage for such a wider air campaign.[72] Had the attacks indeed intensified to force-related targets, the Bosnian Serb position on the ground would have been seriously compromised and the VRS would have risked a quick defeat in ground combat by the opposing Croatian and Bosnian forces.[73]

The Croatian–Bosnian land campaign

Ultimately, however, it was more likely the impact of the gains on the ground by the Croatian–Bosnian alliance which in and of itself was the key factor in convincing the Bosnian Serbs to seek an end to the war quickly. The Croatian push in western Bosnia which led to the encirclement of Knin and facilitated the subsequent Operation Storm against the Krajina Serbs in August, as well as against Bosnian Serb positions, revealed the impressive new potential of the Croatian Army, as well as the brittleness of the Serb position, and the limits of likely help from Belgrade.[74]

[70] According to the Belgrade press, Milošević was said to have impressed the visiting Bosnian Serb leadership that, as Holbrooke had warned them, the bombing would continue indefinitely until they signed a ceasefire. Robert Čoban, 'Hronika propuštenih prilika' [Chronicle of missed opportunities], *Svet*, 1 September 1995, p. 3.

[71] Eric Schmitt, 'Nato commanders face grim choices', *New York Times*, 14 September 1995; Rick Atkinson, 'Nato weighs risks of attacking more targets', *Washington Post*, 16 November 1995. The Official Bosnian Serb press itself identified a list of potential targets if the campaign escalated. Željko Cijanović, 'Genocid s neba' [Genocide from the sky], *Javnost*, Pale, 16 September 1995.

[72] Rick Atkinson, 'In almost losing its resolve, NATO Alliance found itself', *Washington Post*, 16 November 1995.

[73] Lt-Col General Milan Gvero, deputy commander of the VRS general staff, attributed Bosnian Serb reverses to the fact that 'NATO attacked our vital targets in co-operation with the Muslims and Croats', Violeta Marčetić, 'Koncert se odlaže?' [The concert is being postponed?], *NIN*, 13 October 1995.

[74] When Radovan Karadžić was asked, after the fall of Krajina in Croatia, whether he thought Serbia would come to the Bosnian Serbs' aid, he replied: 'No one can

When the combined Croatian–Bosnian forces, for the first time not hampered by a gross inferiority in equipment, attacked and put the VRS to the test, the latter's lack of cohesion and other internal problems made it vulnerable to battlefield defeat. There is compelling evidence to suggest that the VRS, rather than making any planned withdrawal to accommodate new maps to be negotiated, was simply outfought on the ground by an enemy force with essentially no air cover and relatively still markedly underequipped. In a phased campaign of well-planned and executed attacks beginning with the consolidation of their positions in the Bihać pocket, the combined force within a relatively short time was able to wrest control of some 4,000 kilometres of land previously held by the VRS.

There were indications of a lack of resistance and an early pull-back in some cases. Other VRS units simply crumbled with little resistance after being put in an operational dilemma by the advancing enemy.[75] According to Arkan, who personally commanded units of his paramilitary Serbian Volunteer Guard in northern Bosnia in 1995, the VRS in that campaign behaved 'without organization or discipline', and he claimed that cities such as Šipovo, Grahovo, and Ključ had fallen 'without a single shot'.[76] When the VRS fled from Jajce before the advancing Croatian Army in September 1995, a VRS security officer described the retreat as resembling 'a madhouse' and called the fleeing VRS units 'an army in chaos'.[77]

Even those units that stood and fought initially were defeated, as their adversaries outmanoeuvred them, acting faster than the VRS could respond, penetrating their brittle defences, and outflanking static positions. Lt-Col General Manojlo Milovanović, in fact, claimed that although the civilian authorities had indeed pulled the population out of numerous areas early, the VRS itself had left only after being defeated in battle, and after having suffered heavy combat casualties.[78] In another interview, he openly stated that 'we lost the western part of the Republika Srpska above all because of the enemy's military power'. Speaking of the VRS units, he

be sure of anything any more', Vladana Stojanović, 'Srbima su potrebne legende' [Serbs need legends], *Telegraf International*, Belgrade, 23 August 1995.

[75] The Bosnian Serb vice-president Nikola Koljević noted that the withdrawals had not been ordered by higher headquarters, but by officers lower down the chain of command, indicating a breakdown of command and control under stress. Nenad Kovačević, 'Ukroćena goropad' [The taming of the shrew], *NIN*, Belgrade, 20 October 1995.

[76] Interview with Željko Ražnatović by Cvijeta Arsenić, 'Nismo izgubili ni jednu bitku' [We have not lost a single battle], *Srpsko Jedinstvo* [Serb Unity], Belgrade, July 1996, p. 6. According to one VRS soldier, Jajce fell after only 13 shells were fired on it, enabling the Croatian forces to enter on buses. Batić Bačević, 'Pogrešna strana jelovnika?' [The wrong side of the menu?], *NIN*, 22 September 1995.

[77] 'Hrvati piruju na izlazu iz Jajca' [Croats celebrate on the exit from Jajce], *Telegraf International*, 27 September 1995.

[78] Interview with B.M. 'Bez jasnih ciljeva' [Without clear objectives], *Evropske Novosti*, 8 November 1995.

concluded: 'They were simply overwhelmed by the system of a steamroller and curtains of fire, and only one who does not know what it means to be subjected daily to nine or ten thousand shells on one's positions and population centres can speak of quitting by the military.'[79] As Lt-Col General Milan Gvero, deputy chief of staff of the VRS, grudgingly acknowledged later, 'the last military actions showed that the balance of power, just before the end of combat operations, had not only been reached [by the VRS's opponents] but in some areas, thanks to the support that our opponents were receiving, was even in their favour'.[80]

Although the VRS did deal the Croatian Army significant casualties on occasion, such as in the defence of Drvar in August 1995, and at the Una, this had stopped the Croatian offensive only momentarily.[81] The official Bosnian Serb magazine *Javnost* described the disintegrating and panicked units of the VRS, during the resumed 8 October 1995 offensive by the Croatian Army that led to the fall of the town of Mrkonjić-Grad, and the resulting psychological impact, thus: 'The exhausted and disorganized units of the Serb army retreated in panic toward Manjača and Banja Luka. Along with the demoralized army came horrendous news, which poured into Banja Luka, about the great number of dead and captured Serb soldiers.'[82]

For a time, it appeared that the withdrawal might not be controllable and that Banja Luka itself might fall, and rumours were rampant in the city of its potential abandonment, leading to near-panic.[83] The situation apparently became so bad that General Mladić issued a proclamation to

[79] Interview with Borislav Đurđević, 'Još nije kraj rata' [The war is not over yet], *Srpska vojska*, 3 November 1995.

[80] Interview with Colonel Milovan Milutinović, 'Mudrost i oprez' [Wisdom and caution], *Srpska vojska*, 22 March 1996.

[81] At the battle on the Una, Croatian carelessness and overconfidence were the main contributory factors for casualties. The Croatians, operating with the mistaken intelligence that the VRS had already withdrawn, advanced during daytime in a presumed unopposed pursuit without taking adequate precautions, and when engaged gave the order to withdraw, exposing themselves to heavy fire. See interview with the former chief of general staff general Janko Bobetko, 'General poslije rata' [The General after the war], *Nacional*, 23 April 1997.

[82] Dušan Marić, 'Tri žive rane' [Three open wounds], *Javnost*, Pale, 22 June 1996. The situation was so insecure that that VRS pushed into the battle its military cadets in Banja Luka in order to resist the tide, but they got such beatings at the first contact that they had to withdraw. Dušan Marić, 'Banjalučani bežali glavom bez obzira' [The people of Banja Luka fled in panic], *Dnevni Telegraf*, Belgrade (electronic edition), 12 September 1998, Url: http://www.dtelegraf.co.yu/izdagaoliporaz06.html (accessed on 12 September 1998).

[83] Đoko Kesić and Zoran Lukić, 'Banja Luka slučajno izbjegla sudbinu Knina' [Banja Luka missed Knin's fate by chance], *Telegraf International*, Belgrade, 27 September 1995; Perica Vučinić, 'Raspamećeni grad' [The insane city], *Vreme*, Belgrade, 25 September 1995.

his troops to the effect that 'There is no cause for panic or for upsetting the population as, unfortunately, many spreaders of panic, who are in the direct service of our enemies, want to do.'[84]

Banja Luka, the decisive point whose loss would have unhinged the entire Bosnian Serb position, since some two thirds of the Serbs lived in that region, was at immediate risk.[85] According to a senior official in the Bosnian Serb secret police, all that had been left to cover the approaches to Banja Luka were some police and Arkan's militiamen, since even the VRS officers had fled.[86] Arkan's deputy in western Bosnia, Colonel Mihajlo Ulemek, confirmed the rapidly deteriorating situation, with the crumbling of entire VRS units. In fact, one of his main tasks, in cooperation with special police who had deployed from Serbia, was to force fleeing VRS personnel back to the front.[87]

VRS forces immediately available for the defence of Banja Luka amounted to some 22,000 troops with some 270 tanks.[88] However, this presented a dilemma, since, on the one hand, it did not seem that these forces could save the city while, on the other, defence of the city meant shifting VRS heavy forces from the Posavina Corridor, thereby exposing another decisive point to potential attack, especially since the bulk of the Croatian Army was still positioned in Croatia facing the Posavina Corridor, the Serb main artery.[89] Two brigades from the 1st Krajina corps were sent to support the defence of Šipovo in September 1995 but, instead of taking up positions against the incoming enemy forces, proceeded to loot the deserted Serb houses.[90] While that was going on, Banja Luka was already

---

[84] General Ratko Mladić, 'Jedinstvo i odlučnost' [Unity and resolve], *Javnost*, Pale, 21 October 1995.

[85] At the 14–16 October session of the Bosnian Serb parliament, General Milovanović stated bluntly that if the Croatians or the Bosniaks took one of three points – Banja Luka, Trnovo or the Posavina Corridor – 'Republika Srpska would cease to exist.' Quoted in Cvijanović, 'Muke oko Banja Luke' [Distress over Banja Luka], *Javnost*, Pale, 21 October 1995.

[86] Interview with Petko Budiša, 'Pljačke Titove bande' [Looting by Tito's gang], *Intervju*, Belgrade, 3 November 1996.

[87] Interview with Gordana Jovanović, 'Srbin sam; tim se dičim' [I am a Serb and proud of it], *Intervju*, Belgrade , 3 November 1995.

[88] Željko Rogošić, 'Bitka za Banja Luku' [The battle for Banja Luka], *Globus*, Zagreb, 22 September 1995; Miroslav Lazanski, 'Kako skratiti front' [How to shorten the front], *NIN*, Belgrade, 25 August 1995.

[89] According to Serb estimates, the Croatian Army had deployed 50 tanks, 30 APCs and 80 large-calibre artillery pieces to the western, Bosnian theatre, but left 100 tanks, 60 APCs and over 180 large-calibre artillery pieces and multiple rocket launchers facing the Posavina corridor. Jovan Janjić, *Srpski general Ratko Mladić* [The Serb General Ratko Mladić], Novi Sad, p. 214.

[90] Dušan Marić, 'Sa tri tenka držali front – hiljade se izležavala u pozadini' [With three tanks they held the front while thousands lay about in the rear], *Dnevni Telegraf* (electronic edition) (see note 82 above), 15 September 1998.

within artillery range and Croatian forces were confident they could take the city.[91]

In effect, the Bosnian Serb leadership was facing a military defeat with potentially far-reaching consequences, as several of them have acknowledged subsequently.[92] As Biljana Plavšić admitted later, 'the moment for the liquidation of Republika Srpska was very near'.[93]

The front stabilized largely as the result of significant US pressure.[94] Croatian President Tuđman also ordered a halt to the offensive and co-operation with the ARBiH. He was reportedly also wary of contributing to a stronger position for the Bosnian government and was indifferent to trying to capture additional territory which he had been told by international negotiators would revert to the Bosnian Serbs in any case.[95] In hindsight, had the combined ground campaign continued, especially with further NATO air strikes, the entire Bosnian Serb position could well have

[91] In the Croatian Army's official account, General Ante Gotovina stresses that 'entry into Banja Luka was possible, since the enemy defence had been broken', but that this was not done because of 'the higher interests of international and Croatian policy'. *Napadajni bojevi i operacije HV i HVO (Hrvatskih snaga)* [Offensive battles and operations by the HV and the HVO (Croatian Forces)], Knin 1996, p. 110. Bobetko, 'General poslije rata', pp. 499–500.

[92] For example, General Milan Gvero later stated that 'continuing the war under the conditions in which we and our enemies found ourselves could have involved very easily something about which I do not wish to talk publicly'. Interview with Slavica Jovović, 'Mir nas je zatekao' [Peace has caught us unawares], *Intervju*, Belgrade, 1 December 1995. Speaking of the Dayton Accord, Biljana Plavšić also noted that 'we accepted the peace agreement ... when we had been defeated militarily ... The Dayton Accords were made when we were losing ... We gained 49 per cent of territory – Serb territory, mind you ... Republika Srpska was proclaimed in public by that document. That was, let me tell you, almost unthinkable in the situation in which we found ourselves then ... The front was getting closer by the hour. People were leaving Banja Luka. The war was being decided here, in the western territories.' Interview with Slobodan Uparić, 'Moj lobi je narod' [The people is my lobby], *Nezavisna svetlost*, Belgrade, 29 May 1997.

[93] Biljana Plavšić speaking to a Serb group while visiting Hamilton, Canada, in 1998. *Glas srpski*, Banja Luka, 18 May 1998, electronic edition at URL:http//www.srpska.com/index.html (accessed 22 May 1998).

[94] The Belgrade media reported that an unnamed higher US offical told Tuđman that 'the red light is on; go back to the negotiating table'. Batić Bačević, 'Pogresňa strana jelovnika', The fact that the Yugoslav air force was allowed to fly over Bosnia-Herzegovina and attack Croatian forces meant that the USA no longer upheld the 'no fly' policy, which must have sent a clear message to Zagreb. The Serbian MiGs which took part in this operation could be seen on ITN television screens. See Albert Wohlstetter, 'A photo-op foreign policy', *Wall Street Journal*, 23 October 1995. The United States also put pressure on the Bosnian government not to attempt to break the siege of Sarajevo while the VRS was in retreat. Daniel Williams, 'Serbs suffer major defeat in W. Bosnia', *Washington Post*, 14 September 1995.

[95] Holbrooke, *To End a War*, pp. 160, 166, 193–5.

crumbled quickly, thus allowing the international community to dictate terms and avoiding much of the ambiguity of the subsequent peace deal and the problematic prospects for its implementation and for a stable end-state.

COST OF ESCALATION AND THE DECISION TO NEGOTIATE

At the same time, the Bosnian Serbs' strategic centre of gravity – the link with Belgrade – was also being tested and seemed to be neutralized. Milošević apparently found it counter-productive to provide the needed military balance, which might have proved inadequate even if he had been willing to do so. While Milošević did send Arkan and his militiamen to the Banja Luka area, and later continued to provide military aid to the VRS, he faced a basic dilemma of whether or not to escalate to a degree needed to make a difference. In the end, Milošević decided to terminate the war quickly.

The limits of Belgrade's commitment

Why did Milošević choose not to escalate or even continue his policy of confrontation at this time, especially as US observers were convinced almost until the end that Belgrade would intervene in force in both Croatia and Bosnia if the situation on the battlefield deteriorated?[96]

Given the changing situation on the ground in Bosnia, Belgrade would probably have had to make a significant commitment of forces, not just the odd brigade, and with a clearly defined objective in order to make a difference. The Yugoslav Army would have found itself hard-put to engage directly in a long-drawn-out war against a well-armed adversary, leading potentially to high casualties and an unpredictable military quagmire. Serbia had not been primed for a long war, which would have been even more costly than the proxy war it had waged, both in economic terms and casualties, both with a high political cost. Direct involvement in a major

---

[96] For example, Secretary of Defence William J. Perry, in a letter to US Congressman Lee H. Hamilton in 1994, warned that if Croatia used force to reassert its control over the Krajina 'it is possible and perhaps likely that Serbia would intervene'. Likewise, he thought that in Bosnia were 'the situation on the battlefield to change, the Serbian government could be prompted to intervene on behalf of the Bosnian Serb brethren'. Quoted by the recipient, 'Arms embargo against Bosnia', *Congressional Record* 23 May 1994, Washington, DC: Government Printing Office, p. E1024. Richard Holbrooke, who later called this 'flawed intelligence', claims this attitude was pervasive, for example, in the US intelligence community, even as late as the September 1995 offensive against the VRS. *To End a War*, p. 159.

war, indeed, could have threatened to tear asunder the very fabric of Serbian society. According to the Yugoslav Army's former spokesman, dismissed in early 1995 after making this complaint in a letter to Yugoslavia's federal president, 'the personnel, moral, and technological situation of the Yugoslav Army is catastrophic in relation to the objective threat of war which the state faces'.[97]

Fear of ending up in Bosnia, according to the Yugoslav military's interpretation, was mainly responsible for the reluctance of reservists to answer call-ups to exercises, for problems with the response of draftees, and for the decreasing number of candidates to military schools.[98]

One of the SPS vice-presidents, Boško Perošević, summed up what had apparently become the prevailing government cost–benefit analysis:

> On the one hand you have shouting that the people want to go to war, while on the other we have such a [low] response to mobilization. All of that had to be balanced with a wise policy, and I believe that the SPS completely succeeded in doing so.[99]

Mihajlo Marković also highlighted the leadership's awareness of low domestic commitment:

> Suddenly, massive defeatism has spread ... I fear that now there are too many people who are not prepared to fight for any objective whatsoever. It is very naive to think that those who will not defend Herzegovina and Eastern Slavonija will defend Bačka and Boka. Defeatists and pacifists do not become patriots overnight.[100]

When Krajina fell in August 1995, Serbian politicians were surprised by the extent of public apathy in Serbia, and compared the lack of reaction unfavourably with the emotions which led to an anti-Greek riot in Belgrade at that time, sparked by an incident during a basketball

---

[97] Letter from Colonel Ljubodrag Stojadinović, published in *NIN*, Belgrade, 10 February 1995.

[98] See, for example, Lt-Col Mišo Bojović, 'Pomlađivanje kadra' [Rejuvenating the officer corps], *Vojska*, Belgrade, 12 January 1995, p. 5; Mladen Marjanović, 'Obezbeđena brža mobilizacija' [A rapid mobilization is assured], ibid., 12 January 1995, p. 18; Gen. Risto Matović, 'Rado u vojnike' [Gladly into the army], ibid., 19 January 1995, p.18; interview with Col. Milojko Pantelić 'Regruti drumom rezervisti šumom' [Recruits by road, reservists to the forest], ibid., 22 June 1995, pp. 8–9.

[99] Interview with Boško Perošević, 'Kapital se vraća na mesto zločina' [Capital returns to the scene of the crime], *Duga*, Belgrade, 14–27 October 1995, p. 12.

[100] Interview with Mihajlo Marković 'Akademik Mihajlo Marković: istina je, kritikovao sam Miloševića' [Academician Mihajlo Marković: it is true that I criticized Milošević]', *Telegraf International*, Belgrade, 20 September 1995, p. 7.

tournament in Athens. Perhaps most indicative of the Serbs' disposition was an internal poll within Serbia's police, supposedly Milošević's most loyal supporters, which found that 92 per cent opposed serving outside of Serbia.[101]

Given the weight of the negative factors, it seems that Milošević assessed the cost of a full-scale war might be so high as to potentially de-stabilize his government. As Yugoslavia's President Zoran Lilić underlined in August 1995, after the Krajina had fallen,

> The Federal Republic of Yugoslavia will not permit itself to be dragged into a war. That is the desire of many of our enemies, seeking thus to nullify all our victories up to now in the defence of freedom and the historic rights of our people.[102]

Radmilo Bogdanović, another senior Serbian official, likewise defended Belgrade's reluctance to embark on a full-scale war by maintaining that this could lead to defeat and that Serbia was the Serbs' last bastion and thus had to be preserved: 'They [Serbs from outside Serbia] provoke us and [try] to drag us into a war, but where would we go [in case of defeat]? What, will the Bulgarians or Rumanians take us in?'[103] Borisav Jović like-wise estimated that if the Yugoslav Army had become involved in Bosnia against NATO, the Croats, and the Muslims, a conflict would have resulted 'in which we probably would have suffered the same fate as Iraq and been flattened to the ground'.[104]

Underlying this entire decision-making process was the Serbs' sense of strategic isolation, based on an acute awareness throughout the Serbian political class of Russia's weakness and inability to provide a counter-weight to the West. Typically, Yugoslavia's then-foreign minister, Vladislav Jovanović, on a visit to Moscow had acknowledged that, despite its desire for peace, 'Russia, however, does not have that influence which would be sufficient to stand up to the great powers which are interested in

---

[101] Milovan Brkić, '"Oluja" oduvala "Pauka" ['*Storm*' blew away 'Spider']', *Srpska reč*, Belgrade, 11 September 1995, p. 47.

[102] 'Ništa preče od sudbine naroda' [Nothing more important than the people's fate], *Evropske Novosti*, Belgrade, 22 August 1995, p. 2.

[103] 'Knin je mogao da se brani barem još dva meseca' [Knin could have defended itself for at least another two months], *Telegraf International*, Belgrade, 23 August 1995, p. 8. Tomica Raičević, a minister without portfolio in the Yugoslav govern-ment and a high-ranking SPS official, echoed this sentiment: 'No one has the right to drag the Federal Republic of Yugoslavia into such an adventure with cata-strophic consequences.' Interview with Milan Ćulibrk, 'Srbima je dovoljno pola Bosne' [Half of Bosnia is enough for the Serbs], *Duga*, Belgrade, 10–25 September 1995, p. 4.

[104] 'Ko je tenkista' [Who is the tank soldier]?, *NIN*, Belgrade, 17 November 1995, p. 22.

prolonging the war and maintaining the sanctions.'[105] Even when it seemed that the United States might lift the arms embargo on the Bosnian government unilaterally, Aleksandr Zotov, President Boris Yeltsin's special envoy to former Yugoslavia, admitted that Moscow's long-standing threat to unilaterally break UN sanctions on Belgrade in retaliation was not being considered seriously.[106] Indeed, Russia had been unable to prevent the NATO air strikes.

Domestic political considerations

Ultimately, however, the domestic impact on his government of continuing or terminating the war was probably the paramount consideration for Milošević. Avoiding a potential backlash such as might follow an escalation or even just a prolongation of the war was probably a key consideration. The engagement of the Yugoslav Army in Bosnia could have made it difficult for Milošević to deal with the revived opposition in Serbia or with a revived resistance in Kosovo. Milošević and his top officials, in any case, had never officially delineated how big Serbia should be, leaving the contours of the end-state conveniently vague, giving sufficient flexibility to claim even reduced gains as a victory.[107]

In ending the war, Milošević could count on the support of his primary constituency: the Serbs of Serbia. There was something of a popular backlash in Serbia against the *prečani* (Serbs from outside Serbia), who were blamed for miring Serbia in an unwanted war, for the general economic misery which ensued, and for expecting Serbia to fight while they often left for safety. The Belgrade government sought to exploit this rift to consolidate its home base.[108] For example, when Belgrade promoted the Contact Group Plan despite Bosnian Serb opposition in 1994, Serbia's premier Mirko Marjanović played on the anti-*prečani* mood in a speech in favour of the plan, claiming that:

> A great number of those refugees have been successful in Serbia [achieving] a higher material standard and status than they had in the

[105] 'Nazyvayte menya bratom' [Call me brother], *Rossiyskaya Gazeta*, Moscow, 11 September 1993, p. 6. The Serbian opposition too believed that Russia was too weak to help. See, for example, Vojislav Koštunica, president of the Democratic Party of Serbia, in 'Petokratka sa ružom' [The five-pointed star with the rose], *NIN*, Belgrade, 2 December 1994, p. 16.

[106] 'Russia, Germany slam embargo vote', *Washington Times*, 3 August 1995.

[107] Asked where the borders should be, Borisav Jović typically replied: 'We shall pull back the border to where the majority population believes it must remain in Yugoslavia. I personally do not know where that border will be.' See 'Nikoga nismo terali da ostane' [We did not force anyone to remain], *Intervju*, Belgrade, August 1994, p. 57.

[108] On this antagonism see note 4, pp. 338 below.

former Bosnia-Herzegovina, and many of them have profiteered from their emigration. The citizens of Serbia have seen that, and were often unhappy about it, and justifiably so.[109]

Recouping at the negotiating table

The deteriorating military position notwithstanding, Milošević probably continued to believe that he could achieve his objectives, at least in part, through negotiations, and more easily there than on the battlefield, given the shifting correlation of forces. The Serbian leadership also believed that, because of the pressure to clear Bosnia from the agenda before the impending presidential electoral campaign, the United States would be willing to make significant concessions to the Serbs in any negotiations. Looking forward to the start of the 'peace process', Milošević was hoping to establish at least the foundations of a small Greater Serbia. In September 1995, Mihajlo Marković gave the following prognosis regarding Serbia's future expansion:

> The borders of Serbia will never be those of the Krajina, as one could have expected in the 1991–1995 period. However, within a few years they could be the borders of the Republika Srpska, if the present peace process and the partition of Bosnia which it envisions are taken to their conclusion. Over time, the confederation between Serbia and the Republika Srpska would be transformed into a federal state.[110]

Moreover, if Milošević was now accepted by the international community as a peacemaker, the added legitimacy would boost his domestic standing, as well as reduce the likelihood that he would be liable in any pending proceedings by the International Criminal Tribunal.

The Bosnian Serb decision

In the end, for the Bosnian Serb leadership, it was the dire operational situation, as seen above, and their ultimate dependence on Belgrade for the war effort which provided sufficient leverage for Milošević to impose his views. Earlier, the Bosnian Serb leadership, even if unrealistically, had thought they could hold out on the battlefield but, in the wake of the defeats on the ground, they became painfully aware of their limited room

---

[109] Branislav Radivojša, Rade Ranković and Dragoljub Sevanović, 'Vanredno zasedanje Narodne Skupstine Srbije' [Emergency session of Serbia's Parliament], *Politika*, Belgrade, 27 August 1994, p. 1.

[110] Marković, 'Da, kritikovao sam Miloševića', p. 6. And he added: 'It is better for him [Clinton] to be rid of this problem once for all. This is why Frasure will be empowered to make certain concessions to the Serbs.'

for manoeuvre. Reflecting the perception of the influence the Bosnian Serb leadership could exert in negotiations in light of the military situation, and preparing the Bosnian Serb public for a feared negative outcome, the official weekly *Javnost* asked rhetorically:

> What can the Republika Srpska do if an American peace agreement in which even its minimum demands are not respected is adopted in Dayton against its will? Theoretically, the Parliament of the Republika Srpska could probably challenge or even reject such a document, but, given the present conditions and balance of power, the practical likelihood that such an answer would be given is minimal, not to say completely ruled out.[111]

Bosnian Serb leaders, however, also began to see the possibility of achieving their territorial and political objectives, albeit in a reduced form, if they could get the international community to accept partition, at least in practice. Not surprisingly, the Bosnian Serbs came up with additional demands before the start of the Dayton talks to maximize their options if and when final partition took place. Despite protests by US officials that these new conditions were 'a misrepresentation' of the baseline 26 September agreement reached in New York, in the end some of these demands, such as the retention of the name Republika Srpska, control over their own borders, and Serb retention of Brčko pending a final decision, were granted.[112] Overall, as Biljana Plavšić concluded, 'In 1995, we were defeated. However, that said, things did not look all that bad around the negotiating table ... The people were saying: "It's good; we could have come out worse."' [113]

CONCLUSION

The Serb war effort and the timing and manner of war termination in both these wars provides material for several lessons.

First, the military balance does matter, and is relevant to when a war ends and what the end-state looks like. Trying to differentiate between a 'peaceful' or 'political' solution to a conflict and a 'military' one leads to

---

[111] Kolja Besarović, 'Mirovni samit u Sjedinjenim Američkim Državama' [Peace summit in the USA], *Javnost*, Pale, 4 November 1995, pp. 5–6.

[112] Momčilo Krajišnik concluded that 'the partition amounts to a Serb victory', since this would facilitate 'our foremost goal', which was 'to form a Serb state on the Serb ethnic space'. In 'Oduvek sam bio za mir' [I have always favoured peace], *Intervju*, Belgrade, 13 October 1995, p. 15.

[113] 'Nisam stala na pola puta, ići ću do kraja' [I did not stop half way; I will carry on to the end], interview in *Duga*, Belgrade, 7–20 June 1997, p. 14.

a rather artificial conceptual distinction. Foreign mediators, in particular, often insisted that there could be no military solution in either Croatia or Bosnia, but only a political one, and sought to ignore the military situation. This approach stems from a rigid paradigm in which obtaining a settlement is seen as uppermost, with the provisions flowing from such a deal often being almost an afterthought. On the contrary, the military balance and war termination are usually inextricably linked. In general terms, the two phenomena of conflict and political negotiation are not mutually exclusive. Rather, they are complementary and interactive parts of a single process, for, as the Prussian military thinker Carl von Clausewitz observed, war is 'a continuation of politics', albeit in an extreme form.[114] Wars are fought for political ends, and virtually all wars end 'politically', with a negotiated settlement. Military success, however, can be key in determining when and with what results a war ends. What a stronger military position and combat may do is to ensure better terms for an eventual political solution. That is, a nation's war-ending negotiating position, and its diplomacy in general, is far more likely to succeed if its military position is strong compared to that of its opponent, and likely to erode if that balance deteriorates or is expected to deteriorate. It is perhaps self-evident that, all other things being equal, the better a belligerent's military situation, the more likely he is to seek and achieve more favourable terms in the negotiations leading to an end of the war, as belligerents weigh the likely costs and benefits of continuing or ending a war. In particular, both cases confirmed that when a one-sided military advantage – in this instance Serb – was reversed and a different military balance achieved, this increased the likelihood of a war terminating rather than being prolonged. Such a revision in the correlation of forces on the battlefield earlier – by, for example, adopting the much-debated 'lift-and-strike' option in Bosnia – would very likely have led to a quicker and more just war termination, with fewer victims, and, ultimately, to a more stable end-state.

Second, the Serb level of commitment was a vulnerability, as many were not willing to fight and die for the goals which their leadership presented to them. This had a clear negative impact on military effectiveness, although Western assessments chronically overestimated both Serb commitment and fighting power.

Third, the available evidence indicates strongly that both Milošević and the Bosnian Serb leadership were rational in their decision making, although their assessments and political goals may certainly have differed, and that both were responsive to a cost–benefit (or probability of victory) calculus. The assessment of past combat is a central element in this respect for the policy-maker, as he calculates what the future cost is likely to be.

---

[114] Carl von Clausewitz, *On War*, Princeton, NJ: Princeton University Press, pp. 87–8.

To a great extent, combat may have its greatest impact on war termination by shaping a belligerent's expectations of *future* military results. As Pillar posited accurately, the conclusion which a belligerent draws about the likely cost of continuing a war is more important than the actual cost paid up to then.[115]

Fourth, as a caveat, however, although a military advantage enhances a belligerent's achievement of its political goals, or, conversely, is detrimental in case of defeat, this is by no means automatic. Skilful diplomacy, if favoured by other international factors, may off-set some of the disadvantages. In this case, Belgrade and the Bosnian Serbs, thanks to other considerations, quite ill-founded in the long run, which prevailed in the international community, were able to obtain a better deal in the ensuing peace negotiations than their deteriorating military position warranted. In particular, in Bosnia, helped by an international desire for a rapid and cheap solution, as well as parallel plans by Croatia's President Tuđman to carve up Bosnia, the Serbs managed to come away with a better deal than the military balance suggested.

Fifth, the domestic political component in waging and terminating a war is significant, and often dominant. Like other aspects of foreign policy, this too is intimately linked to internal affairs and to the implications that a decision for continuing or ending a war will have for the fortunes of a government with its own population. That factor was a key consideration for Milošević's calculations. Although the ordinary Serbs in Serbia, Bosnia and Croatia paid a high price, for Milošević the war proved to have been a highly successful strategy for remaining in power. Gauging the extent of domestic support for policy is key to a statesman's success. Here, one can give Milošević high marks for recognizing the limits of backing for war and even for turning that factor to his advantage. Milošević has proved to be a calculating pragmatist, not a rigid ideological visionary, and a strong argument can be made that what matters most to him is his personal political position. If and when the cost, in terms of that core interest, increases to what he interprets as an unmanageable level, he could be expected to sit down and negotiate, not escalate. The experience from the wars in Bosnia and in Croatia suggests that discontent in Serbia is quick to emerge if there is a risk of heavy casualties in a conflict not seen as vital to the national interest. Such broad-based discontent threatened Milošević's own political position and, very likely, was a key element in leading him to end the war quickly.

Finally, war termination is a process whose actual consideration ought to begin as soon as the decision is made to go to war. As Clausewitz has observed: 'No one starts a war – or rather, no one in his senses ought to do so – without first being clear in his mind what he intends to achieve by

---

[115] Pillar, *Negotiating Peace*, pp. 196 and 197.

that war and how he intends to conduct it.'[116] In retrospect, Milošević and the regional Serb leadership miscalculated grossly in thinking that they could achieve their goals quickly and cheaply, and end the war at the point they desired. Ultimately, Milošević's luck in getting off relatively easy in the end should not obscure his basic blunder of not having crafted a more successful war termination strategy or, more basically, of not having assessed whether one was possible, before setting down the path to confrontation in both Croatia and Bosnia.

[116] Clausewitz, *On War*, p. 579.

Discussion: The War in Bosnia-Herzegovina
(Chaired by Vladimir Bilandžić)

Stjepan Mesić

Professor Mahmutćehajić's presentation has clarified many things, but I should still like to ask a question. I had a conversation with a highly placed official from the international community about Srebrenica, during which he told me that there was a tape recording made in Srebrenica when the town had fallen and the rest of the population and the soldiers from the ARBiH were surrounded. General Mladić and his officers lined up the troops and said: 'Now we're going to take our revenge on the Turks.' My informant told me that international politicians knew there was going to be a massacre. When I asked him why they had not reacted, why they had not threatened to strike the Serb command positions, concentrations of mechanized troops or artillery sites, of which they knew the precise locations, he explained: 'If we had submitted a request for action to the United Nations, if we had requested a session of the Security Council, then while the Council was in session and while we were justifying and documenting our request, those people in Srebrenica would have ceased to exist anyway. And that's why there was no intervention.' As far as I am concerned, that is no explanation at all. I thought then and still think now that there were political reasons behind such behaviour, reasons which he did not refer to. So I would like to ask you, who have been involved in the war in Bosnia-Herzegovina in all its aspects, how you explain the case of Srebrenica.

Rusmir Mahmutćehajić

There are many interpretations, and I personally think that within the context of the war against Bosnia-Herzegovina, the case of Srebrenica needs to be systematically examined. I will refer here only to published evidence relating to those events. There are people from Srebrenica who have stated publicly that they were invited to accept an exchange of territory – the

Serb-held suburbs of Sarajevo for Srebrenica – and that the Bosniak political leadership took part in such meetings. There have been accounts of this in the press. One of the key people in the defence of Srebrenica, Hakija Meholjić, publicly testified that there had been discussions about it with him when, at Izetbegović's invitation, Srebrenica's wartime government sent a nine-member delegation to Sarajevo in September 1993. This was at the time when the Bosniak Assembly was being held, at which there was a debate about the *Invincible* peace plan for Bosnia-Herzegovina as a union of three ethno-national republics. It was obvious to him that there were very big issues at stake here, since this was the first time that two helicopters were sent to enable them to leave Srebrenica, while UNPROFOR transporters took them from Sarajevo airport to the Holiday Inn. Naturally, Meholjić wondered how it was that they were ready just then to ensure safe passage for the delegation, when, ever since they had been proclaimed a demilitarized zone, no one from the state government had been able to get to them. It was then that the explicit offer of an exchange of territory was made.[1]

I know and I insist that what should have been done for the defence of Srebrenica was not done. I have given these details as demonstrating the theory that there was some kind of agreement behind the Srebrenica drama. This passive stance over a long period led to serious demoralization in Srebrenica itself; people lost the will to defend it, which as I see it was one of the key problems in Bosnia. Meholjić says that 'people in Srebrenica were disillusioned', so that the members of the delegation agreed on their return 'not to tell the people that we had been offered this exchange, because they would understand that we had been written off. ... It was all quite clear to us.' When, after the fall of Srebrenica, he called for the formation of a state commission to investigate the responsibility of the Presidency, the international community, the general staff, and everyone else, he was asked what was to be gained from it?[2]

---

[1] According to Meholjić, at the time chief of police in Srebrenica, Izetbegović asked them immediately after greeting them, 'What would you think about exchanging Srebrenica for Vogošća?' There was a silence, and then Meholjić said, 'Mr President, if you have invited us for a *fait accompli*, you didn't need to, since what has to be done is to go back to the people and accept the burden of their decision.' They rejected the idea without discussion, whereupon Izetbegović said: 'You know, in April 1993 [after the fall of Cerska and Konjević Polje] Clinton proposed to me that we should let Chetnik forces get into Srebrenica and massacre five thousand Muslims, after which there would be military intervention.' They had already been told that Izetbegović would receive them again the following day, but it did not happen, although he received all other such delegations. See Hasan Hadžić: '5000 muslimanskih glava za vojnu intervenciju – razgovor s H. Meholjićem' [5000 Muslim heads for military intervention – a discussion with H. Meholjić], *Dani*, 78, Sarajevo, 22 June 1998.

[2] Ibid.

There are many indications that there was a special agreement behind what happened in Srebrenica and Žepa, since those two towns were among the most important obstacles to the agreements to partition Bosnia-Herzegovina. In the case of Srebrenica there is absolutely nothing that could explain why there was no international intervention. Nor was there intervention when appalling camps where people were killed existed for a whole year by Tuđman's authority, though there is no doubt that there could have been intervention within 24 hours of their existence being known. Nor was there intervention in the case of the systematic destruction of towns such as Stolac; which was not even recognized as a crime. As you all know very well, there are also the cases of Mostar, Prozor, Gornji Vakuf, etc.

The theme could be developed endlessly, so I merely draw attention to a few details which could serve as some kind of an answer.

Jovan Divjak

I attended the negotiations on Srebrenica in April 1993. The situation was critical, and on the very first occasion we made contact with him Mladić brought some sort of agreement for the surrender of Srebrenica, which Sefer Halilović was supposed to sign. Mladić was sure that he was about to enter the town, since at that time, like Žepa, it was completely cut off; a few days earlier Konjević Polje and other surrounding residential areas had been occupied. The first day's negotiations lasted fourteen hours, the second the same. Mladić called for a break every two hours, convinced that at any moment he would receive the news from his people on the ground that the ARBiH had at last raised the white flag, while Halilović was calling his headquarters in Srebrenica every other two hours to find out what the situation was. Since the ARBiH did defend Srebrenica and Mladić did not succeed in entering the town at that time as he had imagined, what was finally signed was an order – directly imposed by NATO – to establish a safe area.[3]

When these matters are discussed nowadays, those who were in a sense responsible for the fall of Srebrenica in 1995 insist that it had really fallen already in 1993. But I can state that it was militarily defended and that what Mr Mahmutćehajić has said is true: from 1993 to 1995 nothing was

---

[3] The concept of *safe area*, a variant on the term *safe haven* from the time of the air campaign in Iraq, gave international protection to certain 'Muslim' towns which were being shelled by Serb artillery; it was based on Chapter VII of the UN Charter. UNPROFOR was to supervise the withdrawal of Serb military and paramilitary units so as to create a demilitarized area around these towns. UN Security Council Resolution 819, of 16 April 1993, applied the concept to Srebrenica, then extended it to Sarajevo, and Resolution 824, of 6 May, established another four *safe areas*: Tuzla, Žepa, Goražde and Bihać.

done which could have strengthened its position, militarily or politically. It is merely laughable when responsible people from the military say to representatives in the Assembly of Bosnia-Herzegovina that two 120mm mortars were sent to the town. Anyone who knows anything about the military know that it means nothing. It is equally laughable when Izetbegović, defending his position, says: 'We sent about thirteen helicopters', when you know that the load-bearing capacity of those helicopters was a tonne and a half or two, by which nothing significant could be achieved.

There were other failings too, but that does not mean that we do not know who is to blame. The guilt lies on Mladić and on Belgrade, i.e. Karadžić and Milošević, who did it on the pretext of revenge for our units having broken out of the town towards Bratunac and massacred some defenceless Serbs. It is also certain that the international community is to blame for not intervening, when it had sufficient evidence that Serb forces were advancing on Srebrenica. It is true that they were not particularly strong forces, but we did not have the resources to oppose them and nor did we know how to use what we had. I am thinking of the Red Arrow system, the latest anti-tank weaponry, which was damaged the very first time it was used and later could not be used at all. There were certainly failings in the ARBiH General Staff too; it made several errors that led to the catastrophe. There was simply no synchronization between the army command and the defence command of Srebrenica. Recently one of the commandants, a month before his death, described how stunned the people were when they realized that they had been abandoned.

All this certainly should not lead to the conclusion that the case of Srebrenica should not be fully investigated, as well as others, for example that of Sarajevo. Three times during 1992 we tried to break the siege of Sarajevo and always came up against obstruction from the HVO, or rather the HDZ authorities, who would not even allow our TO units to take part in the siege-breaking action across territories under their control. And something else about those attempts to break the siege. After each failure, we in the general staff would analyse who was responsible for what, and in most cases we established that the errors lay in the command structure, the elements which had prepared, organized and led the attempts, the one in June and the one in December 1992. It was always said that we would hold a public inquiry into the responsibility for these cases once the war was over, but so far we have not done so. However it may be, we have enough facts to blame these failures on ourselves in the general staff, and on our people who did not carry out the agreed plans.

I have heard here the observation that we did not succeed in lifting the siege of Sarajevo although we had the chance to do so. I have told you what was happening in the city itself. As one of the members of the ARBiH general staff, like everyone else who remained in the city I believed that there were 8,000–10,000 well-armed members of the army on Mount Igman; but when I reached Igman in November 1992 I discovered that there were only 1,000 men along the entire broad front around Sarajevo, and with only one howitzer: everything else was just light weapons.

Attila Hoare spoke on this subject a little while ago, trying to explain why it was not better and more organized. We had a powerful logistics centre in Visoko where it was decided how and where the resources they had acquired should be directed: to break the siege of Sarajevo or to defend some other place. We never knew how they decided. Some day the details about this and other unexplained events will probably become accessible to everyone, since as early as the end of 1995 and early 1996 a group was formed in the ARBiH general staff, now the joint staff of the Federation Army, to investigate the plans and so reveal how the defence of Bosnia-Herzegovina was organized and conducted.

Stjepan Mesić

General Divjak recalled that sick joke about the Serb-Croat border at the Neretva, with the Bosniaks in the Neretva. But it was no joke; it was an actual statement by Mate Boban.

Rusmir Mahmutćehajić

Someone else said it too – Jadranko Prlić, now minister of foreign affairs of Bosnia-Herzegovina. The statement is recorded in the documents, and reads: 'We to the left, you to the right, and the Muslims must choose one side or the other. If they don't want either, then it's down the Neretva with them.'[4]

---

[4] Božidar Vučurević, president of the SDS regional committee for Herzegovina, mayor of Trebinje and ideologue of the attack on Dubrovnik, described during an interview for the Croatian press his first meeting with Mate Boban in Grude, when it seems the sick joke was made and began to circulate. The precise date is not given, but from the context one can see that it was in spring 1992, in any case before the Boban–Karadžić meeting in Graz on 7 May. Vučurević proposed that the Serbs and Croats agree about the borders, Boban asked him where they should run and, according to Vučurević, 'proposed the most natural line – the river Neretva. Croats on the west bank, Serbs on the east.' When the journalist asked 'what about the Muslims?', he explained, 'Boban asked me that too. I told him that the place for that quasi-nation is between us – in the Neretva. Boban and I laughed, drank our coffee and agreed that we would continue to meet and discuss specific issues of interest to our peoples.' See Srđan Šanović: 'O svojim interesima u BiH Hrvati i Srbi nisu pregovarali samo u Grazu' [The Croats and Serbs did not hold negotiations about their interests only in Graz], Nacional, Zagreb, 22 October 1997; partial translation in Bosnia Report, new series 1, November–December 1997. Vučurević also spoke about a later meeting in Njivice near Herceg-Novi, attended by Jadranko Prlić, then president of the government of the Croat Republic of Herzeg-Bosna.

Stjepan Mesić

This is a horrifying sign of a mentality which gained considerable military and political power during the war, and its existence is not unconnected with the question I want to ask. The international community, i.e. its European and global mechanisms, were in favour of the preservation of Yugoslavia. Seeing that this was not possible, they recognized Bosnia-Herzegovina but then did nothing to see that the state survived, instead allowing Milošević and Tuđman to tear it apart like jackals. Though we asked it to become involved, the international community did practically nothing; it did not encourage the opposition in Croatia, which had principled views about Bosnia-Herzegovina, but twice in a row allowed Tuđman to win elections. I am not entirely sure they will not also allow him to change the Constitution, so that he can run and win presidential elections for a third time. So much for the principles of the international community.

As for Bosnia-Herzegovina, this is the only war in history during which the victim of aggression supplied the aggressor with petrol. Fra Pavao Tomislav Duka, who like us finally resigned from the HDZ, told General Špegelj and me how during one of his journeys to central Bosnia he counted 40 fuel tankers in Dretelj, near Čapljina, which were going to Republika Srpska. I even have personal information, easily verified, that INA exported 2 millions tonnes of petroleum to Bosnia during the war. As early as autumn 1993, the independent Croatian media revealed that convoys from Croatia via Serb-occupied territory were delivering 400 tonnes of food and 112 tonnes of petrol a day to Velika Kladuša, which was several times greater than local requirements. It was obvious that the petrol was only formally being sold to Fikret Abdić, who was then forwarding it on. To whom, if not to Serbia and Republika Srpska? That petroleum was fuelling the tanks that were killing our children and Bosnian children.

The international community knew this very well, that is the whole point. If, after introducing sanctions against Serbia, it was able to prevent the entry of petrol from Albania, Greece, Bulgaria, Hungary and Romania, why did it allow this traffic in millions of tonnes of petroleum derivatives here?

Rusmir Mahmutćehajić

You say 'international community'. In my view this is one of the phrases that serve to befog the whole issue. In the case of the war against Bosnia-Herzegovina, only in very rare cases did we deal with what you call the international community. Otherwise it was just a collection of diverse external players, often fundamentally opposed to each other, so that – depending on their view of the region at war and their reciprocal interests

– they behaved effectively as close allies of those who were destroying Bosnia-Herzegovina. We have the same situation to this day, with allies manifestly being sought even among forces such as Republika Srpska, which is the very embodiment of the plan to destroy Bosnia-Herzegovina. Although completely opposed to the very being of Bosnia-Herzegovina and essentially repudiating it, RS is today being put forward as an entirely legitimate and legal creation. But as Professor Cigar says, even if we were to stand on the other side we would see that Republika Srpska is not good for the Serbs either.

Nor is it any secret, or disputed by anyone, that Belgrade is even now financing the officers and army of Republika Srpska, and Croatia the HVO. Why?

Discordant and divided interests within a broad spectrum of forces are today refracted through Bosnia – from Great Britain and France to Germany and Russia, the role of the United States in the future of Europe, the process and nature of European integration, the place of Southeastern Europe, and the issue of the Middle East; all of them essential issues, as Zbigniew Brzezinski says, for the future of the world. All this requires deeper consideration, but in this context one must also look at the direct collaboration of the Croatian and Serbian armies in Bosnia-Herzegovina. It is not just a question of trade in petroleum across a few front lines, but of the exchange of intelligence, the passage of troops across each other's territory, joint combat actions, exchange or loan of weapons, etc. Much has been written about all this, and it is far from unknown.

Dušan Bilandžić

I have one question which is, I think, very important for the future of Bosnia-Herzegovina. Although it is said that the international community is, to put it mildly, obstructing the reconstruction of the country, in Mr Mahmutćehajić's presentation there was a very optimistic vision, both as to the past and as to future developments. But there are some obstacles to this, of which two in particular are evident.

First, some of the people who fled Bosnia-Herzegovina quite simply do not want to return. Even in Croatia, where the situation is generally better, the younger generation is not on the whole returning to the Danube basin but remaining in Zagreb, Istria, Dalmatia, etc. Only older people are returning, while the young have already disowned, if I may put it like that, their homeland in the Danube basin. The same is true of other areas of Croatia from which the population was expelled in 1991–92, and the phenomenon is probably still more marked in Bosnia-Herzegovina.

Second, the dogs of war to whom we refer are also obstructing the return of refugees and displaced persons, with the aim of maintaining the current population distribution. We have heard that in 1991 Serbs and

Bosniaks were living in 95 per cent of the territory of Bosnia-Herzegovina, and Croats in 70 per cent; now those percentage distributions are radically different. Bearing in mind this obstruction, whether on the part of the international community or of those in power in different parts of the Federation and in Republika Srpska, I wonder what the chances are of a more serious start to the return process. Even if it gets started, it is so difficult that it could last for decades.

Rusmir Mahmutćehajić

I agree with your assessment that the process of reconstituting or renewing Bosnia-Herzegovina will be slow, but there is no alternative. Even if we were to accept Milošević's and Tuđman's model for the destruction of the country and try to eliminate all the obstacles on the way, even if we were to act consistently in accordance with their wishes, still nothing would be fundamentally resolved for the future of Croats and Croatia, or of Serbs and Serbia. Try to imagine that you hold in your hands sufficient power to achieve the goals which Milošević and Tuđman discussed in Karađorđevo, and you will quickly realize that such a model could never resolve anything.

But if we try to project the development of Croatia in the next 50 years, we shall see that there is something Croatia cannot do without. I was recently in Zagreb attending a discussion on the future of Croatia, and I was fascinated by the fact that the Bosnian issue was completely overlooked; everyone there was talking about the future of Croatia but completely forgetting that there can be no such future without Bosnia-Herzegovina. There will be no development, no stabilization of democracy in Croatia without a parallel process in Bosnia-Herzegovina. It is simply not possible, but almost no one in Croatia wants to say so out loud. It is also impossible for Croatia to integrate itself in Europe in any real sense, unless the same integrative trends are operating in Bosnia-Herzegovina.

Tuđman's statement that Croatia has nothing to do with its Balkan neighbours is completely illogical. Here is just one example: the development of the Croatian economy and its integration into Europe cannot possibly occur without taking into account the wider economic environment, nor is it possible if Croatia's borders are not defined and controlled in the same way as any other European borders. But Croatia today is *de facto* a country without borders: without any difficulty at all you can import anything whatsoever from Russia into Croatia; and anyone who goes to Stolac and sees the traffic on the road via Berkovići, on the so-called inter-entity boundary line, will see that Croatia only has borders *de jure*, since its 400 border crossings are simply not functioning, as Jacques-Paul Klein recently pointed out. A smugglers' empire and a functioning trading post have been created in Berkovići, which could neither have originated nor continued to operate without political patronage from above. There, under the auspices of Herzeg-Bosna, now the Federation of Bosnia-Herzegovina, and Republika Srpska, Croatia and FRY illegally trade with each other. Solving that problem is a prerequisite for the future of Croatia, and it cannot be done independently of Bosnia-Herzegovina.

I have often heard Tuđman, and the Croatian leadership in general, speak of the demographic catastrophe of Croats in Bosnia-Herzegovina, but I think they are simplifying the problem. Depopulation is affecting the islands too, and many other regions of Croatia, but it does not occur to anyone to say that because the number of Croats is falling in Vis, Hvar or Rab, those towns might sometime cease to matter to Croatia as a whole, as though only a single generation mattered. It is the same with Bosnia-Herzegovina. Unfortunately, people who do not understand Croat history, culture and mental cast as a totality forget that the Croat totality will be difficult to forge if Bosnia is overlooked. However many Croats there may be in Bosnia-Herzegovina – and so far as I'm concerned, pray God there may be many more in the future than there are now – that country is an integral part of the Croat totality, which must not be reduced to the currently dominant, superficial political stratum. Endeavours aimed at consolidating the situation in Bosnia-Herzegovina rather than its dis-memberment are a precondition for the Croat future.

There are forces in Europe and in the world which would like to see Bosnia as the mirror of European disunion. As you know, there are covert and overt differences in regard to the future of Europe, and advocates of various perspectives and actions related to that future try to use the dis-cord in Bosnia-Herzegovina to demonstrate all manner of things connected with NATO, the United States, German-French relations, the future of Russia, and so on.

What I have said here is valid for Serbia too. The precondition for a better future for Serbs in Bosnia-Herzegovina, without whom there is no Bosnia-Herzegovina, is consolidation and normalization of relations between Serbia and B-H. Many of us do not want to hear a word today about regional integration, or about regularizing relations between Serbia, Croatia, Bosnia-Herzegovina, Montenegro, Albania, Kosovo, Bulgaria and so on; but that is the precondition for a better future for Croatia, the precondition for a solution to the Kosovo crisis, the precondition for much more.

As long as states exist whose capacity as instruments for protecting their rights is deficient, they will attempt to maintain an oligarchy in power, as has often been said here, and as Professor Cigar has made very clear today. Problems will arise with amorphous states, in which the ruling oligarchy always declares: 'we shall shape what our ancestors were unable to shape in a thousand years', and uses this self-assigned task to support their mystified model, which was dangerous both for the rule of law and for democracy. You should not be surprised that borders do not exist or are not recognized; this is the way some people acquire for themselves the role of Father of the Nation, Creator of the State: the person who realized the age-old dream that no one else was able to conceive or realize.

The solution to these issues and the precise definition of relations in this region is, of course, a long-term process with many internal obstacles, but there is no alternative. If it really was not possible to destroy Bosnia between 1990 and 1995, it seems to me that it never will be possible.

Tudman's policy in Bosnia was defeated with terrible losses, intolerable for Croatia's demographic strength. Our estimates of Croatian losses in Bosnia-Herzegovina are between 15,000 and 30,000 dead, mostly non-civilian, fighting men. Professor Cigar stated, on the basis of official data from the Bosnian Serbs, that they suffered more than 18,000 dead, while our estimate of their losses is 80 per cent of the most productive part of the population, i.e. 70,000 people, mostly in the army, which means the final extinction of many families. Between 150,000 and 160,000 Bosniaks were killed, of whom between 70 per cent and 80 per cent were civilians. When all this is added up, it is clear that all sides need to sober up and make a fundamental change of direction; but the ideological models dominating the scene in Bosnia, her neighbours and the wider region are a real problem.

Dušan Bilandžić

I agree with your thesis. But the war ended three years ago. What do the statistics say about the return of refugees and displaced persons?

Rusmir Mahmutćehajić

The data I have are as follows. In two years, from the end of March 1996 to the end of March this year, about 240,000 people returned to Bosnia-Herzegovina while 40,000 left. The age structure of the 240,000 returnees is very poor: they are elderly and mostly in need of social welfare; while the 40,000 are the most productive element of the population, in the social sense probably worth a million people over 40. But the war in Bosnia-Herzegovina was of huge dimensions, and it will not be possible to calm the resulting psychological traumas in a mere year or two – or even three, four or five. Bosnia has no long-term vision of reconstruction. We hope that the international community will understand that this only appears to be the most expensive, but is in fact the cheapest project for Bosnia.

Bosnia used to have a uniform university system in Sarajevo, Tuzla, Banja Luka and Mostar. Everyone, on all sides, now engaged in the reconstruction of Bosnia-Herzegovina was educated in it, including Presidency members Alija Izetbegović, Momčilo Krajišnik and Krešimir Zubak. The universities of those days were under the ideological sway of the regime, of course, but at least they were united; whereas now they are separated into four distinct universities under the direct influence of the ruling oligarchies, and the kind of knowledge and mentality produced in them destroys bridges of understanding and widens chasms of mistrust. No university in Bosnia-Herzegovina has any chance of liberating itself from this oligarchic or direct party tutelage. The international community is investing in the revival of the economy, but for the long term it would be better to invest in a modern, European university able to act as an integrative factor. It is the nature of a university to be open, and to take no account of national, religious or ideological affiliations. Our universities are not like that today: Sarajevo university has hardly any Serbs or Croats, Banja Luka no Croats or Bosniaks, and Mostar no Bosniaks or Serbs. This is only one of many issues which must be addressed.

As I have said, Bosnia was not destroyed, and that is the fundamental premise of its reconstruction. I have not been expressing some kind of optimism as a reflection of my feelings, my love for my country as it is; at this moment in Bosnia-Herzegovina there simply is no other way, if we believe that we are people with any kind of future. The forces in Bosnia that are building that future are very frail, but they are the only forces, now that young people are instinctively leaving, capable of offering some kind of defiant construction of a Bosnian future, similar to the undertaking of Polish intellectuals a century ago, when they were faced with a non-existent Polish state, destroyed and divided, but believed that it could arise again from the ashes. It seems to me that Bosnia's case is similar, and that its resurrection is in the best interests of Serbs and Croats as well. Everything else is merely utopian, or an imposition of formulas pushing all these peoples not only towards a possible new war, but into psycho-dramas that prevent us from truly understanding where we are going.

Martin Špegelj

I have two short comments and one question. I should like first to comment on what has been said about Croatia. We in the opposition have already assessed on a number of occasions that nothing is as it should be in Croatia and that the country is functioning irrationally, so we have taken action together with all those who want to support democracy and to change the whole structure, from internal relations in every sector to relations with neighbouring states, especially with Bosnia-Herzegovina, with which Croatia is closely connected. I hope that the irrationality of our government has gone far enough to be visible even to those who until recently were overlooking and ignoring it, and that its time has run out.

Changes are inevitable, and I hope that they will have a positive effect on similar consolidation in neighbouring countries, especially in Bosnia-Herzegovina.

My second comment relates to the role of the superpowers. I have the impression that the superpowers think their historic task was ended at the moment when the Eastern European communist empire began to collapse. During a discussion with Warren Zimmerman I saw how pleased he was that the whole process was occurring without the West having to send in its armies or spend a single dollar. He was convinced that the transition in Yugoslavia would take place far more easily and painlessly than elsewhere, because Yugoslavia had been more liberal than the other Eastern European states. That was a huge delusion, both on the part of Western politicians and among our people, who simply did not pay any attention to the message continually issuing from Belgrade, which went something like this: 'Socialism was brought to the countries of Eastern Europe on the bayonets of the Red Army, while we in Yugoslavia made our own indigenous socialist revolution, paid for it with our own blood and will not allow anyone to destroy it bloodlessly.'

However much the United States, Britain, France or Germany may have been involved in everything, they still had far less impact on events in Yugoslavia than the forces working from within. It was so throughout the war, except at the end of 1993, when there was a real desire to stop the war, and the United States become somewhat more strongly committed. Hence we should not try to justify ourselves by referring to the actions or influence of external forces in conflict situations for which we alone are responsible. Certainly there was plenty of espionage, our region was indeed a training ground for the most diverse intelligence services, but remember that intelligence services of themselves have never created or destroyed anyone's country. One should not immediately look for the covert action of some external power in every instance that is not easily explicable; anyone who does so is giving a clear signal that he does not want to face up to the real answer from within.

My question relates to the role of the 5th corps of the Army of Bosnia-Herzegovina. I have spoken with many people in Sarajevo about the role of that corps, including two of its commanders, Generals Ramiz Dreković and Atif Dudaković, with whom I maintained close contact during the war. It seems to me that their troops played a huge role, which is so suppressed and marginalized in official Croatian analyses of the war that there must be some profound political reason for it. I do not know if it is because of plans linked to Fikret Abdić, or because of the desire – which still has some life in it – that this part of western Bosnia should belong to Croatia. I should be glad if someone in Bosnia-Herzegovina would carry out a complete analysis of the role of the 5th corps from beginning to end. In my view, this corps played an important role in the success of Storm, since it broke the link between the forces occupying our territory and Republika Srpska.

Nor have we touched on the issue of the concluding operations on B-H soil in the late summer and early autumn of 1995, which have political as well as military connotations. These operations have raised a number of political questions concerning both the relations between Zagreb and Sarajevo and those between Belgrade and Sarajevo. An analysis of those events could provide some answers which would be very useful in destroying the policies of Zagreb and Belgrade towards Bosnia-Herzegovina.

Jovan Divjak

I shall talk about operations, not about the political background since from the time I was relieved of my duties much of that background has not been accessible to me. There are two fundamental conclusions: first, the 5th corps saved that part of Bosnia-Herzegovina; second, it thereby made a major contribution to Bosnia-Herzegovina's survival in the sense that Professor Mahmutćehajić has talked about. Imagine what it would have been like in other parts of the country if other units had done what that corps did on its territory.

But it made one error, in 1994, when it attempted to make an independent sortie to the east, got more or less to Martin Brod, and then, having unrealistically assessed its own strength and logistics, had to withdraw with significant losses. In terms of B-H politics, what is more important is that it successfully defended itself against what we may call the internal aggressor, the forces of Fikret Abdić, who was collaborating with Mladić's forces and those of the SVK.

What General Špegelj said about 5th corps actions in the Republic of Croatia during Storm is also important. Unfortunately, they are not given their true worth by the Croatian authorities. Nor, so far as I know, has there been any attempt in Bosnia-Herzegovina to carry out a full analysis of combat actions in the Bosnian Krajina. At the time the Federation Army was formed, while I was still involved in the process, we were beset by anxieties caused by the fact that the Krajina and the 5th corps were cut off from the central part of the country and the rest of our forces. Between the 5th corps, in other words the area of today's Una-Sana canton, and central Bosnia there is a huge area under the control of HZ Herzeg-Bosna, which is still in existence even though it has been abolished on paper.

We have spoken of the obvious collaboration between the HVO and the VRS, but I was surprised to learn that ARBiH too, at times when it was in great difficulties in its conflict with the HVO, collaborated with the VRS, never with the knowledge of the general staff (or perhaps they did know in places where it mattered). It was pure human fraternization.

248

I remember well how in 1992, when there was no food in Sarajevo, the soldiers still had a packet of cigarettes every day. I know that they exchanged those cigarettes for food with Serb soldiers on the front line, but that is just being human, in the same way as it was from human feelings that individual Serb families protected Croats and Bosniaks in areas controlled by Karadžić's forces. Such too had been the relations between the three nations in Bosnia-Herzegovina during the Second World War.

When I first came to Mostar, I learned that during the time when the situation was critical, when it was possible that the HVO supported by the Croatian Army might even cross to the east bank of the Neretva, support from VRS positions was negotiated not so much by Mostar's military as by its political leaders; the VRS even gave ARBiH some arms and ammunition to halt the attack. And when I was in Zenica in October, when the HVO and the Croatian Army were in action in the areas held by the ARBiH 3rd and 7th corps, the chief of staff said to me: 'We don't know what to do. The Serbs from Vlašić have no salt, and they are asking us for two or three lorry-loads and offering in return to fire on the Croatian Army and HVO positions.' I think that in situations where a people's very survival in a particular area is at stake, some kind of cooperation will be sought; it surprised me at the time, but later I understood that it was quite natural. It was not like the collaboration between the commands and staffs of the VRS, HV and HVO, but these two or three examples show that there were moments of cooperation between the ARBiH and the VRS.

Ozren Žunec

I think that all the participants in this seminar who have come from Croatia will agree with me that the presentation by our colleague Mahmutćehajić was a great help to our deliberations and has clarified them. I was just saying today to General Špegelj that we talk all the time about the war in Croatia as inseparable from the war in Bosnia-Herzegovina, and then, when we sit down to write about it, we reduce it all to Croatia alone. So I think that for all of us today's lecture has meant a great deal.

All the same, I shall put one question to Mr Mahmutćehajić relating to Bosnia-Herzegovina as a multicultural society. Your thesis showed brilliantly that to consider Bosnia in this way is a means of breaking it apart, a way of demonstrating its alleged lack of cohesive wholeness, since it suggests that a region where several cultures coexist is a kind of artificial creation, which can be broken up according to anyone's needs, whims, interests or simple malice. I think that what you said relates chiefly to the previous situation in Bosnia, to how Bosnia was viewed before the war. Now the situation is such, so far as I can tell, that one can indeed say that there is almost no cultural life or, if you will, co-existence, since the ravages of war have caused powerful changes and horrifying damage, not only extensive but also long-lasting. So it seems to me that the idea of multicultural Bosnia is an ideal to which we shall simply be unable to convert people, or mobilize them in order to establish that unified Bosnia which all of us here, I believe, stand for.

What worries and discourages me the most is the massive support of the population in the 1996 elections for the forces of destruction. My Bosnian friends like Ivan Lovrenović, or Ivo Komšić who played such a key role in reaching the Washington Agreements, who in the terrible war chaos of 1993 and early 1994 tried to put the pieces of shattered Bosnia back together again, lost catastrophically in those elections. Whereas the HDZ gained overwhelming support among Croats in the elections, as was once again confirmed just a few days ago.

In your presentation you designated two categories of members of society – the elite, and the executors. The problem is clearer as regards the first and offers certain possibilities. If there are academics and intellectuals advocating a destructive programme, their thinking can change, or they can become isolated and lose their influence on the public. But what when so-called ordinary people, *en masse*, obstinately vote for such ideas and such programmes, without regard to all the obvious harm they portend? This is a catastrophe whose elements and roots cannot be gone into now in detail, though I have tried to explain to myself where this persistence comes from, and how all these forces of destruction continue to obtain such mass support.[5]

You have already responded in a way to these doubts in your answer to Professor Bilandžić, and I too believe that the long-term strategies evoked here are probably the only solution, although it would do no harm to examine some short-term and medium-term possibilities from which we might see some progress as soon as possible, at least in certain areas, which might then have a snowball effect in accelerating the entire process. Whence my first question: what is your view on the wider basis of destruction that has been described?

I should like to put a quite different question to Professor Cigar and General Divjak, relating to the conclusion of operations in Bosnia-Herzegovina. The war in Bosnia-Herzegovina came to an end for all three sides. Professor Cigar has shown how the position looked from the Serb angle, and suggested the ways in which the war's end was good for the Serbs. I can see how it was good for the Croatian leadership: if Croatia still wants to partition Bosnia-Herzegovina, some Serbs have to remain in the country or there would be no one to divide it with. We surely shan't divide it with the Bosniaks! So the Serbs must remain. But there is still the question of why the ARBiH allowed itself to be brought to a halt on

[5] See note 1, p. 68 above.

5 November 1995. Was it really, as is widely believed, just because the Croatian side had agreed to halt, so that the ARBiH no longer had support on its flanks and could not go it alone?

Another story says that the US representatives as the new jargon has it, 'Holbrooked' Izetbegović and the B-H military leadership, telling them that if they continued operations their over-extended front would be indefensible in the event of a Serb counter-attack, which would lead to catastrophe. This seems to me quite unconvincing, so I should like to hear your views on why the ARBiH agreed to break off its operations.

Rusmir Mahmutćehajić

There are many examples in European history which could give a credible answer on how to overcome large-scale destruction, not only physical destruction but the destruction of mutual trust. Nations which have behind them long periods of warfare, destruction and killing must, at the end of the day, find a way of replacing the condition of permanent conflict and mutual mistrust with something which is not, and cannot be, a further phase of exacerbating the conflict and mistrust. In Bosnia-Herzegovina there are almost innumerable reasons for, and instances of, a mutual trust that has shown itself to be so steadfast that the two greater-state blueprints, the Greater Serbian and the Greater Croatian, were unable to destroy it. They came up against something in Bosnia which they had not counted on. To the majority of observers who remain within the confines of purely logical modelling, this is incomprehensible and inexplicable.

We are talking of convictions which have developed over a long period in the deep strata of individuals and communities in Bosnia-Herzegovina, which cannot be understood from such a purely logical perspective. During the last 100 years there have been endless attempts to deny the existence of all Bosnian-Herzegovinian cultural, artistic or any other integrative factors. The partition of Bosnia-Herzegovina in the 1939 Cvetković–Maček agreement significantly contributed to the scale of mutual conflict in the Second World War. But the deep foundations of Bosnian life were not destroyed, and sooner or later it will have to be realized that the only rational policy is one which does not deal with the country in that way. Some people may keep returning to the idea of partition, a Tuđman and his Šušak will perhaps again be found who will seek allies to achieve it, but that it is simply unfeasible and impossible is obvious.

After 1945 an ideological structure was established with an almost incomprehensible level of reductionism. Its ideological values completely repudiated the integrative factor in Bosnia-Herzegovina, the 1,000 years of Bosnian culture, making it impossible even to understand that factor.

I say again – B-H was no paradise. But it is a fact that Sarajevo today contains religious monuments belonging to people who could never have achieved them by their own power. This situation arises from deeper layers of being that are hard to understand within the context of ideological models.

The fact that Franciscans remained and survived in Bosnia, for example, cannot be explained by any interests of illusory political and economic power, but only by the deeper layers of individual and group consciousness in Bosnia-Herzegovina. These strata must once again emerge onto the stage of public life and lead to concord between diverse opinions, which is not happening now. B-H culture in its totality is a sacral culture, hence it is possible for a sense of the sanctity of one place of worship to generate a sense of responsibility for the sanctity of another place of worship, which may be different in form, but is in essence the same. It is not possible to explain otherwise the fact that there are no towns in Bosnia-Herzegovina where mosques, churches and synagogues were not built side by side. Of course, for the atheist world-view the secret of life remains unattainable, just as Bosnia remains incomprehensible to the fundamentally atheized ideological world-view.

It is obvious today that something different is taking place, both in our environment and on the world stage as a whole, so even the Catholic Church in Croatia feels apprehensive about the unambiguous clash between a shallow, ideological world-view on the one hand, dangerous for individual and collective alike, and its own universalist world-view on the other. In Bosnia such talk is hard to grasp for most people, but you will see that this is a key issue in the basic expressions of world thought on the relation between liberalism and tradition.

I think Bosnia will free itself or return from its current destruction precisely in this way, if the world as a whole moves towards some better state; or it will fall into ruin together with the world. But separately, as such, it cannot fall into ruin. Moreover, I think that time is working for Bosnia, both in terms of the altered way of thinking of Bosnian people themselves and in terms of this process in the world.

As for your question, the wounds are truly terrible. Never before have there been internal conflicts on such a scale in Bosnia-Herzegovina. There have been conflicts – there are many ugly episodes in Bosnian history – but never on such a scale. So it is up to people who are concerned with their own future and that of their progeny – and who act, therefore, not just after reflection but instinctively – to find a way to heal those wounds. Terrible wounds have appeared in the relations between Bosniaks and Croats in B-H, indescribable wounds that freeze the blood in your veins if you contemplate them, but they are unknown to the public because for four years Croatia has been possessed by an unspeakable propaganda. These wounds must be healed by Croatia in its own interest, by the

Croatian people, by Croatian intellectuals, and in this they must find allies among the people of Bosnia. Otherwise, please tell me what future – be it even our own, if we want to look at everything in purely selfish terms – we can speak of? I am not saying this emotionally at all, but precisely arguing for a cool and rational approach.

I cannot say how things will be in a year or two, doubtless just as hard as today. Perhaps for 13 and perhaps for 30 years, Bosnia will be the scene of terrible anguish in every way, unless somewhere a group of people can be found to offer a breaking of the mould, and for whom these circumstances are suffocating. But such changes in Bosnia are the precondition also for a better future for Croatia. I repeat, because it needs to be repeated constantly: it is unreasonable and stupid to expect any changes in Croatia without changes in the wider region. That is simply impossible.

Jovan Divjak

My response to Dr Žunec's question as to why the ARBiH allowed itself to be brought to a halt is that a diktat was in force – an order not to exceed the 51 per cent of territory that was to be under the control of the authorities in Sarajevo. The whole of 1994 went by in preparations for achieving that ratio of 51 per cent to 49 per cent. Here are two supporting facts.

At that time, in late summer and early autumn 1995, the Sarajevo operation was taking place and the operation to liberate western Bosnia had begun. The order was given, under US pressure, that the ARBiH units around Sarajevo must not move so much as a metre, and that if they did go into action regardless, air action would be taken against them. On the other hand, as you know, ten days later action was taken in the west of the country, as a result of which our units together with the HVO took a large area and entered Šipovo. The map shows clearly what that area looks like now: entering Šipovo went beyond the assigned ratio, and in December 1995 those units had to withdraw far enough to establish the 51:49 ratio. Thus what was recognized on the ground was the previous agreement, rather than what had been achieved in combat. You know that at one point, when the Croatian Army had gone into Bosanski Novi via Otoka, there were air strikes against it and the HVO. The conclusion is obvious: everything was decreed so as to reach the agreed territorial division.

Adrian Hastings

This is a good point for me to come in. I wanted to say that I disagree with one point made by General Špegelj, when he suggested, if

I understood him, that one should not look too much for explanations from outside. Clearly we can't look at everything at the same time, and tomorrow is to be our international day. But I think that we would misunderstand the whole history of this conflict if we left out the intentions of the Great Powers.

I am not sure that I fully understand yet who exactly caused what as between Britain and France, and as between the two of them, Germany and the United States. My own judgement is that Britain was the decisive factor for a long time, though not, of course, at the end: it was precisely the rejection of British policy which brought the war to an end. I have no doubt that strong action on the part of the international community could quickly have brought the war in Croatia to an end and prevented any further war. It could also have brought the war in Bosnia to an end many times. I am convinced that this was not what the British government wanted, nor the international community which followed Britain. I am not sure why British politicians took the position that they did and lied to the extent that they did.

There is no question that, if we wanted to, we could arrest Karadžić and Mladić. But Britain and the United States do not wish to do so. And they do not wish to do so because, if Mladić and Karadžić are put on trial at The Hague, they would give damning evidence about British politicians and others in the West. So we cannot afford to put them on trial.

If the arms embargo had been raised early on, I am sure the war would have come to an end. If arms had been flowing through easily to Bosnia, the Serbs would have been faced with the kind of argument which made them sue for peace in 1995. Arguments in favour of stopping the war would have established their validity very much earlier. But what is important is why Britain was so determined that the arms embargo should not be raised. It was absolutely determined: it did everything possible to stop it being raised. So if you want to understand the history of the war you must not underestimate the secret factors outside your own society, which produced the situation in which the siege of Sarajevo could continue for all those years. All the arguments that were given as to why we couldn't do anything about it proved untrue in 1995. That it was impossible in this sort of country to bomb effectively. That we would kill so many civilians, if we bombed. And so on. I don't think we should underestimate these factors and their psychological effect: that Milošević, who was paying the forces responsible for it all, knew he was safe. The relationship between Milošević and various Western politicians – Carrington, Hurd, Owen, etc. – were such that he felt secure. He knew that the British and the West would close their eyes to the continued support he was giving all through the war, that they would keep up their pretence and denial when we knew what he was doing. I think that the importance of all this is very great indeed and that the war need not have lasted any length of time if the West had wanted it to stop.

Tarik Kulenović

I should like to respond to General Špegelj's question about the 5th corps. I too think that it should be given more consideration. It is worth considering two aspects of the matter: one is the strictly military evaluation of its effectiveness, the other its symbolic significance.

When one considers the effectiveness of the ARBiH at the level of the common soldier, taking into account the resources available to him and the logistical support he enjoyed, his limited equipment and the conditions in which he was fighting, I think one can say that the soldiers of the ARBiH were the best in the recent war. In Croatia, for example, the common soldier received three meals a day throughout the war, guaranteed regardless of all obstacles, meals which might be skipped at most for a day or two during the fiercest battles. What the elite troops of the ARBiH ate for months on end, as they themselves acknowledge, was just a portion of boiled spaghetti per day. So imagine what the common soldiers must have eaten. So while there are debatable points about the ARBiH at the strategic level, one must say without any hesitation that, given the conditions in which they were having to fight, the men showed themselves to be exceptionally fine soldiers.

When it comes to the external appearance of military formations in the Bosnian war, one is first faced with the aggressive propaganda of the VRS, which began with the appearance of Arkan's paramilitaries – modern camouflage uniforms, black hoods covering their faces, full sets of arms including everything from pistols to *zolja* shoulder-launchers – and continued with media insistence on the VRS's armaments and powerful military hardware. Croatian propaganda, meanwhile, presented the HVO as a mixture of soldiers of Christ and Rambo: they were not only well equipped, but adorned with religious symbols (crosses, rosaries, images of Our Lady). The ARBiH never developed an image based on technology, uniforms and general appearance. Their variegated appearance was somewhat reminiscent of the Partisans. But what always struck me, at least, was their faces. This was the only one of the armies in which, even in those tired faces, burned, drained and hardened by the war, one could see people who had transcended the usual dehumanization of an army, expressed in uniforms and the demonstration of technical power. This was not an army where the uniform disguised the person, but one where human beings were wearing uniforms.

The ARBiH is often underestimated by the Croatian media too, with the assertion that Bosnia-Herzegovina was first defended by the HVO, although the facts show that a rather large part of the country was defended where the HVO was not present at all or had only one brigade, usually a combat unit, in the overall defence formation. Moreover, the HVO lost a significant amount of territory at the beginning of the war, such as the part of Mostar east of the Neretva; this was theoretically under HVO control, but Serb forces got right through to the river, and it was only later that General Bobetko organized a counter-offensive, with the assistance of the Independent Mostar battalion of the ARBiH, and regained that territory. The northern part of Bosanska Posavina, too, was formally under HVO control and jurisdiction (or at least, it behaved as though it was), and that territory too was lost. Whatever the various explanations for the withdrawal from Posavina in early autumn 1992, the fact is that the HVO was there at the beginning and now the Serb military and civilian authorities are, except for Orašje. The HVO also lost Kupres very early on, in April 1992. So it does not all add up to any particularly good defence preparations.

The ARBiH, on the other hand, defended a rather large area and almost all the largest towns, though it was said from the start that the war found the Bosniaks completely unprepared, totally lost politically, and as a people unaware in every way. In principle, all towns with a significant Bosniak population – or rather, it would be better to say a Bosnian population, a population that considered Bosnia-Herzegovina its home-land – all these towns resisted being overrun by the VRS. To my knowl-edge, such resistance was broken only by the sheer technical superiority of the VRS, not as a result of any human factor. Of the ARBiH as a whole, it can be said that it was an army that defended itself, that won a defensive war.

What distinguishes the 5th corps from other troops is that it was also an army of liberation, since it liberated most territory in comparison with all the other corps. At the end of 1994 or the beginning of 1995, the chief of staff General Rasim Delić stated in an interview that the ARBiH had won such a tactical and operational position that it was on the verge of liberating most of Bosnia's towns. In 1995 a large number of towns were indeed liberated: Velika Kladuša, Bosanski Petrovac, Bosanska Krupa, Otoka, Kulen Vakuf, Ključ, Sanski Most, Donji Vakuf. Except for Donji Vakuf, which was liberated by the 7th corps, all these towns were liberated by the 5th corps.

What is special about this corps is that, being surrounded and cut off from the rest of the ARBiH, it was in a way fortunate in its misfortune, since it was also cut off from the centre of political events, hence was able to evaluate the situation with less pressure from political influences, to make its assessments on the basis of military evidence. The story went round in Bihać that when Alija Izetbegović woke up in the morning, the first thing he asked was what crazy things those 5th corps people had been doing last night. They were indeed constantly active. It must be said, however, that the 5th corps never went beyond the limits of the military framework; its command did not transform itself into a military junta and the army was always under the jurisdiction of the civilian authorities. But its isolation did help to diminish the influence of high politics on its activities on the ground. I think that is one reason why its soldiers went on behaving like real warriors during the last stage of war, when the conviction grew that the whole war had been a simulation, played out on previously agreed lines.

Completely surrounded as it was, the 5th corps did not have one enemy but three: working for the same ends, but doing so separately. One was the SVK, but that front was largely pacified by 1994, with the main attacks then coming from the second enemy, the VRS. The third enemy was Fikret Abdić, but to begin with there was no military pressure on the 5th corps from that side, probably because there were plans that he should take over political power in the area, as either a Serb or a Croat quisling, or in some third combination with yet other external factors. It was only in 1993, when he failed to take political control of the whole Bihać-Cazin region, with his 'Autonomous Region of Western Bosnia' programme, that operations intensified on all three fronts against the 5th corps, including the all-out attacks on Bihać during 1994.

The Croatian public is convinced that Croatia was providing the 5th corps with huge supplies, and the same opinion is held in other regions of Bosnia-Herzegovina under the control of the Sarajevo government. Whenever I mention the 5th corps, people say: 'It was easy for them, they were getting everything from Croatia!' But the military attaché in the B-H Embassy in Zagreb told me that there were 182 or 183 helicopter flights to Bihać; since a helicopter can carry a load of a tonne and a half, this means that about 300 tonnes of materiel were supplied for 20,000 soldiers, which is not a lot over a period of four years.

For me the most interesting and significant thing about the 5th corps is that they were continually active. It is said that when General Dudaković was asked once if it was true that his officers were forbidden to keep TV sets in the command posts, he replied: 'There is absolutely no reason for them to watch television, when they have observation posts from which they can watch the enemy.'

And now something about Dudaković himself, not only a competent soldier but an indisputably charismatic individual. He was supported by an excellent command, and very competent brigade commanders such as Senad Šarganović, Hamdija Abdić, the late Izet Nanić, Amir Avdić, Mirsad Selmanović, the late Jasmin Kulenović Havarija and others. They were a harmonious team clearly working well together. Since they were mostly JNA-educated officers, they had military experience; their priority was to select people who knew how to fight, regardless of ideological and political acceptability or recommendations.

General Divjak mentioned the unfortunate sortie of the 5th corps towards Kulen Vakuf and Martin Brod. When I asked about this, senior people from the corps assured me that they had been forced to make the sortie, since they had simply nothing left to eat. They had to try to break through and get as far as the Serb stores to obtain food at any cost; but they admitted that they went too far. Once they had broken through the enemy lines, they tried to exploit their success as much as they could, but then came up against a Serb counter-attack and were pushed back to Bihać. But even after withdrawing they held on to the strategic Grabež plateau above Bihać, which they had taken in the foray, and the loss of Grabež caused considerable panic in the Serb ranks.

Finally, it must be said that the actions of the 5th corps greatly raised the morale of all those who were for Bosnia-Herzegovina, setting them thinking: 'So the Serbs are finally getting a beating, someone is showing them what's what at last.' Irfan Ajanović was an SDA official who became vice-president of the SFRY Assembly after the multiparty elections in Bosnia-Herzegovina, and subsequently an official in B-H itself. He was arrested in Žepče during the war by the HVO and handed over to the Serbs. They threw him in gaol, where members of the SDS and soldiers from the VRS interrogated and ill-treated him. As he later wrote in his book, one day in 1994 one of the guards came into his cell and said that 'those fools of yours' were attacking Petrovac. Ajanović, who had been two years in gaol without any news from the outside world, asked which fools he meant, and the guard replied that it was Dudaković from Bihać. Radovan Karadžić's arrival in uniform to calm down the Serb population in Bosanski Petrovac confirms what a shock it had been to the Serbs. I think it was the first time in the war that Karadžić wore uniform. So even the Serb extremists, who looked down on everything Bosniak and arrogantly talked of *balije* and 'Turks' as a worthless lot, were forced to take the 5th corps seriously and to recognize that someone had arisen from somewhere whom they had to respect. Perhaps this psychologically symbolic significance of the 5th corps was sometimes even more important than their actual military successes.

There are many legends woven around Dudaković, and it is not always possible to determine whether they have any basis in reality. They told us in Bihać that in autumn 1994, when the VRS had got to within about 300 metres of the hospital and it was a matter of minutes before the town would fall, General Dudaković himself came to the front line and turned back the defenders, who had already begun to turn tail, threatening that he would personally liquidate them if they did not return to their positions. They did return, and Bihać did not fall. I have asked myself countless times what would have happened if there had been someone like him in Srebrenica, with that sort of courage, in the fateful moments of 1995.

As for the operations of liberation in the second half of 1995 and why the ARBiH stopped, members of the 5th corps have told me that their problem was that they had no second echelon. They pushed their existing brigades to the limit and got to Sanski Most, but the Serb forces there had already launched a counter-offensive. Then General Mehmed Alagić turned up and, according to his own account, reorganized the defence and halted the Serb counter-offensive. But now we are again faced with the problem of the attitude of the ARBiH Command towards the 5th corps. Alagić says that he happened to be in Bihać on his return from Germany, which at once prompts the question why, when the 5th corps was conducting an offensive which altered the balance of power in B-H, the commander of the neighbouring 7th corps, which should have offered the 5th corps maximum support, was allowed to be somewhere other than in his own command post, for whatever reason, let alone to visit Germany in the middle of the war. No one has ever answered this question.

The 5th corps had evidently reached the absolute limit of its strength; its troops had traversed about 120 kilometres on foot, and during the final 10–15 days had been under severe strain. Reinforcements had apparently been sent from Sarajevo, but the HVO did not allow them to cross the territory under its control, so they arrived rather late.

Obviously they had to stop; and then came the usual question of what to do with these charismatic heroes when the war was over. When Dudaković came to Sarajevo for the first time after the fighting stopped, the people came out on the streets to welcome him with ovations. He was certainly the safest man in town, but then an order is supposed to have come from the commander-in-chief of the Federation Army that the general should come at once to HQ, since it wasn't safe for him to be on the streets – something might happen to him! Clearly there were feelings of animosity and jealousy at play here. The fact is that people love and need heroes, especially in wartime. If there had been no real Dudaković to personify the 'Heavenly Force' – as the 5th corps was called – some other Dudaković would have to have been invented. But what distinguishes him from the motley gaggle of Jukas, Cacos, Ćelos and other semi-mythical figures on the Sarajevo streets is, I believe, the fact that he did not consciously work on his own myth: the mythologization came as a result of his effectiveness. Dudaković was primarily a professional soldier, in whom knowledge, talent and, perhaps most important, the good fortune to command an excellent army all felicitously combined. I think that the secret of his success was that, unlike many others, he carried out the tasks which he had taken upon himself honestly and well and without boasting.

Over and above everything else, the essential contribution to the war of the 5th corps and of Dudaković himself was their winning mentality, their psychological and symbolic role. The 5th corps utterly destroyed the myth that the Chetniks were invincible: in panic flight they did not look at all frightening or dangerous, let alone invincible.

Militarily speaking, their most important contribution was that for the first time they were applying what could be called active defence at the operational level. They continually carried out tactical strikes, producing a kind of constant dynamic, so that as a detached observer I can say that they created a picture (perhaps illusory) that we were not involved in political games of which the war was just an aspect, but that this was a genuine war, led by people who knew how to fight one. It is an open secret that Dudaković was in constant telephone contact with General Špegelj in Zagreb and often sought his advice, so the model of active defence may be said to be the result of their collaboration.

Finally, I should like to take this opportunity to ask General Divjak something about the opening phase of the war in Bosnia-Herzegovina. I am interested to know how mobilization was carried out after the TO structure had been activated: was it according to the existing registers or in some other way? How were brigades formed? Was their structure taken over from the TO and Partisan brigades, or did you create your own new structure? And another question, about weapons, which has not yet been mentioned. Since in B-H as in Croatia there were weapons depots, and since you were following the situation in Croatia and seeing that the depots there were being seized, I am interested to know why you did not try to take over the TO and JNA depots. Or did you try, and fail? Or did the JNA get everything out in time? What really happened?

Rusmir Mahmutćehajić

The question of why the depots were not occupied and why there was no action just before the war is also an important comment on another question posed yesterday by General Divjak when he mentioned the Lisbon negotiations. I was one of the participants in those negotiations, and it has often been claimed in the press that I was the author of that agreement from the Bosniak side. To understand the circumstances in B-H during 1991, you must know that it was clear to a small group of people that the republic was in deadly danger. We knew about Milošević's plan and his instructions to Karadžić in spring of that year; we knew about the Milošević–Tuđman agreement, and about the preparations and agreements between members of the secret service on both sides. It was clear to us that the denouement of the so-called Yugoslav crisis would be international recognition of Slovenia and Croatia, and that we would be faced with a battle for Bosnia-Herzegovina, which was then generally very fragile and in the eyes of outsiders unsustainable. In any case, it had no chance of defending itself against such external pressure.

So there was a real struggle, from April 1991 onwards, to preserve and safeguard the institutions of Bosnia-Herzegovina, which were in constant danger of simply disintegrating, which would have been in the interest of those planning the war. The governmental bodies were completely blocked, at a time when Belgrade and Zagreb and their offshoots in Sarajevo were assessing how most easily to achieve their aim of destroying these fragile elements of statehood before they could begin to gain strength. Faced with this, we were considering what would be the most effective way to prevent what Karadžić announced at the very beginning of the war: 'Our aim is to break up Bosnia-Herzegovina.'

The strategy formulated that year was that Yugoslavia would disintegrate and Bosnia-Herzegovina be preserved, which is like driving a lorry over a rough, unsurfaced road covered with broken glass, when by simply braking or mildly accelerating one can destroy everything. It really seemed like that. But it was nevertheless clear that this was the route to be followed, so that the government would not collapse, and the Assembly would not collapse, and international recognition would follow, and the response to Milošević and Tuđman who were working to destroy Bosnia-Herzegovina would be as subtle as possible, while neither would be given the opportunity to complete their preparations and actually achieve their ends. Preparations for B-H's defence were carried out in such a sophisticated manner that it is not possible to present them in a single presentation. Without infringing the legal order we set in motion a broad range of preparations which could not be destroyed by any party; it was like a picture which, however you dismantle it, remains complete, a bit less recognizable, but the same picture. And that was how we imagined our defence.

No one can truthfully say today that the Patriotic League and the other organizations we created were para-state organizations or that they existed outside the state institutions. There are some who have written to that effect, but there is no evidence for such assertions. Individual elements of the system were closely linked to the patriotic element in the political leadership and served as a kind of forum in which their connection to the state bodies was analysed and a stable core developed for the preservation of Bosnia-Herzegovina. This was why the TO very quickly went into action. We were trying in these complex circumstances to fulfil the conditions for the international recognition of Bosnia-Herzegovina, and to do nothing that might damage its institutions. For what could the world recognize, if the state structure had already collapsed?

Suppose the Serb insurrection had begun just five days earlier than it did, that insurrection which took the shape of blockading the streets of Sarajevo. We would not then have met the conditions for international recognition, which would doubtless have suited many external players. The Badinter Commission said that Bosnia-Herzegovina would fulfil the conditions for recognition if its citizens voted for it.[6] In that very subtle game we came out as the winners. If the insurrection had begun just five days earlier and as a result the referendum of 29 February and 1 March 1992 had not been held, Bosnia-Herzegovina would not have satisfied the conditions for recognition, while the actual situation in the country would have remained unchanged, with the same JNA ready to attack, the same armed and organized Serb population, the same aims of official policy in Croatia and Serbia, and so on. To have something to defend, it had to have substance, however unwelcome it might be to the international players.

Someone said yesterday that many of the latter were saying: 'Now we have to support Bosnia-Herzegovina overtly, since we have no way out; but covertly we shall work against it.' What made that 'overtly' inescapable was that from 6 April 1992 they were dealing with an internationally recognized state; otherwise it would not have been defensible. Only after that could action to conduct a war of defence be speeded up in Bosnia-Herzegovina. I think the strategy was highly successful. There were many tactical failures, errors and weaknesses, but in its essence it was not flawed, and Bosnia-Herzegovina was defended.

The defence was based on some very clear and immediately formulated elements, one of which was – as was clear to us although we did not want to say so publicly – that the key problem for B-H's defence was Croatia, and Tuđman's attitude towards our state. All the eastern territories were lost or handed over to Karadžić and Milošević because Bosnia-Herzegovina became completely blocked from the south in spring 1993. At the beginning of June 1993 I took part in discussions in Medjugorje,

---

[6] At its meeting in Paris on 10–11 January 1992, the Badinter commission considered the requests for recognition submitted by Slovenia, Macedonia, Croatia and Bosnia-Herzegovina. It was established that the first three had satisfied the conditions that had been set, while in the fourth case it was held 'that the expression of the will of the people of Bosnia-Herzegovina for the creation of a sovereign and independent state of Bosnia-Herzegovina cannot be considered to have been fully confirmed. That assessment could be altered if the republic which has submitted a request for recognition provides guarantees in this respect, perhaps by means of a referendum, in which all citizens of the Republic of Bosnia-Herzegovina should participate, on fully equal terms, and under international supervision.' See 'Sažetak mišljenja Arbitražne komisije o Jugoslaviji (10–11. siječnja 1992)' [Abstract of the opinion of the Arbitration Commission for Yugoslavia (10–11 January 1992)], in: Anđelko Milardović (ed.), *Dokumenti o državnosti Republike Hrvatske* (Documents on the statehood of the Republic of Croatia), Zagreb 1992, pp. 152–3; also Marc Weller (ed.), *The Crisis in Kosovo 1989–1999*, Documents and Analysis Publishing Ltd, Cambridge 1999, pp. 81–2. Slovenia had held a referendum in December 1990, Croatia in May 1991, and Macedonia in September 1991, all three producing affirmative results, while the Memorandum on Sovereignty, which was adopted by the Assembly of Bosnia-Herzegovina on 15 October 1992, was not considered adequate, since it was disputed by the SDS. On the formation of the Commission, see note 11, p. 105 above; on the Memorandum of the Assembly of Bosnia-Herzegovina, see note 2, p. 153 above.

and a senior Croat official, whom I knew well from before, came up to me and said quietly: 'I am really sorry, colleague, I feel great sympathy for you, but the way things are going you simply won't exist as a state in two weeks' time.' Part of the HVO was operating on the basis of the same assessment, those who were blocking the roads and had embarked on a vicious war against the ARBiH to the south. So Bosnia's defence was completely cut off: the country had no access to any of the things that were essential for its defence.

Yet the assessment was entirely wrong. In the following few months the ARBiH reached the peak of its development and things basically did not change thereafter.

Four factors were formulated in our defence strategy, of which two were vital: a war-time energy policy, with which those besieging Sarajevo had not reckoned; and defence manufacturing, which was also completely outside the enemy's calculations and one of the essential reasons for their being unable to achieve their objectives. The war-time director of the *Soko* Military Aviation Institute, a Croat, put together a large group of associates and organized the repair of helicopters and training of pilots in the most difficult circumstances. Such work was possible only because of the engineering cooperatives and establishments which, contrary to all expectations, were set up during the course of our struggle for survival. The deputy head of the directorate for the manufacture of arms and military equipment, which was organized as the technical and technological brains of the defence, was also a Croat. Without many such people, both Serbs and Croats, it would not have been possible to block the plan to destroy Bosnia-Herzegovina.

The same process was going on throughout B-H, but I want to cite just one example from Sarajevo, since we believed that the fall of Sarajevo would be disastrous, however much we might defend other parts of the country. In one year, when the city was completely under siege, 40,000 82mm mortar shells were produced. If you asked any engineer today to calculate this, he would say that it was impossible, that it was a miracle. In the city itself we did not have a single factory equipped for such manufacture, not a single suitable production line, but in volume it was as if forty large trucks had entered the city. To cap it all, part of that production was achieved when the tunnel underneath the runway at Butmir did not yet exist, when 20 young people were killed running across the runway at night carrying bags of sand. Although they were probably half-starved, they did not, or only rarely, carry food, but sand needed for casting the shells in Sarajevo.

I have mentioned just one kind of shell, but General Divjak would be able to tell you much more and better than I, since he was around the battle fronts far more than I was. We had soldiers who sometimes had rifles and absolutely nothing else, who stood in the trenches anticipating an attack at any moment, with nothing to defend themselves. When the industrial production of hand grenades began in Sarajevo, with the inscription *Armija BiH*, many people to whom they were issued kissed them. And behind all that production was a Croat officer, the director of *Soko*, who deserves great credit for his role in the defence of Bosnia-Herzegovina.

When I met some young men with these hand grenades, somewhere near Kladanj, I noticed that they held them as though they were precious gems, for they simply did not have anything else. Although I knew about the whole process, I asked the young men, 'What's that, what kind of grenades are those?', and one replied, 'What, you don't know? They're grenades!' – 'But what grenades? I've never seen any like them. Do sell me one.' – 'I wouldn't give you one of these grenades for all the world.' They were people whose only options were to surrender or to defend themselves, and they were unarmed, trapped in that position. That was how Cerska fell, and Konjević Polje, and eastern Bosnia, all the places that were completely cut off.

Here is another instance that may illustrate the issue. I know personally that there were times when only two days separated Sarajevo from collapsing on its own account, except that Karadžić and Mladić did not know it. When one of Tuđman's prominent people in Bosnia-Herzegovina, higher at that time in the hierarchy than I was, came and asked me for a confidential discussion, the first thing he asked was how much petroleum Sarajevo had. I replied: 'There's enough. Thank God, we don't have a problem there.' – 'But how much have you? – 'I can't tell you that.' – 'If I can't have that information, we can't work together!' And he threatened to demand that I be thrown out of the government, otherwise he would resign himself. I said: 'Go ahead, and be quick about it! As far as I'm concerned, I'll never give you that information; you can put anyone you like in my place, and let him give it to you.' The reserves of petroleum for the defence were just then at their lowest level, while at the same time petroleum was getting through via Stolac, by a route which that same man controlled along with Mate Boban, to the people besieging Sarajevo. There is no end to the number of such details on which the defence of Bosnia-Herzegovina was built; and of course great care was taken, and still is, that they should not become known to those who could have used them to undermine the defence.

Jovan Divjak

I appreciate what Mr Kulenović has said about the 5th corps, but thanks are also due to TV BiH journalist Nada al-Issa, who very successfully conveyed the reality of the situation, both when it was and when it was not critical. When it was critical, we in the general staff would be scared because we did not see how Bihać could be helped. On the other hand, such situations did provide motivation for the 5th corps and in a way strike fear into its attackers.

One detail stays with me from 1994. I happened to be with the commander when news came that Mladić had been wounded, and his briefcase with plans in it had been seized. The commander asked the commander up in Bihać if this was true, and the answer was: 'Not in the least, but give it out, make some kind of positive propaganda of it!'

In the first days of the war we tried to attack the depots where arms and military equipment were stored, and in many places succeeded. The first clash was in March in Bijeljina, although there had already been fighting around Brčko and Bosanski Brod, yet we have just heard from Professor Mahmutčehajić that the whole of April went by in gaining time and trying not to provoke anything. We issued our first directive, in various forms, with hypotheses: 'If such and such happens, do such and such ... if there is movement from the barracks ... if there is an attack ...' And the local commander would then decide to attack, and as I described this morning problems would arise, since Izetbegović would then deny that he had put his signature to it or agreed to any such action. Here are two negative examples from Sarajevo.

I said this morning, and I think Professor Mahmutčehajić would agree, that from the very beginning there were two parallel lines of command. It is not important now whether this was due to mistrust, but the fact is that the relationship between the TO command, or later the newly formed general staff, and the command and political section of the Patriotic League was not fully regularized during the first two months, although the League's political element entered the defence structure without any problems. Some actions in Sarajevo were carried out in such a way that either the TO staff on the one hand or the Patriotic League on the other would know nothing about them.

In the early days there was an attempt, which met with considerable success, to attack the depot in the Pretis factory. This was the largest military installation for the manufacture of munitions for heavy artillery and mortars in former Yugoslavia, and the first attack was really successful: during the night of 17 to 18 April 800 *zolja* and *osa* shoulder launchers were seized. But the position had not been precisely enough gauged. Though a second surprise attack cannot succeed immediately after a first one, a second group was sent in an hour after the successful attack and was caught in an ambush. Safet Hadžić was killed, one of the organizers of B-H's defence and a member of the Patriotic League; his death at this early stage had a really shocking impact on the organization for the defence of Sarajevo.

There was also an attempt to attack the depot in Faletići, where there were arms and munitions sufficient for two brigades, but it revealed the weak organization and lack of synchronization between the city, municipal and republic TO staffs. I recall one of those who took part in the attack saying sadly, when he returned: 'But one can't destroy a bridge with 3 kilos of explosive!' They needed to destroy an access route across a water barrier, for which they really had been supplied with only 3 kilograms of explosive. All the same, they got 40 lorry-loads of equipment out of Faletići that night, while the majority of depots in other places were already under JNA control and were then handed over by the JNA to the SDS. The largest depot of munitions, arms and military hardware was in Hadžići, but the JNA blocked that one right at the beginning. There were successes in Zenica and Tuzla, and those garrisons alone supplied all the tanks that the ARBiH had at its disposal. Our people even stopped a JNA convoy loaded with tanks, which was making for Serbia from Zenica. Seen in proportion it was just an incident, but it brought us benefits which could not be cancelled by any intervention by the federal secretariat for national defence in Belgrade.

Of course, one has to ask whether the arms seized were used effectively, regardless of their quantity. Those *zolje* and *ose* from Pretis played a very important, indeed a decisive role in the defence of Sarajevo and prevented it from being bisected by the JNA's persistent mass tank assaults. But because of the lack of other arms, especially artillery, our soldiers were using those light anti-tank missiles to target individual hot spots and barricaded buildings, in close combat in residential areas, and even to target troops, so that a significant proportion of them were used ineffectively and for purposes for which they were not intended, and not only in Sarajevo. We did everything we could to attain the maximum effectiveness with what was available to us: at one time two or three *zoljas* were driven in a VW Golf from one front line to another, wherever the situation had become critical, with explicit orders to target the enemy tanks with these missiles only after attempts to set them on fire with Molotov cocktails had failed.

You in Croatia were able to organize your resistance to the JNA, since you had a deep rearguard; you were in direct conflict along a front with a depth of 50 or even 100 kilometres, while the entire territory on which the ARBiH was formed was surrounded, so that it had absolutely no possibility of in-depth manoeuvres. We were already cut off in 1992, since the HVO did not want to take part in lifting the siege of Sarajevo. Our people in the city would often say: 'They are afraid that when we get out of this we'll move against them.' However that may be, the HVO and those who directed it did not care that people in Sarajevo were starving.

Finally I should like to say that the whole of Sarajevo, everyone who was in the city, took part in its defence. There was no gas or electricity, but the citizens received a kilo or half a kilo of bread throughout; *Oslobođenje* appeared on the streets throughout, even if it was only two or three pages; the doctors and hospital staff were in the hospitals with the sick and wounded throughout, without any payment. We in the army were getting something at one time: our monthly pay in B-H dinars was the equivalent of two German marks; and during 1993 and 1994 you could see people making gardens on their balconies and windowsills or in front of their buildings, where they grew vegetables. The case of Dobrinje best shows just how difficult the situation was. Those who were suffering at that time, chiefly from snipers, had nowhere to bury their dead except right outside their own windows, and at night; people would come out of their cellars and bury their dead next to their own apartments.

But I must respond to Mr Kulenović's question about the formation and organization of units. There was no reliance on the Partisan experience, although there was a need for it. There simply were not the conditions for it, since Partisan operations imply a combination of frontal and rearguard actions. It can be asked now whether the level of awareness or of military expertise was adequate; but we did not in fact undertake mass diversionary actions on enemy territory, meaning territory the enemy was occupying.

We created our formations on the basis of our own experience, gained in the war itself. They were chiefly brigades linked to some experience of urban warfare. At one time, at the beginning of 1993, we even had people offering us their experience from the wars in the Near and Middle East, and their first question was, why didn't we dig a tunnel through to free territory. They asked me directly: 'Do you know what we did around Basra? Do you know how we extricated ourselves from that?' So our TO was not a copy of the Yugoslav TO, of which we were supposedly the successor. The brigades were different, and varied one from another, depending on where they were formed: some were mountain brigades, and some we called motorized, although they did not have any such equipment, but in structure and numerical strength corresponded to that category. Up to the end of 1993 or early 1994, until a solid organization and formations had been established, everything was changing, we even came down to the level of municipal headquarters.

You also asked about the call-up. It was announced only in June; prior to that people were turning up voluntarily; about 90 per cent of our people were volunteers. As I have said, by 14 April we already had a list of 75,000 volunteers from the whole of Bosnia-Herzegovina and when two, or rather three months later a state of war was proclaimed and mobilization was announced, the only mobilization that took place was what was necessary to complete the units.

Apart from what Professor Cigar spoke about, one of our basic problems was that we did not have enough specialists; we had enough infantry, but we were short of people trained for artillery, anti-aircraft defence, engineers, and we had no one able to handle the equipment we had seized. In November 1992, when we broke out onto Trebević and cut communications between Lukavica and Pale, the soldiers who had seized quantities of arms did not know how to use them, so we lost that position in the Serb counter-offensive.

Rusmir Mahmutćehajić

At that time, and in those circumstances, the question of mobilization was simply not raised. Large numbers of people were appearing every day offering to join the defence in some way, but we had nothing to give them. Mobilization was not possible throughout the whole war, because there was a key obstacle to the south: the Croat leadership, who did not allow us to import light arms. They created the illusion that arms were getting in, so that some trucks with a few artillery shells would be allowed through, which could not have any fundamental impact even if they got to their final destination. Bearing all this in mind, ordinary military measures during the Bosnian war look like an attempt to change something really rough and raw into something of quality.

Stjepan Mesić

We have just heard a fully justified criticism of my president, but I must also mention one useful thing that he did, albeit inadvertently. Some days before the referendum there was an agreement in force between the HDZ leadership in Zagreb and the HDZBiH that the B-H Croats would not vote. It was a very firm position, and I was appalled when I came to know about it a few days later. Since I knew that this decision derived from the agreement with Milošević to partition Bosnia-Herzegovina, I knew that Tuđman could be persuaded to change it only if I used a ruse and made out that I did not know that he himself was behind it. I asked to see him and said, as if astonished: 'Do you know that those Herzegovinians are insisting that the Croats should not take part in the referendum?' He said, 'Yes, I know. The Serbs aren't going to, so why should the Croats?' and I replied: 'Do you realize that Bosnia will remain in Yugoslavia if the referendum doesn't succeed?' Only then did it occur to him that there could be no partition of Bosnia-Herzegovina if it remained part of Yugoslavia, so he immediately called the Herzegovina people to Zagreb and changed his stance. And that's how it was that the Croats took part in the referendum and voted for an independent Bosnia-Herzegovina.

Here is another event which you may not know about. In April 1993 I was visiting Iran and agreed with President Rafsanjani that he would give us – Croatia and Bosnia-Herzegovina – all his arms from the Soviet bloc, with the proviso, naturally, that we would have to take care of their transportation ourselves. They needed modern Western armaments, and the huge quantities of Soviet arms they had were just an embarrassment to them. He said, 'Why are you spending money on arms when we have unlimited quantities of them?' – those were his very words. Not long after, while I was still in Teheran, I got a call to another discussion with Rafsanjani. I went, and he said, 'Look at this! Information has just come through that there has been a massacre in Ahmići. How can we give you arms when you are fighting among yourselves?' This shows that if there had been cooperation between Croats and Bosniaks, it would have been much easier to obtain arms and the war could have been ended much earlier and more successfully.

Part III

The international response –
lessons for the future

10

The International Community's Response to the Crisis in Former Yugoslavia

Paul Williams

The purpose of this contribution is to discuss the international community's objectives and the effectiveness of the international community in dealing with the conflicts in Bosnia and Croatia. I shall also discuss the motivation of the key policy players, the key decision points and what impact the international community actually had on the crisis in former Yugoslavia and whether it was positive or negative. In order to accomplish these tasks I shall first discuss some of the initial objectives of the international community, examine the evolution of these objectives as the conflict intensified, and discuss the various tools which were employed by the international community to try to bring an end to the crisis. I shall only touch upon the military aspects, as Warren Switzer will be dealing with them in greater detail in his contribution. And, finally, I shall take a brief look at the Dayton Accords and how the failures of the international community's policies in former Yugoslavia have led to the crisis that we are currently experiencing in Kosovo.

Two points should be made before I begin. One is that there is no such thing the international community: it is essentially the gang of seven, consisting of the United States, Russia, France, Great Britain, Germany, Italy and the European Union as such. The second is that the gang of seven were overwhelmingly preoccupied with their own interests. So when I go through my contribution today you may scratch your heads a couple of times and think, why are they talking about EU integration or the election of President Clinton or various other issues; but I'm hoping to give you a perspective on a multitude of distractions which unfortunately faced the gang of seven when they were trying to deal with this very serious crisis.

THE DRAMATURGY OF PARTIAL INTERESTS

The primary interest of the United States was in maintaining the status quo and creating a no-risk atmosphere, whatever the status quo might be:

the territorial integrity of the former Soviet Union, the territorial integrity of Yugoslavia, etc. Germany was motivated primarily by economic interests, which were affected by the influx of refugees, whether from Bosnia or, as today, from Kosovo. The United Kingdom was primarily motivated by its interest in retaining its status as a world power. Professor Hastings referred to the historic ties between Serbia and the United Kingdom and the infiltration of Serbian representatives into the British political system. The French were primarily interested in the balance of power within the European continent, which might or might not include Central and Eastern Europe, depending on the French definition. Russia was interested in maintaining its world power status and the Chinese were essentially interested in gathering political chips which they could then trade with the United States on subsequent issues. As the Chinese saw it, they were doing the United States a favour by being forward-leaning in the crisis in former Yugoslavia, a favour which they could call in when discussing most-favoured-nation status in trade matters or human rights in Tibet. The recognition of these interests is essential to the understanding of the broad balance-of-power framework in which the so-called international community operated.

Specifically with respect to the crisis in former Yugoslavia, the overriding interest of the international community was to contain the conflict. We see the same thing today in Kosovo: build a wall round the conflict and let it burn out. Of course, this approach neglects the fact that the process of burning out entails ethnic cleansing and genocide. The other interest was the promotion of state-territorial unity. This was less important to the United States than to states such as the United Kingdom, Spain, France, Italy, Belgium or Canada, all of which have their own secessionist movements.

The European Union was also preoccupied with this enigma called a Common Foreign and Security Policy. At the time when Yugoslavia was burning there was this dream, subsequently a nightmare, of the European Union's need to have a Common Foreign and Security Policy. Importantly, the United States was quite keen on deferring to the European Union and promoting their idea of a Common Foreign and Security Policy, because the United States was interested in sharing some of the burden of what it perceived as unilateral international leadership. The United States was particularly interested in allowing the European Union to demonstrate its effectiveness in the crisis in former Yugoslavia. In late 1991, for instance, the French ambassador to Washington very proudly announced that the United States would deal with the former Soviet Union and Europe would deal with the crisis in former Yugoslavia. At the time I thought that the United States had the more difficult task, but as it turned out that was not the case.

The United States was also interested in enticing the EU into a greater role, into taking on the obligations of international leadership and international responsibility. The United States was also quite willing to allow the Europeans to use the United Nations as a tool for the Common Security and Foreign Policy: to let the EU decide on policy and then work through the UN Security Council and use UN peace-keeping forces to carry out what they had identified as their objectives within the Common Security and Foreign Policy. The United States was thus quite complicit, some would say negligent, in permitting Europe to go about making policy with respect to former Yugoslavia.

Unfortunately, the EU embarked upon the path of rhetoric rather than action. Its first act was to draft guiding principles for recognition of the successor states, and to create a legal arbitration commission to settle questions of succession and recognition.[1] It seems to have believed that if it adopted a set of guidelines calling upon the successor states to adhere to the rule of law, democracy, market reform and the protection of human rights, this would somehow lead to peaceful resolution of the Yugoslav crisis.

THE CONCENTRATION CAMPS SHOCK

As the conflict intensified it caught the gang of seven by surprise. The first reaction of the US government upon becoming aware of concentration camps in former Yugoslavia was that this simply could not be true. There were two reasons: one was that this was Europe, and two, the United States had no policy for dealing with genocide in the 1990s. So the government simply closed its eyes to it and made a policy decision that there was no genocide. The second reaction on the part of the EU, primarily influenced by the British government, was that the solution to this crisis was to partition Bosnia and insert UN peacekeeping forces (using the United Nations as a tool of European policy) into the region to prevent further genocide, further ethnic cleansing.

It is no secret that the Europeans believed this was going to be a ten-days war, and that as long as there were blue helmets on the ground there would be no difficulty in preventing genocide and ethnic cleansing. The difficulty occurred after UNPROFOR was sent in, because they became essentially hostages of the Serbian regime in its aggressive nature and intentions. The United States still had no policy, the Europeans became committed to the UN-orientated policy and to peacekeeping as opposed to peacemaking.[2] So the United States defaulted and supported the arms embargo, since they needed to be seen to be doing something and the one thing they could do was support the embargo, though it was a violation of international law.

---

[1] On the establishment of the commission, see note 11, p. 105 above; on its position on recognition of the new states, see note 6, p. 262 above.

[2] For these concepts see note 9, p. 167 above.

The second thing they did was to work up the Federation Agreement between Croatian and Bosnian parties to the conflict, which eventually became the corner stone of US policy. The idea, as has been discussed here for the last couple of days, was a very positive one: to build this coalition, the Federation. The difficulty is that the agreement itself was actually quite unworkable. The further difficulty is that it formed the basis for the Dayton Accords, which we all agree are also unworkable. The interim agreement for Kosovo which was leaked last week is based on the same principles as the Federation Agreement, which consists essentially in double and triple political vetoes and creates an institutionalized political gridlock.

The US thus worked throughout with the arms embargo and with the Federation Agreement. In working with the arms embargo, I agree with Adrian Hastings that the United States was complicit, a willing supporter of the United Kingdom's policy of keeping the arms embargo and letting the conflict burn out within the borders of Croatia and Bosnia-Herzegovina. Only when confronted with genocide, the continuing genocide, did the United States seriously consider military intervention. And even then, in fact, they did so only at press briefings, when some reporter would raise the idea of mounting a commando raid on one of the camps, and they would patiently explain how there were all sorts of difficulties with any such operation to rescue the people in the camps, although they could not go into more detail. So the policy adopted by the United States was to evade the moral imperative to become actively involved, while presenting that posture as positive and conscientious. Initially the US government took up a policy of misrepresenting to the American people and the rest of the international community the extent of the genocide in former Yugoslavia.

For example, Warren Christopher, after being in office for three months, was called to Capitol Hill to explain what US policy was in Bosnia. After he had listed a series of initiatives which essentially amounted to no formal policy, he was asked by Congressman McCloskey whether or not genocide was occurring in former Yugoslavia. His answer was that ethnic cleansing and the movement of peoples was occurring. When asked again whether that constituted genocide he said: 'Well, some people died in the process of ethnic cleansing.' When asked if that constituted genocide he said: 'Well, all sides are responsible for the atrocities.' When asked if 90 per cent of atrocities were committed by one side, according to the State Department and CIA, and if this constituted genocide, he said: 'Well, ethnic cleansing might in some instances constitute acts of genocide.'

Warren Christopher's statements were the result of a very affirmative policy of dissuading the US Congress from its attempts to become politically and militarily involved in the Bosnian crisis. This worked for about six months. Finally the CNN factor – or the news media in general – filled the moral gap created or left open by the US government. And it became patently obvious to everyone in the United States that genocide and ethnic cleansing were occurring in former Yugoslavia.

In regard to the discovery of the Serb concentration camps it is impossible not to mention Roy Gutman. Since even before the start of the war he had visited Bosnia-Herzegovina and the rest of Yugoslavia, learnt the language and acquired contacts, on 9 July 1992 one of his Bosnian acquaintances, a Bosniak leader from Banja Luka, called him up and informed him of mass deportations of civilians. Gutman then went to Banja Luka and managed to gain permission to visit, on 19 July, the concentration camp of Manjača, a former JNA installation, 25 kilometres south of the city. He published the first of his series of reports, quoting the testimony of several survivors, on 2 August 1992 in *Newsday*, a tabloid with a circulation of more than 800,000 copies in the area of New York and Long Island. The front page had the 2-inch headline: 'The Death Camps of Bosnia'.

The report was immediately transmitted by news agencies and TV and radio programmes in the United States and throughout the world, while secretly made photographs appeared on the front pages of *Newsweek* and the German *Stern*. A few days later a British ITV team managed to film in Omarska and Trnopolje, getting pictures of starved prisoners behind barbed wire. In the month and a half following Gutman's first report some 360 reporters managed to visit the parts of Bosnia under Serb control; they reported that 30,000 Bosniaks and Croats were being kept in camps in the Banja Luka area.[3]

Since these pictures inevitably recalled the Nazi 'final solution', public opinion and humanitarian organizations began to exercise pressure. The United States then reached into its diplomatic bag of tools and imposed diplomatic sanctions: it had 34 diplomats in Belgrade, so it dropped the number from 34 to 32. It continued to enforce the arms embargo, thinking for some reason that it might promote peace in the region. It imposed economic sanctions, creating the Serbian Sanctions Task Force which met every week and pressed states that were trading with Serbia to stop selling oil and other commodities. Lastly, the United States tried to promote negotiations, which were conducted to no real effect by David Owen, Thorvald Stoltenberg and Cyrus Vance.

ESTABLISHMENT OF THE HAGUE TRIBUNAL

In a last breath of desperation, the United States was inspired to create the War Crimes Tribunal, one bright spot in its policy. It was initially very reluctant to create it, because it had not prosecuted Saddam Hussein for

[3] See Roy Gutman, *A Witness to Genocide*, New York 1993, pp. vii–xvi.

war crimes in Iraq and during the invasion of Kuwait. The Gulf War had ended two or three years earlier, but the United States was still focused on that policy as opposed to policy in former Yugoslavia. But it did eventually create the Tribunal.

The International War Crimes Tribunal for former Yugoslavia (ICTY) was finally established, on 25 May 1992, by UN Security Council Resolution 827 on the basis of Chapter 7 of the UN Charter, as an enforceable measure aimed at protecting international peace and security. It was empowered to deal with serious infringements of the Geneva Convention, i.e. with war crimes, ethnic cleansing or genocide, and crimes against humanity. The judges are elected by the General Assembly of the United Nations and the first team was sworn in in November 1993. In February 1994 the office of prosecutor was established and in October of the same year a UN prison complex was made available as part of the Dutch prison complex in The Hague neighbourhood of Sheveningen. In 1998 the court's budget amounted to $64.8 million and this was expected to rise to $94.1 million in 1999.

The rules of procedure were changed several times in order to get a balance between continental European and Anglo-Saxon law. The duties of states to cooperate with the Court were drafted in accordance with Rules of Procedure and Proof, according to which the rules established by Article 29 of the Court Statute override all legal hindrance to extradition of suspects or witnesses derived from national courts or extradition agreements. If a state fails 'in reasonable time' to obey the order of extradition of the indicted persons, the Court is entitled to inform the Security Council via its representative. Up to now 79 persons have been charged and there are a number of secret, i.e. sealed, indictments which can be activated at any time.

The difficulty with the War Crimes Tribunal, however, is that it has essentially ceased to function above low-level and mid-level culprits. Either lack of clear political guidelines or institutional inertia has produced a decision not to indict Slobodan Milošević, Arkan, Šešelj and other leaders in Serbia, who are clearly culpable and who in 1992 were identified by Secretary of State Eagleburger as indictable war criminals (he didn't get around to Tuđman, but that might have been an option as well).[4]

---

[4] Chief prosecutor Louise Arbour, however, announced on 27 May 1999 an indictment charge against FRY president Slobodan Milošević, Serbian president Milan Milutinović, FRY deputy premier Nikola Šainović, FRY army chief of staff Dragoljub Ojdanić, and Serbian interior minister Vlajko Stojiljković. They are charged with crimes against humanity (murders, deportations, persecution) and infringement of wartime conventions in Kosovo. The charge is accompanied by an international arrest order. According to the judge, there were good grounds for holding the indicted responsible for the deportation of 740,000 and the murder of 340 identified Kosovo Albanians. The prosecution also stated that it

HAGGLING AT DAYTON

After a great deal of blood had been shed, the United States finally accepted the necessity of NATO involvement in the crisis in former Yugoslavia. But I again insist that this was brought about not by any pro-active initiative of the government agencies, but by CNN, BBC and public opinion pressure in general. Immediately after the NATO air strikes in Bosnia-Herzegovina, the United States and its European partners convened the Dayton peace talks, and essentially set off on the path of appeasement of the Serbian aggressors. During the Dayton negotiations the interests that I stressed earlier, the primary interests of the various powers, reasserted themselves.

Germany, for example, was interested in a peace deal that would allow it to return Bosnian refugees, and tried to insert into the agreement a proposal that Bosnian refugees should be obliged to return home in order to vote. The idea was that once the Bosnian refugees went home to vote they could no longer qualify for political asylum in Germany, because they clearly *could* return home without fear of persecution – even if this was true not for the areas of B-H where they had lived before the war and actually had their homes, but only areas where their own ethnic group was now in the majority.

The US interest was in re-establishing US leadership. They finally realized after four or five years of conflict that there was not going to be European leadership in Europe. They wanted a peace deal concluded in Dayton under their own leadership. Their primary interest was not to craft a peace package which would actually work for the reintegration of Bosnia, for the protection of human rights, for free and fair elections and for freedom of movement. If those things happened, that was OK, but what the US government really wanted was a peace deal. They wanted three signatures on a piece of paper which would bring an end to the war and permit NATO forces to take up positions in Bosnia. Essentially, the Americans accepted the same theory that the British were promoting, though the British were for a clear partition of Bosnia, using UN forces to keep the conflict damped down. The US government thought it would just smother Bosnia with 50,000 NATO troops, which would bring an end to the conflict, and then see what happened.

So, although there are many provisions in the Dayton Accords relating to freedom of movement, return of refugees, free and fair elections, there are no real means of enforcing their implementation. There are no real

was continuing to investigate Milošević's responsibility for war crimes in Bosnia-Herzegovina and Croatia during 1991–95. It revealed that Arkan had been on a collective international arrest order of the tribunal since 1995, because of crimes committed in Bosnia-Herzegovina. Šešelj remains to be charged.

sanctions for failure to comply. The Bosnian delegation had proposed a series of automatic sanctions against both Serbia–Montenegro and Republika Srpska, if they failed to participate in elections, or did not allow the return of refugees or freedom of movement. These proposals were all rejected by the European Union, which was no longer interested in economic sanctions against FRY, and the United States happily went along with this.

It is also interesting that the role for justice in the Dayton Peace Accords is limited. The Bosnians put forward a series of seven proposals to be inserted into the Accords, relating to the obligation to arrest and extradite war criminals, to cooperate with the Tribunal, to bar indicted individuals from elections, to exclude from the military, the police and public service individuals who might be responsible for war crimes – with automatic sanctions for those failing to comply. All but two of these were stripped from the Dayton Accords by the US and EU governments. They were simply not interested in pursuing a policy of justice, they were interested in getting a peace deal, and the Bosnian proposals were seen as road blocks to this. It is very clear, however, that it is the lack of justice, denial of justice, that is the road block to the integration of Bosnia. Numerous individuals belonging to international bodies in Bosnia-Herzegovina were until a fortnight ago making optimistic statements that the second elections after the signing of the Dayton Accords, held on 12 and 13 September 1998, would bring about a qualitative change in the balance of political forces and, above all, a significant reduction of the power of the nationalist parties. They proved wrong. We can see from the result of the elections this last weekend how the fact that Karadžić, Mladić and other war criminals are still at large in Bosnia makes it nearly impossible to hold free and fair elections or produce a transformation of the electorate that would strip the nationalists of power and influence.

The other element in play during Dayton was a preference for economic incentives as a means of reducing tension. The sanctions were lifted on a staggered basis only six months after the signature of the Accords, and almost immediately thereafter the European Union and the United States began to pour money into Bosnia, at first only into the Federation, later also into Republika Srpska: the US government has made one of its primary aims to flood Republika Srpska with US taxpayers' dollars. There was a brief movement on Capitol Hill – this is somewhat on the side, but it is very telling of US policy – to prohibit USAID from providing funding to communities which harboured indicted war criminals. The Department of State objected to this requirement as an unreasonable interference in the conduct of US foreign policy; and it proceeded to give money to Pale, Banja Luka, Foča and a number of other municipalities in Republika Srpska harbouring war criminals. They are continuing along this path of economic incentives, though they might change their minds after these elections.

KOSOVO: THE STORY REPEATED

This leads us to the Kosovo crisis. I was at the lunchtime presentation with Secretary of State Albright two weeks ago where someone asked: 'What is US policy on Kosovo and have we not learned our lessons from Bosnia?' She answered that we had a three-pronged approach. The first was humanitarian assistance, which sounds similar to Bosnia. The second was to support ongoing negotiations, which sounds similar to Bosnia. And the third was to consider our military options. Someone remarked that we had considered our military options for five years before we did anything in Bosnia. She retorted that Kosovo was not the same as Bosnia. At which point many of us scratched our heads and said: 'Well, you seem to have ethnic cleansing, you seem to be on the verge of genocide, you've got territorial aggression committed by the Serbian regime against an ethnic or religious group for political reasons, and you have the same individual, Slobodan Milošević, carrying out, directing, these atrocities.'

If we had the time, we could discuss Kosovo in more detail. It could be argued that a demonstration or show of force would dissuade the Serbian military from continuing to carry out hostilities against civilians. The only thing which is different is that when you look at the diplomatic bag of tools that were applied in the Bosnian context – the downgrading of diplomatic relations, the relatively weak sanctions – even these tools, ineffective in Bosnia, are not being applied in Kosovo. The only lesson that seems to have been learned in Bosnia is that trying to do anything is a nuisance. And that rather than engaging diplomatically and trying to seek a serious solution to the crisis, e.g. by seeking to delegitimize President Milošević, by recognizing Kosovo's right to self-determination, we are being left with the military option, the use of military force. In my view, the United States and the EU countries have abandoned their political tools and their diplomatic initiatives. They are essentially willing to permit Slobodan Milošević to carry out his political goals, his ethnic aggression, and to continue to act in this manner on the territory of former Yugoslavia – leaving it up to the US and NATO military, at the last moment, either to decide that it is feasible to take some deterrent action to resolve the crisis, or to seek the path of appeasement.

11

International Military Responses to the Balkan Wars: crises in analysis

Warren H. Switzer

The subject of international military responses to the Balkan wars is fascinating and frustrating. The tendency is to go immediately into a detailed analysis of the campaigns, commitments, tactics and techniques. However, such an investigation would be meaningless without understanding the strategic frame of reference for the various participants. This is particularly the case with the late Balkan wars; no international military response occurred except as an extension of larger political considerations. Indeed, even at the lowest tactical level, the actions and reactions of the members of the international force were carefully specified, circumscribed, monitored and controlled. An elaborate communication and control network made individual decisions by members of the international force both rare and unwelcome. Essentially, all significant military decisions (and a great many that were not) were vetted through higher level authorities, often at much expense of time. Not surprisingly, this desire for micro control was simply incompatible with an adequate response to a constantly changing, often dangerous, situation.

PARAMETERS AND CHARACTERISTICS OF THE STRATEGIC MILIEU

Let us begin our analysis by observing that while the war was energized by a number of engines, it was, in the tradition of Clausewitz, an extension of politics. But unlike most major wars in the twentieth century, this conflict was truly a people's war. What is more, it approached a Hobbesian environment of 'war of all against all'. The pre-war Yugoslav strategy, doctrine and organization of Total National Defence ensured that individual weaponry and the associated skills would be widely available. When vociferous propaganda inflamed issues, such as religion, which fundamentally engaged the individual, people found themselves forced to identify themselves in terms of beliefs, history and ethnicity. These two features ensured that combat would be protracted, subject to low levels of order and authority, and more subject to emotional whims than legal constraints.

For many, deciding either-or questions about their own identity was repugnant. For others it simply was not possible: intermarriage, shared concerns and values, common history made such distinctions impossible. Despite much literature propounding the opposite, we have significant evidence that such discrimination was hardly universal or even acceptable. Moreover, since mixed ethnicity (within families) seems to have been more common in cities than in the countryside, a difference between 'cosmopolitan' and 'rural' cultures added a further complicating dimension to the war.[1]

EXTERNAL PERCEPTIONS

One consequence of these many factors was the inability of the international community to sort out the factions and the issues. Indeed, there was difficulty from the beginning in understanding who was in charge of what. Despite assertions of effective autocratic authority by the various combatants, the rapidity with which arrangements were broken and policies or positions changed, and the slow pace of implementing directives, all suggest that control was less than complete.[2]

In part, the difficulty experienced by foreign officials in identifying suitable counterparts for dialogue was caused by the external powers themselves; being used to an international states system, they naturally sought to engage similar entities. But it was often unclear precisely to what degree the visible leadership was in charge, or what was at issue. Partly from frustration and partly because of the prominence of loud, extreme voices, external authorities and officials found themselves dealing with self-appointed charismatic leaders. It is not clear that these individuals truly represented the majority or best interests of those they purported to lead. However, their willingness to use any means whatever to retain power ensured that they would remain factors to be considered. So it was often extremely difficult for external parties to distinguish the 'good guys' from 'the bad guys'. Moreover, determining 'good' and 'bad' depended

---

[1] The city of Tuzla remained united as an entity despite a heterogeneous composition; there was a mixed force (including Serbs) defending Sarajevo, and, most telling, there is the mass of refugees who simply voted with their feet not to make such a choice. Statements to the author by the mayor of Tuzla, July 1997, and by Zlatko Šugra, a member of the ethnic Serb unit defending Sarajevo, May 1997.

[2] See Christopher Bennett, *Yugoslavia's Bloody Collapse: causes, course, and consequences,* New York 1995, pp. 83–155 where he makes a telling case against Slobodan Milošević.

upon the observer. Nor did taking a Procrustean approach suffice; the issues were simply too complex and intertwined to permit unalloyed alignment.

COUNTERPOISING INFLUENCES

Faced with this situation, the alignments of external forces, their policies and the techniques they used reflected issues more germane to parochial domestic politics and national concerns than to the combatants or to strictly Balkan issues. For example, the war in Bosnia became a campaign issue in Bill Clinton's presidential race. In Russia, the stance of the various powers towards what was happening in the Balkans was closely watched for implications in regard to Chechnya. This aspect increased the situation's complexity as the war progressed and more external actors became involved. All the actors (internal and external) had their own objectives and priorities, and these objectives and priorities also affected other actors (current and potential). Thus, external states were forced into balancing their own national objectives against those of the various alignments of which they were a part.

For example, the United States attempted to steer clear of active involvement, particularly military involvement; the divisive effects of Vietnam continued to counsel extreme caution in matters more ideological than economic.[3] But the United States central position in NATO meant that it could not ignore the concerns of other member nations without risking the loss of its leadership, perhaps even the fragmentation of the organization.

Again, NATO could not ignore a war that clearly had multiple ways of spilling over into other areas and involving them. The memory of how the First World War had started remained a sobering consideration. The Balkan situation at the end of the twentieth century did not seem too far removed from that which had generated the seemingly prescient remark attributed to Otto Von Bismarck in the nineteenth, that war in Europe could easily result from 'some murky business in the Balkans'.

[3] See testimony of Lt-Gen. Barry McCaffrey before the Senate Armed Services Committee, 11 August 1992. He cautioned that operations in Bosnia-Herzegovina would be a 'tremendous challenge', involving control of 'the most mountainous and inaccessible fortresslike' heartland against an enemy whose strategy 'borrows more from Giap than from classical Western military thinking'. Such caution (and an estimate that 100,000 troops would be required) could hardly fail to discourage elected officials, all of whom were witnesses to the turmoil generated by the Vietnam War. This testimony essentially doomed US involvement at that time. This reaction comes in stark contrast to the Persian Gulf War, where the combination of economic interests (oil) and favourable terrain augured well for a limited involvement wherein military prowess would dictate negotiating conditions.

Neither could Russia, then in considerable difficulties, pursue its historical affinity with the Serbs without imperilling the Western support needed to revamp its economic, political and military structures. But neither could Moscow ignore the issue, as the ramifications were ominous if applied to Russia's breakaway region of Chechnya.

Germany too could ill afford to ignore the situation, despite an historical animus associated with the region. Berlin, in the midst of reunification problems, was already dealing with the multifaceted problem of largely Islamic 'guest workers'. Berlin's difficulties were exacerbated by the influx of refugees, including many Muslims, and nor were the problems associated with refugees Germany's alone. In varying degree, other nations faced similar problems. For example, French chauvinism, already active, was building momentum as a popular political issue and focusing its frustrations on refugees both from former French colonies and from the Balkans. In Britain, the presence of yet more refugees added to tensions caused by immigration from former British colonies.

The only universal agreement was that everyone wanted the 'Bosnian problem' to go away quickly, quietly, inexpensively and with all refugees back where they came from. There has been no change in this desire.

THE UNCONTAINABLE PROBLEM AND POLARIZING OPTIONS

During the conflict, this was impossible. The war spilled over in refugees, in the media, in testimony, in religion and in implications – particularly in fearful implications. And, as it intruded, it involved external parties, despite their desire to avoid such entanglements. Facing muddled issues and an expanding, constantly changing milieu, the external powers seemed confronted by the uncomfortable choice either of staying completely free of the worsening situation, or of entering it and attempting to resolve it. Neither seemed promising.

To choose strict non-involvement would imply an acknowledgement of the conflict as acceptable. But this was very difficult. Widespread knowledge of 'ethnic cleansing' could not be ignored. Moreover, attempting to ignore the situation was dangerous, as it became an open question whether the ideals of international organizations or Western countries could sustain more erosion and retain their legitimacy and effectiveness. If the atrocious spectacles of Cambodia's killing fields and of the butchery in various African conflicts could be endured (and generally kept off TV screens), similar practices in the Balkans could not be so easily managed or ignored.

Disturbing as these images were, there was a larger, darker and more sinister spectre: the chance of a general European war. Throughout the Cold War period and into the transition that followed, the interests of the major powers had been balanced. Common interests had been the subject of trans-national teamwork. None of these powers was interested in upsetting the balance or sacrificing the progress made towards achieving common objectives. This inclined them to inaction and non-involvement. But such passivity meant that initiative, including that for restraint, passed to the combatants; which was hardly reassuring for containing the conflict and maintaining that larger balance, particularly as the war continued.

As the conflict evolved, the various external powers found aspects of it aligning with or opposing one or another of their own goals. The pre-war arrangements serving to maintain a web of balanced tension were disturbed by the Balkan wars, and induced shifts portending a much greater danger should affairs begin sliding out of control. The Balkan wars became of concern to external powers not so much as a localized conflict, but because of the way that those powers' own circumstances and the entire fabric of Europe might be affected.[4] As President Mitterrand put it: 'Don't add war to war.'

Moreover, the cost of involvement would be significant, and would ultimately have to be borne by the countries involved, at the expense of other, usually social, programmes.[5] Political figures certainly viewed such costs as being of dubious value to their own political agendas. The large number of 'involved' nations, the number and complexity of the intertwined issues, and the worsening milieu combined to reinforce the opinion of those who advocated a 'hands off' approach.

The alternative choice of entering the conflict and attempting to resolve it had its advocates. Taking issue with the moral indefensibility of doing nothing in face of the barbarity of 'ethnic cleansing', refuting the estimates for military requirements and pointing out the dangers of inaction, these persons perhaps took their historical lessons from the catastrophic results of Chamberlain's acquiescence to Hitler at Munich. In their view, a quick, powerful, 'surgical'[6] operation would sober the combatants, relieve the situation, restore order and, through an international mandate, prescribe the post-conflict arrangements. The dangers of escalation would be bypassed by employing a combined force under international leadership.

Advocates of the interventionist approach asserted that greater danger lay in inaction, since escalation could and would occur as each of the combatants manoeuvred to gain external support. They stressed the overwhelming

---

[4] See David Rhode, *End Game*, New York 1997, p. 24.

[5] Although the thrust of this paragraph is on financial costs, there were internal and external political costs, dislocations, casualties and a host of other expenditures, none of which were likely to be popular.

[6] This unfortunate term was abandoned quickly by military personnel, who decried it as meaningless and misleading. However, political figures were inclined to use it as a means to assuage public anxieties that military involvement might involve significant numbers of casualties (friendly and non-combatant).

military capability of the West, the economic strength that could parallel military activities with economic ones, and the West's pre-eminent leadership position (especially that of the United States), as the means to 'make things come out right'. Rejecting parallels between Vietnam and Bosnia as false analogies, debunking the myth of Serb military prowess and outraged that inaction was a *de facto* endorsement of aggression, they took their campaign onto TV screens, to humanitarian organizations and into public representative bodies. Assuring their listeners that 'appeasement' and 'imprudent hesitation' would only cause a longer casualty list, greater costs, and reduced cooperation, they strove for a robust intervention to 'separate the combatants and broker a peaceful, negotiated settlement'.

Thus the same elements that drove some to advocate involvement drove others to the opposite conclusion. Not surprisingly, the leaders of the external powers found themselves in a confusing, polarizing and divisive situation, in which no course seemed propitious. All courses were unsure, all promised difficulty. Not only would the dangers of escalation exist with either course of action, but also the mere presence (or absence) of military forces would seem to place those forces on one side or the other. Taking any active role to separate the combatants would probably be viewed by one or the other as taking sides.

FEAR AND COMPLEXITY BREED RESTRAINT

But the greatest barrier to taking any course of action (except inaction) was that none of the states that had the ability was willing to bear the costs (and risks) of the force required to impose a cessation of the conflict or to endure the length of time its forces would have to be committed. There have been several estimates, but, significantly, the widely published figure of 100,000 troops for an indeterminate period was never rebutted. It was even less likely that force would be used to roll back the combatants to pre-war positions as an object lesson to would-be aggressors. Moreover, having watched the puzzling fragmentation and tragic self-destruction of a socialist state in transition (one that had been deemed especially capable of an economic 'soft landing'), there were grave doubts that negotiations *could* prove effective, even with an imposed 'military solution'.

The question of military involvement naturally paralleled the international political stance. Unable to come down squarely on one side or the other, involvement grew by degrees as the issue was neither resolved by the combatants nor attenuated by attempts at compromise. Plainly, the number and complexity of the interrelated issues, compounded by the number of involved states, required any solution to be a compromise, but the attitudes of the major combatants hardly suggested compromise. For their part, the external powers temporized and attempted to make adjustments 'on the margin'.

MISPERCEPTIONS RESULTING FROM INACCURATE ANALYSES

The external powers

The external parties assumed that some sort of modest compromise would be acceptable. They failed to understand that Serbs, Croats and Muslims would endure the trials and risks of war rather than surrender their goals.[7] Having undertaken violence as a means to their perceived ends, the combatants were not settled on peace, but upon whatever course might allow them to realize their ends. To them, negotiations were part of the arena of struggle, not a path to peace.

To illustrate this point, throughout the course of the conflict, each stage of international involvement was characterized by negotiated 'agreements' which were broken almost as soon as they were announced. As signals and tests of international commitment, each agreement or pronouncement had to be and was challenged by one or more of the combatants.[8] Thus, warnings, security guarantees (as for safe havens) and any international presence were challenged and, when found wanting, disregarded by the combatants, especially the Serbs.

Having a considerable military advantage from the outset, and needing less external assistance, the Serbs probably felt that they could achieve their goals if there were no significant external intervention. Assessing the struggle chiefly through a military calculus, 'significant' equated to military force. This calculation was precisely what the external powers sought to avoid. It does not seem to have occurred to them that the Serbs' strategy and tactics *required* them to challenge every foreign presence, particularly foreign military personnel, and if finding them insubstantial, deal with them in any expedient manner. Significantly, the Croat and Muslim forces were under the same necessity, if from slightly different motivations. Thus, perversely, the Serb challenges to external organizations such as UNPROFOR served Croat and Muslim ends, while simultaneously placing the Serbs in an adversarial posture with respect to the Western powers.

Yet those powers continued to vacillate. When the combatants perceived a continued reluctance to become involved, they began matching

[7] Commentary by Col Andrei Demurenko, chief of staff for Sector Sarajevo, as found in Elena Kalyadina, 'Colonel Demurenko's Bosnian Confession', *Komsomolskaya Pravda*, Moscow, 29 May 1996, p. 6.
[8] Since the combatants used a strategy wherein external involvement was crucial to the course of the war, both those opposed to and those eliciting external intervention (regardless of which side might be favoured) had to test that commitment.

each other, if not in scale, certainly in increasingly barbaric forms and techniques. This was partly because of a perception that the external powers would not forcefully intervene. Or, if intervention did come, the map dividing the territory would probably reflect the battle lines at the conflict's end. Thus the deliberate practice of 'ethnic cleansing' was accelerated to realize revanchist aspirations, to terrorize and burden opponents (real and potential), and to break the will of those who saw their salvation in terms of external intervention.[9]

The combatants

The misperceptions and flawed analyses made by external entities were matched by two commonly held by the combatants. First, they failed to realize that the central goals of *all* the external powers were to avoid entanglement, to contain the war and its effects, and, insofar as possible, to maintain a united front in dealing with the conflict. Second, they failed to see that if the conflict could not be contained at some endurable level, those powers *would* act to resolve the issue *to their own satisfaction.*

The first criterion (keeping distance) suggested that assistance would come reluctantly, and only after other means had been exhausted and frustrations were evident. The second suggested that external intervention would come on terms other than whole-hearted support. Intervention would aim at reducing the conflict to some lower order of intensity, but the goal of achieving a permanent solution would not be the *only* acceptable solution for either action or negotiation. Indeed, while a permanent peaceable solution was *preferred* by the external powers, *to avoid the dangers of entanglement, some interim status would suffice.* Military action by external powers would be primarily to contain the conflict and prevent a wider, more dangerous development.

Thus, although all the combatants aimed at involving external powers in their behalf, the misperception of the external powers' goals and priorities led to grave results.

First order consequences

Desperately seeking to conclude the conflict on their own terms as the war continued to grind ever deeper into the people, the combatants read into

---

[9] There were baser reasons. Soldiers often banded together for simple robbery, to evict home-owners and seize their property (usually, but not always, those of differing ethnicity). Out of control of their military commanders, sometimes with the connivance of the police and often in open defiance of their own courts, such sad spectacles are characteristic of the destruction of the basic order of society.

the pronouncements and 'on-off' actions of external powers what they wished to believe.[10]

The combatants seem to have been under a common impression that the external powers would act separately to achieve their own goals at the expense of unity. While under this impression and frustrated at the war's evolution, the combatants attempted to force *both* a decision on the battlefield *and* the supportive intervention of external powers by ratcheting up the violence. They were disappointed on both counts. For the external powers, lack of unity was a far greater risk than any issue unique to the Balkans. Fear of disunity prevailed among the external powers despite attempts to separate them from each other and obtain their support.

Reality deflates erroneous perceptions

Thus, the perceptions of both the combatants and the external powers were based on fundamental misperceptions. Only when the iron logic of destruction, suffering and exhaustion convinced the combatants that military means would be uncertain in result but certain in ruin was there a sufficient change in attitude to allow *some* degree of compromise. And only when the iron logic of continued conflict, with its continually spreading, worsening effects, bankrupted sundry low-risk measures, did the external powers move to resolve the war. Even then they made their military moves with restraint, taking the lowest order of risk commensurate with the mission. In short, they sought to end the fighting, but temporized on the peace. The goal remained containment, not resolution.

UNDERSTANDING THE DIALOGUE OF CONFLICT

It would be easy to assign the lack of a true peace treaty to a half-hearted, uncommitted set of external powers (particularly the United States). But this would be unfair. Much of the impossibility of achieving a 'military decision', enabling a prescription of peace terms, resulted from the nature of the war. The deliberate campaign of 'ethnic cleansing' had had considerable effect. The Serb policy of driving out the Bosniaks in order to gain control over territory was both difficult to achieve and dirty in execution; virulent ethno-nationalism was necessary as a motivating engine. This shifted the military target from military forces or political

---

[10] They can be excused some degree of naivety, given statements such as that made by General Philippe Morillon, 'You are now under the protection of the United Nations ... I will never abandon you ...' From an impromptu address given at the post office in Srebrenica, 8 July 1995.

'centres of gravity' to the people themselves. The inability of the Serbs (or anyone else) to force a military decision reinforced this effect.

In consequence, there was a subtle shift in strategy, from accepting the risks involved in seeking outright military victory to hedging one's bets by ensuring that the other side could not win. The policies of hatred promulgated by the extremists were not incidental to the conflict, but a deliberate part of a protracted campaign aimed at ensuring the ultimate failure of compromise solutions.[11] A common misperception was that the people were incidental to the violence. In fact, they were both a military objective and the core of this true 'people's war'. The policies of hatred *had* to be effective at the *individual* level. Catastrophic individual trauma was to be the tool for polarizing that great body of persons to whom compromise might have been acceptable. It is no surprise that organized rape was seen as an 'ideal' method of 'ethnic cleansing'. At the individual, psychological level it ensures a level of revulsion lasting a lifetime. Sadly, the victims of these policies were precisely those to whom compromise solutions would perhaps have been acceptable. This shift in military focus also made international military involvement far more complex and problematical.

The conflict changed from one in which the battlefield determined the political outcome to one where the war in all its forms was but a stage in a struggle of indeterminate dimensions and duration. Deliberately generated hatred and fear were to be the motive forces to sustain the conflict through periods of 'lower operational activity'. Without hatred and fear the struggle might be marginalized, dissipated and resolved.[12] At this stage the battlefield was being defined in ways other than those 'normally' used.

External hesitancy a product of both Balkan and historical experience

It is not surprising that the external powers found elements of the conflict alarming and assessed the probabilities of permanent success through a forced military solution as low. Indeed, the Yugoslav doctrine of Total National Defence raised the spectre of an endless military commitment. If the United States was fearful of another Vietnam-like experience, the examples of Afghanistan, Northern Ireland, the Arab–Israeli struggle,

---

[11] It also cemented the extremist leadership with a visceral bond composed of fear, hatred and guilt. The extremists thus hijacked the force of ethnic feeling and exploited it for personal gain. It is an open question whether the primary reason for such policies was the retention of power or a military strategy.

[12] Had this been allowed to happen, as well it might given the long history of intermarriage and accommodation, extremist positions would have been abandoned by the people and the extremists themselves would have become anachronisms. Aside from the sacrifice of whatever ideals there may have been, the prospect of losing power, of being blamed for misjudgements and sacrifice, and the possibility of being brought before an international war crimes tribunal, ensured that the extremists would go to any lengths to avoid such consequences.

Angola, Algeria, and a host of other unfortunate experiences served to dissuade other would-be participants.

When, at any of several stages, an external power advocated a more forthright, forcefully direct and assertive role, others would object and thus emasculate the response. Sometimes this would occur even within a foreign country. For example, on 10 January 1993, after Amnesty International published a report of vile conditions in the detention camps, French Foreign Minister Dumas said that France was prepared to act alone to free civilians from the camps, only to have Defence Minister Joxe say later that his colleague's words had been 'misinterpreted'.

It is now possible to understand the international military responses to the conflict in Bosnia as generally fearful reactions to a complex, evolving, expanding, multidimensional crisis. It is also easier to see why the international military involvement was reactive, hesitant, reluctant and generally ineffective for much of the conflict. Since all choices seemed bad, there were deliberate attempts to ignore, play down, and muddle along in the vain hope that the situation would somehow solve itself, or so change that a path to success might be more discernible.[13]

The net effect was to do little, and that, perhaps, too late.[14] The 'lowest common denominator' approach was inefficient, but it was supported because all other approaches seemed even more problematic and risk-laden. Cautious of their footing on the slippery slope of involvement, the external powers displayed an aggregate response of choosing between muddled and equally distasteful alternatives. Thus each step along the path to active military involvement was reluctant, made with the minimum of resources and hazarding the lowest degree of escalatory engagement. The assumption was that gains would be low and losses high.

PARADOXES

Cooperation

The lack of international cooperation and coordination partly resulted from attempting to present a solid front while disagreeing over the

---

[13] Conflicts normally become entropic; exhaustion ensues and the conflict grinds to a halt. The contesting parties accept that military operations cannot gain their objectives, and conflict ceases without an announced political solution. The Yugoslav military doctrine of Total National Defence virtually ensures entropy, yet at the same time indefinitely protracts the conflict. If external powers correctly sensed that years of conflict were stretching the combatants to exhaustion and thereby shortening the war, they may have underestimated the residual stamina and capability for violence at the individual level.

[14] It could be argued that the violent entry of NATO under US leadership came too

appropriate roles and missions of the forces being engaged. For example, the UN application of sanctions against Yugoslavia was a low-risk technique aimed at limiting and containing the fighting. But it provoked Russia, the Ukraine and Romania into demanding international compensation for losses suffered through the sanctions. Less-than-identical objectives caused awkwardness in integrating missions, rules and techniques, abetted by misunderstandings over everything from definitions to contingency planning.[15] Only after some humiliating experiences were these difficulties sufficiently clarified and resolved to permit a coordinated (if incomplete) effort.

Terminology

For example, the type, extent, role(s) and authority of foreign forces introduced into Bosnia varied, including limited function observers, members of the International Police Task Force, United Nations Protection Force, UN 'Peacekeeping', 'Peacemaking', 'Peace-building', 'Nation-building' and 'Implementation Force' elements, selected NATO forces and sundry 'private' entities.[16]

Indeed, there is a pattern that suggests great reluctance to use force until personally faced with the reality of the situation. Commanders of the various foreign military formations in Bosnia showed a marked initial reluctance to opt for force, suggesting both an awareness of the dangers of escalation and, perhaps, a conviction that they could succeed where others had failed in the use of moral suasion. Realizing later that such moral suasion was insufficient and even dangerous, they called for combat support, i.e. air strikes. Their reactions to being denied such support suggest both an underestimate of the reluctance of their political

---

late to prevent the establishment of a Hobbesian environment and that this action, not being accompanied by parallel programmes offering alternatives to revanchism, has failed to prevent recidivism.

[15] See Timothy L. Thomas, 'Russian Lessons Learned in Bosnia', *Military Review*, Fort Leavenworth, KA, vol. 76, no. 5, September–October 1996, pp. 38–40, and interview with Lt-Col Hochne, United States, SHAPE chief media officer, Mons, France, 18 December 1996, as found in Wentz (ed.), *Lessons From Bosnia: The IFOR Experience*, Institute for National Security Studies, Washington, DC 1998, p. 453.

[16] These entities often enjoyed quasi-official recognition and support. For example, a number of so-called 'international fighters' arrived from Islamic states, ostensibly to observe the fighting, but actually to train Bosnian Muslims, transfer military equipment and (to a limited extent) take part in the fighting. A more limited role was played by Western organizations, such as Military Professional Resources, Inc., who undertook to train Croatian officers. This was later extended to Bosnian Muslims under the provisions of a Congressionally mandated programme for training and equipping Bosniaks for self-defence.

masters and an overestimate of their own credibility with those masters.[17]

Moreover, the choice of descriptive titles, the definitions applied to these forces and the roles imputed to them confused combatants, external observers and even the participants themselves. Titles such as 'UN Protection Force' (UNPROFOR) were misnomers, since these soldiers had no authority to protect anyone (nor, very often, the ability to do so had they tried). Their mission was to restore peace, under the very vague mantra of 'restoring stability', but UNPROFOR members found that there was an irreconcilable contradiction between the ultimate basis of their authority (coercion through armed force) and an operational strategy of restraint. Even in terms of self-protection they were hampered, a point made embarrassingly plain when the Serbs took UN peacekeepers hostage for use as human shields against NATO air strikes (350 in May 1995 and 55 Dutch in July). Similarly, the term 'safe haven' inaccurately suggested that the United Nations would protect such places. In fact, as late as 1995, no such protection was offered, not only because the means was inadequate, but more specifically because the peacekeepers were ordered to remove themselves if fighting broke out; rather than protecting civilians and imposing order, their primary task was to preserve themselves, and so prevent the United Nations from becoming involved. When challenged by armed force, as at Srebrenica, the true situation quickly became apparent and tragedy resulted.[18]

Other military assistance

As for the presence of other military elements, their significance was on the whole minor and remained so. None of the neighbouring states wanted the conflict to spread into their territory and the major powers were united in their desire to contain the conflict. Paradoxically, although very reluctant to be involved, the external powers were even less willing to allow others to enter and perhaps expand the conflict (or, perhaps, resolve it in ways unsuited to mutual cooperation). So various surrogates, 'volunteers', cross-border safe havens and external sponsors had very little effect.[19]

[17] See commentary of General Janvier before UN Security Council in Rohde, *End Game*, pp. 73–4. This pattern seems to hold true at several levels in the various military formations.

[18] See commentary by Major Robert Franken, then Deputy UN commander in Srebrenica, Captain Jelte Groen and Lt Leen Van Duijn, all Dutch officers on the scene, on the events surrounding the tragedy, in Rohde, *End Game*, pp. 378–9.

[19] For example, there were Russian volunteers on the Serb side (less than 1,000), but they were in such a sad state that it is questionable whether they were an asset. The presence of so-called 'international fighters' from Islamic states was unsettling to those who feared the intrusion of Islam into Europe. They may even have been a catalyst for greater Western involvement, aimed at displacing foreign Muslim

Why 'soft' techniques resulted in 'harder' solutions

As the war developed, international attention and military responses went through several stages. It is not difficult to see that moral suasion, political negotiations and economic pressure were the international community's preferred tools for re-establishing stability. Such methods obviously entailed lower costs and risks. As military resources were increasingly called upon, the pattern is one of reluctance, restraint, relaxation and moderation in their use. What is puzzling is the refusal to realize that ineffective 'soft' techniques only increased the combatants' obstinacy, which generated a need for 'harder' techniques. What was worse, the appearance of paralysis invited contempt and rejection, extending to all other efforts.

Yet, despite the clear ineffectiveness of soft measures, attempts to use other than military methods were never wholly abandoned, only augmented with combat power late in the war. The rotation of leading foreign officials, together with their personal predisposition to avoid use of the military instruments, reinforced the strategic interest in avoiding military engagement. This combination produced a repetitive cycle of naivety, frustration, embarrassment, disillusionment, reappraisal and coercion. The combatants, of course, were not subject to any such rotation. Their behaviour suggests that they used their knowledge of this cyclic process to improve their own positions. Unsurprisingly, when their efforts proved successful (as they often did), two results were inflation of the leadership's egos and reinforcement of its legitimacy. At the same time, it made later peacekeeping activities, restraint and negotiations still more problematic.

FRUSTRATION, ACTION AND CONTAINMENT

Eventually the war's escalating violence, growing exhaustion and mounting frustration generated a rapidly fluctuating milieu, but it was not one which promised an outcome acceptable to all the external parties. So, while the combined Croat and Muslim forces drove back the Serbs and NATO air power struck from above, considerable pressure was applied to limit the gains and preserve the possibility of compromise.

The war did not end with peace terms dictated by the victors; there were no victors.[20] There was a signed agreement, which was perhaps perceived as the best that could be achieved given the present and projected

presence and influence. As it turned out, the United States was eventually to turn a blind eye to arms shipments from the Middle East destined for Bosniak forces.

[20] This is not quite accurate. Criminals (both official and otherwise) profited, and some people control property which should not belong to them. But the biggest 'winners' are those who would have been the next victims, and whose lives were saved by stopping the fighting. Of course, the net result for society has been a horrific loss of blood, treasure, time and self-confidence.

circumstances. Nevertheless, agreement on the meaning of the Dayton Peace Accords remains elusive. Fundamental issues were not resolved, nor were the underlying causes of the conflict addressed. Much of the language seems deliberately ambiguous, allowing the parties to read into the document whatever interpretations they wish. As indeed they must. Like exhausted fighters leaning on each other in the ring, the leaderships of the combatants found themselves deriving support from what their followers were against or feared, not from what they themselves had been able to do to improve the lot of their constituencies. The language of Dayton is significant in that it allows each to 'declare victory' (to some extent), to stop fighting and to retain power. Revanchist attitudes have been banked, but not extinguished.

SELECTED EXAMPLES

Having discussed the characteristics, misperceptions and resulting evolution of the conflict, it may be useful to examine a few key military-related developments. To those involved directly in military operations, the key factor is how higher level analyses affect their operations.[21] The Balkan wars give us considerable opportunity to discuss specific operations across a wide spectrum. Below are three examples – a 'passive' (essentially defensive) military operation: the arms embargo; an 'active' (essentially offensive) military operation: the use of air strikes; and a 'civil relief' (essentially collateral) military operation: humanitarian assistance. The first two are well understood as 'military' operations. It took some time for humanitarian assistance to be recognized by the external powers as another arena of military consequence.

The arms embargo

The arms embargo was one example of how changes on the battlefield caused a reflexive reaction. Starting from the French notion of 'not adding war to war', the imposition of an arms embargo was to go through several stages. The embargo's first result was to ensure a considerable initial advantage to the Serbs and to place the Croats and the Bosniaks at a disadvantage. There was a pronounced disparity. The bulk of the former Yugoslav Army became a Serb force; the curtailing of arms shipments to the region prevented the other combatants from gaining anything approaching equity in military hardware. The disparities were especially pronounced in heavy weapons (tanks, artillery, aircraft). Moreover, the

---

[21] It must be understood that any one of the issues next discussed is complex, deserving detailed research focused on it alone. Further, in the absence of original sources, the assertions and conclusions must remain to some degree speculative.

geographical aspects of the conflict further isolated the combatants (especially the Bosniaks).

However, a series of conditions prevented the Serbs from successfully using their advantage in military hardware to force a military decision. Among these were the interrelated difficulties in bringing their advantage in equipment to bear, the dispersed nature of the conflict, and Serb shortages in manpower.

The war dragged on, and with international public awareness of 'ethnic cleansing' and the shelling of civilians in places such as Sarajevo, assistance began flowing in limited amounts to Muslim forces from a number of sources. Some of these sources were Islamic countries such as Iran and Turkey, which provided their support out of a sense of Islamic brotherhood. The United States could not without considerable risk take issue with Turkey, its NATO ally, nor oppose Iranian assistance, since this would give the impression that it was siding against Islam. Further, the United States found its declared political ideal of 'self-determination' to be at cross purposes with its desire to avoid entanglement. There was another significant consideration. US support for the introduction of arms would run counter to the wishes of its allies (France and Britain) and to Russia's desire to support the Serbs.

Operationally the arms reaching the Muslims increased the Serbs' difficulties, particularly with respect to built-up areas, which require considerable amounts of infantry in a protracted, high-casualty operation. Armoured vehicles are far more vulnerable and artillery can be counter-productive, since rubble still gives cover and concealment, while making the attacking force more vulnerable. At the same time these weapons served to hearten the Muslim defence.[22]

Moreover, the arms embargo was not entirely effective. All the combatants needed military supplies, and there were all sorts of entities who were pleased to sell them arms: Middle Eastern states (including Israel), European states (Eastern and Western) and 'private' organizations. Sensing considerable profit, these entities exploited the situation until reined in by some authority. There were overland routes that allowed arms and other supplies to flow to the Muslims as well as to the Croats and Serbs. In this conflict of incongruities, there were places where a tacit understanding between combatants permitted some arms and other supplies to get through, the rest being confiscated by those who let them through. Such arrangements have been documented between Croats and

---

[22] From statements made to the author by Muslims who fought around Sarajevo and Mostar. One commented: 'It was a relief to fight the Serbs man to man after being shelled for so long. And when we broke up an attack and drove them out, the sight of their dead increased our confidence. And we know it hurt theirs.'

Serbs, and between Muslims and Croats; it would be surprising if they did not occur also between Serbs and Muslims. It has been alleged that *military* persons were engaged in smuggling arms and made considerable fortunes. There were aircraft deliveries, airdrops and even some shipments by river and sea. There were few of these, however. The two-year naval presence of the United States and others (Operation Sharp Guard) was sufficient to thwart most attempts. Of the 31,400 ships challenged and 2,550 boarded, only 643 were sent to Italian ports for further inspection. Of these only a very small number (less than 10) were found to be carrying illegal arms. Perhaps more telling was the fact that the Muslims, who had the most severe arms shortages, had almost no access to the sea, while the combination of rough terrain and limited surface transportation networks made cross-country movement extremely difficult.

But if the arms embargo was not wholly effective, the shipments that did get through were little more than stop-gap. The Bosniaks never acquired enough weapons to equip their forces, and heavy weapons were particularly scarce. They also had little capability for effective training in the use of such weaponry, for supporting it and for integrating it with their other, largely homegrown resources. Croatian forces were much better able to integrate such capabilities, having a higher percentage of professional military personnel in their ranks. The Serbs, with a higher percentage of heavy weapons, suffered from chronic support difficulties for their weapon systems. This led to tactical situations where Bosniak forces remained on the defensive in areas (e.g. built-up areas) where Serb mechanized elements could operate only with considerable difficulty. A general stalemate existed for some time when Serbs could not operate inside such areas, while Bosniaks had difficulty operating outside them.

The inability of the Muslim forces to relieve the siege of Sarajevo or protect outlying areas from 'ethnic cleansing' was plain. Less obvious was Serb inability to force a capitulation of Sarajevo without dangerously weakening their forces. The Serb shortage in manpower meant that they dared not compromise their ability to take and/or hold key areas (all of which had to be retained), which made protracted operations, such as reducing Sarajevo through battle, impractical. It also meant that Serb forces in these other areas were under such pressure that they could not reinforce each other. This caused grave difficulties for the Serbs late in the conflict. As the war became less coherent, as dysfunctional social aspects eroded popular support among the Serbs, and as the combined Bosniak–Croat forces continued to improve, this operational isolation became a strategic vulnerability. The Serbs simply did not have sufficient force to be strong everywhere, but they had to be strong in key areas. Brčko, Banja Luka, Vukovar and Goražde could not be left isolated. Loss of any of these areas (particularly Brčko) risked the dismemberment and dissolution of the Bosnian Serb state.

Meanwhile, there was an acceleration of the campaign in the media. Stressing the plight of civilians, the inability of the Muslims to respond to Serb artillery and tanks and their stubborn resistance as unfairly handicapped 'underdogs', a successful lobbying campaign was launched on the lines of 'send arms for the Muslims to defend themselves'. So successful was this campaign in the US Congress that it generated a major clash between the Clinton administration and their political foes. The results were first the abandonment by the United States of enforcing the arms embargo, and eventually the US acquiescenced in a flow of arms, training, and other support. By the time NATO was committed, a basic, limited *de facto* support structure was in place for the combined Croat and Muslim forces. The post-Dayton period has seen the Congressionally mandated 'train and equip' programme.[23]

Humanitarian assistance

Strange though it may seem, the provision of humanitarian assistance, particularly food, was a significant international military factor in the conduct of the war. Although many of the military implications of humanitarian assistance are plain (particularly to logisticians), this issue has not received much attention. It is unclear why this should be so. Most observers are well aware that the shipments of food to refugees were routinely stopped, raided and delayed for reasons germane to the interests of the combatants. There have been assertions that were it not for humanitarian aid, which functioned as a logistics support system for the combatants, the ability to sustain combat operations would have been significantly restricted, and the war would have ground to a halt. This has two aspects. The Serbs had a goodly supply of equipment, but the requisite support structure to maintain their forces in the field (including fuel, ammunition, spare parts, trained mechanics, tools and food) was inadequate. So perhaps their ability to maintain major, coherent, 'regular' formations would have been greatly diminished, and arguably this could have changed the character of the conflict. But it is unlikely that the conflict could have been terminated through terminating humanitarian aid. The war did not start with a grand offensive, but by slowly accelerating violence. In such a confused people's war, shortage of supplies may reduce the tempo of operations, but is hardly going to terminate them.

---

[23] This unilateral US programme is administered by a private company (Military Professional Resources, Inc.) under US government oversight, and provides military equipment and training to both Bosnian Croat and Bosniak military elements. Carefully measured, the aim of the programme is to provide sufficient capability for defence, but not enough to conduct a successful major offensive. From commentary made by special ambassador for Bosnia James Pardew to the author, Sarajevo, June 1997.

On the other hand, were it not for that humanitarian aid, Sarajevo (and other places) could not have successfully withstood siege. So, it has been asserted, without humanitarian aid the war might have been concluded much earlier by Serb military action. This brings to the surface the perceptual difficulty that faced the external powers at the outset. Most thought that this conflict would be over in weeks or months, that it would be internally resolved, and that external interference would be ill-advised (essentially immaterial and dangerously entangling). Less attention was given to the Serbs' difficulties in conducting the war effectively and efficiently, let alone bringing it to a successful conclusion. When the conflict was not quickly resolved, not only did this misperception become clear, but the need to assuage human suffering had become starkly apparent.

The proponents of this view have argued that a quicker end to the war by a Serb victory would not only have saved lives, but contributed to achieving a permanent solution. This argument is mentioned here only because some authors have sought to portray the combatants as equally guilty and the situation as beyond any external resolution. I do not concur with this assessment, which presupposes the Serbs' ability to control a considerable area and population, discounts the pre-war 'total national defence' doctrine, and assumes a centrality of control on the part of the combatants which seems unsupported by other indicators. Serbian inability to prevent the successful secession of Slovenia suggests that Serb capabilities were less than overwhelming, even for a much smaller area and population. One telling point is the small percentage (less than 20 per cent) of former JNA officers who were willing to serve in the Serbian forces throughout the conflict.

At the same time, the delays imposed by those interfering with the relief convoys are also significant. Those intercepting the convoys had several objectives. First, the delay placed the needs of the destitute population squarely on the back of whatever humanitarian or peacekeeping forces were present, inducing them to make concessions to the intercepting force.

Second, the delays induced the population to believe that international aid was a fading hope. Not only did this strike at general morale, it degraded social order and the ability of international (or any other) organizations to develop and execute orderly processes.

Third, the delays were an easy means of testing international resolve and capability. Tactical risks were low. Not only were the convoy elements essentially hostages (actually or potentially), but any response in the shape of military assistance would have a difficult time dealing effectively with roadblocks. The food convoys were led by officials having little real authority, highly conscious of their tactical vulnerability, and very cautious about being dragged into an uncertain but potentially escalating affair. They generally lacked sufficient moral authority or control of military assets to accomplish their mission.

Fourth, convoy interception was politically flexible. The interceptor could back away from the confrontation with limited negative political or military exposure and minimal effort. Even if forced to retreat, the interceptor was well aware that other convoys would be required; the effects of hunger are cumulative, and the costs of pushing supplies through were progressively higher, and thereby harder to justify.

Fifth, the delays allowed those imposing them to time the development of a situation to their tactical advantage. For example, by delaying food convoys, the hunger of the population becomes such that there is no food available to combatants, or if provided to combatants there is insufficient food for the civil population. This places the forces and those they protect in competition for the available resources, weakening the resistance both by physical hunger and by internal division.

Humanitarian relief, as a facet of international military reaction, resulted in international vulnerability and delayed resolve. By attempting to portray themselves as non-aligned, peaceful and yet militarily potent, the function of foreign military elements became so confused that their mere presence was a contradiction. There seems to have been a plain failure to understand that in the absence of lawful order, the military is the law, its legitimacy based on coercive force. The reluctance, even inability, of international military elements to act according to this principle was disastrous.[24] Paradoxically, the disastrous effects served to convince many that military force was an absolute necessity. Otherwise the combatants would be supported as well as the victims, and the result would simply be better-fed victims. Thus, while the tactical, short-range effects clearly benefited the interceptors, the longer-term effects told against them.

The earlier approach was eventually abandoned, with the military accepting the role of security guarantor for humanitarian efforts of all kinds. Not surprisingly, those military formations that had supplied themselves from humanitarian aid convoys quickly weakened, soon losing their unit coherence and capacity for sustained operations. From a military operational perspective, humanitarian relief functioned much as terrain or weather; the force that controlled it or used it most successfully gained advantages. The force that ceded it suffered a reduction in capabilities.

Air strikes

Air strikes, one part of the air campaign, are another example of the influence of external political considerations. Considering the reluctance

---

[24] This is not universally true. General Lewis MacKenzie was ready to use force, without being compelled to rely on air power or 'dual key' authority (see note 2 on p. 310 below), and his resolution was effective.

of the external powers to become engaged, air power was a logical, if less than completely effective military tool. There were advantages to the external powers. For example, the Serbs had almost no military ability to counter such strikes, seeking instead to use hostages as shields, or negotiations to delay, mitigate or deflect strikes. No direct Serb retaliation was possible, as the air bases were located far from Serbian ability to reach them.

The allies saw that the use of air strikes would be low in friendly casualties, thereby avoiding negative domestic public reactions. The strikes could be controlled at a high level and executed with great speed, avoiding the problems inherent in a slower, less centralized ground operation. There were also disadvantages, including targeting, expense, collateral damage and the concerns of nearby countries.

The result was restraint and much stop-and-go in the use of air strikes. For example, the French made a deal with the Serbs that they would veto air strikes on certain locations if the Serbs would free a number of French soldiers they had taken hostage. Air power was not used in certain areas to avoid retaliation against French and British elements located nearby, and an extremely tight political authorization for strikes was imposed. This led to some embarrassment when on-scene ground commanders called for strikes in support of their units, only to find their requests vetoed by non-military persons far from the scene and focused on another agenda. This was to occur several times in confrontations between UNPROFOR and the Serbs. When the air campaign was finally launched, it still showed marks of restraint, with a very limited number and type of targets being selected.

Significantly, the air campaign could have been far more destructive. For example, attacks were not made against major troop concentrations, because such attacks would have been devastating in terms of Serb casualties. Indeed, since Croat and Muslim forces were advancing at the time, which prevented the limited Serb manpower from being shifted, the air campaign was abated, perhaps to give the Serbs a chance to seek negotiations. The targets chosen were largely ones with a longer-range effect, such as an ammunition factory, suggesting that tactical support on the battlefield was not generally provided. Few targets of immediate tactical impact were struck. Yet it is clear that the Serbs began to negotiate seriously only *after* the air and ground campaigns began in earnest, suggesting that Serb perception of the air campaign was not primarily focused on the damage the strikes *had done*, but on what they *would do* and their effects on future developments.

This is important. Coming late in the war, the effectiveness of the strikes cannot be assessed in isolation. Serb forces were tired, on the defensive, facing a growing numerical disparity on the battlefield, and suffering serious morale and discipline problems. The combination of changes in the fortunes of war, economic distress, general international isolation, erosion of discipline and the firm signal that the intervention of external forces would only make everything worse, forced Serbian acceptance of negotiations. A moment in the conflict had arrived when a compromise might be reached, without anyone dictating the terms. The air campaign helped to convince the Serbs that the West was committed and continued conflict would be counter-productive, which is to say that air strikes were strategically effective rather than operationally.

IMPLICATIONS AND POSSIBLE LESSONS

In retrospect, it seems that combatants and external powers alike were deficient in analytical rigour and sense of judgement. If the external powers did not underestimate the extent to which the combatants would persist in their goals, they did overestimate the effectiveness of moral suasion and 'soft' techniques. Their persistence in maintaining these perceptions is remarkable. In an arena of violence, where the most basic elements of humane conduct have been abandoned as a matter of policy, persistently clinging to demonstrably bankrupt notions seems fatuous. Only when the 'Balkan problem' intruded unacceptably into other areas did the external powers come to realize the need for intervention, and then they argued among themselves over who would do it, how it would be done and who would pay for it.

For the combatants, the same sorts of perceptual and analytical diffi-culty were evident. Determined to realize a particular ethno-political goal, each underestimated the persistence and determination of others similarly motivated. More ominously, each was willing to use violence to realize that goal, albeit with differing motivation. Where ethnic homogeneity was a professed goal (despite its impossibility and impracticability), the use of violence and the policies of hatred became a necessary mode. There seems to have been little analytical consideration of the vortices which such violence and such policies would generate, particularly those which would serve to frustrate or undo the goal itself. There also seems to have been an unrealistic estimation of the threshold at which external powers would feel compelled to intervene and a corresponding overestimation of the extent of that intervention if it did occur.[25] There also seems to have been a notion that external powers could be played off against each other, as in Yugoslavia's foreign affairs during the Cold War.

Nor is that all. The difficulty all combatants had in identifying key military objectives, effectively and efficiently marshalling military effort,

---

[25] This is particularly true of the Bosniaks. The Serbs were quite good at reading and using Western reluctance to intervene until the last year of the conflict.

and executing an integrated political-military strategy, suggests a process less grounded in objective analysis and more on subjective, instinctual reaction. There is a pervasive tone of reacting to developments, rather than guiding or controlling them. True, war is the province of chance, but the science of war suggests that success is usually the result of planning based on sound appraisals. The more complex the environment, the greater the need for analysis. Moreover, the efficient prosecution of war requires coherent effort. This is usually expressed as 'unity of command' and 'co-ordination'. Historically, armies have always had difficulty in maintaining coherence and control when operating across broad fronts or in a de-centralized fashion. The recent Balkan wars are no exception. The inherently fragmented nature of the forces, the policies which decentral-ized their activities and simultaneously eroded their discipline, and the low level of professionalism all suggest that considerably more attention should have been given to scaling major factors and exploring second and third order effects.

It seems that far greater rigour in analysis and the use of available tools to forecast outcomes and develop contingency plans would have been highly useful. It is unclear whether any such steps were taken. Indeed, the results suggest that the war began to develop its own momentum, control became more difficult, opportunities were lost, casualties increased and risks expanded. Much of this was unnecessary. As with the external powers, the means were available (as they still are) for delimiting the problems, whether it is a matter of force-on-force calculations, logistics requirements, or political-military policy formation. The same techniques can reveal difficulties, illuminate alternatives, disclose opportunities and develop plans. Gaming seminars, computer-assisted models and simula-tions all serve to train personnel in near-real circumstances that can be revisited at will. In short, many of the sorts of problems that character-ized and vexed the past conflict can be avoided, perhaps precluding un-fortunate future developments.

Discussion: The International Response
(Chaired by Adrian Hastings)

Adrian Hastings

Clearly, the war we have been looking at has four participants: Serbia, Croatia, Bosnia-Herzegovina and the international community. This last was often the side that did nothing; but of course if you can do something and don't, that is doing something. It is quite certain that the international community could have stopped the war at any time, that it manifestly had the power to do so. If the war went on for four years, it was because the international community allowed it to go on, whether out of ignorance, stupidity, deliberate choice or whatever.

The truth is that we cannot understand this conflict without paying attention to its most enigmatic participant, the international community, which is particularly difficult since it consists, in fact, of the United States, Great Britain, France, Germany, the European Union, NATO and the United Nations, so that when we say 'the international community' we mean an awful lot of different things, given also that we often find the same people wearing different hats at different moments, or pretending to.

There is a double contrast between the British and US attitudes to this war. The first is that Britain controlled the first phase of the process and America the last. As our two American colleagues have stressed, the initial US policy was to leave this problem to Europe, which effectively meant leaving it to Britain. The second contrast is that Britain knew what it wanted and America did not. Britain had a very clear policy from beginning to end. It could not quite admit what its policy was, but it has never changed it – in contrast to France, which had a divided policy: different French politicians wanted different things. Basically speaking, British politicians all shared the same view, which, until the United States decided to intervene and take control, was the decisive one. It is not enough to say that Britain's policy was to keep its world power status, since this of course could have been done equally well by following Margaret Thatcher's pro-intervention position.

It is necessary to recall here how Britain controlled the first phase of the war. In the crucial early stage it held the presidency of the European Community (later Union), while the initial and most important international negotiators were two British diplomats, Peter Carrington and David Owen. The Foreign Office, headed by Douglas Hurd, controlled the negotiating process for several years by maintaining a close relationship with them. The British position can be summarized in the following seven points. First, they thought that the Serbs had a very good case and the Serbian view was hence allowed to prevail.

Second, since unfortunately for the Foreign Office the Serbs were behaving very badly and something had to be done, they initially denied that the Serbs were behaving badly and, though they knew about the concentration camps, kept it to themselves. When the camps were revealed, they said: 'Well, we have to do something', but it did not alter their basic view that the Serbs were right. The British view was and has remained completely Belgrade-oriented. We don't have to understand why – it was done for a series of reasons: personal, traditional, etc.

The third point is also crucial. They were convinced that the Serbs were going to win and very quickly at that. Of course, the longer they did not win the more awkward the British position became. But the initial view was: 'Well anyway there's nothing we can do except rush in and we certainly can't do that; we can't stop a Serb victory.' Sarajevo in their view was not going to last, and once Sarajevo collapsed Bosnia too would collapse. They did not believe in Bosnia. Most people in Britain, moreover, had never heard of Bosnia. They knew about Serbia and some knew about Croatia, but hardly anyone knew about Bosnia.

The fourth point is that there is no British interest in Bosnia.

The fifth is that there is an anti-Muslim feeling, albeit not a very strong one. The interest in Serbia, by contrast, is very strong indeed. The idea of Serbia's defeat or humiliation goes against the whole of Britain's traditional policy in the area. Serbia was a good thing to have, and if one could not have a Serbia-dominated Yugoslavia, then one must have a Greater Serbia. That is British policy.

Sixth, there is a preference for partition: when you have a big problem you divide countries. Britain divided Ireland very successfully, also India, Cyprus, Palestine. The British preference for partition as a solution is deeply ingrained.

And seventh, they found a very clever secret weapon – and not by accident. Faced with news about the terrible humanitarian crisis, they had to do something. The secret weapon was a combination of insistence on the arms embargo with a military presence to protect humanitarian aid. So they could always say: 'If you raise the arms embargo, we will take our troops out; and if we take our troops out, then humanitarian aid will not get through. Do you really want those people to die? Will the lifting of the arms embargo make much difference anyway?' This was a very clever argument. It was consistently used to prevent military intervention and the lifting of the arms embargo.

The use of its military to protect the convoys became the crucial piece in British non-intervention and non-opposition to Serbia, while saying: 'But we are concerned.' When things got very bad, at very bad moments, they would say: 'Perhaps we have to think again.' Douglas Hurd would say again and again: 'Perhaps we shall have to think about raising the arms embargo, but it will have big implications.' So you wait and wait, and go to Washington and tell the Americans things mustn't change. Britain held this line successfully, right up to 1995. British policy only failed because the Bosnians were obstinate and refused to be defeated.

The Foreign Office always argued that bombing was too difficult anyway, since it would kill a lot of civilians, which is exactly what the Serbs said. Every time we in Britain argued for that kind of intervention, saying that ground troops were not necessary, that the balance could be altered by careful intervention from the air, which would make it unpleasant for the Serbs to carry on, they would say: 'No, no, no. That's impossible. It's completely impracticable.' People working in the Foreign Office later admitted to me that they were wrong, that their whole policy had been wrong.

Stjepan Mesić

I have one comment and one question. We are all saddened when we see how the international community has behaved. I see that we were right when we called for international troops to be positioned on the borders between Serbia and Croatia, and between Serbia and Bosnia-Herzegovina. Bosnia-Herzegovina, in any case, had the right to call for the forces of any friendly state to help her guard her borders. That would certainly have prevented the aggression, and a political solution would have been found. When confronted with the behaviour of the international community, we also see how justified was General Špegelj's proposal that every JNA depot in Croatia be taken over within three days of the start of hostilities in Slovenia. Their garrisons would then have been left without arms and ammunition, and the possibility that Serbia would go to war would have been eliminated. If troops of that army had nevertheless been sent against us from Belgrade, Užice and Novi Sad, we would have had something with which to answer them, although all indications are that they would not then have been despatched. This, however – and again I come back to the Karađorđevo agreement – would not have suited Tuđman, since in that case there could have been no partition of Bosnia-Herzegovina.

Although there were indubitably several factors involved in all this, there is no excuse for the international community's actual behaviour. It cannot justify its passivity with assertions that little Balkan dictators wanted this or that, that they had this or that objective, since it itself should have had the objective of preserving peace in this part of Europe and, at the very least, of not permitting genocide. It chose, however, to do neither the one nor the other.

And I wonder now what will happen with Kosovo. True, we are meeting here under the auspices of the Bosnian Institute, so Bosnia-Herzegovina is the focus of our attention. But the war had its origins and is now having its sequel in Kosovo. The events there were the main generator of the crisis which preceded the outbreak of the war, and none of its causes has been eliminated in the meantime. So what will happen next? When I was in Albania and met the then President Sali Berisha, I proposed to him that if the Serbian Army went into action in Kosovo, he should cross the border with his forces. That would be a challenge to the international community, which would then have to become involved. Otherwise massacres will continue with no end in sight and eventually, it seems to me, there will be international intervention anyway; but in the meantime there would be perhaps 100,000 killed, the economy would be destroyed, the entire country would be devastated and all bridges between the Balkan peoples would be destroyed.

Marko Attila Hoare

Just to pick up on some points that Adrian has made. I think that one of the weaknesses on the Bosnian side in its relationship to the West was that they believed that the West represented a kind of moral high ground, or certain democratic values. They also believed that the Western powers represented a kind of legitimate authority in world affairs, whereas they – the Bosnian or Croatian governments – saw themselves as representing essentially subject peoples, almost like village heads in relation to an emperor. It is not that democratic rule is not to be valued, but it tends to be only for domestic consumption, while international relations seem to be subject to the law of the jungle regardless of the political order at home.

Several speakers have stressed that Western powers were not motivated by any desire to save Bosnia, but rather by a desire to partition it. If they failed to partition Bosnia-Herzegovina completely, this was due to Bosnian resistance, which thus deserves all credit. The conflict between the US on one hand and Britain and France on the other was really over methods rather than goals, because all of them – the Clinton administration, Britain and France – they all wanted to partition Bosnia. The only difference was whether you achieve this with the consent of Serbia or by coercing Serbia. It was consequently better for the Bosnians that this international policy did break down. In autumn 1994, for example, the failure of the West and NATO to defend Bihać prompted Croatia to begin preparations for the defence of Bihać, which it could not allow to fall. In the summer of 1995, it was the Serbian conquest of Srebrenica, the renewed attack on Bihać, and the complete failure of the West to react, which led to the Split agreement between Sarajevo and Zagreb, the liberation of Krajina and the breaking of the blockade of Bihać. When Western policy collapsed, the Bosnian and Croatian governments were forced to behave in a statesman-like manner. It seems to me there is a lesson here: you have to act for yourself and not rely in your basic policy on any kind of expectation of support from abroad.

Norman Cigar

When one considers foreign policy in the USA and every other country, one can see that it is often an extension of domestic policy. As far as Kosovo is concerned, we must all realize that American foreign policy will most probably be paralysed for the foreseeable future because of domestic concerns, especially the Clinton–Lewinsky affair and the investigation which the president is facing. American attention is always directed more to domestic than to foreign issues, which is particularly true at present. With hindsight, I think that even in the Bosnian case domestic concerns were very important. President Clinton's focus has always been on domestic issues: health reform, the reform of the military, the issue of homosexuality in the military, etc. – all more important to him than foreign issues. There is no doubt that for the current administration foreign issues are only a means to be used when there is a need to distract public attention from something internal. The result is a minimalist approach: it is a success if there is no outcry, i.e. silence is the final measure of success.

I think that many people in this region failed to understand this, starting with President Tuđman. At the beginning of August 1991, he told the US ambassador to Yugoslavia, Warren Zimmermann, that a general offensive against the JNA and Serb paramilitary forces was being prepared; and when the latter expressed his lack of confidence that such a plan would succeed with an army that had only just been formed, Tuđman replied: 'Well, your country will leap to our assistance with your military strength.' Zimmermann assured him that there was no hope of that, and that he should not get carried away by such calculations, to which Tuđman retorted: 'Perhaps I know a little more about your country than you do, Mr Ambassador.'[1]

---

[1] See Warren Zimmermann, *Origins of a Catastrophe*, Random House, New York 1996, p. 154.

It is important to understand the international community's mis-perceptions of the region. It is equally important, as Marko suggests, for regional players to develop a realistic appreciation of the failings, limitations and often stupidities of countries composing the international community.

To take up the question of Kosovo, there are no UN soldiers there to be taken hostage, there is no real humanitarian mission in danger, nor a dual control by UN. All of the usual excuses fall by the way, and yet we see pretty much a repetition of the Bosnian policy. I should like to hear whether anyone knows why this is so.

Paul Williams

Norman has mentioned a number of reasons for not intervening in Bosnia which are absent in Kosovo. I don't know the fundamental reasoning for not intervening in Kosovo, but I do find it surprising that the same arguments are being trotted out, even though we don't have a dual-key system or UN peacekeepers as potential hostages.[2] A couple of weeks ago I had a meeting with a US senator who had just returned from Kosovo. Representatives from other NGOs and myself were trying to convince him of the need to support US military action, and what he said was that while there he was shown hillsides where refugees were located, with heavily armed Serbian military and paramilitary forces along the roads below. He was told that the moment NATO engaged in air strikes, these paramilitary forces would move up the hillside and kill the civilians. So they have created essentially the same argument as with UN hostages.

Of course we asked him why, given that these individuals were willing to kill unarmed civilians for the goals of their regime, we were negotiating with that regime? Why were we proposing an interim accord which would keep Kosovo within Serbia and which does not provide the right of self-defence or the right of self-determination? I think what it comes down to, as Professor Hastings has pointed out, is that the British government is still pursuing its policy of the need for a Greater Serbia, while the US government feels exhausted by the Bosnian crisis. The Clinton administration, in

---

[2] The dual key system originally pertained to the 1992 deployment of UN forces in the occupied areas of Croatia, when the Serbian paramilitary army was supposed to place its heavy armour under UNPROFOR control; transformed into a local police force, it kept one key to the depots, while the other was held by the UNPROFOR commanders. During the war in B-H, however, the dual key formula meant that NATO could conduct air strikes against Bosnian Serb positions only when permitted by the head of the civilian wing of the UN operation, Yasushi Akashi. This provision was finally suspended in the wake of the fall of Srebrenica, when VRS forces moved against Goražde. Faced with the possibility of another massacre, foreign ministers of the countries with soldiers serving in UNPROFOR, at a meeting in London on 21 July 1995, empowered NATO to strike on the direct request of the commander of UN ground forces.

particular, has had very few victories in foreign policy. So Bosnia has been declared a US foreign-policy success, which of course is not true. Clinton is afraid that any intervention in Kosovo might unravel or endanger the US foreign-policy 'success' in Bosnia. So we are hearing all over again different versions of the same arguments from people in Congress and public life that we heard for non-intervention in Bosnia. I fear that we shall witness a new genocide, albeit one carried out this time by Mother Nature in the shape of the bitter Kosovo winter, and this will force US and NATO forces to go in under less than ideal circumstances in mid winter. But the fact is that, instead of a purely reactive policy like that followed in Bosnia, they are beginning in Kosovo to apply a pro-active policy which, had it been in operation all along, would have prevented many of the horrors that have occurred in the meantime.

Adrian Hastings

British policy has not changed in substance. The Foreign Office thinks about Kosovo exactly as it did about Bosnia – it still wants to build up Serbia and do nothing against it. It thinks that Serbia now has a stronger case indeed, in that, unlike Bosnia, Kosovo has not been recognized as an independent state. There is very little difference on this issue between the Labour and Conservative governments, although the Labour Party is less linked with Serbian interests. The only person who was really prepared to disregard the Foreign Office was Margaret Thatcher – she never trusted it.

Warren H. Switzer

I would like to make a point on the military side here. The fact that the military component used to end the Bosnian war was effective makes it, in my view, likely that military force will be used much more quickly than it has been in the past, if only because of simple frustration and a desire to get things done as quickly as possible. This does not seem to fit with what is happening now, but it is nevertheless an option. One important thing that has happened, at least within military circles, is that the myth of Serbian military prowess has been dispelled. I think that the fragility of the Serbian military machine really has been made apparent. The combination of improved Croatian and Bosnian military capabilities with NATO's presence on the ground in Bosnia suggests that if the military component is used it is likely to be much more efficient than it has been in the past, and will not be limited strictly to air action.

Rusmir Mahmutćehajić

I should like to ask Dr Williams two questions. Taking his considerations into account, maybe we can logically establish a hierarchy of factors in the whole region according to their importance. At the top are Serbia and Milošević; he was able to carry out his strategy only because he encountered weak resistance. It is obvious that he could not have survived without some kind of American support and without being accepted as the most important player. The Kosovo situation can be taken as proof of this. I should like to know what you can tell us about America's long-term strategy in relation to Serbia.

Second, we can take it that the concentration camps were organized and run completely autonomously within the Serb ethno-national project. Is it true that this would not have been done if there had not been some kind of tacit permission? If so, if it was done in the context of the Serbian plan, then we have a paradox. Croat extremists established, undoubtedly without US permission, the same kind of internment camps in Herzegovina (Gabela, Dretelj, Mostar and so on), which were organized under the direct control of Zagreb. At the beginning some representatives of US policy in Bosnia were informed of this, in the obviously naïve belief that they did not know what was happening there. My question is this: is it possible that the American leadership did not know about the internment camps? And if they did know, was their silence a kind of support for such activities?

Paul Williams

Something about US policy and its dynamic that must be realized, if we are to understand the US failure in its dealings with Serbia, is that it is very personality based. The US is enamoured of Richard Holbrooke, a very powerful personality; Richard Holbrooke is enamoured of President Milošević. And when we look at Serbia, what do we see as an alternative to Milošević? Who are the other personalities? Šešelj, Drašković, Đinđić? We see no alternative. This is a flaw in US policy. We should not be looking at the democratic movement in Serbia as a combination of these three leaders, but as a broad-based movement for democracy, without worrying too much about which individual will replace Milošević.

This would be a three-step process. The first step is to stop negotiating with Milošević: you cannot dance with the devil and expect to promote peace in former Yugoslavia. The second is to ensure that the Tribunal indicts Milošević for the crime of genocide. When in December 1992 Secretary of State Eagleburger identified Milošević as a war criminal, presumably he had enough evidence to do so.

Before the secretary of state goes on national television and identifies an individual as a war criminal, he asks his lawyers whether there is sufficient evidence or not. Then why has the US government not turned this evidence over to the Tribunal? And the third step is to promote democratic reform, by publicly delegitimizing Milošević and supporting the democratic opposition, financially or otherwise. The reason why the United States continues to support Milošević is somewhat similar to the British attitude. They are interested in promoting regional stability, and good relations between Greece and Turkey in particular. That is the focal point of US long-term strategy, and they see instability in Serbia as leading to instability in Macedonia, with a follow-on affect on Greece and Turkey. But Milošević is really the one who is promoting instability in Serbia and the Balkans, and hopefully some of the perspectives which are being worked on within the Department of State may prevail, so that we see a change in US policy over the winter. I should point out that the US government is not a monolith. There are a number of people in the foreign service and on the National Security Council, and even a few in the Department of Defense, who realize that US policy has failed and that we need to cease our interaction with Milošević and begin to delegitimize him. Hopefully we shall see changes in this regard.

As for the second part of your question, the US government knew about the concentration camps. We were fully aware of their existence, we had horrific reports, we had information, but we sat on it and did not release it to the media or the public. The reason was that it would have created a moral imperative to intervene. If Warren Christopher, or before him Margaret Tutweiler, had announced that there were concentration camps in Bosnia-Herzegovina, the next question would have been: 'And what is the US government doing about it?' And the answer would have been: 'Nothing'. And since this was an unacceptable answer for political reasons, we simply didn't make the public aware of the concentration camps.

Under the international convention on genocide, all states are obliged to intervene and punish the crime of genocide, since to be complicit in the commission of genocide is itself a crime. A very clear legal case could be made that the United States and other governments, particularly our friends the British, are complicit in genocide; and if their role in the genocide in former Yugoslavia cannot be brought under the jurisdiction of the Tribunal, it should be investigated by a Truth Commission or similar mechanism.

Adrian Hastings

It is very noticeable that nobody in the British government would ever use the word 'genocide', because under the genocide convention there was a legal obligation to act. If somebody put a question about genocide in parliament, it was always answered in other terms: the government never admitted that anything like genocide was taking place in Bosnia.

Norman Cigar

Terminology was indeed very important. The expression *concentration camp* was never to be found either. When General Barry McCaffrey, then chief planner responsible for Bosnia-Herzegovina, and now leader of the Federal anti-drugs trade programme, was asked in November 1993 at an open meeting at which I also participated, about the camps and genocide, he insisted that there was no genocide. There were 100,000 murders, but no genocide. Radovan Karadžić, of course, had always claimed that there was no ethnic cleansing in Bosnia-Herzegovina, only 'ethnic transfers'. But it was not just the Serb political elite that tried to trivialize the concept of genocide and the general situation on the ground. Representatives of the international community regularly used interesting euphemisms, as though they never understood what was happening before their very eyes. Thus the Canadian, Barry Frewer, spokesman for the UN forces in Sarajevo, asserted in mid August that the siege was already over and that the Serbian artillery and tanks around the city constituted only an 'encirclement' and a 'tactically advantageous position', while UNPROFOR commander General MacKenzie, during a CNN appearance three months earlier, spoke not of ethnic cleansing but of the more benign 'population redistribution'.

A certain number of observers in media and academic circles in the West persisted in saying that what was happening, although undoubtedly deplorable, was in no sense genocide. Their argument ranged over a wide area, but always with the purpose of downplaying the severity of the situation. One author, fairly typical of that school of thought, stated in the *Washington Post* of 28 February 1993 that to call the events in Bosnia genocide would cheapen or distract from the Holocaust. To that end, he held that 'the comparison [of the Bosnian Muslims to Nazi-era Jews] exaggerates the crimes of the Serbs and diminishes those of the Nazis ... Such references not only exaggerate the problem and inject emotional terms into the debate, they also hold the Serbs to a standard of evil that they may be unwilling or unable to meet.' Genocide is an attempt to eradicate a people, but what happened in Bosnia was 'something else – an effort to rid certain Bosnian areas of Muslims'. The author concluded that the decisive difference was that the Bosniaks were not totally defenceless, while the Jews had had neither an army nor a state.[3]

---

[3] For these and many other examples, see Norman Cigar, *Genocide in Bosnia: the policy of 'ethnic cleansing'*, Texas A & M University Press: College Station, TX 1995, pp. 88, 115–17, etc. For the debates being held in German intellectual circles with the same motive, whether it was appropriate and morally admissible to compare the Bosniak and Jewish tragedies, see Richard Herzinger: 'Srebrenica i Nova Njemačka' [Srebrenica and the New Germany], *Vijenac*, Zagreb, 7 November 1996 (originally published in the periodical *Merkur*, Heft 5, May 1996). On the applicability of the concepts 'genocide' and 'apartheid' to the situation in B-H, see

Paul Williams

I shall be brief. Bearing in mind that the United States was quite happy to bring numbers of Nazis to the United States, scientists who helped with various nuclear and similarly advanced scientific experiments, it is not inconsistent that the US government is keen to work with indictable or potentially indictable war criminals to promote the Federation of Bosnia-Herzegovina, the US policy success. I think you can see a shift in the policy of the Tribunal. Judge Arbour has refused to focus on Milošević, Tuđman or other potentially indictable high-level or even mid-level leaders. She realizes that the US government doesn't want her to go after these people, so she is going to work on those 26 individuals whom the Tribunal has in custody.

We are not likely to see much activity in this area. It is wrong, it is not ethical, it is not justice, it is not going to promote peace in the region, but that is the policy. In the case of the KLA, Milošević was given the green light to take out the KLA for many reasons. When the US government looks at the negotiations now, it sees two factors. There are the very, very weak Kosovo Albanians, who will basically sign whatever is put in front of them if they are told to, and there is Milošević, who is a far weightier and stronger factor. But if the KLA succeeded in controlling some territory, exercising local power, you would then have two weighty factors. Rugova would be involved in any talks, requesting protection of human rights, some degree of self-determination, autonomy, etc., and the KLA would have its own people on the ground, so would have to be involved as well as Rugova. The Kosovo Albanians' position would be stronger and negotiations would be much harder. So the West was only too happy to have one weak party and one strong one to deal with. If both were strong and one put up some resistance, it would make it more difficult to achieve a peace deal, to get signatures on a piece of paper. The KLA complicated the peace negotiations so they wanted it removed.

Jovan Divjak

I can confirm that ordinary people, who cherished hopes at the beginning because of the appearance of UNPROFOR, soon came to feel the effects

---

the reflections of Freimut Duve in the book *O ratu u duši. Obziri jednog Nijemca* [On war in the soul. Reflections of a German], Zagreb 1997. In their book *Postmoderna i genocid u Bosni: 'etničko čišćenje' – velika prevara našeg doba* [Postmodernism and genocide in Bosnia: 'ethnic cleansing' – the great deceit of our time], Zagreb 1997, Bartol and Slaven Letica give a good survey of the terminological manipulation, euphemisms and semantic substitutes for the terms 'genocide', 'ethnic cleansing', 'crime against humanity', 'war crime', 'Holocaust', with numerous examples and an exhaustive bibliography that also covers the Internet.

of the two-faced policies of European governments towards Bosnia-Herzegovina, just as our friends Williams, Switzer and Hastings have described. We realized that the UN secretary general's special envoy Yasushi Akashi, and all the UNPROFOR commanders from MacKenzie via Morillon and Rose to Janvier (and including the exceptionally decent Generals Briquemont and Smith), were putting into effect the policy of their own governments, so we did not trust them. But that made no difference.

At a seminar on 5 August 1998 I had an opportunity to ask NATO Secretary General Javier Solana why there had been no reaction so far to Kosovo, to which he replied: 'We have no diplomatic strategy for regions of emerging crisis.' That is, first the crisis has to occur, and then they look for some kind of strategy. But we all know that a crisis will arise in Kosovo. Indeed, we prayed to God that it would break out as early as 1993, so as to alleviate the situation in Bosnia-Herzegovina for the Bosniaks and all those who were for the country's preservation. We knew that a crisis in Kosovo was inevitable and were astonished that Europe did not step in to frustrate Milošević's plans then.

A little while ago, Dr Williams, you replied to a question about The Hague and Milošević, but in Bosnia-Herzegovina there is much talk these days of moves in Congress, or perhaps only in the US Senate, to charge Milošević. I should like to ask you how much impact that could have on Milošević in the coming months.

Dr Switzer spoke very evocatively about the wars in the Balkans. But in his presentation of the war in Bosnia-Herzegovina, while he spoke of 'warring parties' and 'civil war', I did not hear him mention the aggression against our country. For us in B-H it was aggression, initially supported by the JNA. During the whole war military units were coming from Serbia and Montenegro, with commanding officers and personnel who were paid and are still being paid by Belgrade. Throughout the war logistical support was reaching the VRS from FRY. What is your opinion of our view that aggression was committed against Bosnia-Herzegovina?

One more question for you. The Chinese military theoretician Sun Tze argued that to succeed in war you must know yourself and your opponent. In Bosnia-Herzegovina we had serious problems because, among other reasons, we respected neither the experience of others nor the theoretical principles of conducting war. We had no time to prepare ourselves. During the war we had, above all, to preserve the territory on which we could carry out actions. I should like you to give us some more detail on how you see the war, in the military-technical sense, in Croatia and Bosnia-Herzegovina.

Paul Williams

I am glad you have brought up the initiative of the Senate and the House of Representatives to put pressure on the US executive branch to indict

Slobodan Milošević. This is one of the initiatives that the coalition of NGOs has been working on, and it is two-fold. One is to embarrass the Tribunal, i.e. Judge Arbour, into acknowledging that there can be only two reasons for not indicting Slobodan Milošević. Either the Tribunal is being instructed politically not to do so, which they have denied, or they are incompetent. And this initiative of the US Congress is beginning to demonstrate this fact, in order to apply political pressure. The second aim is to embarrass and apply political pressure on the US executive branch, which is insisting on negotiating with Milošević. There is some movement afoot in the US government to delegitimize Milošević and the Serbian regime, and working through Congress is one way of achieving that.

The second question is whether it was aggression and an international conflict. From the legal point of view, it was clearly an international conflict. The Tribunal in the case of Duško Tadić found that it was not, but that is now on appeal.[4] Judge Gabrielle Kirk MacDonald, who is an American judge, is of the opinion that it was an international conflict. Hopefully the Appeal Chamber will find the same. But when I was in the US government service we always considered that it was an international conflict, and the basis for the various Security Council resolutions and other actions was that this was a war between Serbia and Bosnia, and to a certain extent between Croatia and Bosnia.

---

[4] Duško Tadić, a Bosnian Serb from the Prijedor region, was the first person to be arrested and charged after the formation of the Hague Tribunal: he was arrested in Germany, extradited to the Tribunal, and in 1997 sentenced to 20 years' imprisonment for torturing prisoners in the Serb concentration camps Manjača and Keraterm. The court argued in its judgment that after 9 May 1992, when the JNA withdrew from Bosnia and the Bosnian Serbs formed the VRS, there existed only internal conflict, which meant there was no legal basis for applying the Geneva convention on protecting civilians, nor for charging FRY with responsibility for the war in Bosnia-Herzegovina, since it was not proved that Belgrade had *operational* control over the VRS formations.

The prosecution appealed, the Appeal Court accepted its argument and on 15 July 1999 decided that the war in Bosnia-Herzegovina was an international armed conflict. Regardless of the JNA's formal withdrawal, three criteria remained for understanding the war as an international conflict in which FRY was involved, i.e. behaved as an aggressor: 1. one side in the conflict (VRS) was *dependent* on an external state (FRY) and its armed force (VJ); 2. one party to the conflict (the Bosnian Serbs) and the external state (FRY) had a *single* or *common* political aim – the creation of a Greater Serbia including B-H territory; 3. Belgrade had a *general* control over VRS activity and the RS leadership, since the VRS command maintained direct contact with the VJ, the VRS structure was the same as that of the VJ, and there is clear evidence of a single hierarchy of command originating in Belgrade and operating throughout the war in Bosnia-Herzegovina.

Warren Switzer

Since I am not a lawyer I will not speak of the legal aspects, but rather about the military point of view. The Serbs' objective was a Greater Serbia defined in terms of Serb people wherever they might be. To realize that kind of state they had to assume an offensive, i.e. an aggressive, strategy. The Bosnian and Croatian strategy required, from the military point of view, that the Serbs fail, since in that case they would themselves have a piece of territory, a state. The Serbs were under extraordinary strategic pressure and in strategic jeopardy once Slovenia separated off successfully, because that set a precedent that could lead to a landslide, i.e. to the complete disintegration of former Yugoslavia. So the Serbs initiated an offensive strategy, one which had to be carried out by aggression. They could not sit still. So my answer is: of course it was a war of aggression, it had to be a war of aggression.

I should like to say something about regression in the status of warfare. Military force was used in this war to extend the scope of the conflict and at the same time to lower its intensity. The technique of military art over the centuries, with certain notable aberrations, has been to refine the 'forces on forces' approach and leave civilians out of conflict. That was the business of the law on warfare, originally initiated by Grotius and others; it is what the Geneva and Hague conventions are all about. Though during the Second World War there were some atrocious departures from law, basically the military profession seeks to refine the business of warfare so that it is conducted among fellow professionals. This particular conflict, on the contrary, brought everything down to individuals, concentrated on individuals. I am speaking of the use of the military in ethnic cleansing, in a manner very reminiscent of what happened in certain places in Europe under Nazi control. That is damaging not just to the military profession but to the fabric of civilization itself. It is a very dangerous tendency and applies not only to the war in Bosnia. The war in Bosnia is not just a matter of local genocide but constitutes an attack on what human civilization is all about.

Martin Špegelj

I should like to clarify my intervention yesterday on the role of international factors in the recent war. I maintain that, if one compares the significance of external and internal factors during the entire period of the genesis, course and conclusion of the war, it was the latter that were crucial. Perhaps external factors should have played a crucial role, but unfortunately they did not. They did act, but not to such an extent as to prevent internal factors from operating right to the end. When the political elite in Belgrade, Zagreb or even Sarajevo speak of international forces or

318

international policies, they commonly do so as a justification for their own policies, though they never really took them into account nor were much afraid of them. Otherwise, I fully agree with the final assessment of external factors.

The question was raised whether American, British and French global politics were really familiar with the SFRY and its internal structure, whether they really knew about the relationship between the peoples and the social situation, etc. I believe that they knew everything. We often say scornfully that they hadn't a clue where Bosnia was, if indeed it existed at all. That is true of the greater part of the general public, but those who were involved in politics, regional relations and military planning were fully informed about what we were in reality. In 1991, as a senior official of the Croatian Army, I was in the Pentagon, where I spoke about the Pivska mountains in north-western Montenegro, about the positions of Zvornik, Bijeljina and Ilok, about the great bend of the Danube and a whole lot of other geographical and topographical details about which the colleagues in the Pentagon knew everything they needed to know without any help from me. I do not believe that their knowledge was not readily accessible to the politicians. But the issue was what you yourself mentioned: opportunism, and speculation about what would happen. 'Nothing was known' about the camps, because if they had been known about, it would not have been possible to do nothing. Just as they knew then, so today too they know everything about the events in Kosovo, but they restrict that knowledge to controlled doses so that they can also control the dosage of action.

I should like to confirm what Stipe Mesić said. It is no longer a secret that the Pentagon had an exhaustively detailed plan for blocking Serbia on the Drina–Danube line, so that things would fall into their right places within Bosnia-Herzegovina and Croatia. For various reasons it did not happen, but I shall mention only that seven days after my visit to the Pentagon, Secretary of State Warren Christopher stated that what was happening to us was not aggression by Serbia against another Yugoslav republic, or rather a sovereign state, but a civil war, and that one should not meddle in such wars. And that is one of the reasons why a less costly and much easier end to the crisis was not reached in former Yugoslavia – cheaper both in the financial sense and in terms of human and technical resources. Perhaps it would have been possible then to influence Serbia to stop its repression of Kosovo and give it greater autonomy, so that what is now happening there would not have happened.

Far too much political ammunition was expended on the embargo issue too. I had gone to the United States precisely in order to talk about the procurement of weapons, and we were already close to agreement – indeed, the first contract had been prepared – and then came the message that an embargo was to be introduced. I did not get angry about it, nor was I particularly anxious whether the contract would be fulfilled or not, since in my understanding of arming and conducting the war, ammunition, arms and other resources were not outside Yugoslavia but within the Federation itself. All I needed was stage one, light weapons, and we resolved that the very same year.

Allow me to quote some numbers in this connection, even if they are only approximate. SFRY had about 3.5 million modern infantry firearms, about 11,000 large-calibre artillery weapons (100 mm or more), 18 up-to-date anti-aircraft units, with both traditional and missile-firing equipment, and about 3,500 tanks, with another 30 modern T-84 tanks being manufactured monthly. There was a sufficient quantity of ammunition and other so-called consumables in the depots for two years of intensive warfare, without any additional manufacture; and almost all the republics had their own production capacity of the entire spectrum of military hardware, including infantry weapons, mines, and ammunition of various calibres from the smallest to the largest. In the last ten or so years of its existence the military industry complex in SFRY had expanded so much that all the republics were overflowing with arms; so much so that the problem arose of how and where to store them!

Hence the embargo meant nothing from the military point of view, just as it means nothing now, except that it acts against the Albanians in Kosovo, since that was one region where not much in the way of arms was located. (All the same, they no longer have a big problem in obtaining what they need.) But it was the internal factor that destroyed the possibility of establishing a favourable balance of power in which there would be neither diktat nor war. As I have already mentioned, Tuđman rejected any kind of arming of Croatia and every defence plan for the country between November 1990 and September 1991. That is why I submitted my irrevocable resignation as commander of the ZNG forces.

If Tuđman had behaved differently, the embargo would have meant nothing, since we would have reached a balance of military power from our internal sources such that it would not have paid anyone in Yugoslavia to go to war. A negotiated agreement in accordance with the constitutional borders would have become possible, which would have been beneficial to all, including Serbia.

This was not done, because it would have made altering the borders impossible, not only those of Bosnia-Herzegovina but also others which the Serbian and Croatian merchants had put on the table – one buying, the other selling. But then their haggling ended when they concluded that it was better not to touch their mutual borders, but to settle their accounts at the expense of a third party – Bosnia-Herzegovina. I agree with Professor Mahmutćehajić that Serbia and Croatia attacked Bosnia-Herzegovina in order to destroy it, and that they acted in coordination.

I have the impression that the desire of the international community was to end the war in Bosnia-Herzegovina at any cost, and thus it was done: the war was brought to an end with political and legal discrepancies which suited absolutely no one. Whenever I find myself in a position to talk with political and military leaders from the West, they confirm that their only and absolute objective was to stop the shooting, on the grounds that US and other interests could not allow lasting instability in South-Eastern Europe. But perhaps there are also other reasons for the Dayton Accords, which is unjust and an obstacle to a better solution, so that the problems will continue for many years to come and no one knows how everything will finally be resolved.

Jovan Divjak

In my view, the embargo robbed Bosnia-Herzegovina, and the Bosniaks in particular, of the right to self-defence. It is as simple as that. We spoke yesterday about how Croatia and Bosnia-Herzegovina are a single strategic region, with which I agree. So if you, General Špegelj, had passed on to us the arms which you had in your possession, seeing that we form a single strategic region with you, things would certainly have gone very differently. And another thing: I do not know why you had to procure arms from outside, when you say that you had quite enough.

Stjepan Mesić

But they didn't allow us to take them.

Martin Špegelj

I was speaking only about the initial quantity of arms necessary to enable us to take the rest.

Jovan Divjak

But the fact remains that our right to self-defence was denied to us.

Martin Špegelj

But the whole of Bosnia-Herzegovina was a military base! You had more arms than any other republic!

Rusmir Mahmutćehajić

What General Špegelj was talking about, and what we are analysing here – a coordinated war waged by Serbia and Croatia against Bosnia-Herzegovina – was essentially preplanned and merely initiated at the agreed moment. In that context, the question of the arms embargo and that of international community support becomes comprehensible. Interpretations to date of the entire phenomenon come down to attempts to justify the lack of success of the two blueprints – Greater Serbia, Greater Croatia. Or rather their incomplete success, and from my perspective failure.

Daniele Conversi

I apologize for interrupting this interesting discussion, especially since I do not understand military matters. All the same, I should like to quote something said by Emma Bonino, one of the most tenacious advocates of Bosnia-Herzegovina in the EU. She claims that foreign policy is the last resort for the collapsing power of national states. I share her opinion that in some countries geopolitics appears as a new discipline attractive both to nationalists and to those of strongly pro-European disposition.

Since we in Italy have a very interesting example of this kind of development, I should like to broaden the theme a little so as draw attention to lesser regional actors, among which I count Italy, since even at the peak of its military-political power it remains very weak. Traditionally completely subordinate to US leadership, it has now visibly altered its policies towards Bosnia-Herzegovina. As you will recall, at the beginning Italy, along with Germany, Austria, Hungary and a few others, was one of the greatest advocates of recognizing Croatia and Slovenia; but we are now seeing a definite swing in Serbia's favour.

Paul Williams says that US foreign policy was not monolithic, and Adrian Hastings suggests that the Foreign Office is open to changing course provided it comes under sufficiently strong pressure from Washington. I have for a long time been researching the role of lobbying in foreign policy and I believe that no course can be truly changed unless there is someone on the side of change who is able to influence policy. It is widely known that Clinton, who is no expert in any kind of foreign policy, was influenced by Robert Kaplan's *Balkan Ghosts*.[5] Our discussion should

---

[5] Robert D. Kaplan, *Balkan Ghosts: A Journey Through History*, New York 1993, whose message is that the Balkan countries and peoples labour under dark collective passions which from time to time erupt uncontrollably (Romania 1989, Yugoslavia 1990–91); that they are intersected by unbridgeable civilizational divisions, and are incapable of rational understanding of their own historical and social reality. President Clinton read the book as soon as it came out in 1993, at the time of the debate on whether the arms embargo should be lifted for Bosnia-Herzegovina, and Serbia be threatened with air strikes. He was powerfully influenced, it seems, by the author's suggestive portrayal of different peoples who, ever since the battle of Kosovo, have remained embroiled in hopeless conflict in which it was pointless to intervene. In consequence he changed his mind about the decision that was about to be made. The book was also read by Hillary Clinton, and parts of it by General Colin Powell, chief of staff of the US Army. On this see Elisabeth Drew, *On the*

therefore include an account of how various external political actors, especially in the United States and Great Britain, were exposed to lobbying, pseudo-academic opinion-formers, and so on.

Adrian Hastings

British, i.e. Foreign Office, policy has not altered at all. It will not be significantly affected by lobbies in Britain, but only by strong US pressure. What is important is the degree to which the Foreign Office controls British state policy, and this rather depends on the incumbent minister. In my view its influence was greatest when Douglas Hurd was foreign secretary. The Foreign Office, naturally, if it has to choose between Washington and Belgrade, will choose Washington; but if it can pull Washington along because Washington is not interested, then it will. While the Foreign Office at present does not want to do anything about Kosovo, if the United States wants to it will go along. Robin Cook, having announced his ethical foreign policy, will go along. I think it will be difficult for the international community not to act in Kosovo sooner or later, because the problem will not go away and something will happen sooner or later which will force the international community to act.

Norman Cigar

I should like to hear how people who were directly involved in the war see the international humanitarian presence, because it was really the core

Edge: The Clinton Presidency, New York 1994, pp. 157–8; also Brian Hall, 'Rebecca West's War', The New Yorker, 14 April 1996.

On Western stereotypes of the Balkans, and the wider cultural and historical context for Kaplan's thesis, see Maria Todorova, Imagining the Balkans, New York and Oxford 1997, pp. 53, 119, 134, 157, 187.

See too Misha Glenny, The Fall of Yugoslavia: the third Balkan war, London 1992, 1993, which likewise promotes a stereotype of transgenerational, ineradicable hatreds. Implying that the only solution for the Western democracies is to isolate the Balkans and leave the region to its fate, the book largely ignores the social and political context of the Yugoslav crisis and the propaganda activities of the Serbian political and cultural elite in preparing for the war: see Attila Hoare, 'Misha Glenny and the Balkan mind', Bosnia Report, new series, no. 3, March–May 1998, pp. 17–19. Various pro-Serb lobbies have made considerable use of Glenny's book, and one key international mediator from 1992–95 has commended it as 'an essential text for any serious researcher': see David Owen, Balkan Odyssey, Indigo, London 1996, p. 327, where he also states that the US special envoy Richard Holbrooke was 'milking information' from Glenny. Glenny's theses have also been taken up by ethnological studies not primarily concerned with the 1991–95 war; for one such example, see Ivo Žanić, 'Hercegovački rat i mir', Erasmus, Zagreb, 23, 1998, pp. 84–92, translated as 'War and peace in Herzegovina', The Budapest Review of Books, vol. 8, no. 3–4, 1998, pp. 125–35.

of the failure of Western policy, while the West itself felt satisfied and happy because of it. I think that this is a very important question, because this will also be the core of its Kosovo policy. The question must have been difficult for anyone directly involved in the war, but I think the policy-makers found it an easy thing to busy themselves with.

Rusmir Mahmutćehajić

I believe that the Bosnian experience is proof that Western countries had neither a strategy for, nor an understanding of, the role of humanitarian aid in the situation in Bosnia-Herzegovina. The result was that humanitarian aid helped the forces which were destroying the country and prolonged the conflict. Humanitarian aid must always be linked with some realistic military and political objective.

The start of humanitarian aid to Sarajevo clearly demonstrated that the war could have been stopped right at the beginning and that there was no need for the suffering and casualties in the years that followed. Once the airlift had been established from Italy, Frankfurt and elsewhere, it became clear that the city could be relieved and the war could be stopped. But the Serbs agreed to open Sarajevo airport and not obstruct the airlift only on condition that no action would be taken against them. So the humanitarian aid really fed the aggression. It was one of the reasons, too, why the HVO and HZ Herzeg Bosna were established, which, since the only land communication between the Sarajevo–Zenica–Tuzla region and the Adriatic ports passed that way, proceeded to impede, halt and even loot the convoys, thus draining our internal resources. The result was that this ill-conceived humanitarian aid nourished the HVO and its anti-Bosnian activities.

A systematic examination of all these experiences would be very valuable, since in the current discussions about the Kosovo problem it would be possible to refer back to the experiment with humanitarian aid in Bosnia-Herzegovina. Sending humanitarian aid without parallel military action will not resolve but prolong the Kosovo conflict and tragedy. Such aid must be a channel for imposing a ceasefire and eliminating the aggressive behaviour of Serbian military forces in Kosovo. Otherwise it will merely contribute to a situation such as occurred in Bosnia, which means the continuation of war, more casualties, more destruction.

Jovan Divjak

Just a few memories of what the aid looked like. When there was no water in Sarajevo, which was always the greatest problem, nor electricity nor anything else, it seemed that any aid was welcome. I remember that we were getting only 30 per cent of daily needs for children, and 60 per cent for the rest of the population. One pack contained 200 grams of oil,

10 grams of salt, 300 grams of rice, 300 grams of beans, 2 kilos of flour and one item of tinned food. Whoever got that was rich.

The biggest problem, and as it turned out the greatest insult to the citizens, was medicines. They came in by the thousands of tonnes, and after the war they had to be incinerated, or more accurately dumped since there was nowhere to incinerate them nor anyone who knew how it was done. Among those consignments there were medicines 20 or even 30 years past their use-by date, and in 1993 we even received about 10 tonnes of quinine, for treating malaria. We had all sorts of diseases, but not malaria; I think there must have been a malaria epidemic in the offices of those international humanitarian organizations. People who brought in humanitarian aid made huge amounts of money by it. This was an appalling experience and must never be repeated.

What is worse, we were not permitted to distribute humanitarian aid to the army. Try to imagine the situation when a soldier comes home on leave, after spending 24 hours in the trenches or battling for ten days without respite to defend the city, and then finds nothing to eat, or only what others have been able to save for him from their own rations, since the family could not receive anything in his name but only for the other family members. And as regards the embargo, I repeat that Bosnia-Herzegovina did not try to get offensive weapons, but only defensive ones; not ground-to-ground missiles, but anti-tank missiles.

Rusmir Mahmutćehajić

I shall tell you an interesting story about humanitarian aid, not so as to explain anything but to bring a little brightness to this sombre tale. Aid was arriving at Butmir airport, which was under the control of the French military, and it would take one day to transport it through the Sarajevo suburbs under Karadžić's control, while during the second or third day it would be taken to various places in the parts of Sarajevo held by the defence. As those humanitarian aid vehicles were not under close supervision, we had made a double floor in one of them, a real storage space, so that the French soldiers, who were doing quite enough to hinder the liberation of the city, were also transporting from the suburbs to the interior what the defence needed: arms and ammunition, which were being manufactured, often to a high level of sophistication, on free territories. This went on for a month: at night, when the vehicle was parked in the suburbs, we would load it; and the next morning the material would arrive, along with the humanitarian aid, in Sarajevo, where during the day it would be carefully removed from the double bottom, which would then be closed again. So the French soldiers were actually doing what they did not want to do: opening supply lines that they themselves were keeping closed or helping the Serbs to keep closed.

Stjepan Mesić

From the point of view of humanitarian aid too, the international community displays double standards. In the case of the sanctions against Iraq, no one minded that children were dying as a result of the embargo, whereas with us something quite different was happening: most of the humanitarian aid was actually going to the aggressors. The aid was not differentiated or protected against anyone, so the people who should have been punished were getting it, and the defenders were only getting just enough not to die of hunger.

Adrian Hastings

We have now reached the end and what remains for me to do is to thank everyone here for their valuable contributions. It has been a small conference, but small conferences are often by far the best, since one gets the closest concentration on specific issues. We have, naturally, missed those whom we would have liked to have here with us, but the themes of our concern have been well covered from various angles and by people with real expertise, and there has been great overall consensus and shared understanding. Finally, one more very big word of thanks to our hosts and the Institute for Southeastern Europe. Without them, without their help, we could not possibly have put on this conference. Budapest, of course, was a very good place for it, since historically and in their character Budapest and Sarajevo have much in common. We are immensely grateful to our hosts, who amply deserve to have the last word.

Vladimir Bilandžić

Thank you for your kind words. We have worked very hard to make this seminar a success. But we ourselves are grateful to The Bosnian Institute for its initiative, since our contribution has been relatively modest. We hope that our collaboration will continue, for together we can achieve much. You mentioned that Budapest is an appropriate place for this discussion. I entirely agree with that – the city, you know, has a square with a Bosnian name, and between Bosnia and Hungary there exist clear cultural and civilizational links, as those who deal with history are very well aware.

Part IV

Addendum

12

Who Wants to be a Soldier?
The call-up crisis – an analytical overview of media reports

Ofelija Backović, Miloš Vasić and Aleksandar Vasović

The call-up crisis of 1991 was one of the key events in the destruction of Yugoslavia.[1] This assertion is not made lightly. The refusal of such a large number of Serbs and Montenegrins to take part in a fratricidal war of conquest caused a trauma after which nothing was ever the same again. The call-up crisis affected all subsequent key events, and its impact is still evident today. Paradoxically, it was one desperate, openly astonished general who captured the essence of the matter when he asked: How was it that western Serbia with its 'glorious tradition from four victorious wars', now all of a sudden refuses to go and fight on the Vukovar battlefield? There was no answer to that fundamental question, yet it was so obvious. 'As soon as Serbia itself comes under attack, we will be ready', was the reply of a reservist from Valjevo. The father of Draža Marković [for many years a communist official in Serbia], a teacher in a village below Kopaonik, wrote in his memoirs of the First World War that in 1914, after its victories at Cer and the Kolubara, the Serbian Army did not want to cross the Sava in pursuit of the Austrians, since the land on the other side of the Sava was not theirs. On breaching the Salonica front in 1918 that same army began kissing the ground only when it had reached Vranje and Leskovac. One could see again in 1991 that the Serbian people knew the difference between what was theirs and what belonged to others.

[1] This text has been adapted from a report in the Belgrade independent journal *Republika*, Year X, no. 198–9, 1–31 October 1998. As the authors state, their analysis was completed at the end of July 1995 and was based on 'the following media sources: the daily newspapers *Politika*, *Borba*, *Politika ekspres* and *Večernje novosti*; the weekly *Vreme*; the news agency Tanjug. It drew also on those rare issues of the weeklies *Vojska* and *NIN* and the bi-weekly *Intervju* that dealt with this topic. The electronic media, especially the regime ones, relied almost exclusively on Tanjug.' The text is somewhat condensed here; brief technical clarifications, or explanations of abbreviations in the original, have been added in square brackets to the text itself, while more extensive explanations are provided in the notes.

Everyone seems to have felt the shock: the dumbfounded government and the army, which did not dare to go in pursuit of deserters and mutinous reservists; the embarrassed regime propagandists and media, which shrank from facing the problem; the nationalist opposition, which closed its eyes to such an obvious expression of the will of the people. In the besieged barracks in Slovenia and Croatia, the JNA discovered that its effectiveness depended on the support of local resources: human, logistical, transport. In Serbia it discovered that it is not possible to make war without the consensus of the entire population.

Milošević's regime took good care not to reveal its war aims when it embarked on open hostilities in Slovenia at the critical moment, at the end of June 1991 (special operations in Croatia had intensified since summer 1990). Propagandist slogans about the 'defence of Yugoslavia' fell on stony ground among the Serbian public, already primed with the anti-Yugoslav propaganda of Serbian nationalism. In such political circumstances, national consensus, at least among Serbs and Montenegrins, was hard to achieve. Milošević never ceased to lay the responsibility for the war on the rest of Yugoslavia and the JNA, since he insisted that 'Serbia is not at war'. Mutinous reservists repeatedly asked, in autumn 1991, to be told what the war aims were; they never received an answer.

Passive resistance was strong from the beginning, despite the unprecedented warmongering campaign in all the regime's media and the zealous efforts of the 'pillars of Serbdom' – the Serbian Orthodox Church, the Writers' Association, the Serb Academy of Sciences and Arts, the [football club] 'Red Star' – to spread hatred and chauvinism. It took various forms: avoiding receipt of military call-up papers; sleeping away from home; caution in public places because of the frequent police raids. Parents invented excuses: claiming that their son had joined one of the paramilitary units was a fairly effective one. The military authorities resorted to various ruses so that the conscripts would not catch on that they were being called up; for example, a young girl would be sent to ring the doorbell, and so on. People were escaping abroad, even by illegal channels.

The greatest loser in the call-up crisis of 1991 was the Serbian opposition, which allowed itself the fatal error of not making use of the powerful political charge and motivation among military conscripts, the stratum of the male population in the prime of life, which was increased manifest by the emotional charge of their families. But the Serbian opposition was primarily a nationalistic opposition, trying to beat Milošević on his own ground of Serbian nationalism by being even more radically nationalist; they were for war, and against Milošević, not understanding that it was Milošević's war.

The trauma of the military conscripts is the greatest and – from the human perspective – the most significant. These people either came back from the war with bitter memories, some of them crippled, some of them disturbed, or joined the great exodus of the young and capable to the West. Those who were called up, those who mutinied while in uniform and returned home (about 40,000 of them), the draft-dodgers (100,000 to 200,000 of them): all of them, and all their families and the families of those who were killed, remained marked by it, without an answer to the question: 'Why?'

JULY 1991: THE MONTH OF SHOCKS

Psychologically the call-up crisis was prepared by the famous nine-day war in Slovenia, when the captive media concentrated on bemoaning 'our children without ammunition whom the corrupt *deželaši*[2] are shooting in the back', or shouting 'Treachery, treachery!', and so on. The reputation of the JNA was seriously damaged in the media.

It all led to a movement of soldiers' parents – the prelude to the call-up crisis. First Milan Kučan, president of Slovenia, publicly called upon the presidents of the other Yugoslav states to recall their JNA recruits from Slovenia, because he could not guarantee their security, and called on all Slovenes – officers and men – to leave the JNA and join the Slovenian Territorial Defence (TO). Then the 1st army began a limited call-up of reservists on 30 June, which came up against political resistance in Bosnia-Herzegovina: the SDA and HDZ advised their members to 'judge for themselves on the spot whether it was necessary to respond or not', and the SDS to 'proceed according to the law'. On 2 July the Presidency of Bosnia-Herzegovina officially called for suspension of the call-up, referring to the constitutional provisions according to which only the Federal Presidency could order mobilization. Lt-Col Vehbija Karić, then spokesman of the Sarajevo JNA corps, complained in a statement to *Vreme* that 'never before have we had such a high level of non-response' and accused the nationalist parties of 'working on' the reservists to that end.

The shock of the war in Slovenia broke up with unexpected speed the system of values and civic discipline and the perception of Yugoslavia as a homeland worth defending. The families of recruits in JNA units that were blockaded in Slovenia reacted spontaneously. The media, especially the press, gave detailed reports: on 2 July some 300 furious parents surged into the Assembly of Serbia with cries of 'treason' and curses. They booed at Prime Minister Dragutin Zelenović. The vice-president of the government, Budimir Košutić, spoke to them of 'genocide', and told them to trust the army, but General Adžić had already told them that he could not return

---

[2] A pejorative expression for Slovenes, derived from the word *dežela*. For the political connotations which this Slovenian term gained in the late eighties, see note 15 on p. 121 above.

their children to them. Many parents demanded that Milošević, like [president of Macedonia, Kiro] Gligorov, should issue a call for Serbian soldiers to return to Serbia.

That same evening, newly mobilized soldiers from Serbia set off for the border of Vojvodina and Croatia. The following day the citizens of Loznica surrounded a called-up reservist unit. The Valjevo reservists did not get further than Šabac; there the entire armoured-mechanized battalion stopped and complained of lack of training, the poor condition of the equipment and weapons and – the five-pointed star on their caps. They continued only after they had been promised that they would not go to the Croatian 'land-of-no-return'. Two weeks earlier, in Tuzla, two reserve units had refused to take part in 'exercises', laid down their arms and equipment in front of the municipality and dispersed to their homes. The captive press started to make threatening noises, and the state agency Tanjug published a commentary against the Albanian minority, containing an allusion to the intention of young Albanians to 'desert and join the Ministry of Interior of Croatia'.

In Belgrade there was mass draft dodging, while the nationalist opposition was trying to form its own paramilitary units, waving volunteers' membership cards, and screaming about a 'Serb army' which would do all this far better than the JNA. News was coming from Montenegro that the response to the call-up was 'unexpectedly thin'; there were references to 'units at half strength'. President Momir Bulatović was the first to mention in public the 'order that military conscripts *make it clear* [our italics] whether they are ready to fulfil the appointed tasks and that, if they are not, they leave their units'. Certain units were left with only 10 per cent capacity – Montenegrins, Albanians and Muslims alike were leaving, but the Podgorica captive press launched a chauvinistic campaign exclusively against the national minorities. The possibility of choice offered to the Montenegrin reservists enabled the 'patriotic' press to differentiate between 'patriots' and 'traitors', creating thereby still more bad blood. There were curses and fights, and people pulled guns at the call-up points. In the pages of the Podgorica daily *Pobjeda* the 'patriots' upbraided the 'traitors'; some firms began to dismiss people for 'treason', and finally Colonel Božidar Babić, the Montenegrin minister of defence, had to intervene and condemn such behaviour. The Belgrade weekly *NIN* covered this exhaustively at the end of July.

It was all known, then, and everything was in the newspapers. Parents were roaming about Croatia and Slovenia, looking for their children. General Života Avramović, the new commander of the 5th army, scolded the parents who had come to Zagreb to collect their children: 'I suppose you would like your children to eat, fuck around and make war on their own doorsteps.'

And then the decision was taken to withdraw the JNA from Slovenia. The regime media hailed the news, while the public was again shocked. The call-up continued, but so did desertions. The Hungarian authorities in Széged opened a reception centre for refugees after about 20 Vojvodina Hungarians fled there; it was a farsighted move. At some border crossings the Serbian authorities began to return the men despite their having valid passports. The SSNO [Federal Secretariat for National Defence] asserted that this was not their concern: they could ban travel only if a state of emergency or general mobilization was declared. In mid July reservists sent on holiday demonstrated in Pančevo: they were demanding everything, from the annihilation of the mosquitoes where they were located to the dismissal of the JNA high command. They complained about nervous breakdowns and uncertainty; demanded to be told whether the JNA existed at all, whether they were the only ones defending the country or also reservists from other republics, and so on. At a peace rally in Podgorica, under the banner 'Heroism today is to avoid war!,' about 5,000 people protested against the war, and were addressed by the president of Montenegro's Partisan War Veterans' Association, Vlado Kapičić, Partisan hero Komnen Cerović and others. *Pobjeda*, on the other hand, published a letter from women who offered to occupy the vacant places in the units and show the men how to fight.

AUGUST 1991: WAR IN CROATIA

The war-mongering hysteria of the regime media grew. Dobrica Ćosić issued a statement with the message that 'at this time pacifist rhetoric is senseless'. *Politika* published a headline: 'A member of the municipal government in Pančevo deserts' – giving his name and address and, to make it all perfectly clear, stating that he was 'of Croat nationality'.

At the beginning of August it became publicly known that in mid July Minister of Defence General Kadijević had signed an order that incompetent officers be dismissed from the army, that deserters should be dealt with according to the laws of war, but also that the classic call-up should be suspended in favour of voluntary mobilization with, at the same time, the dismissal of 'waverers, defeatists and those who do not want to fight' from the army. The estimated number of these who never even got to the army reached around 50,000 at the beginning of August. General Kadijević's order would not be obeyed in any single respect: incompetent officers did not leave, nor were deserters dealt with according to the law, nor was mobilization suspended, nor were 'waverers, defeatists and those who did not want to fight' dismissed from the JNA. Volunteer members of paramilitary units were, however, given the status of full members of the armed forces (though this was not to be known to us until October).

SEPTEMBER 1991: WAR LORDS

Marshal Yazov's unsuccessful *coup d'état* of 19 August 1991 destroyed the last hopes of the Milošević regime and the leading men in the JNA that they might obtain external support for their own counter-revolution in Yugoslavia. Milošević had to fall back on his reserve plan: the 'anti-fascist' propaganda rhetoric of the JNA and the regime began to change into Greater Serbia rhetoric, and the term 'Ustashe' was increasingly used to mean all Croats rather than just the 'HDZ regime'. The JNA units deployed in July on the border between Vojvodina and Croatia moved into an attack for territory and not – as had been anticipated – to depose the HDZ from power in Croatia. The political platform for the war was changed into an ethnic one. The independent media reported on resignations from the JNA as well as the statements of senior officers that the army 'would carry out its tasks with professionals' – officers, NCOs and civilians serving in the JNA. The JNA was slowly becoming a Serb army albeit under the sign of the five-pointed [Communist] star, but officers in the Slavonian theatre of operations complained that they had to 'sleep with their pistols in their hand' for fear of a new insurrection among the reservists. Various local Serb authorities in Croatia – in Knin, Banija and the 'Serb Autonomous Regiona of Slavonia and Baranja' – proclaimed their own call-up.

In September the parents' movement shook even the areas of Yugoslavia where there was as yet no war. A delegation of parents from Serbia, Bosnia and Macedonia appeared in Belgrade; there was a nationally based division between the mothers of Serb recruits and the mothers of Muslim and other recruits in Bosnia-Herzegovina. The Serb mothers issued a telegram condemning the 'rallies designed to break up the JNA ... which is not an army of occupation in any part of Yugoslavia, but a people's army in the true sense of the word'.

Notwithstanding talk about 'professionals', a new wave of mobilization began on 5 September, accompanied by new draft-dodging, protests and mutinies. Public opinion, however, was slowly coming round to the war option. In September the call-up crisis finally reached a tragic dimension: on 20 September, during a revolt in a unit of reservists from Gornji Milanovac located in Slavonia somewhere between Šid and Tovarnik, reservist Miroslav Milenković found he could not decide between his friends who refused to go to war and the pressure of officers harrying him to do so; standing between the two columns, between 'traitors' and 'patriots', Milenković put a bullet in his head.

This Gornji Milanovac reserve was raised during the night of 16 and 17 September; they were told they were going to Sandžak, but they found themselves in the Ruma region in the guise of 'an elite detachment of volunteers for cleansing remaining pockets of resistance as soon as Vukovar falls'. They were given arms with which they were unfamiliar; there was no medical inspection, so that there were diabetics and people with heart disease alongside the healthy; the range-finders of the sniper rifles they were given had not been set. The officers told them that they would pass through Tovarnik smoothly, in inter-city buses, but they were listening to the radio and the radio said that Tovarnik – although it had several times been 'liberated' on TV-Belgrade – was full of Croatian troops. The same day *Politika ekspres* published on its front page a statement by Slobodan Milošević that 'there is not a single Serb soldier of the Territorial Defence in Croatia, and Serbia is not at war with anyone'. When they asked their officers some logical questions, they were denounced as 'traitors' and 'cowards'. After Miroslav Milenković chose the 'heavenly kingdom', the entire unit returned to Gornji Milanovac, buried their comrade and organized a rally at which they asked: who had dubbed them 'volunteers' and why? who should lead the war and how? against whom should they be making war and why? There was no answer.

Reservists from Čačak and Pranjani were told that they were going to Srijem, but after a two-day journey they found themselves in Lipik. The seeds of mutiny spread more widely: the Kragujevac 'people's army' (some 2,000 of them) returned home from Šid, the centre of chaos in the Slavonian theatre of operations; the Valjevo reservist Vladimir Živković climbed into an APC and drove it to the Federal Assembly building as a mark of protest (the Valjevo armoured-mechanized battalion later returned home, after it had been bombed in error by the Yugoslav air force); another few thousand reservists came back from the front during September. At the end of September an anonymous general stated to the Belgrade daily *Borba* that 'people simply don't want to go to war' and that 'it's better for those who want to leave their units to do so – because of the others'. He said it was better that way and that people who chose to leave should not be prosecuted, since Serbia was not at war and general mobilization had not been announced; in any case, 'where would we imprison them all?' In his opinion, 'the major problem is those who stay but don't want to go on'. At the same time, 'weekend warriors', and 'proven' volunteers were given the right to claim paid leave, annual holidays and sick leave – which went unrecorded (municipalities of Lučani, Gornji Milanovac, Užice, Čačak, Požega).

At the end of September court martial judges were mobilized in Vojvodina and given ranks without any formalities (these courts martial, however, never began to function). The only thing that the Serbian government could do with the reservists was to send – of all people! – Minister of Faiths Dragan Dragojlović to Valjevo. His speech to the reservists has gone down in history, since the minister recognized – for the first and only time – that Serbia was indeed at war: 'Serbia, ostensibly, is not at war, in order not to be labelled as an aggressor, so it does not have its own army, either; but it has one within the JNA. ... You mustn't leave your units, because other people will say that Serbs are not what they used to be, and then the Muslims and Albanians will rise up too.' The reservists were not impressed by this argument.

In a closed session of the Assembly of Serbia, it was announced that the response of reservists in Serbia as a whole was 50 per cent, but in Belgrade only 15 per cent. Internally, things were getting worse: reservists from Kosjerić, furious because of poor organization and reception, did not even go to the assembly points; instead, they dismissed the municipal authorities and nominated their reserve captain as president of the municipality. They demanded that General Kadijević be dismissed and that a 'Serbian Defence Force' be established, which would not fight outside Serbian borders. At the same time, hundreds of reservists were returning from the assembly area of Šapac to Smederevska Palanka, Kragujevac, Rača, Knić, Topola, Bogatić and elsewhere.

General Blagoje Adžić, the JNA chief of staff, permitted himself to lash out at exhausted soldiers who had fought honourably. According to Rade Andrić, a reservist from Valjevo: 'When General Adžić visited us, I brought a dead and massacred comrade who was a shapeless mass; he had been bombed by our own air force. I said to him: "General, the Ustasha may be killing us, but why is our own air force killing us too?"' He reached for his pistol and said: "Shut up, you idiot, that's a lie!" There was a lieutenant there who said: "General, it's not a lie." But he wanted to arrest the lot of us.' *Politika* reported the event correctly, but without details. However, in regard to the return of 600 Valjevo artillerymen from Herzegovina, it reported only the statement of the Užica corps, which spoke of cowardice, influence of the opposition parties and the press. More and more awkward questions were being publicly asked: 'Whose war is this – Serbia's or the JNA's?' (a reservist from Novi Sad); 'What are refugees of military age from Croatia doing?', and so on. For his part, General Kadijević complained in an interview for Sky News (transmitted in all the media) that it was difficult to force reservists to serve when the army did not have the authority that would derive from the proclamation of a state of war.

OCTOBER 1991: TO DUBROVNIK!

During October the JNA became stuck in the 'victorious campaign' in the Slavonian mud and the Herzegovinian karst, while one by one the garrisons in Croatia came under siege. The proclamation of a 'state of immediate threat of war', on 3 October, did not help at all: no one was ready to stand by an anti-constitutional act passed by a 'half-presidency' of four members.[3]

[3] The expression 'half-presidency' (or 'rump presidency') refers to the fact that of

Politika ekspres published a memorable front-page headline: 'Dubrovnik waiting to be liberated'. The Assembly of Serbia debated the reports of reservist mutinies. The situation was described by *Vreme*'s reporter thus:

> They have been running away and returning in these chaotic times into which Serbia has been drawn. The dynamic of these mutinies is strange: some are fleeing because they don't want to go to war, some because they don't think the war is being waged with enough vigour. ... Not one Serbian political party has stood up for the mutinous reservists who most seriously, conceptually and at very great personal risk are threatening the strategy of the Serb political leadership.

Mutinous reservists from Pazova shouted slogans in the streets of Belgrade: 'Treason at the front!', 'We won't have the Ustasha [i.e. General Kadijević]!', 'We want Adžić!'.

Valjevo remained the centre of resistance: several thousand reservists who did not want to take part in a fratricidal war returned from Šid, Tovarnik and Nevesinje. Reservists who came from Herzegovina were disgusted by the looting, the targeting of mosques, the ill-treatment of Muslims and the intention to occupy Dubrovnik. People from Valjevo came under JNA artillery and air attack near Tovarnik. The regime immediately accused the municipal leadership of Valjevo (at that time run by the opposition) with 'spreading defeatism and aiding and abetting reservists leaving the JNA'. There was a patriotic campaign in Valjevo where the opposition parties called on the people of Valjevo to stand ready to 'defend the Serb people in Croatia'. Only 6 per cent of reservists returned at once to their units, where they were met with threats of dismissal, interrogations, etc. *Večernje novosti* continued its anti-Hungarian campaign, welcoming the notices of dismissal issued to Hungarians in Bačka who were refusing to go to war and quoting the statement of the military authorities of Subotica that 500 Hungarians had already fled across the border. The same newspaper published a Tanjug news under the headline 'Possibility of death penalty' for desertion.

Prosecutions began too: in Niš a military court pronounced a sentence of four to six months' imprisonment against six soldiers from Leskovac

the former eight constitutional and legal members of the SFRY Presidency, four had resigned or been effectively excluded from decision-making: the representatives of Slovenia (Janez Drnovšek), Croatia (Stjepan Mesić), Bosnia-Herzegovina (Bogić Bogićević) and Macedonia (Vasil Tupurkovski). There remained the representatives of Vojvodina, Kosovo and Montenegro, completely insignificant political figures who had been Milošević's puppets from the start, and the representative of Serbia, Borisav Jović, as Milošević's exponent. He manipulated this now illegitimate body to legitimize the JNA's actions, and to preserve the illusion of SFRY's continued existence, particularly in the eyes of the outside world.

who had left their units in Croatia (these were regular recruits, not reservists). Two reservists from Aleksinac were arrested in Dalj (Croatia) and charged with leading a mutiny in which between 150 and 200 soldiers left the front and went home. The Serbian minister of military affairs General Tomislav Simović announced that it was 'regrettable that the awareness of defending Serbs is not sufficiently developed, even in my own Šumadija'. One member of the central office of the Serbian Renewal Movement (SPO) responded: 'Serb children are again going to be killed so that the Sixth Lika and Seventh Banija brigades can come again to Dedinje and once again execute reactionaries in Belgrade.'[4]

The command of the Užica Corps again accused the Valjevo troops who did not want to go to Dubrovnik of 'cowardice'. Repression continued in Valjevo against rebellious reservists: a new wave of call-up papers was successfully delivered to only 250 addresses out of 1,800; the remainder went into hiding (in the first mobilization, 5,693 call-up papers were delivered out of 6,460). Reservists were saying more and more loudly: 'We will not be an aggressor army.' By as early as the third week hundreds of candles for the war dead were burning every night outside the Assembly of Serbia.

---

[4] Allusion to events at the end of the Second World War, when members of these two Partisan brigades, mainly made up of Serbs from those parts of Croatia, were expressly overrepresented in the new military and political elite of Yugoslavia, especially in Belgrade itself, where the population for the most part had anti-communist and monarchist leanings, i.e. was 'reactionary'. Dedinje is a residential quarter of Belgrade, where the wealthiest strata of the population lived between the two world wars; after 1945 the new elite settled there, having first carried out expropriations and political or even physical executions of its 'class enemies'. The metaphor cited is a symbol of latent antagonism between Serbs from Serbia itself and 'those from the other side', i.e. Serbs living in areas on the far side of the Drina, the Sava and the Danube.

This traditional antagonism increased in the nineties, since it was evident that the most militant ideologists of the Greater Serbia project and of the war were born outside Serbia: the writer and neo-Chetnik ideologue, president of the Serbian Renewal Movement and political patron of the paramilitary Serbian Guard, Vuk Drašković; the president of the Serbian Radical Party and Chetnik leader Vojislav Šešelj; the writer and pamphleteer Vojislav Lubarda; the historian Milorad Ekmečić; Generals Kadijević and Adžić; Admiral Mamula; Vice-Premier Budimir Košutić; the president of the Serbian National Renewal and leader of the para-military White Eagles, Mirko Jović; and so on. Milošević himself comes from northern Montenegro, as does the poet Matija Bečković and the leader of the para-military Tigers, Željko Ražnatović Arkan. To these one must add SDS leaders in both Croatia and Bosnia-Herzegovina (Rašković, Karadžić, Plavšić, Krajišnik), who as a rule behaved arrogantly towards the inhabitants of Serbia proper, especially those from Belgrade, describing them as 'lukewarm' Serbs. In fact, the only significant exceptions – among people in public view – were Dobrica Ćosić and Borisav Jović.

NOVEMBER 1991: VUKOVAR AND THE GLORIOUS WAR

At the beginning of November men were forbidden to travel without a permit from the military department. It would be learned that the decision was passed by the military command of the city of Belgrade, which was trying to raise some reserve units, but the response was scandalously low. In the Belgrade 4th July barracks there was a new reservists' mutiny; this time because the reservists were demanding that the entry in their army books should show that they were at war, and not 'on exercises'. The Belgrade reservists, a whole armoured battalion, demanded for days that someone should receive them and ensure they would be replaced at the front. *Borba* printed a touching story about them, with many direct quotes: 'It wasn't clear to any of us why we were there, or what we were fighting for'; 'We understood that we were nobodies. Even the Serbian government told us so.' Reservists from Preljina and Čačak blocked the Ibarska highway. When the police arrived, shots were fired in the air, and after a MUP armoured vehicle also arrived, an anti-tank missile was fired into a parked trailer ('so that they know what's waiting for them', said the reservists). The police then withdrew. No one among the mutinous reservists would be called to account. In Vojvodina it was believed (and never denied) that of the total of 140,000 mobilized troops in Serbia, 82,000 were from that region.

In November 1991 the results were published of a public-opinion poll carried out in August of that year: 80 per cent of those questioned were for 'preserving the peace in any way'; 54.9 per cent stated that they did not want to go to war, 'but if it has to be, what can one do'; 23.3 per cent that 'this is not my war, let the people wage it who started it, I won't take part in it'. A repeat of the research showed that 48 per cent of those questioned now opposed the war policy of the Serb regime and 52 per cent supported it; however, 83 per cent circled the response 'The refugees are hiding, and we're fighting for them.' On the basis of age groups, 55.6 per cent of those aged between 18 and 36 opposed Milošević's policies. At the same time, Academician Mihailo Marković, the vice-president of Milošević's SPS, said that the Hague agreement must be rejected because 'with large-scale mobilization of our forces we can gain strength'.[5]

Then on 19 November Vukovar fell. The bloody, senseless war showed its true face; there was a sense of anti-climax, without triumph except among the most extreme warmongers; the effective 'loss' of western

---

[5] At its 4 November 1991 session in The Hague, the Peace Conference on former Yugoslavia, chaired by Lord Carrington, considered the proposal of the European Community to resolve the Yugoslav crisis on the basis of accepting the republic borders as the borders of new states and of respect for human rights. Serbia rejected the plan, as later Montenegro did also.

Slavonia at the end of November passed unnoticed. The Dubrovnik operation ended in disgrace and withdrawal.

DECEMBER 1991: SOBERING UP

> Our young people were not psychologically prepared for war. Young people have been living comfortably, dreaming of a *Dynasty*-like future, and now they are faced with the shock of having no choice but to put on a uniform, take up arms and go to fight. (Mihajlo Marković)

The professor and former dissident was late with his psychological analysis of our spoiled youth. Those who wanted to pull out, pulled out; those who didn't, didn't. The SPO estimate at the time was that at least 200,000 young, educated people had fled Serbia and the war and would never return. The JNA never published the true figures of losses in the war in Croatia. General Simović refused the demand to provide substitutes for the reservists at the front, because there was a shortage of some skills, and it was reckoned that they might need them if the 'southern front' were to open up. Reservists who had returned from the fighting in Slavonia were getting new call-up orders. There were protests in Požarevac, where reservists surrounded the municipality assembly, and the police surrounded them. The chief of the military section conveyed to them the message of General Vlado Stojanović of the 1st army that 'all who did not want to go to the war areas, i.e. join their war units, were at liberty'. The general was trying to save the honour of the JNA with the explanation that there were more and more volunteers, including women.

In Serbia, 50,000 people signed a petition for peace and for conduct of a referendum on whether the country should go to war, i.e. whether soldiers from Serbia should fight outside their own republic. The petition organizers – peace movements and organizations – estimated, on the basis of their own research, that 150,000 people had fled Serbia, that 50,000 reservists were at that time in hiding from the call-up, and that criminal proceedings had been instituted against about 10,000 people.

At the end of December, participants in the reservists' revolt in Obrenovac explicitly refused to talk about 'substitution'; they wanted an end to the war, and did not want Serbian youth to fight outside their own borders. On 15 December, Belgrade reservists said that they had had enough; they referred to chaos, incompetent officers, looting ('you would not believe how good the Mirkovac people are at stealing!'), and that this was why they had come back from Slavonia: 'we won't have anything more to do with this crazy war'. The Ivangrad criminal court fined 400 reservists who, it was said, had not responded to the call-up although all these reservists had confirmation of service on the front.

340

JANUARY 1992: THE FALL OF KADIJEVIĆ

In an unexplained incident an aircraft of the Yugoslav air force shot down a European mission helicopter.[6] General Kadijević tendered his resignation, and general Blagoje Adžić became acting minister. Reservists who had come back from the front after the acceptance of the Vance Plan sat around the barracks and despaired. They were not allowed to take off their uniforms, and their army books with the record of their having been to war were not returned to them until they had returned the very last item of equipment.

At the end of January, the most serious mutiny of reservists since the beginning of the war occurred in southern Serbia and the Timok region. There was unrest in Sokobanja, Zaječar, Negotin, Niš, Knjaževac, Aleksinac and Svrljiga. In Knjaževac alone, 4,000 reservists gathered, demanding to know why they were being called up now and what were the objectives of the war. The vice-president of the government, Zoran Aranđelović, was hit on the head with a clod of earth when he tried to explain. In Sokobanja, reservists refused to believe that there were 10,000 Kurds on the Bulgarian border intending to invade Serbia, as the regime press claimed. The president of the municipality joined them and promised them that nobody from Sokobanja would go to the war in Croatia before it was officially proclaimed that Serbia was at war. He was later taken in for interrogation.

The tone of the regime media changed. *Večernje novosti* published a statement by lawyer Milenko Radić that

> the real culprits, where desertions from the war is concerned, are not those several thousand people against whom military courts in Serbia are taking proceedings and who abandoned the front as victims of the JNA's incompetence and treachery, but those who are hiding behind them: military officers, members of the former SFRY Presidency and the Serbian leadership.

Attorney Branko Stanić proposed in *Borba* an amnesty for Croat [!] JNA officers and men.

THE QUESTION OF AMNESTY: 1992–95

NIN, in its issue of 21 February 1992, opened the question of amnesty for 'deserters' and others who had fled the army. It did so with the rhetorical question: 'So many brave soldiers have been killed, injured and disabled;

---

[6] The helicopter, clearly bearing the insignia of the peace mission, was shot down by two FRY warplanes above Varaždin in northwest Croatia, killing the French pilot and four Italian observers.

so many children have been orphaned – and the deserters are calling for amnesty! The right to desert does not exist. Dimitrije Tucović did not run away.'[7] It quoted the estimate that about 12,000 people had been charged on the basis of the Law on Military Service during the seven months of the war, and that between 100,000 (government estimate) and 150,000 people had left the country because of the war. Attorney Đorđe Mamula, member of the Democratic Party's legal committee, proposed an amnesty; the Centre for Antiwar Action drafted a proposal for the law and sent it to what passed for the Yugoslav Presidency and to the Assembly of Serbia. Jovan Buturović, until 1 January a colonel and judge of the Supreme Military Court, and now an attorney, published his text in the 28 February issue of *Borba*: 'Amnesty – at once, and for all.' His argument was legal, political, moral and practical (10,000 candidates for criminal prosecution).

At the beginning of March 1992, however, the Belgrade military court found four reserve officers from Aranđelovac guilty, and sentenced them each to two and a half years' imprisonment. The case was exceptionally interesting, since on 31 October 1991 the four had refused to take part in an operation and led their soldiers, 67 out of total of 81, from Bač back to Aranđelovac. It was an operation which in fact never came about – forcing the Danube at Vukovar. It was abandoned, as would later be learned from senior active JNA officers. At a tumultuous meeting of the local operative group command there was a fierce clash between the commanders proposing to force the Danube and those who were against the idea; when the meeting heard that projected casualties were 60 per cent some commanders, with comments that are not printable, even refused to discuss the matter any further and walked out of the meeting.

At this time General Marko Negovanović, Serbian minister of defence, stated in Gornji Milanovac: 'There can be no question of any kind of amnesty, since those who have committed criminal acts against the armed forces must be held to account, especially those who incited and organized desertions.' At the beginning of April, the Belgrade weekly *Intervju* published a correct and balanced article on amnesty, while *Politika* reported on research by the Centre for Higher Military Studies into 230 soldiers and 80 officers of a mechanized guards unit which had been in the Vukovar field of operations. A third of the soldiers had not been sure of their role and tasks on the ground; only 100 soldiers felt that they had been adequately trained to carry out their tasks; a mere 13.9 per cent of the soldiers were 'very satisfied' with their officers; and so on. At

---

[7] Dimitrije Tucović (1881–1914) was the founder of social democracy in Serbia, author of a series of lucid papers on the political situation in Serbia and the Balkans, a critic of the Greater Serbian idea and an anti-militarist. When Serbia was attacked in summer 1914 he responded to the call-up and was soon killed.

the beginning of the same month *Večernje novosti* began a 'contact series' with the headline 'Deserters in our midst', which lasted several days. In an editorial which called on readers to send in their views on evasion of military service, *Novosti* also stated: 'The virus of desertion, originating in Vojvodina, primarily among the Hungarian population, has rapidly spread ... More than 25,000 people from Vojvodina (mainly Hungarians), fled to Hungary ... Many of the fugitives regret their conduct', etc.

At the beginning of May the educational council of Belgrade University voted by 16 votes out of 25 to propose to the Serbian government that it open proceedings with the relevant bodies to enable the unconditional return of young people who had left the country because of the war. The council divided along the same 'patriotic' and 'peacenik' lines. In September 1992 a member of the Serbian Assembly Aleksander Tasković (SPO) called on the Assembly to order the court authorities to abandon prosecutions of 'deserters' (*Večernje novosti* now put the word in quotation marks) until a decision had been reached on whether there should be an amnesty or not.

The 6 November 1993 issue of *Borba* reopened the issue of deserters and amnesty. The newspaper cited the immigration services of many countries and the International Red Cross, according to which there were between 90,000 and 100,000 young people from FRY who had fled from military service to the United States and Europe (officially registered; the number of illegals is unknown). It mentioned that, according to military sources, the treatment of reservists was different from one military sector or municipality to another; in the case of the majority of mutinies there was an attempt to separate 'leaders' from 'led', etc. – all of which brought disorder into the methodology. The information of the general staff and of the Federal government sent to the Assembly of FRY was quoted as saying in early 1993 that the Law on Amnesty could cover 13,672 people, of whom 8,448 or more were not FRY citizens or were abroad; there were 4,976 criminal acts of desertion from the armed forces, and the perpetrators were mainly soldiers (7,191), and less often civilians (5,625); this number, it was said, was based on prosecutions initiated up to the end of 1992.

On 28 October 1993 the European Parliament unanimously adopted the Resolution on Deserters from Former Yugoslavia, of which *Borba* published the entire text in its 13 November 1993 issue. The essence of the resolution consisted in demands that the international community adopt regulations on the protection of deserters; that member states of the European Community should accept deserters, give them legal status and not permit them to be expelled (especially from Denmark, which had the intention of doing so). At the same time, a campaign began in 16 European countries to sign an 'Appeal for support for deserters from former Yugoslavia', with Anatole France's words 'To disobey criminal orders is beautiful.'

In mid March 1995 the daily press reported on the proposal for a Federal Law on Inheritance; the law proposed that 'servicemen who have left the country in order to avoid fulfilling their defence obligations, and who have not returned to the country by the time of the legator's death' should lose their right of inheritance. This formulation replaced the previous one, in which the prohibition of inheritance related also to 'citizens of Yugoslavia who have fled the country to avoid conviction for felony or to avoid military service, or who have committed enemy acts against SFRY' (the proposal was rather old). In other words, of these categories, only one, military deserters, was retained, while criminals and 'state enemies' were privileged by comparison. This was yet another proof of the widespread assertion that the objective of the regime was actually to prevent the return to the country of the young, the educated, the competent and the honourable.

MOBILIZATION OF REFUGEES FROM BOSNIA AND CROATIA IN SERBIA

On 11 June 1995, the police in Serbia began to place men aged between 18 and 60 who were born in Croatia or Bosnia-Herzegovina, or who were listed there in the military records, under house arrest. In the following days the police began raiding public places and checking identities. Everyone who was caught in that way was put in transit camps (military and police buildings), and kept under armed guard, sometimes by the military and police of RSK, who had orders to fire (in at least one incident, in Sremska Mitrovica, one person was seriously injured while trying to escape). The police gave no explanation, other than that they were carrying out orders and that matters would become clear 'on the scene'. The place of birth on an identity card, refugee status or even the wrong accent were sufficient reason for arrest. People who were born in FRY and whose documents were in order were also picked up from the streets and from their apartments; the explanation was that they had once lived and worked in Croatia or Bosnia and thus had been listed in the military records there. It was interesting that the government of Montenegro officially refused the request of Radovan Karadžić to extradite men of military age from Bosnia-Herzegovina, and that there were no such cases in Montenegro.

According to reports from the field, from the Republic of Serb Krajina and Republika Srpska, at least 6,000 to 7,000 people were extradited from Serbia to those two trans-Drina Serb areas (as stated by Colonel Vojin Karamarković of the RS office in Belgrade), and at most about 25,000 (sources from Republic of Serb Krajina, the Bihać area and Pale).

From the legal perspective, this campaign of the Serb authorities was a criminal act and an extremely serious violation of all international treaties and conventions signed and recognized by former Yugoslavia of which FRY was its aspiring successor. Only the independent media reported on this campaign. The captive media ignored the whole thing completely, with the exception of *Politika ekspres* which, in a confused and feeble-minded commentary, accused the 'traitorous' independent media of imagining the whole affair in order to prevent the lifting of UN sanctions against FRY, which had almost happened. The very next day, the command of the Serb Krajina Army hailed the 'influx of volunteers' and the cooperation of the Serbian authorities in this regard. The FRY Minister of Interior Vukašin Jokanović stated, however, that he knew nothing about the whole thing while the Minister of Interior of Serbia issued a statement that this was a 'routine check of the identities of people who do not have properly registered residence in Yugoslavia'. One must remember that Milošević's regime had given these same refugees the right to vote in the elections of December 1993. Now he no longer needed them. He had indeed to get rid of them, since in the meantime they had come to understand that the Greater Serbia project was abandoned, that they had suffered needlessly, and as a result had become potential voters for the opposition.

Part V: Appendix

Chronology 1985–1995

1985

23 May Assembly of the Serbian Academy of Sciences and Arts (SANU) decides to draw up a study of 'current social issues', the future SANU Memorandum.

1986

2 September Zagreb newspaper *Vjesnik*, which had criticized the Greater Serbian approach of Vuk Drašković among Serb diaspora in the United States and Canada, receives his *Letter to the Editor* with the slogan *'Serbia was, is and will be wherever there are Serb pits, Serb gallows and Serb graves'!*

24 October Widest circulation newspaper in Yugoslavia, the Belgrade *Večernje Novosti*, publishes the SANU Memorandum, which states that Serbs in Yugoslavia are continually under threat and economically exploited, and calls for (re)centralization of the Federal state and/or revision of its internal borders.

1987

24 April Group of Kosovo Serbs, systematically creating tensions in Kosovo under auspices of Serbian secret service, invite Slobodan Milošević, visiting Kosovo, to meeting in Prishtina suburb of Kosovo Polje. After inciting Albanian police to intervene by throwing stones, Serbs gathered outside the building call on Milošević for help with the words 'They are beating us!', and he responds from balcony, 'No one should dare to beat you!' That phrase serves captive media as a start to creating the cult of Milošević as 'defender of Serbs'.

3 September In JNA barracks at Paraćin in Serbia, a deranged Albanian conscript from Kosovo kills four fellow soldiers and wounds five. In Serbia

346

the event is officially interpreted as 'organized attack against Yugoslavia and brotherhood and unity', and used to reinforce anti-Albanian campaign.

23–24 September Eighth Session of CC of Serbian League of Communists, at which Milošević is victorious over rivals Ivan Stambolić and Dragiša Pavlović and takes over full control of the republican party organization.

1988

29–30 May First conference of LCY within the JNA (75,924 members, of whom 54 per cent are officers on active service). The conference opts overwhelmingly for ideological rigidity and centralism.

28 June (St Vitus' Day, anniversary of Battle of Kosovo.) Reliquary of Prince Lazar, canonized participant in the 1389 Battle of Kosovo, starts on its journey from Serbian Orthodox monastery of Ravanica across Yugoslavia in order that the Serbs 'will be inspired to return to their religious and national roots'. During summer the procession visits Zvornik–Tuzla Eparchy in Bosnia-Herzegovina. Gatherings are dominated by a mood of 'historic tragedy of the Serb people, which is experiencing a new Kosovo', and by ever more explicit nationalistic statements and Chetnik iconography.

9 July First mass arrival of militant Kosovo Serbs in Novi Sad, organized by Serbian secret service. A series of rallies follows in Vojvodina, which rapidly results in the fall of the provincial government and the appointment of politicians subservient to Belgrade.

17 July Start of trial in Ljubljana of three journalists and a JNA captain, accused of revealing military secrets. Its background is the ideological conflict in Slovenia between the JNA and majority public and political opinion on such issues as doing military service in one's own republic and the right to use non-Serb languages in the army.

1989

10 January In a series of coordinated rallies, culminating in Titograd/ Podgorica (50,000), Milošević overthrows the Montenegrin government and appoints a regime loyal to him.

14 February Albanian miners in Trepča (Kosovo) begin strike, demanding that autonomy of Kosovo be respected as set out in 1974 Constitution of SFRY. They are supported by students of Prishtina University. Miners' protest soon escalates into hunger strike in pits (1,500 miners).

28 February Demonstrations in Knin (about 2,000 strong) ostensibly in support of Belgrade's 'settling accounts with the counter-revolution in Kosovo', but in fact the start of Greater Serbian insurgency in Croatia.

16 March SFRY Assembly elects new Federal government, led by Ante Marković, who sets in motion a programme of transition to mixed economy and controlled political pluralization.

28 March Assembly of Serbia proclaims new constitution for republic, which revokes autonomy of Kosovo and Vojvodina, but retains their representatives in SFRY Presidency and other Federal organs. Serbia thus gains three votes in these bodies, and together with satellite representative of Montenegro is able to block all Federal institutions. In Kosovo, police fire on Albanian demonstrators (19 dead, 49 injured). A huge crowd in Belgrade shouts anti-Albanian slogans, cheers Milošević and calls for arrest of Albanian leaders. Following day Azem Vllasi is arrested.

20 May Social Liberal Alliance, first non-communist party in Croatia, founded in Zagreb.

17 June Croatian Democratic Community (HDZ) founded in Zagreb, with Franjo Tuđman as president.

28 June In speech as part of celebrations of 600th anniversary of Battle of Kosovo, Milošević announces that 'armed conflict is not excluded' as solution to state crisis.

27 September Assembly of Slovenia proclaims constitutional amendment giving republican laws priority over federal laws in event of conflict, and declares that state of emergency cannot be pronounced without agreement of republican assemblies.

29 November Slovenian government bans planned rally of Kosovo Serbs in Ljubljana, and following day Serbian government calls upon firms and institutions in republic to break off relations with Slovenia. For first time in history one unit within a federation introduces economic boycott of another.

6 December Milošević elected president of Serbia.

8–25 December On model of protests in other Eastern European countries, citizens light candles in Zagreb city centre and sign petition calling for multiparty elections.

25 December After reform wing of Ivica Račan gains predominance in Croatian League of Communists, its CC sends Assembly Initiative for the Election of Assembly Bodies of the Socialist Republic of Croatia, thereby effectively recognizing political pluralism, later legalized by the Assembly.

1990

20–22 January At the 14th Extraordinary Congress of the LCY, attempt to establish Serbian domination fails; Slovenian delegation walks out of the meeting, followed by Croatian delegation, effectively marking end of the LCY.

7 February Janez Drnovšek, Slovenian member of SFRY Presidency, announces that Slovenia will begin process of separation from Yugoslavia.

17 February Serbian Democratic Party (SDS) founded in Knin; president Jovan Rašković.

21 February State of emergency declared in Kosovo; tanks and armoured units on streets; killing of 33 Albanian demonstrators.

24 February First general assembly of HDZ in Zagreb; radical nationalists and returning *émigrés*, along with statement by Tuđman *de facto* legitimizing NDH, give tone.

4 March Greater Serbia rally on Petrova Gora: retired JNA general Dušan Pekić calls for arrest of non-communist politicians in Croatia and Slovenia, and crowd shouts 'We want arms!'

7–8 April Parliamentary and presidential elections in Slovenia – government formed by coalition of five non-communist parties, Democratic Opposition of Slovenia (DEMOS), with 50.9 per cent of votes and 55.1 per cent of seats. Leader of reformed communists, Milan Kučan, elected president of republic.

22–23 April First round of elections in Croatia (second round 6–7 May). HDZ victory, with 41.5 per cent of votes and 68.8 per cent of seats.

13 May In Zagreb, fans of Belgrade *Red Star*, led by Arkan, smash up fittings and attack spectators. Fans of local *Dinamo* hit back.

14 May JNA leadership passes decision to disarm republican Territorial Defence (TO), aimed at Slovenia, Croatia and Bosnia-Herzegovina, excepting municipalities with Serb majority.

26 May Party of Democratic Action (SDA) founded in Sarajevo; president Alija Izetbegović.

30 May Peaceful transfer of authority in Croatia; new multiparty Assembly elects Tuđman president of Croatia.

28 June Proposal of Federal government to legalize multiparty elections at federal level (for SFRY Assembly) vetoed by Slovenia, fearing limitation of extent of sovereignty already gained by elections, and by Serbia, fearing confederal option will be strengthened.

27 June Decision in Knin to found 'Community of municipalities of northern Dalmatia and Lika with Serb majority', first step towards establishing SDS authority in part of Croatia.

2 July Assembly of Slovenia adopts Declaration of Sovereignty. Serbian police prevent Albanian delegates to Assembly of Kosovo from entering building; 114 of 123 delegates hold street session and adopt Constitutional Declaration proclaiming Kosovo a republic within the Yugoslav Federation.

5 July Assembly of Serbia annuls Assembly and government of Kosovo and takes over their powers.

12 July Serbian Democratic Party (SDS) founded in Sarajevo; president is Radovan Karadžić.

25 July Big SDS meeting in Srbo (in Lika, Croatia), at which Vojislav Šešelj receives ovation.

29 July Federal Prime Minister Marković announces formation of his own party, Alliance of Reform Forces.

12 August First openly armed guards in Serb villages in northern Dalmatian hinterland. JNA and part of police linked to SDS distribute arms to Serb population.

17 August Armed Serb extremists block traffic in Knin Krajina and southern Lika, abusing and looting vehicles. Two helicopters of Ministry of Interior of Croatia set off to take control of police stations in Obrovac, Benkovac and Knin, which have revoked obedience to authorities, but are intercepted by two MIGs of Yugoslav Air Force and forced to return to Zagreb.

18 August HDZBiH founded in Sarajevo; after short-lived mandate of D. Perinović, Stjepan Kljuić becomes president.

7 September Assembly of Kosovo meets secretly in Kaçanik (southern Kosovo) and adopts Constitution of Republic of Kosovo.

10 September Slovenia and Croatia propose confederal model for peaceful reorganization of Yugoslavia; representatives of government and press in Serbia and Montenegro ridicule it.

5 October Members of JNA forcibly occupy general staff of Slovenian TO.

8–11 October Croatia imports 20,000 machine guns from Hungary.

17–18 November First round of free elections in Bosnia-Herzegovina (second round 1–2 December) – SDA: 29.6 per cent votes, 33.1 per cent seats; SDS 23.5 per cent votes, 26.5 per cent seats; HDZ 14.4 per cent votes, 16.2 per cent seats. The three parties share power: president of presidency, Alija Izetbegović (SDA) (Presidency constituted 20 December); president of Assembly, Momčilo Krajišnik (SDS); president of government Jure Pelivan (HDZ).

19 November Communist League – Movement for Yugoslavia (SK-PJ) founded in Belgrade; led by retired and active JNA generals, with ideology of rigid communism and programme of centralization.

8–9 December First round of multiparty elections in Serbia and Montenegro; the only two republics in which communists are victorious.

22 December New Constitution of Croatia adopted.

23 December Plebiscite in Slovenia on sovereignty and independence; 93.2 per cent turn-out, of which 86 per cent vote Yes.

28 December Serbia illegally raids primary currency issue of National Bank of Yugoslavia.

1991

9 January SFRY Presidency issues order to disarm all 'paramilitary formations', aimed at the ZNG in Croatia. In Bosnia-Herzegovina, the start of a year-long commemoration of Serb victims of Second World War, organized by Serbian Orthodox Church, SDS and Vuk Drašković's SPO.

9–25 January Martin Špegelj, Croatian minister of defence, forced to resign and go into hiding after JNA leadership accuses him of planning armed insurrection.

25 January SFRY Presidency, despite pressure from Serbia and Montenegro, passes decision not to permit military intervention by JNA in Croatia. Assembly of Macedonia issues Declaration of Sovereignty and Independence; no reaction from Belgrade.

30 January JNA military court in Zagreb issues order to detain Croatian minister of defence Martin Špegelj for investigation, but government contests its legality.

21 February Croatian Assembly proclaims that republican law has precedence over Federal law, and adopts resolution on initiating proceedings to withdraw from SFRY.

28 February Serb National Council of Serb Autonomous Region of Krajina adopts Declaration on 'Separation' from Croatia. It states that 'the Serb Autonomous Region of Krajina remains within the state of Yugoslavia' with Serbia, Montenegro, 'and the Serb nation in Bosnia-Herzegovina and other nations and republics that accept a common state'.

1 March In Pakrac Serb policemen occupy the police station but are forced to flee by regular Croatian police.

4 March Feigned evacuation of women and children from Serb villages in Danube basin in Serbia, to create impression that they are threatened with massacre and to mobilize Serbian public.

12–13 March Attempt at extraordinary session of the SFRY Presidency to declare state of emergency fails to gain majority (4–4, with Bosnia-Herzegovina, Croatia, Macedonia and Slovenia opposed).

14 March Borisav Jović announces resignation as president of SFRY Presidency; Milošević states that he does not recognize decisions of an incomplete Presidency, so as to permit JNA to take over the government. Military leadership desists and Jović withdraws resignation.

15 March Independence of Serb Autonomous Region of Krajina proclaimed in Knin.

16 March Milošević announces that Serbia will no longer be bound by Federal bodies and that 'Yugoslavia is finished.'

25 March Meeting between Tuđman and Milošević in Karađorđevo, with agenda of collaboration to bring down Federal government and partition Bosnia-Herzegovina.

30 March At founding Assembly in Belgrade of Association of Serbs from Bosnia-Herzegovina, statement by Karadžić and Serbian Orthodox Bishop Amfilohije Radović on creation of a 'united Serb state' met with ovation.

31 March Police units of Croatian MUP attacked in Plitvice by Serb paramilitary units; one policeman killed, injuries on both sides.

1 April Serb Autonomous Region of Krajina adopts decision to join Serbia.

15 April Tuđman and Milošević renew their discussions at Tikveš.

2 May 12 Croatian policemen killed in ambush in Borovo Selo; under pretext of ending clash, JNA conducts itself as sponsor of local Serb paramilitary units. Also during this month, first meeting of all representatives of military wing of B-H Patriotic League, on Mount Trebević near Sarajevo.

15 May Serbian bloc on SFRY Presidency obstructs regular annual rotation of post of president (Croatian representative Stjepan Mesić was due to take over).

19 May Referendum in Croatia: 84.94 per cent turnout, of which 93.24 per cent vote for 'sovereign and independent state', and 5.38 per cent to 'remain in Yugoslavia as a single federal state'.

28 May ZNG publicly announced in Zagreb; commander-in-chief Martin Špegelj.

6 June Izetbegović and Gligorov propose so-called asymmetric (graduated) federation as a solution to the crisis.

10 June Council for National Defence of the Muslim Nation, with Patriotic League as its military wing, founded in Sarajevo under auspices of SDA at meeting in Sarajevo of 356 leading Bosniak public figures from throughout Yugoslavia.

12 June Meeting between Izetbegović, Milošević and Tuđman in Split, without results.

15 June Meeting in Ljubljana of delegations from Croatia and Slovenia to agree on harmonization of moves towards independence.

17 June Rašković founds Homeland Front, ostensibly to unite the Serb Autonomous Region of Krajina and Bosanska Krajina in 'a single federal unit if Yugoslavia breaks up'.

21 June In Belgrade, US Secretary of State James Baker states Bush administration's opposition both to use of force to preserve Yugoslavia and to Slovenian and Croatian independence.

25 June Assemblies of Croatia and Slovenia proclaim sovereignty and independence.

26 June Federal government proclaims independence declarations illegal, prohibits changes to signs at international border crossings, and authorizes Federal police and JNA to take control of Federal borders, upon which delegations of the two republics walk out of Federal Assembly.

27 June JNA forces move into Slovenia, as well as into western Croatia. Slovenian police and TO set up road blocks, and first clashes occur between JNA and Slovenian TO. Despite previous agreement, Croatia declares its neutrality. General Špegelj presents plan for defence of Croatia to Tuđman, who rejects it in belief that JNA will not attack.

30 June–1 July Under pressure from three-member delegation of European Community, Mesić is elected president at midnight session of SFRY Presidency.

2 July About 300 families of conscripts serving in Slovenia enter Serbian Assembly and call for their return to Serbia. Resistance to call-up in Serbia grows.

5 July EC introduces arms embargo against SFRY and freezes all financial aid.

7 July Negotiations under EC auspices in Brioni formally end war in Slovenia; Slovenia and Croatia accept three-month moratorium on implementation of independence decisions.

8 July US government, which on 2 July had announced that it did not support use of force for preservation of SFRY and that it would accept independence of republics if gained by peaceful means, joins EC embargo.

10 July Serb paramilitary units loot and burn village of Ćelije near Vukovar and expel all its Croat inhabitants.

18 July Massacre of Croat population in Dalje on Danube; following day, expulsion of remaining Croats from there and also from Aljmaš, Erdut and Sarvaš.

2 August All parties represented in Croatian Assembly sign agreement to form government of democratic unity for effective defence of Croatia, premier is Franjo Gregurić.

14 August Serb police loot and burn Croat villages around Petrinja (Croatia) and expel population.

16 August In Psunj (western Slavonia), JNA arms and trains some 2,000 Serb paramilitaries; following day armoured units of JNA's Banja Luka corps cross river Sava on pontoon bridges to support insurgents in region, especially in attacks on Pakrac.

21 August Vice-President of Serbian government, Borisav Košutić, announces that internal borders of Yugoslavia – especially Serbia's own – are not legitimate and must be altered.

23 August JNA and Serb paramilitaries occupy Baranja.

25 August Seven officers and five soldiers (two Croats, two Serbs, 1 Albanian) who have fled from JNA barracks, not wanting to participate in aggression, give themselves up to police in Ogulin.

26 August JNA and Serb paramilitary forces destroy village of Kijevo, near Knin.

30 August Mothers of JNA soldiers from Croatia, Bosnia-Herzegovina and Macedonia come to Belgrade to demand that their sons be released from army.

7 September Peace Conference for Yugoslavia, chaired by Lord Carrington and held under EU auspices, opens in The Hague. Basis for negotiations: inalterability of internal borders by force, ensuring rights of minorities. Between 25 June and this date, 569 officers have resigned from JNA.

8 September JNA and Serb police attack Pakrac. Referendum in Macedonia: more than 70 per cent vote for independence; Albanians boycott the vote.

10 September Bosnia-Herzegovina invites EC to send observers to its territory.

11 September In Mirkovci (near Vinkovci), group of conscripts from Serbia (30 Hungarians, 1 Serb), with two armoured vehicles and a lorry, give themselves up to Croatian forces.

12 September In Trebinje SDS proclaims Serb Autonomous Region of eastern Herzegovina, beginning the process of formation of parallel Serb authorities in B-H. During second half of 1991 the Republic of Bosnia-Herzegovina MUP repeatedly stops lorries transporting arms to Serb villages, but is obliged under JNA pressure to let them pass.

14 September All JNA barracks in Croatia blockaded; ZNG and police take over large depot near Ploče containing Croatian TO arms.

17 September In Igalo, under auspices of EC mediator Carrington, Tuđman, Milošević and Kadijević accept immediate ceasefire; fierce fighting on Šibenik and Vukovar access roads; start of surrender of series of JNA barracks.

18 September President of Federal government Ante Marković calls for resignation of Kadijević and his deputy Brovet, which they ignore. Culmination of JNA and Serb police attacks on many Croatian towns. Large group of 'reservists' from Montenegro comes to JNA barracks in Mostar and terrorizes civilians; more and more Bosniaks flee eastern Herzegovina. Tuđman appoints Gojko Šušak, until then minister for the diaspora, as Croatia's defence minister.

19 September Start of large-scale JNA invasion of Croatia from Serbia.

20 September On TV, Belgrade General Kadijević announces 'military action' against Croatia, in an explicit declaration of war. At this time JNA in Croatia has four infantry corps deployed in Croatia, half the air force and almost the entire navy. Independent Podgorica weekly *Monitor* states that during summer, 52 per cent of Montenegrin reservists have rejected call-up and JNA has killed seven Montenegrin soldiers unwilling to go to war.

21 September Formation of chief of staff of Croatian Army: commanding officer General Anton Tus, members Generals Petar Stipetić and Franjo Feldi, Colonel Imra Agotić, Admiral Stevo Letica, Frigate Captain Davor Domazet and others. In mysterious circumstances, police kill vice-president of Croatian Party of Right (HSP), A. Paradžik, advocate of Croat–Bosniak alliance and B-H integrity, political creator of HOS, whose volunteers in Croatia are merged into HV.

22 September JNA barracks at Varaždin surrenders to Croatian forces.

25 September UN Security Council Resolution 713 imposes arms embargo, prohibiting supply of weapons and military equipment to all republics of SFRY.

1 October JNA and Montenegrin paramilitary troops begin to attack Dubrovnik. JNA barracks at Bjelovar taken by Croatian forces, with considerable matériel.

2 October Croat village of Ravno, south-west of Trebinje, destroyed and population killed or expelled in first explicit act of war on Bosnian soil.

3 October JNA mounts general sea blockade of Croatian ports; Dubrovnik, Zadar, Sisak, Vinkovci, Osijek and other towns shelled.

7 October Three-month moratorium having elapsed, Slovenia activates its declaration of independence, and JNA decides to begin withdrawal from the republic on 25 October. Two Yugoslav Air Force fighter aircraft fire missiles at presidential palace in Zagreb, where Tuđman, Mesić and Marković are at the time.

8 October Assembly adopts decision that 'Republic of Croatia abrogates state–legal relations on the basis of which along with the other republics and regions it until now formed SFRY', and 'repudiates the legitimacy and legality of all bodies of the former Federation'. Cyrus Vance appointed as personal envoy of UN secretary general.

10 October Hand-to-hand combat in Vukovar. Intense attack on Sisak, fighting in Pakrac, Croat villages round Drniš burned and their inhabitants expelled.

14–15 October During session of B-H Assembly, Karadžić states that Muslim (Bosniak) nation could 'disappear' if the republic seeks independence. Assembly adopts declaration on Bosnia-Herzegovina as a 'sovereign and indivisible state of equal nations'.

17 October JNA expels non-Serb population (Croats and Slovaks) from Ilok and surrounding villages.

18 October EC plan, presented at Hague Conference, provides for Yugoslavia to be community of sovereign states cooperating in financial and trade issues and security. Republics so desiring would be recognized as independent with existing borders. Minorities would be permitted dual citizenship. Serbia refuses; Montenegro accepts, then withdraws acceptance; remainder accept.

24 October Delegates to B-H Assembly from nationalist Serb parties found Assembly of the Serb People in Bosnia-Herzegovina.

8 November EC Council of Ministers introduces trade sanctions against SFRY, which *de facto* no longer exists, and proposes to UN Security Council imposition of oil embargo. Yugoslav Navy again blockades Croatian ports.

9–10 November In referendum organized by SDS, 'the Serb people in Bosnia-Herzegovina votes to remain in Yugoslavia with all those who wish to do so'.

11 November New JNA attack on Dubrovnik.

12 November Under leadership of vice-president of HDZBiH, Mate Boban, secret meeting held in Grude of 22 local party leaders from Herzegovina and Central Bosnia. Conclusion, with reference to agreements of 13 and 20 June with Tuđman in Zagreb, 'calls for formulation and publication of legal and political documents (proclamation of Croatian Banovina in Bosnia-Herzegovina, holding referendum on joining Republic of Croatia as first stage on road to final solution of the Croat issue, and creation of a sovereign Croatia within its ethnic and historical (now possible) borders'. The 'Croatian Community of Bosanska Posavina' formally established as para-state entity for north-Bosnian Croats.

16 November Croatian Navy and coastal artillery damage or sink some Yugoslav Navy ships around central Dalmatian islands and Pelješac peninsula.

17 November Macedonia adopts Constitution establishing it as sovereign and independent state.

18 November JNA, Serbian TO and Serb police occupy Vukovar – some civilians flee, some are killed, some are taken to camps in Serbia. JNA Knin Corps kills civilians in Škabrnje (81) and Nadin (18) in the northern Dalmatian hinterland.

In Grude, Croatian Community of Herzeg Bosna (HZH-B) proclaimed as 'political cultural, economic and territorial unity' of Croats in Bosnia-Herzegovina (comprising 38 municipalities in which Croats are in majority or where HDZBiH won elections, but also some not meeting those criteria): seat in Mostar, president Mate Boban. Community will 'respect the democratically elected authorities of the Republic of Bosnia-Herzegovina as long as B-H retains state independence from the former or any future Yugoslavia.'

20 November Bosnia-Herzegovina requests UN troops.

30 November JNA Banja Luka corps makes foray towards Virovitica, Croatian Army halts and repels it.

2 December Meeting between Izetbegović and Patriotic League commander, Sefer Halilović, in Sarajevo suburb of Hrasnica, on organizing defence of Bosnia-Herzegovina.

3 December Blockade of all Croatian ports except Dubrovnik lifted. Fiercest attack yet on Dubrovnik follows; 10,000–13,000 people protest in Cetinje, organized by Liberal Alliance of Montenegro: 'Forgive us, Dubrovnik!' Other major protests: Cetinje, 1 February; Podgorica, 23 February, 13 July and 25 August 1992.

9 December Arbitration (Badinter) Commission of EC submits report to Peace Conference in The Hague with conclusion that SFRY is in process of dissolution.

13 December In B-H Assembly, families of JNA soldiers demand that their sons be withdrawn from battlefield in Croatia.

17 December EC invites all republics wishing to do so to submit request for international recognition by 24 December, to be considered by Arbitration Commission. Slovenia, Croatia, Bosnia-Herzegovina and Macedonia, as well as Kosovo, respond, while Serbia and Montenegro reject the Arbitration Commission view that SFRY is in dissolution, declare that certain republics are in fact seceding, and claim sole right to succession.

19 December Serb Autonomous Region of Krajina proclaims itself state, with name Republic of Serb Krajina (RSK), with Knin as capital and Milan Babić as president. Paramilitary, TO and JNA units on its territory to be called Serbian Army of Krajina (SVK).

20 December Marković tenders resignation as president of Federal government.

21 December Assembly of Serb People in B-H adopts decision to form Serb Republic of B-H on territory hitherto proclaimed as Serb Autonomous Region, including almost all of Sarajevo, with Radovan Karadžić as president.

23 December Germany announces recognition of Croatia and Slovenia, decision to take effect on 15 January 1992.

25–26 December Tuđman, against all military logic, halts successful counter-offensive of Croatian Army in western Slavonia.

30 December At New Year press conference in Zagreb, Tuđman tells journalists that a three-way partition of Bosnia-Herzegovina 'best suits the long-term interests of all three peoples' and wider regional stability. Yugoslav General Staff orders JNA to begin arming Bosnian Serb TO units

1992

2 January Gojko Šušak and JNA General Andrija Rašeta sign agreement in Sarajevo on unconditional ceasefire in Croatia. JNA pulls back troops into territory of RSK and Bosnia-Herzegovina, deploying them on strategic routes and around major towns.

8 January UN Security Council authorizes UN peace force (UNPROFOR: 10,000 troops envisaged) as part of Vance Plan for Croatia.

9 January SDS proclaims Republic of Serb People in B-H and Karadžić states that 'united Bosnia-Herzegovina no longer exists'. Milošević issues secret order for all JNA officers born in Bosnia-Herzegovina to return there.

9 January Serb Republic of B-H proclaimed.

14 January Zagreb newspaper *Vjesnik* publishes Open Letter written by six Croat intellectuals from Bosnia-Herzegovina warning that Tuđman's New Year statement is expression of 'political irresponsibility', with likely catastrophic consequences for Bosnia-Herzegovina, Croatia, Bosniaks and the entire Croat people.

15 January European Union (EU) recognizes Slovenia and Croatia, defers recognition of Macedonia due to opposition from Greece, and calls upon Bosnia-Herzegovina to hold a referendum on independence.

25 January B-H Assembly, in which SDS and SPO delegates no longer sit, decides to announce referendum on independence.

2 February At Široki Brijeg, Stjepan Kljuić replaced as president of HDZBiH by Mate Boban, puppet of the Zagreb HDZ centre.

7–8 February Military conference of Patriotic League regional and national commanders in Mehurići near Travnik; Sefer Halilović's introductory statement will be basis for later official Directive for Defence of B-H Sovereignty.

14 February International Conference on Bosnia-Herzegovina begins in Sarajevo under EU auspices; chaired by Jose Cutilleiro.

16 February In RSK, Babić dismissed for refusing to accept Vance Plan.

21 February UN Security Council Resolution 743 establishes UN Protection Force (UNPROFOR) which, on basis of Vance Plan, is deployed on Croatian territory controlled by Serb para-authorities, organized into four sectors.

25 February General Staff of Patriotic League, meeting in Hrasnica, near Sarajevo, adopts Directive for Defence of B-H.

27 February Two days before referendum in Bosnia-Herzegovina, secret meeting held in Graz between representatives of Croatian government (president's adviser Zvonko Lerotić, head of Office for Protection of Constitutional Order Josip Manolić) and Serbs from Bosnia-Herzegovina (Karadžić and B-H Presidency member Nikola Koljević).

29 February–1 March Referendum on independence of Bosnia-Herzegovina.

1–2 March SDS sets up barricades around Sarajevo to prevent ballot boxes from being collected. Bosnians set up counter-barricades. Izetbegović agrees to formation of joint patrols by JNA and Bosnian police to dismantle barricades.

3 March Results of referendum published: 63.4 per cent turnout, 92.68 per cent affirmative votes, 0.19 per cent negative. Government of Republic of Bosnia-Herzegovina proclaims independence and open aggression begins: 7 March, attacks on villages around Čapljina; 8 March, JNA artillery from Tuzla moves towards Sava; 15 March, Serb paramilitary units attack suburbs of Bosanski Brod; firing in Bosniak villages around Goražde; 19 March, Serb artillery fires on Neum.

13 March Government of Bosnia-Herzegovina defers further service in JNA for recruits from Bosnia-Herzegovina.

18 March Lisbon Agreement (Cutilheiro Plan) provides for respect for borders of Bosnia-Herzegovina with administrative decentralization; national majority in certain municipalities appears for first time among criteria for such decentralization, and will remain a constant of all international plans.

24 March Assembly of Serb People in B-H, meeting in Pale, declares against independent and sovereign Bosnia-Herzegovina.

25 March In heaviest bombardment so far, about 2,000 rocket-launched projectiles fired at Bosanski Brod.

27 March 'Serb Republic of Bosnia-Herzegovina' formally established.

28–29 March Congress of Serb intellectuals (about 500 participants) in Sarajevo, organized by SDS, speaks openly about partition of Bosnia-Herzegovina on ethnic basis. Declaration states that the only solution for Bosnia-Herzegovina is 'a tripartite union in which the Serbs will be sovereign within their own borders'.

1–3 April Arkan's Serbian volunteers, under auspices of JNA, occupy strategically important town of Bijeljina: at least 500 Bosniaks killed, remainder expelled from town. Members of B-H Presidency, Biljana Plavšić and Fikret Abdić, and defence minister Jerko Doko visit Bijeljina. Plavšić thanks Arkan 'for protecting the Serb people'. By end of the month Bosniaks from entire Podrinje region killed and expelled (Zvornik occupied 10 April, Višegrad 13 April).

3 April Izetbegović sanctions JNA occupation of Bijeljina to end terror against Bosniaks. JNA bombardment of Mostar. Bosnian Croat paramilitary forces take control of Kupres. Croatian Army in Slavonia, under General Gorinšek, launches offensive against Serbian-occupied Baranja, terminated on orders from Tuđman.

4 April SDS militia attack police academy of Republic of B-H MUP in Vraca (Sarajevo). B-H Presidency orders general mobilization, whereupon Plavšić and Koljević tender resignation. JNA and armed detachments of SDS take over power in Banja Luka.

5 April SDS sets up street barricades in Sarajevo with armed, masked guards.

6 April EU recognizes Bosnia-Herzegovina; United States recognizes B-H, Croatia and Slovenia. Serbian terrorists fire on peaceful anti-war protesters outside B-H Assembly in Sarajevo (four dead, six wounded); elements of special police loyal to legal government (commanding officer Dragan Vikić) discover series of snipers' nests in the city. JNA occupies Sarajevo airport.

7 April Croatia recognizes Bosnia-Herzegovina within its existing borders, while offering Croats option of dual citizenship.

8 April B-H Presidency proclaims state of immediate threat of war and establishes General Staff of Territorial Defence of Republic of Bosnia-Herzegovina (GSTORBiH): commander Colonel Hasan Efendić, chief of staff Colonel Stjepan Šiber, deputy chief of staff Colonel Jovan Divjak, members include Abdulah Kajević (communications and mobilization system), Franko Plećko (logistics), Kerim Lučarević (military police).

In Grude (Herzegovina), HVO founded as 'sole institutional form of defence' of Croats in Bosnia-Herzegovina; large number of Bosniaks also join it. Under auspices of Croatian Party of Rights, HOS also formed, of mixed composition.

JNA expels Croat forces from Kupres. Zvornik is attacked by Arkan's Tigers, Šešelj's Chetniks and JNA's Užice Corps and occupied two days later.

9 April Bosnian Presidency declares unification of all armed forces on the territory of Bosnia-Herzegovina.

11 April Bosnian TO commander Efendić publishes appeal to JNA in Bosnia-Herzegovina to establish a joint command with TO, in hope that JNA might be included within the future armed forces of the Republic of B-H (OSRBiH).

13 April Efendić appeals for individual JNA officers to put themselves at disposal of B-H defence. Višegrad occupied by Užice Corps, in conjunction with TO forces from Užice (Serbia), Chetniks and White Eagles.

15 April Republican Staff of Bosnian TO formally assumes command of all armed units in B-H formed on political platform of Patriotic League: Bosnian Army officially born.

16–19 April 187 JNA officers, mainly Bosniaks, Croats and Albanians, come over to TORBiH.

26 April Izetbegović signs agreement on withdrawal of JNA from Bosnia-Herzegovina with B. Kostić, representing illegitimate Presidency of Yugoslavia.

27 April Federal Republic of Yugoslavia (FRY) proclaimed in Belgrade, compromising Montenegro and Serbia (with Vojvodina and Kosovo). Izetbegović orders JNA withdrawal from Bosnia-Herzegovina.

2–3 May JNA seizes Izetbegović at Sarajevo airport on his return from negotiations in Lisbon; JNA attempt to bisect Sarajevo defeated; Izetbegović exchanged for commanding officer of Sarajevo corps General Kukanjac; JNA column retreating from Sarajevo attacked by Bosnian forces; attempts by Bosnian forces at Visoko to break siege of Sarajevo successfully obstructed by HVO stronghold in Kiseljak.

In Bosnian Krajina, particularly in Banja Luka and Prijedor region, mass killings and expulsions of non-Serb population begin. Concentration camps set up (Manjača, Keraterm, Trnopolje, Omarska). Bosniak villages (Kozarac, Hambarine) and Croat villages (Ivanjska, Trn) looted, burned and destroyed, as well as Islamic and Catholic religious buildings and monuments. In Brčko, massacre of Bosniaks and Croats in Luka camp lasting several days. JNA occupies Doboj.

4 May Bosnia-Herzegovina proclaims Serbia aggressor and calls for international intervention.

4–20 May Some 14,000 JNA troops not officially natives of B-H are withdrawn from the country.

6 May Boban and Karadžić discuss in Graz an end to 'armed conflict of Croats and Serbs on the entire territory of Bosnia-Herzegovina', but cannot agree on 'redrawing borders of the Serb and Croat peoples in Bosnia-Herzegovina by agreement' (e.g. in Herzegovina SDS demands border along Neretva, while HDZ demands all Mostar and Stolac).

8 May HVO General Staff declares HVO to be only legal armed force on territory of HZH-B.

10 May HVO takes control of Busovača from TO.

15 May Ratko Mladić, commander of Knin Corps, appointed commander of Bosnian Serb Army (VRS), formed of elements of JNA and TO with paramilitary units of SDS. JNA garrison in Tuzla destroyed while attempting to evacuate city. UN Security Council Resolution 752 calls for 'JNA units and elements of the Croatian Army' to withdraw from Bosnia-Herzegovina or place themselves under control of authorities in Sarajevo. United States withdraws its ambassador from Belgrade.

16 May In meeting at Split, Croatian and Bosnian representatives discuss power-sharing and confederal arrangements. JNA outside Sarajevo attacks Pofalići with the aim of capturing Hum, linking up with the besieged Marshal Tito Barracks and cutting the city in half along the line Pofalići–Vraca, but is repelled.

20 May B-H Presidency takes decision to form OSRBiH. Croatian Army launches operation to liberate Dubrovnik hinterland.

23 May Halilović appointed chief of staff of Bosnian armed forces in place of Efendić. Croatian Army liberates Križ hill near Zadar, from which SVK is firing on Zadar and Adriatic highway.

27 May First major massacre of civilians in Sarajevo: from VRS positions, three shells land on bread queue (about 20 dead and 100 injured). VRS artillery fires across Sava at children's playground in Slavonski Brod (three dead).

30 May UN Security Council Resolution 757 imposes sanctions on FRY, stating failure to respect Resolution 752; Croatian Army no longer mentioned, since it is now in parts of Bosnia-Herzegovina (Posavina, Herzegovina) by agreement with authorities in Sarajevo, as ally of Bosnian armed forces. Yugoslav navy evacuates Vis island.

31 May Yugoslav navy evacuates Lastovo island.

6 June JNA withdraws from Marshal Tito Barracks in Sarajevo.

8 June UN Security Council gives approval for peace forces to take over control of Sarajevo airport from VRS, to establish air lift for delivery of humanitarian aid. Successful defence of Žuč hill by ARBiH prevents VRS bisection of Sarajevo.

15 June Dobrica Ćosić elected president of FRY.

16 June Croat and Bosniak forces launch counter-attack in Mostar, liberating town in following days and forcing aggressor back towards Trebinje. As part of operation, HOS units reach abandoned Trebinje, but are halted by political pressure from HDZ and HVO.

20 June B-H Presidency proclaims state of war, orders general mobilization and adopts platform for Presidency functions during state of war. HVO and Bosnian TO clash at Novi Travnik.

21 June Croatian Army liberates part of Drniš.

28 June French President Mitterrand comes to Sarajevo, symbolically 'opening' airport. Parallel command lines of Croatian president, separate from general staff of Croatian Army, order withdrawal of Croatian Army and HVO from parts of Bosnian Posavina despite favourable military conditions. This enables VRS forces from the Banja Luka and Bijeljina areas to link up and form 'corridor' between Serbia and parts of Croatia and Bosnia-Herzegovina under Serbian control. VRS occupies Derventa, Modriča, Odžak and Bosanski Šamac.

3 July HZH-B announces that, because of breakdown of state adminis-tration, 'provisional executive governance is established in liberated and defended territories', but this 'in no way calls into question the sovereignty and integrity of Bosnia-Herzegovina'; HVO is 'considered an integral part of the united defence forces under the Presidency of Bosnia-Herzegovina'.

4 July By decree of B-H Presidency, TORBiH renamed Army of Republic of Bosnia-Herzegovina (ARBiH).

6 July Envoys of HDZBiH and SDA meet in Međugorje to discuss forms of decentralization of country, but no agreement is reached.

7 July Croatian Army, after four-day battle, breaks siege of Dubrovnik.

8 July VRS takes Derventa in northern Bosnia.

12 July Authority over general staff of Bosnian armed forces shifted from Ministry of Defence, headed by HDZ member, to B-H Presidency.

21 July Izetbegović and Tuđman sign agreement recognizing HVO as legal military force, forming with ARBiH the Armed Forces of the Republic of B-H, and announcing military cooperation at state level. HZH-B formally recognizes authority of Sarajevo government.

2 August Military police of HVO kill HOS commanding officer Blaz Kraljević, advocate of Croat–Bosniak alliance, near Mostar. HOS breaks up: Croats join HVO, Bosniaks ARBiH. US and British media publicize existence of Serbian concentration camps in B-H.

3 August Izetbegović calls on UN Security Council to permit Bosnia-Herzegovina to acquire arms on basis of Article 51 of UN Charter, which guarantees right to self-defence to states under attack. UNPROFOR command, headquartered in Belgrade, begins to operate from Zagreb.

12 August Serb Republic of Bosnia-Herzegovina changes name to Republika Srpska (RS).

17 August Confrontation between ARBiH and HVO at Stup, in Sarajevo.

26–27 August Final declaration of London Conference formulates conditions for political resolution of crisis: all former republics must recognize Bosnia-Herzegovina, borders may be altered only by agreement of all interested parties, national communities and minorities must be guaranteed all rights, and all refugees and displaced persons have right to return. Provides for creation of international peace force, under UN Security Council auspices, to maintain ceasefire and supervise troop movements. Stated aim is to 'take all necessary measures to establish mutual confidence'.

3 September New permanent conference on Yugoslavia begins work, chaired by David Owen (for EU) and Cyrus Vance (for UN). Fifth Corps of ARBiH formed by decision of B-H Presidency.

14 September UN Security Council Resolution 776 authorizes sending of peace forces to Bosnia-Herzegovina.

6 October Izetbegović and Boban meet at Split and agree on joint ARBiH–HVO command.

7 October HV and HVO withdraw from Bosanski Brod.

8 October VRS takes Bosanski Brod; occupies entire Bosnian bank of Sava except Orašje. Since southern parts of Brčko and Gradačac municipalities have been successfully defended, southernmost part of 'corridor' is only 5 km wide; but it will remain to conclusion of war, continually the focus of covert political and diplomatic games that prevent it being cut. At meeting with Izetbegović, Boban demands replacement of Halilović.

9 October UN Security Council Resolution 781 imposes ban on flights in B-H airspace.

First half of October 7th Muslim brigade formed within structure of 3rd corps in Zenica, the first large unit of ARBiH that explicitly declares its aim to be 'fight for the faith'. Volunteers from Near and Middle East also appear in this region, terrorizing local Serb, Croat and Bosniak population.

18 October ARBiH–HVO clashes at Vitez and Novi Travnik.

20 October Yugoslav Army withdraws from Prevlaka.

25 October HVO carries out surprise attack on ARBiH troops in Prozor and expels Bosniaks from town.

28 October Negotiations in Geneva formally reject partition of B-H into three ethnic republics, calling for country to be restructured into 7–10 provinces with high level of autonomy, but internal borders subject to further negotiation. Central government would be located in Sarajevo, with responsibility for defence, foreign policy and trade. Presidency would have protocol function and be based on principle of rotation and representation of all peoples. HVO withdraws from Jajce.

29 October VRS occupies Jajce; about 25,000 Bosniaks and Croats flee towards Travnik. Break-up of joint Croat–Bosniak defence, largely provoked by political intrigues of HDZBiH.

13 December VRS advance halted at Maglaj.

18 December HVO takes over power in areas it controls: disbands legal municipal assemblies, dismisses mayors and members of local government who oppose confrontation with Bosniaks, and disarms remaining Bosniak soldiers (except in Posavina).

20 December Alija Izetbegović's second one-year mandate as president of B-H Presidency expires; Constitution provides for rotation (Croat is next in line, meaning realistically member of HDZ); SDA refuses, justifying stance by war circumstances; Izetbegović remains in post until end of war.

29 December FRY Assembly passes no confidence vote in premier Milan Panić.

1993

2 January Owen and Vance present plan to structure Bosnia-Herzegovina as state composed of 10 provinces; central government would have nine members (three Bosniaks, three Croats and three Serbs) and decide by consensus; composition of local authorities would maintain national structure based on 1991 census.

15 January B-H defence minister Bozo Rajić (HDZ) orders ARBiH troops in operational zones of proposed provinces 3, 8 and 10 (Posavina, Herzegovina, part of central Bosnia with Travnik and Lašva) to be placed under HVO general staff, which ARBiH refuses.

22–25 January Croatian Army liberates part of northern Dalmatian hinterland (Maslenica bridge, Zemunik airport and Peruča dam near Sinj).

10 February US government expresses reservations about Vance–Owen plan as legitimizing ethnic cleansing. In central Bosnia war flares up between ARBiH and HVO. In this 'war within a war', mass expulsions, burning of villages and killings of civilians take place.

11 March Major VRS offensive against Srebrenica, its prewar population swollen by tens of thousands of refugees.

31 March UN Security Council Resolution 816 authorizes NATO air force to shoot down aircraft violating flight ban over Bosnia-Herzegovina.

March–April Although by agreement with ARBiH it is to receive 25 per cent of consignments, HVO in Grude blockades 25 lorries with arms for Tuzla and defence of Srebrenica, which is in critical state.

12 April Fifty-six civilians killed by VRS bombardment of Srebrenica.

16 April UN Security Council Resolution 819 proclaims Srebrenica, about to fall into VRS hands, a 'safe area'. HVO massacres over 100 Bosniak civilians at Ahmići in Central Bosnia.

25 April HDZBiH and SDA representatives meet in Zagreb and agree to cooperate on implementation of Vance–Owen Plan.

25–26 April SDS leaders reject Vance–Owen plan, accepted by leaders of HDZ and SDA.

27 April Strongest UN Security Council sanctions thus far against FRY enter into force.

5 May Thorwald Stoltenberg replaces Cyrus Vance as co-chair of International Conference on Former Yugoslavia.

6 May FRY announces suspension of military aid to VRS, because of SDS rejection of Vance–Owen plan. UN Security Resolution 824 creates 'safe areas' of Sarajevo, Tuzla, Žepa, Goražde and Bihać.

8 May Ceasefire between ARBiH and VRS.

9 May HVO and HV begin general attack on eastern Mostar, systematically destroying the town. HVO expels Bosniaks from part of Mostar under its control, or deports them to camps where they are starved, tortured and killed (Heliodrom near Mostar, Dretelj, Gabela, Ljubuški). HVO passive on all fronts with VRS, or collaborating with it (except in Orašje, Usora and Bihać, where alliance with ARBiH is maintained). During remainder of year, Tuđman retires most competent and best-educated senior HV officers, opponents of conflict with ARBiH; General Janko Bobetko appointed chief of staff.

18 May Međugorje meeting to arrange HVO–ARBiH ceasefire and implementation of Vance–Owen plan. Boban forced to promise dissolution of HZH-B in this event.

22 May United States, Russia, Britain, France and Spain present plan providing for: deployment of international observers on B-H borders with Serbia and Croatia; presence of UNPROFOR in 'safe areas'; formation of International War Crimes Tribunal; increase in number of international observers in Kosovo; and peace force for Macedonia.

25 May UN Security Council Resolution 827 founds International Tribunal for War Crimes Committed on the Territory of Former Yugoslavia (ICTY) with headquarters at The Hague.

30 May Croatian parliament recognizes unity and sovereignty of Bosnia-Herzegovina.

4 June UN Security Council Resolution 836 authorizes sending additional troops to protect 'safe areas', and gives them mandate to use force in event of VRS attack.

6–7 June ARBiH expels HVO from Travnik.

8 June B-H Presidency appoints General Rasim Delić to command ARBiH, replacing Halilović who formally remains chief of staff.

14–16 June ARBiH expels HVO from Kakanj.

15–16 June Milošević and Tuđman agree on partition of Bosnia-Herzegovina into 'three national constituent units' in loose confederation.

20 June EU foreign ministers state that B-H's territorial integrity must be respected, while simultaneously discussing with Owen creation of three 'entities' within the country. Izetbegović rejects offer to join negotiations between Serbia and Croatia until VRS ceases to surround 'safe areas'.

7 July Assassination attempt on Halilović.

9 July B-H Presidency rejects Serb–Croat proposal to structure country as confederation of Serb, Croat and Bosniak republics.

11–12 July VRS expels ARBiH from Trnovo.

27–30 July In Geneva, plenary session on Bosnia-Herzegovina: Owen, Stoltenberg, Milošević, Tuđman, Izetbegović and Bulatović, as well as Boban and Karadžić; first time Izetbegović sits at same table with Karadžić, *de facto* recognizing him as legitimate negotiator. Debate on plan defining Bosnia-Herzegovina as union of three republics with limited central government. ARBiH takes Bugojno from HVO.

4 August VRS drives ARBiH from Mount Igman.

9 August Geneva negotiations broken off when Izetbegović refuses to take part until VRS withdraws from mounts Igman and Bjelašnica. NATO approves in principle military action in Bosnia-Herzegovina, in form of air strikes to protect UNPROFOR and weaken siege of Sarajevo; final decision remains with UN Security Council.

15 August Under this threat, VRS withdraws from Igman and Bjelašnica.

18 August Karadžić, Boban and Izetbegović reach agreement on Owen–Stoltenberg proposal: provisional status of Sarajevo as demilitarized zone under two-year UN administration, agreement to enter into force if overall peace accord reached.

20 August Owen and Stoltenberg present constitutional framework and territorial dispositions as package for partition of Bosnia-Herzegovina into three republics: Serbs to have approximately 53 per cent of territory, Bosniaks about 30 per cent and Croats slightly under 18 per cent. Sarajevo would have special status under UN administration, and Mostar under EU administration. SDS accepts, HDZ announces it will accept only if other two parties do so. B-H Assembly, by now overwhelmingly Bosniak, rejects plan but decides to continue negotiations.

21–22 August Meeting of general staff and senior commanding officers of ARBiH in Zenica, at which Halilović sets out plan of operation *Neretva '93*; objective to break through to southern Neretva valley and defeat HVO in Herzegovina.

28 August In Grude, HZH-B proclaims Croat Republic of Herzeg Bosna (HRH-B) as state of Croats in Bosnia-Herzegovina, with Mostar as capital, Boban as president.

7 September Croatian parliament recognizes HRH-B as one possible form for sovereignty of Croats in Bosnia-Herzegovina.

7–8 September ARBiH massacres 35 Croat civilians at village of Grabovica, near Mostar.

8 September Izetbegović, in Washington, fails to secure assurance from President Clinton that United States is ready for military intervention in Bosnia-Herzegovina.

9 September Croatian Army liberates Medak pocket in Lika, from which SVK was shelling Gospić; systematic destruction of Serb villages and atrocities against Serb civilians.

14 September ARBiH massacres at least 19 Croats at Uzdol, near Prozor.

20 September At meeting on British aircraft carrier *Invincible* in Adriatic, international mediators with consent of Tuđman and Milošević present plan which effectively partitions Bosnia-Herzegovina (Serbs 53 per cent, Croats 17 per cent, Bosniaks 30 per cent).

24 September Croatian Assembly calls on UNPROFOR to disarm and disband Serb paramilitary units in 'pink zone'.

27 September B-H Presidency member Fikret Abdić withdraws loyalty to central government and proclaims 'Autonomous Region of Western Bosnia' in Velika Kladuša and parts of Cazin municipality. His forces attack 5th corps of ARBiH and collaborate with SVK and VRS, as well as with Croatian authorities.

29 September Assembly of Bosnia-Herzegovina rejects *Invincible* plan.

21 October Boban signs agreement in Zagreb on cooperation with Abdić; next day in Belgrade Abdić signs declaration on cooperation with Karadžić. Coup by HVO extremists in Vareš.

23 October HVO massacres over 80 Bosniak civilians at Stupni Do near Vareš.

26 October Operation Trebević: destruction of military-criminal fiefdoms of Sarajevan warlords Ramiz Delalić-Ćelo and Musan Topalović-Caco, commanders of 9th and 10th brigades, by regular Bosnian Army and police. Topalović killed. Halilović blockaded in his headquarters during operation and subsequently dismissed as chief of staff.

28 October Reconstitution of Bosnian government; removal of HDZ ministers from key posts; Haris Silajdžić becomes prime minister.

2 November Secret negotiations between Croatian government and RSK begin in Oslo.

6 November Forcible incorporation of HVO's 'King Tvrtko' brigade in Sarajevo into 1st corps of ARBiH. Sarajevo branch of HDZ denounces Bosnian government 'aggression'.

4 November ARBiH expels HVO from Vareš.

9 November HVO destroys Old Bridge at Mostar.

29 November EC presents Action Plan, in effect variant of plan for B-H as union of three republics and *Invincible* plan.

1994

31 January General mobilization in Republika Srpska.

3 February UN Security Council calls for withdrawal of Croatian Army from Bosnia-Herzegovina.

5 February Mortar shell from Serb positions kills 68 people at Markale marketplace in Sarajevo.

6 February Assembly of B-H Croats in Sarajevo, with more than 400 representatives of political parties, cultural and professional societies, Church and prominent individuals opposed to ethnic partition and HDZ policies. Declaration states that Bosnia-Herzegovina is also homeland of Croats, who must participate in governmental bodies and negotiate on ways to decentralize country.

8 February HDZBiH leaders meet at Livno; Boban replaced by Krešimir Zubak.

9 February NATO issues ultimatum to Serb forces to withdraw heavy weapons from positions around Sarajevo (to 20 km from current line), which they begin to carry out on 17 February.

23 February ARBiH and HVO reach agreement on ceasefire.

26 February Under US auspices, negotiations begin on creation of Federation of Bosnia-Herzegovina (FBiH), to cover area of Bosnia-Herzegovina with Bosniak and Croat majority, but with possibility of being joined subsequently also by territory with majority Serb population.

11 March Bosnia-Herzegovina and Croatia sign agreement in Split on formation of joint military command.

18 March Agreement on FBiH signed in Washington; end of Croat–Bosniak war.

c. 7–23 April Full-scale VRS assault on Goražde.

10–11 April First NATO air strikes, against VRS positions around Goražde.

26 April First meeting of Contact Group (United States, Britain, Russia, Germany, France), formed with aim of reaching agreement between leaders of FBiH and RS. Principles: Bosnia-Herzegovina as single state with two 'Entities', whose relations are to be defined by agreed constitution.

30 April Founding congress in Zagreb of Croatian Independent Democrats, party of HDZ dissidents opposed to Tuđman's Bosnian policy.

12 May US Senate votes to lift arms embargo against Bosnia-Herzegovina; next day Russian Duma votes to end sanctions against FRY.

13 May Contact Group ministers clarify principle of internal partition of Bosnia-Herzegovina: 51 per cent of territory to FBiH, 49 per cent to Serb 'Entity'.

16 May Joint general staff of Federation army formed (ARBiH + HVO), with aim of creating joint armed forces.

31 May Constitution-forming Assembly of FBiH elects Zubak president of Federation, Ejup Ganić vice-president and Haris Silajdžić prime minister.

6 July Contact Group presents maps for internal territorial division of Bosnia-Herzegovina.

7–9 July ARBiH 5th corps inflicts heavy defeat on Abdić's troops in Operation Tiger.

13 July Milošević accepts Contact Group plan, but RS rejects it; FRY proclaims sanctions against RS.

18 July Government of FBiH accepts Contact Group plan.

21 August ARBiH 5th corps, commanded by General Atif Dudaković, occupies Velika Kladuša; Abdić and population (about 20,000) flee to Croatian territory held by RSK.

6–7 September Contact Group proposes to UN Security Council to ease sanctions against FRY, since its government has purportedly broken off political and economic relations with Bosnian Serbs because of their rejection of proposed territorial ratio (VRS holds approximately 70 per cent of territory of Bosnia-Herzegovina at this time).

12 September Failed VRS and VRSK offensive against 5th corps in Bihać pocket.

6–10 October ARBiH crosses demilitarized zone on Mount Igman to strike at VRS positions. UN forces expel ARBiH from Igman; UN commander Michael Rose threatens ARBiH with air strikes.

18 October Croatian officials announce that a delegation of 15 US Army officers will shortly be arriving in Sarajevo to assist in training the senior staff of FBiH Army.

23–31 October 5th corps offensive Grmec '94 results in string of victories.

29 October–3 November Successful ARBiH offensive to the south of Sarajevo; liberation of Mount Treskavica and part of Igman.

3 November In first joint action after Washington Agreements, HVO and ARBiH liberate Kupres.

4–27 November Successful VRS and VRSK counter-offensive against 5th corps threatens Bihać.

10–11 November In accordance with decision of US Senate, US government announces that it will no longer participate in monitoring arms embargo against Bosnia-Herzegovina. Move condemned by European powers.

15–16 November Owen and Stoltenberg present draft agreement on economic cooperation between Croatia and RSK. Relates to future electricity supply and the opening of oil pipelines and routes between Zagreb and Belgrade.

18 November Croatian Army prepares to intervene to defend Bihać.

21 November NATO bombs Udbina airport, from which RSK aircraft have been attacking Bihać.

23 November NATO strikes hit three VRS missile sites in north-western Bosnia.

24 November 250 UN troops taken hostage by VRS in vicinity of Sarajevo.

29 November Šušak threatens Croatian intervention to defend Bihać. US Defence Secretary William Perry signs 'memorandum on cooperation' with Šušak.

30 November HV and HVO begin offensive against Serb positions in Livanjsko polje; objective is to enter Knin from north and relieve and link up with ARBiH 5th corps in Bihać.

2 December Croatian government and RSK sign Agreement on Economic Issues in Zagreb, co-signed by US and Russian ambassadors to Croatia.

9 December UN General Assembly resolution recognizes Croatia's borders and describes VRSK-held areas as 'occupied'.

17 December VSRK and Abdić forces retake Velika Kladuša.

1995

1 January After mediation by former US President Jimmy Carter who had visited Pale, ceasefire signed between VRS and ARBiH.

12 January Croatia rejects extension of UNPROFOR mandate after expiry of current mandate on 31 March.

30 January EU, United States, Russia and co-chairs of International Conference for Former Yugoslavia present Plan Z-4, which would make RSK a *de facto* state within the state of Croatia, but RSK rejects it. Bosnian Presidency condemns politicization of ARBiH along party political and Bosniak-nationalist lines; Izetbegović rejects its right to do so.

20–28 March ARBiH liberates Mount Vlašić, gaining strategic control of large area.

31 March UNPROFOR mandate in Croatia expires. UN Security Council adopts three Resolutions defining UN mission in successor states of SFRY. UNPROFOR to be divided into three organizational and military units: UNCRO in Croatia, UNPROFOR (UN Protection Forces) in Bosnia-Herzegovina, and UNPREDEP (UN Preventive Deployment) in Macedonia.

24 April International War Crimes Tribunal in The Hague begins criminal investigation on Karadžić and Mladić.

1–2 May Croatian Army liberates remainder of western Slavonia in Operation Flash.

2–3 May SVK fires rockets at Zagreb and other Croatian towns in retaliation (seven dead), and with entire civilian population under its control in western Slavonia flees into Bosnia-Herzegovina.

25 May VRS shells central square in Tuzla (71 dead), and continues shelling Sarajevo. When NATO threatens air strikes against its positions around the city, VRS takes more than 350 members of peace forces hostage for use as human shields.

26 May NATO air strikes destroy six bunkers in Pale.

June Croatian Army completes occupation of Dinara range, giving it position of strategic superiority *vis-à-vis* Knin.

3 June NATO adopts decision to form Rapid Reaction Force.

12 June EU appoints Carl Bildt as its official mediator after Owen's resignation on 29 May.

June–July Unsuccessful ARBiH offensive to break siege of Sarajevo.

11 July VRS and units of VJ under Mladić occupy 'safe area' of Srebrenica. Defenders and population attempt to break through to Tuzla; in and around the town Mladić's forces massacre over 7,000 civilians.

19 July VRSK begins assault on Bihać enclave.

21 July Western allies, on US initiative, decide that NATO must take decisive action and announce heavy air strikes on VRS if it continues to attack 'safe areas'.

22 July Izetbegović and Tuđman in Split sign agreement on military cooperation.

25 July VRS occupies Žepa, killing and expelling Bosniak population.

26 July US Senate votes for proposal of Senators Dole and Lieberman for unilateral lifting of arms embargo against Bosnia-Herzegovina (69 votes for, 29 against).

28–29 July HV and HVO take Bosansko Grahovo and Glamoč. Serb population pulling out everywhere, along with VRS; Knin half surrounded.

1 August Congressmen in US House of Representatives vote for unilateral lifting of arms embargo against Bosnia-Herzegovina (298 votes for, 128 against). Possibility of direct conflict between legislative and executive branches.

3 August Silajdžić resigns as Bosnian premier, following power struggle and policy differences with Izetbegović.

4–7 August In Operation Storm, HV liberates entire territory of Croatia except strip along Danube (eastern Slavonia), and links up on border with ARBiH 5th corps, thus lifting blockade of Bihać. Complete exodus of SVK (about 30,000) and Serb population (at least 100,000) from former occupied territories (RSK). Exodus of Bosniaks (about 20,000) from Velika Kladuša, after 5th corps enters town. Few remaining Serbs, mainly elderly, on territory of former RSK exposed during following weeks to looting and general terror, including many murders. Mass expulsions of remaining Croats and Bosniaks from Bosnian Krajina (about 20,000).

11 August President Clinton vetoes unilateral lifting of arms embargo against Bosnia-Herzegovina, and appoints Richard Holbrooke to begin new peace initiative.

12 August Russian Parliament passes law unilaterally ending sanctions against FRY.

18 August HV and HVO units threaten Trebinje in eastern Herzegovina, but then local ceasefire is signed with VRS.

28 August Mortar shells from VRS positions kill 41 civilians in Sarajevo, at Markale marketplace.

30 August NATO begins systematic air strikes on VRS positions.

8 September In Geneva, under auspices of Contact Group, foreign ministers of Croatia, Bosnia-Herzegovina and FRY agree principles for accord: Bosnia-Herzegovina to retain international personality; internal partition to respect ratio of 51 per cent for FBiH, 49 per cent for RS.

12 September and following days, Croatian forces take Drvar, Šipovo and Jajce, B-H forces take Donji Vakuf, Bosanska Krupa, Bosanski Petrovac, Ključ, Sanski Most; 5th corps draws near to Prijedor, and HV comes to within 25 km south of Banja Luka. VRS in disarray, and entire population of RS west of corridor begins to flee towards Serbia.

19 September Under pressure from Western powers, especially USA, offensive is halted, since ARBiH and HV advance threatens agreed territorial ratio between 'entities'. Failed HV operation across Sava at Bosanska Dubica is additional factor persuading Zagreb to cease operations.

26 September Contact Group announces further principles for accord: joint institutions, free elections, freedom of movement and protection of human rights. Clinton and Izetbegović reach agreement that lifting arms embargo be deferred for 4 to 6 months.

10 October After resisting counter-attack of VRS threatening Ključ and Bosanska Krupa, ARBiH reinforced in Sanski Most and HV enters Mrkonjić Grad.

12 October After UNPROFOR confirms that military action has ceased, Holbrooke announces that negotiations will begin on 31 October and last until agreement is reached. NATO Council adopts decision to send troops to Bosnia-Herzegovina as soon as accord is signed.

1 November Negotiations begin at Wright-Patterson air base in Dayton, Ohio.

12 November Croatian authorities and local Serbs from eastern Slavonia sign agreement on peaceful return of that area (former UN 'Protected' Eastern Sector) to Croatian authority.

21 November Accord on Bosnia-Herzegovina reached, covering 'entity' borders, electoral procedures, instruments for protection of human rights, return of refugees and displaced persons. Bosnia-Herzegovina (FBiH plus RS) to have joint institutions of two-chamber Parliament, three-member Presidency, Council of Ministers, Constitutional Court and Central Bank.

14 December Tuđman, Izetbegović and Milošević formally sign Dayton Accord in Paris, in presence of representatives of Contact Group countries.

Index

377